D0149132

Debating Immigration

Debating Immigration presents 20 original and updated essays, written by some of the world's leading experts and preeminent scholars, that explore the nuances of contemporary immigration in the United States and Europe. This volume is organized around the following themes: economics, demographics and race, law and policy, philosophy and religion, and European politics. Its topics include comprehensive immigration reform, the limits of executive power, illegal immigration, human smuggling, civil rights and employment discrimination, economic growth and unemployment, and social justice and religion. A timely second edition, *Debating Immigration* is an effort to bring together divergent voices to discuss various aspects of immigration often neglected or buried in discussions.

Carol M. Swain is an award-winning political scientist and member of the James Madison Society at Princeton University. She is the author or editor of eight books. Her highly acclaimed *Black Faces, Black Interests: The Representation of African Americans in Congress* won three national prizes, including the Woodrow Wilson Foundation Award for the best book published in the U.S. on government, politics, or international affairs. Dr. Swain has been cited by the U.S. Supreme Court and profiled in major publications and documentaries. She regularly makes guest appearances on numerous national and international radio and TV shows. Her opinion pieces have been published in major national and international newspapers.

"Carol M. Swain has a knack for identifying important issues of social welfare policy before other analysts. From her background and research, she sees issues, trends, and perspectives in an important way. Hers is a voice that needs to be part of any conversation on immigration."

James F. Blumstein, University Professor of Constitutional Law
and Health Law and Policy, Vanderbilt Law School
and Medical School

"This collection of reasoned and informed articles is a welcome intervention in the politically toxic and shrill debate on immigration. It should contribute to a balancing of conflicting interests for the common good."

Herman Daly, Emeritus Professor, School of Public Policy,
University of Maryland

"Some Americans favor immigration, some oppose it, and most academics are all-too-united in defending it. Carol M. Swain and her contributors treat the divisions clearly and fairly. She achieved that in the first edition of *Debating Immigration*, and now she has done it again. This book is engrossing and disturbing, because the subject is. America's future is on the anvil."

Lawrence M. Mead, New York University

"The timely publication of this second, updated, edition of *Debating Immigration* is a welcome event. In this volume, editor Carol M. Swain has gathered an impressively knowledgeable and ideologically diverse set of contributors, who comprehensively address the immigration issue in all of its moral, legal, economic, and political complexity. As an added bonus, Professor Swain provides her own trenchant and, to this reader, persuasive critical assessment of how the interests of rank-and-file black Americans are ill-served by the positions taken on this issue by liberal elites."

Glenn C. Loury, Merton P. Stoltz Professor of the Social Sciences,
Brown University, Rhode Island

"Thoughtful. Challenging. Wide-ranging. The updated edition of *Debating Immigration* offers new and dynamic perspectives on one of our nation's most important issues. Readers from across the political spectrum will see their most cherished ideas effectively elucidated and constructively interrogated. Professor Swain has assembled a magnificent group of thinkers whose efforts combine deep philosophical debates with powerful calls to action. A critical and highly valuable contribution."

Arthur Lupia, Hal R. Varian Collegiate Professor of Political
Science, University of Michigan

Debating Immigration

Edited by
CAROL M. SWAIN
James Madison Scholar, Princeton University

CAMBRIDGE
UNIVERSITY PRESS

CAMBRIDGE
UNIVERSITY PRESS

University Printing House, Cambridge CB2 8BS, United Kingdom

One Liberty Plaza, 20th Floor, New York, NY 10006, USA

477 Williamstown Road, Port Melbourne, VIC 3207, Australia

314–321, 3rd Floor, Plot 3, Splendor Forum, Jasola District Centre, New Delhi – 110025, India

79 Anson Road, #06–04/06, Singapore 079906

Cambridge University Press is part of the University of Cambridge.

It furthers the University's mission by disseminating knowledge in the pursuit of education, learning, and research at the highest international levels of excellence.

www.cambridge.org
Information on this title: www.cambridge.org/9781108470469
DOI: 10.1017/9781108556606

© Cambridge University Press 2018

This publication is in copyright. Subject to statutory exception and to the provisions of relevant collective licensing agreements, no reproduction of any part may take place without the written permission of Cambridge University Press.

First published 2018

Printed in the United States of America by Sheridan Books, Inc.

A catalogue record for this publication is available from the British Library.

ISBN 978-1-108-47046-9 Hardback
ISBN 978-1-108-45467-4 Paperback

Cambridge University Press has no responsibility for the persistence or accuracy of URLs for external or third-party internet websites referred to in this publication and does not guarantee that any content on such websites is, or will remain, accurate or appropriate.

Contents

Figures

Tables

Contributors

Philip Cafaro, Professor of Philosophy, Colorado State University, affiliated faculty member of CSU's School of Global Environmental Sustainability and President of the International Society for Environmental Ethics.

Steven A. Camarota, Ph.D., Research Director for the Center for Immigration Studies.

Elizabeth Cohen, Associate Professor, Syracuse University.

James R. Edwards, Jr., Fellow at the Center for Immigration Studies, Washington, DC.

Amitai Etzioni, University Professor and Director of the Institute for Communitarian Policy Studies at The George Washington University.

Nathan Glazer, Professor Emeritus of Sociology and Education at Harvard University.

Sara Wallace Goodman, Associate Professor of Political Science, University of California at Irvine.

Randall Hansen, Professor of Political Science and Canada Research Chair in Global Migration at University of Toronto.

Marc Morjé Howard, Professor of Government and Law at Georgetown University.

Stephen Macedo, Laurence S. Rockefeller Professor of Politics and Director of the Center for Human Values at Princeton University.

Susan F. Martin, Donald G. Herzberg Professor of International Migration at Georgetown University.

Douglas S. Massey, Henry G. Bryant Professor of Sociology and Public Affairs, Woodrow Wilson School, Princeton University.

Camilo Pardo, Graduate Research Assistant, Terrorism, Transnational Crime and Corruption Center of the Schar School of Policy and Government at George Mason University.

Noah Pickus, Associate Director of the Kenan Institute for Ethics and Adjunct Associate Professor of Public Policy at the Sanford Institute of Public Policy at Duke University.

Karen A. Pren, Project Manager, Office of Population Research, Woodrow Wilson School, Princeton University.

Louise Shelley, Omer L. and Nancy Hirst Endowed Chair as well as a University Professor in the School of Policy, Government and International Affairs and the founder and Director of the Terrorism, Transnational Crime and Corruption Center (TraCCC) at George Mason University.

Peter Skerry, Professor of Political Science at Boston College.

John Skrentny, Professor of Sociology, and Director of the Yankelovich Center for Social Science Research, University of California, San Diego.

Rogers M. Smith, Christopher H. Browne Distinguished Professor of Political Science at the University of Pennsylvania.

Carol M. Swain, James Madison Scholar, The James Madison Program in American Ideals and Institutions, Princeton University.

Virginia Yetter, Associate Attorney, Bass, Berry, and Sims, Nashville, TN.

Karen Zeigler, Demographer, Center for Immigration Studies, Washington, DC.

Preface to the Second Edition

Carol M. Swain

More than a decade ago, we published the first edition of *Debating Immigration*. It received much attention and was used in classrooms around the world. Readers praised the stature of the contributors, the diversity of perspectives, and the book's readability for non-experts.

In this revised edition, we strive to maintain the same high standards of the first book. Readers will encounter some new voices as well as updates of recurring chapters and new chapters written or co-authored by me.

Many major developments occurring since 2007 have affected migration worldwide, especially in the United States. It has been more than thirty-five years since Congress has passed major legislation affecting immigration. American presidents, most notably Barack Obama, used executive powers to make changes at the margins. President Obama's efforts, however, have encountered opposition and in some cases reversal since the election of Donald J. Trump, an outsider candidate who campaigned in 2016 as a restrictionist. In the year since his election, President Trump has taken actions consistent with many of his campaign promises and has begun to use executive action and agencies to make some substantive changes.

Significant events that have helped shape immigration laws and practices include:

- Donald Trump's 2016 election as president and his efforts to implement a travel ban affecting nations suspected of sponsoring terrorism.
- The expansion and restriction of immigration federalism. Such involvement dictates what state and local governments can and can't do to assist the federal government in undertaking its role to enforce immigration laws.
- The unprecedented use of executive actions and prosecutorial discretion to bypass Congress and enact policies that have slowed deportation of illegal immigrants and expanded immigrant rights.

- A surge in border crossings of illegal aliens from Central American asylum seekers.
- The rise in unaccompanied youth crossing the border.
- An increase of refugees from majority-Muslim states.
- A steep decline in the percentage of working-age Americans in the labor force, either employed or unemployed, which was at a thirty-six-year low (62.4 percent) in September 2015, but had risen to 63.1 percent by September 2017.[1] In this edition of *Debating Immigration*, we cover most, if not all, of these issues. We also expand the section on European migration to examine globalization, human trafficking, citizenship for immigrants, and the reality of terrorism.

NOTE

1. Bureau of Labor Statistics, 2007–2017, https://goo.gl/p440d7; "United States Labor Force Participation, 1950–2017," *Trading Economics* https://tradingeconomics.com/united-states/labor-force-participation-rate, accessed February 12, 2018.

Preface to the First Edition

The origins of this volume lie in a conference I organized at Princeton University in January 2005 on the theme: "Contemporary Politics of Immigration in the United States." With the sponsorship of the James Madison Program and the close assistance of program manager Reggie Feiner, we convened a diverse group of well-known activists, scholars, and journalists, most of whom had taken highly visible public positions on various aspects of immigration policy. Conference participants included Tamar Jacoby of the Manhattan Institute; Peter Brimelow of VDARE; Amitai Etzioni of George Washington University; Stephen Camarota of the Center for Immigration Studies, Washington, DC; Stephen Macedo of Princeton University; Philip Kasinitz of City University of New York; Jane Junn of Rutgers University; Ken Masugi of Claremont University; Rogers Smith of University of Pennsylvania; Linda Bosniak of Rutgers University Law School; Elizabeth Cohen of the Maxwell School at Syracuse University; Lina Newton of Hunter College, Noah Pickus of Duke University; Peter Skerry of Boston College; and Charles Westoff of Princeton University.

Our group spent two days together, grappling with some of the more troubling aspects of the current immigration situation in America. At the top of the list was the issue of the nation's estimated 11–14 million illegal aliens. Other topics treated included the history of American attitudes toward newcomers, and the impact of large-scale immigration on current United States citizens, especially poor minorities. A major goal of the conference was to bring together people who rarely converse with each other and create a place where they could have a vigorous conversation that might allow them to find common ground on certain aspects of these issues. To their credit, the participants were cordial and civil to one another, even though they often had quite divergent viewpoints. What emerged from that conference forms the core of the following anthology, which examines from a variety of ideological perspectives the current realities and projections about immigration in the U.S.

Some of our participants were unable to contribute chapters to the volume. In order to achieve balance and to ensure coverage of a number of issues not specifically addressed by the conference, including the biblical perspective on immigration, and immigration's impact on certain historically disenfranchised groups, we invited Nathan Glazer of Harvard University; Randall Hansen of the University of Toronto; Marc M. Howard of Georgetown University; Peter Schuck of Yale University; James R. Edwards, Jr. of the Hudson Institute; and Jonathan Tilove of Newhouse News Service to contribute additional chapters. One of my own chapters also appears here. The resulting volume is a timely, multifaceted interrogation of a highly visible and pertinent issue in contemporary America and one that includes the viewpoints of some of the most distinguished thinkers and activists in the world.

Foreword

Nathan Glazer

I write as someone who has studied problems of immigration for seventy years or more, but also as the child of immigrants, as so many Americans are, raised in East Harlem and the South Bronx during the 1920s and 1930s, when these areas were parts of the poorest Congressional districts in the nation. For over a century and a half now, we have grappled with problems of immigration and immigration policy. In 1984, in a book I edited titled *Clamor at the Gates,* I described America as a "permanently unfinished country," founded by settlers and pioneers long before the establishment of an independent nation, and long before we began to call newcomers "immigrants" or had any need to think of immigration laws and debates about whom to admit and whom to exclude. We still deal with these issues, and how to develop a workable immigration policy that balances the values and needs of the nation with the pleas of the many seeking to enter.

The second edition of *Debating Immigration* is being published at a time very different from ten years ago. Then, we were still in a stage in which immigration was celebrated for the most part as a distinctive contribution to making the United States a great nation, and it had been so celebrated by every president since John F. Kennedy. Today, a new president is in office, who has promised in his campaign the most radical changes in immigration policy since 1965 and a return to the most restrictive policies on immigration since the early 1920s. This has already transformed our consideration of what has been considered the most important and difficult problem in immigration policy: how to handle the large number of undocumented or illegal immigrants, ten million or more, integrated into American life and the economy, and related to American citizens by birth or marriage. In this second edition, some new contributors appear and older ones offer fresh insight from their updated chapters. We find excellent research, particularly on the economic effects of recent immigration – not that we all agree or can be expected to agree on the conclusions of this research, especially its impact on the most vulnerable Americans: blacks, poor whites, and Hispanics. There is also a good deal of research, by its nature more difficult to conduct, on the various dimensions of the assimilation and integration of immigrants into American society, and the conclusions of this research are also disputed. We have had extended debate and a good deal of legislation with respect to illegal or undocumented immigration, universally considered the most serious issue in current immigration, but it has not seriously curtailed illegal entry or presence in the United States. Scholars like Doug Massey and Karen Pren would argue we have made things worse through our restrictive legislation.

As we struggle with this issue in the first decades of the twenty-first century – just as we struggled with it in the 1980s and 1990s of the last century – it is clear we have come to no generally accepted and politically realizable conclusions as to what, if anything, can and should be done. Or, are we to consider the tossed-off remarks during a political campaign of a historically unique candidate, who lost the majority of the popular vote, but gained a victory in the Electoral College, such a generally acceptable and realizable policy? He certainly thinks so, but the judicial and legislative branches of the government may not agree. Yet we know it is a problem crying out for a solution. Fears of terrorism and growing pressure to admit refugees from Third World nations, some known to breed terrorism, further complicate the dilemma we face.

This edition tells us some familiar things about current immigration and brings to our attention some of the recent research, particularly on economic effects, but its true value is to raise some new questions. In view of how difficult it has been to resolve disputes over immigration in the past thirty plus years, some new thoughts and ideas may well be just what we need. While every chapter has something to tell us that is helpful, I would point to two issues from the previous edition that are brought to our attention in these chapters with a degree of forcefulness that has not characterized these themes in the past.

The first of what I consider as these new thoughts is the focus of two of the chapters on the ethical and moral bases that should guide our immigration policy. One point of view that is particularly significant for American politics today is that of evangelical Christians, which generally enters political discussion in the form of demands from one side and denunciations on the other and almost never appears in reasoned policy discussion. But here it warrants an interesting and important inspection. What is the biblical point of view, insofar as it can be drawn from the Hebrew and Christian Bibles? This perspective is developed in the essay by James R. Edwards. It is supplemented by a sophisticated piece by Stephen Macedo in which recent thinking in moral philosophy, in particular the influential work of John Rawls and Michael Walzer, is brought to bear on the immigration issue. I will develop below my reasons for thinking moral and ethical issues are beginning to, and will continue to, play an increasingly important role in discussions of immigration, even though such considerations will be in abeyance as long as the period initiated by the victory of Donald Trump prevails.

The second of these new thoughts, to my mind, is developed in the chapter by Noah Pickus and Peter Skerry. It attacks what has politically become the central issue in the immigration debate: the distinction between legal and illegal immigration. They ask, "Is this really the problem? Do not many of the consequences that concern us when we consider immigration, consequences affecting the economic interests of various groups, for example, result from legal immigration, which is, after all, by far the greater part of immigration, as well as from illegal immigration? Is not much that we applaud and approve among immigrants evident among illegal immigrants, too?" It is time to rethink the distinction, and explore what light this may throw on immigration issues. Likewise, Philip Cafaro makes an enlightened case for reducing immigration by pointing to the impact of large-scale immigration on progressive goals to achieve a more economically just and ecologically sustainable society.

Clearly the moral issues raised by Edwards and Macedo are relevant here, too. We find, I believe, that the ideas of natural justice, and moral and ethical concerns more generally, play an increasingly relevant role in political thinking and, until very recently, in international affairs. Such a development has to throw some doubt on the significance of the difference between legal and illegal immigrants. Both come for the same reasons, escaping the same countries and attracted similarly to the realm of free countries with greater opportunities. Can we be so absolute in erecting a wall between them, with rights for those on one side and no rights at all for those on the other?

Furthermore, this book pays a significant amount of attention to the changes in race and ethnicity of immigrants in recent decades, devoting an entire section to it and placing particular emphasis on the question of how the issue of immigration interacts with the place and fate of black Americans. Of particular interest is a chapter by John Skrentny that shows the continuing effect of race and racism in employer decisions about whom to hire and what types of jobs they should be assigned to. His study of factories shows how low-skilled whites and blacks frequently lose out to employer-preferred Latino and Asian immigrants. This occurs despite the Civil Rights Act of the 1960s that makes such ethnic preferences illegal.

Another issue to which I would point is spelled out by Rogers Smith. Smith, more than most of the others, suggests to us that a look back at the history of immigration in the United States may be helpful. It reminds us that there are possibilities in immigration policy that are not evident on the horizon today. We do not see much reference to the past in these chapters, and it may well be argued that so much has changed in the United States in the past fifty years that there is no point to looking at the history of immigration policy, much of which is disreputable. But history reminds us of one important lesson: The mantra that this is, has always been, and always will be an immigration society is as much ideology – the ideology of the past half-century in particular – as a proper evaluation of the actual role of immigration in American society.

We should recall that in large stretches of American history – and indeed in some of its most formative periods – immigration was low and not much considered a central and shaping element in American society. I would point to two such periods in particular. Consider the sixty years from the time of the American Revolution to the 1840s. Revolution and war played a major role in keeping immigration low during much of this period. The Napoleonic Wars did not end until 1815 and even after the return to peace, immigration remained low. During this entire period, and for a few decades thereafter, there was no national legislation on immigration; as Elizabeth Cohen reminds us, it was a matter then for the states, and few bothered to exercise their rights on the subject. Tocqueville, traveling through the United States in the 1830s, did not think of the United States as a country being shaped by immigration. To him, it was a country of Anglo-Americans, and he didn't expect that to change. He was happy to make contact with French immigrants, but they were few. The problematic minorities – to use current terminology – in the American population were Indians and blacks, not immigrants.

Consider another lengthy period, from the 1920s to the 1960s, forty years covering the growth of the twenties, the Great Depression, the four terms of FDR, World War II, and postwar prosperity. During that entire period, immigration was kept low by the Depression and war and by law if these did not suffice. National sentiment, as expressed in Congress, was strongly anti-immigration. Even efforts to bring in threatened Jewish children or concentration camp survivors who could find no home in Europe met fierce political resistance. Indeed, when immigration law was finally changed in 1965, it was only because no one expected that immigration would rise much. A degree of family reunification for some Europeans was expected and made possible, and a bow to the anti-racism which we had formally espoused in the war against Hitler twenty years before permitted the elimination of the ban on Asians. But not many of them were expected.

America has changed since, and one of the chief ways in which it has changed is in our acknowledgment of responsibilities and duties, to some degree, to the entire world – another example of the role of the ethical and moral concerns to which I earlier alluded. Such an acknowledgment has to raise the question of what kind of claim people in poor or war-ravaged countries, or in countries brutalized by dictators, have to the assistance of richer and more fortunate countries in escaping from terrible conditions. We have seen the emergence of an international ethic according to which it has become an obligation of rich countries to provide aid to poor countries, even to those for whose poverty they bear no particular responsibility. The idea of aid to poor countries as an obligation of the richer countries was certainly no part of international thinking before World War II; the idea may have arisen with decolonization after World War II, but it has since become a general obligation. For various poor countries, there is a club of donors, most of whom have no previous colonial relation to the country in question. The United States is a willing participant in these clubs, or has been until now. Things may change under President Trump.

The United States, despite its prickly insistence on untrammeled sovereignty, does accept obligations set by international organizations, such as the right to asylum, under which many immigrants come. Initially, this was sharply circumscribed: we accepted asylees insofar as they furthered our Cold War with Russia or our conflict with Cuba, or insofar as their desperate condition owed something to American policies, such as the failure of American foreign and military policy in Vietnam. But, as mentioned before, the obligation has become more general over time.

Yet another oddity of our immigration policy illustrates the increasing hold of the idea of international obligation on this proud and independent country. Consider the "diversity" provision in immigration law. We know why it came into effect; the immigration law of 1965, which favored relatives of citizens, also disfavored immigration from countries from which immigrants had come a long time ago and for whom close family relations had frayed, and this affected Ireland particularly. The "diversity" provision, which permits persons in countries that provided few immigrants to apply for visas in an international lottery, was designed to make it possible for more Irish to come. Its effect over time, however, has been to make it possible for more Bangladeshis, Nigerians, and other Africans and Asians to come. This was no part of its intention, but the law has not been changed or abandoned as a result. It becomes an exemplification of the idea that all peoples have a claim on entering the United States and becoming part of the country, a claim which cannot be limited by differences of religion or race or by lack of connection to the ethnic and religious groups that have played a central role in the making of the United States.

These disparate policies and changes bear the common characteristic that we increasingly accept the idea that we have an obligation to the poorest of the globe and that we are bound by an emerging moral and ethical code in dealing with the peoples of the world. How this actually works itself out in policy would take us far afield, and many find the expression of this commitment to universal ethical and moral standards and international human rights hypocritical, but the fact remains that the words expressing such a responsibility were pronounced until recently by the most authoritative voices representing America, our Presidents. This had to reflect itself in our immigration policy, and thus we, and other democratic and free countries of the developed world, increasingly abandoned the right to choose immigrants for the purpose of molding or controlling the racial and ethnic character of the country. This is a surprising development indeed.

The increasing weight of a regime of international human rights, raised for all people whatever their legal status or citizenship, must also affect our thinking about the difference between legal and illegal immigrants, the issue raised in the chapter by Pickus and Skerry. Our two chapters on the moral and ethical aspects of immigration both agree that a limited political community with its own defined rules, and a fundamental obligation to its own members, is a morally and ethically legitimate social form, not simply a means of selfishly excluding others outside it. But as the Pickus–Skerry chapter indicates, it is hard to consider the overwhelming majority of illegal immigrants – who come to seek work in industries and areas eager to employ them, to provide sustenance to families back home, and to escape difficult economic and political conditions, and so many of whom establish families and in effect become good citizens, even without the status of citizenship – as simply criminals and lawbreakers, and even those specifically employed to enforce the law and control the borders do not often so consider them.

Contemplate another change which both bears on the issue of the steady expansion of moral and ethical concerns and which may also affect our thinking about illegal immigrants. We have seen in the last few decades a surprising change in our conception of and the legal status of citizenship. We think properly of American citizenship as a treasured and exclusive status. The oath of citizenship specifically gives up all previous allegiances, yet we increasingly recognize the status of dual citizenship, not only the dual citizenship that is the result of being born in the United States to immigrant parents whose native countries grant citizenship to the children of their nationals born abroad, but also the dual citizenship of mature individuals who have maintained their citizenship in their native country. Many nations allow their citizens to maintain citizenship even when they become citizens of the United States.

In effect, we recognize today not only the sentimental and familial ties that inevitably bind immigrants to their native countries, but we also recognize – if their native countries permit it – the legal status of citizenship in a foreign country, even when that person has become a citizen of the United States. Depending on the country, such citizenship may permit voting in its elections, even though that dual citizen also votes in elections in the United States, and may include running for and taking office in the native country.

This development is often a subject of outrage by those following it, and indeed were these possibilities of dual citizenship embodied in legislation it is hard to believe Congress would accept them. The expansion of the status of dual citizenship and the ability without danger to American naturalization to take up duties of citizenship in a foreign nation (serving it in elected or appointed positions, serving in its armed forces, voting in its elections, etc.) is the result of Supreme Court decisions which have rejected the harsher and more exclusive version of American citizenship – decisions which Congress has not seen it necessary to overrule, as it probably could.

I mention this development and its possible bearing on our thinking about the difference between legal and illegal immigrants because it reflects, to my mind, the ascendancy of more complex ideas of citizenship and how people might relate to their mixed allegiances than we often find in the stark contrast of legal versus illegal immigration. Among illegal immigrants, there is certainly criminality aside from the specific fact of breaking the laws on entry or remaining, and that should and does concern us (whether there is more or less than among legal immigrants is not a question I have seen addressed). But many illegal immigrants we know are visitors who have overstayed the legal period of their stay, students who are not in the specific status of studenthood that makes them legal, and persons caught in the complexities of immigration law. Many of those who apply for the immigration diversity lottery are in residence in the United States in some status short of legal residency, and apply for the lottery in the distant chance that they may win and legalize their status. (If they are so lucky, I believe the previous condition of illegality does not affect them as winners entitled to legal residency.)

Of course, the major impact in our thinking about illegality comes from the disappointment of the hopes of the 1986 Immigration Reform and Control Act. We thought that granting amnesty to the existing illegal immigrants, only three million or so at the time, and imposing restrictions on the employment of illegal immigrants would dry up the supply and bring the problem to an end. It turned out that our amnesty was successful, with 2.7 million foreigners put on the path to U.S. citizenship, but our constraints on the employment of illegal immigrants were full of holes. Employers benefiting from the labor power of illegal immigrants had enough influence to prevent really effective restrictions on their employment. And did the rest of us – the American people – really want such controls? Did we not benefit from them as gardeners, painters, roofers, handymen, nannies, and the like? Is it not clear that the only solution to the illegal immigrant problem, if there is any, is in effect to legalize the illegal? I believe our more tolerant society will not deport 10 million illegals, or any substantial part of them, many of whom are the parents and husbands and wives of American citizens. Despite President Trump, I believe we will not accept the costs, in the form of a huge increase in numbers of border police, and in a huge increase in inconvenience for the millions of citizens, immigrants, and visitors crossing the borders daily, or in the costs of building a two-thousand-mile wall, that a really serious effort to effectively seal the borders would require. We once did deport hundreds of thousands, but our sense of the proper and legitimate behavior of government has changed, and I believe we will not accept, as a people, the inevitable cruelty and heartlessness that the physical removal of illegal immigrants would cause or the economic losses and inconvenience that such a radical reduction in the labor force working the fields and hotels and restaurants and homes and factories would cause.

What do Americans really want in immigration? The ideology – see the inscription on the *Statue of Liberty* – which welcomes the unfortunate and the striving – says "more." The pragmatic judgment as to personal self-interest generally says, for many of us, "more." But there are strong motivations to say "less" when we consider the impact of immigrants on any neighborhood and the inevitable conflict between the known, the stable, the expected, and the changes that immigration brings. This leaves aside the still-powerful, if minority (and somewhat underground), point of view that America should remain a white man's country and that its ethnic and racial composition should not undergo radical change.

The conflict is, in strictly comprehensible political science terms, between those with a strong interest in more immigrants, for economic reasons or for reasons of familial sentiment or group attachment, and a more diffuse general feeling that the United States has enough immigrants, and less would be better. In such a situation, the specific and powerfully motivated interests overwhelm the diffuse opposition. But this balance may change. One reason it may change – and indeed is already changing to some degree – is the sharp rise in fears of terrorist attack following 9/11 and the subsequent attacks on American soil in Chattanooga, San Bernardino, Orlando, and other U.S. cities. The impact of this quantum jump in security concerns is not discussed in these chapters, but it has already affected the number of students coming from abroad to study in the United States, an important source of immigrants that has shown the first substantial drop since World War II as a result of the greater difficulty in getting visas to study here. It has also undoubtedly reduced the number of visitors – some part of whom overstay and become illegal immigrants and some part of whom become legal immigrants in the end – because of the increased difficulty in getting visas. Muslims coming from many countries are under specific suspicion, but less understandably our immigration authorities are not very good at making distinctions, and a turbaned Sikh or a distinguished Parsee Indian author responding to an invitation to lecture in an American university, and indeed almost anyone seeking to enter the United States today, is likely to find as much difficulty as a potential Egyptian student.

The balance between pro- and anti-immigration forces is delicate and shifting. In the 1990s, we saw some legislation affecting the public benefits immigrants could receive. Many thought that this signaled a new anti-immigration phase, but it did not: Neither legal nor illegal immigration dropped, and benefits were restored for many immigrants. I believe the changes I have referred to above, in the form of the greater power in international affairs of concern for the poor and the abused, and the greater tolerance and reduction of racist attitudes within the United States, are permanent changes, with a permanent impact on our immigration policies. But they do not mean the ebb and flow of attitudes affecting immigration policy has ceased, as we have seen in the election of President Trump. These will respond to large events, such as an increase in terrorism and an awareness of the dangers of extremism among some part of immigrants, or to large changes in the economy. We see this conflict in attitudes not only between different groups and interests, but in the same people: The homeowner who is happy to find immigrant workers who will paint his house for less will also be annoyed at the group of day laborers in the center of town waiting for those who would employ them for the day. The American who says, "Deport illegal immigrants" will also say, "Not the one who comes to take care of my children." This matter will play itself out, and will be influenced by changes in our sense of security and in our economy, but I think we will continue to be affected by a long change in attitudes which is reducing the boundaries between "us" and "them," those within the polity and those outside it, those deserving rights to decent human treatment and those to whom we owe no obligation.

Acknowledgments: First and Second Editions

SECOND EDITION

I am deeply grateful for the many people who encouraged me to produce a second edition of *Debating Immigration*. Since I edited the 2007 volume, a number of changes have occurred, including the retirement of my long-term Cambridge University Press editor, Lewis Bateman, who skillfully guided me through three earlier projects. The second edition could not have been published without the support of people like Nathan Glazer, who at age 94, wrote the Foreword. I am indebted to the collaborators and the secretaries and research assistants who worked on various aspects of the project. These include Renee Hawkins, Julie Gillespie, Ingrid Laubach, and Lori Ungurait at Vanderbilt University Law School. In addition, the following former Vanderbilt University Law students co-authored or rendered considerable research support: Gwendolyn Hauck and Virginia Yetter. Mike Towle, Dr. Mary Poplin, and Dr. Jeanie Roberson offered feedback on some of the chapters. Lastly, Jaymee Cole Westover, a *summa cum laude* graduate of Vanderbilt University's class of 2017, worked tirelessly during the final stages of this book. Ms. Westover, a political science and Spanish major, who plans to pursue graduate education at a major research university, provided research and editorial assistance.

FIRST EDITION

Carol M. Swain

This book is a collaborative enterprise made possible through the support of several organizations and a number of good people. Foremost amongst those to whom I am especially grateful is Lew Bateman, my friend and editor at Cambridge University Press. Lew's unflagging support and his wise and steady guidance saw this project through to completion. Equally indispensable to the completion of this project has been the generous support of Robert P. George, Director of the James Madison Program in American Ideals and Institutions at Princeton University. I want to thank Vanderbilt University students and faculty assistants who helped with the project. Lastly, I want to express my deep gratitude to the authors of the essays who produced work of the highest quality and substance.

Introduction

Déjà Vu

Carol M. Swain

Unfortunately, immigration lends itself to lawlessness. The benefits are great; the tickets are scarce; administrative discretion is wide; political intervention is commonplace; and the judicial system governing immigration is slow and often lacking in credibility – Lawrence Fuchs, 1985.[1]

For it is hardly likely that the American people and its representatives will live indefinitely with the present situation in which no effective measures to control illegal immigration exists and we are divided on the question of what principles should govern our efforts to control immigration. No policy set by Congress, or the Executive, or even the courts – though their interventions have affected policy deeply – now truly control "whom we shall welcome" – Nathan Glazer, 1985.[2]

"The more things change, the more they stay the same" comes from a French proverb. It captures well an aspect of the political complexity surrounding efforts to reform United States' immigration law and policy. Lawrence Fuchs and Nathan Glazer penned the words in the epigraph after the Reagan Administration era's Simpson/Mazzoli bill failed to survive the conference process. Simpson/Mazzoli was supposed to fix the problems caused by the previous grand effort of 19 years earlier to reform immigration. It failed.

Before delving into background material and an overview of the current immigration situation, it is useful to review the language and terminology that shapes immigration discussions in the United States and, in some cases, other parts of the world. Readers of this volume will encounter different terminology from the scholars, activists, and policy experts who have contributed their expertise to this volume. In my chapters, I have chosen to use the official United States government designations to refer to individuals in the country without proper documentation.[3] Other contributors have made different decisions about how they refer to various populations. The Department of Homeland Security's definitions below depict how the government characterizes the population:

Alien
Any person not a citizen or national of the United States. "Foreign national" is a synonym and used outside of statutes when referring to noncitizens of the U.S.

Illegal Alien
Also known as an "Undocumented Alien," is an alien who has entered the United States illegally and is deportable if apprehended, or an alien who entered the United States legally but who has fallen 'out of status' and is deportable...

Lawful Permanent Residents
Also known as "green card" holders, are noncitizens who are lawfully authorized to live permanently within the United States.

In this volume, I use the government designation of illegal alien to refer to non-green card holders who are in the country without legal papers. Other contributions might refer to these as undocumented immigrants, unauthorized foreigners, undocumented citizens, or just plain immigrants. Legally, the term immigrant refers to a person who enters another country for the purpose of taking up permanent residence. The U.S legally admits foreigners by granting them one of two types of visas: immigrant and non-immigrant.

The terms "asylee" and "refugees" have their own special meanings as described below:

Asylee
A foreign national in the United States or at a port of entry who is unable or unwilling to return to his or her country of nationality, or to seek the protection of that country because of persecution or a well-founded fear of persecution. Persecution or the fear thereof must be based on religion, nationality, membership in a particular social group or political opinion.

Refugee
Generally, any person outside his or her country of nationality who is unable or unwilling to return to that country because of persecution or a well-founded fear of persecution based on the person's race, religion, nationality, membership in a particular social group, or political opinion. For a legal definition of refugee, see section 101(a)(42) of the Immigration and Nationality Act (INA).

Now that we have addressed terminology, we can return to an overview of immigration history and politics since the turn of the last century. We have had mixed success with resolving immigration challenges in America and abroad.

After more than a century of grappling with immigration problems and successfully passing only three major legislative Acts (the 1924 National Origins Act, the 1965 Immigration and Nationality Act, and the 1986 Immigration Reform and Control Act), our nation still contends with many direct and indirect problems related to the presence of millions of illegal aliens who reside within our borders. We face an ever-expanding set of concerns related to criminal behavior, national security, refugee and asylee policy, family reunification, birthright citizenship, guestworker programs, human trafficking, and birth tourism. At the state and federal level, we fight over how to treat the children of these illegal aliens: How should we treat the American-born children of illegal aliens who have deportation orders, and how should we treat the foreign-born children of illegal aliens who attend our schools, churches, synagogues, and mosques? Should unaccompanied minors and foreign-born children of illegal aliens be immune from deportation? Should they receive in-state tuition and admission preferences at public colleges and universities?

The list of immigration-related concerns and issues seems endless. It touches many areas, including tax policy and entitlement programs such as Social Security and Medicaid. Among the perennial problems is that no one knows with certainty how many illegal aliens reside in the United States. Writing more than 30 years ago, Lawrence Fuchs noted that a commonly repeated guesstimate was twelve million, a number he dismissed. Fuchs concluded: "There are currently no reliable estimates of the number of illegal aliens in the country or the net volume of illegal residents in the United States." That about sums up the situation in the second decade of the twenty-first century as well. We still conveniently throw out guesstimates of 11 or 12 million illegal aliens when we attempt to guess how many people reside in the country without legal authorization.

Since the publication of this volume's first edition, Congress in 2005, 2006, 2007, and 2013 failed to pass major immigration reform bills, originating from different houses of Congress. The House Border Protection, Antiterrorism, and Illegal Immigration Control Act (H.R. 4437) was approved in 2005; but not taken up in the Senate. The Senate approved the Comprehensive Immigration Reform Act (S2611) on a 62–36 vote on May 25, 2006, but failed to approve the Comprehensive Immigration Reform Act of 2007 (S 1348) in 2007. The Senate in June 2013 approved the Border Security, Economic Opportunity, and Immigration Modernization Act of 2013 (S 744). The failure of immigration reform to move forward in Congress led President Barack Obama to push the limits of executive power with the implementation of Deferred Action for Childhood Arrivals (DACA) and, later, Deferred Action of Parents of Americans (DAPA) in 2014 (Swain, Chapter 12).

AN OVERVIEW OF A SHIFTING LANDSCAPE

In November 2016, the immigration landscape shifted once again with the election of Donald J. Trump as the incoming president. Trump campaigned as an immigration restrictionist, who promised to have Mexico pay for the construction of a border wall between Mexico and the United States. Trump also vowed to protect American citizens from terrorists and criminal aliens. Statements made during his historic campaign even came back to haunt him as he attempted to follow the pattern of executive action and prosecutorial discretion instituted by President Obama. Federal court injunctions against an executive "travel ban" led the Trump Administration to appeal to the Supreme

Court, which granted a measure of relief, allowing the most vital parts of his executive order pertaining to selected Muslim nations to stand.

The following is a list of major developments that have shaped immigration procedures and practices since 2006.

- The election and re-election of Barack Obama in 2008 and 2012 as a liberal, activist president.
- Both the expansion and restriction of immigration federalism, which dictates what state and local governments can and cannot do to assist the federal government in undertaking its role to enforce the nation's immigration laws.
- An unprecedented increase in the use of executive action and prosecutorial discretion to bypass Congress and implement rules and practices that slowed deportation and expanded immigrants' rights.
- A surge in unaccompanied minors crossing the southern border.
- Chaos in the Middle East and a destabilization that has led to an increase in refugees from Arab nations to Europe.
- A rise in Islamic terrorism within the United States and around the world.
- A steep decline in the percentage of working-age Americans in the labor force, either employed or unemployed, which was at a 36-year low (62.4 percent) in September 2015, but had risen to 63.1 percent by September 2017.[4] The record low was 58.10 percent in 1954.
- The election of Donald J. Trump in 2016 as an immigration restrictionist president.

As I show in Chapter 12 of the Law and Policy part of this edition, President Obama established a precedent of using executive actions to implement his policy goals. Acting unilaterally, he expanded presidential power in areas related to healthcare and immigration reform. Most prominently, at least in the area of immigration, was the creative use of executive powers to bypass Congress and unilaterally institute the Deferred Action for Childhood Arrivals (DACA) Program in 2012 and Deferred Action of Parents of Americans and Lawful Permanent Residents (DAPA) in 2014. Challenged in the courts, DAPA has been withdrawn by the Trump Administration.

Federalism refers to the constitutional division of power between the national government and the sovereign states. As I edited the first edition of this book, states and localities had begun taking action to resolve the problem themselves. However, immigration federalism came to a screeching halt in 2012 after the U.S. Supreme Court reaffirmed the position of federal dominance in its ruling in *Arizona* v. *United States*.[5] In reaction to broad legislation passed by the state of Arizona, which raised concerns about civil rights and civil liberties violations, the Court reaffirmed the federal government's broad power over immigration and alien status (Swain and Yetter, Chapter 11).

During the Obama Administration, we saw an increase in executive actions and prosecutorial discretion that affected the status of legal and illegal aliens as well as refugees and asylees. The Administration used its discretion to implement policies such as "catch and release." This allowed the border patrol to apprehend and release persons caught entering the U.S. illegally and to shift resources that allowed it to improve some of the conditions affecting persons in the country illegally. In addition, after the failure of the Schumer/Rubio Senate bill, thousands of unaccompanied minors, mostly from the Central American countries of El Salvador, Guatemala, and Honduras, streamed into the U.S., and most were allowed to remain. Data from the Center for Latin American and Latino Studies capture the magnitude of the problem:

During fiscal year (FY) 2014, U.S. Customs and Border Protection (CBP) reported the apprehension of 68,541 unaccompanied minors – a striking 77 percent increase from the previous fiscal year and a 429 percent increase from just 15,949 UAC apprehensions in FY2011. Family unit apprehensions along the southwest border also skyrocketed 461 percent, from 14,855 in FY2013 to 68,445 in FY2014.[6]

Unfortunately, the placements of these minors were not always with parents and relatives in the U.S. Since some of this influx occurred in late spring and summer, one can only imagine the strain placed on local school budgets as administrators adjusted to the challenges of having to accommodate unexpected pupils and language barriers.

Chaos related to the 2010 Arab Spring that destabilized parts of the Middle East has had a profound impact on America. It created a critical need to address the refugee crisis that came out of the violent unrest in that part of the world. Under President Obama, a record number of Muslim refugees came to the United States in 2016, constituting 46 percent of the total[7] number of refugees entering the U.S. Fear of Islamic terrorism on American soil affects how some Americans view Muslims. It explains their receptivity to presidential candidate Donald Trump's vow to institute a Muslim ban until refugees could be properly vetted.

Since 9/11, and particularly in recent years, there has been an increase in Islamic terrorism in the U.S. and in Europe. Political scientist John Mueller compiled an extensive dataset on attacks in the United States since 9/11.[8] High-profile attacks at the Boston Marathon (2013), and in large and small cities such as Chattanooga, Tennessee (2015), Orlando, Florida (2016), San Bernardino, California (2016), Saint Cloud, Minnesota (2016), and Fort Lauderdale, Florida (2017), along with the attacks in European nations, have fueled national security concerns. In Chapter 9, Rogers Smith points out that U.S. officials have taken many actions to reassure those who fear immigrants for cultural or national security reasons, yet have not taken many substantive actions likely to lead to significant declines in immigration.

After the November 2015 attacks in Paris killed 130 people and wounded 368, Trump called for a database of Muslims entering the United States. A few weeks later, a terrorist attack in San Bernardino killed 14 and critically wounded 22. Trump quickly called for a temporary ban on all Muslims entering the United States. His controversial stance evoked criticism from foreign leaders and led some to argue that his remarks should disqualify him from serving as president. These words would later haunt the newly elected president when they were cited in a legal brief challenging the then-president's executive orders that placed a temporary ban on Muslims from seven nations. Injunctions from lower federal courts led to a Supreme Court intervention which affirmed presidential power.

The American workforce is undergoing dramatic demographic changes, with fewer native workers participating in the labor force. The final job report for the Obama Administration, released in December 2016, revealed that more than 95 million Americans are no longer in the labor force. Labor force participation stood at 62.7 percent, barely up from a 38-year low of 62.4 percent in September 2015. Some of the labor force dropouts have given up on looking for work and others have chosen not to participate in the labor force. For those who would like to work, the outlook is far from rosy.

Research by Steven Camarota and Karen Zeigler (Chapter 3) shows that a third of the net new jobs created between 2000 and 2017 went to immigrants, and that the native population has never recovered from job losses associated with past recessions. In addition, research by John Skrentny (Chapter 1) presents further unsettling news about employment discrimination and its impact on low-skilled white and black native workers. Skrentny found that employers nationwide preferred immigrants over native workers because they believe job skills vary based on race and ethnicity. Employers preferred Asians and Hispanics over white and black workers. Other unsettling news for native workers comes from data showing a decline in the percentage of Americans willing to work. Charles Murray has found a growing percentage of white working-class men who prefer to stay home rather than work. Murray reports in his study of Fishtown that, between 1960 and 2000, the percentage of able-bodied white men who were not in the labor force grew from 9 percent to 30 percent. Much of the problem came from men not interested in working.[9] His findings are echoed in a similar study by Nicholas Eberstadt, *Men without Work: America's Invisible Crisis*.[10] Eberstadt reports that about 10 million men between the ages of 25 and 54 have left the labor force and are now addicted to drugs, porn, and/or television and video games. Of course, we have no way of knowing the size of this population and how many were never in the workforce. Their lifestyle is made possible by government entitlement programs and the generosity of relatives. These men resemble the poverty-stricken, lower-class whites described in J. D. Vance's *Hillbilly Elegy*, which portrays a value system and a reality of hard-core unemployable whites who have no interest in living by the rules and norms of most of society. There are clearly jobs, some of them decent-paying, available for men who want to work.[11]

Indeed, both white and black Americans find themselves confronting new realities, such as the possibility that elites have little concern about the realities of the native population. A new reality for white Americans, which undoubtedly played a small role in President Trump's election, is a higher mortality rate for whites and a growing sense of hopelessness. Anne Case and Angus Deaton referred to these early deaths as "deaths of despair." According to their findings:

Around the turn the century, after decades of improvement, all-cause mortality rates among white non-Hispanic men and women in middle age stopped falling in the US, and began to rise... By 2014, rising mortality in midlife, led by these "deaths of despair," was large enough to offset mortality gains for children and the elderly.[12]

In addition, the authors surmise:

[D]eaths of despair come from a long-standing process of cumulative disadvantage for those with less than a college degree. The story is rooted in the labor market, but involves many aspects of life, including health in childhood, marriage, child rearing, and religion. Although we do not see the supply of opioids as the fundamental factor, the prescription of opioids for chronic pain added fuel to the flames, making the epidemic much worse than it otherwise would have been.[13]

Clearly, this is a new and changing environment for Caucasian Americans who now face greater uncertainty about their future and that of their children and grandchildren as they adapt to changing circumstances in a nation that once offered Anglo-Americans enormous privileges.

THE GENESIS OF THE IDEA

In 2005, I was new to the study of immigration. My interest in the subject was piqued in the late 1990s and early 2000s as I conducted research for my book *The New White Nationalism in America: Its Challenge to Integration* (2002), in which I forecast the rise of what now brands itself as the alt-right movement.[14] I commissioned interviews of key figures in what has variously been styled as the white nationalist, white supremacist, white protest, or white rights movements in America. I was interested in exploring the background of these individuals, how they came to hold their views, and their positions on key race-related issues of the day. Repeatedly, the interviewees offered harsh commentary on the high level of legal and illegal immigration flowing into America from "Third-World nations" and the failure of the U.S. government to stem this tide – a development the interviewees perceived as a threat to Euro-American values and culture. Although many of the views expressed were openly racist, the respondents did not seem to care how critics might perceive them.

After listening to their arguments and watching events unfold in border states (such as the formation of the Minute Men and other militia groups), it became increasingly clear that a situation was developing in America in which the racist right was framing the debate on serious and potent issues regarding immigration and naturalization. Although these issues are of great concern to many Americans, they were largely ignored; an open debate was being suppressed by many people in the mainstream who feared being dismissed as racist. Accordingly, a very limited public discussion was being monopolized by a small minority on the racist right. This was effectively silencing legitimate conversations that ought to have taken place in the public realm among more mainstream thinkers. Those mainstream conversations would be about the changing demographics of the nation and the continued existence and embracing of immigration policies that many Americans believe placed the needs and concerns of new immigrants above those of the native-born.

My instincts about these issues were seemingly confirmed in November 2005, when I received an e-mail from a stranger that I refer to here as "Martha."

Martha described herself as a 65-year-old white woman who had recently joined the California Minute Men. This was a group of citizens organized to help stem what Martha described as an invasion of her beloved country. Martha wrote me to lament the fact that a 15-year friendship with a black neighbor ended on the day that she asked her black friend to join her at the border. With horror, disdain, and anger, the black friend exclaimed: "I don't do anything to help white people." Martha was crushed. She is not a racist, she explained to me in her e-mail. She does not hate Mexicans – her husband of 23 years is Mexican-American. Rather, her e-mail expressed rage at illegal immigration and at the failure of blacks to join the fight against it. After all, she argued, it is their country, too, that is being invaded.

Martha's frustration had risen to the point where she was willing to stay up all night patrolling the border in the belief, or hope, that her lone act, multiplied by the acts of several hundred others, might actually reduce illegal immigration. Her e-mail expressed fear about not wanting her children and grandchildren to be forced to learn Spanish in order to live and work in their own country. She decried the 14th Amendment's guarantee of citizenship by birth for those who entered the country illegally. Martha also lamented the drain on local goods and services that she claims have forced hospital emergency rooms in Los Angeles to close. She ended her e-mail with the capitalized words: GOD BLESS AMERICA.

Martha's fears might appear extreme, but they are not without some foundation. Immigration is and was a growing concern for many Americans. Moreover, it remains a critical issue even today.

Announcing his entry into the 2016 presidential contest, Trump brought immigration to the forefront of public discussion when he said he would build a wall to keep illegal aliens from entering the country. In that same speech, Trump threw political correctness to the wind by accusing some Mexicans of coming to the U.S. for nefarious purposes:

When Mexico sends its people, they're not sending their best. They're not sending you. They're not sending you. They're sending people that have lots of problems, and they're bringing those problems with them. They're bringing drugs. They're bringing crime. They're rapists. And some, I assume, are good people.[15]

The murder of Kate Steinle, on July 1, 2015, served to bolster support for Trump, and it forced other candidates to address the immigration crime problem. Her shooting death on Pier 14 in San Francisco led Congress to introduce and debate a bill called Kate's Law, which would add an additional mandatory prison sentence to illegal aliens who return to the U.S. to commit crimes after they have been deported.[16] As of July 2017, Kate's Law (H.R. 3004) has passed in the House of Representatives and is awaiting Senate action, along with a companion bill, "No Sanctuary for Criminals Act" (H.R. 3003), that would make it more difficult for sanctuary cities to flourish.[17]

A BRIEF OVERVIEW

Figure 0.1 depicts immigration growth between 1965 and 2015, and key legislative efforts, as well as the births of DACA and DAPA in 2012 and 2014, respectively, which occurred without legislative action. A sense of déjà vu comes from our knowledge that Congress has attempted to address the immigration problem with mixed results. In 1986, Congress passed the Immigration and Reform Control Act (IRCA),[18] and four years later it passed the 1990 Immigration Act.[19] Next came the Illegal Immigration Reform and Immigrant Responsibility Act of 1996 (IIRIRA).[20] Lastly came President Obama's executive orders giving temporary legal status to some classes of illegal immigrants. His orders have been blocked or rescinded by the Trump Administration. So far, each congressional Act or executive action has brought numerous unintended consequences. Douglas Massey argues that congressional policy since 1986 has been filled with contradictions. Rather than fix the problem, U.S. policies toward Mexico have made it less likely that illegal migrants from Mexico will return home of their own accord.[21] Massey and Pren, Chapter 8, provide an in-depth analysis of immigration from Latin America.

A close perusal of the graph further shows no real fluctuations between 2007 and 2015, despite the national recession that caused massive unemployment and layoffs for native workers.

THE IMMIGRANT PROTESTS OF THE 2000S

The 109th Congress tried to fix the immigration problem with a bill that could not muster the support needed to become a law. Repeatedly, members of Congress have introduced measures that have died in one or both houses of Congress. Momentum for the 2007 bill grew after hundreds of thousands of legal immigrants and illegal aliens engaged in mass protests during the spring of 2006. Breathtakingly large public demonstrations first occurred in April 2006, and again on May 1, 2006, when organizers ratcheted up the stakes by arranging a national boycott touted as "A Day Without Immigrants," intended to bring the U.S. economy to a crawl. Although the impact of the

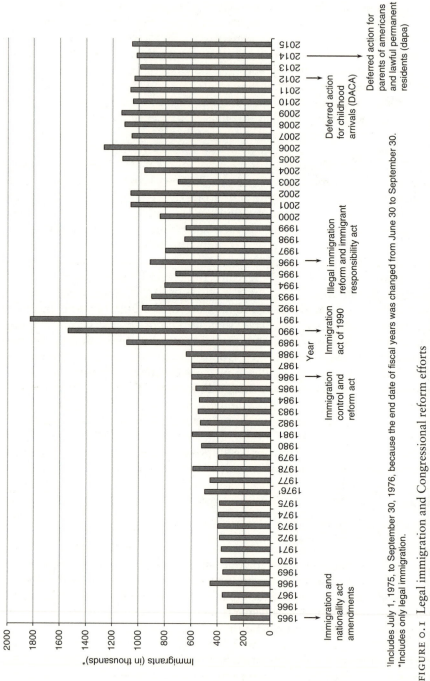

FIGURE 0.1 Legal immigration and Congressional reform efforts

Source: *Yearbook of Immigration Statistics 2015*, Available at www.dhs.gov/immigration-statistics/yearbook/2015

boycott was minimal, the new assertiveness made the immigration issue one that members of Congress could no longer ignore, especially after media images of angry protesters – many waving homeland flags – were broadcast into the homes of formerly indifferent Americans. The assertive image of illegal aliens demanding legal status stood in direct contradiction to media portraits of them as a frightened, docile people, cowering behind locked doors, not knowing if the next knock would bring deportation.

The initial politicization of illegal immigrants came with the Freedom Rides of October 2003, which mimicked the Black Freedom Rides of the 1960s. Thousands of protesters traveled to Washington, DC, to press their demands for better treatment. Many immigrants were upset about the perceived foot-dragging and promise-reneging in the interactions between President George W. Bush and then Mexican President Vicente Fox. What was once an auspicious climate for immigration reform had changed overnight in the wake of the terrorist attacks of September 11, 2001.

The 9/11 attacks, which killed almost 3,000 people, halted momentum for creating a new guestworker program with Mexico. National attention was shifted to border control and national security.[22] In 2003, the Immigration and Naturalization Service (INS) became part of several different units absorbed into a new Department of Homeland Security. Later, an activist Congress passed the Real ID Act of 2005, which created restrictions on political asylum, increased enforcement mechanisms, restricted some due process rights, and imposed federal restrictions on state driver's licenses for immigrants, making it more difficult for illegal aliens to utilize certain programs.

Following these events, the 2006 protests seemingly led to a backlash – although some argued they persuaded the Senate to pass a bill with amnesty in June 2006. Instead of making Americans more sympathetic to the plight of immigrants and aliens, the mass protests seemingly had the unintended consequence of directing public attention to negative economic and social spillover effects, such as the displacement of American workers, drains on public services, and overcrowded housing. Within days of the April 2006 protest, the Department of Homeland Security made headlines when it announced the arrest of eleven hundred illegal workers in a Texas pallet supply shop in Houston.[23] Since then, crackdowns, arrests, and mass deportations have frequently garnered headlines.

A March 2006 national survey, taken before the mass demonstrations of April and May that year, showed Americans conflicted over the immigration issue.[24] Fifty-two percent of Americans agreed that "immigrants today are a burden on our country because they take our jobs, housing, and healthcare." A majority of the public (also 52 percent) said that illegals should be made to go home; 40 percent of this group said they would support a program that would allow illegals to stay temporarily with a legal status.

Almost half of all Americans would have liked to see increased border patrols and tougher penalties for employers who violate the law by hiring illegals. The least amount of enthusiasm (9 percent) was shown for building walls along the border, and the most (76 percent) was shown for a proposal to create a national database that employers could use to check for employment verification and eligibility. Perhaps in recognition of Congress's past failures to improve the situation, 56 percent of Americans expressed more confidence in local government's ability to reform immigration than they did in (then) President George W. Bush (42 percent) and the major political parties. The Republican and Democratic Parties earned ratings of 45 and 53 percent, respectively, in answer to the question of who is best suited to reform immigration.

After the mass demonstrations, Hispanics reported a greater frequency of ethnic discrimination. Over half of all Hispanics surveyed (54 percent) by the Pew Hispanic Center reported an increase in discrimination as a result of the policy debate. While there might have been some backlash from the public, 63 percent of Hispanics thought that the pro-immigration marches signaled the beginning of a new social movement that would spur higher Hispanic voter turnout.[25] Although some immigrants spoke of the 2006 protests with pride and believed the protests advanced their cause, public opinion polls and the passage of numerous restrictive laws and ordinances in cities and states across the nation suggested otherwise (Swain and Yetter, Chapter 11; Pickus and Skerry, Chapter 10).

More recently, a 2017 Gallup poll revealed a persistent American worry about illegal immigration that was heightened among Trump voters, who were significantly more concerned about illegal immigration than Democrats.[26] Gallup reported that 59 percent of Americans said they worry "a great deal" or "a fair amount" about illegal immigration. The report stated this is typical of American attitudes over the past 17 years, except for the period between 2006 and 2011, when "roughly two-thirds of Americans expressed worry."

CHAPTER OVERVIEW AND STRUCTURE OF THE VOLUME

This edition is divided into four Parts: I Economics, Demographics, and Race; II Law and Policy; III Philosophy and Religion; and IV Cosmopolitanism: European Nations and Immigration.

Part I, Economics, Demographics, and Race, seeks to answer a number of pressing questions: In Chapter 1, John Skrentny asks, "How real is discrimination in the workplace? Do employers prefer immigrant labor to the labor of native-born blacks and whites? Are civil rights laws and protections adequate to protect working-class Americans?" In Chapter 2, Peter Skerry explores how we should view illegal aliens: Are they victims of economic and political failures? Are they criminals or would-be welfare recipients, or are they responsible agents who have made decisions in a complicated and risky environment? In Chapter 3, Steven Camarota and Karen Zeigler examine long-term employment growth between 2000 and 2017. They query, "Who were the losers and winners in the job competition?" In Chapter 4, Carol M. Swain looks at the Congressional Black Caucus and its representation of African Americans by asking, "How well are they doing in representing the preferences of the black rank-and-file?" In Chapter 5, Amitai Etzioni inquires whether Hispanic and Asian immigrants are doing more to reshape America in positive ways than blacks ever did.

Part II, Law and Policy, covers a myriad of issues involving legal and illegal immigrants, refugees, state and federal actions to address different aspects of the problem, and the increasing use of executive actions to bypass Congress.

In Chapter 6, Philip Cafaro examines a host of factors before making a progressive argument for immigration reduction. Cafaro asks, "What would a commonsense immigration policy look like? Would it take into consideration population growth, pollution, surplus labor, and the need to address income inequality?"

In Chapter 7, Carol M. Swain takes a look back at the thinking that surrounded the passage of the 1924 Immigration Act and the major aspects of the Trump proposal, before sharing her thoughts about what a comprehensive immigration reform bill might include. In Chapter 8, Doug Massey and Karen Pren look at the unintended consequences of U.S. immigration policy to Latin America: What explains the patterns of Mexican immigration? Why have we had so many surges since 1965?

In Chapter 9, Rogers M. Smith examines immigration policies and practices in the wake of 9/11 and the national security concerns that followed. Have we created an environment that is discriminatory toward immigrants and their legal rights? What, if anything, is the trade-off between national security and immigrant rights?

In Chapter 10, Noah Pickus and Peter Skerry raise questions about dichotomous terms such as "legal–illegal" and "citizenship–noncitizenship," in which the immigration debate has been framed. Is this approach misleading and does it inhibit creative public policy? Should we be focused on immigrants as good citizens or immigrants as good neighbors? While the current immigration debate asks whether immigrants can be good *citizens*, Pickus and Skerry argue that, to many Americans, the more immediately pressing question is whether immigrants can be good *neighbors*.

In Chapter 11, Virginia Yetter and Carol M. Swain examine federalism as it relates to immigration reform: What role, if any, should the states play when it comes to involvement in immigration politics? Does immigration federalism offer any hope for creative policy solutions for immigrants and citizens?

In Chapter 12, Carol M. Swain examines President Obama's use of executive actions to implement his immigration goals and how this compares with President Trump's efforts to do the same. When is it appropriate to use executive action to bypass Congress? What problems are posed by the creation and expansion of the Deferred Action for Childhood Arrivals (DACA) and the Deferred Action for Parents of Americans and Lawful Permanent Residents (DAPA)?

Part III, Philosophy and Religion, provides historical, religious, and moral guidance. In Chapter 13, James Edwards draws upon his perspective as a Christian congressional staffer to outline the principles that he believes should guide immigration policy. He seeks to answer questions such as the following: How should Christians think about immigration policy? What role does the Bible bestow on civil government when it comes to the preservation of the rule of law? Should the needs of foreigners be placed on an equal level with those of natives?

In Chapter 14, Stephen Macedo discusses the moral issues surrounding immigration in the U.S. and elsewhere. After discussing the debate between a "cosmopolitan" viewpoint that promotes shared citizenship and a universal obligation of distributive justice, he poses a "civic obligations" viewpoint that argues for the existence of special obligations among citizens. Should we adopt the cosmopolitan view or should we focus on fellow citizens in a self-governing political community? What weight should we give to the poorest of Americans as we weigh their needs against the needs of the global impoverished?

In Chapter 15, Elizabeth Cohen asks why America has not developed a coherent public philosophy to undergird its approach to immigration. What impact did the British common law have on American policymakers? What kinds of policy outputs can we expect in the future?

Part IV, Cosmopolitanism: European Nations and Immigration, examines different aspects of the new and changing reality for European nations:

In Chapter 16, Marc Morjé Howard and Sara Goodman examine citizenship policies and politics in Western Europe, asking "How important is political contestation to citizenship policy, and what role should political parties play in political mobilization?"

In Chapter 17, Susan F. Martin places international migration trends, causes, and consequences into the context of broader aspects of globalization: What is the relationship between movements of people and other facets of globalization, such as movements of capital and goods? What are the similarities and differences in those three elements of globalization?

In Chapter 18, Randall Hansen discusses the changed attitude, rhetoric, and posture toward immigration evident among major European states. Looking at population growth and the needs of the nation, Hansen asks, "How can Europe ensure the socioeconomic integration of such migrants, given its broad failure to integrate previous waves of migrants economically?" Second, he asks how can Europe ensure that the new migrants embrace the liberal democratic values institutionalized in Europe at the cost of much blood and "treasure"?

In Chapter 19, Louise Shelley and Camilo Pardo examine the large-scale migration into Europe today and which actors are responsible for smuggling human cargo. Questions include: How much does this rely on corruption? How are the migrants paying to be smuggled? Where are they coming from? To what extent are individuals coming as single males or as family members? What financial conditions does this smuggling impose on the migrants when they arrive in Europe?

In Chapter 20, Carol M. Swain gives an overview of the volume and highlights areas of agreement and disagreement. Overall, she emphasizes the importance of continued debate to find solutions that will lead to successful immigration reform.

The second edition of *Debating Immigration* goes beyond the earlier edition to explore new ideas on a perennial problem. Nevertheless, it remains true that a major strength of *Debating Immigration* lies in the willingness of its contributors to tackle such controversial issues as racial discrimination, religion, and the moral basis for immigration restrictions at home and abroad. The volume offers a diversity of viewpoints and backgrounds, and it offers approaches that range from economics to demographics to moral and religious perspectives. In addition, the volume examines new issues related to the president's use of executive orders to bypass a foot-dragging Congress as well as the contested areas of immigration federalism.

Given the many anthologies on immigration, it is appropriate to explain why this updated volume is needed. First, the immigration scene has changed dramatically over the past decade. Race and religion, long neglected in immigration debates, continue to play a more central role in public discussions. This is particularly true concerning the impact of legal and illegal immigration on African Americans and, now, low-wage, low-skilled white Americans. In the past, discussions of immigration and religion have often been focused on the Catholic Church's more universal approach, while ignoring or belittling as racist any restrictionist viewpoints emanating from Protestants.

This volume is a wholehearted effort to address neglected areas in the public debate. It should be noted, however, that the contributors to *Debating Immigration* continue to have widely differing views on a range of issues. We do not pretend to have definitive answers to the questions we raise; rather it is our desire to stimulate an open and vigorous debate about immigration and citizenship. We would encourage more public forums in which opponents could get together and share their views, as we have done here.

NOTES

1. L. Fuchs, "The Search for a Sound Immigration Policy: A Personal View," in Nathan Glazer (ed.), *Clamor at the Gates* (New York: ICS Press), p. 22.
2. N. Glazer (ed.), *Clamor at the Gates* (New York: ICS Press, 1985), p. 11.
3. Official Department of Homeland Security, Glossary Terms. Available at: www .uscis.gov/i-9-central/customer-support/glossary-terms, accessed February 12, 2018.
4. Bureau of Labor Statistics, 2007–2017. Available at: https://goo.gl/p440d7; "United States Labor Force Participation, 1950–2017, *Trading Economics*. Available at: https:// tradingeconomics.com/united-states/labor-force-participation-rate, accessed February 12, 2018.
5. *Arizona* v. *United States*, 567 U.S. ___ (2012). Available at: www.supremecourt .gov/opinions/11pdf/11-182.pdf, accessed February 12, 2018.

6. D. Stinchcomb and A. Hershberg, "The Crisis in Context: UACS and Trends in Central American Migration," Center for Latin American & Latino Studies, 2014, p. 6.

7. P. Connor, "U.S. Admits a Record Number of Muslim Refugees in 2016," Pew Research Center. Available at: www.pewresearch.org/fact-tank/2016/10/05/u-s-admits-record-number-of-muslim-refugees-in-2016/, accessed February 12, 2018.

8. J. Mueller, "Terrorism since 9/11: The American Cases". Available at: http://politicalscience.osu.edu/faculty/jmueller/since.html, accessed February 12, 2018.

9. C. Murray, *Coming Apart: The State of White America, 1960–2010* (New York: Crown Forum, 2012), pp. 220–221.

10. N. Ebenstat, *Men without Work: America's Invisible Crisis* (West Conshohocken, PA: Templeton Press, 2016).

11. J. D. Vance, *Hillbilly Elegy: A Memoir of a Family and Culture in Crisis* (New York: HarperCollins, 2016).

12. A. Case and A. Deaton, "Mortality and Morbidity in the 21st Century," BPEA Conference Draft, 23–24 March 2017, Brookings Institution. Available at: www.brookings.edu/wp-content/uploads/2017/03/6_casedeaton.pdf, p. 3, accessed February 12, 2018; See also, A. Case and A. Deaton, "Rising Morbidity and Mortality in Midlife Among White Nonhispanics Americans in the 21st Century," (December 8, 2015) 112.49 *PNAS*, 15078–83; K. D. Kochanek, E. Arias, and B. A. Bastian, *The Effect of Changes in Selected Age-Specific Causes of Death on Non-Hispanic White Life Expectancy between 2000 and 2014*, National Center for Health Statistics data brief no. 250.

13. Case and Deaton, "Mortality and Morbidity in the 21st Century," pp. 3–4.

14. C. M. Swain, *The New White Nationalism in America: Its Challenge to Integration* (New York: Cambridge University Press, 2002).

15. D. J. Trump, "Announcement Speech," Time.com, June 16, 2015. Available at: http://time.com/3923128/donald-trump-announcement-speech/, accessed February 12, 2018.

16. S. A. Miller and A. Blake, "Congress Gives Kate's Law Another Chance to Crack Down on Deportees who Return to U.S." *The Washington Times*, January 6, 2017. Available at: www.washingtontimes.com/news/2017/jan/6/kate-steinle-kates-law-congress-gets-another-chance/, accessed February 12, 2018.

17. "Pending Legislation," American Immigration Lawyers Association. Available at: www.aila.org/advo-media/whats-happening-in-congress/pending-legislation, accessed July 2, 2017.

18. IRCA included four main provisions designed to address illegal immigration. It instituted employer sanctions on those who hire illegals, legalized long-term undocumented residents, legalized special agricultural workers, and protected US citizens and permanent residents against discrimination that might come from employers seeking to avoid sanctions.

19. The 1990 Immigration Act raised the immigration ceiling to 700,000 and created preferences for relatives of U.S. residents or citizens and foreigners with specialized skills.

20. IIRIRA made it much easier to deport illegal residents by restricting the judicial review of administrative removal orders and by limiting appeal processes.

21. D. Massey, D. Jorge, and N. Malone, *Beyond Smoke and Mirrors: Immigration Policy and Global Economic Integration* (New York: The Russell Sage Foundation, 2002).

22. Legislation passed after September 11, 2001, expanded the grounds for inadmissibility and deportation, allowed for the detention of suspected terrorists or people coming from areas of the country known to harbor terrorists, allowed nationality to play a larger role in decision-making, imposed more restrictions on foreign visitors, imposed new limits and barriers on refugees, restricted public access to removal hearings, and expanded the law-enforcement role of states and localities.

23. E. Lipton, "U.S. Crackdown Set Over Hiring of Immigrants," *The New York Times*, September 21, 2006, p. 1.

24. A. Kohut, R. Suro, S. Keeter, C. Doherty, and G. Escobar, "America's Immigration Quandary," Pew Research Center, March 30, 2006. Available at: www.pewhispanic.org/2006/03/30/americas-immigration-quandary/, accessed February 12, 2018.

25. Kohut, *et al.*, "America's Immigration Quandary," p. ii.

26. J. M. Jones, "In U.S., Worry About Illegal Immigration Steady," Gallup, March 20, 2017. Available at: www.gallup.com/poll/206681/worry-illegal-immigration-steady.aspx?g_source=IMMIGRATION&g_medium=topic&g_campaign=tiles, accessed February 12, 2018.

PART I

ECONOMICS, DEMOGRAPHICS, AND RACE

1

Race, Immigration and Civil Rights Law in the Low-Skilled Workplace

John D. Skrentny

Despite the long-standing national controversies regarding the impacts of immigration on the employment rates of native workers, social science research in this area regularly finds little or no effect. Overall wage impacts are also found to be very small. A recent, high-profile report of the National Academies of Sciences added more weight to this commonly held view that, on the aggregate, the economic impact of immigration is complex, difficult to measure, but nevertheless quite small.[1]

However, the controversies persist, perhaps because no one lives "on the aggregate" – everyone lives their own particular experience. And the same National Academies report noted that, at least in the short term, particular native populations were more likely to experience negative wage effects (specifically, high school dropouts) and reduced employment hours (teenagers).[2] How are we to understand these processes where some of the most economically vulnerable are shown to experience harm from immigration, and why, with a host of employment laws and regulations on the books, do the processes occur?

My contention here is that it is not immigrants themselves who are having the impact. Rather, the problem stems from employers' perceptions – and their acting on these perceptions – which then impacts opportunities in the nation's low-skilled workplaces. Specifically, those whom employers prefer to hire, and the reasons they prefer some workers over others, are a complex mix of perceptions of the value of different racial groups and also immigrant/native statuses, and, at the low end of the market, these perceptions especially limit opportunities for African Americans. Because these perceptions treat each worker's race as a *reality* that is relevant to the day-to-day operation of the workplace, they can be understood to be part of a strategy of management that I call *racial realism*. Relatedly, strategies of management that treat each worker's immigration status as real and relevant I call *immigrant realism*.

In this chapter, I consider these management strategies in low-skilled work contexts across the country but where unions are absent or in decline, and many jobs have become increasingly precarious. My focus is on the racial and immigrant realist perceptions and practices, and how they relate to existing law.

I argue that race- and immigration-status-relevant hiring and placement of workers is occurring in the U.S. today despite the passage of celebrated laws banning discrimination in employment. Title VII of the Civil Rights Act of 1964 prohibits discrimination based on race and national origin in employment (as well as other grounds for discrimination), and Title I of the Immigration Reform and Control Act, passed in 1986, prohibits discrimination based on citizenship status – or, more specifically, knowingly hiring workers who are not authorized for employment in the U.S. As I show below, employers today prefer workers who are Latino or Asian, or prefer immigrants over the native born, and they do so because of stereotypes regarding individuals from these categories. Specifically, employers believe Latinos and Asians will work harder and longer, with more reliability, than white American but especially African American workers, and that immigrants (especially Latino and Asian immigrants) work harder and longer than do natives.

In this chapter, I first describe the conceptual framework for understanding the roles of race and immigrant status in the low-skilled workplace in today's America, defining racial realism and immigrant realism. I then show how race and immigrant status matter in today's workplaces, describing the widespread racial rankings of workers used by employers, the place of immigrants in this ranking, and also whether these racial and immigrant realism strategies are the result of white racism. Next, I describe social science work on the realities behind these perceived realities – the factors that feed into these stereotypes. I then show how courts have been ruling on these practices when challenged under Title VII. I conclude by arguing that reforms are needed to bring workplace practices and American values in line.

**

STRATEGIES TO MANAGE DIFFERENCE IN THE WORKPLACE

There are at least three different strategies for managing racial (and other) differences in the workplace, each with different perceptions of race associated with them. All are prominent in the discourse of employers and their advocates, and all are often openly promoted, but they vary in the meaning or significance that they give to race and also in their goals. Moreover, despite the openness with which some employers discuss them, the strategies vary in the amount or specificity of legal authorization that they enjoy.

The most prominent can be called *classical liberalism*. In this strategy, employers perceive no significance to racial differences, and they therefore do not see any useful management strategy based on racial differences. The idea is to treat workers as employees who vary only in their aptitudes, experience, and perhaps seniority, but nothing else. The purpose of classical liberalism is justice and equal opportunity. Classical liberalism is clearly authorized – and required – by Title VII of the Civil Rights Act of 1964, which prohibits discrimination on the basis of race, national origin, sex, and religion in hiring, firing, and the placement of employees. Workers on contracts are protected by Section 1981 of the Civil Rights Act of 1866, which requires that everyone be granted the same rights to make contracts as enjoyed by white persons.[3]

Also relevant to low-skilled employment in the United States is the Immigration Reform and Control Act, which made it illegal to knowingly employ undocumented immigrants, but also made it illegal to discriminate against persons lawfully in the United States on the basis of citizenship or immigration status. The purpose of this latter provision was to ensure that employers did not avoid hiring *legal* immigrants for fear that they were in fact undocumented.

Classical liberalism is a strategy of managing race that denies that race, national origin or immigrant status have any reality at all. Simply put, an employer is not to consider them when making workplace decisions.

Another prominent strategy for managing race in employment is what I will call *affirmative-action liberalism*. In this strategy, employers perceive significance to racial differences, but they do not perceive racial differences to be useful to them in any way that is related to the performance of jobs or the functioning of the organization. Employers make efforts to ensure that their job applicant pools reflect the racial mix of the qualified population in the relevant area, and also to ensure that applicants are hired and placed as would reflect their availability. As with classical liberalism, the purpose of affirmative-action liberalism is justice and equal opportunity. Employers often undertake this strategy voluntarily, or because the law requires it.

Either way, the law explicitly authorizes affirmative action. Its primary legal basis is Executive Order 11246 and its various implementing regulations, which require affirmative action from firms that have contracts with the federal government. Courts also sometimes order firms to implement affirmative action plans. Firms that wish to voluntarily engage in affirmative action have explicit legal rules to follow, developed by the Supreme Court, so that they are doing it in ways that comply with the law. The legal rules for affirmative action plans require that certain conditions are met: (1) the plans have the goal of remedying an imbalance in the organization's workforce; (2) the plans put no unnecessary limits or bans on opportunities for whites/males; (3) the plans are a temporary fix and cannot be used to maintain the desired racial proportions.[4]

Affirmative-action liberalism is different from classical liberalism in that it does direct employers to perceive some reality to racial and some other differences. However, this occurs in a limited way, directed only at repairing imbalances and ensuring that persons of all races find equal employment opportunities. In the day-to-day operation of the workplace to achieve organizational goals, racial difference must have no reality for employers.

A third strategy for managing race in employment has become increasingly prominent in recent decades. In a strategy that I call *racial realism*, racial differences have both significance and usefulness to employers. Because of this, employers see race as real and relevant to their organizations because it helps them perform better. When using this strategy, employers may see what I call "racial abilities." This is the belief that different racial groups vary in their ability to do particular jobs, or in what they can bring to the organization in any job due to their abilities to perform in particular ways. In high-skilled jobs, racial abilities typically have a racial-matching dynamic, where employers or other advocates believe that persons of particular races should serve customers or citizens of the same race (e.g., African American teachers are better at teaching African American students because they understand their learning styles better). In less-skilled jobs, as I show below, employers perceive certain racial groups, particularly Latinos and Asians, as having better aptitude by virtue of what employers perceive as superior work ethics and attitudes (willingness to work for low wages in often harsh environments) than do white and especially black workers.

A variant of racial realism can be called immigrant realism. It is similar to racial realism except that the relevant status is whether or not employees are foreign-born. Here, employers perceive "immigrant abilities" – the aptitude that immigrants may have to work hard in sometimes harsh environments for low wages. In some cases, employers may perceive superior abilities among undocumented immigrants specifically.

The goal of racial realism and immigrant realism, in contrast to the other two strategies, is organizational effectiveness. Employers consider race or immigrant background not out of concerns for justice or equal opportunity, but because they want more profits, or to achieve other benchmarks of performance.

Another contrast is that racial and immigrant realism have very little basis in law. As I describe below, Title VII flatly forbids the consideration of race as it relates to the performance of an organization. Some courts have ruled in favor of racial realism where it serves the "operational needs" of the organization, but these cases have been limited to law enforcement contexts and police departments, and since these are public employers and Title VII forbids such considerations, these courts have created this legal rationale on the basis of the Fourteenth Amendment's Equal Protection Clause.[5] Thus, even the most benign form of racial realism, when corporate employers seek a racially diverse workforce because they believe it will result in more creativity and better ideas and responsiveness to diverse client bases, has no authorization from the Supreme Court. The Equal Employment Opportunity Commission states only that "Title VII permits diversity efforts designed to open up opportunities to everyone" – suggesting a goal of justice or equal opportunity, and not racial realism's goal of organizational effectiveness.[6]

In the pages in the next section, I describe the most pernicious kind of realism – the stereotyping of workers in low-skilled jobs on the basis of their race and immigrant status. Despite the ostensibly clear violations of civil rights law in these acts, studies by sociologists, economists, and anthropologists suggest they are surprisingly common, and only recently have courts begun to rule against these employers in significant numbers.

THE LOW-SKILLED WORKPLACE TODAY

Rankings of Race

There are now large numbers of social science studies of employers' perceptions of workers, and how they might vary by race or ethnic background. What they reveal time and again is that since at least the 1980s, employers across the country, in cities as well as rural areas, hire and place workers using racial realist strategies, and with a ranking of workers based on race (with Latinos typically considered to be a racial group). In these rankings, it is not whites who are the most preferred. Asians or Latinos are typically at the top. African Americans are typically at the bottom.

For example, in Chicago in the late 1980s, one employer explained, "when we hear other employers talk, they'll go after primarily the Hispanic and Oriental first, those two, and, I'll qualify that even further, the Mexican Hispanic, and any Oriental, and after that, that's pretty much it, that's pretty much where they like to draw the line, right there."[7] A hotel manager in Chicago also saw racial abilities, and believed that blacks lacked them: "I see far more blacks thinking the employer has the obligation to give him a check for doing nothing. There are some whites that think that way, but, far more blacks. Not so much the Hispanics."[8] In New York City, in the 1990s, a warehouse manager stated, "There is a friend of mine who is a carpenter and . . . (he says) that all the Mexican guys he's come in contact with are incredibly good workers. You hear that enough times and then if a Mexican guy came here for work I'd probably hire him based on that."[9] A manager of an Atlanta construction company stated vividly of Latino workers, "To be honest, I love the little fuckers. I mean, they get into their work and shimmy up and down those frames of a house and jump back and forth. Man they work it. [*sic*] . . . And, the whole time they smile and say, 'Need anything else done?' Not, 'It's too fucking hot, I need a break,' or any of that other shit."[10] A manager of a Los Angeles garment factory explained the racial abilities of different groups in the following way: "the work ethic for Hispanics is better than it is for blacks," while Asians also "are very good workers."[11]

Some Los Angeles employers complained about white workers, with one arguing that "it's a little tougher to find today white workers with as high a work ethic as Asians. ... I would say that twenty years ago there were [more]." Another stated more bluntly that "The white factory worker is a whining piece of shit. They [feel that they] never make enough money, they always work too hard, they never want to work over eight hours a day and they feel that, as soon as you hire them, you owe them."[12]

But in this literature, negative comments are most common about African American workers, while laudatory comments about Latinos and Asians are common across the country. Similar racial realist dynamics have been found in places as diverse as rural Florida,[13] Silicon Valley,[14] Boston, and Detroit.[15]

These quotes do not represent the views of a wayward few. In William Julius Wilson's study of Chicago employers, 74 percent of the employers he interviewed held negative perceptions of African American workers' abilities, particularly their lack of work ethic.[16] In a study of Atlanta, Boston, Detroit, and Los Angeles employers, economists Philip Moss and Chris Tilly found that 46 percent of the employers in the study had negative perceptions of blacks' abilities to work at these low-skilled jobs.[17]

These studies tend to rely on interviews and surveys to ascertain the racial realist views of employers, and so there may be a question regarding whether employers actually act on these perceptions. I would argue that these racial and immigrant realist practices are indeed responsible for the negative effects on overall wages of less-educated African American workers found in the National Academies study cited above. It is likely related to the black unemployment rate, which has been consistently double that of whites, as well as higher than Latino and Asian unemployment rates, for years. Other statistics – e.g., the workers who helped rebuild New Orleans after Hurricane Katrina were about 50 percent Latino, though the city was only 3 percent Latino in 2000[18] – also suggest that employers are indeed acting on professed racial realist perceptions, and employing Latinos and Asians at a higher rate than African Americans.

There are also instances of observed, specific behavior. For example, the provocative participant observation of an industrial manufacturer by sociologist Laura López-Sanders, who was hired by the firm and asked to manage black employees in such a way as to lead them to quit so they could be replaced by Latinos, shows the firm preferred Latinos for their racial abilities. Driving off the undesired workers could be accomplished by speeding up assembly lines, adding to existing job descriptions, and breaking up social groups, adding Latinos to existing social groups, and transferring to the dirty or unpleasant jobs. After one year, the plant had about 300 Latino employees out of a total of about 1,000; it had started with just two Latinos.[19] A series of lawsuits, described below, also suggest that racial realism is not only found in discourse, but is a strategy of management that is not uncommon in the U.S.

Racial Realism or Immigrant Realism

It is clear that many employers are viewing race as a real and useful part of employees' backgrounds. But is this really about a preference for immigrants? It appears that it is often about race, often about immigrant status, and often about both – employers express a perception in the superior abilities of immigrants, but they do so in racialized terms. One Atlanta construction manager theorized that "the Mexicans from the mountainous areas of Mexico are short but stout workers. They seem to pick up bags of concrete and heavy shit with little effort."[20] Another distinguished Latino immigrants from Latino Americans, explaining "When (they're) Americanized, they ain't worth a shit."[21] A Boston factory employer saw Asian immigrants as the best workers: "Your Asian workforce, because it's the newest immigrant in the country, and what I've seen with them is they have a completely different work ethic. You need them for seventy-two hours a day, they'll be there for seventy-two hours a day."[22]

Many firms in the meatpacking industry have become almost totally dependent on immigrant workers – a situation that was arguably self-inflicted when they reduced wages, increased line speeds, and built plants in rural areas where there were few workers. Latino populations especially have increased rapidly in towns where the major employers are meatpackers or poultry processors. For example, Benton County, Arkansas, had a 9 percent Latino population in 2000, but the chicken plant was 72.5 percent Latino. Hall County, Georgia, was 20 percent Latino but the chicken plant was 84 percent Latino. McDonald County, Missouri, host of Simmons and Hudson Foods plants, saw a 2107 percent growth in the Latino population between 1990 and 2000.[23]

The intertwining of racial and immigrant realism can be seen when meatpackers mix national origins with pan-ethnic or racial categories ("Koreans and Hispanics are very hard workers – but Koreans are probably the best"), or complain about the Americanization of Latinos and Asians ("Vietnamese and Spanish start working hard when they first get here, but after a while they must get Americanized, because their productivity and attendance fall off"). Many of these firms hire undocumented immigrants, and at least one employer claims that there may even be an undocumented-immigrant realism shaping management of the workforce: "A lot of blacks don't work as hard as Hispanics, but the legalized Hispanics tend to not work as well as when you could hire illegals."[24]

Is Racial Realism in Low-Skilled Workplaces a Story of White Racism?

In the U.S., we are used to hearing of anti-black prejudice as part of a narrative white oppression over blacks. The studies cited above do find many white employers holding negative views of blacks, while valorizing the abilities of

Asians, Latinos and especially immigrant Asians and Latinos. But it is not the case that only white employers use racial realist management strategies in their workforce. Immigrant entrepreneurs from Asia and Latin America tend to prefer co-ethnics for their workers, for example.[25] Moss and Tilly's employer survey found that 25 percent of Latino employers said Latinos are better workers, which was about double the average for all employers. Asians were slightly more laudatory to the racial abilities of Asians, with 29 percent of Asian employers claiming that Asians are better workers, which was more than triple the average. The situation was different for black employers, who showed lower levels of homophily: only 2.6 percent of black employers said blacks are better workers, while the average was 1.7 percent.[26]

Non-white employers in general prescribed to similar rankings of racial abilities as the white employers, showing an aversion to workers with African ancestry. A study of Chinese and Korean garment factory owners in New York found that these employers used racial realist strategies to avoid African Americans, preferred co-ethnics, and preferred Latinos – but not Puerto Rican or Dominican Latinos. Persons of these ancestries were grouped with African Americans. In the words of one Korean employer, "I have friends that [*sic*] own stores who hire blacks, and they are just too lazy. They come to work in the beginning and work hard and then a couple of weeks later, they start coming in late, and [then they start] taking days off. I can't have that kind of person working here. We have deadlines to make. I'm not just selling things."[27]

Even African American employers could valorize the abilities of Latino immigrant workers. As one black construction contractor said of Latino immigrant workers, "You know, they really will just do anything to get paid. I mean they will shovel shit, crawl up under houses, and work like the devil until they're done ... and won't say a damn thing about how hot it is or how they wished they could get off early. Not many other guys would be like that."[28]

Realities Underlying Racial and Immigrant Realism

Are the racial and immigrant abilities described above simply matters of perception, based only on cognitive biases in the minds of employers? Or is there evidence to suggest the employers are latching onto something that is going on in the real world? While racial realism is undoubtedly unfair to individual workers, who should not be judged based on perceptions of groups (see below), there are reasons to believe that there are real differences between workers.

First, migrants typically bring an entirely different attitude to the workplace, accepting temporary conditions that are substandard for the host nation's context because the wage differentials with their homeland make acceptance worth it – and the migrants may perceive the conditions as only temporary anyway.[29] On the other hand, African American workers, the least preferred, have a totally different attitude. As legal scholars Jennifer Gordon and

R. A. Lenhardt have noted, Latino immigrants typically have an "incentive to do whatever the boss asks in order to achieve greater economic and social status outside this country," but African American workers have a "desire to control work pace and conditions in order to ensure a modicum of dignity and respect within the United States."[30]

Illustrative of this process was the response of a poultry processor. Stillmore, Georgia's Crider Incorporated, which lost about three-quarters of its mostly Latino workforce after an immigration raid. The firm, desperate for replacement workers, raised its starting wages more than a dollar to improve to $7 to $9 an hour, offered free transportation to the plant, and sought workers from a state-funded employment office. Blacks became 60 percent of the workforce, while whites made up 30 percent. But the new workers did not last in these jobs, finding the conditions unacceptable, and Crider began to search for (documented) Latino and Asian immigrants to replace them.[31]

Other studies have found that young black workers do have higher absenteeism rates than other workers. However, it may be that workplace dynamics – and perceptions that correspond to racial differences – tend to produce these patterns rather than them being the result of racial abilities that vary before workers walk in the door. For example, a study of low-skilled workers in the 1980s found that absenteeism rates were higher among workers who saw their bosses as biased.[32] Similarly, a study from the 2000s found that black absenteeism was higher than white or Latino, but was correlated with whether black employees perceived their organizations as valuing diversity or not.[33]

Other research provides reasons why employers may perceive Asians and Latinos as superior workers that are not linked to perceptions, however. Specifically, sociologist Frank Bean and his colleagues analyzed data regarding workers in their prime working ages but who have less than a high school education – precisely those that researchers have found to have wages negatively impacted by immigration. They found a series of indicators that showed the disturbing state of less-educated black and white America. For example, their 1996–2008 data showed that for those with less than a high school education and aged 22 to 28, Asians (40 percent) and Latinos (50 percent) were less likely to have been arrested than whites (about 69 percent) or blacks (60 percent), and incarceration rates also favored Asians and Latinos, who were at about 18 percent, while blacks and whites were both at about 27 percent. The vitality of the immigrant workforce is also indicated by their data showing that immigrants are less likely to report being in only fair or poor health (about 9 percent) than are native-born white (15 percent) and black (16 percent) workers at this education level. In addition, only 0.6 percent of immigrants reported that health problems caused limitations on their activities, while 4 percent of whites and 5 percent of blacks reported the same. Finally, the data regarding substance abuse report similar stories. Though Latinos had the highest rates of alcohol use in the late 1970s and early 1980s, in the mid-2000s, about 47 percent of Latinos reported using alcohol in the previous month, while blacks were about 55 percent and whites at 60 percent. Regarding narcotics, whites were mostly likely to use, at slightly more than 30 percent, while blacks were at 20 percent, and Latino use had fallen from a high of 35 percent in 1979 to 15 percent in 2007.[34] Taken together, these data do provide some insight into why, other than pure imagination, so many employers would find Latino and Asian workers, and immigrants in general, to be the most desirable workers. Nevertheless, it is problematic for all workers to be treated as members of groups rather than as individuals, and treating racial and immigrant status as real and relevant to the job is likely to cause employers to run afoul of the law, as I show below.

WHAT DOES THE LAW SAY?

Congress passed Title VII of the Civil Rights Act of 1964 to eliminate race, national origin, sex, and religion from the hiring, promotion, and work assignment decisions of employers. A special concern in this process was the employment rates and opportunities for African Americans. Congress sought to improve opportunities for African Americans by eliminating discrimination in favor of whites.

In the 1960s, there is little record that anyone was contemplating discrimination in favor of non-whites other than African Americans. Perhaps for that reason, many employers seem to believe that preferring Asians and Latinos over blacks is acceptable – and they sometimes brag about it to social scientists and journalists (and some have even defended the practice in court, as shown below). Nevertheless, the laws, and the way they are interpreted, would seem to prohibit any actions based on the stereotyped generalization that some workers are better than others at any workplace task. That racial realism and immigrant realism appear to be so relevant requires some analysis.

Title VII states:

It shall be an unlawful employment practice for an employer:

(1) to fail or refuse to hire or to discharge any individual, or otherwise to discriminate against any individual with respect to his compensation, terms, conditions, or privileges of employment, because of such individual's race, color, religion, sex, or national origin; or
(2) to limit, segregate, or classify his employees or applicants for employment in any way which would deprive or tend to deprive any individual of employment opportunities or otherwise adversely affect his status as an employee, because of such individual's race, color, religion, sex, or national origin.[35]

The most straightforward interpretation of the text of Title VII is the "disparate treatment" theory of discrimination, which involves a finding that an employer intentionally opened or closed opportunities because of a person's race.

Disparate treatment is most easily shown when an employer makes statements similar to those, quoted above, that I used to show how racial realism operates in the nation's workplaces.[36] However, employers are not as willing to advertise their racial realism to employees when they make discriminatory decisions as they are when being interviewed by social scientists or journalists. This may be part of the reason racial realism is so common.

Firms that prefer immigrants are also able to rely on word-of-mouth hiring to bring in the favored Latino and African American immigrant workers. Courts have considered this type of recruitment method to be discriminatory when employers with mostly-white workforces have used it because, given the tendency for segregation in family and personal networks, it tends to reproduce the racial patterns of a workforce. This result is so obvious that at least one court considered it to be disparate treatment discrimination, concluding that the employer must have intended the exclusion of African Americans.[37] Other courts have ruled it as discriminatory under a different theory. That approach to discrimination, "disparate impact," posits that employment actions that have a disparate or adverse impact against a protected group can be discriminatory even if there was not discriminatory intent.[38]

Some more recent cases, however, have carved some room for employers to use word-of-mouth hiring, even when it reproduces racially imbalanced workforces. In two cases involving employers who hired mostly Asian and Latino immigrants, courts ruled that if an employer "passively" relied on word-of-mouth hiring, that is, they hired applicants whom their current employees referred to them, then the practice was acceptable.[39] The climate has changed on this type of recruitment enough that Tyson, the poultry processor, has even boasted publicly that its overwhelmingly Latino immigrant workforce is primarily recruited through word-of-mouth.[40] Given that African Americans are much less likely to aggressively or proactively use word-of-mouth recruitment than are immigrants,[41] it is not likely that these decisions would have any positive impact on black employment opportunities.

Litigants have another option: they can bring a prima facie charge of racial discrimination. Here there are clear, judge-made rules involving four steps. The plaintiff must be able to (1) show he or she is a member of a protected class based on race; (2) the plaintiff lost some employment opportunity; (3) the plaintiff was differently treated on the basis of race; and (4) there is a causal link between the different treatment and the plaintiff's race. Satisfying all four of these requirements, the rules allow the defendant employer to then provide a nondiscriminatory reason for the alleged disparate treatment. The plaintiff then has the opportunity to "rebut" that supposedly nondiscriminatory motivation for the denial of opportunity.

It is not easy for plaintiffs to win prima facie cases because employers can typically identify some skill the excluded worker lacked and claim that was the nondiscriminatory reason for the employment choice.[42] Employers can also claim that they have workforces that are dominated by Latinos, Asians and/or immigrants because African American or white workers are simply not interested in applying for jobs in significant numbers. In the early years of Title VII, this kind of defense did not fare well, and employers who made it lost 86 percent of the cases, but their loss rate declined to 40 percent between 1978 and 1989.[43]

One employer was bold enough to make the claim that avoiding African Americans while hiring Latinos was not a violation of Title VII. The case involved a hotel operator in the city of Indianapolis. In a pattern that may be occurring across the country, the firm in this case, New Indianapolis Hotels, sought to replace its black housekeepers with Latinos. Rather than firing the undesired workers, the firm hoped to drive them away with fewer hours and lower pay. In court, the firm tried to argue that in a prima facie discrimination case, the plaintiffs must show they are members of a protected class, and this classification was the basis of the discrimination. New Indianapolis Hotels relied on a district court case from Illinois where a black worker was replaced by a Latino, and the court considered this to be fatal to the litigation, reasoning that because one of the African American plaintiffs "was replaced by another member of a protected class, he cannot meet the fourth element of the prima facie case."[44] In this view, one minority is the same as another – even though the firm was clearly preferring one *over* the other. New Indianapolis Hotels lost the case, however, as an Indiana district court noted that most courts have ruled that discriminating in favor of one minority over another is a violation of Title VII.[45]

The employer practice of driving out black workers by assigning them less favorable jobs, or even by purposefully assigning them to work groups where they are isolated from other English-speakers, as has been the case in some employment situations, is also likely a violation of Title VII. The law made it illegal for an employer to "limit, segregate, or classify his employees or applicants for employment in any way which would deprive ... any individual of employment opportunities ... because of such individual's race, color, religion, sex, or national origin."[46] The EEOC Compliance Manual similarly explains, "Race or color should not affect work assignments, performance evaluations, training opportunities, discipline, or any other term or condition of employment ..."[47] This aspect of the law would also seem to prohibit the concentration of Latino workers into the most dirty, dangerous, and difficult jobs, which sometimes occurs because of employers' beliefs in the racial abilities of Latinos or Asians to do this work diligently and without complaint.

With the letter of the law on the side of African American workers, but with great challenges in winning cases – and little incentive to litigate – it is thus not surprising that these practices continue across the country, and employers openly discuss their racial and immigrant realist strategies of management. The EEOC pushed back during the years of the Obama administration, bringing several cases that it categorized as "Hispanic preference" cases – and winning in court or in out-of-court settlements.[48] For example, the EEOC sued a Hampton Inn franchise for allegedly replacing white workers with Latinos, based on the stereotype that the white workers were "indolent."[49] The EEOC also sued a Georgia farm for retaining Mexican workers while firing African American workers, and providing "lesser job opportunities to American workers by assigning them to pick vegetables in fields which had already been picked by foreign workers, which resulted in Americans earning less pay than their Mexican counterparts."[50]

Some workers initiate the litigation themselves. African American workers in the Chicago area filed a suit on their own against a job placement agency, MVP Staffing, and some of its clients for preferring Latino workers and avoiding African Americans. The attorneys in the case argued that the clients were employers who sought to shield themselves from litigation by using the staffing agency. African Americans complained that they could sit in the MVP Staffing office all day and not be assigned, while Latino workers would get assignments. A former employee of MVP Staffing admitted that the firm used code words for white and black workers, calling them "guapos," or "handsome ones" (meaning that they didn't want to work hard and get their hands dirty), while they labeled Latinos "feos," or "ugly ones," meaning the opposite. Another way clients sought Latino workers and to avoid non-Latinos was to say they wanted workers who listened to 107.9 FM, a Chicago radio station that broadcast in Spanish.[51]

The Immigration Reform and Control Act (IRCA) made it illegal to discriminate against legal immigrants – or in favor of them – and made it illegal to hire undocumented immigrants. It states that "It is unlawful for a person or other entity to hire, or to recruit or refer for a fee, for employment in the United States ... an alien knowing the alien is an unauthorized alien."[52] It also states that discrimination on the basis of "citizenship status" is also illegal.[53] And so it obviously would be illegal to *prefer* undocumented immigrants, or immigrants in general. Yet immigrant realism, like racial realism, appears to be quite common. Why should this be the case? First, most of the preferred immigrants discussed above are documented, so no Homeland Security enforcement mechanisms would affect this hiring. Second, IRCA requires the government to prove that a firm *knowingly* hired undocumented immigrants. All they must do to evade a charge of discrimination is hire only undocumented immigrants with false papers, and then claim to not know the difference. When the Justice Department sued Tyson after an investigation of 2.5 years (involving the combined efforts of the Immigration and Naturalization Service, the Social Security Administration, and the Department of Agriculture) when it was discovered that one branch was paying recruiters to bring undocumented workers from Mexico, the government lost. While the local plant managers at the center of the investigation took the fall, the government targeted the Tyson headquarters, which demanded certain profit margins from its various plants. The government could not prove that the Tyson headquarters knew of the heavy reliance on undocumented workers at many of its plants.[54] In short, the requirement that employers be shown to have known that their employees were undocumented has proven to be a major obstacle to successful litigation – a significant issue since the federal government has been inconsistent in its enforcement of the law.[55]

CONCLUSION

Racial realism does not only exist in the low-skilled labor markets, though the management strategy has some differences when used with more educated workers. Racial realism in low-skilled jobs does share with racial realism in high-skilled jobs a perception that the racial background of employees can be useful for the functioning of an organization. In skilled jobs, however, it can create opportunities for *all* groups, because many employers believe that persons of particular racial backgrounds are the best at providing services to those of similar backgrounds, and this can benefit African Americans, who remain America's most disadvantaged group, along with Latinos and Asian Americans. Similarly, "diversity" policies, designed to leverage the creativity and dynamism that is thought to result from racially and otherwise diverse workforces, can benefit all racial groups. While these practices can limit opportunities if employers believe that particular racial groups can only serve the needs of racially concordant clients or citizens, it remains the case that this form of racial realism may benefit all Americans. It is also the case that immigrant status does not matter in skilled employment. As I have argued elsewhere,[56] the law also gives little authorization for these practices, but in many cases, civil rights advocates actually argue for them.

In low-skilled jobs, however, racial realism is about hierarchy. It is the practice of preference of particular groups over others based on stereotypes of superior ability. Moreover, the preferred groups – typically Latinos, Asian Americans, or immigrants from these and other groups – are exploited. If anything, the wages and conditions in these jobs are lower when immigrants are concentrated in them.

This brings us back to the themes of this volume. Employers tend to perceive as real abilities that vary by race, national origin, and immigrant status. Even though some courts have weakened them, the laws on the books would seem to prohibit racial and immigrant realism. But law restricts actions only when there is litigation and enforcement. Given the lack of incentives for workers themselves to litigate for these usually low-paying jobs, providing true equal opportunities, and preventing the exploitation of immigrants, will require much more government effort than has thus far been provided.

NOTES

1. National Academies of Sciences, Engineering, and Medicine, *The Economic and Fiscal Consequences of Immigration* (Washington, DC: The National Academies Press, 2016), doi: 10.17226/23550.
2. National Academies, *Consequences of Immigration*, p. 205.
3. Congress passed this statute during Reconstruction, but it was not used for a century. It states: "All persons within the jurisdiction of the United States shall have the same right in every State and Territory to make and enforce contracts, to sue, be parties, give evidence, and to the full and equal benefit of all laws and proceedings for the security of persons and property as is enjoyed by white citizens, and shall be subject to like punishment, pains, penalties, taxes, licenses, and exactions of every kind, and to no other." 42 USC § 1981.
4. *United Steelworkers* v. *Weber*, 443 U.S. 193 (1979); *Johnson* v. *Transp. Agency*, 480 U.S. 616 (1987).
5. See the Equal Employment Opportunity Commission's *Compliance Manual* as it relates to affirmative action. Available at: www.eeoc.gov/policy/docs/race-color .html#VIC, accessed February 9, 2018.
6. See www.eeoc.gov/policy/docs/race-color.html#VIC, accessed February 9, 2018.
7. Joleen Kirschenman and Kathryn M. Neckerman, "'We'd Love to Hire Them, But ... ': The Meaning of Race for Employers," in Christopher Jencks and Paul E. Peterson (eds.), *The Urban Underclass* (Washington, DC: Brookings Institution, 1991), pp. 203–232, 228.
8. W. J. Wilson, *When Work Disappears: The World of the New Urban Poor* (New York: Knopf, 1996), pp. 112–113.
9. Philip Kasinitz and Jan Rosenberg, "Missing the Connection: Social Isolation and Employment on the Brooklyn Waterfront," *Social Problems* 43(1996): 180–196, 189.
10. Cameron D. Lippard, "Racialized Hiring Practices for 'Dirty' Jobs," in Cameron D. Lippard and Charles A. Gallagher (eds.), *Being Brown in Dixie: Race, Ethnicity, and Latino Immigration in the New South* (Boulder: FirstForumPress, 2011) pp. 201–235, 219.
11. P. Moss and C. Tilly, *Stories Employers Tell: Race, Skill, and Hiring in America* (New York: Russell Sage Foundation, 2001), p. 119.
12. R. Waldinger and M. I. Lichter, *How the Other Half Works* (Berkely, CA: University of California Press, 2003) p. 158.
13. James W. Button, Barbara A. Rienzo, and Sheila L. Croucher, *Blacks and the Quest for Economic Equality: The Political Economy of Employment in Southern Communities in the United States* (University Park, PA: The Pennsylvania State University Press, 2009), p. 59.
14. Edward J. W. Park, "Racial Ideology and Hiring Decisions in Silicon Valley," *Qualitative Sociology* 22 (1999): 223–233, 229.
15. Moss and Tilly's study was part of larger Russell Sage Foundation study that looked at low-skilled employment in Atlanta, Boston, Detroit and Los Angeles.
16. Wilson, *When Work Disappears*, p. 112.
17. Moss and Tilly, *Stories Employers Tell*, p. 153.
18. Laurel Fletcher, Phuong N. Pham, Eric Stover, and Patrick Vinck, "Rebuilding After Katrina: A Population-Based Study of Labor and Human Rights in New Orleans,"

Human Rights Center Reports, Paper 2006_06 Rebuilding Katrina. Available at: repositories.cdlib.org/hrc/reports/2006 06Rebuilding-Katrina, accessed August 13, 2009.

19. Laura López-Sanders, *Trapped at the Bottom: Racialized and Gendered Labor Queues in New Immigrant Destinations*, (Working Paper 176, Center for Comparative Immigration Studies, University of California, San Diego, 2009).

20. Lippard, "Racialized Hiring Practices," p. 222.

21. Lippard, "Racialized Hiring Practices," p. 226.

22. Moss and Tilly, *Stories Employers Tell*, p. 117.

23. Leticia M. Saucedo, "The Browning of the American Workplace: Protecting Workers in Increasingly Latino-ized Occupations," *Notre Dame Law Review* 80 (2004): 303–332, 322–323.

24. David Griffith, "Consequences of Immigration Reform for Low-Wage Workers in the Southeastern U.S.: The Case of the Poultry Industry," *Urban Anthropology* 19 (1990): 155–184, 169–173.

25. Tarry Hum, "The Promises and Dilemmas of Immigrant Ethnic Economies," in Marta López-Garza and David R. Diaz (eds.), *Asian and Latino Immigrants in a Restructuring Economy: The Metamorphosis of Southern California* (Stanford, CA: Stanford University Press, 2001), pp. 77–101, 80–81.

26. Moss and Tilly, *Stories Employers Tell*, p. 132.

27. Margaret M. Chin, *Sewing Women: Immigrants and the New York City Garment Industry* (New York: Columbia University Press, 2005), p. 86.

28. Lippard, "Racialized Hiring Practices," p. 219.

29. Michael J. Piore, *Birds of Passage: Migrant Labor and Industrial Societies* (New York: Cambridge University Press, 1979).

30. Jennifer Gordon and R. A. Lenhardt, "Rethinking Work and Citizenship," *UCLA Law Review* 55 (2008): 1161–1238, 1222.

31. Evan Perez and Corey Dade, "An Immigration Raid Aids Blacks – For a Time," *Wall Street Journal*, January 17, 2007. Available at http://online.wsj.com/news/articles/SB116898113191477989, accessed August 13, 2009; Jennifer Ludden, "Hmong Fill Jobs Left Empty by Immigration Raid," *NPR.org*, May 29, 2007. Available at http://www.npr.org/templates/story/story.php?storyId=10461104, accessed August 13, 2009.

32. Ronald Ferguson and Randall Filer, "Do Better Jobs Make Better Workers? Absenteeism from Work Among Inner-City Black Youths," in Richard B. Freeman and Harry J. Holzer (eds.), *The Black Youth Employment Crisis* (Chicago: University of Chicago Press, 1986), pp. 261–298, 292.

33. Derek R. Avery, Patrick F. McKay, David C. Wilson, and Scott Tonidandel, "Unequal Attendance: The Relationships between Race, Organizational Diversity Cues, and Absenteeism," *Personnel Psychology* 60 (2007): 875–902. Also see Patrick F. McKay and Michael A. McDaniel, "A Reexamination of Black–White Mean Differences in Work Performance: More Data, More Moderators," *Journal of Applied Psychology* 91 (2006): 538–554.

34. Frank Bean, Susan K. Brown, James D. Bachmeier, Zoya Gubernskaya, and Christopher D. Smith, "Luxury, Necessity and Anachronistic Workers: Does the United States Need Unskilled Immigrant Labor?" *American Behavioral Scientist* 56 (2012): 1008–1028; John D. Skrentny, After Civil Rights: Racial

Realism in the New American Workplace (Princeton: Princeton University Press 2014), pp. 240–244.

35. 42 USC § 2000E–2(a).
36. *Slack* v. *Havens*, 522 F.2d 1091 (Ninth Cir. 1975).
37. *Parham* v. *Southwestern Bell Tel. Co.*, 433 F.2d 421, 427 (8th Cir. 1970).
38. *Robinson* v. *Lorillard Corp.*, 444 F.2d 791, 798 n. 5 (4th Cir. 1971); *Barnett* v. *W. T. Grant Co.*, 518 F.2d 543, 549 (4th Cir. 1975); *Brown* v. *Gaston County Dyeing Machine Co.*, 457 F.2d 1377, 1383 (4th Cir. 1972); *United States* v. *Ga. Power Co.*, 474 F.2d 906, 926 (5th Cir. 1973).
39. *EEOC* v. *Chicago Miniature Lamp Works*, 947 F.2d 292, 299 (7th Cir. 1991); *EEOC* v. *Consolidated Service Systems*, 989 F.2d 233 (7th Cir. 1993).
40. The company was defending itself from a charge that it intentionally hired undocumented immigrants, stating in a press release that "Virtually all of our immigrant laborers have come to us as a result of word-of-mouth from friends and families, not recruiters," John D. Skrentny, *After Civil Rights*, p. 258.
41. Sandra Susan Smith, *Lone Pursuit: Distrust and Defensive Individualism among the Black Poor* (New York: Russell Sage Foundation).
42. Leticia M. Saucedo, "The Employer Preference for the Subservient Worker and the Making of the Brown Collar Workplace," *Ohio State Law Journal* 67(2006): 961–1021, 984–985.
43. Vicki Schultz and Stephen Petterson, "Race, Gender, Work, and Choice: An Empirical Study of the Lack of Interest Defense in Title VII Cases Challenging Job Segregation," *University of Chicago Law Review* 59 (1992): 1073–1181, 1098.
44. *Pollard* v. *Azcon Corp.*, 904 F.Supp. 762, 773 (N.D. Ill. 1995).
45. *EEOC* v. *New Indianapolis Hotels*, 2011 U.S. Dist. LEXIS 2658 (S.D. Ind. 2011) at 4.
46. Section 2000e-2.
47. See www.eeoc.gov/policy/docs/qanda_race_color.html, accessed February 9, 2018.
48. For example, see *EEOC* v. *Propak Logistics Inc.*, No. 09–00311 (W.D.N.C. Aug. 6, 2010); *EEOC* v. *Paramount Staffing Inc.*, No. 2:06–02624 (W.D. Tenn. settled Aug. 23, 2010); *EEOC* v. *Little River Golf, Inc.*, No. 1:08CV00546 (M.D.N.C. Aug. 6, 2009). These and other cases are listed at an EEOC website under the "Hispanic Preference" heading. Available at: www1.eeoc.gov/eeoc/initiatives/e-race/caselist.cfm, accessed February 9, 2018.
49. EEOC Newsroom Press Release, "EEOC Sues Hampton Inn Franchise for Race and National Origin Bias," October 3, 2011. Available at www.eeoc.gov/eeoc/newsroom/release/10-3-11b.cfm, accessed February 9, 2018.
50. EEOC Newsroom Press Release, "Hamilton Growers to Pay $500,000 to Settle EEOC Race /National Origin Discrimination Lawsuit," available at www.eeoc.gov/eeoc/newsroom/release/12-13-12.cfm, accessed February 9, 2018.
51. Liam Stack, "Black Workers' Suit Accuses Job Agency of Favoring Hispanic Applicants," *New York Times*, December 6, 2016, available at: www.nytimes.com/2016/12/06/us/lawsuit-alleges-discrimination-against-blacks-at-national-job-agency.html?_r=0, accessed February 9, 2018.
52. 8 U.S. Code § 1324a.
53. 8 U.S. Code § 1324b.

54. See Skrentny, *After Civil Rights*, pp. 259–262, and Steve Striffler, *Chicken: The Dangerous Transformation of America's Favorite Food* (New Haven, CT: Yale University Press, 2005).

55. Hiroshi Motomura, *Immigration Outside the Law* (New York: Oxford University Press, 2014), pp. 47–49; Peter Brownell, "*The Declining Enforcement of Employer Sanctions*," *Migration Information Source*, September 2005. Available at: www .migrationinformation.org/usfocus/display.cfm?ID=332, accessed February 9, 2018.

56. Skrentny, *After Civil Rights*.

2

Comprehensive Immigration Confusion*

Peter Skerry

One of the more challenging aspects of teaching undergraduates about immigration is getting them to consider that the biggest winners in the process are the immigrants themselves. Even when presented with the evidence, my students are extremely reluctant to view immigrants as risk-takers making rational choices. They prefer to see them as victims of global forces beyond their control.

Still more challenging is getting undergraduates from affluent backgrounds to consider that the other big winners are people like themselves – upper-middle-class Americans for whom a huge influx of unskilled immigrants has been a boon. Instead, immigrants become the focus of sincere sentiments of compassion and demands for "social justice." Yet for their fellow citizens who complain about or even denounce immigrants, my students have virtually no compassion. They readily dismiss them as racists and bigots – all the more so since Donald Trump's arrival in Washington.

To be sure, this admixture of limited information, self-interest, and moralism is hardly unique in our politics. And in the context of immigration policy, there is also a conservative variant. I have certainly endured some frustrating discussions with students convinced that illegal immigrants are simply criminals who must be sternly punished. Yet such young people remain steadfastly untroubled by employers who routinely break the law by hiring workers that they have good reason to believe are undocumented. In any event, such views are clearly in the minority at selective institutions, as well as among political and intellectual elites more generally.

Republican elites have not been shy about wielding lofty rhetoric about the national purposes served by immigration. Yet their policies have been firmly rooted in mundane clientelist politics, leaving party leaders in thrall to well-organized business interests addicted to low-skilled immigrant labor. Meanwhile, working- and lower-middle-class whites have grown increasingly

---

* This article orginally appeared in *National Affairs*, Fall 2016, pp. 3–23.

restive. Slow to be aroused and now difficult to appease, such constituencies are long past the point of being soothed by rhetoric about the *Statue of Liberty*.

Instead, these Americans have been drawn to bombast about "building a wall" – even though many undocumented immigrants arrive with valid papers, and then either overstay their visas or get tripped up by complex rules administered by a notoriously incompetent bureaucracy. Impatient with such policy details, fed-up Americans are drawn not only to simplistic nostrums but also to the apparent clarity of legalistic bright lines and drastic remedies, including challenges to the constitutional basis of birthright citizenship.

Yet we ought not gainsay the concerns expressed by so many Americans, who have long felt ignored and condescended to by the very elites who overwhelmingly benefit from mass immigration. The specific claims and complaints articulated by ordinary citizens typically miss their mark and may get expressed in off-putting and downright offensive ways. But this is because they have not had the benefit of tribunes with the temperament and skills to articulate popular anxieties in more reasonable, policy-relevant terms.

Democrats have had an easier time of it. They have been better positioned to wield the rhetoric and symbols of our immigrant history to sustain support for high levels of unskilled immigration. Unlike Republicans, liberals have been able to maintain a relatively costless entente with business interests. And their position has been bolstered by free-market enthusiasts, led by the *Wall Street Journal*, and by the dispassionate if bloodless analyses of most economists. Finally, the liberal position has been supported by Americans like the parents of my students: affluent suburbanites and professionals whose high-minded convictions are implicitly undergirded by their self-interest as consumers of the goods and services provided by cheap immigrant labor.

All of this comes together to make the politics of immigration in America deeply dysfunctional, with grave results for our political culture. Overcoming that dysfunction will require at least three things: First, we need a much better grasp of the actual motivations of immigrants – illegal as well as legal – and how these shape immigration and assimilation in America. Second, we need to see how some of our most intensely held – and intensely debated – notions about immigration are a function of the politics of civil rights and race in our country, and how this distorts our immigration debates in curious and poorly appreciated ways. And third, we need to understand that the policy nostrums to which we have been wedded – the bright line between legal and illegal immigrants, the obsession with border control, and the mirage of guestworker programs – obscure more than they reveal about the challenges and the promise of immigration in America. Seeing these dynamics more clearly can help us dispel the fog that envelops immigration politics, and points away from so-called "comprehensive immigration reform" toward incremental steps in the direction of more constructive policy initiatives.

REFUGEES OR IMMIGRANTS?

At the Jesuit University where I teach, the dominant pro-immigrant ethos is reinforced by the teachings of the Catholic bishops. Unfortunately, the Church's pronouncements on this topic serve mostly to exacerbate the confusion that my students share with other Americans. For example, in his remarks at the Mass celebrated along the U.S.–Mexican border in February 2016, Pope Francis failed to draw any distinctions as he criticized the United States for denying entry both to Mexican migrants seeking to work or join relatives here and to Central American women and children fleeing gang violence and civil disorder, a crisis for which the U.S. arguably bears considerable responsibility.

Such rhetoric overlooks the critical distinction in law between immigrants and refugees. Yet the Pope and his bishops have hardly had a monopoly on sowing such confusion. Recall these lines from the Emma Lazarus sonnet, "The New Colossus," now affixed to the pedestal of the *Statue of Liberty*:

> Give me your tired, your poor,
> Your huddled masses yearning to breathe free,
> The wretched refuse of your teeming shore.
> Send these, the homeless, tempest-tost to me...

Lazarus, the assimilated daughter of a well-established New York Jewish family, wrote these out of concern over the plight of her co-religionists fleeing pogroms in Tsarist Russia. These were the "huddled masses" to whom the "Mother of Exiles" lifted her "lamp beside the golden door!"[1]

So, too, after World War II did Liberty greet – however belatedly and begrudgingly – Jews and other "displaced persons" fleeing a ravaged Europe. She was somewhat more welcoming of those fleeing communist oppression after successive popular uprisings in Hungary, Czechoslovakia, and Poland. Then of course she reached out to Soviet Jews during the closing years of the Cold War. If she had been standing in the 1840s, Lady Liberty would no doubt have welcomed those fleeing famine in Ireland.

But again, none of these were, strictly speaking, immigrants. Instead, they were what we now refer to as refugees: individuals who, according to the UN Refugee Convention, have been forced to flee their country because of persecution, war, or violence. To be sure, in practice the line between immigrants and refugees can be difficult to draw. And according to today's legal framework, the Irish fleeing famine were not in fact refugees. But, like the words of Pope Francis at the border, Lazarus's well-known poem only blurs the line further. So, too, did the remarks of President Lyndon Johnson when in October 1965, at the base of the *Statue of Liberty*, he signed the Hart-Celler Act, repealing the reviled national-origins quotas that had been the basis of U.S. immigration policy since the 1920s. For at that ceremony Johnson also announced a new program to receive refugees fleeing Castro's

Cuba. As historian John Higham has noted, "Emma Lazarus would have approved."[2]

So would today's refugee advocates, who routinely blur the distinction between *refugees* motivated, again in the language of the Refugee Convention, by "a well-founded fear of persecution for reasons of race, religion, nationality, membership in a particular social group, or political opinion"; and *immigrants* motivated by a desire to reunite with family, to work hard and earn money, or simply to seek their destiny. And this is because, from the perspective of advocates, refugees may have stronger moral claims, but immigrants have greater political clout.

Indeed, it is remarkable how few Americans display curiosity about what leads individuals to incur the considerable inconvenience and risk of moving here, especially illegally. As economic historians remind us, only a tiny fraction of the world's population has ever left home in search of economic gains. This remains true even today, when the rewards are high and the costs relatively low.

Unlike refugees, immigrants do not face a stark binary choice: Leave home or stay and face persecution – or worse. On the contrary, the decision to emigrate is often marked by hesitation, ambivalence, and profound misgivings. Indeed, historians report that many of those who arrived here from Europe in the late nineteenth and early twentieth centuries did not stay. Particularly during the years before World War I, when steamship travel made the journey shorter, safer, and cheaper, many so-called "birds of passage," mostly men, came intending to work, save money, and then resume their lives back in the old country.[3] For example, it is estimated that half of Italian migrants to the United States during that period returned home.[4]

Today, the motivations of Irish, Mexican, and many Central American migrants are not dissimilar. Focusing specifically on the undocumented from Mexico, anthropologist Leo Chavez refers to "target earners."[5] As Chavez and others have shown, the intention to return home shapes the behavior of migrants – such that a reasonable observer might conclude that they "exploit themselves." They put up with unpleasant, even dangerous working conditions.[6] They skimp on expenses and crowd into substandard living quarters to maximize their savings. And while it is true that many end up remaining here, the process has often been difficult and drawn out, with frequent journeys back and forth across the border – at least up until the Great Recession and then more recently the Trump administration's bellicose rhetoric and more stringent, albeit episodic, enforcement efforts.

A frequent result of such migrant motives is concentrations of unattached males living in urban settings. And the social consequences can be problematic, occasionally explosive. In *There Goes the Neighborhood*, a study of transitional Chicago neighborhoods during the 1990s, sociologists William Julius Wilson and Richard Taub comment on how "litter and graffiti … mar the formerly pristine streets" of a neighborhood once dominated by "European Americans" but subsequently populated by Mexican immigrants whose "perceptions of the neighborhood as a temporary haven meant that many residents did not invest in their homes."[7]

In East Los Angeles during the late 1980s, I heard similar complaints from Catholic priests and community organizers trying to build up parish life in the face of what they bemoaned as transience, not just of single men but also of entire families.[8] Demographers Ira Lowry and Peter Morrison make a similar point about the 1992 Los Angeles riot, which resulted in 55 deaths. Unlike the 1965 Watts riot, which involved only blacks, the 1992 disturbances led to arrests of about equal numbers of blacks and Hispanic immigrants, overwhelmingly adolescent and young adult males.[9]

During this same period, political scientists Wesley Skogan and Susan Hartnett report that Chicago police had a difficult time involving Hispanics in community-policing efforts.[10] After all, as a police lieutenant in the predominantly immigrant Mexican city of Santa Ana, California (the county seat of Orange County), once put it to me bluntly but not harshly, "How do you do community policing when there is no community?" This aspect of immigrant neighborhoods is also well understood by social-service providers, but is rarely talked about, for fear of stigmatizing immigrants and being denounced as racist.

More than actual violations of the law, it is typically behaviors associated with such transience that most offends or angers ordinary Americans.[11] But their responses invariably get misinterpreted in policy debates, where the distinction between legal and illegal immigrants is invariably drawn – a distinction that may make it easier for many Americans to talk about their anxieties about immigration, but that does not necessarily speak to the sources of those anxieties.

ARE UNDOCUMENTED IMMIGRANTS CRIMINALS?[12]

When Americans link immigrants with "crime," what they have in mind is the social disorder that even sympathetic analysts associate with immigrant communities.[13] Consider, for example, Robert Putnam's reluctant finding that "in the short run ... immigration and ethnic diversity tend to reduce social solidarity and social capital."[14] And of course Putnam's insight is consistent with James Q. Wilson's "broken windows" hypothesis.[15]

Consider also the complaints routinely lodged against undocumented immigrants. Apart from breaking immigration laws, these include not learning English, not paying taxes, depriving American workers of jobs, and imposing fiscal burdens on schools, hospitals, and other social services. Not all of these charges withstand scrutiny, although several do. But however well-grounded they turn out to be, these complaints pertain generally to immigrants in America today, not just the undocumented.

For as immigrant advocates continually – and not incorrectly – remind us, illegal and legal immigrants (many of whom become U.S. citizens) live in the same communities, often in the same households. So, the social disorder that alarms many Americans is not unfairly associated with large numbers of economically marginal newcomers, regardless of their legal status.

Further, it should be noted that while the number of lawful permanent residents (so-called green card holders) admitted annually now hovers around one million, the number of non-immigrants admitted on visas to live and work (as students, exchange visitors, intra-company transferees, diplomats, temporary workers, and their family members) has most recently been more than seven million. And this does not include the 67.5 million tourist- and business-visa-holders admitted, for example, in 2014.[16]

These numbers might seem to dilute or dwarf the impact of 11 million undocumented immigrants.[17] Yet to disgruntled Americans feeling ignored and denigrated by elites, they might plausibly have the opposite effect, sensitizing them to the scale and dynamism of contemporary migration and coloring it negatively. Perhaps this is why, when asked by pollsters, Americans greatly exaggerate the undocumented as a proportion of all immigrants.[18]

In sum, the legal status of the undocumented has become a highly visible but imperfect surrogate for broader concerns that run very deep. Reviewing the spate of local ordinances prohibiting landlords from renting to illegals, and denying city contracts to companies that hire them, Cristina Rodriguez of Yale Law School points out that many such ordinances have included declarations affirming English to be America's "official language," which would also pertain of course to legal immigrants. As she concludes, the "concern is not exclusively over immigration of the illegal variety." Such ordinances "arguably represent part of a larger struggle to adapt to and resist immigration more generally."[19]

This is not a conclusion gratifying to our elites. Immigration advocates often respond with statistics showing lower crime rates among immigrants than among non-immigrants,[20] and so ignore or sidestep their fellow citizens' underlying or poorly articulated concerns. Immigration skeptics and critics respond with legalisms, blaming the undocumented for "breaking the law," and so conveniently overlook that many employers do the same. And while the affluent continue to employ legal and illegal immigrants as gardeners, house painters, au pairs, house cleaners, waiters, and factory laborers, most Americans can neither afford such help nor easily insulate their neighborhoods from the transience and disorder generated by mass immigration. In the end, whatever their ideology, pro-immigration elites get their way. And many Americans feel dismissed, either as chumps or as bigots – or sometimes as both.[21]

And so, to pro-immigration forces on both the right and the left, it has proved politically useful to draw a sharp line between legal and illegal immigrants and to focus on the latter as the source of all problems. The shrewd and insightful analysis of Kenneth Lee, author of *Huddled Masses, Muddled Laws*, highlights how this tactic was perfected during the 1994 debate over California's Proposition 187. As he writes, attacking illegal immigration "insulated pro-immigration legislators from potential public backlash for their votes against legal immigration reform, because they could at least point to the harsh measures against illegal immigration as a symbol of their determination to 'get tough.' "[22] More than twenty years later, this tactic may be played out. For as Professor Rodriguez observes, illegal immigration has come to dominate the agenda to such an extent that it risks turning large segments of the American public against immigration altogether. Nevertheless, the enduring utility of the legal–illegal dichotomy to activists, policy wonks, and politicians favoring sustained high levels of unskilled immigration is striking.

THE ORDEAL OF ASSIMILATION

"Why aren't they assimilating?" This frequently heard question also reflects anxieties about immigrants in general, not just the undocumented. And while assimilation is debated more passionately than immigrant motivation, it is just as poorly understood. However earnestly Americans call for assimilation, very few realize that it leads to new social and political challenges. Assimilated immigrants, and especially their children, can be our most strident and demanding co-workers, neighbors, and fellow citizens. Norman Podhoretz understood this once.[23] Donald Trump certainly does not. As for liberals, they are mostly too preoccupied with denouncing "assimilation" to bother looking at how it actually plays out in contemporary America.

One reason for the popular perception that immigrants aren't assimilating can be traced to the intellectual hegemony of the multiculturalist critique of the concept. The orthodoxy among immigrant activists, advocates, and their allies in the academy is that America has required immigrants and their offspring to reject all ties to the cultures of their homelands.[24] In response, social-service providers and policymakers have advanced "integration" as a goal more compatible with multiculturalism. Yet this neologism has also come in for criticism.

In any case, the distinction between "assimilation" and "integration" is truly one without a difference, rooted in the multiculturalists' misreading of our history. With some exceptions, such as the treatment of ethnic Germans during World War I, American practices and policies have been remarkably accommodating of immigrant cultures – certainly more so than the systematically coercive policies of contemporary France, for example. And as Nathan Glazer has remarked about assimilation in this country, "The word may be dead, the concept may be disreputable, but the reality continues to flourish."[25] American society is still remarkably tolerant and absorptive, allowing newcomers from around the world to pursue their own goals while retaining much, though hardly all, of their home cultures. And over time, most adapt to and embrace those values and habits critical to our way of life.

Yet if immigrants are in fact assimilating, at least in most important respects, why do Americans insist they are not? Well, we seem not to understand some key points about assimilation. First and foremost, we fail to appreciate that it can be a contentious process. When immigrants get involved in politics, for example, the result is inevitably competition, even conflict with other groups. And when immigrant-origin youth get mobilized politically, they tend to do so as native-born citizens who assert their rights far more strenuously than their parents ever could, or would. Note how even undocumented youth, the so-called Dreamers, have made bold claims on America's conscience that their parents, who brought them here illegally, have typically not dared to do.

Assimilation is also a process that unfolds in various dimensions: social, economic, cultural, and political. Each proceeds at its own rate and rather independently of the others. For example, historian John Higham describes how nineteenth-century Jewish immigrants to America, especially those from Germany, assimilated economically but not socially. For as they succeeded in business and the professions, these immigrants encountered barriers raised by Gentile elites, especially at private clubs and organizations.[26] Similarly today, Muslims tend to be highly assimilated into business and the professions, but less so socially or culturally.

Then, too, not all assimilation is benign. Some immigrant children "assimilate down" to gang or other disaffected subcultures. And as sociologist Christopher Jencks reminds us, many immigrant youth assimilating to America's "laissez-faire culture" get caught up in dysfunctional behaviors resulting in teen pregnancy, drug addiction, or obesity.[27]

These distinctions get ignored when Americans expect immigrants to "assimilate" *tout court*. What is expected is that immigrants "speak English" (or perhaps avoid speaking their mother tongue, especially in situations where monolingual English-speakers feel ignored or excluded) and "fit in" (without causing any commotion or making any demands on the rest of us). In this regard, the multiculturalists have a point: Today's popular understanding of assimilation relies on a standard that is ahistorical, unrealistic, and unfair.[28]

Nevertheless, Americans are hardly misguided when they express concerns about immigrants changing and even disrupting their communities. Yet they do fail to understand that such challenges typically arise precisely because immigrants and their children *are* assimilating. Still, when immigrant advocates and their allies reject "assimilation" in favor of a provocative and equally ill-informed multiculturalism, they fail utterly to speak to the legitimate concerns of their fellow citizens.

THE RACIALIZATION OF IMMIGRATION

Multiculturalism reflects a deeper, little noted shift in how Americans have been induced to think about immigrants, which points to the profound changes in our politics wrought by the civil rights movement and its progeny. To be sure, these changes are widely, if not universally, recognized as critically important to African Americans. And over time their applicability to immigrants, especially Hispanics and to a lesser extent Asians, has come to be taken either for granted, or simply dismissed as inappropriate for any and all minority groups. Seldom asked, however, is whether immigrants merit the same benefits and protections that have been afforded, however begrudgingly or controversially, to the descendants of slaves and the victims of Jim Crow.

Yet Hispanic leaders and their allies routinely claim the mantle of the black civil rights movement. To cite one striking example, in 2003 a coalition of foundations, churches, labor unions, and civil-rights organizations sponsored the Immigrant Workers Freedom Ride, described by political scientists Daniel Tichenor and Janice Fine as "a national mobilization meant to evoke the 1961 freedom rides of the Civil Rights movement."[29] Other rides have followed, including the UndocuBus, which traveled from Arizona to the 2012 Democratic National Convention in Charlotte, North Carolina. On the 50th anniversary of the original Freedom Rides, Congressman John Lewis, a veteran of that historic effort, denounced efforts "to demonize the Latino population" and called for "a real movement to resist this attempt to say that people who come from another land are not one of us."[30]

When a civil rights icon like Lewis takes such a stand, it merits scrutiny. For he is articulating the basis of a surprisingly effective "black–brown coalition" predicated on overcoming, even denying, the virtually unavoidable competition between African Americans and Hispanic immigrants for jobs, social services, and visibility. This competition is straightforwardly depicted by Wilson and Taub in their study of Latinos and blacks in Chicago: "The flow of immigrants ... to American urban neighborhoods not only exacerbates tensions between Latinos and whites, but also between Latinos and blacks."[31]

Yet this reality is seldom acknowledged, much less articulated, by minority leaders and their allies. To be fair, this reflects an effort to avoid enflaming tensions between these groups. But such concerns have long since ossified into denial, and we are now at the point where any possible implications for immigration policy are never even considered.

Once again, we encounter a misreading of history. Whatever mistreatment, humiliation, and unfair dealings Mexicans have experienced at the hands of Anglo-Americans, these never included anything remotely resembling the institutionalized cruelty of slavery or the systematic humiliation of *de jure* segregation. For example, the 1848 Treaty of Guadalupe Hidalgo (ratifying America's conquest of half of Mexico's territory) designated Mexican-origin individuals as eligible for U.S. citizenship at a time when this status was restricted in custom and in law to whites.[32] Indeed, Mexicans were eligible for citizenship at a time when blacks were not. This may help to explain why, though a substantial minority of Mexican-origin individuals self-identify on the U.S. census as "other race," a majority has for decades consistently identified as "white."

Similarly, in the continuing controversy around Black Lives Matter, it is rarely noted that Hispanics have different criminal histories and less fraught relations with the police than African Americans. Reflecting on this point, as well as on Hispanics' generally superior standing on most social indicators, syndicated columnist Esther Cepeda is a lone voice when she refers to "the mirage of the rainbow coalition."[33] Indeed, Black Lives Matter can be sympathetically interpreted as an effort by African Americans to recapture their prominence on the agenda after more than 15 years of national preoccupation with issues – terrorism and immigration – that have focused attention on Muslims and Hispanics.

Nevertheless, this template – classifying blacks and Hispanics as similarly situated and deserving racial minorities – has powerfully shaped the prevailing interpretation of America's immigrant history. In this view, this "nation of immigrants" has experienced many episodes of anti-immigrant hysteria: the Alien and Sedition Acts in the 1790s, mob violence against Irish Catholics in Boston in the 1830s and 1840s, anti-Chinese movements in California in the post-Civil War era, anti-German sentiment during World War I, and the Red Scare of the immediate postwar years. From this perspective, what we are experiencing today is just the latest chapter in a long and ugly story.

That we have had such bouts of racism, nativism, and xenophobia and that these have led to restrictionist policies is undeniable. But it is too easy to regard such policies as driven by raw ignorance and hatred and in no way as rational responses to actual – or reasonably perceived – competition, challenges, or threats. To be sure, such distinctions can be difficult to delineate. But our political and intellectual elites have long since stopped trying. Instead, they have grown accustomed to treating all negative reactions to immigrants – in the present as well as the past – as "racist, nativist, and xenophobic."

Here, it is worth noting that in 1955 John Higham published the definitive treatment of American nativism, *Strangers in the Land: Patterns of American Nativism 1860–1925*, and then spent the remainder of his distinguished career recanting it.[34] As early as 1957, he called for a halt to "the bad habit of labeling as nativist any kind of unfriendliness toward immigrants," and urged his fellow historians to focus less on the irrational ideas, prejudices, and "frenzies of the mob," and more on "basic structural realities." Admonishing his colleagues "to recognize that our divergent and unequal backgrounds are causes, not just results of our difficulties," he ruefully noted that "it is more comforting to think that everyone is pretty much alike and that our differences are foisted upon on us by myths and stereotypes."[35]

Yet at no point did Higham ever deny that irrational forces have played a role in our immigration history. He merely argued for a more balanced account. As he wrote in 1999, commenting on the notoriously restrictive legislation of the 1920s: "In the passage of the 'national origins' law of 1924 an intensely racialized nativism was an important factor *but not the only one*. The new law, for all its extravagant unfairness, was an essential building block in the slow construction of a welfare state" (emphasis added).[36]

Perhaps Higham, however renowned, was idiosyncratic. It is all the more important, therefore, to consider briefly the work of economic historians Timothy J. Hatton and Jeffrey G. Williamson, particularly their compendious volume, *Global Migration and the World Economy: Two Centuries of Policy and Performance*. Building on findings by Harvard economist Claudia Goldin, Hatton and Williamson focus on the determinants of immigration restriction in the post-World War I era. Arguing that global economic forces were at work well before the onset of war, they emphasize the declining literacy and occupational status of immigrants arriving in increasing numbers from Southern and Eastern Europe.[37]

In a strikingly balanced account reminiscent of Higham, Hatton and Williamson assert that "perhaps the Immigration Commission [the much criticized Dillingham Commission, chartered by Congress from 1910 to 1914] was right in suggesting that those who arrived most recently were in some respects 'inferior' to previous immigrants."[38] While acknowledging the racial basis of the late nineteenth-century exclusion of Asians, the authors stipulate that in the pre-World War I period, "[t]here is no compelling evidence that xenophobia or racism was driving immigration policy..."[39] Instead, they point to labor-market fundamentals and conclude, "New World governments [the United States, Argentina, Australia, Brazil, and Canada] acted to defend the economic position of unskilled labor ... by restricting immigration."[40]

The political and policy implications here are subtle but important. If resistance to immigrants is rooted in fundamentally irrational prejudice, it cannot and should not be pandered to. But if it is grounded in more rational sources, then it cannot be so easily ignored. In the context of today's post-civil rights regime, there are powerful incentives to "fight prejudice" and not yield to "restrictionist sentiment." Those incentives are all the more potent if the principled forces fighting ignorance and racism also happen to benefit from immigration.

PUBLIC INTEREST POLITICS

Religious zeal and moral certainty have frequently plagued American politics. To be sure, such fervor helped sustain the civil rights movement itself in its darkest hours. But since the 1960s, these tendencies, and the rigidity and inflexibility associated with them, have become pervasive and institutionalized. And in our decades-long debate over immigration, these political dynamics have encouraged immigration advocates to not take their opponents seriously, indeed to cavalierly dismiss them.

A key factor here has been the emergence of public-interest organizations. John Gardner, founder of Common Cause, the paradigmatic such organization, had profound misgivings about this terminology. As political scientist Andrew McFarland highlights, Gardner preferred something akin to what McFarland terms "civic balancing."[41] Yet today, our civic and political life is seriously out of balance, and public-interest organizations are often part of the problem. Certainly, they have exacerbated the already challenging task of formulating immigration policy in the national interest.

Of major concern is the heavy reliance of these organizations on controversy and contention to generate the publicity they need to demonstrate to donors (individual as well as institutional) that their contributions are making a difference, particularly in public-policy domains where success is seldom easy to measure. A related challenge is what James Q. Wilson has referred to as "vicarious representation."[42] Public-interest entrepreneurs may seek to fill the political vacuums left by unorganized, unarticulated interests. But inevitably, they risk being more accountable to third-party funders than to the people they claim to represent.[43]

Consequently, public-interest entrepreneurs tend to engage not so much in the negotiation and compromise that lead to immediate, concrete outcomes demanded by dues-paying members capable of voting with their feet; but rather in the hard-bargaining and posturing that result in stalemate acceptable to or even sought by third-party contributors focused on long-term programmatic or ideological agendas. This dynamic has certainly been evident in immigration politics, where the interests being represented include those of individuals who are not citizens, not here legally, and perhaps not even here physically.

The paradigmatic example is the Mexican American Legal Defense and Education Fund (MALDEF), a public-interest law firm established by, and long dependent on, the Ford Foundation. MALDEF's policy analysts and lawyers have played a prominent role in immigration policymaking over the last few decades. They were particularly visible in the debate culminating in the Immigration Reform and Control Act of 1986, which simultaneously instituted sanctions on employers hiring undocumented workers and offered amnesty to millions of illegal immigrants.[44]

But MALDEF's role in this debate was not very constructive. As political scientist Christine Marie Sierra has chronicled, Latino and allied organizations in Washington during the 1980s faulted MALDEF for its "purist politics" and "no compromise" posturing. They complained that, because MALDEF "did not represent a mass-based constituency" and was "answerable only to a board of directors, the organization could afford to pursue uncompromising stands."[45] Sierra reports, not surprisingly, that MALDEF eventually lost credibility with Congress. Today, the organization's visibility and clout are greatly diminished. Yet the dilemmas raised by the inevitable demands to represent immigrants who are either poorly situated or simply unable to speak for themselves continue to confront all of us.

More recently, Philip Schrag, a professor of public-interest law at Georgetown who has advocated before Congress on behalf of refugees, published a revealing and compelling account of these challenges. Commenting on the difficulties encountered by his coalition of immigrant and refugee organizations, Schrag notes that "public interest advocates are often concerned about legitimacy."[46] He then relates this concern directly to their resistance to compromise:

For advocates, the most difficult moments of the legislative battle involve the development, timing, and exposure of fallback positions. Part of the problem is the sense of stewardship that public interest advocates feel for the interests of constituents they represent, most of whom do not choose their representatives... *Public interest advocates perpetually doubt their right to take less than an absolutist position*, even when it is clear that advocating an absolutist position will result in worse legislation than seeking a compromise. (emphasis added)[47]

WHAT CAN BE DONE?

To be clear, I am not proposing a renewed debate about affirmative action, or even about public-interest politics. In the current environment, the first would be too rancorous and explosive, and it is doubtful that Republicans could wage it effectively. The second is too taken-for-granted, and too little understood, to be tackled right now. Yet for those concerned about the sorry state of our immigration policy and debate, there are initiatives that could lead us toward a genuinely comprehensive approach. This is not going to happen overnight, but it is worth making a start.

The beginning of wisdom here is to stop exaggerating the importance of the line between legal and illegal immigration. If Americans now obsess about illegal immigrants, it is because they have been conditioned to do so by our political elites, liberal and conservative alike, who have discovered that harping on this distinction is a useful way to simplify a tricky issue. The public's anxieties and outrage should be taken seriously, but it must also be acknowledged that as Americans we are all complicit in the dilemmas presented by the 11 million undocumented in our midst.[48]

We should also stop chasing the illusory remedy of guestworker programs. America has a long history with guestworkers. This includes a few small, targeted programs currently in place: an underutilized program for agricultural laborers (H-2A) and an over-subscribed program for "hi-tech workers" (H-1B). But these are like band-aids on a festering wound: They help a bit, but the problems are getting worse.

Historically, our largest such initiative was the Bracero Program, which from 1942 to 1964 brought approximately 4.6 million guestworkers here from Mexico.[49] To their credit, such programs typically acknowledge and actually try to work with the transience of low-skilled migrants, especially from nearby countries. But decades of experience, both here and in Europe, have shown that most such "guests" end up staying and bringing in their friends and families. Among migration experts there is virtual unanimity that the Bracero Program established the migratory patterns that eventually resulted in the torrent of illegal immigration across our southern border.[50]

Acknowledging these realities, policymakers are now proposing to offer guestworkers – after a specified period of residency – the possibility of permanent legal residency and eventual citizenship. Yet it strains credulity for legislators and advocates to refer to such initiatives, though they certainly do, as "guestworker programs."[51] If the challenge of mass immigration involves the strains associated with increasing numbers of newcomers settling here, then guestworker programs are not an answer – or at least not an honest one. If the waters are to be calmed and any progress in addressing our immigration dilemmas is to be made, we will need to refrain from this kind of double-talk.

Finally, we must stop obsessing over border security. During the recent presidential campaign, candidate Trump supercharged this trope, but he hardly pioneered it. Here again, our political and policy elites have found this a convenient simplification. During the 1980s and 1990s, when the border with Mexico really was out of control, our responses were halting at best. For example, the original border fence was easy to climb over – not necessarily on account of design flaws, but because, among other things, the Border Patrol did not want to be burdened with migrants falling and injuring themselves.[52] "Controlling the border" will always necessitate ongoing efforts to man and monitor whatever physical barriers and electronic devices are in place. But for some time now, "border security" has been little more than distracting political rhetoric.

In recent years, Republicans in particular have obsessed over border security. Yet once again, avoiding the more challenging or controversial aspects of immigration enforcement has been the name of the game. One such involves monitoring not just the millions of individuals who arrive here yearly (which is now done rather effectively), but also the millions who depart (which we do not at all attempt, because it is logistically daunting, expensive, and perhaps ill-advised).[53]

Obsessing over border security also allows Republicans (and many Democrats) to avoid imposing burdens on employers. For almost 30 years, it has been clear that America's immigration law is virtually unenforceable at the workplace, primarily because the documents required to prove legal status are easily forged. As a result, employers cannot fairly be held legally responsible for judging the validity of documents presented to them by employees.

The underlying issue, which we have only recently begun to address, is the sustainability of high levels of unskilled immigration.[54] This is not the venue to focus on it, except to note that economists calculate that prevailing policy, taking into account illegal as well as legal immigrants, contributes at most a few tenths of 1 percent of GDP annually to native-born Americans (the overwhelming share of GDP attributable to immigration goes of course to immigrants themselves!).[55] Because such analyses do not take into account the burdens placed on local and state social-service providers, we will at some point have to grapple with the realization that what's good for the landscaping contractors of America (and their customers) may not be good for America.[56] Or, in the wry observation of agricultural economist Philip Martin, "In the long run, there is nothing more expensive than cheap food."[57]

Yet if we should stop pursuing such policies, then what should we start doing instead? Short of a genuinely comprehensive approach to immigration reform, which looks to remain politically elusive, there are a few incremental measures that follow from these reflections.

A good first step would be a general implementation of meaningful employment verification. For many years, efforts to enforce the law in the workplace were stymied by privacy concerns and the specter of a "national identity card." But immigration officials persisted through various pilot programs and developed a reliable internet-based system that allows employers to rely on social-security numbers. E-Verify is not without problems, including false positives (causing legal residents, even citizens, to be mistakenly identified as illegal). And of course the program inevitably imposes burdens on employers. Yet such concerns have been minimized to the point where, after years of opposition, the U.S. Chamber of Commerce now endorses E-Verify's wider implementation.[58]

To be sure, many small businessmen will still object, and immigrant advocates will continue to raise concerns about false positives. Others will ask how such an effort would be coordinated with any future program offering relief to America's 11 million undocumented without encouraging abuse and more illegal immigration.[59] These are serious concerns, but they are manageable. It is time to make the reliable verification of all employees' immigration status standard practice.

Another initiative to be undertaken sooner rather than later involves helping immigrants to assimilate. America is an open and absorptive society, but it is also a large and pluralistic one that gives many divergent and confusing cues to newcomers. And there are some aspects of our society that immigrants – and especially their children – would do well to avoid. If many of us need to recognize and acknowledge America's continuing assimilative capacities, others among us must not take them for granted – or treat them like a free good. Instead, we should assume a more active stance in guiding and promoting assimilation.

This doesn't necessarily mean a renewed emphasis on citizenship instruction or even naturalization classes. Though important components of civic and political assimilation, right now these are too fraught with disagreements over content and goals, and too easily burdened with various political agendas. Instead, we should begin by pursuing a serious, sustained, coordinated effort to teach adult immigrants to speak English. This would reassure Americans that a critical component of their cultural heritage is not being threatened by mass immigration – and is being supported by elites. At the same time, encouraging adult immigrants to learn to speak English would not only benefit them directly but also provide a clear signal to them and their children about the need to adapt to their new home. If such an undertaking demonstrated initial success, it could be expanded to include English literacy.

Some may say we do this already, but our current efforts are meager and ineffective. English as a Second Language (ESL) classes have long been notoriously underfunded and oversubscribed. And in recent years, though the need has hardly abated, both funding and enrollments have been declining. The latest available data indicate total enrollment of about 734,000 individuals in adult ESL courses supported by the federal government's principal program.[60]

Besides our overall ineptness at teaching languages, certainly by European standards, ESL programs are frequently orphans, typically offered at community colleges where the needs of non-traditional, immigrant students compete with those of more acclimated and younger American students. Wherever offered, ESL classes are predominantly no- or low-fee, non-credit courses with "open-entry/open-exit" and are taught by underpaid, part-time instructors. Not surprisingly, adult immigrants with work and family responsibilities have a difficult time attending regularly. Most students start with no or very little English, and soon drop out. Those who stick with it make, according to the available evidence, minimal progress speaking English.[61]

Whether in a crowded rec room in a Brighton Beach apartment building for elderly Russian Jews or a classroom in a Polish American center in Chicago, classes I have observed are inspiring but disappointing. At a time when language learning has been revolutionized by digital technology, ESL programs seem caught in a time warp. Apart from the occasional inspired instructor, such programs do not convey to immigrants that America places a high priority on or feels much pride in their learning (or our teaching them) English.

But if we are to invest more in such programs, they will need to be more focused and demanding than current efforts. Forrest Chisman of the now-defunct Council for Advancement of Adult Literacy (CAAL) has argued for increased funding for ESL programs – but not "unless they more clearly define what their goals should be."[62] Indeed, Chisman's research highlights the nettle of inappropriate, competing, and confused objectives of ESL administrators and students alike. The former need to clarify not only what level of English proficiency is the target, but also in what context – family, work, public schools, or civic life – English-language skills are deemed critical. But, as Chisman also emphasizes, any such endeavor points directly to the confused, unrealistic, and generally low expectations of immigrant students, who nevertheless grossly underestimate the commitment required of them to make meaningful progress in learning English. As Chisman concludes, ESL "programs should make much greater efforts to help students expand their personal goals ... nurture a culture of success that expects faculty and students to strive for the largest possible learning gains, even though all will not achieve this goal."[63] Toward this end, Chisman suggests that ESL programs examine the possibility of charging students modest fees to "increase persistence in noncredit classes."[64] More generally, Chisman's analysis suggests that adult ESL is a program in urgent need of the energy, direction, and focus that only a highly visible national campaign could give it.

The perennial, if at times exaggerated, complaint that immigrants are not learning English reflects many Americans' real and enduring concerns that newcomers are not being encouraged to participate in the mainstream of our national life. Meanwhile, bilingual ballots and bilingual education, however necessary or helpful in specific instances, have only exacerbated such concerns. So, too, has the rhetoric of immigrant advocates and multiculturalists.

But if a new national ESL initiative were undertaken, how would we pay for it? One possibility would be a tax on employers who hire substantial numbers of immigrants, or perhaps a tax incorporated into the visa fees that businesses already pay to gain access to various categories of temporary workers. Fees on visas for high-skilled and professional employees might make particular sense. No doubt there would be resistance and pushback from employers. But if they reap the benefits of immigrant labor, then it is not unreasonable to ask them to share the burdens.

At the same time, there is considerable room here for private initiative. Foundations and wealthy entrepreneurs might well underwrite the cost of new, online curricula to teach English to native speakers of diverse languages. Such courses could be pursued by individuals at home and supplemented by class meetings. Indeed, community-based programs afford enormous opportunities for volunteer instructors. With his fellow immigrants in mind, Andrew Carnegie jump-started the free public library. Why couldn't a philanthropist today support such a contemporary version of that vision? Should this idea arouse opposition from multiculturalists claiming that it would diminish diversity by marginalizing the languages and cultures of immigrants, that would be a debate worth having – and it could be won!

TAKING IMMIGRATION SERIOUSLY

"In this volatile transitional situation, where the best and worst are equally possible in our racial relations and attitudes, the very worst thing that journalists, analysts, and commentators can do is to misinform the white majority that it is losing its majority status ..."[65]

The black sociologist Orlando Patterson voiced this concern back in May 2001. He was criticizing media hype surrounding the release of 2000 census data that America was turning into a "majority minority nation" in which whites were fast becoming the new minority. On the contrary, Patterson argued, "even with the most liberal of assumptions, there is no possibility that whites will become a minority in this nation in this century." Echoing a point I had made some years earlier,[66] Patterson went on to the point that among Hispanics driving the numbers, about half consistently identify racially as white and indeed that "second-generation Hispanic whites are intermarrying and assimilating mainstream language and cultural patterns at a faster rate than second generation European migrants of the late 19th and early 20th centuries."[67]

Today, as the 2020 decennial census approaches, these and other aspects of Hispanic assimilation are still very much in evidence. Yet America is in a very different place. We all live in the aftermath of 9/11, the Great Recession, and a long, rancorous debate over immigration. Large numbers of Americans – whites but also many non-whites – have lost ground economically and feel America to be in decline. Populist currents threaten elites on both sides of the Atlantic, and Donald Trump is in the White House. The dysfunction of our political institutions has been nowhere more apparent than in our doomed efforts at "comprehensive immigration reform."

Patterson's point – and my point here in this chapter – is that it need not be this way. Much that we have been struggling with concerning immigration is a function of our perverse post-civil rights political institutions and culture. Understanding this won't resolve the genuine dilemmas posed by immigration policy, but it does underscore the futility of "comprehensive immigration reform" – at least as we have conceived of it.

Instead, incremental steps are now the order of the day. And focusing on English-language acquisition is a feasible and constructive place to begin. *Andale!*

NOTES

1. John Higham, "The Transformation of the Statue of Liberty," in *Send These To Me: Jews and Other Immigrants to Urban America* (New York: Atheneum, 1975), pp. 78–80.
2. Higham, "Transformation of the Statue of Liberty," p. 87.
3. See Michael J. Piore, *Birds of Passage: Migrant Labor and Industrial Societies* (Cambridge: Cambridge University Press, 1980).
4. Mark Wyman, *Round-Trip to America: The Immigrants, Return to Europe, 1880–1930* (Ithaca and London: Cornell University Press, 1993), pp. 10–11.
5. Leo R. Chavez, *Shadowed Lives: Undocumented Immigrants in American Society*, Third Edition (Belmont, CA: Wadsworth Learning/ Cengage, 2013), p. 34.
6. For a revealing account of the challenges confronting labor activists attempting to organize immigrant workers, see Jennifer Gordon, *Suburban Sweatshops: The Fight for Immigrant Rights* (Cambridge: Harvard University Press, 2005).
7. William Julius Wilson and Richard P. Taub, *There Goes the Neighborhood: Racial, Ethnic, and Class Tensions in Four Chicago Neighborhoods and Their Meaning for America* (New York: Knopf, 2006), pp. 104–105.
8. Peter Skerry, *Mexican Americans: The Ambivalent Minority* (Cambridge: Harvard University Press, 2005).
9. Peter A. Morrison and Ira S. Lowry, "A Riot of Color: The Demographic Setting," in Mark Baldassare (ed.), *The Los Angeles Riots: Lessons for the Urban Future* (Boulder: Westview Press, 1994), pp. 19–46.

10. Wesley G. Skogan and Susan M. Hartnett, *Community Policing, Chicago Style* (New York: Oxford University Press, 1997), pp. 117–119, 158–160.

11. For a case study of precisely this dynamic, see Peter Skerry, "Immigration and Social Disorder," in Norton Garfinkle and Daniel Yankelovich (eds.), *Uniting America: Restoring the Vital Center to American Democracy* (New Haven and London: Yale University Press, 2005), pp. 124–138.

12. For an extended analysis of this question, see Peter Skerry, "Splitting the Difference on Illegal Immigration," *National Affairs* (Winter 2013): 3–26.

13. See Noah Pickus and Peter Skerry, "Good Neighbors and Good Citizens: Beyond the Legal–Illegal Immigration Debate " in this volume.

14. Robert Putnam, "*E Pluribus Unum*: Diversity and Community in the Twenty-First Century," *Scandinavian Political Studies* 30 (2007): 137.

15. George L. Kelling and James Q. Wilson, "Broken Windows: The Police and Neighborhood Safety," *The Atlantic* (March 1982).

16. *U.S. Department of Homeland Security, Yearbook of Immigration Statistics: 2014* (Washington, DC: U.S. Department of Homeland Security, Office of Immigration Statistics, 2016), pp. 65–66.

17. Jeffrey S. Passell and D'Vera Cohn, "As Mexican Share Declined, U.S. Unauthorized Immigrant Population Fell in 2015 Below Recession Level," *FactTank* (Washington, DC: Pew Research Center 2017), April 25.

18. Seth Mydans, "Poll Finds Tide of Immigration Brings Hostility," *New York* Times (1993), June 27, A1, A16.

19. Cristina M. Rodriguez, "The Significance of the Local in Immigration Regulation," *Michigan Law Review* 106, (February 2008): 594.

20. For a review of this literature, see Walter A. Ewing, Daniel E. Martinez, and Ruben G. Rumbaut, *The Criminalization of Immigration in the United States: Special Report* (Washington, DC: American Immigration Council, July 2015).

21. It is striking that long before Donald Trump campaigned against free trade and "open borders," a few attentive public opinion researchers highlighted the unprecedented gap in attitudes toward trade and immigration between U.S. elites and workers. See Kenneth F. Scheve and Matthew J. Slaughter, *Globalization and the Perceptions of American Workers* (Washington, DC: Institute for International Economics, 2001), March and *Worldviews 2002: American Public Opinion and Foreign Policy* (Chicago: Chicago Council on Foreign Relations, 2002); also Peter Skerry, "The Real Immigration Crisis," in Robert Faulkner and Susan Shell (eds.), *America At Risk: Threats to Liberal Self-Government in an Age of Uncertainty* (Ann Arbor: University of Michigan Press, 2009), pp. 174–192.

22. Kenneth K. Lee, *Huddled Masses, Muddled Laws: Why Contemporary Immigration Policy Fails to Reflect Public Opinion* (Westport, CT: Praeger, 1998), p. 145.

23. See his discussion of "the ordeal of assimilation" in Norman Podhoretz, *Making It* (New York: Bantam Books, 1969).

24. See Peter Skerry, "'This Was Our Riot, Too': The Political Assimilation of Today's Immigrants," in Tamar Jacoby (ed.), *Reinventing the Melting Pot: The New Immigrants and What It Means to Be American* (New York: Basic Books, 2004). For an extremely thoughtful analytical review and critique of the academic literature on assimilation, see Ruben G. Rumbaut, "Assimilation and Its Discontents: Ironies and Paradoxes," in Charles Hirschman, Philip Kasinitz, and

Josh DeWind (eds.), *The Handbook of International Migration* (New York: Russell Sage Foundation, 1999), pp. 172–195.

25. Nathan Glazer, *We Are All Multiculturalists Now* (Cambridge: Harvard, 1997), p. 119.

26. John Higham, *Send These to Me*, pp. 116–195.

27. Christopher Jencks, "Who Should Get In? Part II," *New York Review of Books* (December 20, 2001).

28. For a recent example of this perspective, written by the American-born son of Syrian Muslim immigrants, see M. Zuhdi Jasser, "Americanism versus Islamism," in Zeyno Baran (ed.), *The Other Muslims: Moderate and Secular* (New York: Palgrave Macmillan, 2010), pp. 175–191.

29. Janice Fine and Daniel J. Tichenor, "A Movement Wrestling: American Labor's Enduring Struggle with Immigration, 1866–2007," *Studies in American Political Development* 23 (April 2009), 107.

30. Quoted in Cynthia Gordy, "Rep. John Lewis: Immigration Is the New Civil Rights Battle," *The Root* (May 2, 2011). Available at: www.theroot.com/rep-john-lewis-immigration-is-the-new-civil-rights-ba-1790864033, accessed June 22, 2017.

31. Wilson and Taub, *There Goes the Neighborhood*, p. 182.

32. For one analysis of this complicated, fraught story, see Mae M. Ngai, *Impossible Subjects: Illegal Aliens and the Making of Modern America* (Princeton: Princeton University Press, 2004), pp. 50–55.

33. Esther Cepeda, "The Mirage of the Rainbow Coalition," *Washington Post Writers Group* (March 15, 2015).

34. See John Higham, *Strangers in the Land: Patterns of American Nativism, 1860–1925* (New York: Atheneum, 1975); and then John Higham, "Another Look at Nativism," in Higham, *Send These to Me*, pp. 102–115.

35. Higham, "Another Look at Nativism," pp. 107–108.

36. John Higham, "Cultural Responses to Immigration," in Neil J. Smelser and Jeffrey C. Alexander (eds.), *Diversity and Its Discontents: Cultural Conflict and Common Ground in Contemporary American Society* (Princeton: Princeton University Press, 1999), p. 52.

37. Timothy J. Hatton and Jeffrey G. Williamson, *Global Migration and the World Economy: Two Centuries of Policy and Performance* (Cambridge: MIT Press, 2005), pp. 155–179.

38. Hatton and Williamson, *Global Migration and the World Economy*, p. 83.

39. Hatton and Williamson, *Global Migration and the World Economy*, p. 178.

40. Hatton and Williamson, *Global Migration and the World Economy*, p. 179.

41. Andrew S. McFarland, *Common Cause: Lobbying in the Public Interest* (Chatham, NJ: Chatham House, 1984), pp. 40–43.

42. James Q. Wilson, "The Politics of Regulation," in James Q. Wilson (ed.), *The Politics of Regulation* (New York: Basic Books, 1980), pp. 370–372.

43. For an enlightening discussion of such issues, see Neil K. Komesar and Burton A. Weisbrod, "The Public Interest Law Firm: A Behavioral Analysis," in A. Burton, Joel Weisbrod, F. Handler, and Neil K. Komesar, *Public Interest Law: An Economic and Institutional Analysis* (Berkeley: University of California Press, 1978), pp. 42–79.

44. See Skerry, *Mexican Americans*, pp. 323–330.

45. Christine Marie Sierra, "Latino Organizational Strategies on Immigration Reform: Success and Limits in Public Policymaking," in Roberto E. Villarreal and Norma G. Hernandez (eds.), *Latinos and Political Coalitions: Political Empowerment for the 1990s* (New York: Greenwood Press, 1991), p. 74.

46. Philip G. Schrag, *A Well-Founded Fear: The Congressional Battle to Save Political Asylum in America* (New York: Routledge, 2000), p. 251.

47. Schrag, *Well-Founded Fear*, p. 251.

48. For an extended exposition of this perspective, see Skerry, "Splitting the Difference on Illegal Immigration."

49. Ngai, *Impossible Subjects*, pp. 138–166.

50. See Philip Martin, "Guest Workers: New Solution or New Problem?" *University of Chicago Legal Forum* (2007): 289–315.

51. See, for example, the proposal presented in Jeb Bush and Clint Bolick, *Immigration Wars: Forging an American Solution* (New York: Threshold Editions, 2013), pp. 27–28.

52. Peter Skerry, "How Not to Build a Fence," *Foreign Policy* (September/October 2006), 64–67.

53. See David Martin, "Resolute Enforcement Is Not Just for Restrictionists: Building a Stable and Efficient Immigration Enforcement System," *Journal of Law and Politics* 30 (2015): 432–435.

54. For an unusually encouraging example of just such an effort, see the recent legislation introduced by U.S. Senators Tom Cotton (R-Arkansas) and David Perdue (R-Georgia), the Reforming American Immigration for Strong Employment (RAISE) Act, which would begin to reorient U.S. policy away from family-based admissions and toward more employment-based criteria.

55. See George Borjas, *Immigration and the American Worker: A Review of the Academic Literature* (Washington, DC: Center for Immigration Studies, April 2013).

56. On the fiscal impacts of our immigration policy, see Hatton and Williamson, *Global Migration and the World Economy*, pp. 288–311.

57. Philip L. Martin, *Promise Unfulfilled: Unions, Immigration, and the Farm Workers* (Ithaca and London: Cornell University Press, 2003), p. 162.

58. See Steven Greenhouse, "Business and Labor Try to Unite to Alter Immigration Laws," *New York Times* (February 7, 2013).

59. See *Breaking the Immigration Stalemate: From Deep Disagreements to Constructive Proposals*, A Report from the Brookings-Duke Immigration Policy Roundtable (Washington, DC: The Brookings Institution and Durham, NC: The Kenan Institute for Ethics, 2009), pp. 9–11.

60. *Adult Education and Family Literacy Act of 1998: Annual Report to Congress-Program Year 2011–2012* (Washington, DC: U.S. Department of Education; Office of Career, Technical, and Adult Education, July 2015), p. 11.

61. See Forrest P. Chisman and JoAnn Crandall, *Passing the Torch: Strategies for Innovation in Community College* ESL (New York: Council for Advancement of Adult Literacy, February 26, 2007) and Forrest P. Chisman, *Findings in ESL: A Quick Reference to Findings of CAAL Research on ESL Programs at Community Colleges* (New York: Council for Advancement of Adult Literacy, July 22, 2008).

62. Chisman, *Findings in ESL*, p. 21.

63. Chisman, *Findings in ESL*, p. 14.
64. Chisman, *Findings in ESL*, p. 13.
65. Orlando Patterson, "Race by the Numbers," *New York Times* (May 8, 2001).
66. Skerry, *Mexican Americans*, pp. 15–18.
67. Orlando Patterson, "Race by the Numbers."

3

Who Got the Jobs?: Two-Thirds of Long-Term Employment Gains Have Gone to Immigrants, 2000–2017

Steven A. Camarota and Karen Zeigler

Researchers have tried to estimate immigration's effects by making assumptions about the U.S. labor market. But such analysis is highly dependent on what assumptions one makes about the substitutability of workers or the interconnected nature of local labor markets. In this analysis, we simply look at who actually got the jobs over the last 17 years. The findings show that, among the working-age population (ages 16 to 65), nearly two-thirds of the net gain in employment from 2000 to 2017 has gone to immigrants (legal and illegal), even though natives accounted for almost two-thirds of the increase in the working-age population. Since the first quarter of 2007, before the Great Recession started, only 26 percent of employment gains have gone to natives, even though they accounted for 62 percent of population growth among the working-age.

While the employment rate (share working) has improved and native-born Americans have made significant job gains in recent years, the rate has not returned to its level before the 2007 recession and is much lower than in 2000. The labor force participation rate (share working or looking for work) of natives remains persistently low; and the number of working-age (16 to 65) natives not in the labor force in the first quarter of 2017 remains well above levels in 2000 and 2007. The long-term deterioration in employment among the native-born has impactions for almost every race, age, education level, and gender.

The enormous number of working-age people not in the labor force is an indication that there is no general labor shortage, which is a primary justification for the large increases in immigration (skilled and unskilled) in the Schumer-Rubio bill (S.744) that passed the U.S. Senate in 2013. Moreover, the decline challenges the argument that immigration increases job opportunities for natives – nearly 18.3 million working-age immigrants arrived in the last 17 years.

INTRODUCTION

Congressional Budget Office projections indicate that if the Schumer-Rubio bill (S.744) had become law, the number of new legal immigrants allowed into the country would have roughly doubled to 20 million over the next decade, adding to the 40 million immigrants (legal and illegal) already here.[1] This increase is in addition to the legalization of illegal immigrants already in the country. The primary argument for this dramatic increase is, as Republican Paul Ryan (R-Wisconsin) has argued, that without it the country will face "labor shortages." The National Restaurant Association, National Association of Home Builders, National Association of Manufacturers, Business Roundtable, U.S. Chamber of Commerce, and numerous other companies and business associations have all argued that immigration should be increased because there are not enough workers in the country, both skilled and unskilled.[2] This analysis examines employment trends for immigrants and natives to see if potential workers are, in fact, in short supply.

The findings show that employment growth has been weak over the last 17 years and has not kept pace with population growth and new immigration. Among the working-age population (16 to 65), about two-thirds of employment growth has gone to immigrants (legal and illegal). This is striking because natives accounted for almost two-thirds of the overall population growth among the working-age population.[3] Employment, of course, fluctuates with the economy, but two-thirds of the net increase in employment among the working-age has gone to immigrants from the first quarter of 2000 to the first quarter of 2017, partly because natives never fully recovered from the 2001 recession and a disproportionate share of employment growth went to immigrants. Further, natives were somewhat harder hit by the 2007 recession and immigrants have recovered from it faster than have natives. Immigrants made gains throughout the labor market over the last 17 years with about half of that growth among those with a bachelor's degree or more.

PRIOR RESEARCH: IMMIGRATION AND BLACK WORKERS

This analysis focuses on employment and the possibility that immigration is reducing the employment opportunities for the native-born. While economists have generally focused more on immigration's potential impact on wages, there is research indicating that immigration negatively impacts native employment. In a 2010 article, Borjas, Grogger, and Hanson found that immigration reduces the employment of less-educated black men and increases their rate of incarceration.[4] Their conclusions are similar to a 2010 academic study by Shihadeh and Barranco, which found that Latino immigration raises black violence by first increasing black unemployment.[5] These findings are supported by earlier work that showed immigration reduced black employment and wages.[6]

IMMIGRATION AND ALL WORKERS

Other studies have also found that immigration reduces job opportunities for natives. In its 1997 study of California, the Rand Corporation concluded that, in that state alone, competition with immigrants for jobs caused between 128,200 and 194,000 native-born workers in the state to withdraw from the workforce.[7] A more recent analysis by Federal Reserve economist Christopher Smith (2012) found that immigration reduces the employment of U.S.-born teenagers.[8] This is consistent with research in 2005 work by Sum, Harrington, and Khatiwada.[9] The Congressional Budget Office cost estimate for the Gang of Eight immigration bill (S.744) indicates that just the increases in legal immigration in the bill will increase unemployment by about 150,000 through the year 2020.[10] Although there is evidence that immigration reduces employment opportunities for natives, there remains a debate among economists about the extent of the job displacement.

METHODS AND DATA SOURCE

This analysis is based on the "household survey" collected by the Census Bureau for the Bureau of Labor Statistics. The survey, officially known as the Current Population Survey (CPS), is the nation's primary source of information on the U.S. labor market.[11] The CPS survey does not include those in institutions such as prisons. We concentrate in this analysis on the first quarter of each year 2000 to 2017 because comparing the same quarter over time controls for seasonality. We also emphasize the economic peaks in 2000 and 2007 as important points of comparison.

We focus on the share of working-age people holding a job or looking for work, referred to by economists as the labor force participation rate. Also, we examine the employment rate, which is the share of working-age people holding a job. Labor force participation and the employment rate are measures of labor force attachment that are less sensitive to the business cycle than the often-cited unemployment rate. The standard measure of unemployment, while useful in some contexts, is a very limited way of thinking about attachment to the labor market. To be considered officially unemployed in the CPS, respondents must indicate that they are not working, but have looked for a job in the four weeks preceding the survey. If a person has not looked for a job in the last four weeks, he or she is not considered unemployed.

OVERALL TRENDS AMONG THE WORKING-AGE POPULATION: THE 16- TO 65-YEAR-OLD POPULATION

Comparing the number of immigrants working (ages 16 to 65) in the first quarter of 2000 to the number working in the first quarter of 2017 shows an increase of 7.7 million. In contrast, the number of working-age (16 to 65)

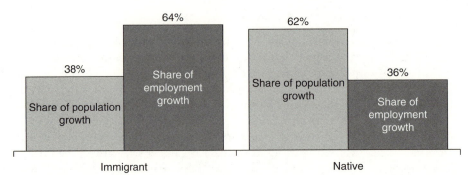

FIGURE 3.1 Natives accounted for nearly two-thirds of the increase in the working-age population (16 to 65), but only one-third of the increase in employment gains, 2000 to 2017. Source: Public-use files of the Current Population Survey for the first quarters of 2000 and 2017. All figures are for those 16 to 65.

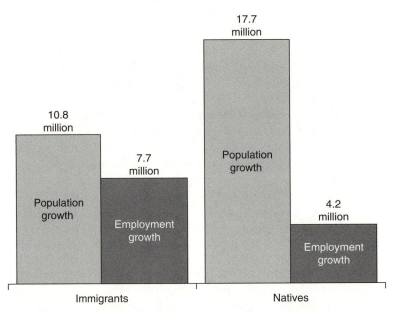

FIGURE 3.2 Employment growth for natives has not kept pace with population growth among the working-age (16 to 65) 2000–2017.
Source: Public use files of the Current Population Survey for the first quarters of 2000 and 2017. All figures are for those 16 to 65.

natives holding a job was only 4.2 million more from the first quarter of 2000 to the same quarter of 2017, even though the number of working-age natives overall increased by 17.7 million. This 17.7 million represented 62 percent of the overall growth in the working-age population. (See Figures 3.1 and 3.2 and Table 3.1) Since growth in the number of working-age natives greatly exceeded

TABLE 3.1 *Labor force status of natives and immigrants 2000–2017*

(Thousands)

	Age 16+					Ages 16 to 65		
	Natives 16+ working	Immigrants 16+ working	Natives working	Natives unemployed	Natives not in the labor force	Immigrants working	Immigrants unemployed	Immigrants not in the labor force
Q1 2000	118,061	17,424	114,827	5,255	35,740	17,115	836	6,562
Q1 2001	117,757	18,881	114,436	5,509	36,380	18,584	943	6,708
Q1 2002	116,149	18,910	112,852	7,420	37,907	18,578	1,336	6,870
Q1 2003	117,160	19,214	113,679	7,583	39,383	18,813	1,468	7,235
Q1 2004	117,684	19,649	114,036	7,467	40,756	19,262	1,282	7,418
Q1 2005	118,922	20,258	115,179	7,053	41,679	19,851	1,095	7,573
Q1 2006	120,540	21,542	116,666	6,337	42,143	21,007	1,049	7,478
Q1 2007	122,119	22,573	118,117	6,111	42,089	22,020	1,060	7,898
Q1 2008	122,313	22,441	118,071	6,525	43,075	21,877	1,331	7,745
Q1 2009	118,916	21,208	114,413	10,970	43,927	20,625	2,237	7,716
Q1 2010	116,188	21,144	111,611	12,875	45,845	20,479	2,672	7,855
Q1 2011	116,479	21,739	111,529	11,777	47,053	21,066	2,358	8,176
Q1 2012	118,005	22,675	112,793	10,675	48,124	22,000	2,251	8,634
Q1 2013	119,035	23,145	113,519	10,096	48,615	22,414	1,971	8,894
Q1 2014	120,626	23,624	114,700	8,774	49,195	22,814	1,663	8,872
Q1 2015	122,377	24,724	116,245	7,354	48,937	23,871	1,414	9,583
Q1 2016	124,489	25,456	118,139	6,683	48,474	24,489	1,231	9,709
Q1 2017	125,836	25,747	119,068	6,172	48,248	24,768	1,265	9,308

Source: Public-use files of the Current Population Survey for the first quarter from 2000 to the first quarter of 2017.
Note: Those unemployed are not working and have looked for work in the prior four weeks. Those not in the labor force are neither working nor looking for work.

growth in the number working or looking for work, the *share* of working-age natives holding a job or in the labor force was much lower in the first quarter of 2017 than the same quarter of 2000. The falloff in the employment and labor force participation rates of natives began before the 2007 recession. The employment rate of natives fell from 73.7 percent in 2000 to 71 percent at the peak of the last expansion in the first quarter of 2007. In the first quarter of 2017, the rate was 68.6 percent. The share of working-age natives in the first quarter of 2000 in the labor force was 77.1 percent, 74.7 percent in 2007, and 72.2 percent in 2017.

Of course, not all the 54.4 million non-institutionalized, working-age natives without a job want to work or even can work. But this has always been the case. It is for this reason that it is necessary to look for a trend over time. There is simply no question that the general decline in the employment rate of natives is both long-term and large. If the employment rate of natives (16 to 65) in the first quarter of 2017 were what it was in 2000 (73.7 percent), 8.8 million more natives would have been working. If the share working were what it was in the first quarter of 2007 (71 percent), 4.1 million more natives would have a job today. Among immigrants, their employment rate in the first quarter of this year is higher than the first quarter of 2000, but to match the employment rate in 2007, 360,000 more immigrants would be working. Both the situation in 2007 before the recession and the situation today represent a significant deterioration from what had been the employment rate of natives as recently as 2000.

POPULATION GROWTH OUTPACED JOB GROWTH

One way to think about the last 17 years is that employment growth did not come close to matching natural population growth and the number of immigrants allowed to settle in the country – legally and illegally. The total working-age population (immigrant and native) grew 9.4 percent from the economic peak in 2000 to the economic peak in 2007, while the number of working-age people actually employed increased only 6.2 percent. Over the entire 17-year period from 2000 to 2017, the working-age population grew by 28.5 million (15.8 percent), while employment grew only about 9 percent (Table 3.1, Figure 3.3). At a basic level, it is this gap between natural population growth and immigration-induced population growth, on the one hand, and employment growth on the other hand, that created such a large increase in the number of working-age people not working, primarily natives. Of course, the gap is only a description of what happened. By itself it does not explain why it happened or provide an answer as to why such a disproportionate share of this gap was absorbed by natives.

NEW ARRIVALS

In addition to identifying the native- and foreign-born, the CPS also asks when individuals arrived in the United States. The CPS from the first quarter of 2017 shows that there were 21.2 million immigrants (legal and illegal) who indicated that they had arrived in the country in 2000 or later.[12] This is a reminder of how large the scale of immigration has been over the last 17 years. It is worth pointing out that the Current Population Survey, like all Census Bureau data of this kind, tends to under-count immigrants generally, and new arrivals in particular; therefore, the actual number of new immigrants is higher than the estimates from the CPS.[13]

The Center for Immigration Studies, as well as other researchers, has found that the level of new immigration post-2007 is below the record levels it was a decade ago.[14] Even with this decline, in the first quarter of 2017 there were 10.9 million new immigrants in the CPS who indicated they had arrived in 2008 or later, despite the economy. Of the 10.9 million post-2007 arrivals, 5.4 million were of working-age and had a job in 2017 – 5.8 million were in the labor force. Over the same time period, the number of working-age natives holding a job

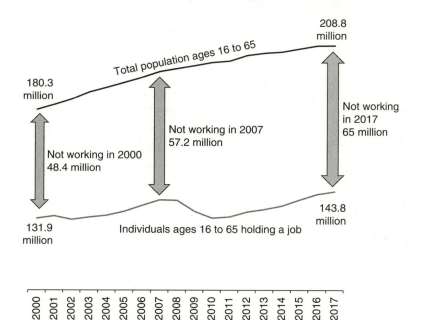

FIGURE 3.3 Natural population growth and new immigration have greatly exceeded employment growth, 2000–2017.
Source: Public-use files of the Current Population Survey from the first quarter of 2000 to the first quarter of 2017.Notes: Those not working are either unemployed (looking for work) or not in the labor force (not working nor looking for work).
Figures are for natives and immigrants ages 16 to 65.

only increased by about 950,000. Although immigration is below its prior peak, the large number of immigrants who arrived 2008 to 2017 is an indication that immigration can remain quite high even in the face of a weak job market. This is because the United States remains a very attractive place for immigrants to settle even during a severe economic downturn. Also, despite the economy, there has been no significant change in U.S. immigration policy, which is among the most generous in the world.

IMMIGRANT GAINS BY OCCUPATION

Unfortunately, the occupational categories used by the Census Bureau in the CPS were changed significantly between 2000 and 2017, so direct comparisons by occupation are difficult. However, the occupations from 2003 forward are defined in a way that allows some direct comparison with the 2017 data. Table 3.2 shows the number of working-age immigrants and natives holding a job by broad occupational categories in 2003 and 2017. The table also reports the number of immigrants in 2017 who indicated that they had arrived in 2000 or later by occupation. There were a total of 12.1 million immigrants who arrived in 2000 or later who were of working-age and employed in 2017. The number of working-age immigrants holding a job increased by six million from 2003 to 2017.[15] The reason the two numbers are so different is partly because they are for different periods. One shows only 14 years of growth, the other is for 17 years of arrivals. More important, they measure very different things. The six million growth figure represents a net increase; the arrival number is a flow of new immigrants. New arrivals are offset by deaths, return migration, and those who age out of the 16 to 65 cohort. Thus, the net increase is substantially less than number of new arrivals.

In terms of the top five occupations for immigrant employment growth 2003–2017, three might be considered traditionally immigrant and lower-skilled: building cleaning and maintenance, construction and extraction, and personal care and service, which includes barbers and nail salon employees. Two were higher-skilled: management and computers and mathematical science. But immigrants also made significant gains in more middle-skilled jobs, such as healthcare support, office and administrative support, and sales. In terms of new arrivals, one out of six immigrants found work in just these three middle-skilled occupations. Clearly immigrants took jobs in occupations throughout the economy. All the occupational categories where immigrants made their biggest gains employ millions of native-born Americans. As we will see, even when we examine occupations at the highest level of detail, it is clear that millions of natives work in the occupations where immigrants are concentrated.

TABLE 3.2 *Immigrant and native employment by occupational category*

	2003		2017		Immigrant growth by occupation 2003–2017[*]	Immigrants in 2017 who arrived 2000–2017[**]
	Native	Immigrant	Native	Immigrant		
Management	12,559	1,335	14,323	2,154	819	888
Construction & extraction	5,759	1,593	5,042	2,321	728	1,185
Computer & mathematical science	2,607	572	3,419	1,207	635	742
Grounds, cleaning & maintenance	2,900	1,380	3,178	1,983	603	982
Personal care & service	3,390	632	4,197	1,180	548	578
Healthcare practitioner & technical	5,633	868	7,408	1,274	406	509
Business & financial operations	4,784	550	6,237	899	349	411
Transportation & material moving	6,567	1,411	6,975	1,753	342	869
Education, training, & library	7,210	641	8,038	955	314	494
Food preparation & serving	5,551	1,555	6,268	1,857	302	1,106
Architecture & engineering	2,177	403	2,410	600	197	312
Installation, maintenance, & repair	4,366	581	4,102	753	172	315
Office & administrative support	17,427	1,695	14,829	1,859	164	782
Healthcare support	2,382	487	2,696	639	152	328
Sales & related	13,444	1,755	13,066	1,901	146	923
Life, physical, & social service	1,082	208	1,006	305	97	191
Arts, design, entertainment, sports, & media	2,288	277	2,723	350	73	159

(continued)

TABLE 3.2 (*continued*)

	2003		2017		Immigrant growth by occupation 2003–2017[*]	Immigrants in 2017 who arrived 2000–2017[**]
	Native	Immigrant	Native	Immigrant		
Farming, fishing, & forestry	571	311	663	379	68	210
Legal	1,323	82	1,438	138	56	39
Protective service	2,393	163	2,669	201	38	95
Community & social service	1,938	176	2,189	206	30	90
Production	7,326	2,137	6,192	1,854	(283)	889
Total	113,678	18,812	119,068	24,768	5,956	12,098

Source: Public-use files of the Current Population Survey (CPS) for the first quarters of 2003 and 2017.

Notes: *Occupational codes do not match prior to 2003.

**Based on the year of arrival question from the CPS in the first quarter of 2017.

JOBS AMERICANS DON'T DO?

As we have seen in Table 3.2, immigrants made gains across the labor market. Looking at broad occupations as shown in that table makes clear that there are tens of millions of natives employed in the occupational categories where immigrants have found jobs in the last 17 years. Thus, part of the reason immigration is likely to adversely impact the employment of some natives is that, contrary to the assertion of some, immigrants often do the same jobs. In other research, we examined all 472 civilian detailed occupations as defined by the Department of Commerce. We found only six were majority immigrant (legal and illegal). These six occupations account for 1 percent of the total U.S. workforce. Many jobs often thought to be overwhelmingly immigrant are, in fact, majority native-born. For example, 51 percent of maids and housekeepers are U.S.-born, as are 63 percent of butchers and meat processors. It is also the case that 64 percent of grounds maintenance workers are U.S.-born, as are 66 percent of construction laborers and 73 percent of janitors.[16] It is simply not the case that there are jobs that Americans do not do.

WHY HAS ALL EMPLOYMENT GROWTH GONE TO IMMIGRANTS? A DETERIORATION FOR NATIVES BEFORE 2007

As we have seen, the period 2000 to 2007 was not particularly good for the native-born. The number of natives holding a job increased just 2.9 percent from the first quarter of 2000 to the first quarter of 2007; in contrast, the number of immigrants with jobs increased 28.7 percent. The share of working-age natives holding a job was lower at the economic peak in the first quarter of 2007 than the prior peak in the first quarter of 2000. Figure 3.4 shows that natives 16 to 65 once had a higher employment rate than immigrants, but by 2007 the rate for natives had fallen while it had increased for immigrants. Figure 3.5 shows that labor force participation was also lower in 2007 than in 2000, which is not the case for immigrants. Thus, when we compare the economic peak in 2000 to the peak in 2007, immigrants clearly fared better.

A FASTER RECOVERY FOR IMMIGRANTS

Figure 3.4 shows that the employment rate for working-age natives declined somewhat more than for immigrants after 2007, hitting a low of 65.5 percent in the first quarter of 2010. The number of working-age natives not working increased by 10.5 million (21.8 percent) from the first quarter of 2007 to the first quarter of 2010, when employment bottomed out. Among immigrants, it increased 17.5 percent over the same time period. Thus, in terms of relative job losses, natives were hit somewhat harder by the Great Recession than immigrants.

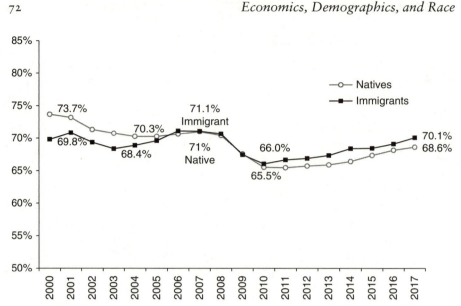

FIGURE 3.4 The employment rate of natives (16 to 65) never fully recovered from the 2001 recession; and the rate remains below the 2007 level.
Source: Public-use files of the Current Population Survey for the first quarter of 2000 to the first quarter of 2017.
Note: The employment rate is the share of a given population holding a job.

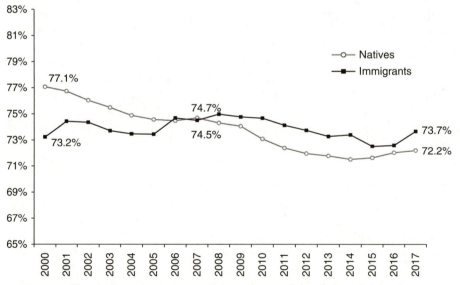

FIGURE 3.5 Despite some improvement in recent years, labor force participation among natives (ages 16 to 65) has looked dismal over the last 17 years.
Source: Public-use files from the Current Population Survey from the first quarter of 2000 to the first quarter of 2017.
Note: Labor force participation is the share of the working-age (16 to 65) population working or looking for work.

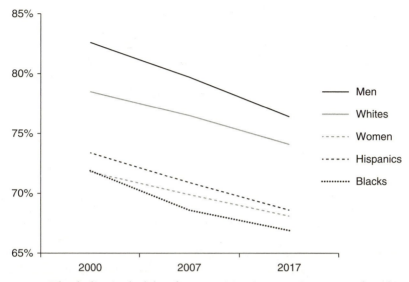

FIGURE 3.6 The decline in the labor force participation rate since 2000 of working-age natives has impacted both genders, whites, blacks, and Hispanics.
Source: Public-use files of the Current Population Survey for the first quarters of 2000, 2007, and 2017.
Notes: Labor force participation is the share of the working-age (16 to 65) population working or looking for work.
Figures for whites and blacks in 2007 and 2014 are for single race; in 2000 it was not possible to select more than one race.
Hispanics can be of any race and are excluded from the figures for blacks and whites.

Equally important, immigrants have recovered more quickly from the recession than natives. The employment rate for working-age natives has increased 3.1 percentage points from the bottom of the recession in the first quarter of 2010 to the first quarter of 2017, but it has improved 4.0 percentage points for immigrants over the same time period. Since 2010, the number of working-age natives actually working increased just 6.7 percent, while the number of working-age immigrants working increased 20.9 percent. Even in the last year (2016 to 2017), the employment rate for immigrants increased by a full percentage point, while increasing less than half a percentage point for natives. The different ways that the recovery has played out for immigrants and natives partly explains why a disproportionate share of jobs went to immigrants in the long term.

LABOR FORCE PARTICIPATION FOR THOSE AGED 16 TO 65

The labor force participation rate is similar to the employment rate except that it is calculated by including unemployment in the numerator. To be considered as participating in the labor market, one has to either be working or have looked for a job in the four weeks before the survey was taken. The number of working-age (16 to 65) natives not in the labor market has increased from 35.7 million in 2000 to 42.1 million in 2007 to 48.2 million in 2017. Thus, the 12.5 million (93.2 percent) of the 13.4 million increase in the number of working-age natives not working from 2000 to 2017 is due to an increase in the number not in the labor force rather than an increase in unemployment.

AN AGING IMMIGRANT POPULATION

The age profile of immigrants has changed over the last 17 years, but this does not seem to explain why they have done better than natives. The decline in the number of new arrivals in recent years means that fewer young immigrants have been added to the foreign-born population – on average immigrants arrive in their mid to late twenties. As a result, 30 percent of working-age immigrants were 29 or younger in 2000; but only 20 percent were in 2017. Among natives (16 to 65) the share under age 30 has increased slightly since 2000. Young people (immigrant or native) have the lowest labor force participation rates (see Table 3.3). Therefore, as the share of working-age immigrants who are young falls, the overall share of working-age immigrants in the labor force should rise.

However, excluding the young still shows that a disproportionate share of labor force growth went to immigrants. From 2000 to 2017 natives accounted for 46.3 percent of the growth in the total population aged 30 to 65, but only 27.9 percent of the net increase in labor force participation. The labor force participation rate for natives aged 30 to 65 fell from 2000 to 2007, while it rose for immigrants in this age group. Over the entire period 2000 to 2017, the labor force participation rate for natives aged 30 to 65 fell by 3.6 percentage points, while it remained the same for immigrants. Furthermore, the labor force participation rates of immigrants and natives by detailed age cohort in Table 3.3 show that immigrants fared better than natives from 2000 to 2007 and from 2007 to 2017 for those in their thirties, forties, and fifties. (Among those aged 60 to 65, natives did better.) Thus the decline in the share of immigrants who are young does not explain the pattern of immigrants doing better than natives in terms of labor force participation rates. It also does not seem to explain why a disproportionate share of labor force growth has gone to the foreign-born.

WHY IMMIGRANTS HAVE FARED BETTER

There are many possible reasons why immigrants did better than natives in the labor market from 2000 to 2007 and in the recovery from the Great Recession. Perhaps some employers are prejudiced against native-born workers, particularly U.S.-born African-Americans. Certainly, the labor force participation of native-born minorities has declined somewhat more than for

TABLE 3.3 *Labor force participation rates of natives and immigrants by age, 2000 to 2017*

All natives

Year						Ages				
	16–19	20–29	30–39	40–49	50–59	60–65	16–24	25–54	18–65	16–65
2000	49.7%	82.3%	85.7%	85.8%	76.3%	44.1%	64.5%	85.2%	79.0%	77.1%
2001	48.5%	81.8%	85.5%	85.5%	76.1%	45.1%	64.0%	84.9%	78.7%	76.7%
2002	45.1%	80.5%	85.4%	85.0%	76.2%	46.8%	61.6%	84.4%	78.2%	76.0%
2003	43.1%	79.2%	84.7%	84.8%	76.4%	48.4%	60.3%	83.9%	77.8%	75.5%
2004	41.3%	78.8%	84.2%	84.3%	76.5%	48.4%	59.3%	83.5%	77.2%	74.9%
2005	41.3%	78.8%	84.3%	84.2%	75.7%	48.2%	59.1%	83.4%	76.9%	74.6%
2006	41.2%	78.3%	84.3%	84.2%	76.2%	48.7%	58.4%	83.4%	76.9%	74.5%
2007	39.5%	79.2%	85.2%	84.3%	76.6%	50.2%	58.1%	83.9%	77.2%	74.7%
2008	37.6%	78.9%	84.6%	83.9%	77.2%	51.4%	56.6%	83.7%	76.9%	74.3%
2009	36.1%	78.5%	84.3%	83.8%	77.5%	52.8%	55.9%	83.4%	76.7%	74.1%
2010	33.1%	76.6%	84.4%	83.4%	77.2%	52.4%	53.2%	83.1%	75.8%	73.1%
2011	31.9%	76.3%	83.5%	83.0%	76.1%	51.7%	53.2%	82.3%	75.1%	72.4%
2012	31.4%	76.2%	83.6%	82.4%	75.6%	52.3%	53.1%	82.1%	74.6%	72.0%
2013	32.3%	76.0%	83.0%	81.9%	75.6%	52.0%	53.4%	81.6%	74.4%	71.8%
2014	31.1%	76.0%	83.5%	81.7%	74.4%	52.7%	53.3%	81.6%	74.1%	71.5%
2015	32.5%	75.9%	83.2%	82.1%	74.4%	52.8%	53.5%	81.7%	74.2%	71.6%
2016	33.3%	76.3%	83.3%	82.8%	74.5%	53.5%	54.0%	82.1%	74.6%	72.0%
2017	33.6%	77.1%	83.7%	82.6%	74.8%	52.9%	54.4%	82.3%	74.7%	72.2%

(continued)

TABLE 3.3 (*continued*)

Immigrants

Year	Ages									
	16–19	20–29	30–39	40–49	50–59	60–65	16–24	25–54	18–65	16–65
2000	39.1%	72.7%	80.2%	82.1%	72.7%	47.8%	57.6%	79.4%	74.7%	73.2%
2001	41.9%	74.6%	80.8%	82.5%	72.5%	48.7%	61.3%	80.1%	75.6%	74.4%
2002	40.9%	74.4%	79.4%	82.5%	73.6%	49.7%	61.6%	79.8%	75.4%	74.4%
2003	35.0%	73.7%	79.2%	80.9%	75.0%	50.3%	59.2%	79.0%	74.9%	73.7%
2004	34.9%	71.2%	79.9%	82.3%	74.2%	47.8%	58.3%	79.1%	74.7%	73.5%
2005	32.8%	71.4%	78.4%	81.6%	76.1%	50.0%	56.1%	78.8%	74.7%	73.4%
2006	37.1%	74.0%	79.8%	81.8%	75.1%	53.0%	58.9%	79.7%	75.8%	74.7%
2007	34.7%	73.2%	78.3%	83.2%	76.0%	52.3%	58.2%	79.7%	75.7%	74.5%
2008	35.1%	72.8%	79.1%	83.3%	77.1%	53.9%	57.2%	80.1%	76.1%	75.0%
2009	28.3%	71.1%	79.9%	83.3%	77.4%	52.3%	54.4%	80.3%	75.9%	74.8%
2010	28.3%	72.0%	79.3%	82.9%	77.0%	53.9%	54.8%	80.0%	75.7%	74.7%
2011	26.6%	72.3%	77.9%	82.0%	78.1%	55.6%	55.0%	79.3%	75.3%	74.1%
2012	27.7%	70.1%	78.4%	81.3%	77.7%	56.7%	52.2%	79.0%	74.8%	73.7%
2013	26.1%	69.4%	78.1%	81.7%	77.1%	54.9%	52.0%	78.6%	74.3%	73.3%
2014	26.1%	69.0%	78.9%	81.1%	76.7%	54.2%	51.3%	78.8%	74.5%	73.4%
2015	27.4%	67.7%	77.0%	79.9%	77.6%	55.6%	51.5%	77.6%	73.7%	72.5%
2016	24.8%	68.1%	77.2%	80.2%	77.1%	56.7%	49.0%	78.0%	73.7%	72.6%
2017	26.3%	70.6%	78.3%	80.9%	76.8%	59.1%	50.8%	78.9%	74.7%	73.7%

Source: Public-use files of the Current Population Survey from the first quarter of 2000 to the first quarter of 2017.
Note: Labor force participation is the share of the working-age population working or looking for work.

native-born whites or for immigrants (Figure 3.6). Moreover, there are ways in which the immigration system makes immigrant workers more attractive than natives. For example, the Summer Work Travel Program (part of the J-1 visa program) allows employers to hire temporary workers without having to make the Social Security and Medicare payments that employers would be required to make on behalf of native-born workers. Another example of the way the immigration system makes foreign workers more attractive to employers is that those who enter under the H1-B or H2-B visa programs cannot change companies easily, making them more captive to their employers.

Immigrants, having often come from much poorer societies with less social order, may be more willing to work off the books, for lower pay, or endure worse working conditions than natives, causing employers to prefer them as workers. Immigrant social networks may tend to shut natives out of jobs because employers come to rely on these networks to fill vacant positions to the exclusion of natives. For example, once an employer has a few immigrant workers, he may become less likely to advertise jobs widely, preferring instead to use the informal social network of his immigrant workers to fill positions. Immigrants may also be more mobile. By coming to this country, immigrants almost always see substantial improvement in their standard of living, no matter where in the United States they settle. This may make them more willing to move wherever there is job growth in the United States. Natives, on the other hand, may need significant wage incentives to move, which, because of the availability of immigrant labor, businesses are unwilling to offer. All of these factors, and perhaps others, likely explain why so much of the limited employment growth in the last 17 years has gone to foreign-born workers.

LITTLE RECENT IMPROVEMENT IN LABOR FORCE PARTICIPATION

Despite significant employment gains by natives in recent years, the labor force participation rate for working-age natives is actually slightly below the 2010 rate, when the jobs recovery began. The number of working-age natives not in the labor force was 2.4 million larger in the first quarter of 2017 than in first quarter of 2010. To some extent the economic recovery pulled the unemployed back into jobs, but not those outside the labor market. Also, some of the fall-off in unemployment was caused by those who left the labor market entirely. The long-term decline in the labor force participation of working-age natives would seem to be powerful evidence that there is no labor shortage.

WHEN WILL THE LABOR FORCE PARTICIPATION RATE RECOVER?

Between 2014 and 2017, the labor force participation rate of working-age natives improved seven-tenths of a percentage point, nearly one-quarter of a percentage point a year on average. If we optimistically assume a 0.25 percentage-point improvement each year moving forward it would take ten years (until 2027) for the labor force participation rate for natives to return to the 2007 level. For the native labor force participation rate to return to the 2000 level, it would take ten more years, to 2037. If there is another recession before either date, which given the average length between recessions in the post-war World War II period seems almost certain, then the rate will fall again, never having returned to the prior peak. As for the employment rate for working-age natives, between 2011 and 2017 the employment rate of working-age natives improved 3.2 percentage points, about half of a percentage point a year on average. If we assume a 0.5 percentage-point improvement each year moving forward, it would take five years (until 2022) for the employment rate for natives to return to the 2007 level. For the native employment rate to return to the 2000 level, it would take six more years, to 2028.

AGE, RACE, AND EDUCATION: BROAD DECLINE BY AGE

If we divide the population by different age groups, we still find the same decline in the share in the labor force. Table 3.3 reports different age groups for immigrants and natives. Among young natives 16 to 24 years old, the share in the labor force was 10.2 percentage points lower in 2017 than it was in 2000. In 2000, 64.5 percent of this age group worked; in 2017 it was only 54.4 percent. Looking at the labor force participation rate for those aged 20 to 29 shows it was 5.2 percentage-points lower in 2017 than 2000. The decline in the employment rate for younger natives under age 30 was larger than the 4.9 percentage-point decline for all working-age natives. Thus, there is no question that young natives have been harder hit by the relatively weak economy 2000 to 2007 and the Great Recession.

Immigrants are new entrants into the labor market and most natives begin their working life in their teens and twenties. It is likely that if immigration is reducing the job prospects for natives, younger natives would be more adversely affected. Older workers who are more established in the labor market are less likely to be impacted by newly arrived immigrants. The fact that those under 30 have seen a larger decline in their labor force participation rates is certainly consistent with the possibility that immigration explains a significant share of the decline in work among this population.

Although younger workers experienced the biggest decline in work, older workers have also had a difficult time in the labor market. The labor force participation rates for natives in their thirties, forties, and fifties all declined as well. In terms of the 12.5 million increase in the number of working-age natives not in the labor force, slightly less than half were among those under age 30. This means a disproportionate share of those leaving the labor force were young because they account for less than half of all working-age people. Nonetheless, more than half of the decline was among workers aged 30 and older. In short, native employment declined across virtually every age group.[17]

YOUNG NATIVES STILL HAVE HIGHER LABOR FORCE PARTICIPATION

We often worry in the United States about the work ethic of our young people. In private, many advocates for immigration will argue that immigrants have a better work ethic than natives, especially younger natives. However, teenage immigrants (16 to 19) are actually less likely to participate in the labor force than natives of the same age. This was the case in 2017 and in 2000. The same is true for those aged 16 to 24, though the difference is smaller. Of those in their twenties, natives again have a higher labor force participation rate. No matter how we define "young," natives have a higher labor force participation rate than immigrants. Therefore, if there is a work ethic problem among young natives in 2017, then the problem is even more pronounced among young immigrants, at least when measured by labor force participation.

LONG-TERM EFFECT OF YOUNG PEOPLE NOT WORKING

In some ways, the decline in work among the young is the most troubling because there is good evidence that not working when one is young has significant negative impacts on an individual's long-term employment patterns. Research indicates that those who do not work in their youth often do not develop the skills and habits necessary to function well in the labor market, such as respecting authority, showing up on time, and following instructions. The very large decline in work among those under age 30 may have significant negative consequences for those individuals as they age.[18] The failure of young people to gain work experience earlier in their adult lives may also have negative implications for the larger American society.

BROAD DECLINE BY RACE

Black Americans have long had lower labor force participation rates than other groups. But the last 17 years show that the labor force participation rate for working-age, native-born blacks declined 5.0 percentage points, compared to 4.4 percentage points for native whites and 4.8 percentage points for native-born Hispanics. The gap between whites, blacks, and Hispanics remains large through 2017.

BROAD DECLINE BY EDUCATION

The labor force participation rate of native-born high school dropouts, high school graduates, those with some college education, and those with at least a bachelor's degree all declined from 2000 to 2007 and from 2007 to 2017. (Education figures are only for those aged 18 to 65.) The decline in the share participating in the labor force has been most pronounced for those with some college education or less. The broad decline in work began before the Great

Recession, including those with at least a bachelor's degree. The share with at least a bachelor's degree in the labor force declined from 87.7 percent in the first quarter of 2000 to 86.2 percent in the first quarter of 2007, even though those were the peak years of the last expansions. In the first quarter of 2017, it was 85.5 percent. Figure 3.7 shows the decline for labor force participation by educational attainment.

As the share not in the labor force has increased, the number not in the labor force has also increased for all educational groups. The number of adult natives (aged 18 to 65) with no more than a high school education not in the labor force was 2.1 million larger in the first quarter of 2017 than at the start of 2000; the number with some college education not in the labor force was up 5.3 million; and the number with at least a bachelor's degree not working was up 3.1 million. In the first quarter of 2017, there were a total of 34.1 million adult natives aged 18 to 65 without a bachelor's degree not in the labor force as well as 7.7 million with at least a bachelor's degree.

The potential supply of workers for employers to draw upon at every education level is seemingly very large. It should be noted that the total size of the working-age native population with less than a high school education (working and not working) declined by 4.5 million. But the share in the labor

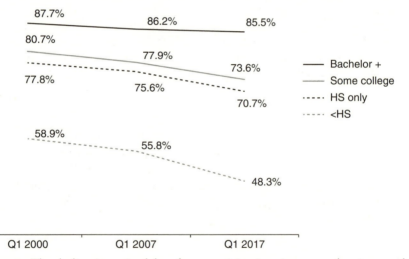

FIGURE 3.7 The decline in native labor force participation since 2000 has impacted every education level.

Source: Public-use files of the Current Population Survey for the first quarters of 2000, 2007, and 2017.

Notes: Labor force participation is the share of the working-age working or looking for work.

Because the analysis is by education it is restricted to those aged 18 to 65.

See Table 3.3 for all years 2000 to 2017.

force declined so much there was still a decrease in the labor force participation rate from 2000 to 2017. Among immigrants, the total number of adults with less than a high school education not in the labor force peaked in 2007 and has been trending downward since; though the total number is still higher than in 2000. Most of the labor force growth among immigrants was among those with at least a high school education.

DOES IMMIGRATION MAKE SOCIETY YOUNGER?

Ratio of Workers to Non-Workers

Because immigrants mostly arrive young and want to work, the argument is often made that immigration increases the ratio of workers to non-workers, helping to pay for government and improving economic growth. Of course, for this to be true immigrants have to actually work; simply being in the country or of working-age does not improve the share of the population that are workers. In the first quarter of 2017, 47.5 percent (151.6 million) of the nation's total non-institutionalized population of 319.4 million worked. If we remove all the 21.2 million post-2000 immigrants and their 5.7 million U.S.-born children, 47.5 percent of the population is working.[19] This means that immigration in the last 17 years has not changed the share of the population that is comprised of workers. One reason immigration over the last 17 years did not improve the share of the population that are workers is that only 57.7 percent of post-2000 immigrants actually had a job in 2017. This fact, coupled with the children they had after they arrived, who are too young to work, means that immigration increases the number of workers and the number of non-workers in roughly equal proportions.

By comparison, every one million persons already in the country shifting from not working to working increases the share of the population that is comprised of workers by 0.3 percentage points. Moving even one million people already here into jobs has a much larger impact than the last 17 years of immigration because it moves people out of one category (non-worker) to another category (worker), thereby increasing the numerator, but not the denominator. Immigrants, on the other hand, arrive at all ages, and, as with any human population, some work and some do not. If we are concerned about not having enough workers to grow the economy or to pay for government, then moving some of the tens of millions of working-age people already here who are not working into jobs is a much more effective way of improving the ratio of workers to non-workers than is immigration.

CONCLUSION

Over the last 17 years, employment growth has not matched natural population growth and the number of immigrants allowed to settle in the country – legally and illegally. Among the working-age, of the employment growth there has been, two-thirds has gone to immigrants. This is the case even though natives accounted for nearly two-thirds of the growth in the working-age population (aged 16 to 65). Though there has been significant recovery from the Great Recession, there are only 950,000 more working-age, native-born Americans holding a job in the first quarter of 2017 compared to the same quarter of 2007 before recession began. The number of natives not working was 54.4 million in the first quarter of 2017, 13.4 million larger than in the first quarter of 2000. There were also 10.6 million working-age immigrants not working at the start of 2017. These workers are of every education level. If employers are looking for college graduates; young workers; less-educated workers; older, more experienced workers; or practically any other type of worker, the potential supply would seem to be enormous.

Some may think that immigrants and natives never compete for jobs. But a majority of workers in virtually every occupation are native-born. Moreover, immigrant gains have not been confined to a few immigrant-heavy occupations, they have taken lower-, middle-, and higher-skilled jobs across the labor market. Thus the idea that there are jobs Americans don't do or that immigrants and natives never compete for jobs is simply not supported by the data.

While the extent to which immigrants displace natives from the labor market is debated in the academic literature, there are several things we can say based on the last 17 years. More than one million new immigrants arrived in the country every year since 2000. The long-term decline in labor force participation among natives is certainly supportive of the research showing that immigration reduces employment among the native-born. There is certainly no question that high levels of immigration have gone hand in hand with a profound deterioration in native-born labor force participation.

NOTES

1. *S.744 Border Security, Economic Opportunity and Immigration Modernization Act*, Congressional Budget Office cost estimate 2013. Table 2, p. 14 reports that by 2023 there will be 10.4 million additional U.S. residents if the bill passes, 1.2 million of whom will be the U.S.-born children of these new immigrants who will enter the country if the bill passes. See www.cbo.gov/sites/default/files/113th-congress-2013-2014/costestimate/s7444.pdf, accessed February 10, 2018.

2. The National Restaurant's position on the need for more foreign workers can be found at: www.restaurant.org/advocacy/Immigration

   The National Association of Home Builders letter on S.744 can be found at: www.nahb.org/~/media/Sites/,-w-,NAHB%20Tagging/Tagged-Comment-Letters-and-Testimony/RickJudsonTestimonyforWVisaPanelFinal_20130422100634.ashx. Their general view on the need for more immigration can be found at: www.nahb.org/en/research/nahb-priorities/immigration.aspx and at: www.nahb.org/en/advocate/policy-resolutions/workforce-and-labor/comprehensive-reform-of-immigration-laws.aspx

The National Association of Manufacturers letter on S.744 can be found at: www
.nam.org/Issues/Workforce-and-Immigration/Workforce-Development/NAM-and-
SEIU-Letter-to-Senate-on-S_744/. Their general views on the need for more
immigrant workers can be found at: www.nam.org/Communications/Articles/2013/
01/Manufacturers-Comprehensive-Immigration-Reform-an-Absolute-Necessity.aspx

This report provides an overview of the Business Round Table's call for increasing
immigration. Available at: http://businessroundtable.org/sites/default/files/legacy/
uploads/studies-reports/downloads/20130405_Taking_Action_on_Immigration.pdf

The Chamber of Commerce's press release, testimonies, and reports on immigration
can be found at: www.uschamber.com/immigration/testimony#timeline

A statement by the chamber's president on the need to increase immigration
can be found here: www.uschamber.com/blog/time-now-immigration-reform
and at:

http://immigration.uschamber.com/reforms/lesser-skilled-work-visa-reform

The Agriculture Workforce Coalition includes most of the major associations
representing farmers, landscapers, nurseries, and horticulture. Here is a report put
out by the Coalition on the need for more workers: http://migrationfiles.ucdavis.edu
/uploads/cf/files/2009-may/regelbrugge.pdf

Here is the coalition's statement on S.744: www.nmpf.org/files/AWC-Statement-
on-Senate-Committee-Immigration-052213.pdf

Compete America is a prominent coalition primarily of technology companies
and related associations that has lobbied for S.744 and other increases in higher
skilled immigrants, see www.competeamerica.org/. All websites were accessed on
February 10, 2018.

3. Table 3.1 reports employment for working-age (16 to 65) immigrants and natives
   for the first quarter for every year since 2000. It also reports the number of people
   working aged 16 and older. Comparing the first quarter of 2000 to the same quarter
   in 2017 for the working-age shows that two-thirds of the net increase in
   employment has gone to immigrants. However, looking at all workers aged 16-
   plus shows that natives over age 65 did make sizeable employment gains. As a result,
   there are 7.8 million more natives of all ages working in 2017 than in 2000 (3.5
   million of those gains were to natives over age 65). Thus, of the employment gains
   made by natives, a substantial portion were to those over age 65. Employment
   among immigrants aged 65-plus has increased to 670,000 since 2000.

4. George J. Borjas, Jeffrey Grogger, and Gordon H. Hanson, "Immigration and the
   Economic Status of Black Men," *Economica* 77(2010): 255–282.

5. Edward S. Shihadeh and Raymond E. Barranco, "Latino Employment and Black
   Violence: The Unintended Consequence of U.S. Immigration Policy Social Forces,"
   Social Forces 88 (March 2010): 1393–1420.

6. Augustine J. Kposowa, "The Impact of Immigration on Unemployment and
   Earnings Among Racial Minorities in the United States," *Racial and Ethnic
   Studies* 18 (1995):605–628.

7. Kevin F. McCarthy and Georges Vernez, "Immigration in a Changing Economy:
   California's Experience" (Santa Monica, CA: Rand Corporation,1997).

8. Christopher L. Smith, "The Impact of Low-Skilled Immigration on the Youth Labor
   Market," *Journal of Labor Economics* 30 (January 2012): 55–89.

9. Andrew Sum, Paul Harrington, and Ishwar Khatiwada, "The Impact of New Immigrants on Young Native-Born Workers, 2000–2005," Center for Immigration Studies, September 2006.

10. *S.744 Border Security, Economic Opportunity and Immigration Modernization Act*, Congressional Budget Office cost estimate. Available at: www.cbo.gov/sites/default/files/113th-congress-2013-2014/costestimate/s7444.pdf, accessed February 10, 2018.

11. We do not use the "establishment survey," which measures employment by asking businesses, because that survey is not available to the public for analysis. Equally important, it does not ask if an employee is an immigrant. Like all Census Bureau surveys, the CPS is weighted to reflect the size and composition of the nation's population. There are breaks in the continuity of the survey and this could slightly impact comparisons over time. This is due to periodic re-weighting done by the Census Bureau to better reflect what it believes is the actual size of the U.S. population, such as after the decennial census. Any long-term studies of poverty, wages, health insurance, and other socio-demographic characteristics that use Census Bureau surveys have this issue. However, the re-weighting affects both the native and immigrant populations and is done to make the data more accurate as new information becomes available. For 2000 to 2002, we use the revised weights that were issued by the Census Bureau after the 2000 Census revealed that the original weights assigned to the CPS were too low – mainly because the Bureau had underestimated immigration. If we use the original weights it does not meaningfully change the results. In our view, and the view of most immigration researchers, using the revised weights makes the data slightly more accurate and improves the continuity of the data. For a technical discussion of how the Census Bureau believed the re-weighting improved the data, see Mary Bowler, Randy E. Ilg, Stephen Miller, Ed Robison, and Anne Polivka, "Revisions to the Current Population Survey Effective in January 2003," Bureau of Labor Statistics, 2003.

12. This figure is from the public-use files of the Current Population Survey for January, February, and March 2017. The survey asks immigrants when they came to the United States. The figure includes both legal and illegal immigrants.

13. The Department of Homeland Security estimates an undercount of post-1980 immigrants (foreign-born) in the American Community Survey, which is similar to the CPS used in this analysis, of 5.8 percent. See Table 2 in Bryan Baker and Nancy Rytina, "Estimates of the Unauthorized Immigrant Population Residing in the United States: January 2012," Department of Homeland Security, March 2013, p. 4. Available at: www.dhs.gov/sites/default/files/publications/Unauthorized%20Immigrant%20Population%20Estimates%20in%20the%20US%20January%202012_0.pdf, accessed February 10, 2018.

14. Steven A. Camarota and Karen Zeigler, "*A* Shifting Tide: Recent Trends in the Illegal Immigrant Population," Center for Immigration Studies, July 2009; Steven A. Camarota and Karen Zeigler, "Homeward Bound: Recent Immigration Enforcement and the Decline in the Illegal Alien Population," Center for Immigration Studies, July 2008; Jeffrey Passel, D'Vera Cohn and Ana Gonzalez-Barrera, "Net Migration from Mexico Falls to Zero and Perhaps Less," Pew Hispanic Center, April 23, 2012.

15. As already discussed, if we use 2000 as a starting point, the number of immigrants working increased by 7.7 million.

16. Steven Camarota and Karen Zeigler, "Are There Really Jobs Americans Won't Do? A detailed look at immigrant and native employment across occupations," Center for Immigration Studies, May 2013.
17. It should be pointed out that the only age group of natives under age 66 that has seen an improvement in their labor force participation rate is those aged 60 to 65. Also, natives over age 65 increased their employment by 3.5 million between 2000 and 2017.
18. For a review of this literature, see Steven A. Camarota and Karen Jensenius, in "A Drought of Summer Jobs Immigration and the Long-Term Decline in Employment Among U.S.-Born Teenagers," Center for Immigration Studies, May 2010, pp. 4–5.
19. These figures come directly from the Current Population Survey for the first quarter of 2017. The total non-institutionalized population figures from the CPS do not include the roughly four million people in institutions such as nursing homes and prisons. We estimate the number of children born to post-2000 immigrants by looking at immigrant families that arrived in 2000 or later and counting the number of U.S.-born children in those families aged 17 or younger.

4

The Congressional Black Caucus and Immigration Reform

Carol M. Swain

Who speaks for African Americans when it comes to United States immigration policy? I contend it is not the 49 members of the Congressional Black Caucus (CBC) who vociferously purport to represent the interests of 38.9 million African Americans. A perusal of the CBC website and press releases shows that immigration has rarely been listed among its legislative priorities, nor has the organization, traditionally concerned with jobs and education, acknowledged the negative impact that high immigration has had and is continuing to have on their constituents. Surprisingly, the organization has not taken an official position, despite conditions in black communities and surveys that show Americans in agreement about the need for major reform. In this policy area, African Americans have been left without a strong black voice in Congress on a topic that affects them deeply given their high unemployment rates and historic struggle to get quality housing, healthcare, education, and other goods and services that often pit them in direct competition with the immigrant population.[1]

In this chapter, I discuss black representation from black members of Congress before exploring the impact of high levels of immigration on black communities. After presenting data on the employment situation of blacks in high-immigrant areas, I argue that the best representation for African Americans will not come from the CBC. Instead, it must come from conservative Republicans who have taken decisive leadership roles on this issue. I conclude that black representation emanating from the collective institutional body will always trump dyadic representation between black legislators and black constituents, largely because the self-interest of CBC members and their elite status prevent them from effectively representing their black constituents. Robert Weisberg has demonstrated that a given representative's failure to represent his or her constituency's interests could be corrected, or cancelled out, by the actions of other legislators elected outside the district.[2] In the case of immigration reform, African Americans must look beyond the CBC for effective representation. Ironically, Republican House members in the 115th Congress have been more of a voice for working people than the CBC, which operates out of what I would describe as elitist self-interest and a liberal leftist ideology that causes its members to embrace a politics of symbolism and grandstanding through vigils and media press conferences with exaggerated claims of racism rather than working diligently with Republicans and Democrats for substantive relief.

WHAT DOES IT MEAN TO REPRESENT BLACKS?

Hanna Pitkin argues that representing means "acting in the interest of the represented, in a manner responsive to them."[3] By examining objective conditions and standards, one can gauge the quality of black representation on the issue. When one considers the socioeconomic situation of black communities with their high rates of poverty, crime, unemployment, and disease, their need for effective political representation takes an added sense of urgency. Black representatives are widely perceived as being more likely than white representatives to discern and act in the interests of African Americans.[4] This might be true on some issues, especially if we equate representation with position-taking and rhetoric on issues such as jobs, education, healthcare, housing, social justice, and denouncements of racism. However, if we move beyond rhetoric and position-taking to efforts to actively shape debates on issues like immigration reform, it becomes clear that a disjuncture exists between the needs and preferences of the people and what CBC members do. Historically, the CBC has not been out front shaping immigration policy by seeking employer sanctions for hiring illegal workers, developing provisions designed to stem the flood of illegals, or encouraging illegals to engage in civic education and naturalization at higher rates.[5] In fact, when the CBC had been more actively involved during the 1980s and 1990s, it weakened legislation designed to stem the flow of illegal residents.[6]

Whether the issue is education, poverty, housing, healthcare, or unemployment, blacks remain clustered at the bottom of the ladder in the most desperate of situations.[7] Therefore, their need for representation is ongoing – the more vigorous, the better for them. CBC members bring descriptive representation in the form of shared skin color between the representative and the constituency, but their actions as a collective body do not ensure substantive representation on critical bread-and-butter issues. Substantive representation can only take place when a legislator identifies and actively champions the policy interests and preferences of constituents.[8]

Such substantive representation has not been forthcoming with regard to immigration. The CBC webpage, for example, lists press releases put out by the organization and news articles mentioning the group going back to January of 2008. While it is easy to spot the numerous documents pertaining to African American unemployment, it is much more difficult to find any mention of immigration. In fact, of the nearly 550 press releases and news articles listed on the site, only 20 even mention immigration in any way – and most of these are only passing remarks. The CBC's lack of discussion regarding this issue is especially surprising considering its increasing salience in recent years.

Indeed, in the 114th and 115th Congresses, the debate over the issue of immigration has been raging. A search for the keywords "immigration reform" on the U.S. House of Representatives' website yields no less than 102 legislative proposals for the 114th Congress and 27 for just the first six months of the 115th Congress (as of June 2017). These bills include ones supporting or condemning sanctuary cities, disqualifying "anchor babies" born on US soil to noncitizens from automatic citizenship, endorsing increased border enforcement measures, reexamining patterns of chain migration, reexamining the importation of foreign workers, reexamining interior enforcement, clarifying designations for refugees and asylum, and defining the criteria and numbers for visa lotteries. As this list exemplifies, there has been very little agreement in Congress about what should be done about the increasingly complex immigration situation in the country. Consequently, very few immigration policy bills have passed either house of Congress in recent years, a fact that seems unlikely to change in the near future.

As the debate rages on, members of the CBC should be openly discussing the negative impact that illegal immigration is having on black communities and deciding which bills are best suited to reverse that impact. However, despite the heightened attention immigration reform is getting from Congress, the CBC still has only listed it as a legislative priority for one session of Congress as of July 2017 (the 113th Congress). Because of the lack of action, immigration remains unreformed and the special needs of America's black communities remain unaddressed.

The question arises: Why is there not greater substantive representation coming from the CBC? The failure of the organization to act assertively on immigration reform may relate to how the representatives see their constituencies. Increasingly, black members of Congress represent districts with growing numbers of Hispanic and Asian residents. In some of these districts, the percentage of blacks and whites is rapidly decreasing relative to other groups, especially as reverse migration takes place and urban and Midwestern blacks return to the South. These recent demographic shifts mean that CBC members are confronting new realities and new incentives. Since 2002, Hispanics, a group that includes Cubans, Dominicans, Mexicans, Puerto Ricans, Guatemalans, and Salvadorans, has surpassed African Americans as the nation's largest minority group.[9]

No fewer than 14 CBC members currently represent districts with greater than 10 percent Hispanic voting-age population (VAP).[10] The growth of Hispanic residents in CBC member districts has already increased inter-group competition and conflict around a number of issues, including legislative redistricting.[11,12] The fact that CBC members have large numbers of Hispanic constituents should encourage them to actively work at framing immigration initiatives that will work to the benefit of the district majority rather than assume a reactionary posture towards proposals advanced by other groups. The organization follows, rather than leads, despite the growing diversity of many CBC districts.

Unfortunately, the CBC has offered black America an inadequate quality of representation on immigration issues that goes back to the Immigration Reform and Control Act of 1986, when it joined with members of the Congressional Hispanic Caucus and other liberal Democrats to gut the employer sanctions provisions of the Simpson/Mazzoli immigration reform bill.[13] Because of the loopholes and concessions in the legislation passed in 1986 and the changes made in the 1990 Immigration Act, illegal immigration is a greater problem today than it was before the reforms began.[14] Douglas Massey noted that the immigration reform bills passed in 1986 and 1990 provided enforcement at specific entry points along the U.S.–Mexico border where large amounts of illegal immigrants entered the U.S.[15] However, while this prevented immigrants from entering at those specific points, all the legislation really did was cause immigrants to enter at points along the border where enforcement was more lax. This meant that immigrants crossed into the U.S. at rural entry points, which in turn meant that they would be less likely to be caught by Border Patrol. In addition, immigration became a more widespread problem as immigrants found themselves traveling to new parts of the country because of the increased enforcement at traditional entry points. Moreover, the CBC has continued to offer meager representation for black Americans on immigration policy issues in more recent years, as well. Even when focusing on immigration reform during the 113th Congress, the stated goals and actions of the organization focused more on African immigrants and the rights of immigrants as a whole than on the needs of the African American community more generally.[16] As the evidence presented below shows, this lack of emphasis on protecting the interests of black workers in the immigration debate may have disastrous consequences.

THE ECONOMIC IMPACT OF IMMIGRATION ON BLACKS AND OTHER LOW-SKILLED AMERICANS

The CBC consistently includes job procurement among its most pressing legislative priorities. To draw attention to the issue, it sends out press releases whenever the Labor Department releases its new numbers. As Figure 4.1 shows, African American rates of unemployment are consistently higher than other groups. Consider the fluctuation in the unemployment rate between June 2009 and June 2011. In June 2009, the overall unemployment rate was 9.5 percent, with white unemployment at 8.7 percent, black unemployment at 14.8 percent, and Hispanic unemployment at 12.1 percent. By June 2011, the economy as a whole seemed to be improving somewhat, as the overall unemployment rate dropped to 9.1 percent. However, the employment situation for blacks did not

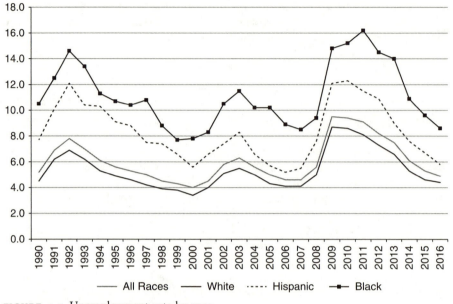

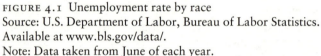

FIGURE 4.1 Unemployment rate by race
Source: U.S. Department of Labor, Bureau of Labor Statistics.
Available at www.bls.gov/data/.
Note: Data taken from June of each year.

improve. In fact, black unemployment actually increased to 16.2 percent, up from 14.8 percent in 2009. So, while white unemployment dropped from 8.7 percent to 8.1 percent and Hispanic unemployment dropped from 12.1 percent to 11.5 percent, blacks saw their unemployment rate actually rise, while members of other groups enjoyed substantial job gains. Although most mainstream media accounts focus on the low rates of unemployment for whites, the CBC points out the persistent disparities between blacks and whites.

Among the black unemployed are a disproportionate percentage of black high school dropouts and graduates. In fact, following the recession of 2007 to 2009, almost 75 percent of blacks had less than a college degree.[17] This contributed to especially poor outcomes for African Americans during this period, as the recession especially affected workers with less education.[18] Even when job gains have occurred for blacks, they have been disproportionately in dead-end, low-sector jobs. Furthermore, a study published by the Pew Hispanic Center also found significant employment gains for Hispanics in newly created low-wage jobs, although these gains were offset by reduced earnings for the newer immigrants who were suffering a two-year decline in wages.[19] In Chapter 3, Steven Camarota and Karen Zeigler show that most of the longer-term employment gains between 2000 and 2014 went to immigrants.

The high black and Hispanic unemployment rates can be partially attributed to the oversupply of low-skilled immigrants arriving since 1990, increasing the supply of labor by 25 percent for the kinds of jobs traditionally taken by high school dropouts and graduates.[20] While immigrant workers constitute only 16.9 percent of the U.S. labor force, they are a whopping 53 percent of workers without high school diplomas.[21] The greatest competition, therefore, occurs among people at the margins of society, a multiracial group that includes poorly educated blacks, whites, and Hispanics competing against each other and against new immigrants for low-wage, low-skill jobs. No wonder it is members of the working classes and not highly educated Americans that are most upset about immigrant labor; many of the other Americans parrot the refrain that immigrants merely take "unwanted jobs."[22] Within this group, racial and ethnic discrimination play a significant role for low-skilled whites and blacks. Despite civil rights laws, John Skrentny (Chapter 1) has revealed employer discrimination against both whites and blacks, with employers showing a clear preference for Asians and Hispanics.

The best research on the impact of immigration on native workers has found that immigrant competition for jobs hurts natives by holding down wages and reducing employment opportunities for native workers at different occupational levels.[23] Dustmann, Frattini, and Preston find that immigration especially lowers wages in the lower 20th percentile of the wage distribution.[24] In Los Angeles, CA, for example, immigrants fill more than half of the unskilled, blue collar jobs, but hold no more than one-fifth of the managerial and professional jobs.[25] Central city workers have found it harder and harder to find alternative employment when old jobs have been lost, ostensibly, to growing immigrant populations.[26] The availability of cheap labor causes employers focused on the bottom line to neglect the needs of native workers by failing to work at improving their productivity or by procuring higher wages. Too often the big business focus is on increasing the labor supply, which works to the detriment of native workers by depressing their wages.[27] George Borjas has further found that when immigration increases the supply of workers in any skill category, the wages of native workers decrease.[28]

Greater immigrant competition for low-wage, low-skill jobs has made it easier for Congress not to address the needs of the working poor. The federal minimum wage has been $7.25 an hour since 2009, with Congress unwilling to raise it any higher, presumably because the number of adults actually earning that rate constitutes only a small percentage of the population.[29] But it is the case, however, that in parts of the South adult men and women work at low-wage, low-skill jobs earning $7.25 to $9.00 per hour, even though most analysts target $15.00 per hour as a living wage.[30] In some industries and regions of the country, illegal residents are able to command wages of $12.00 to $18.00 an hour for jobs American workers routinely performed in the past and continue to do in places where immigrant competition is weak. This includes jobs within the construction, landscaping, hotel, and restaurant industries. This

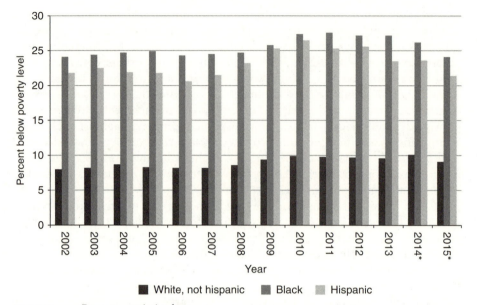

FIGURE 4.2 Poverty statistics by race
Note: *The Current Population Survey gathering data for these years used redesigned survey questions to determine income.
Source: United States Census Bureau, Current Population Survey.
Available at www.census.gov/programs-surveys/cps.html.

whole situation is now complicated by data such as those found in Nicholas Ebenstat's study cited in the Introduction to this volume which shows a declining interest in work among a portion of the native population.

Figure 4.2 shows poverty rates by race. Since 2002, poverty has been growing in America, especially among African Americans and Hispanics. But starting in 2008, the poverty rate for whites also increased. Overall, the plight of poor people in America is likely to worsen. No one seriously expects illegals to be asked to return home. More people of lower socioeconomic status will compete for fewer opportunities. When Congress gets around to legalizing millions of illegal residents, it will increase the ranks of those eligible to compete for the full range of social welfare programs, many of whom will use more of these services than native residents.[31]

Although education has largely been seen as an equalizer, cuts in governmental programs like student loans and Federal Pell Grants have made it more difficult for lower-middle-class and inner-city students to get the kinds of support needed to prepare themselves for higher-paying jobs. What is at risk is a permanent underclass of disgruntled people who live off the dole or are only qualified to work as low-wage service providers. Their situation and that of their children worsens even more because of the poor quality of public schools in some areas of the country. Of course, this situation also affects America's poor whites and second-generation Hispanics who find themselves trapped as well.

Many African Americans firmly believe that the U.S. government favors newly arrived immigrants over them in the administration of government benefits and opportunities for advancement.[32] Affirmative action issues come into play. Some African American citizens feel threatened by surges of immigrants because of their impact on affirmative action. A source of disjunction between African American civil rights activists and immigration advocates is the preference for opposing roles for government. Civil rights activists seek an expanded regulatory state, while immigration reformers want to dismantle a tight regulatory regime.[33]

Ricky Gaull Silberman, the vice-chairman of the Equal Employment Opportunity Commission in 2002, labeled immigrant participation in affirmative action as "the ultimate nightmare of affirmative action. It is its Achilles heel."[34] In recent years, tensions have emerged between African Americans and immigrants over its benefits. Historian Hugh D. Graham has stated:

For the Black urban poor, whose lives were largely untouched by affirmative action programs, the economic effects of large-scale immigration have been overwhelmingly negative. On balance, immigrant participation in affirmative action programs has been destabilizing. Historically, African American leaders, such as Frederick Douglass, Booker T. Washington, and W.E.B. Du Bois, had opposed importing cheap foreign-born labor to compete with native-born workers. But the 1960s encouraged a new "people of color" solidarity that paid political dividends for a generation. The immigrant success ethos, however, with its emphasis on hard work, merit, and social assimilation, clashed with hard affirmative action's emphasis on historic victimhood, reparations, and racial entitlement.[35]

What is at once puzzling and disconcerting for many black residents is that immigrants often achieve economic success without having to acculturate. These feelings often boil over into antipathy and sometimes lead to black boycotts of immigrant-owned businesses. Sociologist Jennifer Lee has captured this tension between African Americans and immigrant groups in New York and Philadelphia. She has found that as Jews moved out of black neighborhoods, and other new immigrants moved in, blacks began to see these groups as getting ahead of them and achieving the success that eluded so many of them. Seared into many minds is the image of new immigrants invading their communities, taking the businesses, and leaving at night with the community's money.[36] In the case of Hispanics, many of them crowd into the low-income neighborhoods formerly occupied by blacks, creating much resentment and increased acts of ethnic violence among minority groups.

Additionally, the impact of immigrant competition is now national in scope. The competition was once confined to a few key states such as California,

New York, Illinois, and Texas, but it has spread to more distant southern places such as Georgia, Mississippi, North Carolina, South Carolina, Virginia, and Tennessee, where more than 55 percent of the nation's black population resides.[37] Blacks from urban and rural places and poor whites have seen their high-paying, unskilled union jobs (e.g. janitorial services, textiles, meatpacking, and construction) either disappear or be given over to non-unionized immigrants. Although some scholars have argued that immigrants have not had negative economic impacts on particular communities, research by economists Borjas, Freeman, and Katz tells a different story for the nation as a whole.[38] These scholars have found that comparisons by geographical areas *understate* the potential effect that immigration-induced increases in the labor supply have on lowering native wages. When the nation as a whole is examined, there are greater depressant effects than what is found by confining the analysis to single metropolitan geographical areas.[39] The impact is also national in scope because of evidence that high immigrant populations affect internal migration by causing some native-born workers with low skill levels to migrate to other regions of the country in an effort to flee immigrant competition.[40]

Often neglected in discussions of illegal immigration is the impact of the oversupply of labor on the earning capacities of older immigrants and legal residents who find themselves adversely affected by the influx of newcomers. Borjas has found that the average wage for legal migrant workers in rural areas is $9.54, compared with illegal residents who are willing to work for $5.98.[41] This makes illegal residents more attractive to employers focused on the bottom line. Indeed, one of the most strident supporters of tougher immigration laws and more secure borders in recent years has been the United Farm Workers Union, once led by the great labor activist and Mexican immigrant César Chávez. In 1966, Chávez led a melon worker strike in an attempt to bring wages over $1 an hour, but the company simply hired workers straight from Mexico, harming the earnings of those immigrants already in the country.[42] Beyond these effects, newly-arrived immigrants also decrease the wages received by these older immigrants; Ottaviano and Peri, for example, find that newly-arrived, low-skilled immigrants depress the wages of more established immigrants by up to 6.7 percent.[43] The undercutting of immigrant wages by immigrants competing with immigrants may be happening on a much grander scale than imagined, as well. In 1992, an Agriculture Department study found roughly one million farm-worker jobs and 2.5 million potential farm workers during the peak season, many of whom were newly arrived immigrants.[44]

Moreover, the oversupply of labor is not confined to dead-end jobs. It also includes the technology sector, where foreign workers compete with more highly educated Americans. While the number of highly skilled immigrants pales in comparison to the number of unskilled and uneducated ones, the oversupply of labor creates similar problems that lead employers to justify paying lower wages for longer hours. In 2001, it was reported that one in four research personnel at IBM's Yorktown Heights Lab and two in five researchers at Bell Labs were new immigrants brought in on work visas, leaving many native engineers and programmers either unemployed or underemployed. Some employers openly expressed a preference for immigrant laborers because they were willing to work longer hours for less pay with fewer complaints than American workers.[45] The United States' immigration policy provided both a means and an incentive for companies to use the H1-B work visa program to create competition for American technical workers.

In a survey of Chicago-area employers, William J. Wilson finds that Third-World immigrants are preferred by many employers because they are willing to tolerate harsher work conditions, lower pay, fewer upward trajectories, and other job-related characteristics that would deter native-born workers.[46] Immigrants were also perceived as exhibiting a much better "work ethic" than blacks. In fact, Calavita quotes former Secretary of Labor Ray Marshall as commenting that undocumented residents were more likely to "work scared and hard."[47] Perhaps as a consequence, African Americans suspect quite correctly that some employers would rather hire new immigrants than give them a chance.

In short, a need exists for aggressive action to address the negative effects of immigration on American workers. Steven Camarota has argued in favor of two sets of policy options that might address the needs of U.S. workers.[48] One proposal would take aggressive steps to enhance the position of native-born workers employed in low-skill jobs by increasing the minimum wage or by expanding the Earned Income Credit. He notes, however, that taking such an action without reducing the levels of illegal immigration would most likely make matters worse for the native-born workers by increasing their unemployment levels. A second proposal actively works at reducing the percentage of unskilled legal and illegal immigrants in the country. As he points out, only 12 percent of legal immigrants are admitted on the basis of their education skills and training. Two-thirds of the immigrants are coming for family reunification purposes. Unskilled illegal immigration could be tackled by greater enforcement provision in the interior of the country. Rather than governmental deportation of millions of illegal residents, Camarota argues that reduction can be achieved by attrition simply through the enforcement of existing laws that would encourage and pressure many illegals to go home voluntarily by self-deportation.

Clearly, there are both moral and ethical issues of social justice involved in how the nation addresses the situation. The voice of the CBC is needed on this issue because it affects all low-wage, low-income workers, especially blacks. It is also needed because its members present themselves to the world as representing blacks and other downtrodden people. The latter concern and the presence of well-organized and funded interest groups seem to block effective policy reform.

THE CBC'S MISPLACED PRIORITIES

The CBC decries unemployment. An April 2015 CBC press release states that "African Americans are struggling and continue to face high rates of persistent poverty, unemployment and long-term unemployment as well as significantly lower incomes and slower wealth accumulation than white households."[49] Given the CBC's concern with unemployment and social justice, as is highlighted on its website and in its press releases, it would seem reasonable for them to be actively involved in shaping immigration laws. The oversupply of labor hurts blacks more than other groups because of negative stereotypes and other factors surrounding blacks' work habits and perceived dependability and honesty, which even affects an employer's willingness to accept their job referrals.[50]

The CBC, however, is struggling to define its mission. In the early 2000s, the CBC website stated a mission to:

Close (and, ultimately, to eliminate) disparities that exist between African Americans and white Americans in every aspect of life. These continuing and troubling disparities make it more difficult, and often make it impossible, for African Americans to reach their full potential. In pursuing the core mission of the CBC, the CBC has been true to its motto that "the CBC has no permanent friends and no permanent enemies, just permanent interests."[51]

The updated mission on the 2017 website omits the mention of white Americans. Its mission now, as reported in a recent press release, is to "empower America's neglected citizens and to address their legislative concerns," as well as to be "the voice for people of color and vulnerable communities in Congress" with a commitment to use "the full Constitutional power, statutory authority, and financial resources of the Government of the United States of America to ensure that everyone in the United States has an opportunity to achieve their version of the American Dream."[52]

Similarly, in 2017, the specific mission mentioned by the organization on their "About the CBC" page also speaks specifically about African Americans *and* other marginalized communities:

[U]sing the full Constitutional power, statutory authority, and financial resources of the federal government to ensure that *African Americans and other marginalized communities* (emphasis mine) in the United States have the opportunity to achieve the American Dream.[53]

This shows a clear shift in focus in recent years.

Consider that the above statements represent an especially ambitious goal that the organization is unlikely to achieve given that African Americans surpass every other racial and ethnic group when it comes to poverty, unemployment, crime, and incarceration rates. If the CBC wants to correct disparities, it should begin by identifying measurable goals that encourage the active involvement of their constituents. Whether we examine the CBC's history on immigration or its votes on other issues that affect low-income people (such as the 2005 Bankruptcy Reform bill where ten CBC members voted in favor of a bill that benefited big business at the expense of working people), we find too many of its members failing to live up to the mantle they have claimed for themselves and for their organization.

Unless something dramatically changes in the body, black representation on immigration will not be forthcoming from the CBC. Fortunately, however, a broader conceptualization of representation that focuses on the performance of the institution as a whole offers a possibility for more vigorous representation on the issue coming unexpectedly from the Republican side of the aisle, where a number of legislators have staked out positions conducive to the interests of working people and sensitive to the needs of new immigrants. Because many citizens and legal residents are adversely affected in different ways by the failure of existing immigration policy, it becomes more likely that multiracial and multi-ethnic coalitions can be formed if enough legislators are willing to bypass narrow self-interests in re-election to focus on the needs of the nation. Although the immigration reform proposals of the past have been dismal failures, it is sometimes possible for Congress to formulate legislation that achieves its stated intent to the benefit of the nation. Since immigration reform affects all Americans, the most beneficial reform approaches will include strategies that make it costlier for employers to discriminate against native-born workers, create incentives for them to train and hire new workers, create a tamper-proof social security card, and include concrete plans to protect and expand the gains of members of historically disadvantaged populations such as American Indians, Appalachian whites, legal Hispanics, and black descendants of slaves.

NOTES

1. B. DeBose, "Blacks, Whites View Immigration Similarly, Poll Says Think U.S. Should Limit Number," *The Washington Post*, November 17, 2005, p. A12; J. Diamond, "African American Attitudes Towards Immigration Policy," *Internal Migration Review* 32 (Summer 1998): 451–470; Gallup Poll News Service, "Gallup Poll Social Series Governance," Field survey (09/12/2005–09/15/2005), Qn42.

2. R. Weisberg, "Collective Versus Dyadic Representation in Congress," *American Political Science Review* 72 (1978): 535–547.

3. H. F. Pitkin, *The Concept of Representation* (Berkeley: University of California Press, 1967), p. 210.

4. K. A. Bratton and K. L. Haynie, "Agenda Setting and Legislative Success in State Legislatures: The Effects of Gender and Race," *Journal of Politics* 61 (1999): 658–679; D. T. Cannon, *Race, Redistricting, and Representation: The Unintended Consequences of Black Majority Districts* (Chicago: University of Chicago Press, 1999); K. Tate, *Black Faces in the Mirror: African Americans and their Representatives in the U.S. Congress* (Princeton: Princeton University Press, 2004);

K. Whitby, *The Color of Representation: Congressional Behavior and Black Interests* (Ann Arbor: University of Michigan Press, 1997).

5. L. H. Fuchs, "The Reactions of Black Americans to Immigration," in V. Vans-McLauglin (ed.), *Immigration Reconsidered: History, Sociology, and Politics* (New York: Oxford University Press, 1990), p. 304; Diamond, "African American Attitudes," 460–462.

6. When non-elected black leadership such as Jesse L. Jackson, Sr., and Reverend Al Sharpton have weighed in on the issue, more often than not it has been to denounce racist statements or negative portrayals of blacks by the Mexican government and not to advance mutually beneficial policy proposals that take into consideration the needs of American workers who compete with immigrants for basic services and goods (C. Stillwell, "Racism Rears its Ugly Head in Mexico," *The San Francisco Chronicle*, August 3, 2005. Available at: www.sfgate.com/politics/article/Racism-Rears-Its-Ugly-Head-in-Mexico-3171753.php, accessed July 3, 2017; "Fox 'Regrets' Remarks About Blacks," CNN, May 17, 2005. Available at: www.cnn.com/2005/WORLD/americas/05/16/mexico.fox/, accessed July 3, 2017).

7. C. M. Swain, *Black Faces, Black Interests: The Representation of African Americans in Congress* (Cambridge: Harvard University Press, 1993), pp. 3–19.

8. Pitkin, *The Concept of Representation*, p. 210.

9. L. Clemetson, "Hispanics Now Nation's Largest Minority," *The New York Times*, January 22, 2003. Available at: www.nytimes.com/2003/01/22/national/22CENS.html/, accessed July 3, 2017; A. Portes, "From South of the Border: Hispanic Minorities in the United States," in D. Jacobson (ed.), *The Immigration Reader: America in a Multidisciplinary Perspective* (Washington, DC: Blackwell Publisher,1998), pp. 113–143.

10. "Mapping the Latino Electorate by Congressional District," Pew Research Center, 19 January 2016. Available at: www.pewhispanic.org/interactives/mapping-the-latino-electorate-by-congressional-district/, accessed July 3, 2017.

11. L. F. Estrada, "Making the Voting Rights Act Relevant to the New Demographics of America: A Response to Farrell and Johnson," *North Carolina Law Review* 79 (June 2001): 1283; B. Grofman and L. Handley, "Minority Population Proportion and Hispanic Congressional Success in 1970s and 1980s," *American Politics Quarterly* 17 (October 1989): 436–445.

12. The new demographics establish a different playing field. When, for example, New Jersey experienced a vacancy in its U.S. Senate seat after its Democratic senator Jon Corzine became its governor-elect, Corzine nominated Representative Robert Menendez as the State's first Hispanic senator, even though the state has never had an African American senator. Given that there was only one black member of the U.S. Senate during the 109th Congress and two Hispanics, Corzine could have easily justified nominating black representative Donald Payne (D-NJ). The fact that he found it politically expedient to name a Hispanic senator points to the growing influence of Hispanics in the state.

13. Diamond, "African-American Attitudes," 451–470; Fuchs, "Reaction of Black Americans."

14. D. Massey, J. Durand, and N. J. Malone, *Beyond Smoke and Mirrors: Mexican Immigration in An Era of Economic Integration* (New York: Russell Sage Foundation, 2002); H. Calavita, "Gaps and Contradictions in U.S. Immigration Policy: An Analysis of Recent Reform Efforts," in David Jacobson (ed.),

The Immigration Reader: America in a Multidisciplinary Perspective (Washington, DC: Blackwell Publisher, 1998), pp. 92–107.

15. D. Massey, "Borderline Madness: America's Counterproductive Immigration Policy," in C. M. Swain (ed.), *Debating Immigration* (New York: Cambridge Press, 2007), pp. 129–138.

16. "CBC Outlines Policy Agenda for the First Session of the 113th Congress," Congressional Black Caucus, February 5, 2013. Available at: https://cbc.house.gov /news/documentsingle.aspx?DocumentID=72, accessed July 3, 2017; "CBC Chair Marcia L. Fudge's Statement on President Barack Obama's Executive Action on Immigration," Congressional Black Caucus, 21 November 2014. Available at: https://cbc.house.gov/news/documentsingle.aspx?DocumentID=238, accessed July 3, 2017.

17. "The African-American Labor Force in the Recovery," United States Department of Labor, February 29, 2012. Available at: www.dol.gov/_sec/media/reports/ blacklaborforce/, accessed July 3, 2017.

18. "The African-American Labor Force," United States Department of Labor.

19. R. Kochbar, "Latino Labor Report, 2004: More Jobs for Immigrants but at Lower Wages" (Washington, DC: Pew Hispanic Center) p. 18.

20. S. A. Camarota, Testimony for U.S. House Committee on Education and the Workforce, November 16, 2005.

21. Bureau of Labor Statistics, "Foreign-born Workers: Labor Force Characteristics – 2016," United States Department of Labor, 18 May 2017. Available at: www.bls .gov/news.release/pdf/forbrn.pdf, accessed July 3, 2017.

22. Peter Katel, "Illegal Immigration: Do Illegal Workers Help or Hurt the Economy?," *CQ Researcher* 15 (May 2005): 394–419.

23. G. Borjas, R. Freeman, and L. Katz, "Searching for the Effect of Immigration on the Labor Market" *American Economic Association Papers and Proceedings* (May 1996): 246–251.

24. C. Dustmann, T. Frattini, and I. P. Preston, "The Effect of Immigration along the Distribution of Wages," *Review of Economic Studies* 80 (2013): 145–173.

25. W. H. Frey, "Immigration, Domestic Migration, and Demographic Balkanization in America: New Evidence for the 1990s," *Population and Development Review* 22 (December 1996): 741–763.

26. W. H. Frey, "Central City White Flight," *American Sociological Review* 44 (1979): 425–448.

27. M. Brown, *Shapers of the Great Debate on Immigration* (Westport, CT: Greenwood Press, 1999).

28. G. Borjas, "The Labor Demand Curve is Downward Sloping: Reexamining the Impact of Immigration on the Labor Market," *Quarterly Journal of Economics* 118 (November 2003): 1335–1374.

29. "Minimum Wage," United States Department of Labor. Available at: www.dol .gov/whd/minimumwage.htm, accessed July 3, 2017.

30. C. Nadeau, "New Data: Calculating the Living Wage for U.S. States, Counties and Metro Areas," Massachusetts Institute of Technology, August 19, 2016. Available at: http://livingwage.mit.edu/articles/19-new-data-calculating-the-living-wage-for-u-s-states-counties-and-metro-areas, accessed July 3, 2017.

31. J. Richwine, "The Cost of Welfare Use by Immigrant and Native Households," Center for Immigration Studies, May 2016. Available at: http://cis.org/Cost-Welfare-Immigrant-Native-Households, accessed July 3, 2017.

32. K. Taylor-Clark, *Synthesis of Research Findings: Public Opinion on Immigration*, The Opportunity Agenda, May 2008. Available at: https://opportunityagenda .org/explore/resources-publications/synthesis-research-findings-public-opinion-immigration, accessed July 3, 2017.

33. H. Graham, "Unintended Consequences: The Convergence of Affirmative Action and Immigration Policy," *American Behavioral Policy* 41 (April 1998): 901.

34. Graham, "Unintended Consequences," 899.

35. Graham, "Unintended Consequences," 910.

36. J. Lee, *Civility in the City: Blacks, Jews, and Koreans in Urban America* (Cambridge: Harvard University Press, 2002).

37. "Immigrant Population by State, 1990–Present," Migration Policy Institute. Available at: www.migrationpolicy.org/programs/data-hub/charts/immigrant-population-state-1990-present?width=1000&height=850&iframe=true, accessed July 3, 2017; S. Rastogi, T. D. Johnson, E. M. Hoeffel, and M. P. Drewery, *The Black Population: 2010*, United States Census Bureau, September 2011. Available at: www.census.gov /prod/cen2010/briefs/c2010br-06.pdf.

38. Borjas, Freeman, and Katz, "Effect of Immigration," 247.

39. Borjas, Freeman, and Katz, "Effect of Immigration," 250.

40. Frey, "Immigration, Migration, and Balkanization"; W. H. Frey and J. Tilove, "Immigrants in, Native Whites Out," *The New York Times*, August 20, 1995.

41. G. Borjas, *Friends or Strangers* (New York: Basic Books, 1990).

42. Brown, *Great Debate*, p. 241.

43. G. I. P. Ottaviano and G. Peri, "Rethinking the Effect of Immigration on Wages," *Journal of the European Economic Association*, 10 (2012): 152–197.

44. R. Beck, *The Case Against Immigration: The Moral, Economic, and Environmental Reasons for Reducing U.S. Immigration Back to Traditional Levels* (New York, NY: Norton, 1996), p. 121.

45. K. Bredemeier, "Work Visas Swell Area's Tech Corps," *Washington Post*, December 1, 2000, p. E1.

46. W. J. Wilson, *When Work Disappears: The World of the New Urban Poor* (New York: Knopf, 1996), p. 141.

47. Calavita, "Gaps and Contradictions," 95.

48. Camarota, Testimony for U.S. House.

49. "CBC Chairman G. K. Butterfield on the Impact of Persistent Poverty in the African American Community," Congressional Black Caucus, April 30, 2015. Available at: https://cbc.house.gov/news/documentsingle.aspx?DocumentID=275, accessed July 3, 2017.

50. K. S. Newman, *No Shame in My Game: The Working Poor in the Inner City* (New York: Alfred A. Knopf and the Russell Sage Foundation, 1999); M. Waters, *Black Identities: West Indian Immigrants and American Realities* (Cambridge, MA: The Russell Sage Foundation at Harvard University Press, 2001).

51. This press release is no longer posted. "November Jobless Rate," Congressional Black Caucus, December 2, 2005.

52. "114th Congress, 1st Session: Year in Review," Congressional Black Caucus, 2015, p. 7. Available at: https://cbc.house.gov/uploadedfiles/2015_cbc_year_in_reviewfinal .pdf, accessed July 3, 2017.

53. "About the CBC," Congressional Black Caucus. Available at: https://cbc.house .gov/about/, accessed July 3, 2017.

5

Will Hispanic and Asian Immigrants Save America?*

Amitai Etzioni

INTRODUCTION

The claim that large waves of 'non-white' immigration will have a significant effect on the American creed, identity, and society is not without foundation. Immigration waves have continually changed American society since its earliest days. However, these immigrants have made their mark not by undoing the established creed, and thus leaving a normative vacuum and sewing societal dissent, but by *recasting the framework that holds America together and often making it the better for it*. This same process of societal reframing is occurring in the current stage of American history. Large numbers of immigrants, many from Mexico and South American countries (and to a lesser extent from Asia), are making America more communitarian than it has been in recent decades by fostering stronger commitment to family, community, and nation, as well as respect for authority and moderate religious-moral values. Like other immigrant groups, they have proved themselves to be industrious and achievement-oriented. Furthermore, by virtue of their young age, many of these immigrants will help to protect the U.S. from the demographic malaise that is diminishing European and Japanese populations. And, least noted but of much importance, these same immigrants are going to modify American society, changing a country often depicted as divided along immutable racial lines between whites and blacks – a society in which many of the latter continue to see themselves as victims – to an increasingly varied society in which more

---

* In drafting this chapter, I drew on several previous works, including: *The Monochrome Society* (Princeton: Princeton University Press, 2001), *The New Golden Rule: Community and Morality in a Democratic Society* (New York: Basic Books, 1996), and the Diversity Within Unity Platform. For additional information on these titles, please see www.communitariannetwork .org, accessed February 9, 2018. I am indebted to Jessica Roberts Frazier for research assistance and numerous editorial suggestions.

fluid ethnic groups will play a greater role and in which victimhood will play an ever-smaller role. Their high intermarriage rate serves as but one example of this positive modification; for, through intermarriage, Hispanic and Asian immigrants help to ensure that the most intimate ties – those of family – will prevent American society from breaking down along ethnic lines.

I do not claim that all the effects of recent (or previous) immigrants have been salutary. However, most of the troubling effects are temporary and limited, and they pale in comparison to the constructive ones. American society is light years ahead of most other societies, which have yet to learn how to incorporate large numbers of immigrants without losing their own core values or abusing the immigrants.

ASSIMILATION, MULTICULTURALISM, OR DIVERSITY WITHIN UNITY?

Three Competing Paradigms – Their Definitions and Affiliated Metaphors

Examinations of the effects of immigrants draw implicitly or explicitly on competing paradigms. The paradigm through which a study of immigration is approached in turn affects the findings and conclusions drawn. Regrettably, after centuries of debate on these issues (issues that have been contested since the colonial days), there are still no agreed-upon terms through which one can frame the discussion. Several terms are used to refer to the same phenomena, and the same terms are used to refer to different developments. I follow here those who use the term *assimilation* to refer to the full immersion of immigrants into the existing culture, bleaching out all distinctions. I employ *multiculturalism* to indicate the views of those on the other end of the spectrum who prefer to break up the American framework and have the land occupied by a variety of ethnic and racial groups – each acting as a societal whole, in effect as a nation unto itself. (Some who embrace the multicultural paradigm also refer to the American society as a "multiracial society."[1]) And finally, the *integration* paradigm encompasses the perspectives of those who think immigrants ought to become incorporated into American society but should simultaneously maintain some differences that may benefit both them and society as a whole. A model that I refer to as Diversity Within Unity (DWU) serves as a particular form of the integration paradigm.[2]

Affiliated with each of these paradigms are various metaphors that serve to illustrate further the distinctions between the three approaches. For example, one image frequently associated with the assimilation paradigm is that of the *melting pot* – a cultural caldron in which all groups are stripped of all their distinctive characteristics and are assimilated into one homogeneous amalgam. Those preferring the paradigm of multiculturalism often invoke a rainbow as their emblem, with the diversely hued bands connoting the various people of different colors "arranged" next to one another in a multicultural America.³

The image of a mosaic, if properly understood, well captures the integration approach and more specifically the DWU model to which I earlier referred. A mosaic is enriched by a variety of elements of different shapes and colors, but it is held together by a single framework. Yet to what sociological concepts do these two parts of the mosaic, the individual pieces and the framework, connect and what is their implication for American society? One can fairly easily conclude that the pieces of the mosaic symbolize the country's diverse populations or communities. Yet selecting the appropriate sociological concept for the shared framework proves a bit more involved. Some call it a "creed," which prejudices the discussion by assuming a tightly and clearly demarcated set of shared beliefs. Others use the term "culture," which brings to mind art and music, as well as values and habits of the heart – a very open-ended term. I refer to the mosaic's framework as a "core of shared values" to stress that there are some values – important, normative ones – we all embrace and adhere to, while there are others, not part of the core, on which we may well differ.

Thus, in light of this understanding, the mosaic symbolizes a society in which various communities (the pieces) maintain their cultural particularities, ranging from religious commitments and language to cuisine and dance. But while they are proud and knowledgeable about their specific traditions, these distinct communities also recognize that they are integral parts of a more encompassing whole.

This is not to say, however, that the framework of the mosaic remains static. It can be, and has been throughout American history, both reinforced and recast by immigrants – a point that cannot be stressed enough as reference is often made only to the enrichment that the addition of pieces brings to the American mosaic (or society) by providing greater diversity through the incorporation of a growing range of cuisine, music, and holidays. Certainly, the mosaic has been made more varied. But of equal importance are the changes made to the framework of the mosaic – to what unites us and makes us Americans.

Which Paradigm Should Guide the Analysis?

The extent to which large waves of immigration, especially if they differ significantly from previous ones, are viewed as straining American society depends in part on what one considers a sound societal condition. For example, two people might make the same observations of society; however, the person expecting assimilation might find what he or she sees much more troubling than the individual who seeks only to maintain unity in the face of growing diversity. Multiculturalism "solves" the problem by denying unity exists; if there is no, one, unified American society and none is desired, then increased cultural and social differences matter not.

Throughout American history, and again recently, alarms have been sounded when immigrants did not seem to assimilate (or do so quickly enough) and continued to maintain subcultural distinctions. As a result, various coercive measures have been advocated, both to stop additional immigration and to deal with those immigrants already in the country. (For example, Hispanic children were prohibited from speaking their native language even in school playgrounds,[4] and laws have been enacted in several states that require all ballots, street signs, and official transactions to be English only.[5]) But these, to a significant extent, have reflected the alarmists' measuring rod and not the scope of the problem. Generation after generation of immigrants who were first viewed as undermining American society and its core of shared values have become an integral part of it, including Jewish immigrants and immigrants from Catholic countries (especially Ireland and Poland), without giving up their subcultures and ethnic identities.

I join with those who see that there are no compelling reasons, sociological or other, to assimilate immigrants into one indistinguishable American blend. There is no need for Greek-Americans, Polish-Americans, Mexican-Americans, or any other group to see themselves as plain Americans without any particular distinction, history, or subculture. Similarly, Americans can, if they so choose, maintain their separate religions (from Greek-Orthodox to Buddhism) and their subcultures (including distinct tastes in music, dance, and cuisine) without constituting a threat to the American whole. Indeed, American culture is richer for having an introduction to jazz and classical music, the jig and polka, Cajun and soul food, and so on. In her essay, "What It Means to Be American in the 21st Century," Tamar Jacoby addresses the introduction of these diverse, cultural enhancements into the American mainstream of mid-twentieth-century, writing, "If anything was different, it was the hybrid culture that had evolved through the decades. From African-American music to Jewish humor, from the German work ethic to Irish eloquence: more and more of what it meant to be American was something that had been brought here by an outsider and then ... gradually seeped into the mainstream."[6]

The sociological challenge posed by recent immigrant waves is basically the same as that of previous ones: to maintain the uniquely American societal formations of DWU, which leave considerable room for the enriching particulars of autonomous subcultures and communities, and still sustain the core of shared values and societal bonds.

DIVERSITY WITHIN UNITY: THE KEY ELEMENTS

Diversity Elements

In line with the DWU concept, while immigrants are expected to buy into the shared core of American values, they, like all Americans, are free to diverge on many other values. They are free to differ when it comes to which country of origin they hold especially dear, have a sense of loyalty to, maintain social bonds with, send remittances to, and choose to learn more about and visit more often; which second languages they learn; which religion they adhere to, if any; and which subcultural traditions they uphold, as reflected in preferences for cuisine, music, dance, and holiday rituals.

I turn next to list the key elements of unity, the core of shared values, that immigrants are expected to embrace, i.e. those values that are so essential that a lack of adherence to them by immigrants would pose a serious threat to the American society, polity, and indeed to its future as a nation. Several individuals who have previously written about integration of the DWU kind have underscored that it is difficult to specify the elements involved. Others have provided a rather brief list of the components, including Diane Ravitch and Lawrence Fuchs.[7] I draw here on their work, as well as that of others, to try to draft a fairly specific list of those core American values that must be shared. One may, of course, disagree about one or more of the items, but the merit of having such a clearly delineated list is that it allows for a stronger assessment of the effects that new waves of immigration have on the American society.

Shared Elements

Democracy as a Core Value
Proceduralists view democracy as a mechanism; communitarians see it as a core value that must be shared. The basic reason is that if democracy is viewed merely as an arrangement or procedure, it may be abandoned when it comes into significant conflict with a major interest group or with the values of one of the major contesting subgroups.

Democracy is not a lifestyle option – a political format adhered to by some while others prefer to follow rules set by rabbinical courts or a national authoritarian regime or some other kind. It is a core value that all those who seek to join our community and polity must embrace.

There is no indication that Hispanic and Asian immigrants are seeking a different form of polity. On the contrary, they are actively participating in the democratic process by fielding candidates, voting, and so on. Certainly, much disagreement exists over the large body of voting data. Some scholars point to statistics showing lower voting rates for Hispanics and Asians than for other Americans.[8] Other scholars argue that when accounting for socioeconomic factors, these immigrants vote largely at the same rate as other Americans. Usually these data do not take into account what one might call the "newcomer factor," a factor that has been highlighted by Linda Chavez.[9] It refers to the fact that when one compares an immigrant group that has many members who came to the U.S. recently to groups whose number of new immigrant members has stemmed, the group with many newcomers will look less integrated. A valid comparison would "deduct" this factor. The result would be a vast improvement in the voting and other acculturation scores for Hispanics and Asians.

The Constitution

The Constitution embodies the core values that guide the American polity and society. It is the embodiment of the shared conceptions about the ways in which liberty will remain ordered, of the basic individual and minority rights that hold the government at bay. The Constitution defines the relationship between the individuals and communities that constitute the society and the society at large. It does so by drawing a line between the decisions that individuals and communities can make and those that are framed by the overarching society. This balance is manifested in the distinction between those numerous matters in which the majority rules and those in which the majority cannot reign because of the need to guarantee minority and individual rights. For instance, no majority (local or otherwise) can vote to allow individuals to be sold as slaves, to be denied the right to vote or speak freely, and so on. On the other hand, the majority is entrusted with deciding the level of taxes that will be exacted, the allocation of these funds among various competing demands, and so on.

Although the line between legitimate majority decisions and those from which the majority is excluded does not *necessarily* parallel the line between community-particulars and the societal common (the pieces and the framework of the mosaic), it often does. Most policies concerning education, transportation, and similar issues are set locally in each of the 50 states. The policies that local and state governments pursue often reflect values that particular communities seek to uphold. This is the reason for stricter anti-drug policies in Houston, Texas, than in New York City; immigrants are treated more harshly in Southern Californian communities than in those of Maine; and so on. In each of these communities, local or state majorities set their particular course. However, all of these communities must act within the values embodied in the Constitution. This prevents communities from following their particular values in those specified areas in which the society at large has agreed that shared values are to take precedence. Foremost among these values are various freedoms, such as the freedom of speech, association, and assembly that prevent communities from banning speakers whose views a given community finds offensive, from outlawing troubling books, or from discriminating against a given racial or ethnic group. Here the Constitution, speaking for the shared values of the society at large, upholds universals in the form of limits on local policies. All those who seek to become members of the American community must agree to honor the Constitution, as reflected in the oath they take when they become American citizens.

Some Jewish and Muslim immigrants (as well as some Native Americans) have preferred to deal with matters such as divorce, estates, and conflict resolution through their respective religious institutions. However, there is no evidence that Hispanic or Asian immigrants seek extra-constitutional treatments. Moreover, the Latino National Political Survey conducted in the early 1990s revealed that by and large Hispanic immigrants (of all nationalities) did not believe that immigrants from their own countries of origin should be given any special legal considerations when it came to immigration law.[10] Most relevantly, no one has presented systematic data to show that Hispanic and Asian immigrants and their descendents are less supportive of American constitutional conceptions than other immigrant families who have been established in the U.S. for the same period of time and who occupy the same socioeconomic status (income, education, etc.).

Respect for the Law and Universalism

The normative conception that no one is above the law, that all are equal before the law, and that laws must be respected, is a profound part of the American core of shared values – although these values are not always respected in the streets and courts of the Nation, to put it carefully.

Whether or not immigrants adhere to these values is a particularly key test for their successful integration into American society because many immigrants – Hispanics, Asians, and others – come from cultures in which the government is often corrupt to the point that it cannot be trusted. In such cultures, working around the law is the norm, and particularistic loyalties to one's family, friends, and community take precedence over observing the law. It is particularly important that immigrants from such countries shed these notions and habits.

There is no evidence that Hispanic and Asian immigrants are slower to incorporate these values than the waves of other immigrants that came from traditional, particularistic societies. Indeed, many Hispanic immigrants identify the cronyism, corruption, and favoritism that permeate the political systems of their countries of origin as the source of many of the problems facing those countries. For instance, take the overwhelming agreement among Latino National Political Survey interviewees that corruption within the Mexican government proved responsible for the majority of that nation's internal quandaries.[11] And results from the same study also reveal that Hispanic immigrants' greatest concerns are those illicit activities that deviate from American law and endanger communities, such as drug use and crime.[12]

Societal Values

Trumping Loyalty

To maintain the proper equilibrium between the particular, constituting communities (many of which are ethnic and immigrant based) and the overarching American community (the Nation), a *layered loyalty* must be fostered in which commitment to the overarching community takes precedence in matters concerning political action. The DWU approach is based on a split loyalty, divided between commitment to one's immediate community and to the Nation, and according priority to the Nation on key but select matters.

In recent years, much has been made of the fact that some immigrants (and some American-born citizens) have dual citizenship or dual nationality. Peter Salins takes umbrage with the notion of dual citizenship, warning that such continued loyalty to a country of origin cheapens the value of American citizenship.[13] Others worry that the loosening of restrictions on citizenship by foreign powers thinly veils these countries' desire to gain access to and power in American politics. Although far from an alarmist, Nathan Glazer does note this possibility: "... it [the alteration of the Mexican Constitution to allow for dual nationality] would help Mexican-Americans serve as an interest group in defense of Mexican interests in the United States with respect to trade and immigration."[14]

However, experience and data show that these fears are vastly exaggerated. Actually, dual nationality often merely reflects a matter of convenience, making travel easier. Sometimes it might indicate a mild sentimental attachment to the country of origin and, in some cases, an unresolved conflict of loyalties, largely limited to the first generation.[15]

Drawing on findings from two comprehensive studies, de la Garza concludes that Mexican-Americans not only harbor negative sentiments about the Mexican government but also display little interest in following the political machinations of their original homeland. He writes, "Although [Mexican-Americans] have positive feelings for Mexico as a nation, their feelings toward the United States are much stronger. More significantly, they have little interest in Mexican politics, and they are extremely critical of the Mexican government."[16]

Mutual Respect

For the American community to be sustained, immigrants need to combine their appreciation of and commitment to their own particular traditions, cultures, and values with respect for those of others.[17] James Hunter argues that the criteria should be tolerance, which does not mean accepting all views as equally valid as one's own but rather learning to live peacefully next to those with whom one disagrees.[18] The term "tolerance," however, implies considerable distancing. It implies that one will put up with such views out of good manners or for the well-being of society, while actually judging them to be inferior. Respecting subcultures other than one's own, so long as what is at issue are particulars and not mores and values that concern the "framework," seems more communitarian. Respect means that one would have no normative objections to others holding values which one would not personally hold.

There appears to be no evidence that Hispanic or Asian immigrants are less tolerant or respectful of others than previous groups of immigrants or American-born citizens. True, there have been a few incidences of inter-ethnic conflicts (and even violence) involving Cambodian and Vietnamese immigrants and others. But these have been few and far between. Moreover, all the cases that I could trace concerned first-generation immigrants. By and large, it seems that Hispanic and Asian immigrants overall demonstrate levels of respect at least comparable to that of other groups of immigrants.

Openness

One of the key elements of the American shared framework is the relative unimportance attached to social distinctions. Indeed, American society has few sharp, insurmountable class (let alone caste) lines. And those divisive, largely immutable lines that do exist, especially those between the races, are considered lines that should be overcome rather than valued. True, in American society there are very great differences in wealth; however, these are fluid in the sense that the wealthy can end in poverty and the poor can overcome meager beginnings. (At least this is what the creed strongly holds.) Where do Hispanic and Asian immigrants fit into this aspect of the framework?

Although attempts have been made to treat Hispanic-Americans as a distinct race ("brown") or as black[19] and to view Asians as a race, they behave much more like ethnic groups and are so treated – a concept underscored in Peter Skerry's work on Mexican-Americans.[20] This is most evident in the very high rates of intermarriage for Hispanic (and Asian) immigrants. Indeed, these rates provide strong evidence that these two groups are accepting the core American value of openness and living up to its tenets. When accounting for all generations, data from 1998 show that cross-racial or cross-ethnic marriage reached 16.7 percent for Hispanics and 15 percent for non-Hispanic Asians.[21] Studies that look beyond first-generation Hispanic and Asian immigrants to subsequent generations reveal even higher numbers.

As a result, Hispanic and Asian immigrants will help to encourage a sense of connectedness. Americans will be linked across, not in spite of, ethnic and racial lines, with families consisting of individuals of varied ethnic backgrounds.[22] Not only will this sense of interconnection reinforce America's core value of social and economic mobility and limited social distinctions and decrease racial tensions, but it will also mute fears of tribalism, equally divisive and destructive. As I noted in *The Monochrome Society*, "If one must find a simple image for the future of America, Tiger Woods, or Hawaii, as I see it, seems more appropriate than a view of a country in which Louis Farrakhan and his followers and the Aryan Nation are threatening one another."[23] Nothing refutes the notion that Hispanics will form a separate nation more conclusively than their high rate of intermarriage.

One Shared Language?

Many societies – such as Belgium, Switzerland, Canada, Israel – debate whether one set language should comprise part of the shared framework or whether several can coexist. In the U.S., some have used the commitment to English as the official language (the only one in which government documents can be issued, voters guides published, etc.) as a code-word for nativism and anti-immigrant sentiments.[24] Some of these groups have been associated with a movement to keep immigrants out and America white and Aryan.[25] Most recently it has been suggested that Mexican-Americans are slow to learn English, which, it was argued, is one sign that they are refusing to assimilate and are thus endangering the American creed.[26] Some on the Left have used the existence of racist, pro-English groups as proof that to favor English as a core language seeks to rob immigrants of their culture.

However, after stripping away such emotive overtones, the following facts stand out: most immigrants, including Mexican-Americans, are keen to learn English and do not view learning English as an attack on their culture or something forced upon them. According to the Latino National Political Survey, over 60 percent of Mexican-Americans agree that both U.S. citizens and residents should acquire English.[27] And Alejandro Portes and Richard Schauffler conclude from their research in South Florida that "[c]hildren raised in the core of the Spanish-speaking community in Miami (those attending bilingual private schools) are actually the most enthusiastic in their preference for the language of the land."[28] Moreover, most second-generation Hispanics have a full command of English, and most third-generation Hispanics know little Spanish.

Most importantly, only an assimilationist viewpoint suggests that to maintain a distinct subculture, including speaking a distinct secondary language, say Turkish for German-Turks, is a sign of trouble. From a DWU perspective, this is completely acceptable.

In light of the foregoing discussion, it may be said that there is every indication that Hispanic (and Asian) immigrants are integrating into American society without altering its framework as a result of their presence. It may be true that integration is slower in areas with an unusually high concentration of immigrants of the same ethnic background, especially if there is a continuous flow of additional immigrants into these areas. However, there is no convincing evidence that even in these parts, integration will not take place, albeit at a slower pace.

I suggest that Hispanic and Asian immigrants *do better than merely buy into an existing unity-preserving framework*; they *seem to have a rehabilitation effect on the American core of shared values and the institutions embodying them*. This will become evident once this examination is extended to encompass a facet of society often not included in such analyses: the communitarian balance.

CORRECTING A COMMUNITARIAN IMBALANCE:
THE REHABILITATION EFFECT

I have argued elsewhere that societies flourish when they maintain a carefully crafted balance between liberty and social order, between individual rights and social responsibilities.[29] There are those who have characterized American society as centered around rights and individualistic values, a Lockean nation. Various historians, including Louis Hartz, J. G. A. Pocock, Isaac Kramnick, and Rogers Smith, have espoused the centrality of this liberal individualism to the American society.[30] In his writings about American "exceptionalism," Seymour Martin Lipset also sees American society's emphasis upon individual rights and liberties as the defining quality of the "civic culture." The values that he perceives as the main components of the American creed are individualism, anti-statism, populism, and egalitarianism.[31]

As I see it, this characterization of the core American values is an accurate but only partial one – and one that makes America's core values and character seem much more self-centered, more Lockean, than they actually are. I join with those who see the American society as constantly struggling to balance these values of liberty with commitments to community, to forming a "more perfect union," to advancing the common good, and to shoring up shared values and communal bonds.

The special normative standing accorded to the common good in American society is reflected in the high value historically attributed not only to the nuclear and extended family (common in other societies) but also to communities.[32] Many of these communities are not of the traditional and receding kind (traditional villages and small towns) but modern, voluntary communities (the Toucquevillian elements of America), including prominently those of various ethnic and also religious groups.

Throughout American history there has been a continuous struggle between the Lockean and the pro-community elements. Up to the 1960s, the pro-community elements were rarely highlighted, as they were powerful and by and large not contested. Indeed, one may well argue that despite normative commitments to the contrary, Lockean elements were short. Much of the history of the Nation can be depicted as an attempt to scale back authoritarian elements and excessive community controls and to expand the liberties and rights of people without property, of minorities, and of women and other groups, and to free the market forces from excessive interventions by special interests (not necessarily the government). But as communitarians have often pointed out, as of the 1960s individualism expanded, as reflected first in the expressive individualism of the sexual revolution and the counterculture and then in the 1980s in the instrumental individualism of the Reagan/Thatcher era.[33] As of 1990, communitarians pointed out that this excessive tilt toward individualism had resulted in several dysfunctional effects, including an increase in the neglect of children, withdrawal from other familial commitments, self-centered behavior, white collar and violent crime, drug abuse, litigiousness, a strong sense of entitlement but a reduced sense of responsibility for the common good, and a rejection of all forms of authority.[34] I hence called for a pro-community correction, which to some extent did take place in the decade and a half that followed.[35]

The values that most Hispanic and Asian immigrants subscribe to are supportive of this rehabilitation of the American society. That is, in matters concerning a restoration of the communitarian balance, these immigrants by and large do not recast the framework, do not modify it, but reinforce one of its cardinal elements: the pro-community element, broadly understood as including a sense of responsibility for children, family, ethnic group, and nation.[36]

Because this thesis has not been subjected to significant amounts of social science research, there seem to be little data to support it. Yet the research that does exist largely supports this view. Hispanic-Americans have a relatively low divorce rate. Around 73 percent of "Mexican-origin" immigrants are married – a figure matched only by "whites" who have marriage rates of 80 percent.[37] The number of single parent homes among Hispanic immigrants remains low, as does the birthrate for children born out of wedlock – especially when compared to African Americans.[38] Also the Latino National Political Survey reports that "[m]ore than half of Mexican and Puerto Rican and 40 percent of Cuban respondents engaged in school-related activities."[39] When I served as the staff director of a commission that investigated nursing homes, we found very few Hispanic and Asian senior citizens in these homes. We were told that these ethnic groups are strongly inclined to take care of their elders in their own homes. Furthermore, these immigrants possess a strong work ethic. According to Pachon and DeSipio's 1994 study, most immigrants of Hispanic descent hold full-time jobs, and most eschew any form of government aid.[40] As Chavez notes, "Family members are expected to help each other in times of financial or other need, which some analysts believe explains why so many Mexican-origin families shun welfare even when their poverty makes them eligible for assistance."[41]

Religion too plays a role in the lives of Hispanic and Asian immigrants, with estimates that Hispanics will comprise over half of the U.S.'s Catholic parishioners in the near future.[42] According to Peggy Levitt, integral spiritual tenets find expression within and beyond the church walls of the Hispanic community in the United States from "lighting candles in a church to establishing private altars within the home."[43]

All said and done, to the extent that data allow one to gain a preliminary impression, Hispanic (and Asian) immigrants are reinforcing the weakened communal elements of the American society and are thus helping to rehabilitate it by restoring a communitarian balance.

I do not argue that the communitarian rehabilitation of the American synthesis of communal and individualistic elements, which these immigrants foster, will necessarily result in the perfectly balanced mix. Each element must be examined in its own right, which in turn may point to various desired public education campaigns (for instance on women's rights). However, as I see it, out of this renewed synthesis, for instance, when these immigrants' element of authoritarianism blends with recent American tendencies to be disrespectful of authority, and when their strong sense of gender differentiation mixes with current American trends toward de-gendering (if not androgyny), American society will move closer to the desired communitarian balance.

THE NORMALIZATION OF POLITICS

The move from separatism and identity politics to "normal" politics of interest groups, which accepts the basic societal framework, is one important effect of Hispanic (and Asian) immigration not often discussed. This is occurring as a direct result of the increase in Hispanics and the *relative* decline of African Americans in the total demographic and political picture.

The Census Bureau has projected that the African American population, which made up 13 percent of the total U.S. population in the year 2000, will grow to approximately 15 percent in 2050, where it will remain steady until 2100.[44] In contrast, the Hispanic population, which made up approximately 12 percent of the total U.S. population in 2000, is projected to rise to approximately 24 percent of the total U.S. population in 2050 and approximately 33 percent in 2100.[45] Often reference to race relations still evokes the opposition of black and white, while other groups are mentioned only as an afterthought, if at all. This will change in the future as the number of Hispanics continues to grow, along with their political awareness and organization. (The same holds true, although to a lesser extent, for Asian immigrants.)

The current and forthcoming changes in the composition of American society are especially consequential because African Americans have been much slower to intermarry and to be otherwise absorbed into American society than other minorities. And although some African Americans, particularly middle-class blacks, tend to be moderate, on average their leadership has been less moderate and more given to identity politics than the leaders of other minority groups.

One may wonder whether Hispanic leadership may be driven to less moderate, identity politics. This is hard to predict; however, one notes several factors that agitate against such a development: the strong tendency to intermarry, movement up the economic and social ladders, and the growing Hispanic middle class. The same holds true for Asian-Americans. (The fact that members of these ethnic groups act like earlier immigrants and unlike African Americans was reflected in the 2004 elections, when African Americans continued to vote largely for one party – albeit less so than in previous years – while Hispanic and Asian-Americans distributed their support more evenly between both parties.)

All said and done, one should expect that Hispanic- (and Asian-) Americans will contribute to the depolarization of American society. They will replace African Americans as the main socially distinct group and will constitute groups that are either not racial (many Hispanics see themselves as white or as an ethnic group and not as a member of a distinct race, black or brown) or are of a race that is less distinct from the white majority (as in the case of Asian Americans). By increasing the proportion of Americans who do not see themselves as victims and who intermarry with others, these immigrants will continue to "normalize" American politics.

RECASTING THE FRAMEWORK

Societies are constantly in flux, as the framework that holds them together is recast. Part of maintaining the framework is to uphold the fiction that no changes to it are being made – as continuity, tradition, and following the founders carry a measure of legitimacy. This tendency to claim that one ought to follow the old and true *veritas* is particularly highlighted in the treatment of the Constitution (and the shared values ensconced in it) but is also evident in the respect accorded to traditional conceptions of marriage, authority, and the core values. But actually, instead of rigidly adhering to traditional conceptions that are no longer adaptive as economic, technological, environmental, and international conditions change, one must realize that over time certain modifications to the core values and to the societal institutions that embody them prove a requirement for continued societal stability and adherence to those values. Such modifications, however, should remain within the deeper meaning of the original framework. In that sense, meta-stability requires low-level change. Thus, allowing people without property to run for office was a change, yet it did not undermine the original concept of democracy but instead deepened it; the same of course holds true for extending voting rights to women and ensuring that African Americans can exercise theirs. And adding the right to privacy to the other rights enumerated in the Constitution modified the Constitution but reflects its core conception that the people need to be protected from excessive intrusion by the government. I am not suggesting that historically every change to American institutions has been in line with America's core values but that alteration can be made to these institutions and to the core values themselves without undermining them.

It is difficult at this point to determine if Hispanic and Asian immigrants will not only reinforce the American framework but also modify it because the large waves of these immigrants have been occurring only recently and because this matter has been so little studied. However, there are some indications that Hispanic and Asian immigrants help to reorient American society's traditional focus on Europe toward a more mindful and informed focus on Asia and, to some extent, on Latin America. Also, Hispanic immigrants make the American character more expressive and less instrumental; in this sense, they join immigrants from Southern Europe in modifying extreme American elements of self-restraint and in providing for greater psychological openness, easier forms of empathy, and maybe a dash of fatalism.[46] This is one of the least studied and arguably less predictive matters concerning Hispanic and Asian immigration.

Further analysis along these lines would require taking into account that both categories, that of Hispanic and Asian, are convenient simplifications;

there are significant and relevant differences within each group – for instance, between Cuban- and Mexican-Americans and between Japanese- and Cambodian-Americans. The essence of prejudice is to assume that all the members of one group have the same traits, attributes, views, and feelings or that they all conduct themselves in the same way. However, one simply cannot conduct a study of the issues at hand without noting that *statistically* speaking, *many* members of the same group conduct themselves in a similar fashion and in a fashion different from that of members of other groups. Keeping these reservations in mind, I hold that when such detailed analyses are conducted of the various ethnic subgroups of immigrants currently lumped together under the terms "Hispanic" or "Asian," they will show that the conduct and values of the overwhelming majority of the members of these groups not only far from undermine the American core of shared values and the institutions based on them but also help to shore them up – albeit not by returning American society to its founding days, but to its deeper ideals as adapted to the current history.

NOTES

1. Martha Farnsworth Riche, "We're All Minorities Now," *American Demographics* 13 (October 1991): 26.
2. For further discussion of the diversity within unity paradigm, refer to: Amitai Etzioni, *The New Golden Rule*; Amitai Etzioni, "Diversity within Unity," in Howard F. Didsbury, Jr. (ed.), *21st Century Opportunities and Challenges: An Age of Destruction or an Age of Transformation* (Bethesda, MD: World Future Society, 2003), pp. 316–323; Amitai Etzioni, "In Defense of Diversity Within Unity," *The Responsive Community* 13 (Spring 2003): 52–57; www .communitariannetwork.org for the Diversity Within Unity platform and for a list of those who have endorsed it.
3. Sheldon Hackney, former Chairman of the National Endowment for the Humanities, suggested that "jazz [is] the ideal metaphor for America.… As befits a democratic society, it was created from the bottom up, is non-hierarchical in both its performance and appeal …" (Sheldon Hackney, "Organizing a National Conversation," *The Chronicle of Higher Education*, 20 April 1994, A56). See also Roberto Suro, *Remembering the American Dream: Hispanic Immigration and National Policy* (New York: Twentieth Century Fund Press, 1994).
4. Personal communication with Raul Yzaguirre, National Council of La Raza.
5. Rosalie Pedalino Porter, *Forked Tongue: The Politics of Bilingual Education* (New York: Basic Books, 1990), p. 211 (Table). Six states have English-only constitutional amendments, and 11 have statutes or resolutions to that effect.
6. Tamar Jacoby, "What it Means to Be American in the 21st Century," in Tamar Jacoby (ed.), *Reinventing the Melting Pot: The New Immigrants and What It Means to Be American* (New York: Basic Books, 2004), p. 306.
7. In an effort to define the shared framework, Fuchs identifies three concepts as key to the foundation of "civic culture." The ability of people to self-govern responsibly through officials chosen by the polity and the right to equal participation in "public life" comprise two of the inherent ideals integral to the formation of the civic

culture. But the third proves the most interesting for its implications for the DWU model. Fuchs writes, "... and third, that individuals who comport themselves as good citizens of the civic culture are free to differ from each other in religion and in other aspects of their private lives ..." thus demonstrating that an acceptance of a certain amount of cultural diversity indeed exists as one of the values shared within the very framework. Lawrence H. Fuchs, *The American Kaleidoscope: Race, Ethnicity, and the Civic Culture* (Hanover, CT: Wesleyan University Press, 1990). Diane Ravitch proves slightly more general in her assessment of those values implied within a shared framework or civic culture, but she too emphasizes the preeminence of both "tolerance and liberty," as well as "responsibilities of citizenship," Diane Ravitch, "The Future of American Pluralism," in Lamar Alexander and Chester E. Finn, Jr. (eds.), *The New Promise of American Life* (Indianapolis: Hudson Institute, 1995), p. 85.

8. As stated, various data have been published that scholars on both sides of the issue of Hispanic and Asian voter turnout utilize. Refer to the following publications for additional information about some of the studies on voter turnout for these groups: Carol A. Cassel, "Hispanic Turnout: Estimates from Validated Voting Data," *Political Research Quarterly* 55 (June 2002): 391–408; Rodolfo O. de la Garza, Louis DeSipio, Martha Menchaca (eds.), *Barrio Ballots: Latino Politics in the 1990 Elections* (Boulder, CO: Westview Press, 1994); Rodolfo O. de la Garza, Louis DeSipio, F. Chris Garcia, John Garcia, and Angelo Falcon (eds.), *Latino Voices: Mexican, Puerto Rican, and Cuban Perspectives on American Politics* (Boulder, CO: Westview Press, 1992); Louis DeSipio and Harry Pachon, *New Americans by Choice: Political Perspectives of Latino Immigrants* (Boulder, CO: Westview Press, 1994).

9. Linda Chavez, *Out of the Barrio: Toward a New Politics of Hispanic Assimilation* (New York: Basic Books, 1991), pp. 106, 134.

10. de la Garza et al., *Latino Voices*, pp. 100–101.

11. *Ibid.*, p. 102.

12. *Ibid.*, pp. 87–89.

13. Peter D. Salins, "The Assimilation Contract: Endangered but Still Holding," in Jacoby, *Melting Pot*, p. 107.

14. Nathan Glazer, "Assimilation Today: Is One Identity Enough?" in Jacoby, *Melting Pot*, p. 70.

15. DeSipio and Pachon, *New Americans by Choice*, pp. 93–96.

16. Rodolfo O. de la Garza, "Interests Not Passions: Mexican-American Attitudes toward Mexico, Immigration from Mexico, and Other Issues Shaping U.S.–Mexican Relations," *International Migration Review* 32 (Summer 1998): 406.

17. William J. Bennett, in John Leo, "Cash the Check, Bob," *U.S. News and World Report*, September 18, 1995, 43.

18. James Davidson Hunter, *Before the Shooting Begins: Searching for Democracy in America's Culture War* (New York: Free Press, 1994).

19. Etzioni, *Monochrome*, pp. 18–19.

20. Peter Skerry, *Mexican Americans: The Ambivalent Minority* (New York: The Free Press, 1993), pp. 16–17.

21. Etzioni, *Monochrome*, p. 25.

22. Etzioni, *Monochrome*, p. 27.

23. *Ibid.*

24. Porter, *Forked Tongue*, pp. 214–216.

25. *Ibid.*, pp. 193–221.

26. Samuel P. Huntington, "Mexican Immigration and Hispanization," in *Who Are We?: The Challenges to America's National Identity* (New York: Simon & Schuster, 2004), pp. 221–256.

27. de la Garza, *Latino Voices*, 98.

28. Alejandro Portes and Richard Schauffler, "Language and the Second Generation: Bilingualism Yesterday and Today," in Alejandro Portes (ed.), *The New Second Generation*, (New York: Russell Sage Foundation, 1996), p. 28.

29. Etzioni, *New Golden Rule*.

30. Louis Hartz, *The Liberal Tradition in America: An Interpretation of American Political Thought since the Revolution* (New York: Harcourt, Brace, 1955); J. G. A. Pocock, *The Machiavellian Moment: Florentine Political Thought and the Atlantic Political Tradition* (Princeton, NJ: Princeton University Press, 1975); Isaac Kramnick, *Republicanism and Bourgeois Radicalism: Political Ideology in Late Eighteenth-Century England and America* (Ithaca, NY: Cornell University Press, 1990); Rogers M. Smith, "Beyond Tocqueville, Myrdal and Hartz: The Multiple Traditions in America," *American Political Science Review* 87 (September 1993): 549–566.

31. Seymour Martin Lipset, *American Exceptionalism: A Double-Edged Sword* (New York: Norton, 1996).

32. For further discussion of the common good, refer to Amitai Etzioni, *The Common Good* (Cambridge: Polity Press Ltd, 2004).

33. Robert Bellah, *Habits of the Heart: Individualism and Commitment in American Life* (Berkeley, CA: University of California Press, 1985).

34. The following works address in greater detail the repercussions of the excessive individualism manifested in America during the 1990s. Refer to: Bellah, *Habits of the Heart*; Francis Fukuyama, *The Great Disruption: Human Nature and the Reconstitution of Social Order* (New York: The Free Press, 1999); Mary Ann Glendon, *Rights Talk: The Impoverishment of Political Discourse* (New York: The Free Press, 1991); Amitai Etzioni, *The Spirit of Community: Rights, Responsibilities, and the Communitarian Agenda* (New York: Crown Publishers, Inc., 1993); Etzioni, *New Golden Rule*. Robert Putnam also followed this line of analysis and provided considerable data to support it, *Bowling Alone: The Collapse and Revival of American Community* (New York: Simon and Schuster, 2000).

35. Amitai Etzioni, *My Brother's Keeper: A Memoir and a Message* (Lanham, MD: Rowman and Littlefield Publishers, Inc., 2003); Etzioni, *New Golden Rule*.

36. Francis Fukuyama, "Immigration," in Alexander and Finn, *The New Promise of American Life*, p. 105. For additional perspectives on how immigrants reinforce the American framework through the strength of their "traditional" values, refer to: David Reimers, *Unwelcome Strangers: American Identity and the Turn Against Immigration* (New York: Columbia University Press, 1998), p. 114; Raymond Rocco, "Citizenship, Culture, and Community: Restructuring in Southeast Los Angeles," in William V. Flores and Rina Benmayor (eds.), *Latino Cultural Citizenship: Claiming Identity, Space, and Rights* (Boston: Beacon Press, 1997), p. 120.

37. Chavez, *Out of the Barrio*, p. 108. Note, as I discussed in *The Monochrome Society*, I do not find acceptable the use of the word "whites" to distinguish between Hispanic and Non-Hispanic Americans (refer to Chapter 1).
38. *Ibid.*
39. de la Garza, *Latino Voices*, p. 117.
40. DeSipio and Pachon, *New Americans by Choice*, pp. 33–34.
41. Chavez, *Out of the Barrio*, p. 109.
42. Peggy Levitt, "Two Nations under God?: Latino Religious Life in the United States," in Marcelo M. Suárez-Orozco and Mariela M. Páez (eds.), *Latinos Remaking America*, (Berkeley: University of California Press, 2002), p. 150.
43. *Ibid.*, pp. 153–154.
44. Data extrapolated from figures in Population Projections Program, Population Division, Census Bureau, Projections of the Total Resident Population by 5-Year Age Groups, Race, and Hispanic Origin with Special Age Categories: Middle Series, 2050 to 2070; and Population Projections Program, Population Division, Census Bureau, Projections of the Total Resident Population by 5-Year Age Groups, Race, and Hispanic Origin with Special Age Categories: Middle Series, 2075 to 2100. Available at: www.census.gov/population/projections/nation/summary/np-t4-h.txt. Accessed March 8, 2000.
45. Data extrapolated from figures in Population Projections Program, Population Division, Census Bureau, Projections of the Total Resident Population by 5-Year Age Groups, Race, and Hispanic Origin with Special Age Categories: Middle Series, 2050 to 2070; and Population Projections Program, Population Division, Census Bureau, Projections of the Total Resident Population by 5-Year Age Groups, Race, and Hispanic Origin with Special Age Categories: Middle Series, 2075 to 2100. Available at: www.census.gov/population/projections/nation/summary/np-t4-h.txt. Accessed March 8, 2000.
46. The conclusions drawn in one study, the Latino National Political Survey, suggested optimism from Hispanics regarding their future.

PART II

LAW AND POLICY

6

The Progressive Argument for Reducing Immigration into the United States

Philip Cafaro

I teach philosophy at a large public university in the western United States, and like many of my fellow academics I'm a political progressive. That means I value economic security for workers and their families and support a much more equal distribution of wealth. I favor strong and well-enforced environmental protection laws and the creation of an ecologically sustainable society. I support ending racial discrimination in the United States. I want to maximize the political power of common citizens and limit the influence of large corporations. My political heroes include the three Roosevelts (Teddy, Franklin, and Eleanor), Rachel Carson and Martin Luther King Jr.

I also want to reduce immigration into the United States. If this combination strikes you as odd, you aren't alone. Friends, political allies, even my mother the social worker shake their heads or worse when I bring up the subject. I've been called a nativist and a racist (thankfully not by Mom) and had close friendships strained by discussions of this topic. Yet the more I've learned about the economic and environmental impacts of mass immigration, the stronger my conviction has grown that reducing immigration is necessary to achieve progressive political goals and create more just and flourishing societies at home and abroad.

That said, I can understand why many progressives embrace mass immigration. Immigration is not an easy issue for those of us looking to create fairer, more egalitarian societies, precisely because vital interests are at stake and no set of policies can further all of them. Consider two stories from among the hundreds I heard while researching a recent book on immigration ethics.[1]

THE DILEMMA

It's lunchtime on a sunny October day and I'm talking to Javier, an electrician's assistant, at a home construction site in Longmont, Colorado, near Denver.[2] He is short and solidly built; his words are soft-spoken but clear. Although he apologizes for his English, it is quite good. At any rate, much better than my Spanish.

Javier studied to be an electrician in Mexico, but could not find work there after school. "You have to pay to work," he explains: pay corrupt officials up to two years' wages up front just to start a job. "Too much corruption," he says, a refrain I find repeated often by Mexican and other Central American immigrants. They feel that a poor man cannot get ahead there, can hardly get started.

So, in 1989 Javier came to the United States, undocumented, working various jobs in food preparation and construction. He has lived in Colorado for ten years and now has a wife (also here illegally) and two girls, aged 7 and 3. "I like USA, you have a better life here," he says. Of course, he misses his family back in Mexico. But to his father's entreaties to come home, he explains that he needs to consider his own family now. Javier told me that he's not looking to get rich, he just wants a decent life for himself and his girls. Who could blame him?

Ironically one of the things Javier likes most about the United States is that we have rules that are fairly enforced. Unlike in Mexico, a poor man does not live at the whim of corrupt officials. When I suggest that Mexico might need more people like him to stay and fight "corruption," he just laughs. "No, go to jail," he says, or worse. Like the dozens of other Central American immigrants I interviewed for my book, Javier does not seem to think that such corruption could ever change in the land of his birth.[3]

Do immigrants take jobs away from Americans? I ask. "American people no want to work in the fields," he responds, or as dishwashers in restaurants. Still, he continues, "the problem is cheap labor." Too many immigrants coming into construction lowers wages for everyone – including other immigrants like himself.

"The American people say, all Mexicans the same," Javier says. He does not want to be lumped together with "all Mexicans," or labeled a problem, but judged for who he is as an individual. "I don't like it when my people abandon cars, or steal." If immigrants commit crimes, he thinks they should go to jail, or be deported. But "that no me." While many immigrants work under the table for cash, he is proud of the fact that he pays his taxes. Proud, too, that he gives a good day's work for his daily pay, a fact confirmed by his co-workers.

Javier's boss, Andy, thinks that immigration levels are too high and that too many people flout the law and work illegally.[4] He was disappointed, he says, to find out several years ago that Javier was in the country illegally. Still, he likes Javier and worries about his family. He is trying to help him get legal residency.

With the government showing new initiative in immigration enforcement around the time of our interview – including a well-publicized raid at a nearby meatpacking plant that caught hundreds of illegal workers – there was a lot of worry among undocumented immigrants. "Everyone scared now," Javier says. He and his wife used to go to restaurants or stores without a second thought;

now they are sometimes afraid to go out. "It's hard," he says. But: "I understand. If the people say, 'All the people here, go back to Mexico,' I understand."

Javier's answer to one of my standard questions – How might changes in immigration policy affect you? – is obvious. Tighter enforcement could break up his family and destroy the life he has created here in America. An amnesty would give him a chance to regularize his life. "Sometimes," he says, "I dream in my heart, 'If you no want to give me paper for residence, or whatever, just give me permit for work.'"

It's a few months later and I'm back in Longmont, eating a 6:30 breakfast at a café out by the Interstate with Tom Kenney.[5] Fit and alert, Tom looks to be in his mid-forties. Born and raised in Denver, he has been spraying custom finishes on drywall for twenty-five years and has had his own company since 1989. "At one point we had twelve people running three trucks," he says. Now his business is just him and his wife. "Things have changed," he says.

Although it has gone through some more ups and downs since then, residential and commercial construction was booming when I interviewed Tom. One of the main "things that have changed" is the number of immigrants in construction. When Tom got into it almost thirty years ago, construction used almost all native-born workers. Today estimates of the number of immigrant workers in northern Colorado range from 50 percent to 70 percent of the total construction workforce. Some trades, like pouring concrete and framing, use immigrant labor almost exclusively. Come in with an "all-white" crew of framers, another small contractor tells me, and people do a double-take.

Tom is an independent contractor, bidding on individual jobs. But, he says, "guys are coming in with bids that are impossible." After all his time in the business, "no way they can be as efficient in time and materials as me." The difference has to be in the cost of labor. "They're not paying the taxes and insurance that I am," he says. Insurance, workmen's compensation and taxes add about 40 percent to the cost of legally employed workers. When you add the lower wages that immigrants are often willing to take, there is plenty of opportunity for competing contractors to underbid Tom and still make a profit. He no longer bids on the big new construction projects, and jobs in individual, custom-built houses are becoming harder to find.

"I've gone in to spray a house and there's a guy sleeping in the bathtub, with a microwave set up in the kitchen. I'm thinking, 'You moved into this house for two weeks to hang and paint it, you're gonna get cash from somebody, and he's gonna pick you up and drive you to the next one.'" He seems more upset at the contractor than at the undocumented worker who labors for him.

In this way, some trades in construction are turning into the equivalent of migrant labor in agriculture. Workers do not have insurance or workmen's compensation, so if they are hurt or worn out on the job, they are simply discarded and replaced. Workers are used up, while the builders and contractors higher up the food chain keep more of the profits for themselves. "The quality of life [for construction workers] has changed drastically," says Tom. "I don't want to live like that. I want to go home and live with my family."

Do immigrants perform jobs Americans don't want to do? I ask. The answer is no. "My job is undesirable," Tom replies. "It's dirty, it's messy, it's dusty. I learned right away that because of that, the opportunity is available to make money in it. That job has served me well" – at least up until recently. He now travels as far away as Wyoming and southern Colorado to find work. "We're all fighting for scraps right now."

Over the years, Tom has built a reputation for quality work and efficient and prompt service, as I confirmed in interviews with others in the business. Until recently that was enough to secure a good living. Now, though, like a friend of his who recently folded his small landscaping company ("I just can't bid 'em low enough"), Tom is thinking of leaving the business. He is also struggling to find a way to keep up the mortgage payments on his house.

He does not blame immigrants, though. "If you were born in Mexico and you had to fight for food or clothing, you would do the same thing," Tom tells me. "You would come here."

HARD CHOICES

As my interviews with Javier Morales and Tom Kenney suggest, any immigration policy will have winners and losers. If we enforce our immigration laws, then good people like Javier and his family will have their lives turned upside down. If we reduce the numbers of immigrants, then good people in Mexico (and Guatemala, and Vietnam, and the Philippines...) will have to forgo opportunities to live better lives in the United States.

On the other hand, if we fail to enforce our immigration laws, or repeatedly grant amnesties to people like Javier who are in the country illegally, then we forfeit the ability to set limits to immigration. And if immigration levels remain high, then hard-working men and women like Tom and *his* wife and children will probably continue to see their economic fortunes decline. Economic inequality will continue to increase in America, as it has for the past five decades.

In the abstract, neither of these options is appealing. When you consider the people most directly affected by our immigration policies, the dilemma becomes even more acute. Still, these appear to be the options we have: enforce our immigration laws, or don't enforce them; reduce immigration levels, increase them, or hold them about where they are.

Acknowledging trade-offs – economic, environmental, social – is the beginning of wisdom on the topic of immigration. We should not exaggerate such trade-offs, or imagine conflicts where none exist. But neither can we ignore them, or pretend that they are only a function of our benighted fellow citizens' racial biases or cultural fears. Here are some other trade-offs that immigration decisions may force us to confront:

- cheaper prices for new houses vs. good wages for construction workers;
- accommodating more people in the United States vs. preserving wildlife habitat and vital environmental resources;
- more opportunities for foreigners to work in the United States vs. greater pressure on foreign elites to share wealth and opportunities with their fellow citizens.

The most ethically justifiable approaches to immigration will make such trade-offs explicit, minimize them where possible and choose fairly between them when necessary. Which brings me to the progressive argument for reducing immigration into the U.S.

ECONOMIC IMPACTS: STAGNATING WAGES

Consider first the economic impact of current immigration policies, starting with some key numbers. Since 1965, Congress has repeatedly increased overall immigration levels, raising legal immigration into the United States from 250,000 to 1.1 million people annually. That is three and a half times higher than any other country on Earth. Contrary to popular belief, most immigration into the U.S. is *legal* immigration, occurring at levels set by Congress. Add in illegal immigration and *total* annual immigration has fluctuated recently between 1.25 and 1.5 million.

Crucially, in recent decades, immigration into the U.S. has been concentrated among less-skilled, less-educated workers. Again, this is a matter of deliberate policy choice (Canadian immigration policy, for example, employs a points system that brings in a greater percentage of highly skilled and well-educated workers). According to one study, from 1980 to 1995 immigration increased the number of college graduates in the U.S. workforce by 4 percent, while increasing the number of workers without a high school diploma by 21 percent.[6]

The upshot has been flooded labor markets for less-skilled workers, with results that might have been predicted by anyone who passed Econ 101. Wages have been driven down. Benefits have been slashed. Employers have broken labor unions, often helped by immigrant replacement workers (my book explores union busting in the meatpacking industry, where average wages have declined an astonishing 44 percent between 1970 and the present). Long-term unemployment among poorer Americans has greatly increased, as available jobs have instead gone to immigrants. Amazingly, although native-born Americans accounted for two-thirds of the growth in the nation's working-age population between 2000 and 2014, "there were fewer working-age natives holding a job in the first quarter of 2014 than in 2000, while the number of immigrants with a job was 5.7 million above the 2000 level."[7]

Mass immigration is not the only cause of these negative economic trends, but many economists believe it has played an important part in driving them.[8] Harvard economist George Borjas, a leading authority on the economic impacts of immigration, contends that during the 1970s and 1980s each immigration-driven 10 percent increase in the number of workers in a particular job field in the United States decreased wages in that field by an average of 3.5 percent.[9] More recently, studying the impact of immigration on African-Americans, Borjas and colleagues found that a 10 percent immigrant-induced increase in the supply of a particular skill group reduced the wages of black workers in that group by 4 percent, lowered the employment rate of black men within that group by 3.5 percent and increased the black incarceration rate by almost a full percentage point.[10]

Immigration-driven competition has been strongest among working-class Americans, while wealthier, better-educated workers have mostly been spared strong downward pressure on their incomes. According to an analysis by the Center for Immigration Studies, immigrants account for 35 percent of workers in building cleaning and maintenance, but only 10 percent in the corporate and financial sectors; 24 percent of workers in construction, but only 8 percent of teachers and college professors; 23 percent among food preparation workers, but only 7 percent among lawyers.[11] As Table 6.1 shows, high percentages of immigrant workers strongly correlate with high unemployment rates within particular economic sectors.

Poorer Americans are more likely to be rendered unemployed or underemployed due to mass immigration – a simple function of their more direct and intense job competition with immigrants. In a recent study, Steven Camarota and Karen Zeigler found that in occupations in the United States where immigrants fill 25 percent or more of the jobs, unemployment from 2009 to 2011 averaged 14 percent, compared to 8 percent unemployment for occupations with lower percentages of immigrants. "In high-immigrant occupations," they write, "59 percent of the natives have no education beyond high school, compared to 31 percent of the rest of the labor force."[12] These are precisely the people for whom even relatively brief spells of unemployment can be economically devastating.

Meanwhile, wealthier Americans benefit more, in absolute terms, from the lower costs for goods and services made possible by low wages. No wonder wealthy Americans and a bipartisan political elite that serves their interests typically support high levels of immigration. Doctors, lawyers and Wall Street bankers have done pretty well in recent years in America. Truck drivers, construction workers, backhoe operators and meat-packers? Nurses, secretaries, cleaning women and supermarket checkout clerks? Mechanics, roofers, janitors, waiters, day laborers and garbage men? Not so well. Reducing immigration would tighten labor markets for these hard-working fellow citizens – including many previous immigrants – and help them secure employment and income gains.

TABLE 6.1 *Immigrants' occupational share by economic sector in the United States, 2004*

	Share of jobs filled by immigrants	Native unemployment rate
Farming, fishing & forestry	36%	11.9%
Building cleaning & maintenance	35%	10.9%
Construction & extraction	24%	12.7%
Food preparation	23%	9.3%
Production manufacturing	22%	7.2%
Computer & mathematical	19%	5.0%
Healthcare support	17%	6.6%
Healthcare practitioner	12%	1.5%
Sales	12%	6.1%
Arts, entertainment & media	11%	5.9%
Management	10%	2.6%
Business & financial	10%	3.3%
Education & training	8%	1.3%
Legal occupations	7%	2.7%

Source: Steven Camarota, "A Jobless Recovery? Immigrant Gains and Native Losses." Center for Immigration Studies, 2004.

ECONOMIC IMPACTS: GROWING INEQUALITY

Reducing immigration could help reverse five decades of ever-increasing economic inequality in the United States. Mass immigration's biggest economic winners among U.S. citizens are the very wealthy: those who hire workers, or whose incomes come disproportionally from capital gains and stock price increases (which rise more quickly in a rapidly growing economy, which is fostered by immigration-driven population growth). Immigration's biggest losers are found disproportionately among the nation's poor: people whose incomes come primarily in the form of wages rather than stock gains or capital appreciation, and who consume far less than the rich (and hence benefit less, in absolute terms, from lower prices for goods and services).[13] Reduce immigration and you reduce one of the leading drivers of increasing economic inequality in the U.S.

At this point, though, some readers may protest that we are throwing the baby out with the bath water: historically, one of the most persuasive arguments for continuing mass immigration is that it helps fuel economic growth. Tamar Jacoby put this pro-growth case well in an article published several years ago in *Foreign Affairs*. Although "immigrants' overall contribution to economic growth is hard to measure," she writes:

There is no doubt among economists that newcomers enlarge the economic pie. Foreign workers emerging at the end of the day from the meatpacking plant or the carpet factory buy groceries and shoes for their children; on Saturday, they buy washing machines and then hire plumbers to install them. The companies where they work are more likely to stay in the United States, rather than move operations to another country where labor is cheaper. Readily available immigrant workers allow these businesses to expand, which keeps other Americans on the job and other US businesses, both up- and downstream, afloat ... no one disputes that [this] results in a bigger, more productive economy.[14]

Jacoby is right that economists disagree on the relative importance of demographic increases to economic growth. All else being equal, however, it seems clear that more people means more workers and more consumers, leading to increased economic activity and a larger economy.

Yet a little reflection might cause progressives to question the value of immigration-driven economic growth. The two graphs below show changes in annual income among wealthier and poorer Americans in recent decades and the distribution of total wealth among different economic classes. Taken together, they suggest how rapid productivity growth *worsens* economic inequality in the context of a system where poorer workers cannot garner their fair share of a growing economic pie. Under our current economic system, *the more we grow, the more inequitable our society becomes.*

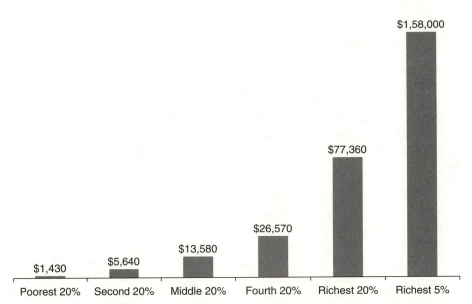

FIGURE 6.1 Changes in annual family incomes in the U.S., 1970 to 2005, by quintile
Source: U.S. Census Bureau, "Current Population Survey, Annual Social and Economic Supplements." Available at: www.census.gov, accessed January 2009.

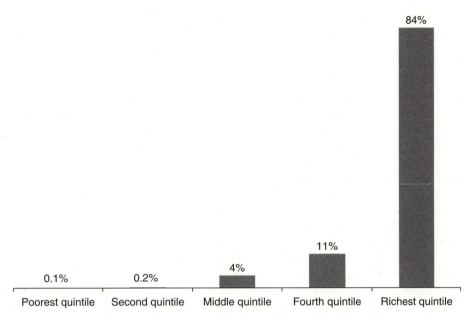

FIGURE 6.2 Distribution of total wealth in the U.S. in 2010, by quintile
Source: Dan Ariely, "Americans Want to Live in a Much More Equal Country (They Just Don't Realize It)." *Atlantic*, August 2, 2012.

Our current era of gross economic inequality, stagnating wages and persistently high unemployment among less-educated workers would seem like a terrible time to expand immigration. Yet strikingly, an immigration reform bill passed by a Democratic Senate in 2013 would have nearly doubled legal immigration levels. All the Democratic candidates for President in 2016, including the eventual nominee, supported large increases in already historically high immigration levels. Not surprisingly, large numbers of working-class voters deserted the Democrats in the general election, with many holding their noses and voting for a Republican presidential candidate who promised to rein in immigration.

Political progressives concerned about growing inequality and the economic well-being of American workers – including recent immigrants – should instead support immigration reductions. After all, Congress can decrease immigration levels as well as raise them. Perhaps a moratorium on non-essential immigration is in order, until the true unemployment rate declines below 5 percent and stays there for several years in a row. Perhaps non-essential immigration could be halted until real wages for the bottom half of American workers increase by 25 percent or more. Tightening up labor markets worked post-World War II, during the golden age of the American labor movement. It seems worth trying today. Given progressive leaders' failure to forcefully advocate for direct wealth redistribution, it is particularly important to get labor markets working for American workers. And it's possible – if we are willing to curtail immigration.

FAIRNESS AND EQUITY

Under our current immigration system, the less our fellow citizens can afford it, the larger the burden we ask them to shoulder in paying the inevitable costs of mass immigration. On its face, this seems unjust.[15]

I'm a progressive. My view is that regardless of who performs them, *all* jobs in America should be as safe as possible and carry high wages and comprehensive benefits. Well-off professionals whose work is intrinsically rewarding should be especially grateful to people like meat cutters, garbage men and cleaning ladies, who do society's tough, dangerous, or monotonous work. We know this work needs to be done. We know that many of our less-educated fellow-citizens wind up doing it and *need* to do it, to earn a living and to secure their own self-respect. So, we should do all we can to improve wages and working conditions in these jobs. With labor unions weak and Democratic politicians confused and timid, perhaps the best thing we can do for our fellow workers is to help tighten labor markets, so they can negotiate the best possible wages and working conditions for themselves. That means reducing immigration (and probably paying a little more for goods and services).

Now I realize the value of those same tough, dangerous, monotonous jobs to new immigrants from Mexico or Cambodia, even at significantly lower wages. I realize the value of their remittances to relatives back home. It's only honest to acknowledge that if we lower immigration levels, some would-be immigrants and their families will lose out.

However, as Americans, it seems to me that our first responsibility is to create an economically just society that provides decent opportunities for all our fellow citizens. If our economy also creates jobs that benefit new arrivals, so much the better. But we have no right to pursue immigration policies that sacrifice the vital economic interests of poor Americans in order to help poor foreigners. There is something morally obtuse in a view that says, "let's spread *your* (native working-class workers') wealth around to poor immigrants, while *I* (successful, well-educated professional) reap the benefits of cheaper gardeners, nannies, lawn-care service and restaurant meals – all while enjoying a profound feeling of superiority for my enlightened views about immigration."[16]

America is a relatively wealthy nation. Arguably, Americans should look for ways to share our wealth so that it benefits poor people overseas. *But we shouldn't do it on the backs of those least able to afford it here in our own country.* That is unjust to our fellow citizens, who have a special claim on us to set policies that increase their welfare. And in the case of mass immigration, it is helping create a less egalitarian society, with an ever-widening gap between rich and poor. If we're not careful, the United States may end up looking like the crummy plutocracies from which so many immigrants are fleeing. At least for progressives, the economic case for reducing immigration seems clear.

ENVIRONMENTAL IMPACTS: MORE POLLUTION AND LESS OPEN SPACE

Turning to mass immigration's environmental impacts, the key issue is immigration's contribution to U.S. population growth. If they think about overpopulation at all, most Americans see it as a problem for countries in the developing world. But at 330 million people the United States is the third-most-populous nation on Earth and given our high per-capita consumption rates and outsize global ecological footprint, a good case can be made that we are the world's most overpopulated country right now.[17] Worse, our near-1 percent annual growth rate – higher than many developing nations, including Jamaica, Thailand and Uruguay – has America on track to double its population by the end of this century.

Whether we look at air pollution or wildlife habitat losses, greenhouse gas emissions or excessive water withdrawals from western rivers, Americans are falling far short of creating an ecologically sustainable society – and our large and growing numbers appear to be a big part of the problem.[18] Put simply, more people put greater stress on natural systems and make it harder to share habitat and resources fairly with other species.

Consider one important example: sprawl, defined as new development on the fringes of existing urban and suburban areas. Over the past three decades, stopping sprawl has become a leading goal for environmentalists across the United States. Sprawl is an environmental problem for many reasons including increased energy and water consumption, increased air and water pollution, and decreased open space and wildlife habitat. Since habitat loss is a leading cause of species endangerment, it's no surprise that some of the nation's worst sprawl centers, like southern Florida and the Los Angeles basin, also contain large numbers of endangered species.

Between 1982 and 2012, the United States converted over 43 million acres of forest, cropland and pasture to developed uses. That's an area the size of Washington state. The average annual rate of land conversion increased from 1.4 million acres to about 2 million acres over this time.[19] In other words, the problem is big and it's getting worse.

What causes sprawl? Transportation policies that favor building roads over mass transit appear to be important sprawl generators. So are zoning laws that encourage "leapfrog" developments far out into the country and tax policies that allow builders to pass many of the costs of new development on to current taxpayers rather than new home buyers. Between 1970 and 1990, these and other factors caused Americans' *per capita* land use in the country's hundred largest metropolitan areas to increase by 22.6 percent. In these same areas during this same period, however, the amount of developed land increased 51.5 percent.[20]

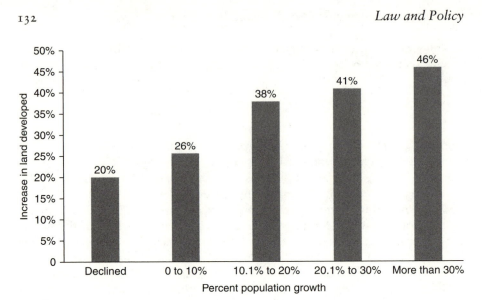

FIGURE 6.3 State sprawl rates, 1982–1997

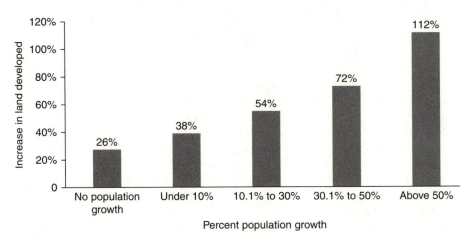

FIGURE 6.4 City sprawl rates, 1970–1990
Source: Roy Beck, Leon Kolankiewicz, and Steven Camarota, *Outsmarting Smart Growth: Population Growth, Immigration, and the Problem of Sprawl* (Center for Immigration Studies, 2003), page 5.

What accounts for this discrepancy? *Population growth*, which is by far the single most important cause of sprawl. New houses, new shopping centers, and new roads are being built for new residents. As Figures 6.3 and 6.4 illustrate, in recent decades, cities and states with the highest population growth rates have also sprawled the most.

One very thorough study of the causes of sprawl in the United States analyzed several dozen possible factors. Grouping together all those factors that can increase per-capita land use and comparing these with the single factor of more "capitas," more people, it found that in America between 1982 and 1997, 52 percent of sprawl was attributable to population increase while 48 percent was attributable to misguided policies that increased land use per person.[21] A more recent study found that 70 percent of recent sprawl in the U.S. can be attributed to immigration-driven population growth.[22]

Some "smart growth" advocates resist the conclusion that population growth is an important sprawl generator, partly because they do not want to obscure the need for good planning and land use policies, but mostly because they are uncomfortable talking about immigration-driven population growth. They point out that several metropolitan areas that lost population in recent decades exhibited significant sprawl, including St. Louis, Detroit, and Pittsburgh. Of America's 100 largest metropolitan areas, 11 lost population between 1970 and 1990, yet they sprawled by an average of 26 percent (see the previous figures). This shows that poor land use planning and bad transportation, zoning, and tax policies are indeed important in generating sprawl. Population growth is not everything.

On the other hand, cities with growing populations sprawl a lot more than ones with stable or declining populations. Several states that managed to decrease per capita land use in recent decades also sprawled, due to high rates of population growth. From 1982 to 1995, Nevada decreased its per capita land use 26 percent while sprawling 37 percent, due to a whopping 90 percent population increase. Arizona decreased per capita land use 13 percent while its population increased 58 percent, generating a 40 percent increase in developed land.[23]

The facts are clear: population growth causes sprawl and "smart growth" will not stop it, unless we also end population growth. We will not stop sprawl if we simply accept population increase as inevitable, when the best research shows that it now accounts for most of the problem. Nor are Americans likely to solve our other important environmental problems without stabilizing or reducing our population. The impacts of population growth are just too powerful.

EFFICIENCY ISN'T ENOUGH

In the early days of the environmental movement, back in the 1960s and 1970s, there was a popular slogan that went: "Any cause is a lost cause, without population control." Subsequent events have borne out its truth. For a variety of reasons, in recent decades environmentalists in the U.S. have grown afraid to discuss population matters (discomfort with talking about immigration has certainly played a role).[24] Instead, we have focused almost exclusively on efficiency improvements: in land use, water use, energy use and other areas.

The upshot of this narrowing has been that the efficiency improvements we have achieved have mostly been plowed back into supporting increased growth, with little real environmental improvement. If environmentalists are ever going to win our important battles, rather than just find ways to lose them more slowly, we need to recognize the way efficiency improvements tend to be swallowed up by growth.

Consider an example that has been much in the news in recent years: California's drought, which has spurred proposals to meet chronic water shortages by building new dams and taking more water out of the state's rivers. Reading news stories about the drought, you might never learn that per-capita water use declined by 50 percent in California over the last 40 years, due to extensive conservation efforts. That's because *total* water use is as high as ever, due to an immigration-fueled doubling of the state's population over the same period.[25]

Long-time California river conservationist Tim Palmer recently discussed what I call the "efficiency paradox." "After thousands of dams had been built through the 1960s," Palmer writes:

People began to realize the tremendous detrimental effects on rivers, fish, and whole landscapes, and a movement grew to protect the best rivers that remained. A powerful political alliance was driven away from the old pork barrel politics and spending on dams. The demand for water was still enormous and expanding with no end in sight, but rather than make more water available via new dams or take it from other people, a strategy was pursued to make improved use of the water we already had. These efficiency efforts paid off and use of water, *per capita*, declined by 20 percent nationally between 1980 and 1995. In California, per capita use was halved over 40 years.

But here's the catch: population growth has rendered the savings almost meaningless. In the same fifteen-year period, the national population increased by 16 percent, and in California's last 40 years the population nearly doubled. Water shortages have increased and they require unpopular adjustments by farmers and consumers, while still spelling ruin to whole ecosystems from the Sacramento Delta to Apalachicola Bay.

Even though much of the low-hanging water-saving fruit has been picked, we can probably cut the current use in half once again. But by the time we do that the population is likely to double for a second time. With the numbers of people outstripping the amounts of water saved, we'll be back in the same place where we started, except with less potential for further conservation and with a lot more people waiting in line for water. In the end, we will not have protected wild rivers, spared endangered species, or saved public money as we had intended, but will have principally served to make more population growth possible. Then, the momentum to grow will be even greater....The point here is that many people sought to do something good in conserving water, something of lasting value. But nothing can truly be protected if the source of the threat continues to grow.[26]

Palmer is not arguing against efficiency improvements. His point is that efficiency improvements must be combined with limits to what we demand from nature if we hope to achieve real, lasting environmental protection.

Because every additional person puts *some* additional demands on the environment, ending population growth is a necessary condition for ecological sustainability.

The story is similar when we turn from water use and river conservation to energy use and climate change, or land use and urban sprawl. Efficiency without an "enough" somewhere only facilitates more growth, uses up any margin of error and locks in a belief in the possibility and goodness of perpetual growth.[27] All this makes it harder, not easier, to create genuinely ecologically sustainable societies. Environmentalists continue to ignore this lesson at our peril.

DEMOGRAPHY: THE GOOD NEWS AND THE BAD

The good news is that, in recent decades, Americans have freely chosen a path toward population stabilization. From a peak of three and a half children per woman at the height of the baby boom in the mid-1950s, fertility rates in the United States have declined to two children per woman today: right around "replacement rate" for a nation with modern sanitation and healthcare. That means that if we reduced immigration rates to the levels that prevailed 50 years ago, America's population would very likely peak and then stabilize by midcentury.

The bad news is that just as America's citizens have chosen to cut back on family size, succeeding Congresses have increased immigration, thus keeping our country on a path of rapid population growth. Consider the graph below of U.S. population growth to 2100 under three different immigration scenarios (with fertility and mortality rates held steady).[28]

Starting in 2010 from a population of 310 million, the graph shows population growth for the rest of this century with 250,000 immigrants annually (roughly the rate 50 years ago), 1.25 million immigrants annually (about the current rate), and 2.25 million annual immigrants (roughly the level that would have resulted under the Senate's 2013 "comprehensive immigration reform" bill). Under these three scenarios, by 2100 we could see relatively modest population growth (to 379 million people), an increase of more than 200 million Americans (to 524 million), or a doubling of our population (to 639 million).

Note how relatively small annual differences in immigration numbers quickly cumulate to huge differences in overall population size. Each additional half million annual immigrants adds about 70 million people to the U.S. population by century's end. Note, too, that reducing immigration would allow Americans to stabilize our population by mid-century, while continuing or increasing mass immigration instead commits us to further massive population increases beyond 2100 (imagine each of those three lines in the graph with a little arrow on the end).

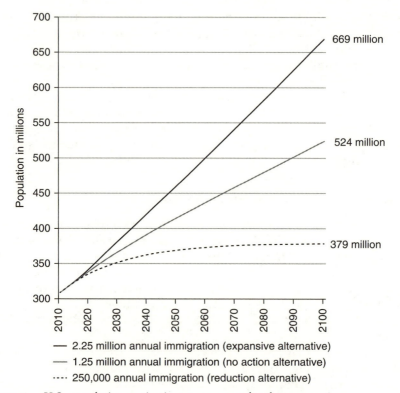

FIGURE 6.5 U.S. population projections to 2100 under three scenarios
Source: Philip Cafaro, *How Many Is Too Many? The Progressive Argument for Reducing Immigration into the United States* (University of Chicago Press, 2015), chapter 6.

Given Americans' failure to create an ecologically sustainable society with 330 million people, creating one with hundreds of millions more inhabitants is very unlikely. And even if we manage to stumble to 2100 with 500 million, 600 million, or 700 million people, our unpromising trajectory with continued mass immigration would be for further immense population growth in the following century. Consider population projections out to 2200 under those same three immigration scenarios (again holding other factors steady across all scenarios).

Only when contemplating this last graph are we considering the demographic implications "seven generations out" of current U.S. immigration policy. Doing so allows us to see how that policy could limit Americans' environmental options down the road and doom any efforts to create a sustainable society. Only by *not* pondering these numbers can serious environmentalists ignore immigration-driven population growth.

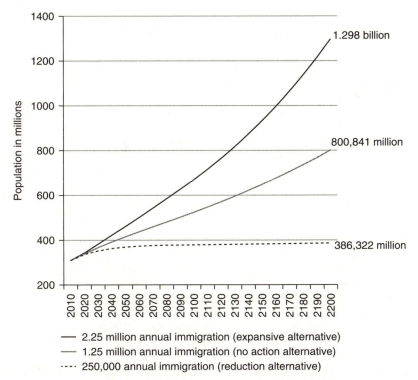

FIGURE 6.6 U.S. population projections to 2200 under three immigration scenarios
Source: Philip Cafaro, *How Many Is Too Many? The Progressive Argument for Reducing Immigration into the United States* (University of Chicago Press, 2015), chapter 6.

CONCLUSION

Fortunately, such overpopulation, like flooded labor markets, is not inevitable. Americans can stabilize our population by reducing immigration (not ending but simply *reducing* it). That, in turn, could help revitalize the American environmental movement which, like organized labor, these days spends most of its time in a defensive crouch, trying to protect past accomplishments rather than achieving new ones.

An environmental movement with the demographic wind at its back would be much more likely to secure the reductions in greenhouse gas emissions necessary for Americans to do our part to help avoid catastrophic global climate change. It would be much more likely to create new national parks and protected areas, preserving opportunities for future generations to appreciate wild nature; much more likely to find a way to keep some water in California's rivers rather than draining them dry; and, in general, much more likely to move America toward real ecological sustainability.

Similarly, a labor movement working within a context of tight labor markets could organize workers more effectively. It could negotiate wage and benefits improvements from a position of strength; fortify its role as an important player in Democratic party politics; and hopefully, move an agenda designed to decrease economic inequality and spread society's wealth more fairly throughout the U.S.

I don't say that reducing immigration into the U.S. will guarantee that progressives achieve these political goals. My claim is that continued mass immigration makes achieving them impossible. For that reason, reducing immigration should be part of the progressive political agenda going forward

NOTES

1. Philip Cafaro, *How Many Is Too Many? The Progressive Argument for Reducing Immigration into the United States* (Chicago: University of Chicago Press, 2015).
2. Author's interview with Javier Morales, September 2007. All personal stories related in this chapter actually occurred; all quotations are reported verbatim. Full citations can be found in Cafaro, *How Many Is Too Many?*
3. Jorge Castañeda's *Mañana Forever? Mexico and the Mexicans* (New York: Knopf, 2011) discusses the causes of this fatalism and some potential cures.
4. Author's interview with Andy Moore, August 2007.
5. Author's interview with Tom Kenney, October 2007.
6. George Borjas, *Heaven's Door: Immigration Policy and the American Economy* (Princeton, NJ: Princeton University Press, 1999).
7. Karen Zeigler and Steven Camarota, "All Employment Growth Since 2000 Went to Immigrants" (Washington, DC: Center for Immigration Studies, 2014).
8. Vernon Briggs, *Mass Immigration and the National Interest: Policy Directions for the New Century* (Armonk, NY: M. E. Sharpe, 2003); Steven Shulman, editor, *The Impact of Immigration on African Americans* (Piscataway, NJ: Transaction, 2004).
9. George Borjas, "The Economic Benefits from Immigration," *Journal of Economic Perspectives* 9 (1995): 7.
10. George Borjas, Jeffrey Grogger, and Gordon Hanson, "Immigration and the Economic Status of African-American Men," *Economica* 77 (2010): 255.
11. Steven Camarota, "A *Jobless Recovery? Immigrant Gains and Native Losses*" (Washington, DC: Center for Immigration Studies, 2004).
12. Steven Camarota and Karen Zeigler, "Are There Really Jobs Americans Won't Do? A Detailed Look at Immigrant and Native Employment across Occupations" (Washington, DC: Center for Immigration Studies, 2013). Camarota and Zeigler also note: "A number of politically important groups tend to face very little job competition from immigrants. For example, just 10 percent of reporters are immigrants, as are only 6 percent of lawyers and judges and 6 percent of farmers and ranchers."
13. For a more detailed analysis see Cafaro, *How Many Is Too Many?*, chapter 4.
14. Tamar Jacoby, "Immigration Nation." *Foreign Affairs* (November/December 2006): 55.

15. For further discussion, see Stephen Macedo, "The Moral Dilemma of U.S. Immigration Policy: Open Borders vs. Social Justice?" in this volume.

16. For more on the need for progressives to make public policy to benefit working-class Americans rather than wealthy professionals, see Thomas Frank, *Listen, Liberal: Or, What Ever Happened to the Party of the People?* (New York: Metropolitan, 2016).

17. Dave Foreman, *Man Swarm and the Killing of Wildlife* (Durango, CO: Raven's Eye Press, 2011).

18. Philip Cafaro and Eileen Crist, editors, *Life on the Brink: Environmentalists Confront Overpopulation* (Athens, GA: University of Georgia Press, 2012).

19. Natural Resources Conservation Service, "National Resources Inventory 2012" (Washington, DC: U.S. Department of Agriculture, 2012).

20. Roy Beck, Leon Kolankiewicz, and Steven Camarota, *Outsmarting Smart Growth: Population Growth, Immigration, and the Problem of Sprawl* (Washington, DC: Center for Immigration Studies, 2003), p. 5.

21. *Ibid.*

22. Leon Kolankiewicz, Roy Beck, and Anne Manetas, "Vanishing Open Spaces: Population Growth and Sprawl in America" (Washington, DC: NumbersUSA, 2014).

23. Beck *et al., Outsmarting Smart Growth*, pp. 68–69.

24. Leon Kolankiewicz and Roy Beck, *Forsaking Fundamentals: The Environmental Establishment Abandons U.S. Population Stabilization* (Washington, DC: Center for Immigration Studies, 2001).

25. Kate Linthicum, "Group says California immigration policies contributed to drought," *Los Angeles Times*, May 24, 2015.

26. Tim Palmer, "Beyond Futility," in Cafaro and Crist, *Life on the Brink*, pp. 98–100.

27. Herman Daly, *Beyond Growth: The Economics of Sustainable Development* (Boston: Beacon Press, 1997).

28. See Cafaro, *How Many Is Too Many?* chapters 2 and 6 for a full discussion of these population projections.

7

What Should Comprehensive Immigration Reform Encompass?

Carol M. Swain

We should insist that if the immigrant who comes here in good faith becomes an American and assimilates himself to us, he shall be treated on an exact equality with everyone else, for it is an outrage to discriminate against any such man because of creed, or birthplace, or origin. But this is predicated upon the person's becoming in every facet an American, and nothing but an American. . ... There can be no divided allegiance here.

—President Theodore Roosevelt, 1919.[1]

When President Theodore Roosevelt expressed the ideas in the epigraph, America was about to initiate a new area of policymaking designed to bring order to what had started to emerge as a potential problem for a nation that was becoming a magnet for people from different parts of the world. At the time, the country was majority Anglo Saxon and no one flinched at the fact that decision makers would take into consideration the racial and ethnic balance of the nation and the perceived attributes associated with different groupings of people, even if this meant that some races, ethnicities, and religions might be systematically disadvantaged.

The language used by Roosevelt was not explicitly racist, and it reaffirmed the idea of the nation being one that was not based on particular bloodlines or nationalities. In a 1916 speech, "America for Americans," Roosevelt argued that,

Americanism is not a matter of creed, birthplace, or national descent, but of the soul and spirit. If the American has the right stuff in him, I care not a snap of my fingers whether his ancestors came over in the Mayflower, or whether he was born, or his parents were born, in Germany, Ireland, France, England, Scandinavia, Russia, or Italy or any other country. All I ask of the immigrant is that he shall be physically and intellectually fit, of sound character, and eager in good faith to become an American citizen.[2]

Of course, we have changed quite a bit over the years. American policymakers no longer express any serious expectations that newcomers, whether refugees or immigrants, would want to become fully American. Whether they decide to learn the English language or acquire a deeper understanding of the U.S.

Constitution, the Declaration of Independence, or other such founding is largely a personal decision beyond what is required for naturalization. We have traded the imagery of Israel Zangwill's metaphor of America as a melting pot, where people of different races and ethnicities come together to become one, for the non-blendable mix of ingredients found in the salad bowl.

As Nathan Glazer and others have documented, the "United States was open to immigrants from all over the world without restriction for its first hundred years of its national existence."[3] Glazer points out this might not have been the case if the immigrants were not from the "British Isles and Northwestern Europe." After World War I, national leaders decided to pass legislation seeking to preserve what was then the prevailing racial and ethnic composition of the United States. Although immigrants could still come with the hopes of becoming Americans, their numbers were greatly reduced from the million entering annually before World War I.[4]

As we think about comprehensive immigration reform, we should not lose sight of the debates that informed earlier generations of policymakers. I believe we can learn much from Theodore Roosevelt's ideas about the kinds of newcomers he thought would thrive best in America and the need for them to have a desire to become fully American by embracing its ideals, which would certainly include its Constitution. Although there is nothing overtly racist about Roosevelt's speech, it had the unfortunate timing of preceding the passage of the Immigration Act of 1924 (Johnson-Reed Act) by several years, which is widely viewed as a governmental decision to integrate racial criteria into immigration law. Calvin Coolidge was President of the United States when the controversial legislation was enacted. The Act established national origin quotas as a basis for immigration policy and it restricted the number of incoming immigrants from each country to 2 percent of the number of residents from that country already living in the United States. The policy, which favored immigrants from Britain, Ireland, Germany, and Scandinavian countries, discriminated against immigrants from Asia and Africa.

In this chapter, I briefly share some of my ideas about what I think comprehensive immigration reform should look like. Even as I write these words, I am not optimistic about Congress's ability to craft an immigration policy that will improve the current situation. Interest group politics and the quest for partisan advantage regularly seem to block thoughtful bipartisan legislation.

COMPREHENSIVE IMMIGRATION REFORM DISSECTED

Congress has been talking about comprehensive immigration reform for more than a decade, but what exactly do they mean by "comprehensive"? When members of Congress and interest group leaders throw around phrases like "comprehensive immigration reform," it is commonly associated with supporters of amnesty, open borders, and liberal guestworker programs.

It comes across to conservatives as a buzzword or a concept that might have emerged from a focus group. Because of this, the concept has lost its meaning. Proponents of "comprehensive immigration reform" argue it is necessary to bring undocumented persons "out of the shadows" and give them an "earned path to legalization." Conservatives and liberals debate whether the "earned path to legalization" is an amnesty, since it potentially places the undocumented population above that of foreigners awaiting various visas.

The imagery of illegal aliens living in the shadows, huddled behind locked doors, and cowering in fear is at odds with the numerous immigrant marches and public forums where the public has been greeted, at least since the early 2000s, with immigrant activists and supporters. Repeatedly, the public has seen some very articulate spokespersons who openly proclaim themselves to be undocumented and show no fear of marching in front of law enforcement, testifying before Congress, and giving media interviews, sometimes with a backdrop of flags from other nations. The reality of the protests and the sense of entitlement run counter to the carefully crafted narrative of exploited people cowering in fear. What's more, the advocates for the illegal aliens far dwarf the activists who speak on behalf of America's poor.

Immigration is not a win–win for the United States. There is a zero-sum aspect to it that harms the most vulnerable Americans, whether it is through the diversion of public resources or the loss of an admissions slot at a state university that goes to someone in the country illegally. Congress cannot reform the issue until it seriously assesses the full impact of immigration on American citizens who live at the margins and who find themselves in direct competition with low-wage, low-skill immigrants for a dwindling supply of jobs. The diversion of resources in local schools is real, and it has an impact on the citizens who live in the neighborhoods where new immigrants cluster. We need to reform immigration while keeping in mind that if mass legalization is done incorrectly, it could easily increase poverty, drain state and local resources, and encourage more migration from foreigners who come illegally hoping to take advantage of the next legalization effort.[5]

President Trump understood the salience of this issue, and his election can be partially attributed to his skillful use of it. Some of what he said resonated with enough Americans to ensure his election. Trump campaigned on a plan to make America great again though immigration reform. His campaign stressed a few core principles. He argued that (1) "A nation without borders is not a nation"; (2) "A nation without laws is not a nation"; and finally, (3) a "nation that does not serve its own citizens is not a nation."[6] His plan emphasized building a wall across the southern border of Mexico, enforcement of existing laws and regulations until new ones could be passed, and a commonsense reform approach that would seek to improve the employment opportunities, wages, and security of American citizens. Specifically, he pledged to defend the laws and Constitution of the United States.

According to the Trump "Make America Great Again" plan, he would triple the number of ICE officers, institute a national E-Verify employment system to ensure all workers were eligible for employment, return criminal aliens to their home nations, end President Obama's controversial "catch-and-release" policy for persons apprehended at border crossings, strip sanctuary cities of their funding, increase the penalties for those who overstay their visas, work with police on eliminating gangs, and bring an end to birthright citizenship. As of July 2017, the Administration began implementing some parts of the President's stated agenda.[7] What he would accomplish remained uncertain because he was operating in an environment of intense opposition to the ideas he represented and because of his status as an "outsider" with no previous political experience.

Over the years, I have given a lot of thought to what a truly comprehensive immigration policy might look like. Below is a sampling of my ideas with brief commentary in those places where it overlaps or meshes with the Trump proposal:

Specific Policy Recommendations[8]

1. Increase border security and complete a fence on the United States' southern border. This agrees with President Trump's call for an increase in ICE agents and the construction of a wall along the southern border that would deter border crossings and save lives.

2. Pass a law that requires all illegal aliens to register their presence in the United States within 12 months. Anyone failing to do so would be subject to immediate deportation. This is important because national security requires a nation to have reliable data on foreigners residing within its borders.

3. Since 40 percent of illegal aliens entered on a valid visa, impose stiffer penalties for anyone overstaying his or her visa as a student, tourist, or worker.

4. When admitting professional and highly skilled guest workers, ensure their backgrounds have been thoroughly examined. This might help avoid embarrassing episodes such as Operation Paperclip, where inadequate screening resulted in the U.S. employment of Nazi scientists.

5. Reform guestworker programs. Require all guestworker visas to be short term and nonrenewable. This is an important component of creating more job opportunities for native workers. It is difficult to understand why America would continue to bring in low-skilled laborers through the H-2B visa. Yet, this is one of the programs the Trump Administration has sought to expand.

6. Mandate and enforce employer participation in E-Verify, a federal program that allows employers to check Social Security cards online against a national database with 96 percent accuracy. The Trump

Administration includes a proposal for national reform and, I presume, mandatory E-Verify among its immigration goals.

7. Punish employers of illegal aliens with stiffer fines and jail sentences for repeat offenders.

8. Return the family reunification definitions to the pre-1965 categories of spouse, children, and parents. This would end the problem of chain migration where a newly naturalized person can begin sponsoring dependents, siblings, and other extended family members beyond just their spouses, children, and parents. Vaughn reports that "[O]ver the last 35 years, chain migration has greatly exceeded new immigration. Out of 33 million immigrants admitted to the United States from 1981 to 2016, about 20 million were chain migration immigrants" (61 percent).[9]

9. Reform when and how birthright citizenship should apply. Section I of the 14th Amendment states: "All persons born or naturalized in the United States, and subject to the jurisdiction thereof, are citizens of the United States and the state wherein they reside." The Amendment was ratified in 1868 to grant citizenship to the newly freed slaves. It now forms the basis of birthright citizenship for the offspring of non-diplomats.[10] Granting automatic citizenship to the more than 300,000 babies born to parents in the country illegally creates mixed-status households that place the children in awkward situations. As long as our nation automatically awards citizenship to every child born in the United States, we will continue to have mixed-status families, the heartbreaking trauma of deportations, and guestworkers who start families and refuse to leave.

10. Make it a felony, triggering automatic deportation, to present fake identification and Social Security cards.

11. Offer financial subsidies for illegal aliens who want to voluntarily leave America. Mass deportation and mass legalization are not the only choices we have. There can be enforcement of existing laws and incentives to make the transition easier.

12. Provide financial assistance for any illegal alien who would like to relocate to a willing third-party country.

13. Give border states the latitude to develop laws and procedures that enable them to protect their citizens by helping the federal government enforce immigration laws.

14. End federal assistance to sanctuary cities and jurisdictions that refuse to cooperate with the Department of Homeland Security and other federal agencies seeking to enforce existing immigration laws and regulations. In 2017, the Immigrant Resource Center published a map that listed 633 jurisdictions that refused to cooperate with federal officials.[11] This also aligns with President Trump's plan.

15. Reform the Deferred Action for Childhood Arrivals (DACA) as part of a more comprehensive immigration reform package. In Congress, this

directive is known as the Development, Relief, and Education for Alien Minors Act (DREAM Act). This meshes with President Trump's executive order in September 2017 that ended DACA and called for Congress to pass such reforms.[12]

RESPECTING THE RULE OF LAW

Whatever we do with immigration reform, it should include a healthy deference to the rule of law. The rule of law embraces the idea that nations need predictable and enforceable rules and regulations that apply equally to all individuals. Enforcement of laws separates civilized nations from barbaric ones.[13] Laws can separate trustworthy governments from abusive and terroristic regimes. In *The Leviathan,* seventeenth-century philosopher Thomas Hobbes warns that life without law is necessarily "solitary, poor, nasty, brutish, and short."[14] This idea is ancient, dating back to Plato and the Old Testament. The Ten Commandments and the Levitical laws distinguished the Israelites from the pagan nations surrounding them. In ancient Israel, there was chaos whenever the people broke their covenant law and followed their own hearts. In Judges 21:25, we read that after the deaths of Moses and Joshua, "Everyone did what was right in their own eyes." As a consequence, the nation fell into a predictable decline.

The U.S. Constitution forms the foundation for the rule of law in our country. Our Founding Fathers established a government in which all governing officials – including the President, members of Congress, Supreme Court justices, military officials, and political appointees – are subject to the law, which they affirm by taking a standard oath before they can assume office. No one is above the law. America's sovereignty and its standing in the world are damaged when its leaders fail to abide by constitutional principles and values that have guided previous generations and which they have bound themselves to follow. Failure to enforce our laws and statutes undermines their authority – such failure also weakens the constitutional protections that frame our interactions with fellow citizens and others throughout the world. Illegal aliens who have entered our country without our consent have broken our laws and diminished respect for the rule of law. We must not allow activist judges, lawyers, and other elites to destroy what once distinguished civilized nations from the barbaric and the totalitarian nations of the world.[15]

There is clearly a need for us to engage in a deeper analysis that draws on the accumulated wisdom and mistakes of our forbears. We need to restore meaning to the concept of comprehensive immigration reform by studying how piecemeal changes in one policy area affect other parts of immigration reform. Most importantly, we need to put the needs of American citizens and legal residents at the forefront of the immigration debate. Our present system is driven almost solely by the needs and demands of individuals who have broken existing laws. Such a short-sighted approach to immigration reform creates an incentive structure that only worsens the problem while creating even more of the unintended consequences we have come to expect.

NOTES

1. Quote from a letter written to Richard M. Hurd, president of the American Defense Society, January 3, 1919. Manuscript Division of the Library of Congress. Available at: www.theodorerooseveltcenter.org/Research/Digital-library/Record.aspx?libID=0265602, accessed February 28, 2018.

2. T. Roosevelt, "America for Americans," Speech, May 31, 1916. Available at: www.theodore-roosevelt.com/images/research/txtspeeches/672.pdf,accessed February 28, 2018.

3. N. Glazer (ed.), *Clamor at the Gates* (San Francisco: ICS Press, 1985), 4.

4. Glazer (ed.) *Clamor at the Gates*, 4.

5. C. Westoff, "Immigration and Future Population Change in America," in C. M. Swain (ed.), (New York: Cambridge Press, 2007), pp. 165–172; H. MacDonald, "Say No to Amnesty," June 28, 2010. Available at: www.forbes.com/forbes/2010/0628/special-report-immigration-laws-deportation-mexico-say-no-to-reform.html, accessed February 28, 2018.

6. Trump Campaign, "Immigration Reform that will Make America Great Again." Available at: https://assets.donaldjtrump.com/Immigration-Reform-Trump.pdf, accessed February 28, 2018.

7. Trump Campaign, "Immigration Reform that will Make America Great Again." Available at: https://assets.donaldjtrump.com/Immigration-Reform-Trump.pdf.

8. Some of the ideas expressed in this section were previously published in C. Swain (ed.), *Be the People: A Call to Reclaim America's Faith and Promise* (Nashville: Thomas Nelson, 2011), pp. 11–15; C. Swain, "A Judeo-Christian Approach to Immigration Reform," *The Review of Faith and International Affairs* 9 (Spring 2011): 11–15.

9. J. Vaughan, "Immigration Multipliers: Trends in Chain Migration," September 2017: 1. Available at: https://cis.org/sites/default/files/2017-09/vaughan-chain-migration_1.pdf, September 2017: 1, accessed February 28, 2018.

10. For more information about the debate, please see A. Wyatt, "Birthright Citizenship and Children Born in the United States to Alien Parents: An Overview of the Legal Debate," Congressional Research Service. Available at: https://fas.org/sgp/crs/misc/R44251.pdf, October 28, 2015, accessed February 28, 2018.

11. J. Lee, R. Omri, and J. Preston, "What are Sanctuary Cities?," February 16, 2017. Available at: www.nytimes.com/interactive/2016/09/02/us/sanctuary-cities.html, accessed February 28, 2018.

12. The White House Office of the Press Secretary, "President Donald J. Trump Restores Responsibility and the Rule of Law to Immigration," September 5, 2017. Available at: www.whitehouse.gov/the-press-office/2017/09/05/president-donald-j-trump-restores-responsibility-and-rule-law, accessed February 28, 2018.

13. See Swain (ed.), *Be the People*, pp. 160–162.

14. T. Hobbes, *The Leviathan* (1651); (London: C. J. Clay and Sons, 1904), p. 84.

15. B. Z. Tamanaha, *On the Rule of Law: History, Politics, Theory* (New York: Cambridge University Press, 2004), pp. 4–5.

8

Unintended Consequences and Path Dependencies: Explaining the Post-1965 Surge in Latin American Immigration

Douglas S. Massey and Karen A. Pren

The year 1965 is often cited as a turning point in the history of U.S. immigration, but what happened in the ensuing years is not well understood. Amendments to the Immigration and Nationality Act passed in that year repealed the national origins quotas, which had been enacted during the 1920s in a deliberate attempt to limit the entry of Southern and Eastern European immigrants – or, more specifically, Jews from the Russian Pale and Catholics from Poland and Italy, groups at the time deemed "unassimilable." The quotas supplemented prohibitions already in place that effectively banned the entry of Asians and Africans. The 1965 amendments were intended to purge immigration law of its racist legacy by replacing the old quotas with a new system that allocated residence visas according to a neutral preference system based on family reunification and labor force criteria. The new system is widely credited to have sparked a shift in the composition of immigration away from Europe toward Asia and Latin America, along with a substantial increase in the number of immigrants.

Indeed, after 1965 the number of immigrants entering the country did increase and the flows did come to be dominated by Asians and Latin Americans. Although the amendments may have opened the door to greater immigration from Asia, however, the surge in immigration from Latin America occurred in spite of, rather than because of, the new system. Nations in the Western Hemisphere had never been included in the national origins quotas, nor was their entry prohibited the manner of Africans and Asians. Indeed, prior to 1965 there were no numerical limits at all on immigration from Latin America or the Caribbean, only qualitative restrictions. The 1965 amendments changed all that, imposing an annual cap of 120,000 on entries from the Western Hemisphere. Subsequent amendments further limited immigration from the region by limiting the number of residence visas for any single country to just 20,000 per year (in 1976), folding the separate hemispheric caps into a worldwide ceiling of 290,000 visas (in 1978), and then reducing the ceiling to 270,000 visas (in 1980).

Thus the 1965 legislation in no way can be invoked to account for the rise in immigration from Latin America. Nonetheless, Latin American migration *did* grow. Legal immigration from the region grew from around 459,000 during the 1950s to peak at 4.2 million during the 1990s, by which time it comprised 43 percent of the entire flow, compared with just 29 percent for Asia, 14 percent for Europe, and 4 percent for the rest of the world.[1] The population of unauthorized immigrants from Latin America also rose from something near zero in 1965 to peak at around 9.6 million in 2008, accounting for around 80 percent of the total present without authorization.[2] How this happened is a complicated tale of unintended consequences, political opportunism, bureaucratic entrepreneurship, media guile, and most likely a healthy dose of racial and ethnic prejudice. In this article, we lay out the path dependent sequence of events that culminated in record levels of immigration from Latin America during the 1990s, focusing particularly on the case of Mexico, which accounted for two-thirds of legal immigration and three-quarters of all illegal migration from the region.

THE UNINTENDED LEGACY OF IMMIGRATION REFORM

Paradoxical as it may seem, U.S. immigration policy often has very little to do with trends and patterns of immigration. Even when policies do respond explicitly to shifts in immigration, rarely are they grounded in any real understanding of the forces that govern international migration. Instead, over time, the relative openness or restrictiveness of U.S. policies is more strongly shaped by prevailing economic circumstances and political ideologies.[3] In the United States, especially, immigrants carry significant symbolic weight in the narrative of American peoplehood[4] and how they are framed in the media, portrayed by politicians, and treated legislatively probably reveals more about America's aspirations and hopes – and its fears and insecurities – than anything having to do with immigration itself.[5]

Americans' fears and apprehensions prevailed in the 1920s and led to the passage of the discriminatory quota laws. In response to rising economic inequality, along with new currents of scientific racism, xenophobia, and conservative ideology, the Quota Acts of 1921 and 1924 sought to reduce the number of immigrants entering the United States and shift their origins away from southern and eastern Europe and toward northern and western Europe, while maintaining outright prohibitions on all immigration from Asia and Africa.[6] In contrast, hopes and aspirations were the Zeitgeist of the 1960s and legislators sought to enact liberalizing reforms and introduce greater openness into the immigration system. As the civil rights movement gathered force, discriminatory quotas against certain Europeans and prohibitions on black and Asian immigration came to be seen as intolerably racist and were duly repealed by Congress in 1965.

At that time, the United States was nearing the end of a "long hiatus" with respect to immigration.[7] Indeed, with so few immigrants settling in the United States, the foreign-born percentage in 1970 dipped below 5 percent for the first and only time in U.S. history. As a result, immigration was not a very salient issue in 1965, except to a few conservative senators who actually liked the restrictive quotas. To the extent that legislators were concerned at all, their attention focused mainly on the consequences of opening the door to Asian and African immigration, not immigration from Latin America. Newly elected Senator Ted Kennedy, who served as floor leader for the bill, assured his colleagues that "our cities will not be flooded with a million immigrants annually ... [and] ... the ethnic mix of this country will not be upset.... Contrary to the charges in some quarters, S. 500 will not inundate America with immigrants from any one country or area, or the most populated and economically deprived nations of Africa and Asia" (*Congressional Digest*, May 1965, p.152).

The second order of business for immigration reformers with a civil rights agenda was ending a temporary worker scheme known as the Bracero Program. Originally established in 1942 as a temporary wartime measure, the program was extended by Congress and massively expanded in the 1950s. By the 1960s, however, the Bracero Program had come to be seen as an exploitive labor regime on a par with southern sharecropping, and in 1964 Congress, voted to terminate it over vociferous objections from Mexico.[8] The program was phased out between 1965 and 1967 and the flow went to zero in 1968, the same year the new cap on immigration from the Western Hemisphere took effect.

Immigration was a back burner issue for most Americans in 1965 who concerned themselves instead with civil rights, the war in Vietnam, the sexual revolution, and urban riots. Nonetheless, under the radar of both citizens and politicians, immigration from Latin America had been quietly but steadily growing, especially from Mexico. Owing to the Bracero Program, however, the lion's share of the migration was temporary and circular and, hence, invisible to citizens. During the period 1955–1959, around half a million Mexicans were entering the country each year, with the actual number fluctuating at around 450,000 temporary Bracero migrants and roughly 50,000 permanent residents.[9] Given this huge annual inflow, the sudden elimination of the Bracero Program obviously was going to have dramatic consequences on migration between Mexico and the United States; and owing to the imposition of a hemispheric cap and, eventually, country quotas, the displaced temporary migrants were not going to be accommodated within the system for legal immigration.

In short, as a result of shifts in U.S. immigration policy between the late 1950s and the late 1970s, Mexico went from an annual access of around 450,000 guestworker visas and a theoretically unlimited number of resident visas (in practice averaging around 50,000 per year) to a new status quo in which there were no guestworker visas and just 20,000 resident visas annually.

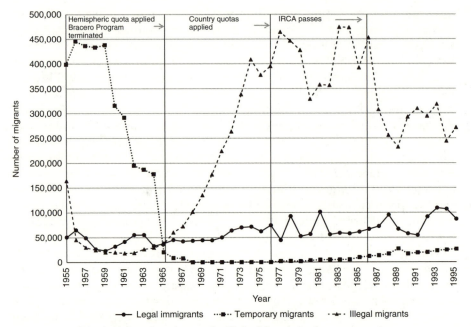

FIGURE 8.1 Mexican immigration to the United States in three categories.

The effect of these new limits on the system of Mexican migration that had evolved during the Bracero era were predictable and illustrated in Figure 8.1, which shows Mexican entries into the United States in three legal categories for the period 1955 through 1995: temporary migrants (Braceros before 1965 and H-visa holders thereafter), legal immigrants (those entering with permanent resident visas), and illegal migrants (proxied here by the annual number of apprehensions per thousand Border Patrol Agents).

The number of apprehensions recorded in any year is a joint function of the number of migrants attempting unauthorized entry and the effort made to catch them, and, as such, raw apprehensions counts are seriously flawed as indicators of the volume of illegal migration. However, once the enforcement effort is controlled, here by dividing the number of aliens arrested by the number of Border Patrol Agents looking for them, the adjusted apprehension counts offer serviceable indicator of *trends* in illegal migration. We do not claim the adjusted count of apprehension actually captures the *true* number of undocumented entries, only that fluctuations over time reflect trends in the volume of undocumented migration.

As already noted, by the late 1950s a massive circular flow of Mexican migrants had become deeply embedded in employer practices and migrant expectations and had come to be sustained by well-developed and widely accessible migrant networks.[10] As a result, when avenues for legal entry were suddenly curtailed after 1965 the migratory flows did not disappear, but simply continued under other auspices, namely without authorization or documents. As shown in the figure, the end of the Bracero Program corresponded exactly in time with the rise of illegal migration. From a figure of around 40,000 in 1965 the number of apprehensions per thousand agents rose to peak at around 460,000 in 1977. It then fluctuated between 330,000 and 460,000 from 1978 to 1986 whereupon it fell into the range of 240,000–320,000 per year after passage of the 1986 Immigration Reform and Control Act (IRCA). IRCA offered legal status to millions of undocumented migrants who before had moved back and forth across the border and contributed to the annual count of apprehensions.

In sum, illegal migration rose after 1965 not because there was a sudden surge in Mexican migration per se, but because the temporary labor program was gone and the number of permanent resident visas had been capped, leaving no legal way to accommodate the well-established flows. With permanent resident visas capped, moreover, the inflow of legal immigrants could not rise and remained below 50,000 through the early 1970s and thereafter fluctuated between 50,000 and 100,000 per year. The number of legal immigrants was able to exceed the annual statutory cap of 20,000 because parents, spouses, and minor children of U.S. citizens were exempted from numerical limitation (more on that later).

RISE OF THE LATINO THREAT NARRATIVE

In the absence of access to any avenue of legal entry, the post-1965 increase in illegal migration was attributable almost entirely to the termination of the Bracero Program, and that once the status quo ante of circular migration had been reestablished under undocumented auspices in the late 1970s, growth in illegal migration ceased and ultimately declined in the wake of IRCA's legalization. The increase in illegal migration from 1965 through the late 1970s is critically important to understanding the dynamics of illegal migration in the years that followed, however, for it was this development that made it possible for political activists and bureaucratic entrepreneurs to frame Latino immigration as a grave threat to the nation.

Chavez[11] has documented the rise of what he calls the "Latino threat narrative" in American media after the 1960s. When he coded national magazine covers on immigration as positive, negative, or neutral he found a steady rise of negative portrayals through the 1970s, 1980s, and 1990s. The rise in the threat narrative occurred during a time of increasing income inequality, of course, and as social psychologist Susan Fiske[12] has shown, "feeling individually deprived ... may alert a person to feeling collectively deprived ... [and] this collective feeling leads to blaming out-groups (immigrants, rich elites, the party in power)."

The most common negative framing depicted immigration as a "crisis" for the nation. Initially marine metaphors were used to dramatize the crisis, with Latino immigration being labeled a "rising tide" or a "tidal wave" that was poised to "inundate" the United States and "drown" its culture while "flooding" American society with unwanted foreigners.[13] Over time, however, marine metaphors increasingly gave way to martial imagery, with illegal immigration being depicted as an "invasion" in which "outgunned" Border Patrol Agents sought to "hold the line" in a vain attempt to "defend" the border against "attacks" from "alien invaders" who launched "banzai charges" to overwhelm American defenses.[14]

In order to capture the rising use the use of such metaphors in the American media, we used the *Proquest Historical Newspaper* files to search for instances in which the words "undocumented," "illegal," or "unauthorized" were paired with "Mexico" or "Mexican immigrants" and the words "crisis," "flood," or "invasion." We focused our analysis on the nation's four leading papers: *The New York Times, The Washington Post, The Wall Street Journal*, and the *Los Angeles Times*. To control for random noise and isolate the underlying trends, we computed three-year moving averages and plotted the results in Figure 8.2. As can be seen, the use of the negative metaphors to describe Mexican immigration was virtually non-existent in 1965, at least in major newspapers, but thereafter rose steadily, slowly at first and then rapidly during the 1970s to reach a peak in the late 1970s, roughly at the same time illegal migration itself peaked. From 1965 through 1977 the correlation between the illegal migration

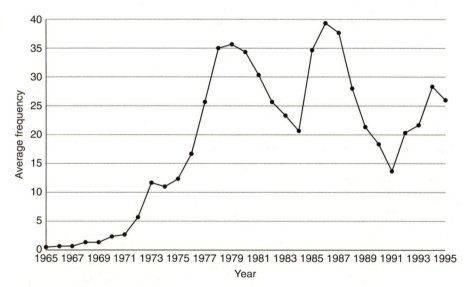

FIGURE 8.2 Frequency of pairing of the terms flood, crisis, or invasion with immigration in five leading newspapers (three-year moving average)

series shown in Figure 8.1 and the negative metaphor series shown in Figure 8.2 is 0.911.

The framing of immigration as a "crisis" and the increasing use of martial imagery was actively promulgated by immigration officials. In 1976, for example, the Commissioner of the Immigration and Naturalization Service (INS) published an article in *Reader's Digest* entitled "Illegal Aliens: Time to Call a Halt!" in which he told readers that "when I became commissioner of the [INS] in 1973, we were out-manned, under-budgeted, and confronted by a growing, silent invasion of illegal aliens. Despite our best efforts, the problem – critical then – now threatens to become a national disaster."[15] Similarly, in 1992 the Chief of the San Diego Sector of the Border Patrol, Gustavo de la Viña, filmed and released a video entitled *Border Under Siege*, which in one dramatic scene showed migrants scrambling over cars and dodging traffic on Interstate 5 to enter the United States without inspection in and around the San Ysidro Port of Entry, then the nation's busiest.[16]

Politicians quickly discovered the political advantages to be had by demonizing Latino immigrants and illegal migration. Ronald Reagan, for example, asserted that illegal immigration was a question of "national security" and in a 1986 speech he told Americans that "terrorists and subversives are just two days driving time from [the border crossing at] Harlingen, Texas" (Kamen).[17] In his 1992 reelection campaign, California Governor Pete Wilson called on Washington to "stop the invasion" and borrowed footage from *Border Under Siege* for a series of attack ads. As images of migrants dashing through traffic rolled, a narrator intoned, "they keep coming. Two million illegal immigrants in California. The federal government won't stop them at the border yet requires us to pay billions to take care of them."[18]

The media discovered that the trope of a border under siege made for dramatic copy and good visuals and happily played handmaiden to aspiring politicians and bureaucrats. Later on, a host of pundits joined the anti-immigrant chorus to attract attention and sell books. Lou Dobbs[19] framed the "invasion of illegal aliens" as part of a broader "war on the middle class." Patrick Buchanan[20] charged it was part of an "Aztlan Plot" hatched by Mexicans to recapture lands lost in 1848, stating that "if we do not get control of our borders and stop this greatest invasion in history, I see the dissolution of the U.S. and the loss of the American southwest" (*Time*, August 28, p. 6). From his lofty Harvard perch, Samuel Huntington[21] warned Americans that "the persistent inflow of Hispanic immigrants threatens to divide the United States into two peoples, two cultures, and two languages .... The United States ignores this challenge at its peril." All these views received extensive coverage in print and broadcast media outlets throughout the country.

EFFECTS ON PUBLIC OPINION

The shift in the legal auspices of Mexican migration thus transformed what had been a largely invisible circulation of innocuous workers into a yearly and highly visible violation of American sovereignty by hostile aliens who were increasingly framed as invaders and criminals. The relentless propagandizing that accompanied the shift had a powerful effect on public opinion, turning it decidedly more conservative not only on issues of immigration, but with respect to social issues more generally. Indeed, the rise of illegal migration remains under-appreciated as a factor in the rightward drift of American public opinion.

To support this argument, Massey and Pren[22] extracted data from the General Social Survey (GSS) from its inception in 1972 to the present and estimated the effect that the annual number of border apprehensions had on the likelihood that a respondent self-identified as conservative, controlling for individual demographic, social, and economic characteristics as well as the nation's overall economic climate. Holding these factors constant, they found that border apprehensions had a very powerful effect on the likelihood of self-identifying as conservative. Increasing the number of apprehensions from its minimum to maximum doubled the likelihood that a respondent self-identified as conservative.

Admittedly, self-identification as conservative does not necessarily predict anti-immigrant sentiment; but annual data on attitudes toward immigration are not available. In order to establish this link, therefore, Massey and Pren[23] used GSS data from 1996 and 2004, two years in which the survey questionnaire had asked questions about attitudes toward immigration that enabled them to create a reliable scale of support for exclusionist policies. They went on to regress this measure on two dummy variables indicating whether respondents rated themselves as slightly conservative or extremely conservative (compared to not conservative at all) while controlling for economic climate and individual demographic, social, and economic characteristics.

Their equation estimates revealed that conservative self-identification strongly predicted support for exclusionist policies. Those self-identifying as slightly conservative had a value on the exclusionist index that was 0.40 points greater than those who did not identify as conservative at all, whereas those self-identifying as extremely conservative had a value that was 0.56 points greater, an effect equivalent to about a third of a standard deviation in individual opinion. Both effects were highly significant and persisted after controls for age, education, income, occupation, race, region, urbanism, and national economic climate were introduced. Other things equal, conservative and exclusionist sentiments are strongly interrelated.

POLICY FEEDBACKS

Not surprisingly, the rise of the Latino threat narrative and the concomitant increase in conservatism was associated over time with the passage of increasingly restrictionist immigration legislation and the implementation of ever more stringent enforcement policies. Table 8.A1 (in the Appendix) offers a cumulative list of 15 restrictive immigration bills passed from 1965 to 2010. As can be seen, over time restrictionist bills come to be passed at an increasingly rapid pace. In the 30 years from 1965 to 1995, for example, only six major immigration bills were enacted whereas in the decade from 1996 to 2006, eight pieces of legislation were signed into law. Table 8.A2 (in the Appendix) goes on to present a list of 16 named enforcement operations launched between 1993 and 2010. They typically were announced with great fanfare, including official releases, press conferences, and saturated media coverage. As can be seen, the pace at which operations are launched becomes increasingly rapid and they became increasingly sweeping in scope, covering locations within the United States as well along the Mexico–U.S. border.

This sustained, accelerating accumulation of anti-immigrant legislation and enforcement operations produced a massive increase in border apprehensions after the late 1970s, when the underlying flow had actually leveled off. Obviously, for any given number of undocumented entry attempts, more restrictive legislation and more stringent enforcement operations generate more apprehensions, which politicians and bureaucrats can then use to inflame public opinion, which leads to more conservatism and voter demands for even stricter laws and more enforcement operations, which generates more apprehensions, thus bringing the process full circle. In short, the rise of illegal migration, its framing as a threat to the nation, and the resulting conservative reaction set off a self-feeding chain reaction of enforcement that generated more apprehensions even though the actual flow of undocumented migrants had stabilized in the late 1970s and actually dropped during the late 1980s and early 1990s.

The dimensions of the paradox are illustrated in Figure 8.3, which contrasts apprehensions standardized for the enforcement effort (i.e. divided by the number of Border Patrol Agents), with total apprehensions (which reflect both enforcement effort and underlying traffic). Controlling for the enforcement effort, we see that illegal migration rose from 1965 to 1977 as the circulation of the Bracero era was reestablished, but thereafter leveled off and fluctuated before ultimately falling. In contrast, the total number of apprehensions kept on growing at an accelerated pace after 1977, peaking at 1.6 million in 1986 before declining to around 900,0000 and then shifting back up to 1.3 million by 1995. As one would expect, temporal variation in the total number of apprehensions is closely related to the use of threatening immigration metaphors. From 1965 through 1995, the temporal correlation between the

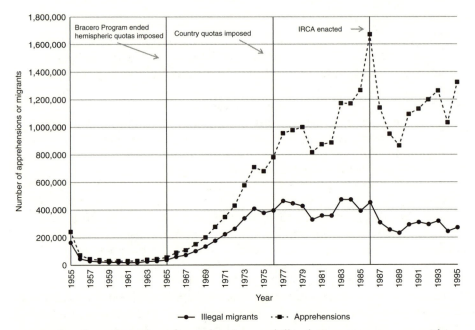

FIGURE 8.3 Annual number of apprehensions and illegal migrants, 1955–1995 (three-year moving average)

frequency of newspaper allusions to crises, floods, and invasions and the total number of apprehensions is 0.956.

After the late 1970s, in other words, anti-immigrant sentiment increasingly fed off itself to drive the bureaucratic machinery of enforcement forward to new heights, despite the lack of any real increase in illegal migration. In Figure 8.4 we model this path dependency using a two-stage least squares estimation strategy on time series data for the 30-year period from 1965 to 1995. Data on apprehensions, the number of Border Patrol Agents, the size of the Border Patrol Budget, and the number of line watch hours spent patrolling the border were obtained from the Office of Immigration Statistics of the U.S. Department of Homeland Security. The cumulative number of pieces of restrictive legislation passed and restrictive operations launched were coded from Tables A8.1 and A8.2.

The exogenous variable, number of undocumented entries, was independently estimated using life history data obtained from household heads interviewed by the Mexican Migration Project (MMP), a binational study that each year surveys Mexicans on both sides of the border and adds the information they provide to create a cumulative database on patterns and processes of documented and undocumented migration (http://mmp.opr .princeton.edu/). At this writing, the database currently contains life histories of 21,475 household heads, and each history includes a complete history of

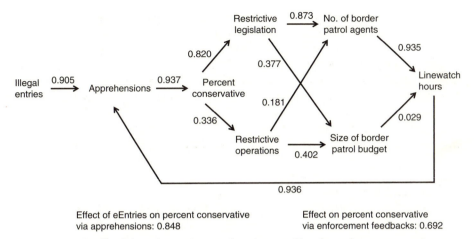

FIGURE 8.4 Feedback loop between apprehensions and border enforcement, 1965–1995

migration that can be used to compute annual probabilities of illegal migration.[24] We then applied these estimated probabilities to annual population counts derived from Mexico's National Institute for Statistics and Geographic Information (the Mexican Census Bureau) to estimate the gross annual inflow of illegal migrants.

Since this number is exogenous to the system of equations that define the policy feedback loop, it offers a suitable instrument to estimate the policy feedback. The causal chain begins with rising undocumented entries, which generate more apprehensions, which are then transformed into a conservative anti-immigrant reaction through the machinations of entrepreneurial politicians, ambitious bureaucrats, and pandering media. This reaction, in turn, generates more restrictive immigration laws and border operations, which increase the number of Border Patrol Agents and the size of the Border Patrol Budget, which ultimately produces more linewatch hours, which generates more apprehensions, which then feedback on the system to increase the conservative reaction independently of the actual number of illegal entries.

Referring to Figure 8.4, we see that the effect illegal entries has in producing a conservative reaction is 0.848 and is achieved through the intervening variable of apprehensions (0.905*0.937), which makes the otherwise clandestine entries visible and politically frameable as threatening, yielding a conservative reaction that itself sets of a chain of policy responses that cumulate to a total effect on the conservative reaction of 0.692 (0.820 * 0.873 * 0.935 * 0.936 + 0.820 * 0.377 * 0.029 * 0.936 + 0.336 * 0.402 * 0.029 * 0.936 + 0.336 * 0.181 * 0.935 * 0.936 = 0.692). Although this feedback effect is not as powerful as the exogenous effect of undocumented entries (0.848), it is nonetheless very strong and powerful enough to sustain an increase in apprehensions even when entries are constant or slightly falling. Of the two principal pathways – the upper one through restrictive legislation and the lower one through restrictive operations – the former is by far the strongest, at ($0.820 * 0.873 * 0.935 * 0.936 = 0.626$) accounting for 90 percent of the total feedback effect ($0.626/0.692=0905$). Thus between 1965 and 1995, rising apprehensions produced a conservative reaction that led to the passage of restrictive legislation, which increased the number of Border Patrol Agents who undertook more linewatch hours to generate more apprehensions, which ultimately exacerbated the conservative reaction.

The end result of this feedback loop is depicted in Figure 8.5, which shows three indicators of the intensity of border enforcement relative to the number of standardized apprehensions, our indicator of the underlying traffic in illegal migrants. Each series is divided by its value in 1977, the year in which undocumented migration reached its peak. Whereas the relative number of apprehensions per thousand agents rose from in the late 1950s to reach 1.0 in 1977 and thereafter fluctuated around 1 before dropping below this value, after 1977 the number of linewatch hours doubles, the number of Border Patrol Agents increases 2.5 times, and the Border Patrol Budget rises by a factor of 6.5. During and after the 1970s, in other words, the border build-up was increasingly on autopilot and disconnected from the actual traffic in illegal migrants.

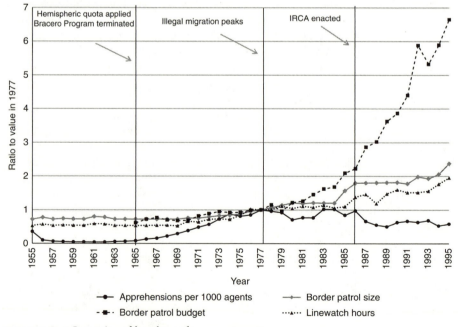

FIGURE 8.5 Intensity of border enforcement, 1965–1995

ENTER THE WAR ON TERROR

The feedback loop connecting apprehensions, public attitudes, legislation, and enforcement was fully established by the 1990s when a series of exogenous terrorist events drove the enforcement cycle to new heights. Major attacks unleashed in the 1990s and early 2000s helped transform the first decade of the twenty-first century into another era of fear and insecurity. Although material and ideological apprehensions were in ample evidence before the 1990s, a string of visible and politically charged terrorist attacks that began in 1993 brought anti-foreign hysteria and xenophobia to new levels. In response to the 1993 attack on the World Trade Center and the 1995 terrorist bombing of the Murrah Federal Building in Oklahoma City, Congress in 1996 passed the Anti-Terrorism and Effective Death Penalty Act as well as the Illegal Immigrant Reform and Immigrant Responsibility Act. Then upon the heels of the 1998 bombing of the USS Cole in Yemen, the 2000 bombings of the U.S. Embassies in Kenya and Tanzania, and the catastrophic attacks on the World Trade Center and the Pentagon in 2001, Congress enacted the USA Patriot Act.

These measures not only increased border enforcement, which had been rising for some time, but more dramatically increased the number of arrests, detentions, and deportations within the United States. Prior to 1996, internal enforcement activities had not played a very significant role in immigration enforcement; afterward these activities rose to levels not seen since the deportation campaigns of the Great Depression.[25] The conflation of the war on terror with the deportation of immigrants is suggested by Figure 8.6, which plots deportations by year from 1965 through 2009.[26] Prior to the mid-1990s the annual number of deportations had not exceeded 50,000 for decades, but with the passage of the 1996 legislation this threshold was breached and by the turn of the century deportations were running at just under 200,000 annually. With the passage of the Patriot Act in late 2001, the number of deportations accelerated once again and reached nearly 400,000 in 2009. None of the terrorist attacks involved Mexicans, of course, and none of the terrorists entered through Mexico. Indeed, all came into the United States on legal visas; yet, as Figure 8.6 clearly indicates, Mexicans nonetheless bore the brunt of the deportation campaign launched in the name of the War on Terror, comprising 72 percent of those removed in 2009.

The dynamic by which this outcome unfolded is summarized by the path diagram shown in Figure 8.7, which uses time-series data from 1965 through 2009 to estimate the effects of the two principal Islamic terrorist attacks on the number of deportations and through them on the conservative reaction, in addition to the ongoing effect through border apprehensions. Data on the budget of the Immigration and Naturalization Service, and its successor agency, Immigration and Customs Enforcement, were obtained from Homeland Security's Office of Immigration Statistics supplemented with other

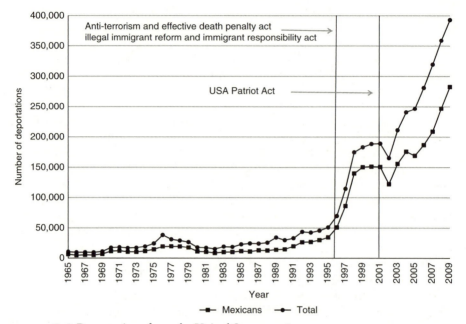

FIGURE 8.6 Deportations from the United States, 1965–2009

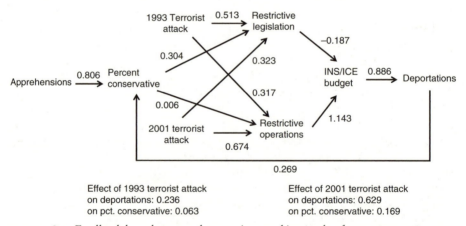

FIGURE 8.7 Feedback loop between deportations and internal enforcement, 1965–2009

sources. The 1993 terrorist attack indicator was given a value of 1 from 1993 onward and zero otherwise, whereas the 2001 terrorist attack indicator was coded 1 during 2001–2009 and zero at earlier dates.

In this model, the effect of apprehensions continues but its influence on the conservative reaction is now much more direct (0.806) than indirect through the feedback loop, which is essentially zero (0.304 * -0.187 * 0.886 * 0.269 + 0.006 * 1.143 * 0.886 * 0.269 = -0.012). In addition, the feedback loop on the percent conservative via enforcement actions is not significant (0.304 * -0.187 * 0.886 + 0.806 * 0.006 * 1.143 * 0.886 = -0.044). The upsurge in deportations arises mainly from the two principal terrorist attacks and the resulting increase in anti-immigrant legislation and enforcement operations. In general, the 1993 attack was less powerful in generating deportations (0.513 * -0.187 * 0.886 + 0.317 * 1.143 * 0.886 = 0.236) than the 2001 attack (0.323 * -0.187 * 0.866 + 0.674 * 1.143 * 0.886 = 0.629), with most of the effect occurring through the rise in enforcement operations in the wake of the Anti-Terrorism and Effective Death Penalty Act.

Though large by usual social science definitions, these effect sizes pale in comparison to the total feedback effect of 0.692 observed in the apprehensions model. Most of the increase in deportations occurred as a response to the two rounds of terrorist attacks.

EXPLAINING THE LATINO IMMIGRATION BOOM

Quite obviously, the massive increase in border enforcement (Figure 8.5) and the exponential increase in deportations (Figure 8.6) were not successful in preventing the entry of millions of unauthorized Mexicans after 1965. From 1980, when Warren and Passel[27] first estimated the number of undocumented Mexicans living in the United States to be 1.13 million, the population grew to 2.04 million in 1990, reached 4.68 million in 2000, and then peaked at 7.03 million in 2008.[28] Most of the remaining growth in the undocumented population came from Central America. When the U.S. intervened on the isthmus in the name of the Cold War during the 1980s, societies were destabilized and the resulting wave of emigrants met with the same restrictions on legal entry that had earlier blocked the entry of former Braceros from Mexico. The sole exception was Nicaragua, whose emigrants had the good fortune to be fleeing a leftist regime and were thus allowed to overstay tourist visas and ultimately adjust status to become legal permanent residents.[29] In contrast, the flows of undocumented Salvadorans, Guatemalans, and Hondurans remained predominantly illegal, accumulating total undocumented populations of 570,000, 430,000, and 300,000, respectively, by 2008.[30] Central Americans and Mexicans together accounted for nearly three-quarters of the increase.

Not only did the massive enforcement effort fail to prevent the entry of unauthorized Latin Americans – in a perverse way it actually accelerated the net inflow. Although the inflow of undocumented Mexicans was largely unaffected by the build-up of enforcement resources along the border, the outflow was drastically curtailed. As the costs and risks of unauthorized border crossing mounted, migrants minimized them by shifting from a circular to a settled pattern of migration, essentially hunkering down and staying once they had successfully run the gauntlet at the border.[31] It was thus a sharp decline in the outflow of undocumented migrants, not an increase in the inflow migrants, that was responsible for the remarkable acceleration of undocumented population growth during the 1990s and early 2000s, and this decline in return migration was entirely a product of U.S. enforcement efforts.[32]

It was not just undocumented migration that grew after 1965. As we have seen, legal immigration from Latin America also grew despite the imposition of caps and quotas. With a country quota of 20,000 visas per year beginning in 1976, the expected number of entries for any nation over a decade is 200,000, yet the number of legal Mexican immigrants, which stood at 442,000 during the 1960s, rose to 621,000 in the 1970s, reached 1 million in the 1980s, and peaked at 2.8 million in the 1990s before dropping back to 1.7 million in the first decade of the new century. Over the same period, legal immigration from the rest of Latin America rose from 544,000 during the 1960s to 734,000 in the 1970s, 935,000 in the 1980s, 1.5 million in the 1990s, and 1.6 million during the 2000s.[33]

The key to understanding the dynamic of this growth again lies with decisions taken by Congress that had unintended consequences: the decision in 1965 to exempt close relatives of U.S. citizens from the country quotas and a series of decisions from 1986 onward that systematically privileged U.S. citizens, limited the rights and liberties of legal residents, and increased the vulnerability of non-citizens to deportation. The quota exemptions by themselves probably would not have led to a dramatic increase in legal immigration from Latin America, but when combined with the rising burden placed on non-citizens by U.S. immigration legislation, they produced a dynamic interplay between naturalization and family reunification that drove legal immigration forward to new heights.

When the citizenship exemption was enacted in 1965, Congress was not really thinking about naturalized citizens. In that year, the typical naturalized citizen was an elderly European who had arrived before 1929 and whose children had been born in the United States. Instead, the prototypical citizen seeking to sponsor an immigrant spouse and children in 1965 was a U.S. serviceman returning from duty in Southeast Asia, or coming home from a deployment in places such as Germany, South Korea, the Philippines, Panama, or other places containing large military bases. In the context of the Vietnam War, Congress certainly did not want to block entry by wives and children of American soldiers. In addition, the Catholic Church, immigrant organizations, and humanitarian groups rallied around the principal of "family reunification" as the moral cornerstone of U.S. policy and succeed in including the parents of U.S. citizens under the quota exemption.

For many years, the quota exemption for citizen relatives had relatively little effect on levels and patterns of immigration. For Latin Americans, there was no special advantage to assuming U.S. citizenship once legal permanent residence had been achieved. Yes, the entry of spouses and minor children was numerically limited, but they were given a high position in the "preference system" of visa allocation; and, with the exception of eligibility for federal employment and the right to vote, there was no particular advantage to naturalization. This calculus began to change in 1986, and in subsequent years the benefits of citizenship only increased as the costs of non-citizenship proliferated.

When Congress passed the Immigration Reform and Control Act in 1986, it authorized two legalization programs, one for farm workers and another for long-time residents, and the terms of these programs for the first time made pre-requisites to citizenship suddenly a requirement for legalization. Prior to adjusting status, legalizing immigrations were required to provide evidence of facility or instruction in English and a knowledge or evidence of instruction in American history. In this way, 2.7 million former undocumented migrants were forced to satisfy the requirements heretofore asked only of people wishing to become U.S. citizens.[34] Five years after regularization, millions of people would suddenly become eligible for naturalization. Having satisfied the language and civic requirements, all they would have to do would be pay an application fee and wait.

The first cohort of persons legalized under IRCA became eligible for citizenship in 1992, with the bulk following in 1993 and 1994. In 1990, Congress undertook the first of a series of actions that began to ratchet up the costs of non-citizenship. In an effort to slow immigration from Latin America and other major immigrant-sending nations, amendments passed in that year sought to limit visas issued for purposes of family reunification by setting an annual cap, but one that could be "pierced" by taking family reunification visas that formerly went to relatives of legal residents and giving them to relatives of citizens. The net effect was to permanently reduce access to legal visas by relatives of legal resident aliens, which dramatically increase their waiting time.[35]

Congress followed up in 1996 with three pieces of legislation, all of which bore down heavily on legal immigrants. The Illegal Immigration Reform and Immigrant Responsibility Act authorized the removal of aliens from ports of entry without judicial hearing and in an effort to restrict family migration still further, required sponsors of legal immigrants to provide affidavits of support that demonstrated a household income at least 125 percent of the federal poverty line. Not only would resident aliens have to wait in a long line to sponsor the entry of a spouse or child – when their turn finally came, they would need more money as well. Meanwhile, the Personal Responsibility and Work Opportunity Reconciliation Act placed new restrictions on legal permanent residents to access public services, barring them from receiving food stamps, Supplemental Security Income, and other means tested benefits for five years after admission.[36]

The legislative trifecta was completed with passage of the Anti-Terrorism and Effective Death Penalty Act, which declared that any non-citizen who had ever committed a crime, no matter how long ago, was subject to immediate deportation. It also gave the federal government broad new powers for the "expedited exclusion" of any alien who had *ever* crossed the border without documents, no matter what his or her current legal status. In addition, the bill granted the executive branch new authority to designate any organization as "terrorist," thereby making all members immediately excludable. At the same time, it severely circumscribed the possibilities for judicial review of deportation orders.[37]

Finally, in response to the terrorist attacks of September 11, on October 26, 2001 Congress passed, without significant debate, the USA PATRIOT Act, which granted executive authorities even more powers to deport, without hearings or any presentation of evidence, all aliens – legal or illegal, temporary or permanent – that the Attorney General had "reason to believe" might commit, further, or facilitate acts of terrorism. For the first time since the Alien and Sedition Act of 1798, Congress authorized the arrest, imprisonment, and deportation of non-citizens upon the orders of the Attorney General without judicial review[38]. These repressive federal laws were not enough to placate the xenophobia unleashed by the Latino threat narrative, however, and recent years have witnessed an unprecedented surge in anti-immigrant measures enacted at the state and local level.[39]

The net effect of this string of legislative acts was to dramatically increase the pressure on non-citizens, regardless of legal status. In response to the rising pressure, more immigrants adopted a strategy of "defensive naturalization" in order to protect themselves and their families from detention and deportation and to guarantee their continued access to public benefits. The trend is most clearly seen among Mexicans, who historically exhibited among the lowest rates of naturalization of any major immigrant group. From 1965 through 1985, the number of Mexicans who naturalized averaged just 8,200 per year. During the immediate post-IRCA period (1986–1995), it grew to 29,400 and in the period just after the 1996 Acts (1996–2001) it mushroomed to 168,500, before finally falling back to 99,000 during the post-9/11 era (2002–2010). If we take the average number of naturalizations per year from 1965 to 1985 as the pre-IRCA norm, then an additional two million Mexicans naturalized after 1986 compared to what would have happened under the old regime.

As the number of newly minted citizens grew, so did the number of Mexicans admitted to the United States outside the quotas as relatives of U.S. citizens, with the number going from an annual average of 24,000 before 1986 to 34,000 during 1986–1995 and 80,000 during 1996–2001 before peaking at 98,000 during 2002–2010.[40] Whereas a legal permanent resident may petition for the entry of a spouse and minor children, their dependents must wait in an increasingly long line for an increasingly scarce allocation of visas. If the same person naturalizes, however, then the spouse, children, and parents can enter immediately without limitation. Each new citizen thus generates more potential

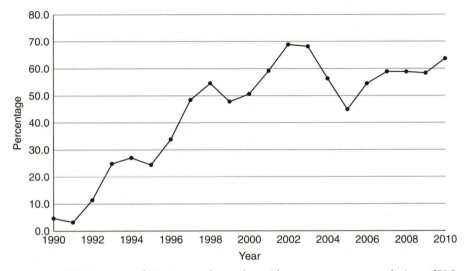

FIGURE 8.8 Percentage of Mexicans admitted outside country quotas as relatives of U.S. citizens

immigrants down the road. By pushing immigrants toward defensive naturalization, Congress in effect increased future legal immigration.

As a result of this dynamic, the share of Mexicans admitted to the United States as relatives of U.S. citizens has steadily increased since 1990, when the costs of non-citizenship began seriously to accumulate. As shown in Figure 8.8, the percentage admitted outside the country quotas rose from just 5 percent in 1990 to peak at 69 percent in 2002 before falling to 45 percent in 2005 and then rising back up to 64 percent in 2010. The more young, naturalized citizens there are in the population, the larger the share of entries by citizen relatives. Indeed, from 1990 to 2010 the correlation between the cumulative total of naturalizations and the percentage entering as citizen relatives is 0.854.

THE NEW AMERICAN DEMOGRAPHY

We have argued that the post-1965 surge in Mexican, Central American, and to a lesser extent South American immigration was not a direct result of immigration reforms that occurred in the mid-1960s, but instead arose indirectly through a complicated path-dependent set of unintended consequences that unfolded afterward. Prior to 1960, a well-established circular flow of migrants between Mexico and the United States had been established under the aegis of the Bracero Program and institutionalized informally through the spread and elaboration of migrant networks, which connected sending communities in Mexico to work sites in the United States. By the late 1950s a circulatory cross-border migration system was entrenched and the annual inflow averaged roughly 500,000 persons per year, with around 90 percent entering on temporary work visas.

A series of immigration reforms enacted beginning in the mid-1960s eliminated the temporary work program while simultaneously imposing new quantitative limits on immigration from the Western Hemisphere. With opportunities for legal entry so constrained, the well-established migratory flow simply continued on informally without authorization. Illegal migration rose steadily after 1965 to peak in the late 1970s. Thereafter it fluctuated in tandem with economic trends north and south of the border. In essence, in 1965, the United States shifted from a de jure guestworker program based on the circulation of Bracero migrants to a de facto program based on the circulation of undocumented migrants.

The substitution of a de facto for a de jure system of labor migration might have been the end of it, were it not for the fact that the associated rise in apprehensions offered aspiring politicians an opportunity to mobilize voters and entrepreneurial bureaucrats the chance to obtain status and resources by framing illegal migration as a grave threat to the United States. They portrayed the undocumented inflow as a crisis, framing it as a "tidal wave" threatening to "flood" the nation and "drown" its society or as an "alien invasion," that threatened national security, defined with reference first to the Cold War and then to the War on Terror. Knowing a good storyline when they saw it, the media embraced the "Latino threat narrative" and the "border under siege" and increasingly deployed threatening marine and martial imagery in newspapers, magazines, and on the air.

The rising number of border apprehensions and the intensifying threat narrative, in turn, had profound political consequences, galvanizing a shift toward conservatism among voters and increasing support for more stringent immigration and enforcement policies, setting off a chain reaction in the public sphere. Rising apprehensions led to greater conservatism, which produced more restrictionist legislation and enforcement policies, which translated into a larger Border Patrol with bigger budgets, which produced more linewatch hours, which boosted apprehensions, which then fed back on conservatism. After 1979, rising apprehensions were driven increasingly by this feedback effect, bringing about a growing disconnect between apprehensions and the actual volume of undocumented migration.

The massive increase in border enforcement that arose from this feedback loop had the perverse effect not of deterring departures but of reducing returns. The volume of out-migration plummeted as the volume of in-migration continued and the net rate of undocumented population growth rose dramatically to bring about an exponential increase in the size of the population during the 1990s and early 2000s. On top of this growth in undocumented migration from Mexico, U.S. intervention in Central America during the Cold War destabilized the region and led to large-scale migration northward. Although Nicaraguan emigres were largely welcomed as refugees from communist tyranny, those from Salvador, Guatemala, and Honduras encountered the same restricted opportunities for legal entry as Mexicans. As a result, most entered without authorization or grudgingly received temporary protected status, only to have it revoked after the Cold War ended. As a result, nearly three-quarters of the 11 million undocumented migrants in the U.S. today are from Mexico or Central America.

In the 1990s the Cold War was replaced by the War on Terror. The Anti-Terrorism Act and Effective Death Penalty Act of 1996 and the 2001 PATRIOT Act contributed to the ongoing surge in border enforcement but, more importantly, brought about an exponential increase in deportations from within the United States, setting off another feedback cycle in which deportations took over from border apprehensions as the visible manifestation of the Latino Threat. Although the resulting feedback loop was not as powerful as the apprehensions-based loop that prevailed from 1965 to 1995, it was potent nonetheless and apprehensions expanded even as apprehensions fell in the decade after 2000.

Led by Mexico, legal immigration from Latin America also rose steadily over the period, especially after 1986 when it came to be powered by a dynamic interplay between rising naturalization rates and the increasing use of quota exemptions by recently naturalized immigrants. Spouses, minor children, and parents of U.S. citizens had long been exempted from the country quotas, but in response to the continuing increase in legal immigration, rising apprehensions about terrorism, and growing xenophobia, Congress began to strip civil, social, and economic rights away from illegal as well as legal immigrants, prompting more permanent residents to petition for citizenship as part of a strategy of "defensive naturalization." This dynamic unfolded just as millions of former undocumented migrants became eligible to naturalize after receiving permanent residence under IRCA, and each new citizen simply created more legal migration down the road. As the number of naturalized migrants grew into the millions, a rising share of immigrants from Mexico and other nations evaded the country quotas as citizen relatives.

The end result of foregoing dynamic processes was a massive transformation of the demography of the United States in the past 40 years. In 1970, the Hispanic population of the United States stood at around 9.6 million and comprised just 4.7 percent of the U.S. population. Over 70 percent were native born, 60 percent were Mexican and just 6 percent were Central or South American, compared with nearly a quarter hailing from the Caribbean. In 2010, after four decades of mass migration, the number of Hispanics had risen to 50.5 million people who constituted more than 16 percent of the U.S. population. The percentage of native born had fallen to a little over 60 percent and the distribution of national origins had shifted, with Caribbeans dropping to around 15 percent while Mexicans rose to 63 percent and Central and South Americans to 13[41] (Ríos-Vargas, and Albert 2011).

Over the past four decades, the legal status distribution was likewise markedly transformed. According to estimates from the Census Bureau[42] and the Department of Homeland Security,[43] a majority of immigrants from Mexico and Central America are present without authorization, including 58 percent of Mexicans, 57 percent of Salvadorans, 71 percent of Guatemalans, and 77 percent of Hondurans. Even when one considers all Hispanic generations together, the undocumented constitute large fractions of these origin groups: 21 percent of all persons of Mexican origin, 38 percent of those of Salvadoran origin, 50 percent of those of Guatemalan origin, and 52 percent of those of Honduran origin. In other words, undocumented migrants are no longer a small share of Latinos in the United States. Never before have so many people been outside the law and never before have the undocumented been so concentrated in such a small number of national origins.

A COUNTERFACTUAL SCENARIO

To say that U.S. immigration policies are a colossal failure is an understatement. From 1970 to 2010 the population of Latino immigrants increased more than 11 times. Owing to mass immigration, the total Hispanic population grew by a factor of five and the percentage of Latinos in the U.S. population more than tripled. All these trends unfolded in spite of – and as we have shown paradoxically also because of – the progressive limitation of opportunities for legal entry, the massive build-up of enforcement resources at the border, the exponential rise in deportations, and the systematic restriction of the civil liberties and social rights of non-citizens. Obviously, if the goal of such actions was to limit immigration from Latin America and prevent the demographic transformation of the United States, they failed miserably.

Might events have worked out differently? Possibly. The crux of the problem is that Congress routinely makes important policy decisions without any real consideration of the underlying dynamics of the social processes involved. That was certainly the case here, for in orchestrating immigration reforms during the 1960s and 1970s, Congress took little notice of the long history of recruitment in the hemisphere; the high degree of circularity that historically had prevailed; the strong connection of flows to the dynamics of labor supply and demand; the key role of networks in sustaining and expanding migration over time; the motivations of migrants and how they change in the course of a migratory career; the structural transformations that occur in sending and receiving areas as a result of mass migration; the likelihood of a migratory response to economic, political, and military intervention; the large size and well-established nature of flows into the United States on the eve of restriction; and most importantly the strong momentum that accrues to migratory flows once they get going.

As this chapter has demonstrated, intervening forcefully in complex social and economic systems without understanding their dynamics is an invitation for unintended consequences and unanticipated policy feedbacks. To be fair, immigration was not a salient issue in the 1960s and 1970s when many of the fateful decisions were taken, and fundamental features of migration processes – network effects, migratory momentum, migrant motivations – are much better understood now than they were four decades ago. Nonetheless, it is possible to imagine a different scenario playing out, particularly if Congress had paused to think about immigration reform as an ongoing social, economic, and demographic process rather than just a domestic civil rights issue to be dispensed with.

Suppose, for example, that in choosing to reform the Bracero Program, Congress had enacted safeguards to improve the wages, working conditions, and treatment of workers instead of shutting the program down entirely. Suppose that in implementing the new system of ethnically neutral country quotas, Congress had granted special, more generous visa allocations to Canada and Mexico as our closest neighbors. Finally, suppose that instead of funding the Contra War in Central America, the Reagan Administration had stood on the sidelines and let events take their course without interference.

Under these circumstances mass migration from Latin America might indeed have been avoided. With the continuation of a reformed temporary labor program and the flow from Mexico, migration would have remained predominantly circular. With a generous country quota for permanent resident visas, Mexican workers who established legitimate ties and wished to settle would have had a legal pathway. Hispanic population growth would thus have been slow, illegal migration would not have risen to high levels and politicians and bureaucrats would have lacked illegal migration as a basis for mobilization. The Latino threat narrative would not have gained traction, fears of an alien flood or invasion would not have pushed Americans toward conservatism, and there would be little support for restrictionist policies. As a result, Mexican migrants would not be caged north of the border to bolster Latino population growth.

At the same time, absent a U.S. intervention in Central America, the Cold War would have wound down of its own accord and the collapse of the Soviet Union would likely have brought down the Sandinista government in Nicaragua and ended insurgencies elsewhere without displacing millions of Central Americans northward. Central Americans would not have contributed so greatly to Hispanic population growth. The illegal population of the United States would consequently have remained rather small, Latinos would still be the nation's second minority after African Americans, and, when the terrorists attacked, the United States would have been a less divided and fractious nation. Ironically, a softer line on restriction, less punitive enforcement, and the exercise of military restraint can often produce fewer permanent immigrants, less undocumented migration, and slower population growth.

APPENDIX TABLES

APPENDIX TABLE 8.A1 *Restrictive immigration legislation enacted by Congress toward Latin Americans, 1965–2010*

1965	**Hart-Cellar Act**
	Imposed first-ever annual cap of 120,000 visas for immigrants from Western Hemisphere
1976	**Amendments to Immigration and Nationality Act**
	Put Western Hemisphere under preference system and country quotas
1978	**Amendments to Immigration and Nationality Act**
	Combined separate hemispheric caps into single worldwide ceiling of 290,000
1980	**Refugee Act**
	Abolished refugee preference and reduced worldwide ceiling to 270,000
1986	**Immigration Reform and Control Act**
	Criminalized undocumented hiring and authorized expansion of Border Patrol
1990	**Amendments to the Immigration and Nationality Act**
	Sought to cap visas going to spouses and children of resident aliens
1996	**Antiterrorism and Effective Death Penalty Act**
	Authorized expedited removal of aliens and deportation of aggravated felons
1996	**Illegal Immigrant Reform and Immigrant Responsibility Act**
	Increased resources for border enforcement, narrowed criteria for asylum, and increased income threshold required to sponsor immigrants
1996	**Personal Responsibility and Work Opportunity Act**
	Declared documented and undocumented migrants ineligible for certain entitlements
1997	**Nicaraguan and Central American Relief Act**
	Allowed registered asylum seekers from Central America (mostly Nicaraguans) in the U.S. for at least 5 years since December 1, 1995 to obtain legal status; prohibited legalization and order deportation for those who lacked a valid visa or who previously violated U.S. immigration laws (mostly Hondurans, Salvadorans, and Guatemalans)
2001	**USA Patriot Act**
	Created Department of Homeland Security, increased funding for surveillance and
	Deportation of foreigners; authorized deportation of aliens without due process
2004	**National Intelligence Reform and Terrorism Protection Act**
	Funded new equipment, aircraft, Border Patrol Agents, immigration investigators, and detention centers for border enforcement

(continued)

APPENDIX TABLE 8.A1 *(continued)*

2005	**Real ID Act**
	Dramatically increased the data requirements, documentation, and verification procedures for state issuance of driver's licenses
2006	**Secure Fence Act**
	Authorized construction of additional fencing, vehicle barriers, checkpoints, lighting and funding for new cameras, satellites, and unmanned drones for border enforcement
2010	**Border Security Act**
	Funded hiring of 3,000 more Border Patrol Agents and increased BP budget by $244 million

APPENDIX TABLE 8.A2 *Restrictive enforcement operations launched by the Immigration and Naturalization Service or the Department of Homeland Security, 1990–2010*

1993	**Operation Blockade**
	Border Patrol's (BP) militarization of the El Paso Sector
1994	**Operation Gatekeeper**
	BP's militarization of the San Diego Sector
1998	**Operation Rio Grande**
	BP program to restrict the movement of migrants across the Texas and New Mexico border with Mexico
1999	**Operation Safeguard**
	BP's militarization of the Tucson Sector
2003	**Operation Endgame**
	Plan launched by Immigration and Customs Enforcement to detain and deport all removable aliens and "suspected terrorists" living in the United States
2004	**Operation Frontline**
	Program launched by Immigration and Customs Enforcement (ICE) to address "vulnerabilities in immigration and trade" by focusing on immigration violators with an "enhanced public safety or national security threat"
2004	**Arizona Border Control Initiative**
	Multi-agency effort supporting Homeland Security's anti-terrorism mission through the detection, arrest and deterrence of all those engaged in cross-border illicit activity.

(continued)

APPENDIX TABLE 8.A2 *(continued)*

2004 **Operation Stonegarden**

Federal grant program administered through the State Homeland Security Grant Program to provide funding to state and local agencies to improve immigration enforcement

2005 **Secure Borders Initiative**

Comprehensive multi-year plan launched by ICE to secure America's borders and reduce illegal migration

2005 **Operation Streamline**

Program mandating criminal charges for illegal migrants, even first-time offenders

2006 **Operation Return to Sender**

Sweep of illegal immigrants by the ICE to detain those deemed most dangerous, including convicted felons, gang members, and repeat illegal migrants

2006 **Operation Jump Start**

Program authorizing the deployment of United States National Guard troops along the United States–Mexico border

2007 **Secure Communities Program**

ICE program to identify and deport criminal aliens arrested by state and local authorities

2007 **Operation Rapid REPAT**

Program Remove Eligible Parolees Accepted for Transfer by allowing selected criminal aliens incarcerated in U.S. prisons and jails to accept early release in exchange for voluntarily deportation

2008 **Operation Scheduled Departure**

ICE operation to facilitate the voluntary deportation of 457,000 eligible illegal migrants from selected cities

2010 **Operation Copper Cactus**

Deployment of Arizona National Guard troops to assist Border Patrol in apprehension of illegal migrants

APPENDIX TABLE 8.A3 Legal and illegal U.S. migration from Mexico and political policy indicators, 1955–2009

Year	Legal migrants (000)	Temporary migrants (000)	Illegal migrants (000)	Appreh-ensions (000)	Deport-ations (000)	Border Patrol agents (000)	Border Patrol bud-get (?)	Linewatch hours (000?)	Percent conserv-ative
	(1)	(2)	(3)	(4)	(5)	(6)	(7)	(8)	(9)
1955	50772	398650	164035.2	242608	1479	NA	919000	NA	1955
1956	65047	445197	45475.2	72442	1593	NA	990000	NA	1956
1957	49154	436049	29812.9	44451	1491	NA	927000	NA	1957
1958	26712	432857	24437.0	37242	1524	NA	947000	NA	1958
1959	23061	437643	20130.7	30196	1500	NA	932000	NA	1959
1960	32084	315846	19846.7	29651	1494	NA	929000	NA	1960
1961	41632	291420	18092.8	29817	1648	NA	1024000	NA	1961
1962	55291	194978	18755.9	30272	1614	NA	1003000	NA	1962
1963	55253	186865	26205.0	39124	1493	NA	928000	NA	1963
1964	32967	177736	29366.4	43844	1493	NA	928000	NA	1964
1965	37969	20286	37116.0	55340	1491	41.7	920000	18.2	1965
1966	45163	8647	60195.2	89751	1491	49.2	930000	19.3	1966
1967	42371	7703	72508.0	108327	1494	52.3	937566	20.5	1967
1968	43563	0	101542.8	151705	1494	47.8	941860	21.6	1968
1969	44623	0	134963.9	201636	1494	46.3	909623	22.7	1969
1970	44469	0	177124.5	277377	1566	47	1148854	23.8	1970
1971	50103	0	224052.8	348178	1554	55.9	1118710	24.9	1971

(continued)

	(1)	(2)	(3)	(4)	(5)	(6)	(7)	(8)	(9)
1972	64040	0	263288.2	430213	1634	60.5	1259430	26	1972
1973	70141	0	338511.2	576823	1704	64.7	1279198	27.8	1973
1974	71586	0	408257.0	709959	1739	62.6	1253191	29.5	1974
1975	62205	0	377366.6	680392	1803	63.1	1465423	30.1	1975
1976	74449	0	394883.3	781474	1979	67.3	1775890	31.7	1976
1977	44646	2011	464160.4	954778	2057	67.9	1740446	31.8	1977
1978	92681	2271	446170.4	976667	2189	78.1	1762616	33.8	1978
1979	52479	1725	427032.9	998830	2339	65.5	1935926	33.9	1979
1980	56680	3323	329097.8	817479	2484	82.6	1815797	34	1980
1981	101268	4719	357787.6	874433	2444	85.6	1929448	33.4	1981
1982	56106	4966	356704.6	887481	2488	98.7	1871173	32.7	1982
1983	59079	5014	473850.4	1172306	2474	110.1	1976162	34.5	1983
1984	57820	5336	473229.2	1170769	2474	114.1	1843179	36.5	1984
1985	61290	9622	392017.0	1266999	3232	141.9	1912895	36.5	1985
1986	66753	12029	452601.7	1671458	3693	150.9	2401575	35.8	1986
1987	72511	13393	307752.1	1139606	3703	194.6	2546397	32.5	1987
1988	95170	16802	255782.9	949722	3713	205.3	2069498	36.7	1988
1989	66933	27168	232417.9	865292	3723	246.4	2570311	32.3	1989
1990	57667	16891	292605.9	1092298	3733	262.6	2781317	36.9	1990
1991	54622	19148	309917.8	1131510	3651	298.7	2638720	32.2	1991
1992	91658	19813	294298.3	1199560	4076	399.3	2642227	34.4	1992
1993	109108	23169	318660.8	1263490	3965	361.7	2713937	36.3	1993

(continued)

1994	107012	24896	244124.0	1031668	4226	400	3073758	37	1994
1995	87073	26512	271297.3	1324202	4881	451.5	3397049	37.1	1995
1996	160138	35949	263674.0	1549876	5878	568	4073542	37.2	1996
1997	144641	35949	205371.1	1412953	6880	717.4	4807669	36.1	1997
1998	129970	66197	194910.5	1555776	7982	877.1	6660692	35	1998
1999	146432	86424	189080.3	1579010	8351	916.8	8740258	34.5	1999
2000	173161	104155	181984.2	1676438	9212	1055.4	8999552	34	2000
2001	205560	116157	131200.3	1266214	9651	1146.5	9802081	34.5	2001
2002	218822	118835	96476.5	955310	9902	1416.3	9183667	35.1	2002
2003	115585	114673	88374.6	931557	10541	1420.3	9457060	36.8	2003
2004	173411	117999	108175.2	1160395	10727	1212.9	9830697	38.4	2004
2005	161445	169786	107069.0	1189108	11106	1525.3	10474078	36.7	2005
2006	173749	225680	86418.8	1089136	12603	1561.8	11562715	34.7	2006
2007	148640	300346	62179.1	876787	14101	2277.5	14055363	35.2	2007
2008	189989	360903	41364.6	723840	17499	3002.2	17852594	35.7	2008
2009	164920	301558	27637.2	556032	20119	3501.3	20657122	40	2009

Sources: Columns 1–8: U.S. Dept. of Homeland Security; Column 9: General Social

NOTES

1. U.S. Department for Homeland Security. 2012. Website of the Office of Immigration Statistics. Available at: www.dhs.gov/files/statistics/immigration .shtm, accessed January 5, 2012.

2. Michael Hoefer, Nancy Rytina, and Bryan C. Baker, *Estimates of the Unauthorized Immigrant Population Residing in the United States: January 2010* (Washington, DC: Office of Immigration Statistics, 2011).

3. Douglas S. Massey, "International Migration at the Dawn of the Twenty-First Century: The Role of the State," *Population and Development Review* 25 (1999): 303–23; Eytan Meyers, *International Immigration Policy: A Theoretical and Comparative Analysis* (London: Palgrave Macmillan, 2004); Ashley S. Timmer and Jeffrey G. Williamson, "Immigration Policy Prior to the 1930s: Labor Markets, Policy Interactions, and Globalization Backlash," *Population and Development Review* 24 (1998): 739–772.

4. Rogers M. Smith, *Civic Ideals: Conflicting Visions of Citizenship in U.S. History* (New Haven, CT: Yale University Press, 1997) and *Stories of Peoplehood: The Politics and Morals of Political Membership* (New York: Cambridge University Press, 2003).

5. Mae M. Ngai, *Impossible Subjects: Illegal Aliens and the Making of Modern America.* (Princeton, NJ: Princeton University Press, 2003); Daniel J. Tichenor, *Dividing Lines: The Politics of Immigration Control in America* (Princeton, NJ: Princeton University Press, 2002).

6. Aristide R. Zolberg, *A Nation by Design: Immigration Policy in the Fashioning of America* (New York: Russell Sage Foundation, 2006).

7. Douglas S. Massey, "The New Immigration and the Meaning of Ethnicity in the United States," *Population and Development Review* 21 (1995):631–652.

8. Kitty Calavita, *Inside the State: The Bracero Program, Immigration, and the INS* (New York: Routledge, 1992); Douglas S. Massey Jorge Durand, and Nolan J. Malone, *Beyond Smoke and Mirrors: Mexican Immigration in an Age of Economic Integration* (New York: Russell Sage Foundation, 2002).

9. Douglas S. Massey, "Epilogue: The Past and Future of Mexico-U.S. Migration," in Mark Overmyer-Velázquez (ed.), *Beyond la Frontera: The History of Mexico–U.S. Migration* (New York: Oxford University Press, 2011), pp 241–265.

10. Douglas S. Massey, Jorge Durand, and Nolan J. Malone, *Beyond Smoke and Mirrors: Mexican Immigration in an Age of Economic Integration* (New York: Russell Sage Foundation, 2002).

11. Leo R. Chavez, *Covering Immigration: Population Images and the Politics of the Nation* (Berkeley, CA: University of California Press, 2001) and *The Latino Threat: Constructing Immigrants, Citizens, and the Nation* (Stanford, CA: Stanford University Press, 2008).

12. Susan T. Fisk, *Envy Up, Scorn Down: How Status Divides Us* (New York: Russell Sage Foundation, 2011).

13. Otto Santa Ana, *Brown Tide Rising: Metaphors of Latinos in Contemporary American Public Discourse* (Austin, TX: University of Texas Press, 2002).

14. Chavez, *The Latino Threat*; Joseph Nevins, *Operation Gatekeeper: The Rise of the "Illegal Alien" and the Remaking of the U.S.–Mexico Boundary* (New York: Routledge, 2001).

15. Leonard F. Chapman, "Illegal Aliens: Time to Call a Halt!" *Reader's Digest*, October 1976, p. 188.
16. Sebastian Rotella, *Twilight on the Line: Underworlds and Politics at the U.S.–Mexico Border* (New York: W. W. Norton, 1998).
17. Al Kamen, "Central America is no Longer the Central Issue for Americans," *Austin American Statesman*, October 21 (1990).
18. Massey *et al.*, *Beyond Smoke and Mirrors: Mexican Immigration in an Age of Economic Integration* (New York: Russell Sage Foundation, 2002).
19. Lou Dobbs, *War on the Middle Class: How the Government, Big Business, and Special Interest Groups Are Waging War on the American Dream and How to Fight Back* (New York: Viking, 2006).
20. Patrick J. Buchanan, *State of Emergency: The Third World Invasion and Conquest of America* (New York: Thomas Dunne Books, 2006).
21. S. P. Huntington, "The Hispanic challenge," *Foreign Policy* (March/April 2004): 1–12. Available at: www.foreignpolicy.com/story/cms.php?story_id=2495, accessed June 15, 2011.
22. Douglas S. Massey and Karen A. Pren, "Origins of the New Latino Underclass," *Race and Social Problems* 4 (2012): 5–17.
23. Massey and Pren, "Origins of the New Latino Underclass," 5–17.
24. Douglas S. Massey and Audrey Singer, "New Estimates of Undocumented Mexican Migration and the Probability of Apprehension," *Demography* 32 (1995): 203–213; Douglas S. Massey, Jorge Durand, and Karen A. Pren, "Nuevos Escenarios de la Migración México-Estados Unidos: Las Consecuencias de la Guerra Antiinmigrante," *Papeles de Población* 61 (2009):101–128.
25. Francisco E. Balderrama, *Decade of Betrayal: Mexican Repatriation in the 1930s* (Albuquerque: University of New Mexico Press, 1995); Abraham Hoffman, *Unwanted Mexican Americans in the Great Depression:Repatriation Pressures, 1929–1939* (Tucson, AZ: University of Arizona Press, 1974).
26. U.S. Department for Homeland Security. 2012. Website of the Office of Immigration Statistics. Available at: www.dhs.gov/files/statistics/immigration.shtm, accessed January 5, 2012.
27. Robert Warren and Jeffrey S. Passel, "A Count of the Uncountable: Estimates of Undocumented Aliens Counted in the 1980 Census," *Demography* 24 (1987): 375–393.
28. Ruth E. Wasem, *Unauthorized Aliens Residing in the United States: Estimates Since 1986* (Washington, DC: Congressional Research Service, 2011)
29. Jennifer H. Lundquist and Douglas S. Massey, "Politics or Economics? International Migration During the Nicaraguan Contra War," *Journal of Latin American Studies* 37 (2005): 29–53.
30. Micahel Hoefer, Nancy Rytina, and Bryan C. Baker, *Estimates of the Unauthorized Immigrant Population Residing in the United States: January 2008* (Washington, DC: Office of Immigration Statistics, U.S. Department of Homeland Security, 2009).
31. Massey *et al.*, *Beyond Smoke and Mirrors*.
32. Steve Redburn, Peter Reuter, and Malay Majmundar, *Budgeting for Immigration Enforcement: A Path to Better Performance* (Washington, DC: National Academies Press, 2011).

33. U.S. Department for Homeland Security. 2012. Website of the Office of Immigration Statistics. Available at: www.dhs.gov/files/statistics/immigration .shtm, accessed January 12, 2012.

34. Massey *et al., Beyond Smoke and Mirrors.*

35. Zolberg, *A Nation by Design.*

36. Lina Newton, *Illegal, Alien, or Immigrant: The Politics of Immigration Reform* (New York: New York University Press, 2008).

37. Stephen H. Legomsky, "Fear and Loathing in Congress and the Courts: Immigration and Judicial Review," *Texas Law Review* 78 (2000): 1612–1620.

38. Zolberg, *A Nation by Design.*

39. Daniel J. Hopkins, "Politicized Places: Explaining Where and When Immigrants Provoke Local Opposition," *American Political Science Review* 104 (2010): 40–60.

40. U.S. Department for Homeland Security. 2012. Website of the Office of Immigration Statistics. Available at: www.dhs.gov/files/statistics/immigration .shtm, accessed January 5, 2012.

41. Sharon R., Ennis, Merarys Ríos-Vargas, and Nora G. Albert, *The Hispanic Population: 2010.* 2010 Census Briefs (U.S. Bureau of the Census, Washington, DC, 2011).

42. Yesenia D. Acosta and G. Patricia de la Cruz, *The Foreign Born from Latin America and the Caribbean: 2010.* American Community Survey Briefs (U.S. Bureau of the Census, Washington, DC, 2011).

43. Michael Hoefer, Nancy Rytina, and Bryan C. Baker, *Estimates of the Unauthorized Immigrant Population Residing in the United States: January 2010.*

9

Alien Rights, Citizen Rights, and the Politics of Restriction

Rogers M. Smith

THE HARSH VIEW OF AMERICAN IMMIGRATION POLITICS

Scholars of American immigration policies have long understood that they characteristically emerge, when they emerge at all, from a "strange bedfellow" politics comprising opposing political coalitions that, in Daniel Tichenor's words, "cut across familiar partisan and ideological lines."[1] Many employers and free market economic conservatives have long supported expansive opportunities for immigration, often in alliance with pro-immigrant cosmopolitan liberals and ethnic American advocacy groups. Cultural conservatives have generally favored restrictive immigration policies, and historically many unions and others on the left often joined them, wishing to protect American workers from competition with cheap immigrant labor – a pattern that has changed in the recent years at the union leadership level, but not nearly so much among rank and file workers, as union household support for Donald Trump in the 2016 election showed.[2] The latter groups – cultural conservatives, less affluent workers, and those who identify with them – have usually greatly outnumbered the former groups among the general public. Consequently, opinion polls have traditionally shown majority support for restrictive immigration policies, though since 2005 attitudes toward immigration have come to be more closely aligned with partisan preferences, and accordingly more polarized.[3]

Even so, the United States has instead usually had relatively generous immigration policies, and at the start of the Trump years it still does so, despite its large numbers of undocumented aliens. I am among the somewhat cynical who have explained this anomaly by arguing that the proponents of more open immigration, especially employers but also in the last quarter-century ethnic advocacy groups, have generally been more intensely active on the issue and more politically powerful than their opponents. Thus they have been able to get their way in substance. The fact that American majorities have favored restrictive immigration, though more diffusely and less intensely, has often only meant that policymakers have set some largely symbolic limits on immigration that could gratify cultural conservatives without much helping American workers. In fact, those limits have often served employer interests instead. Though they did not prevent immigrants from coming to this country, they often did restrict the rights of aliens once here. As a result, in those times when either labor surpluses or the political radicalism of immigrant workers curbed employer desires for their presence, officially restrictive policies often assisted in deporting the nation's troublesome excess immigrant population.

Thus when the intercontinental railroads had been completed and anti-Chinese racism mounted in the late nineteenth century, the U.S. excluded first Chinese laborers, then virtually all Asians. Later in the 1920s, the race-based national origins quota system also kept many southern and eastern Europeans out, with special animus toward Jews. But employers easily replaced their inexpensive Chinese and European laborers with Mexican workers, against whom no restrictions applied except the general ban on immigrants who might be vagrants and public charges – so that when Mexican workers were not needed, they could be deported.[4] Certainly, from the standpoint of would-be Chinese immigrants and, later, many other potential Asian and European immigrants, these restrictions mattered greatly. It is also likely that the history of the U.S., China, and perhaps much more would have been very different if these restrictions had not occurred. But from the standpoint of overall immigration levels and, most pertinently, from the standpoint of employer interests, the bans on Chinese and then on virtually all Asians and the national origins quota system all represented immigration limits that were more symbolic than real.

The pattern of "symbolic restrictions on entry, real restrictions on rights, extensive practical openness for cheap labor" has historically also been visible in the fact that, in relation to its border-patrol responsibilities, the old Immigration and Naturalization Service (INS) was probably the most under-funded, understaffed, demoralized, inefficient, and sometimes corrupt agency in the whole federal bureaucracy.[5] In a kind of perverse functionality, these traits meant that those who sought to immigrate legally, but who lacked political connections, often faced frustrations and delays so great that they sometimes gave up, thereby constraining the total numbers of immigrants. But immigrants who simply sought to slip across the border had little to worry about in the way of either border or in-country enforcement of the immigration laws, so employers still got their workers. And those workers' undocumented status, their lack of any legal right to be in the U.S., made them even more conveniently deportable if they ever sought to be anything more than cheap labor. These patterns often frustrated border guards, many of whom endorsed Trump in 2016; but they often satisfied employers.[6]

This harsh view of American immigration policies and politics may be overdrawn. None should deny that the U.S. has accepted and assisted millions of immigrants in its history, providing many with an asylum from oppression and many more with economic opportunities far beyond any they could dream of having in their home countries. But I lay out the less flattering account at the start in order to be able to ask: Is something like this pattern of immigration politics visible in the last two decades of American politics, a period that saw major immigration laws in 1996; major new executive actions and judicial decisions affecting immigrants after the 9/11 attacks; a wave of state and local laws unfavorable to immigrants in the ensuing years, with gridlock on innovation reforms at the national level; and then the election of a President who promised to build a wall against Mexico that clearly has symbolic significance, but may have less practical impact? Is this pattern likely to characterize American policies and legal doctrines affecting immigrants in the future?

My answer is that many recent developments do fit this pattern, and that the post 9/11 "war on terrorism" resulted in renewed legitimacy for discriminatory policies toward immigrants, reductions in immigrant legal rights, and heightened deportation levels that began during the George W. Bush years, continued under Barack Obama, and promise to increase further under Donald Trump. Many of the anti-immigrant measures from 2008 on were, to be sure, state and local initiatives, some quickly invalidated by federal courts. Even so, the reductions in immigrant rights even prior to Trump's election have been great enough that they have also endangered the rights of American citizens. The heightening of security concerns has contributed to dramatic growth in resources devoted to immigration control as well, a process President Trump will certainly seek to accelerate. Yet in terms of state capacity, the U.S. still does not have the means to patrol its borders effectively or process applications efficiently. The largest contributor to reductions in unauthorized immigration has instead been the Great Recession that began in 2008. The federal government has chiefly strengthened only its legal and administrative powers to detain and deport immigrants, authorized and unauthorized, that the U.S. decides it does not want, and that emphasis may well only persist under Trump. But that is far from inconsequential, since those deportations have often broken up families, leaving citizen children in severe need, if they were not also effectively deported.

In one way, however, the historical pattern of employers always getting the immigrant workers they want, under conditions favorable to employer interests though not necessarily immigrant or citizen rights, has changed in the modern era. Many employers want more high-skilled immigrants, admitted perhaps via adoption of a Canadian- or Australian-style points system. But those proposals have been folded into plans for "comprehensive immigration reform," and despite employer support, efforts by both the Bush and Obama administrations to achieve such reform proved chimerical. After the 2014 midterm elections, Obama appeared to give up on Congress, seeking to bring about change through broad, constitutionally questionable executive orders that still fell short of the sweeping changes many immigration activists have long sought.[7] Legal and political battles over immigration measures, producing gridlock without the more effective controls and greater selectivity desired by many Americans, or the better opportunities for immigrants desired by others, appeared likely to continue.

But as Tichenor and others have shown, immigration politics are complex, and there are factors that may yet counter these tendencies. Going into the 2016 elections, many Republicans like Republican National Committee Chair Reince Priebus saw a real opportunity to increase the GOP (Republican Party) share of the Hispanic vote if the party was not perceived as too anti-immigrant, though the eventual nominee had no such inhibitions, and Priebus served as his Chief of Staff.[8] For a time, GOP congressional leaders sought piece-by-piece rather than "comprehensive" immigration laws, permitting them to restrict more generous measures to those immigrants their constituencies wanted to aid.[9] It is not inconceivable that President Trump will support a similar strategy, given his greater receptivity to, for example, Christian refugees than those he believes more likely to be terrorists.[10] Moving beyond the GOP, many of those seeking to revive the contemporary labor movement have sought to make it more transnational and to make common cause with immigrant workers, rather than opposing them, albeit with mixed results. And the Supreme Court has also made clear that it will not give up its institutional prerogatives in deference to executive security concerns about immigrants, nor will it permit the states to undermine national policies; though whether it will sustain presidential policymaking by executive order, or provide much substantive protection for immigrant rights, as opposed to precedents upholding national congressional authority and the Court's jurisdiction, all remains to be seen.

THE 1996 LAWS: AEDPA, PWOA, AND IIRIRA

Two decades later, it is clear that the trajectory of current immigration policies was set during the first Clinton administration. Polls in the early 1990s suggested some rise in the degree and salience of the longstanding public opposition to the prevailing levels of admissions. Governor Pete Wilson of California, who had supported guestworker programs in the 1980s, championed Proposition 187 in 1994, a referendum proposal that sought to deny public benefits, including education, to undocumented aliens.[11] Journalist Peter Brimelow published various widely read essays and then a 1996 book, *Alien Nation*, devoted to concerns about the "ethnic and racial transformation" that public policies were "inflicting" on the country. He insisted that "race is destiny" in American politics and life.[12] But though Brimelow sold books and Proposition 187 won at the polls, a federal court declared it unconstitutional, and the U.S. did not lower immigration levels. Many observers concluded that the nation's receptive policies and practices had survived another of its periodic spasms of anti-immigrant anxieties.

But that judgment underestimated the fact that Congress passed three laws in 1996 significantly restricting receptive policies and practices and putting "the government seal of approval" on the "wave of widespread anti-immigrant feeling," even though the laws also served employer interests.[13] In June 1996, Congress passed the Antiterrorism and Effective Death Penalty Act of 1996, expediting the exclusion and arrest, punishment, and removal of aliens suspected of terrorism or other crimes by creating a special removal court; limiting judicial review of deportations; limiting the discretion of the Attorney General to grant asylum to suspect aliens; and making many immigration offenses subject to the expansive punitive measures authorized by the Racketeer Influenced and Corrupt Organizations Act (RICO). Its section 439 authorized state and local officials to assist the federal government in immigration enforcement.[14]

In August, President Clinton signed the Personal Responsibility and Work Opportunity Reconciliation Act (PRWORA), replacing the New Deal Aid to Families with Dependent Children (AFDC) program with Temporary Assistance to Needy Families (TANF) block grants to the states. It thereby reduced the federal social assistance rights of all citizens. It also made immigrants arriving after its enactment ineligible for all federally funded means-tested benefit programs like TANF and Medicaid for five years, with a state option to restore them thereafter, and it denied them Supplemental Security Income and food stamps altogether.[15]

In September 1996, the Illegal Immigration Reform and Immigrant Responsibility Act (IIRIRA) increased resources for immigration law enforcement, including detentions, further streamlined procedures to expedite exclusions and deportations, further limited the Attorney General's "parole" authority, banned Social Security benefits for undocumented aliens, authorized states to limit public aid to aliens, mandated new data collection, including requirements that educational institutions report on foreign students, and authorized heightened worksite investigations, among other measures. Its sections 133 and 372 further empowered states to play larger roles in immigration law enforcement.[16]

Collectively, these laws meant that even though the U.S. did not restrict legal admissions during a decade when immigration was rising rapidly, it cut back sharply on the public benefits that immigrants could receive, even as it reduced the social rights of its citizens somewhat less severely. These policies made it more likely that aliens would take any jobs on any terms offered; and if they failed to find employment, the laws made it easier to deport them. Scholars agree that the laws succeeded in sharply reducing the number of immigrants who received various forms of public aid, sometimes with harsh results.[17] These laws also prompted the states to undertake additional financial burdens of immigrant support that many have found difficult to sustain, so that some began enacting their own anti-immigration measures.[18] Even so, the laws did succeed, for a time, in partly satisfying many critics of high immigration levels without jeopardizing the availability of cheap immigrant labor.

THE POST-9/11 INNOVATIONS

Then came September 11, 2001. It showed that, despite the 1996 laws and other measures, the U.S. had failed horrendously to prevent the entry and operations of foreign terrorists. Almost overnight, a wave of new restrictive measures began, with some forms continuing to proliferate up to the present. Administration officials quickly compiled many existing proposals to strengthen the nation's anti-terrorist capabilities into the USA Patriot Act, which Congress passed so rapidly that President Bush signed it into law on October 26, 2001.[19] Section 411 of the Act permitted denials of entry to aliens perceived as having "endorsed" terrorism, and section 412 authorized the warrantless detention of aliens on a renewable basis if the Attorney General had "reasonable grounds," not probable cause, to believe they were engaged in terrorist activities. Then on November 13, President Bush issued an executive order authorizing trials of noncitizens suspected of terrorism in new military tribunals, without most of the procedural protections constitutionally guaranteed in ordinary criminal trials.[20] On January 11, 2002, the administration opened its detention camp for unlawful enemy combatants at the U.S. naval base in Guantanamo, Cuba, where it claimed the right to hold suspected combatants in indefinite detention without the individualized status determinations required by the Third Geneva Convention of 1949.[21] Sometime in 2002, President Bush also secretly authorized the National Security Agency to monitor without warrants the international phone calls and e-mails of those suspected of links to Al Qaeda, aliens and citizens alike; and the NSA also secretly obtained millions of phone call records from several major telephone companies, analyzing calling patterns to identify suspected terrorists.[22]

Then, on the symbolic date of September 11, 2002, the INS began a "Special Registration Initiative" targeted at noncitizens from Arab and Islamic nations, beginning with those from Iraq, Iran, Syria, Libya, and Sudan. The Initiative led to the questioning of roughly 130,000 male immigrants and alien visitors, the deportation of some 9,000 undocumented aliens, the arrest of over 800 criminal suspects, and the detention of 11 suspected terrorists, without any convictions, before it was officially ended on April 30, 2003 (though many of the new practices continued).[23] On November 25, 2002, Congress authorized the creation of the new Department of Homeland Security (DHS) meant to absorb, reorganize and coordinate some 22 federal agencies, including the INS.

In June 2003, an internal report led the Department of Justice's Inspector General to testify to Congress that some immigrant detainees had been treated abusively in ways that amounted to serious civil rights violations.[24] Many private groups and journalists also reported a wide range of discriminatory actions against aliens. In this context, not only civil rights groups but also labor unions began to step up campaigns to protect the rights of immigrants. The AFL-CIO, which had begun emphasizing organizing immigrant workers in the mid-1990s, led a coalition in the summer of 2003 that sponsored the Immigrant Workers Freedom Ride, a bus caravan that traveled across the country to Washington to call for legalization of undocumented farm workers and greater civil rights for noncitizens generally.[25] Perhaps partly in response, on January 7, 2004, President Bush proposed a new temporary workers' program as a means to reduce the immigration backlog that hampered security checks, and he indicated that undocumented aliens in the U.S. with good work histories could be eligible for this program. But Congress did not act, and Bush set immigration issues aside until he felt compelled in 2006 to respond to heightening calls for tighter border security and deportation of immigrants from his own party.[26] The administration's efforts failed to curb the entry of unauthorized immigrants sharply, however, until the dramatic economic collapse of 2008 made the United States a less appealing destination. And comprehensive immigration reform never resurfaced as a practical possibility during Bush's second term. The chief legacy of his later years was to continue the trend toward less receptive immigration policies embodied in the 1996 laws, accompanied by security measures, including detentions and surveillance systems that affected many citizens as well as noncitizens.

A series of Supreme Court decisions did, however, modify these patterns. The initial administration measures aimed at immigrants suspected of terrorism, embodied in the USA Patriot Act, the executive order for military tribunals, and the Special Registration Initiative, all relied on doctrines going back to the *Chinese Exclusion Case* and the *Insular Cases* denying that aliens were entitled to anything more than the most minimal forms of due process rights. But indefinite detentions on the basis of reasonable suspicion alone, without specific charges or evidence and without the detainee having access to an attorney, seemed to many to violate even that undemanding standard; and the administration also soon sought to hold citizens suspected of being involved with terrorism indefinitely in the same fashion. Consequently, executive branch officials came to rely on the previously obscure precedent of *Ex parte Quirin*, 317 U.S. 1 (1942), to justify their measures.

In *Quirin*, the Supreme Court had upheld secret military trials for all persons, whether citizens or noncitizens, who fell in the previously undefined category of "unlawful enemy combatants" – persons engaged in forms of belligerency that violated the laws of war. The unlawful enemy combatants in question were Nazi saboteurs who had landed covertly on Long Island and Florida with the intent of blowing up American weapon production facilities. The Court said that they had no claim to ordinary Fifth and Sixth Amendment procedural guarantees. The Bush administration claimed plausibly enough that all terrorists should be seen as unlawful enemy combatants, so that the Guantanamo detainees, and even U.S. citizens suspected of terrorism, could all be treated like the Nazi saboteurs in *Quirin*. Indeed, in the eyes of the executive branch, the President's national security powers and that precedent virtually precluded any judicial review of the detentions of persons so designated.

The Supreme Court has continued to affirm *Quirin* as a valid precedent. But in cases beginning with *Sharif Rasul* v. *Bush*, 542 U.S. 466 (2004) and including *Hamdi* v. *Rumsfeld*, 542 U.S. 507 (2004), *Hamdan* v. *Rumsfeld*, 548 U.S. 557 (2006), and *Boumediene* v. *Bush*, 553 U.S. 723 (2008), the Court has repeatedly ruled that Guantanamo detainees and others detained as suspected terrorists have statutory and constitutional rights to present habeas corpus petitions to U.S. courts, whether or not they are U.S. citizens. In the Court's view, all detainees who are not nationals of countries at war with the U.S. and who are being detained indefinitely in locations under U.S. jurisdiction are entitled to hearings to determine if they are indeed unlawful enemy combatants, and then to trials that may be conducted by military commissions, but that must meet minimum due process requirements. The propriety of both the combatant status hearings and military commission proceedings, both of which Congress has authorized in subsequent legislation, remain permanently reviewable by the federal courts under habeas corpus. President Obama, like President Bush, claimed inherent executive authority to detain suspected terrorists indefinitely and to engage in extensive electronic surveillance; and Congress provided renewed statutory authority for many of his claims via the 2012 National Defense Authorization Act.[27] Still, his administration did not seek to have the decisions requiring some measure of judicial scrutiny of executive actions overturned. Faced with congressional gridlock on immigration issues, Obama did in his last two years take executive actions to defer deportations of increasing numbers of unauthorized aliens who had violated no laws other than immigration measures, and, to his disappointment, the federal courts invalidated the most sweeping of those measures.[28] The White House revised the executive order to apply only to six predominantly Muslim nations, and in November 2017, the 9th Circuit allowed the revised order to go into partial effect.[29] At this writing it is also not clear whether the U.S. Supreme Court will uphold that ruling. But these precedents suggest that modern federal courts are not averse to finding boundaries to executive powers over aliens as well as citizens, even in national security contexts.

THE RISE OF STATE AND LOCAL IMMIGRATION REGULATIONS

National actions are not the whole story. Even as the Bush administration took strong steps against suspected terrorists, while struggling and failing to deal with unauthorized immigration, many state and local officials began in the first decade of the twenty-first century to address immigration more aggressively. Whereas proponents of immigration restriction once focused almost exclusively on persuading national policymakers, since the mid-2000s, they have increasingly used parallel and often coordinated state and local government actions that seek to transform American national policies "from below" as part of a strategy its proponents have called "attrition through enforcement." The chief aim of this "bottom up" strategy is to reduce the unauthorized immigrant populations by adopting state and local measures (and, when possible, national policies) that make life much more difficult for those populations – in the expectation that many unauthorized immigrants will decide to "self-deport," as presidential candidate Mitt Romney argued in 2012.[30] The most significant development in the "attrition through enforcement" movement came on April 23, 2010, when Arizona Governor Jan Brewer signed into law Senate bill 1070, the "Support Our Law Enforcement and Safe Neighborhoods Act." Section 1 of the act explicitly stated, "The intent of this act is to make attrition through enforcement the public policy of all state and local government agencies in Arizona."[31] Its proponents presented the bill as a means to ensure that all Arizona governmental entities would actively contribute to enforcement of federal immigration laws, rather than abstaining from or even obstructing enforcement, as some local communities have done in Arizona and elsewhere. Among other provisions, the bill required all cities to collect and report information on immigrant statuses to pertinent federal agencies, and to request status information from federal immigration authorities. The law also added state penalties for violations of some federal immigration laws and for the commission of various immigration-related crimes. Most controversially, it authorized Arizona law officers to require proof of immigrant status on the basis of "reasonable suspicion" and to arrest immigration law violators without warrants, so long as police had "probable cause" to believe them guilty of such violations. Latinos believed this provision meant they would need to carry their citizenship or legal resident status papers with them at all times.

The Obama Justice Department immediately challenged the law on the grounds that it represented state interference with national policies concerning the enforcement of immigration laws, and because it might encourage stops, searches, and arrests that amounted to illegal racial profiling. On April 30, the Arizona legislature enacted and the Governor signed a further measure guaranteeing that state prosecutors would not investigate complaints based on "race, color, or national origin." But June 25, 2012, in *Arizona* v. *United States*, the Supreme Court agreed with lower federal courts that the law's criminalization of failure to carry documentation, its ban on unauthorized aliens seeking employment, and its authorization for arrests without warrant were all preempted by federal laws, though it sustained the remainder of the statute. Justice Anthony Kennedy's majority opinion indicated that the requirement for stops based on reasonable suspicion of unauthorized status might also be in jeopardy if it proved to foster invidious discrimination.[32] The Justice Department chose not to pursue issues of racial profiling when arguing the case, since the law had not yet been enforced.

The question of how far SB 1070 would be sustained was urgent because, in its wake, various states began trying to out-do Arizona and each other by enacting the most stringent anti-immigrant attrition through enforcement laws in the nation. Georgia and Alabama quickly passed copycat laws that in fact went well beyond SB 1070, with Alabama making it a crime to give a ride or rent housing to anyone known to be an undocumented alien.[33] Even though SB 1070 was a crucial test case for the constitutionality of attrition through enforcement strategies, the Supreme Court's decision in *Arizona* v. *United States* was not likely to be the last word, since the Court allowed much of the law to stand.

But attrition through enforcement initiatives has never gone uncontested; and after 2010, they suffered some signal defeats. In November 2011, Arizona voters ousted State Senator Russell Pearce, the chief sponsor of SB 1070 as well as a ban on ethnic studies programs in Arizona public schools, in a recall election. Arizona business leaders especially turned against Pearce, arguing that his anti-immigration stance had prompted boycotts that were hurting the state's economy.[34] And even as some state and local authorities sought to prod immigrants to leave, others welcomed them. Major cities including New York, Philadelphia, Chicago, San Francisco, Los Angeles and many more have proclaimed themselves "sanctuary cities" that restrict the ways in which their local law enforcement officials will aid federal enforcement of immigration laws, and California, Rhode Island, Vermont, and Connecticut have adopted similar policies at the state level. In addition to initiating construction of a more extensive wall along the border with Mexico, President Trump in his first month in office also indicated he would cut off significant federal funds to such sanctuary cities and states.[35] The issue of how far states can refuse to cooperate with federal immigration policies, like the issue of how far they may take independent action to enforce them, is likely to be fodder for intensive political contestation and extensive judicial litigation in the years ahead.

CONCLUSION

What do all these somewhat conflicting developments suggest concerning the prospects for immigration politics, aliens' rights, and U.S. citizens' rights in the years ahead?

I believe they provide some continued confirmation of the bleak depiction of American immigration policies sketched at the outset. The 1996 laws took away many rights of immigrants to public benefits, and a whole range of post-9/11 actions made immigrants even more vulnerable to detention and deportation with few procedural protections. Yet the federal government has not restricted immigration levels. It has instead been unable to enact either effective enforcement policies or solutions to the problems accompanying the presence of millions of unauthorized aliens – not even innovations favored by many employers, the one great departure from historic patterns. President Trump has promised to deport all unauthorized aliens with criminal records and to work with Congress on major immigration reforms, but not even he has suggested sharp overall immigration reductions. He has, however, suggested that American citizens of Mexican or Muslim origin, including federal judges, can often be presumed not to be fully loyal to the United States, its laws, and its interests.[36] This rhetoric inevitably makes many legal immigrants and citizens feel their situation in America is vulnerable, even as the nation continues to benefit from their work and skills.

On balance, then, at national, state, and local levels, American officials have taken and are taking more and more actions that seek to reassure, and perhaps will reassure, those who fear immigrants for cultural or national security reasons. They have not as yet, however, taken many actions that are likely to reduce immigration significantly or even to enhance national security against immigrant terrorists substantially, much less improve conditions for immigrants, legal and illegal, who are in the U.S. and those who may yet come. In the process, however, the executive branches of the Bush, Obama and now the Trump administrations have adopted positions that have made aliens and citizens alike vulnerable to indefinite detentions without access to an attorney, on the basis of "reasonable grounds" to suspect that they are engaged in terrorism or even simply material witnesses to terrorist activities. And though it is only aliens who can be the object of more aggressive deportation policies, those measures directly impact many millions of American citizen relatives of those aliens as well.

Clearly, this is not a bright picture from an immigrant rights standpoint, a citizens' rights standpoint, or indeed national security or economic growth standpoints. The condition of Latino immigrants, to be sure, may eventually improve due to the growing number of American Latino voters, although they are not yet swing voters in many states. Islamic and Arab immigrants, however, are not a fast-growing voting base. In post-9/11 America, they remain deeply suspect in the eyes of many, and the anti-terrorist rhetoric of the Trump administration seems aimed at deepening those suspicions. Despite the efforts of civil liberties and ethnic advocacy groups, there has been no definitive official repudiation of the abusive practices and denials of due process rights that have now been elaborately detailed, not only at Abu Ghraib but at Guantanamo and in detention facilities in the U.S. and abroad – with the details provided not only by the administration's international and domestic critics but by internal reports within the executive branch itself. For many Americans, the inescapable reality of the 9/11 attacks makes even extensive infringements of immigrant rights, and the rights of many suspect citizens, reasonable.

If this remains the current political environment, what about the current legal environment? It is very likely that the Court will continue to reject claims that executive branch actions in the war on terrorism are entirely exempt from judicial review. Yet its decisions so far have done more to preserve judicial oversight prerogatives than to end practices of warrantless, indefinite detentions, and the rulings so far have done as much or more to limit executive discretionary powers to aid immigrants as they have done to limit executive discretion to ban groups of immigrants regarded as undesirable.

Consequently, it seems likely that the U.S. will remain a country more open than most to immigrants from impoverished nations seeking significantly improved, though often still relatively meager, economic opportunities. And as the Latino share of the electorate grows, the U.S. may well come to be increasingly shaped by a politics that promotes access to full citizenship, and thus public benefits, for those who prove over time to be productive and law-abiding. Many of these immigrants may also benefit from the advocacy of the more liberal labor unions as well as civil liberties groups and ethnic associations concerned for their rights. But those changes are likely to be long in coming, if they come and at all. In the interim, national, state and local immigration policies are likely to be intensely contested battlefields that will sometimes result in curbs on both aliens' and citizens' due process and equal protection rights, even as they sometimes extend benefits. The U.S. is especially likely to face continuing difficulties with abuse of Islamic, Arab, and Mexican immigrants at the hands of American law enforcement and military forces. The ways they are denied procedural protections may, moreover, continue to rebound to erode the rights of American citizens generally. The harsh picture is therefore not the whole story. But it is enough of the story to ensure that eternal vigilance remains the price of civil liberties, for citizens and noncitizens alike.

NOTES

1. Daniel J. Tichenor, *Dividing Lines: The Politics of Immigration Control in America* (Princeton, NJ: Princeton University Press, 2002), p. 8.
2. Janice Fine and Daniel J. Tichenor, "A Movement Wrestling: American Labor's Enduring Struggle with Immigration, 1866–2007," *Studies in American Political Development* 23 (2009): 106–111; Philip Bump, "Trump got Reagan-Like support from union households," *Washington Post*, November 10, 2016. Available at: www.washingtonpost.com/news/the-fix/wp/2016/11/10/donald-trump-got-reagan-like-support-from-union-households/?utm_term=.949e6624139b, accessed February 20, 2018.
3. Milton D. Morris, *Immigration: The Beleaguered Bureaucracy* (Washington, DC: Brookings Institution, 1985), pp. 24–25; Lee Rainie and Anna Brown, "Americans less concerned than a decade ago over immigrants' impact on workforce," *Facttank: News in the Numbers*, Pew Research Center, October 7, 2016. Available at: www.pewresearch.org/fact-tank/2016/10/07/americans-less-concerned-than-a-decade-ago-over-immigrants-impact-on-workforce/, accessed February 20, 2018.
4. Tichenor, *Dividing Lines*, pp. 87–113; Desmond King, *Making Americans: Immigration, Race, and the Origins of the Diverse Democracy* (Cambridge, MA: Harvard University Press, 2000), 199–236.
5. Morris, *Immigration*, pp. 88–89, 110–121; Committee on Government Operations, "The Immigration and Naturalization Service: Overwhelmed and Unprepared for

the Future," House Report 103–216, Second Report by the Committee on Government Operations (Washington, DC: Congressional Budget Office, 1993).

6. "National Border Patrol Council Endorses Donald Trump for President," *National Border Patrol Council*. Available at: www.bpunion.org/index.php/newsroom/press-releases/1824-national-border-patrol-council-endorses-donald-trump-for-president, accessed February 20, 2018.

7. Michael D. Sheer, "Obama, Daring Congress, Acts to Overhaul Immigration," *New York Times*, November 21, 2014, A1.

8. Eli Stokol, "Reince Priebus' Surrender," *Politico Magazine*. Available at: www .politico.com/magazine/story/2016/07/2016-gop-convention-reince-priebus-donald-trump-214078, accessed February 20, 2018.

9. *The Economist*, "Immigration: Both relieved and worried. Illegal immigrants are confused by the president's order; Republicans are incensed." Available at: www .economist.com/news/united-states/21635006-illegal-immigrants-are-confused-presi dents-order-republicans-are-incensed-both, November 29, 2014.

10. Daniel Burke, "Trump Says US will prioritize Christian refugees," *CNN Politics*, January 30, 2017. Available at: www.cnn.com/2017/01/27/politics/trump-christian-refugees/, accessed February 20, 2018.

11. Tichenor, *Dividing Lines*, pp. 275–278; American Bar Association Commission on Immigration, "American Justice Through Immigrants' Eyes." Available at: www .abanet.org/publicserv/immigration/Due_Process.html, accessed February 20, 2018.

12. Peter Brimelow, *Alien Nation: Common Sense about America's Immigration Disaster* (New York: Random House, 1995), pp. 9–10, 264.

13. Audrey Singer, "Welfare Reform and Immigrants: A Policy Review," (2004): 26. Available at: www.brookings.edu/research/welfare-reform-and-immigrants/, accessed February 20, 2018.

14. See bill. Available at: http://library.clerk.house.gov/reference-files/PPL_104_132_Anti terrorismandEffectiveDeathPenaltyAct_1996.pdf, accessed February 25, 2018.

15. In fact, PRWORA originally made even many immigrants present at the time of its enactment ineligible for SSI and food stamps, but Congress restored eligibility to most pre-enactment immigrants via the 1997 Balanced Budget Act, the 1998 Agricultural Research Extension and Education Act and the Farm Security and Rural Investment Act of 2002. The states have chosen to provide TANF and Medicaid benefits to most pre-enactment immigrants (Singer, "Welfare Reform," pp. 23, 27–28).

16. See statute. Available at: www.uscis.gov/sites/default/files/ocomm/ilink/0-0-0-10948.html, accessed February 24, 2018.

17. For example, see Michael Fix and Ron Haskins, "Welfare Benefits for Non-Citizens" (2002). Available at: www.brookings.edu/research/welfare-benefits-for-non-citizens/, accessed February 24, 2018; Shawn Fremstad, "Recent Welfare Reform Research Findings: Implications for TANF Reauthorization and State TANF Policies" (2004). Available at: www.cbpp.org/1-30-04wel.htm, accessed February 20, 2018.

18. Singer, "Welfare Reform," pp. 29–30.

19. Available at: www.epic.org/privacy/terrorism, accessed February 20, 2018.

20. Available at: https://fas.org/irp/offdocs/eo/mo-111301.htm, accessed February 20, 2018.

21. Human Rights Watch, "United States: Guantanamo Two Years On" (2004). Available at: http://hrw.org/english/docs/2004/01/09/usdom6917.htm, accessed February 20, 2018.

22. James Risen and Eric Lichtblau, "Bush Lets U.S. Spy on Callers Without Courts," *New York Times*, December 16, 2005, A1; Leslie Cauley, "NSA has massive database of Americans' phone calls," *USA Today*, May 11, 2006. Available at: https://usatoday30.usatoday.com/news/washington/2006-05-10-nsa_x.htm, accessed February 24, 2018.

23. Rachel L. Swarns and Christopher Drew, "Aftereffects: Immigrants; Fearful, Angry and Confused, Muslim Immigrants Register," *New York Times*, April 25, 2003, A1.

24. Suleman Din, "Terror City," *ColorLines* 7, No. 3 (2004). Available at: www.colorlines.com/articles/terror-city, accessed February 20, 2018.

25. Maria Panaritis and Jane M. Von Bergen, "Unions Embracing Immigrants," *Philadelphia Inquirer*, September 30, 2003. Available at: www.philly.com/mld/inquirer/news/local/6893203.htm, last accessed July 2006, now available at: www.mombu.com/medicine/t-one-reason-why-immigrant-businesses-are-very-successful-14571179.html, accessed February 24, 2018.

26. Rutenberg, "G.O.P. Draws Line in Border," *New York Times*, May 26, 2006, A1. The story is now available on the *New York Times* website as Jim Rutenberg, "Border Fight Divides G.O.P.," New York Times, May 26, 2006. Available at: www.nytimes.com/2006/05/26/washington/26assess.html, accessed February 24, 2018.

27. The White House, "Statement of the President on H.R. 1540," December 31, 2011. Available at: www.whitehouse.gov/the-press-office/2011/12/31/statement-president-hr-1540, accessed February 20, 2018.

28. Adam Liptak and Michael T. Shear, "Supreme Court Tie Blocks Obama Immigration Plan," *New York Times*, June 23, 2016. available at: www.nytimes.com/2016/06/24/us/supreme-court-immigration-obama-dapa.html?_r=0, accessed February 20, 2018.

29. Jaweed Kaleem, "Federal appeals court allows Trump's travel ban for six Muslim-Majority countries to partially go into effect," *Los Angeles Times*, November 13, 2017. Available at: www.latimes.com/nation/la-na-travel-ban-20171113-story.html, accessed February 24, 2018.

30. David Boroff and Roque Planas, "Romney Says He Favors 'Self-Deportation,'" *New York Daily News*, January 24, 2012. Available at: www.nydailynews.com/news/election-2012/mitt-romney-favors-self-deportation-asked-immigration-gop-debate-article-1.1010812, accessed February 20, 2018.

31. The text of the bill can be found at: www.azleg.gov/legtext/49leg/2r/bills/sb1070s.pdf, accessed February 20, 2018.

32. *Arizona et al.* v. *United States*, U.S. Supreme Court Docket #11–082 (June 25, 2012). Available at: www.supremecourt.gov/opinions/11pdf/11-182b5e1.pdf, accessed February 20, 2018.

33. Daniel Altschuler, "The Georgia and Alabama Anti-Immigration Laws," *Americas Quarterly* (June 24, 2011). Available at: www.americasquarterly.org/node/2611, accessed February 20, 2018.

34. Marc Lacey and Katharine Q. Seelye, "Recall Election Claims Arizona Anti-Immigration Champion," *New York Times*, November 10, 2011, A22.

35. Matthew Green and Jessica Tarlton, "What Are Sanctuary Cities and How Are They Bracing for Trump's Immigration Crackdown?" *The Lowdown: KQED News*, February 7, 2017. Available at: http://ww2.kqed.org/lowdown/2015/07/10/explainer-what-are-sanctuary-cities/, accessed February 20, 2018.

36. Nina Tottenberg, "Trump Questions Neutrality of Muslim and Mexican-American Judges," *NPR Morning Edition*, June 6, 2016. Available at: www.npr.org/2016/06/06/480905889/trump-questions-neutrality-of-muslim-and-mexican-american-judges, accessed February 20, 2018.

10

Good Neighbors and Good Citizens: Beyond the Legal–Illegal Immigration Debate

Noah Pickus and Peter Skerry

PROLOGUE

We wrote "Good Neighbors and Good Citizens" in 2006, when the debate over immigration was stuck in a ditch it had been heading toward for over a decade. Proponents and restrictionists had come to agree that illegal (or undocumented) immigration was a problem that needed to be addressed. Yet they could not agree on either why it was a problem or what to do about it. In 1994, Californians overwhelmingly passed Proposition 187, which, if not struck down by the federal courts, would have denied all variety of public services to the undocumented. So, proponents had come, begrudgingly, to give lip service to the idea of curtailing illegal immigration. Yet these same proponents, mostly liberals but also many business conservatives, persisted in the view that resistance to immigration was driven by nativism and racism. Meanwhile, immigration restrictionists embraced the fight to curtail illegal immigration as a step toward their larger restrictionist goals.

Our argument at the time was that illegal immigration is actually just one of a larger set of concerns about mass immigration that has been riling substantial segments of the American public. While Democratic and Republican political elites of various persuasions were engaged in a Kabuki dance over illegal immigration, we found that many Americans were mainly concerned with the behaviors of millions of unskilled, uneducated immigrants, legal as well as illegal, who had for decades been moving into their neighborhoods, crowding the freeways, sending their kids to local schools, loitering on street corners, and overwhelming hospital emergency rooms. We argued that such concerns were not adequately understood in terms of legalities or formal citizenship requirements, but in more mundane terms having to do with how these newcomers were comporting themselves on a day-to-day basis as neighbors. We further contended that realistic attempts to address these concerns would serve both newcomers and native-born, providing a firmer foundation for a shared social order.

Ten years later, Donald Trump derided Democratic and Republican elites alike for their obtuseness and hypocrisy and rode the issue of uncontrolled immigration to the White House. Now it remains to be seen if that anger and disaffection with globalist elites will morph into a broader restrictionist agenda. If extreme scenarios are to be avoided and America is to maintain its global leadership, our elites must come to a more realistic assessment of the sources of Americans' anxieties and opposition to mass immigration. The focus in our chapter on clarifying the informal bargain by which a common public life is maintained offers one important starting point to achieving those goals.

INTRODUCTION

The year 2006 will go down in history as the year when immigration moved definitively to the center stage of American national politics. For more than 20 years, political elites have been able to contain and marginalize this intractable and emotional issue, dealing with it discreetly and episodically. But over time, the numbers of newcomers – both legal and illegal – have continued to grow and are now reaching historic proportions. Meanwhile, the dispersion throughout the United States of immigrants formerly concentrated in a few gateway states has contributed to the nationalization of this issue.

The politics of immigration changed fundamentally in 2001, when the George W. Bush administration seized on the issue in order to build support among Hispanics and to open a dialogue with Mexico's president, Vicente Fox, one of the few heads of state eager to do business with the new president. This was the rare occasion when a major national political figure did not merely react to events or seek the protective cover of a study commission, but grabbed immigration with both hands to further his own objectives. Sidelined by the terrorist attacks of September 11, 2001, Bush's immigration initiative reemerged in January 2004 with his proposed guestworker program. That proposal jump-started a debate over illegal immigration that was then fueled by tough enforcement legislation passed by the House of Representatives in December 2005. That bill provoked unprecedented demonstrations by illegal immigrants and their supporters in cities across the nation, resulting in a flurry of counter-activity on conservative talk radio. Since then, of course, the debate has hardly subsided.

At the center of this controversy are the approximately 12 million illegal immigrants now living in the U.S. This number is unprecedented, as is the group's homogeneity: almost 80 percent of illegals are Latinos.[1] Further, there is a broad gap in attitudes toward illegal immigration between the vast majority of ordinary Americans and our social, economic, and political elites.[2] Indeed, we believe that part of what is fueling the current reaction is anger among many

Americans that their concerns and complaints about illegal immigrants have for too long been ignored by elites.

We are also critical of our academic colleagues for being insufficiently attentive to the building public outrage over what increasingly looks to be the largest influx of immigrants in our nation's history. More to the point, the American public's anxieties about immigration are not fairly or prudently reduced to racism or nativism. We take our cue here from the late John Higham, the dean of immigration historians and author of the standard work on nativism, *Strangers in the Land: Patterns of American Nativism 1860–1925*.[3] Although his book continues to be widely and approvingly cited by those concerned to underscore the history of prejudice and intolerance toward newcomers in America, Higham himself repeatedly and eloquently distanced himself from such use of his work. In fact, two years after *Strangers in the Land* first appeared in 1955, Higham declared, "I propose that research on the conflicts associated with foreign elements in American society should take a new line. The nativist theme, as defined and developed to date, is imaginatively exhausted."[4] More than 40 years later, Higham was still making this same point.[5]

Following Higham, we believe that a fuller understanding of immigration politics requires moving beyond long dominant academic preoccupations with irrational prejudices and distorting ideologies as the presumed mainsprings of negative reactions to immigrants. Instead, we advocate focusing on the concrete processes and structures of daily life. As Higham acknowledged, this approach entails paying less attention to dramatic and passionate outbursts and more to the mundane contexts of neighborhoods and cities. This is where a myriad of quite rational conflicts of status and interest play out between immigrants and non-immigrants, as well as among various immigrant groups themselves.[6]

Yet this is not to say that the views of Americans – or of the politicians representing them – about immigration should be taken at face value. Even opinions with rational origins can be distorted by perverse political dynamics. Contemporary policy debates often get stuck in frames that politicians and advocates find comfortable, but that do not lead to discussion of meaningful policy options. Immigration is an issue area that seems particularly prone to such distortions.

A case in point is the American public's current preoccupation with illegal immigration. All parties to the current debate share the same unexamined assumption: that legal immigration is benign or even beneficial, while illegal immigration is problematic.[7] Here, we will argue to the contrary that the real challenges do not stem exclusively or even primarily from illegal immigration, but from mass migration itself. Specifically, those challenges involve the social strains and disorder that inevitably accompany any movement of large numbers of unskilled migrants into advanced democratic societies. Were it possible to stop illegal immigration tomorrow, most of the concerns expressed by so many Americans would remain unaddressed.[8]

The high-decibel, popular debate over illegal immigration has proceeded simultaneously with a more muted elite discussion over the meaning of citizenship in contemporary America. Some have expressed concern that immigrants are not naturalizing as quickly or as eagerly as they might. Others are suspicious of the motives of those becoming citizens, in part because of the increased visibility of dual citizenship. Overall, many Americans are convinced that immigrants are "gaming the system" and naturalizing not out of commitment to our values and ideals but for crass, instrumental reasons.

These are different issues, but each reflects widespread anxiety that immigrants are taking advantage of the system, that things are out of control, and that American national identity is being challenged. The parallel debates over illegal immigration and citizenship also both hinge on similar formalistic dichotomies – legal immigrants versus illegal immigrants, citizens versus noncitizens. Now, these categories are hardly incorrect. Indeed, they have intuitive appeal and legal grounding that policymakers ignore at their peril. However, in the contemporary context they get used as legalistic short-hand that obscures the true dilemmas facing us. In our view, rigid adherence to these simple dichotomies has gotten in the way of creative policy responses to the complexities of today's immigration predicament.

In this essay, we will elaborate on the limitations of the legal–illegal and citizen–noncitizen dichotomies; examine why these have nevertheless become so entrenched in the current debate; and offer an alternative way of thinking about these issues that supplements the prevailing preoccupation with the formal, vertical ties between individuals and state institutions with a focus on informal, horizontal relationships. While the current debate asks whether immigrants can be good citizens, we argue that to many Americans the more immediately pressing question is whether immigrants can be good neighbors. To be sure, many communitarians do emphasize this horizontal dimension of civic membership, but they typically neglect the vertical dimension. We argue that both dimensions are critical and that only by paying attention to both can policymakers hope to make rational and fair public policy in this extremely contentious area.

ILLEGAL IMMIGRATION: NUMBERS AND CATEGORIES

The public's anxiety over illegal immigration is hardly unfounded. The Pew Hispanic Center reports that of the 12 million "unauthorized migrants" estimated to be in the U.S. today, 40 percent arrived since 2000. During the first half of the 1990s, about 450,000 illegals arrived here every year. Since 2000, that annual figure has jumped to 850,000.[9]

Over the same period, illegal immigrants have dispersed across the land. In 1990 California had the largest share of the nation's illegals: 45 percent. By 2004 the Golden State still led the nation, but its share had dropped to 24 percent. Meanwhile, the proportion of illegal immigrants ending up in states like North Carolina, Georgia, Tennessee, and other non-traditional destinations more than tripled. As a result, a regional concern has become a national one.[10]

Long before the current furor, it was evident to those who would look that Americans were particularly vexed by illegal immigration. In the early 1990s a *New York Times* poll found that Americans greatly exaggerated the proportion of all immigrants who were in fact illegal.[11] In 1994, California's Proposition 187, which would have banned most public services to illegal immigrants, was passed with support from almost three-fifths of the state's voters, including about one-fifth of Hispanic voters and even greater proportions of Asians.[12]

In 1998, Alan Wolfe reported in *One Nation, After All* that ordinary Americans otherwise uncomfortable with strong moral judgments were not at all reluctant to express moral outrage toward illegal immigrants. Indeed, based on his in-depth interviews across the U.S., Wolfe concluded that the divide between legal and illegal immigrants "is one of the most tenaciously held distinctions in middle-class America; the people with whom we spoke overwhelmingly support legal immigration and express disgust with the illegal variety."[13]

But the watershed event here was Proposition 187. The federal courts eventually gutted this draconian measure. Nevertheless, this was a political earthquake that continues to define the terrain – such that legal immigration is generally regarded as benign, while illegal immigration is seen as the source of most problems.

Before Proposition 187, most politicians – indeed, most officials – studiously avoided the issue of immigration, period. It took a politician as shrewd, tough, and desperate as Governor Pete Wilson to seize on it. Indeed, Wilson salvaged his doomed re-election bid by acknowledging what a majority of Californians felt – that illegal immigration was a critical problem that had to be addressed.

Of course, the price Republicans paid for Wilson's boldness is now political legend. Universally overlooked, however, is that Proposition 187 also chastened immigrant advocates. Before its resounding passage, they vigorously resisted the drawing of any bright lines between legal and illegal immigrants, and rejected labels such as "illegal immigrant" and "illegal alien" in favor of more neutral or positive terms like "undocumented immigrant" and "undocumented worker." But with their backs to the wall after Proposition 187's victory, immigrant advocates retreated to the legal–illegal dichotomy and accepted the fall-back position that attributed negative outcomes associated with immigration to illegals and positive outcomes to legal immigrants. Hence, the still dominant paradigm: "illegal immigrants, bad; legal immigrants, good."

Immigrant advocates are hardly the only ones to have this mind-set. They are joined by skittish politicians and political elites of varied persuasions, who have found this to be a relatively safe way to address a technically complex, emotionally charged issue that they would prefer to avoid completely. For their part, immigration restrictionists went through the obverse process and learned to narrow an array of objections about immigration generally to the problem of illegal immigration specifically. Thus, at some point restrictionists figured out that it was more costly politically to inveigh against Hispanic immigrants than against illegals.

If one must address "immigration," then illegal immigrants – relatively small in number and definitely not well organized or vigorously defended – represent the path of least resistance. To be sure, Proposition 187 taught Republicans that even the illegal immigration card can be overplayed. Nevertheless, illegal immigration – particularly when not explicitly linked to a specific ethnic group – remains the safest way for policymakers and politicians to address this intractable issue.

Now, in recent months immigrant advocates have been arguing for amnesty for millions of illegal immigrants. Does this mean that the line between legal and illegal immigration is becoming less bright? Not really. In fact, the opposite is more nearly true. After all, the case for amnesty has been made on the grounds that illegal immigrants live a separate, second-class existence in a netherworld.

Consider the rhetoric across the political spectrum. A liberal columnist depicts illegals as "living in the shadows."[14] A conservative commentator refers to them as a "huge, subterranean population" that exists in fear of one day being "whisked away by government agents."[15] A Los Angeles religious leader bemoans their exploitation at the hands of "unscrupulous employers" who know they "are reluctant to seek legal recourse."[16] Finally, President Bush has characterized undocumented workers as dwelling "in the shadows of American life – fearful, often abused and exploited."[17]

In a moment, we will argue that such characterizations are misleading, that in fact illegal immigrants are much more integrated into American life than typically understood. But right now, our point is that those arguing for amnesty – to relieve the undeniable burdens on illegal immigrants – actually end up reinforcing that bright line between legals and illegals. And this is just one of many ways that this line gets relied on by political elites.

In fact, the legal–illegal dichotomy makes much more political sense than policy sense. To be sure, illegal immigrants working in remote citrus groves in South Florida[18] or in chicken processing plants in rural Arkansas fit the stereotype. Yet such workers routinely gravitate to urban areas – which is why their employers routinely push for fresh infusions of foreign labor. Once in the cities, illegal immigrants join other immigrants, documented and undocumented alike, in low-paying and arduous service or manufacturing jobs.

One undeniable outcome of this phenomenon is that 59 percent of adult illegals lack health insurance, compared to 25 percent of adult legal immigrants, and 14 percent of natives.[19] Similarly worrisome is the infrequently noted fact (about which immigrant advocates are understandably discreet) that 78 percent of illegals are from Central and South America; 56 percent from Mexico alone.[20] While approximately four-fifths of Latinos are *legal* residents or citizens, the danger nevertheless looms that the public will equate being Latino with being illegal[21]

Despite such troubling indicators, the dominant image of illegal immigrants as a distinctive and isolated group "living in the shadows" is overdrawn. After all, hundreds of thousands have – at least until recent restrictive legislation – applied for and obtained driver's licenses. And how vulnerable could illegal workers be if, as is the case, they have been joining unions in significant numbers? As UCLA sociologist Ruth Milkman observes, undocumented Latinos "have been at the core of the L.A. labor movement's revival."[22]

Similarly suggestive is the number of illegal immigrants who are homeowners. In a study for the American Immigration Law Foundation, Rob Paral presents what he considers a generous estimate of 429,000 undocumented Latino homeowners.[23] A survey of undocumented Mexicans by the Pew Hispanic Center found that at least 10 percent are homeowners.[24] These are necessarily guesstimates. But one way or another, undocumented homeowners number in the hundreds of thousands.

This figure is all the more striking, since mortgages held by illegal immigrants are not, as a matter of policy, purchased on the secondary market by Fannie Mae or Freddie Mac. Pressure from the housing industry to tap into this growing market may change this. But in the meantime, Individual Taxpayer Identification Numbers are being issued to millions of illegal immigrants by the Internal Revenue Service and functioning as an alternative to the social security number necessary to open a bank account and establish a credit rating.[25]

In those homes owned by illegals live many legal immigrants and even citizens. Of the approximately 15 million individuals who live in households where the head or spouse is illegal, about one-fourth are legal. Most of these are children who are U.S. citizens.[26] Looking beyond such households to their relatives and friends, one finds more legal immigrants and citizens, whose presence and support encourage illegals to come here in the first place. In this same vein, the pervasive media image of people sneaking across the Mexican border hardly applies to all 12 million illegals. In fact, as many as 45 percent entered *legally* through a port of entry – as shoppers, workers, tourists – and then overstayed their visas.[27]

On the other side of the ledger, over the decades there have been several amnesties. The last one, in 1986, legalized some 2.7 million aliens.[28] Up until a few years ago, illegal immigrants with children born here (who are therefore citizens) were routinely awarded green cards. Nowadays, every year 50,000 lucky individuals – many of whom are already residing here illegally – win a green card in Homeland Security's Diversity Lottery.[29] Indeed, according to the New Immigrant Survey at Princeton, in a typical year (1996) about one-third of all adult legal immigrants in the U.S. had prior experience here as undocumented immigrants; two-thirds of adult legal Mexican immigrants did.[30]

Then there are the 1–1.5 million among those 12 million illegals whom University of Virginia law professor David Martin estimates to be in "twilight status." Of these, more than 300,000 have Temporary Protected Status (TPS), a category Congress devised in 1990 as a way to avoid either repatriating or granting refugee status to individuals from countries (like El Salvador or Nicaragua) beset by civil war and other unsafe conditions. Some Liberians have been here "temporarily" for 14 years. In any event, those afforded TPS are usually counted among the undocumented.[31]

Martin also points out that as of May 2003, another 617,000 persons were caught up in processing delays waiting to be granted adjustment to "lawful permanent resident" status. All but a small fraction of such persons typically get approved, but they are nevertheless included among the illegals and are technically deportable.[32]

Martin's analysis hardly accounts for all 12 million illegal immigrants in the U.S. today. But it does underscore the fact that a non-trivial number of them are illegal for reasons not entirely of their own making. Indeed, errors and delays by immigration bureaucrats are notorious, and arguably contribute to undermining the rule of law as much as the presence of millions of illegals. In fairness to those bureaucrats, immigration law is a complicated maze of exceptions and deadlines carved out by Congress to accommodate diverse constituencies. These are not only difficult to administer; they are hard to comply with and easy to run afoul of.

Therefore, the conventional understanding of illegal immigrants as conscious law-breakers hardly accounts for all the facts on the ground. While many, indeed most, illegals actively committed a crime – or, to be sure, a misdemeanor – by entering or remaining in the U.S. without authorization, many others have become entangled in a complicated system of rules and regulations that confuses everyone.

BORDER PATROL EMPATHY

There is another, more fundamental source of ambiguity about the line between legal and illegal immigrants. It has surfaced readily and repeatedly in conversations and interviews that one of us has had with scores of Border Patrol agents. Given the opportunity to express their views about the individuals they are charged with apprehending, these federal law enforcement officers routinely volunteer, almost without exception and nearly verbatim: "If I were in their shoes, I would be doing the same thing, coming across that border and trying to better things for me and my family." Ironically, this observation comes from men and women who also readily express frustration about their low status in the federal law enforcement hierarchy and are therefore generally eager to enhance their standing relative to other agencies. Yet just imagine your neighborhood cop similarly empathizing with drug dealers or even petty thieves, and opining that "if I was in that guy's situation, I'd be pushing cocaine, too!"

This ambiguity lies at the heart of our immigration policy dilemmas. How, for example, can one ask Border Patrol agents to risk their lives apprehending illegal immigrants if in an elemental, gut-level sense they and their superiors do not consider the violation in question to be a crime? The answer of course is that one cannot – which is why the Border Patrol long ago abandoned its policy of engaging immigrant smugglers in high-speed pursuits on U.S. highways. Too many serious accidents and fatalities clarified the calculus that the costs far outweighed the perceived benefits from successful pursuits and apprehensions. As a Border Patrol supervisor at a highway checkpoint north of San Diego explained: "The life of one of my agents or of one American citizen is not worth the apprehension of a whole truckload of illegals or of their smuggler."[33]

Border Patrol agents don't need the Catholic bishops or the *New York Times* to tell them that illegal immigrants are not typically criminals.[34] Still, they do their job and detain illegals when they find them.[35] Nevertheless, the trade-offs and moral ambiguities of immigration control pervade all that the Border Patrol does. They clearly contribute to high turnover and low morale at the agency.[36] They also help explain why, for example, agents in the field are so readily drawn into pursuing drug smugglers who operate along our borders – about whose status as *"really* bad guys" there is little or no ambiguity.[37]

If the line between legal and illegal immigration is much fuzzier than it appears, what is bothering Americans? Is it possible that their concerns are both broader and deeper than anyone has bothered to notice? In this connection, it is certainly noteworthy that in one breath Americans denounce illegal immigrants. In the next, they complain about job competition, overcrowded schools, chaotic hospital emergency rooms, and noisy neighborhoods where nobody speaks English – all problems that have more to do with mass migration per se than with its strictly legal component.

Take, for example, the views of independent congressional candidate Jim Gilchrist. Running in a special run-off election in Orange County in December 2005, Gilchrist won 25 percent of the votes in a protest campaign focused exclusively against illegal immigration. But when asked by the *Wall Street Journal* to elaborate, Gilchrist immediately cited concerns about Spanish-speaking newcomers not assimilating, multiculturalism, and overpopulation.[38] Pollsters report similar complaints. Two-thirds of respondents in an April 2005 Fox News poll agreed that illegal immigrants "take jobs away from U.S. citizens," while 87 percent claimed that illegals "overburden government programs and services."[39] In a January 2006 *Time* magazine survey, 63 percent expressed concern that illegals "take jobs away from Americans," and 60 percent agreed that "there are already too many people in the United States."[40]

Whatever their specific merits, none of these or similar problems are unique to illegal immigrants. Indeed, these concerns are explained by readily identifiable factors common to both legal and illegal immigrants: low levels of education and skills, low average age, the strains from the transience of migration, and historically high concentrations of Spanish-speaking immigrants. To be sure, some of these may beset illegal more than legal immigrants. But there is simply no reason to believe that legal and illegal immigrants are starkly different with regard to such salient characteristics. In fact, because there are more legal immigrants than illegal immigrants, the former arguably contribute more to such problems than the latter.

Some of these complaints are wide of the mark in other respects. For example, while immigrants themselves may not be learning as much English as Americans would like, the evidence is that their children and grandchildren certainly are.[41] Neither is there much reason to believe that immigrants are competing directly in the labor market with large numbers of American workers. (The obvious exceptions are low-skilled individuals, including more settled immigrants, especially Latinos, and many African Americans.)[42]

It would be easy therefore to dismiss many such complaints as misguided and ill-informed, even as nativist and racist. Our own reading of the evidence certainly leads us to the conclusion that America is *not* as threatened by the current influx of immigrants as many clearly believe. We do not believe that our society is unraveling.[43]

Yet to cling to expert opinion here is to miss a larger, more important political reality. Both legal and illegal immigrants have become the human face of two sweeping forces: the fraying of local community ties and the decline of national sovereignty. *Bowling Alone*, the title of Robert Putnam's controversial book,[44] has become a national metaphor for the perceived decay of social bonds and traditional institutions that have helped to make a diverse democracy function. At the same time, transformations in communication and transportation have resulted in an increasingly interconnected globe that leaves us unsure about who is part of "our community," as more people live both here and there. However ineptly or even at times harshly they express themselves, large numbers of Americans *do* feel that "things are out of control" and that immigrants are straining the social fabric. Such concerns are not completely unfounded.

Consider day-labor hiring sites, one of the most contentious immigration issues in communities across the nation. For many Americans today, the image of immigrants that most readily comes to mind (aside from shadowy figures running across the border) is of male laborers hanging out near a Home Depot, waiting to be hired by contractors or homeowners. To some, such scenes are evidence of ambition and hard work. But to many others, they represent the annoying, even threatening behavior of unkempt men leering at passing women, darting out into traffic to negotiate with potential employers, drinking and urinating in public, perhaps dealing drugs, and sometimes worse.[45]

Here again, not all such complaints should be taken at face value. Nor should we overlook that day laborers are often mistreated by employers, which is confirmed by findings from the National Day Labor Study at UCLA.[46] That research also indicates that while most day laborers are illegals, one-fourth are legal immigrants.[47]

Yet the UCLA study also confirms that virtually all day laborers are males, more than three-fifths of whom are single or unattached. So, it is not without reason that for many Americans, day laborers have come to personify the transience and social disorder associated with mass migration. At times, such individuals have even been the fodder for civil disturbances that have broken out among immigrants in cities like Miami, Washington, DC, New York City, and of course Los Angeles.[48] Noting that 51 percent of those arrested during the 1992 LA riots were Hispanics, RAND demographers Peter Morrison and Ira Lowry point to "the availability of a large pool of idle young men who had little stake in civil order" as one reason why, in multiethnic states like California, "we ought to expect more riots."[49]

CITIZENSHIP: THE VERTICAL AND THE HORIZONTAL

Similar, though hardly identical, issues arise over the naturalization of today's immigrants. On the one hand, these reflect concerns that the U.S. has reduced citizenship to a thin, one-dimensional relationship, shorn of emotional commitment and focused more on the rights of individuals than on their obligations to the political community. But there is also the perception that immigrants themselves have come to view citizenship in cramped, instrumental terms.

Political scientist Stanley Renshon has written persuasively that in the contemporary world, the real possibility of multiple national memberships renders frequently cited indicators of immigrant economic success insufficient evidence of meaningful attachment to the U.S.[50] The analyst who has raised such questions to the highest visibility is, of course, Samuel Huntington. In his controversial volume, *Who Are We? The Challenges to America's National Identity*, Huntington focuses much of his critical energy on denationalized American elites, who in his view have fostered the weak national commitments that immigrants are now taking advantage of. Notably, Huntington argues that "naturalization is the single most important political dimension of assimilation."[51]

Concerns with the quality of contemporary citizenship are found more among elites than the population at large. They have typically led to calls for more meaningful naturalization ceremonies and more rigorous citizenship exams.[52] Yet the more salient point is that, like popular worries about illegal immigration, elite concerns about citizenship reflect a preoccupation with formal legal categories. Such categories are of fundamental importance, needless to say. But as John Higham reminds us, America's pluralist values call for a "lack of precision in social categories, and a general acceptance of complexity and ambiguity."[53]

Both concerns also reflect the top-down, administrative rationality that the contemporary bureaucratic state inevitably imposes on dense, informal social relations.[54] Thus, when finally compelled to address the issue of immigration, political actors enmeshed in the logic of the administrative state offer responses and "solutions" appropriate for and suited to the tools at their disposal. In the current context, they have focused on refining categories and then policing the new boundaries – whether between legal and illegal immigrants or between citizens and noncitizens.

Such tendencies have been reinforced in recent years by the dramatically increased attention and resources expended on immigration enforcement. Immigration bureaucrats have had to account for themselves. But what if the problems at hand transcend the categories that bureaucrats and politicians have seized upon, or if those problems are not addressed simply by revised citizenship exams and ceremonies? What if they also depend on the horizontal ties between individuals or between individuals and local private or public institutions? Unlike the vertical ties between individuals and the state, which are formal and tend to be episodic, these horizontal relationships are informal, day-to-day, and ongoing.[55]

In our view, the prevailing emphasis on vertical ties overlooks what is at least equally salient to the public about immigrants – regardless of how this public actually articulates its concerns. Most Americans are less worried about immigrants having proper documents or being able to answer questions about American history and politics than their behaving like responsible members of the community. Are immigrants making too much noise? Are they attempting to communicate in English? Are they parking their cars where there is supposed to be grass? Are they crowding too many people into their living quarters? Are they cluttering the neighborhood with abandoned shopping carts or cars? In sum, we believe that when Americans complain about immigrants, their concern is less about immigrants failing to be good *citizens* than about their failing to be good *neighbors*.

Of course, such informal horizontal relations are open to highly subjective, even arbitrary, judgments. They can become the basis of harassment and exclusion of minorities. This is why we are not suggesting that horizontal ties should be looked at exclusively. Indeed, we maintain that citizenship should be defined along *both* the vertical and horizontal axes.

Yet this insight is overlooked by all sides in the current debate. Occasionally, advocates stress immigrants' vertical ties, particularly their paying taxes. More typically, advocates highlight the horizontal ties that immigrants establish, especially good relations with their employers or their children's teachers.[56] But by themselves, these are insufficient. For the matter at hand concerns membership in a political community which can never be reduced simply to social relations.

For their part, immigration critics are preoccupied with the vertical dimension – illegals' lack of formal status. But as we have seen, they are also upset with immigrants' poor horizontal relations. The basic shortcoming of the critics – and of the debate whose terms they have established – is that they ignore the vital distinction between the two dimensions of citizenship, and implicitly collapse all their concerns on to the vertical.

SOCIAL ORDER IN A POLITICAL COMMUNITY

How do we address these constraints? How do we move beyond the unhelpful and misleading formalism and legalism of the current immigration debate toward a meaningful revaluation of citizenship?

A starting point would be to recognize that this is hardly a new problem. Sociologist Philip Selznick reminds us that the liberal theorists who provide the conceptual foundations of our society are heavily reliant on abstractions, including: the state of nature, natural rights, and atomized individuals detached from society, culture, and history. In this same vein, Selznick emphasizes that we are prone to thinking in terms of walls of separation – between individual and society, law and morality, private and public, church and state.[57]

More to the point, Selznick argues for an alternative way of thinking about contemporary society. Reminiscent of Higham, he points out that pluralism necessarily implies a certain messiness: "All societies are composed of different, often contending groups based on kinship, age, occupation, and inequalities of property and power. Pluralism finds in this natural diversity a benign disorder, a vital source of energy and safety."[58] Selznick consequently points to the advantages of boundaries that are *not* bright and rigid: "A common life is furthered when boundaries are blurred – for example, between parenting and teaching, work and recreation, religion and social work."[59] Overarching such specific points is Selznick's broader argument against abstraction in favor of, as he puts it, "the primacy of the particular."[60] He calls for an alternative "conception of individuals as socially embedded persons, products of history and culture, neither idealized nor abstract."[61]

The relative importance of informal horizontal relations over formal vertical ties emerges in varied contexts. The military is a case in point, as underscored by the research of sociologists Edward Shils and Morris Janowitz. In their classic essay, "Cohesion and Disintegration in the Wehrmacht in World War II," Shils and Janowitz found that the effectiveness and cohesion of the German army was traceable not to ideological zeal or indoctrination from above, but to the strong and satisfying primary group relations, especially among infantry and junior officers, fostered by the social dynamics of the German army. As in most settings, the appropriate conclusion is not that formal, vertical relations do not matter. On the contrary, those relations have a lot to do with how well horizontal relationships function. But the broader point is, as Shils and Janowitz noted, that "most men are members of the larger society by virtue of identifications which are mediated through the human beings with whom they are in personal relationships. Many are bound into the larger society only by primary group identifications."[62]

Immigration is the *locus classicus* of these enduring issues. The formalism and legalism of today's complaints about illegal immigrants and citizenship certainly echo those articulated by Progressives in the period leading up to World War I, when the number of immigrants (as a percentage of the population) reached its highest point in our history. Then as now, Americans were alarmed that newcomers were too preoccupied with their own private concerns and were insufficiently attentive to broader community and national goals. Barriers to naturalization were even lower than today, and the process was prone to abuse and corruption. Not unlike today, there were anxieties that citizenship was being devalued and that immigrants were becoming Americans out of the crassest motives. Looming over all such concerns for most Americans was the specter of powerful urban political machines that drew immigrants into the voting booth by catering to their private needs.

Progressive outrage at such abuses led to reforms inspired by a high-minded, dualistic notion of the private and the public. From this perspective, the goal was to reinforce the boundary between the two realms. Requirements for citizenship were raised. So were barriers to electoral politics. Voter registration was instituted as a disincentive to immigrant voting, which remained depressed for a generation until the New Deal. Patronage hiring was curtailed by civil service reforms that reflected the Progressive view that the influence of disinterested, scientific experts housed in legal-rational bureaucracies needed to be enhanced. Not all these reforms were equally effective, but the intellectual ethos that informed them was clear: to cleanse the public domain of petty, private interests. The overall objective of such reforms – sometimes intended, sometimes not – was to exclude immigrants and their families from the civic realm on the grounds that they were inadequately prepared for it.[63] Ultimately, this perspective led many Progressives to advocate immigration restriction.[64]

By contrast, Jane Addams represented a different current of Progressivism. As Jean Bethke Elshtain explains in her biography of the founder of Hull House, Addams was as troubled about the integration of immigrants into American civic life as her fellow Progressives. But unlike many of them, Addams saw the domestic arena as a springboard into wider civic life rather than an inhibition to matters civic."[65] Unlike the principled reformers and dogmatic socialists who either denigrated or just ignored the narrow, even petty, concerns of uneducated immigrants, Addams used those private preoccupations to draw them into the civic arena. Among the immigrant wives and mothers with whom Addams often worked, those preoccupations were strictly domestic and rigidly defined. Nevertheless, Addams taught such women how their families' health and well-being – for example, with regard to garbage collection – depended on much more than keeping their own homes clean.

Accordingly, Addams got embroiled in "the garbage wars" in Chicago's 19th ward, to the point of being appointed garbage inspector. No mere bureaucratic sinecure, this meant getting up at six in the morning to make sure that the garbage collectors were doing their job. Addams did this by enlisting the help of the immigrant women who were her neighbors at Hull House. Over time, the results were impressive. Eventually, the death rate in the ward was reduced.[66]

Yet those efforts definitely clashed with how immigrant women defined their duties and responsibilities. As Addams explained in *Twenty Years at Hull House:*

Many of the foreign-born women of the ward were much shocked by this abrupt departure into the ways of men, and it took a great deal of explanation to convey the idea even remotely that if it were a womanly task to go about in tenement houses in order to nurse the sick, it might be quite as womanly to go through the same district in order to prevent the breeding of so-called "filth diseases."[67]

Such attempts to build bridges between the private concerns of immigrant women and the broader public realm led Addams to her notion of "municipal housekeeping." As Elshtain explains, this did not imply that politics could be replaced by housekeeping on a grand scale. Rather Addams's point was to socialize politics by bringing some of the concerns and virtues of the private realm, especially as experienced by wives and mothers, into the public arena.[68]

In a similar way, Addams resisted the heavy-handed efforts of the Americanization movement, which sought to integrate immigrants and their children by encouraging them to make a sharp break with the history and culture of their country of origin.[69] On the contrary, Addams encouraged immigrants to respect and build on their past while pursuing integration into the American culture.[70] As Addams wrote:

We were often distressed by the children of immigrant parents who were ashamed of the pit whence they were digged, who repudiated the language and customs of their elders, and counted themselves successful as they were able to ignore the past.[71]

To such immigrants, Addams and her Hull House colleagues held up the example of an American like Abraham Lincoln as someone who relied on his appreciation of the past to guide his current and future actions.[72]

Perhaps the most apt support for the point we are making about the importance of informal horizontal ties comes from social scientists who have in recent decades developed an alternative understanding of crime and ways to address it. James Q. Wilson began his 1968 study, *Varieties of Police Behavior*, by observing that "the patrolman's role is defined more by his responsibility for *maintaining order* than by his responsibility for enforcing the law."[73] Written by a conservative in the midst of a nationwide crime wave that was leading to widespread demands for "law and order," this is a striking observation. It suggests that in the midst of today's demands to get tough on illegal immigration, it would be similarly helpful to move beyond the legalistic terms of the current debate. And it once again suggests that the public's anxieties ought not to be dismissed as racist, but neither ought they to be taken at face value. What lurks just beneath the surface of Americans' inarticulate, and sometimes harsh, rhetoric are not unreasonable concerns that record numbers of immigrants are threatening the maintenance of social order.

Twenty years after his initial insight, Wilson and a colleague, George Kelling, published the widely cited article, "Broken Windows."[74] In the subsequent book by that title, Kelling and Coles called for nothing less than the reconceptualization of crime, away from formal status criteria and toward behavioral criteria. They argued that law enforcement should be less concerned with *loiterers* and more focused on *behaviors* that are associated with loitering but are nevertheless specific offenses – such as petty vandalism, public urination, or drunken and disorderly behavior.[75]

These insights about order maintenance and crime suggest to us that we should be less concerned whether immigrants are here legally, or why they are naturalizing. Instead, we should focus more on whether they are *behaving* like responsible, law-abiding members of the political community. For example, are they steadily employed? Are they making sure their children attend school regularly? Are they seriously attempting to learn English? Are they learning about American culture, history, and politics so that they might become knowledgeable, active citizens? Are they involved in local community life? Are they avoiding difficulties with the law? In other words, are immigrants demonstrating through their actions that they intend to become part of the social and political fabric of America; or are they behaving as if they are here provisionally with some other end in view?[76]

Fragments of the perspective being outlined here can be identified in a few programs and proposals. In Chicago, for example, a consortium of predominantly Mexican-immigrant Catholic churches called The Resurrection Project provides housing opportunities – both rental and owner-occupied units – to parishioners. Eager to avoid becoming a mere service provider, the Project requires beneficiaries of its housing programs to meet specific behavioral conditions. In the case of rental housing, these conditions include the protection of the property and attempts to prolong its life. The Project is concerned to develop a stronger sense of commitment, particularly among immigrants who don't always exhibit those traits – either because they are too busy struggling to make ends meet, or because they may be planning to return home to Mexico.[77] As the chief executive officer of the organization put it: "When our residents buy one of our houses, they are buying part of our community."[78]

The State of California's Little Hoover Commission has proposed what would be another example. In a report entitled *We the People: Helping Newcomers Become Californians*, the Commission called for the establishment of "The Golden State Residency Program," in which all immigrants – regardless of their formal legal status – could participate. The guiding principle here would be to commit governmental resources to immigrants who demonstrate through their behavior that they intend to become responsible members of the community. The report mentions several criteria by which to judge immigrant behavior:

- responsibility to the local community, as indicated by a history of paying taxes, remaining in good standing with law enforcement agencies, and where appropriate, being employed or engaged in workforce development and training;
- proficiency in English, as demonstrated by actual skills or enrollment in appropriate programs;
- participation in civic affairs; for example, in public, volunteer and community-based programs;
- responsibility for children and other family members, as demonstrated by care for dependent family members and enrollment of children in school and health plans.

In return for satisfying such criteria, immigrant enrollees would become eligible for benefits that might include: a driver's license, in-state tuition at public colleges and universities, eligibility for public health insurance, and even welfare support.[79]

The Commission even suggests that participants in the Golden State Residency Program be put on track for citizenship – even those who are here illegally.[80] This would clearly be controversial, and perhaps ill-advised. But any such program component could be optional, with specific details tailored to the preferences and values of individual states.

Programs providing benefits to illegal immigrants could even coexist with rigorous enforcement of our immigration laws, especially by federal authorities along the borders and ports of entry as well as at workplaces. We have no illusions that this would be easy. Tensions and inconsistencies would arise. But if efforts like the Golden State Residency Program were allowed to address gnawing but unacknowledged problems, then that would be better than the status quo, which is also rife with inconsistencies.

A further advantage of programs such as those the Little Hoover Commission has proposed is that they would make more explicit the terms of the bargain struck between immigrants and American society. This would be helpful to everyone – immigrants and non-immigrants alike. Immigrants would benefit because such programs would make clear to them what Americans expect of them. Indeed, non-immigrants tend to overlook the confusing signals this diverse society sends out to newcomers. Certainly, in recent decades we have taken a decidedly laissez-faire approach to the integration of immigrants.[81] As one astute immigrant organizer in Chicago put it: "I wish to hell someone would make it clear how we're supposed to act here!"[82]

But endeavors like the Golden State Residency Program would be even more helpful to non-immigrants. If Americans want immigrants to join our political community, then we need to show them how to do that. Yet this is precisely the area where we have the most cause for self-reproach. Contrary to the usual complaints, Americans are not particularly guilty of racial or ethnic prejudice toward immigrants. But we *are* guilty of a certain smug complacency. All too often, we unthinkingly assume that because immigrants have gained an opportunity for which there is clearly an oversupply of takers, they should be content just to be here, and that we have fulfilled our end of the bargain. Initiatives like the Golden State Residency Program require us to turn vague assumptions into conscious choices, and to negotiate an explicit, realistic bargain that asks something of both sides.

In this essay, we have been concerned to highlight the importance of informal, horizontal relations in the current debate over illegal immigration. Ultimately, though, the bargain described here speaks to the *political* community, whose formal, vertical ties of membership benefit from explicit articulation and choice. It would behoove America's newcomers to express clearly both their desire to become members of the American political community *and* their commitment to its terms. But that cannot happen unless those who already belong to that community do a better job of defining just what those terms are.

NOTES

1. Jeffrey S. Passel, "The Size and Characteristics of the Unauthorized Migrant Population in the U.S.: Estimates Based on the March 2005 Current Population Survey," *Research Report* (Washington, DC: Pew Hispanic Center, 7 March 2006), p. 5.
2. *American Public Opinion and Foreign Policy: Global Views 2004* (Chicago: Chicago Council on Foreign Relations, 2004), pp. 12–13, 47–48.
3. John Higham, *Strangers in the Land: Patterns of American Nativism 1860–1925* (New York: Atheneum, 1975).
4. John Higham, "Another Look at Nativism," in John Higham, *Send These To Me: Jews and Other Immigrants in Urban America* (New York: Atheneum, 1975), p. 103.
5. John Higham, "Instead of a Sequel, or, How I Lost My Subject," in *The Handbook of International Migration: The American Experience*, eds. Charles Hirschman, Philip Kasinitz, and Josh DeWind (New York: Russell Sage Foundation, 1999), pp. 383–389.
6. Higham, "Another Look at Nativism," pp. 106–108; see also Higham, "Ethnic Pluralism in Modern American Thought" and "Another American Dilemma," in *Send These To Me*, pp. 196–246.
7. See recent polling data in "America's Immigration Quandary: No Consensus on Immigration Problem or Proposed Fixes" (Washington, DC: Pew Hispanic Center, 30 March 2006), p. 13.

8. This point gets elaborated upon in Peter Skerry and Devin Fernandes, "Citizen Pain: Fixing the Immigration Debate," *The New Republic*, May 8, 2006, 14–16.

9. Passel, "The Size and Characteristics of the Unauthorized Migrant Population in the US," pp. 2–3.

10. Jeffrey S. Passel, "Unauthorized *Migrants: Numbers and Characteristics – Background Briefing Prepared for Task Force on Immigration and America's Future,"* (Washington, DC: Pew Hispanic Center, 14 June 2005), pp. 11–13.

11. Seth Mydans, "Poll Finds Tide of Immigration Brings Hostility," *New York Times*, June 27, 1993, A1, A16.

12. "Demographic Profile of the Electorate: November 8, 1994," *Los Angeles Times Election Poll*.

13. Alan Wolfe, *One Nation, After All* (New York: Viking, 1998), p. 147.

14. Ronald Brownstein, "Bush Needs to Imitate Clinton to Solve Immigration," *Los Angeles Times*, July 23, 2001, A10.

15. Linda Chavez, "Legalizing Immigrants Just Makes Sense," *Chicago Sun-Times*, July 18, 2001, 47.

16. Cardinal Roger Mahony, "Immigrant Workers Deserve Legal Status and Respect," *Los Angeles Times*, June 8, 2000, 13.

17. Quoted in Edward Alden and Scott Heiser, "A Border War: Why America Is Split Over Its Rising Numbers of Illegal Immigrants," *Financial Times*, August 29, 2005, 11.

18. See John Bowe, "Nobodies: Does Slavery Exist in America," *New Yorker*, 21 and 28 April 2003, 106–133.

19. Passel, "Unauthorized Migrants: Numbers and Characteristics," p. 35.

20. Passel, "The Size and Characteristics of the Unauthorized Migrant Population in the U.S.," p. 5.

21. Derived from the numbers cited in footnote 19 and the Census Bureau's 2005 estimate of the total number of Hispanics in the U.S. – 42.7 million.

22. Ruth Milkman, "Immigrant Organizing and the New Labor Movement in Los Angeles," *Critical Sociology* 26 (2000): 59.

23. Rob Paral, "The Potential for New Homeownership among Undocumented Latino Immigrants," prepared for the National Association of Hispanic Real Estate Professionals, no date.

24. Roberto Suro, *Survey of Mexican Immigrants – Part One: Attitudes about Immigration and Major Demographic Characteristics* (Washington, DC: Pew Hispanic Center; March 2, 2005), pp. 10, 23.

25. Marti Dinerstein, "Giving Cover to Illegal Aliens: IRS Tax ID Numbers Subvert Immigration Law," *Backgrounder* (Washington, DC: Center for Immigration Studies; November 2002).

26. Passel, "The Size and Characteristics of the Unauthorized Migrant Population in the U.S.," pp. 6–9.

27. "Modes of Entry for the Unauthorized Population," *Fact Sheet* (Washington, DC: Pew Hispanic Center, 22 May 2006), p. 1.

28. Douglas S. Massey and Nolan Malone, "Pathways to Legal Immigration," *Population Research and Policy Review* 21 (2002): 474.

29. For an instructive critique of this program, see Mark Krikorian, "Taking Chances: The Folly of the Visa Lottery," *Backgrounder* (Washington, DC: Center for Immigration Studies, July 2004).

30. Massey and Malone, "Pathways to Legal Immigration," 477–479, 484–486.
31. David A. Martin, "Twilight Statuses: A Closer Examination of the Unauthorized Population," *Policy Brief* (Washington, DC: Migration Policy Institute, June 2005).
32. Martin, "Twilight Statuses," p. 6.
33. Peter Skerry, field interview notes with the U.S. Border Patrol; February 13–27, 1998.
34. On the Catholic Church's position, see Donald Kerwin, "Immigration Reform and the Catholic Church," *Migration Information Source* (Washington, DC: Migration Policy Institute, 1 May 2006). Also, Roger Mahony, "Called by God to Help," *New York Times*, March 22, 2006, A 19.
35. This is actually a very complicated issue. Like most law enforcement, immigration control is highly discretionary. For a now dated but still invaluable treatment of this question, see Edwin Harwood, *In Liberty's Shadow: Illegal Aliens and Immigration Law Enforcement* (Stanford, CA: Hoover Institution Press, 1986).
36. Stephen Losey, "When Alien Smugglers Go Free, Morale Suffers at Border Patrol," *FederalTimes.com*, June 7, 2006. This has long been a problem for immigration law enforcement; see George J. Weissinger, "Law Enforcement and the Immigration and Naturalization Service: Resolving an Apparent Contradiction," (Ph.D. dissertation, New York University Press, 1982), pp. 74–76.
37. Peter Skerry, field interview notes with the U.S. Border Patrol along the California–Mexico border, 1996–1998.
38. Miriam Jordan, "California Race Highlights Split on Immigration," *Wall Street Journal*, October 18, 2005, B1, B9.
39. FOX News/Opinion Dynamics Poll, April 5–6, 2006.
40. *Time*, January 27, 2006.
41. Richard Alba and Victor Nee, *Remaking the American Mainstream: Assimilation and Contemporary Immigration* (Cambridge: Harvard University Press, 2003), pp. 217–230.
42. See George Borjas and Lawrence Katz, "The Evolution of the Mexican-Born Workforce in the United States," *NBER Working Paper* No. 11281 (Cambridge: National Bureau of Economic Research, 2005).
43. Here we agree with Stanley Renshon, who puts it well when he acknowledges among Americans today "the premature, but not unrealistic, concern of our potential evolution into a country in which separate psychological, cultural, and political loyalties trump a coherent national identity." See Stanley A. Renshon, *The 50% American: Immigration and National Identity in an Age of Terror* (Washington, DC: Georgetown University Press, 2005), p. 144.
44. Robert D. Putnam, *Bowling Alone: The Collapse and Revival of American Community* (New York: Simon and Schuster, 2000).
45. For an early and thoughtful analysis of this problem, see Todd A. Eisenstadt and Cathryn L. Thorup, *Caring Capacity versus Carrying Capacity: Community Responses to Mexican Immigration in San Diego's North County* (Center for U.S.-Mexican Studies, UCSD, 1994).
46. Abel Valenzuela Jr., Nik Theodore, Edwin Meléndez, and Ana Luz Gonzalez, *On the Corner: Day Labor in the United States* (Center for the Study of Urban Poverty, UCLA, January 2006), 14–16.
47. Valenzuela, *On the Corner*, 17.

48. Michael Jones-Correa, ed., *Governing American Cities: Inter-Ethnic Coalitions, Competition, and Conflict* (New York: Russell Sage Foundation, 2001); Patrick D. Joyce, *No Fire Next Time: Black-Korean Conflicts and the Future of America's Cities* (Ithaca: Cornell University Press, 2003).

49. Peter A. Morrison and Ira S. Lowry, "A Riot of Color: The Demographic Setting," in Mark Baldassare (ed.), *The Los Angeles Riots: Lessons for the Urban Future* (Boulder: Westview Press, 1994), pp. 38, 43.

50. See Renshon, *The 50% American*, pp. 222–223.

51. Samuel P. Huntington, *Who Are We? The Challenges to America's National Identity* (New York: Simon and Schuster, 2004), p. 238.

52. See Representative Lamar Smith, as quoted on *Morning Edition*, National Public Radio, March 25, 1997; John Fonte, testimony given at U.S. Senate, Committee on the Judiciary, Subcommittee on Immigration, *Hearing on Naturalization Requirements and the Rights and Privileges of Citizenship* (22 October 1996); John J. Miller, "The Naturalizers," *Policy Review* (July–August 1996): 50, 52; John J. Miller, *The Unmaking of Americans: How Multiculturalism Has Undermined the Assimilation Ethic* (New York: Free Press, 1998), p. 149; and Georgie Anne Geyer, *Americans No More: The Death of Citizenship* (New York: Atlantic Monthly Press, 1996), chapters 2–4. See also Peter Salins, *Assimilation, American-Style* (New York: Basic Books, 1997), p. 215; Noah Pickus, *True Faith and Allegiance: Immigration and American Civic Nationalism* (Princeton, NJ: Princeton University Press, 2005), pp. 175–178.

53. Higham, "Another American Dilemma," in *Send These to Me*, p. 243.

54. James C. Scott, *Seeing Like a State: How Certain Schemes to Improve the Human Condition Have Failed* (New Haven and London: Yale University Press, 1998).

55. A similar point is made in Krishna Guha, "Ethnic Communities Can Be Devout as Well as Good Citizens," *Financial Times*, July 16–17, 2005, 7.

56. For an exploration of these issues in the context of one suburban community, see Peter Skerry, "Immigration and Social Disorder," in Norton Garfinkle and Daniel Yankelovich (eds.), *Uniting America: Restoring the Vital Center to American Democracy* (New Haven: Yale University Press, 2006), pp. 124–138.

57. Philip Selznick, *The Communitarian Persuasion* (Washington, DC: Woodrow Wilson Center Press, 2002), pp. 103, 136–137; Philip Selznick, *The Moral Commonwealth: Social Theory and The Promise of Community* (Berkeley: University of California Press, 1992).

58. Selznick, *The Communitarian Persuasion*, p. 44.

59. Selznick, *The Communitarian Persuasion*, p. 20.

60. Selznick, *The Communitarian Persuasion*, p. 150.

61. Selznick, *The Communitarian Persuasion*, p. 42.

62. Edward Shils and Morris Janowitz, "Cohesion and Disintegration in the Wehrmacht in World War II," in *Edward Shils, Center and Periphery: Essays in Macrosociology* (Chicago and London: University of Chicago Press, 1975), p. 383. See also Morris Janowitz, *The Reconstruction of Patriotism: Education for Civic Consciousness* (Chicago and London: University of Chicago Press, 1983).

63. A recent exploration of this dynamic in the context of the American Southwest can be found in Amy Bridges, *Morning Glories: Municipal Reform in the Southwest* (Princeton: Princeton University Press, 1997).

64. One treatment of this tendency can be found in Daniel J. Tichenor, *Dividing Lines: The Politics of Immigration Control in America* (Princeton: Princeton University Press, 2002), pp. 75–85, 114–149.

65. Jean Bethke Elshtain, *Jane Addams and the Dream of American Democracy: A Life* (New York: Basic Books, 2002), p. 77.

66. Elshtain, *Jane Addams and the Dream of American Democracy*, pp. 168–173.

67. *Jane Addams, Twenty Years at Hull House* (New York: New American Library, 1981), p. 204.

68. Elshtain, *Jane Addams and the Dream of American Democracy*, pp. 161–163.

69. For an informative and balanced analysis of the Americanization movement that contrasts it with the perspective developed by University of Chicago sociologists with whom Addams was in contact, see Janowitz, *The Reconstruction of Patriotism*, pp. 85–94. See also Morris Janowitz, *Last Half-Century: Societal Change and Politics in America* (Chicago and London: The University of Chicago Press, 1978), pp. 305–306, 453–454.

70. For an informative but critical analysis of Addams and her Progressive colleagues, see Rivka Shpak Lissak, *Pluralism and Progressives: Hull House and the New Immigrants, 1890–1919* (Chicago: University of Chicago Press, 1989), especially pp. 157–181.

71. Addams, *Twenty Years at Hull House*, p. 42.

72. Addams, *Twenty Years at Hull House*, pp. 41–42; see also Elshtain, *Jane Addams and the Dream of American Democracy*, pp. 52–53.

73. James Q. Wilson, *Varieties of Police Behavior: The Management of Law and Order in Eight Communities* (Cambridge, MA: Harvard University Press), p. 16.

74. George L. Kelling and James Q. Wilson, "Broken Windows: The Police and Neighborhood Safety," *The Atlantic* 249 (March 1982): 3, 29–38.

75. George L. Kelling and Catherine M. Coles, *Fixing Broken Windows: Restoring Order and Reducing Crime in Our Communities* (New York: The Free Press, 1996).

76. We acknowledge that there is another possible inference about immigration to be drawn from Wilson and Kelling's work. After all, their approach to crime also meant convincing law enforcement professionals to pay more attention to the minor offenses that they traditionally disdained as "social work." Given the ambiguity surrounding illegal immigration that we have emphasized here, one might conclude that Wilson and Kelling's perspective points to waging a campaign to eliminate that ambiguity and persuading law enforcement and the public alike that illegal immigration is an offense worthy of law enforcement's attention. A relevant analogy would be the transformation in public attitudes toward drunken driving wrought by Mothers Against Drunk Driving. Nevertheless, it is our judgment that the ambiguous status of illegal immigration is much more deeply rooted in contemporary American life and not likely to be changed in this way.

77. On the intention of Mexican illegal immigrants to not settle permanently and to return home, see Leo R. Chavez, *Shadowed Lives: Undocumented Immigrants in American Society*, Second Edition (Fort Worth: Harcourt Brace College Publishers, 1998). See also Massey and Malone, "Pathways to Legal Immigration."

78. Peter Skerry, "Citizenship Begins at Home: A New Approach to the Civic Integration of Immigrants," *The Responsive Community* (Winter 2003/04): 30.

79. *We the People: Helping Newcomers Become Californians* (Sacramento, CA: Little Hoover Commission; June 2002), pp. 34–35, 50–54.

80. *We the People*, p. 47.

81. A similar point is made in Renshon, *The 50% American*, pp. 179–181.

82. Skerry, "Citizenship Begins at Home," p. 28.

Federalism and the Politics of Immigration Reform[*]

Carol M. Swain and Virginia M. Yetter

The National Government has significant power to regulate immigration. With power comes responsibility, and the sound exercise of national power over immigration depends on the Nation's meeting its responsibility to base its laws on a political will informed by searching, thoughtful, rational civic discourse. Arizona may have understandable frustrations with the problems caused by illegal immigration while that process continues, but the State may not pursue policies that undermine federal law.

Justice Stevens (Majority)[1]

INTRODUCTION

What happens when the national government fails to do its job? In *Arizona* v. *United States*, the U.S. Supreme Court upheld the federal government's ability to prevent a state from enacting certain types of immigration laws and regulations perceived by the state as necessary to fill a void in federal enforcement. Nevertheless, the Court allowed the state to continue background checks on people detained for other purposes. Immigration would seemingly work best if different levels of government agreed to coordinate their efforts and share enforcement power. Shared and overlapping powers between the federal government and the individual states lie at the heart of constitutional federalism. It is how our political system was meant to work. Malcolm Feeley and Ed Rubin describe federalism as a means of governance "that grants partial autonomy to geographically defined subdivisions of the polity." Accordingly, they explain that a "political entity that is governed by a single central government making all significant decisions cannot be described as federal without abandoning the ordinary meaning of the term.[2] Under a federal arrangement, subunits can have considerable authority in certain spheres that

* Significant portions of this chapter were previously published in Jeffrey Jenkins and Sid Milkus *The Politics of Major Policy Reform in Postwar America* (New York: Cambridge University Press, 2014), pp. 179–202.

overlap with the jurisdictional areas of the central government. Federalism was designed to operate as an important check against the centralized powers of the national government.

The foundation for federalism is found in eight constitutional amendments and in Articles I and VI. Article I, Section 8 lists the enumerated powers of the federal government and contains the "necessary and proper clause," which gives Congress the authority to pass laws that are necessary for it to carry out its enumerated powers. Article VI's Supremacy Clause makes clear that federal laws trump state laws whenever conflicts occur. The 10th Amendment forms the basis for an expansive view of the rights of states to look after the common welfare of their inhabitants. It states that "the powers not delegated to the United States by the Constitution, nor prohibited by it to the States, are reserved to the States respectively, or to the people." In many areas, the state and federal government share concurrent powers. Areas of shared and overlapping power include education, healthcare, and immigration as well as traditional areas such as taxing, borrowing, and spending money; enacting general legislation; and regulating election times and places. In recent years, state activism on immigration reform appears to be pervasive and growing. Nevertheless, it remains a policy area where state governments have lost and continue to lose considerable power to the federal government.

Changes in the percentage of foreign-born and undocumented persons in the United States have no doubt encouraged state and local governments to wade into the controversial waters of immigration reform. With few exceptions, these bills have met with considerable resistance from those who believe that states have overstepped their bounds. In December 2011, the National Conference of State Legislatures reported that state legislators "introduced 1,607 bills and resolutions relating to immigrants and refugees in all 50 states and Puerto Rico." These numbers represented an increase over 2010, when 46 states considered more than 1,400 immigration bills and resolutions. However, most of these bills were not enacted. Eleven percent fewer bills were passed in 2011. Forty-two states and Puerto Rico enacted 197 new laws and 109 resolutions totaling 306 for the year. Fifteen bills that were passed by state legislatures died at the hands of governors who vetoed the bills.[3]

The concept of immigration federalism was birthed during the late 1990s when legal scholars observed the increasing tendency of state and local governments to pass laws and ordinances pertaining to immigration. Clare Huntington argues that by 2008, state activism had become "a central political issue of our times."[4] Much of the discussion surrounding immigration federalism has focused on the constitutionality of state intervention in an area many legal experts say is reserved for the federal government. Other scholars have grudgingly acknowledged a role for state governments even while expressing deeply held fears that state and local governments cannot be trusted to protect the civil rights and civil liberties of racial and ethnic minorities.[5] Although examples of nonfederal involvement in immigration abound, such involvement leaves some legal scholars questioning whether this allocation of authority is justified by our constitutional tradition and the cases surrounding it.[6]

Bosniak argues that there are two distinct questions about immigrants that guide how they should be treated in the regulatory system. There are questions about admission, deportation, and political asylum that clearly fall into the purview of the federal government, and there are other issues that concern how people are treated once they are here.[7] Access to legal rights, criminal procedures, education, healthcare, and welfare benefits fall into the category of alienage law. Alienage law "is a composite of rules and standards set by state and federal law across a wide variety of regulatory domains" where aliens are only one of many potential groups affected by the law.[8]

Bosniak points out that courts have traditionally drawn a sharp distinction between permissible areas of regulation based on the content of suggested policies. If legislation governs removal or admission of immigrants, referred to as "pure" immigration, the federal government controls policy choice; if the legislation governs rights and obligations of noncitizens while in the country, states may jointly govern.[9]

Due to the profound impact of immigration on state and local governmental budgets, these entities often act out of desperation in response to the failure of the federal government to act. Although the federal government has been the dominant force in immigration for more than 100 years, the recent increase in state and local involvement in immigration issues offers a real hope for policy change and innovation.

This chapter provides a historical background of immigration policy that shows federal dominance over the last century. The rise in immigration federalism became particularly pronounced in the late 1990s and the 2000s. We concur with scholars who argue that the Constitution does not forbid state involvement in immigration reform.[10] We believe that state invention can be a positive force for change because it offers new possibilities for innovative policy solutions. In fact, state action can become the needed boost that Congress needs to stop kicking the can down the road and begin to exercise its power under the Supremacy Clause to reform the policy.

If states overstep their bounds, the national government can preempt by statute and by the Supremacy Clause. As recently as 2012, the Court reaffirmed the position of federal dominance in its ruling in *Arizona* v. *United States*.[11] The Court concluded that the federal government's broad power over immigration and alien status rests, in part, on its constitutional power to "establish and uniform Rule of Naturalization," and on Article I, Section 8, Clause 4's acknowledgment of the federal government's inherent sovereign power to control and conduct foreign relations.[12]

HISTORICAL BACKGROUND

For more than 100 years our nation has struggled with its immigration policy. The struggle is evidenced in the public backlash against the Irish in the 1840s, and the Chinese in the 1880s. Early concerns about the foreign-born population particularly the Irish Catholics, led to the birth of the Know Nothing Movement, composed of white Protestant nativists alarmed by the rapidly growing Irish Catholic population.[13] Roger Daniels argues that restrictionist immigration policies were birthed in 1882 with the Chinese Exclusion Act[14] and that it extended through congressional adoption of a literacy test in 1917.[15] These efforts helped determine who could legally enter the United States and on what terms, thereby touching at the core of what shapes and defines an American identity.[16]

At the beginning of the twentieth century, immigrants primarily traveled from Europe; by the end of the century, immigrants were predominantly from Asia and Latin America. Although immigrants in the first half of the twentieth century were motivated by the prospect of employment, immigrants today are often drawn to immigrate in order to be reunited with family and enjoy political freedom.[17] Yet despite the significant shift in the nature of immigration over the years, many of the issues of the past remain constant. Influxes of new immigrants create concern about job competition and the direct and indirect impact on low-wage, low-skill Americans, particularly African Americans, legal Hispanics, and poor whites. In addition, new concerns about the rising cost of entitlement programs and additional burdens unskilled immigrants can place on the strained budgets of local governments can come into play. Public debate about the impact on the nation is tempered by the frequency in which allegations of nativism and racism are hurled against organizations that have argued against unrestricted immigration.

Despite reforms toward the end of the twentieth century, immigration remains one of the most divisive political issues today. No major reform has been enacted into federal law since 1986, and policy preferences have found expression through state action. Although the politics of immigration policy were once dominated by labor unions and policy groups, states have proved essential parties to success in the twenty-first century. The challenges created by expanding legal immigration and the out-of-control growth of illegal immigration demand new solutions to perennial problems.

IMMIGRATION AND NATIONALITY ACT OF 1965 (THE HART CELLAR ACT)

The 1960s was an era of massive social and political change that resulted in the passage of four major civil rights acts: The 1963 Equal Pay Act; the Civil Rights Act of 1964, which outlawed discrimination in public accommodations; the Voting Rights Act of 1965; and the Open Housing Act of 1968, which prohibited discrimination in the rental and sale of houses.[18] Alongside these domestic changes, Congress passed the Hart-Cellar Act, which eliminated racist national-origin quotas that had existed since the 1920s; instituted a family reunification policy that established priority for close relatives of naturalized citizens; and established an immigration policy that favored highly skilled professionals, scientists, and artists along with unskilled laborers for jobs in fields experiencing labor shortage.

A general assumption surrounding the creation of the Hart-Cellar Act was that the volume and nature of immigration would not change with the elimination of nation-based quotas. However, the Hart-Cellar Act had the unintended consequence of radically changing the racial and ethnic complexion of America. The two most noteworthy changes from the act were a significant expansion in legal immigration from Asia and increased movement of undocumented workers across the U.S.–Mexico border. Although the majority of immigrants previous to passage of the law were European, the secondary emphasis on skilled workers allowed for an influx of Asian immigrants. Visas for Asian professionals quickly overwhelmed the quota allotted for skilled workers. As these professionals immigrated, they soon brought their families from abroad.

The Act placed quotas on the Western Hemisphere for the first time, leading to the second unexpected effect of increased border crossings between Mexico and the United States. In a piece of legislation that lifted so many barriers to immigration, this restrictive provision is often overlooked. Previous to 1965, Canada and Mexico had enjoyed unlimited visas as neighboring economies. Following passage of the law, economic crisis gripped Latin America, increasing immigrant flow into the United States. The growing Mexican-American population led to expanding influence for ethnic rights groups, which would play an important role in the immigration reform of the coming decades.

Prior to passage of the law, politicians argued any change in the ethnic makeup of immigration was unlikely. The act permitted immigrants to bring in not only spouses and children, but parents and siblings as well. It was thought that prioritization of family unification ensured the dominance of immigration from Europe. However, the impact of the law quickly disproved these theories: of the ten countries that predominantly sent immigrants in 1965, only two (Germany and Italy) were among the nations the State Department predicted would send the most immigrants in 1969.[19] By the 1980s, immigrants from Asia and Latin America constituted the majority of immigration, which continues to be true today.[20]

Despite the unintentional expansion of immigration following the passage of the Act, the law remained difficult to challenge, resulting in relatively stable immigration policy for the next 20 years. The strength of the law lay in the role of bipartisanship in passing it, the impact of family-based immigration on the electorate, and the reduction of labor contentions for a short space of time. Despite the unexpected impact of the law that rapidly changed the racial and ethnic composition of the nation, politicians were unable to challenge the legislation without being misunderstood as racially-motivated.[21] With a growing immigrant population, attempts to overturn the family unification goal that brought in low-skilled workers in favor of a more skill-based system grew even more difficult.

THE IMMIGRATION AND REFORM ACT OF 1986 (IRCA)

John Skrentny has described IRCA and the bargaining process behind the final passage of the legislation as "one of the great policy failures of American history."[22] IRCA contained a legalization component that offered a form of amnesty to millions of undocumented persons who were offered a pathway to citizenship, and the legislation contained enforcement provisions designed to secure the borders while making it more difficult for undocumented persons to enter and remain in the United States. According to Skrentny, "IRCA's failure to seal the border taught restrictionists not to make any more grand bargains," and it has led to the inability of groups to work together to solve common concerns.[23] IRCA has left behind a legacy of distrust that has contributed to the inability of Congress to make needed reforms.

A crisis was the backdrop for IRCA. By the early 1980s, America faced new immigration challenges that included the presence of large numbers of undocumented workers. The debate over how to address undocumented workers was not salient during the 1960s, but by the mid-1980s it had become an issue too significant to ignore. Labor unions, civil rights groups, employers, and ethnic groups staked out sides on the issue. By the mid-1970s, three major Hispanic groups opened offices in DC, initiating a new era of political activism.[24] Gradually, with a growing legal and illegal population of Hispanic immigrants, the Hispanic policy groups became major actors in policy reform. They eventually cut deals and joined forces with the Congressional Black Caucus and the Leadership Conference for Civil Rights to advance an agenda that gutted employer sanctions and other reforms that might have decreased illegal migration while protecting the jobs of America's most vulnerable populations.[25]

As was true in previous decades, labor unions maintained their concerns about job competition and downward pressure on wages resulting from the oversupply of low-wage undocumented workers. But the importance of labor unions was waning, and immigrants were essential to reviving the weakening institutions. Labor groups eventually began to pressure Congress to address the deluge of illegal workers entering the country, while the National Association for the Advancement of Colored People (NAACP) continued to point out that illegal aliens were depriving lower-income citizens of jobs for which they qualified.[26] Focusing on the need for employer sanctions, the AFL-CIO and groups such as the NAACP, United States Conference for Catholic Bishops, and League of United Latin American Citizens demanded penalties for employers who contributed to the problem by encouraging illegal migration.

By the early 1980s, Congress attempted to address both legal and illegal immigration in a single legislative effort. In their initial attempt to deal with both issues through one piece of legislation, various senators suggested caps on legal immigration, leading to a strong push back from the Reagan administration.

President Reagan had raised America as a "shining city upon a hill," welcoming immigrants to a land of opportunity and freedom. Interpreting any caps on legal immigration as an affront to this ideal, the administration was able to lobby for separation of these portions of the legislation to be dealt with in the future. Thus, the legislative effort was split, with illegal immigration to be dealt with first.

The Immigration Reform and Control Act 1986 was the first stage of the legislation, addressing the rising tide of illegal immigrants in an attempt to close the "back door" to illegal immigration in order to "keep the front door open."[27] Voicing concerns about the possibility of racial profiling and discrimination by employers, Hispanic groups successfully fought against more severe employer sanctions. By the time the employer sanctions were enacted into law, they had been debated for a full fifteen years.[28] But despite the initial alliance between Hispanic groups and western growers to prevent harsh employer sanctions, the debate began to shift to the topic of an agricultural worker program. Once it was determined employers would have an "affirmative defense," releasing the employers from the obligation to check the authenticity of documents provided to them, Western growers shifted their focus to establishing alternative sources of foreign labor. Hispanic policy groups also saw the opportunity for advancing immigrant interests in the offer of amnesty, eventually accepting the trade-off of employer sanctions for the prospect of citizenship. Over time the two most controversial and noteworthy elements of the bill were the issue of amnesty and a future guest-worker program, both of which were divided along ideological lines.

There were lots of hearings, but not on the Schumer compromise that led to SAW (Special Agricultural Worker) and RAW (Replacement Agricultural Worker) Programs; instead, representatives of Western growers, labor unions, and Hispanic interest groups engaged in several rounds of political trading, leading to the compromises of the final legislation. The primary accomplishments of the law were sanctions on employers who knowingly hired illegal immigrants, grants of amnesty for immigrants who had resided in the United States since January 1, 1982, and a path to citizenship for those who had worked as seasonal laborers for a certain amount of time. Many considered the sanctions against employers to be the centerpiece of the law, although the sanctions would prove insufficient to address the uncontrollable flow of illegal immigration. The legislation criminalized the act of knowingly hiring an undocumented immigrant, although it did not require employers to question the authenticity of documents presented to them. The act also established a probationary guestworker program, which granted "earned-stay" rights to special agricultural workers, labeled SAWs. Ultimately, 1.3 million agricultural workers would take advantage of this provision.[29]

THE IMMIGRATION ACT OF 1990 AND THE GEORGE H.W. BUSH ADMINISTRATION

After the passage of IRCA, Congress turned its attention to legislation dealing with legal immigration. In the few years between the legislative enactments, the economy had significantly improved, changing the context of reform. Several studies indicated a skill gap in the workforce, suggesting the possibility of a shortage of skilled labor.[30] The Select Commission on U.S. Immigration and Refugee Policy called for increased admissions of highly trained immigrants that could contribute to American Industry, simultaneously arguing for preservation of existing family-unification goals. Several high-technology companies in the computer and electronic industries, including Microsoft, also joined forces to push for improved access for trained professionals from foreign countries. Republicans were largely in favor of the suggested increase in professional visas, but they opposed the demands of ethnic groups to increase the number of family visas. Democrats, particularly from the Northeast, acted in support of the ethnic groups, lobbying for an increase in visas for family purposes.

More expansive reform would ultimately be determined by the ability to build powerful coalitions among pro-immigration groups. Like the Reagan administration, the George H.W. Bush administration was generally supportive of liberal legal immigration, and their influence won over a large block of Republicans to vote in favor of the legislation. But the most noteworthy coalitions were the business groups and ethnic policy groups, referred to as the "family coalition." As discussed previously, the business groups were driven by a desire to bring in more skilled professionals and improve the ability to recruit temporary employees. Although there was not explicit agreement between the business groups and the family coalition, there was a tacit acknowledgment that they would act in support of each other, and not oppose each other's demands.[31] Another particularly important coalition was between the ethnic groups in favor of family reunification policies and the older immigrant groups who favored a special type of visa for nations in the minority of immigration. As many of the original immigrants no longer had living relatives in their native countries, they were unable to benefit from family-reunification policies, and they demanded an additional "diversity" visa that would permit increased immigration from these nations. Although the two groups arguably had competing interests, their cooperation ensured success for both goals.

Lastly, although forming no new coalitions, labor unions continued to play a powerful role in negotiations over reform. Labor argued aggressively for protection of jobs for native workers, attempting to limit visas for temporary professionals at 65,000 and suggesting a head tax on employers who hired foreign workers, higher standards of proof that business had attempted to recruit American workers, and a requirement that any hiring be linked to state and federal certification of a labor shortage. Eventually the suggested head tax would be eliminated, but the cap on admission of temporary foreign workers was retained as a concession to organized labor.

Largely based on bipartisan support, the Immigration Act passed in 1990. Simpson worked to get a cap on legal immigration of 675,000 a year. The most significant accomplishments of the final legislation included an increase in the total number of legal immigrants allowed into the United States each year, and the creation of diversity visas for countries from which immigration had been low. Eventually, the diversity program would be awarded 55,000 visas a year, and the legislation would increase the visas for non-immediate relatives by 300,000 including siblings.[32]

Despite attempts to limit family-unification policies, the act preserved the visas allotted prior to the legislation. The act also removed homosexuality and AIDS as grounds for exclusion from immigration and provided for exceptions to the English testing process required under the Naturalization Act of 1906. The enactment of this legislation increased annual immigration to the United States by 500,000 additional immigrants.[33]

In an attempt to tighten policy on illegal immigration, the act also significantly strengthened the power and resources of the U.S. Border Patrol. This legislation would eventually lead to the "prevention through deterrence" policy of the Immigration and Naturalization Service (INS) in the early 1990s. In one of the earliest examples of the lessons to be learned from immigration federalism, this particular federal strategy mimicked an attempt by the Texas government to address illegal entry in Operation Blockade. Immigrants who had previously entered through El Paso, the targeted city, were forced into more rural areas as a result of the operation. The Border Patrol adopted the plan on a national level in 1994. With the increased resources granted from the 1990 legislation, the Border Patrol began Operation Gatekeeper near San Diego, using high-intensity floodlights to deter illegal entry. Similar to Operation Blockade, Operation Gatekeeper pushed immigrants into more rural areas, although it is arguable they did little to deter overall migration.

The build-up of resources on the border continued in the Illegal Immigration Reform and Immigrant Responsibility Act of 1996, discussed shortly. Once more, legislation focused on increasing physical obstacles to illegal entry, along with increased Border Patrol agents and the technology available to them. By 2002, the total INS budget was 13 times its 1986 level, and the Border Patrol budget was ten times its former level, with three times as many officers, and eight times as many hours patrolling the border.[34] Formal deportation also grew rapidly, increasing nearly tenfold from 1986 to 2002. Douglas Massey[35] argues that instead of deterring illegal immigration, these policies eventually led to an increased retention of illegal immigrants, as the costs and dangers of making a border crossing rose. Due to increased border security, many immigrants were hesitant to return once they had entered the country, a "perverse consequence" of heavy border enforcement.[36] Thus, the illusion of a "controlled border," begun in the 1990 legislation, may have only exacerbated illegal entry and the greater illegal immigrant population on the whole.[37]

IMMIGRANT RESPONSIBILITY ACT OF 1996 AND THE CLINTON ERA

By the early 1990s, American opinion had turned against illegal immigration. Several highly publicized attempts of illegal migration, including multiple boats from China filled with immigrants attempting to land illegally, renewed attention to the ongoing problem of improper border crossings.[38] There was a sense in place to determine the authenticity of laborers' documents, and an underground industry for false identification was thriving. During this period states began to demonstrate both their frustration with federal attempts to address the issue of immigration, and their ability to sway national politics through their own legislation. Most notably, in California citizens enacted Proposition 187 and elected a Republican governor who ran on the platform of fighting against illegal immigrants in California. The measure passed by 59 percent of the vote in 1994, expressing the deep and desperate frustration of the people of California.[39] As one of the more populous states in the union, California drew attention to the growing problem of illegal border crossings, and the failed attempt by the federal government to restrict the number of illegal migrants entering the county each year. Alongside the events in California, Republicans gained control of both houses of Congress for the first time in 40 years. Part of the victory was a Contract with America, a list of promises and goals to be achieved with a conservative majority. Among other goals, an attempt to address illegal immigration was originally listed in the contract with the people.[40]

In response to the Republican congressional victories and the backlash displayed in California, Senator Alan Simpson and Texas Representative Lamar Smith introduced bills calling for restrictions to be placed on legal immigration alongside limitations on illegal immigration. Although initially it appeared the country was eager for the suggested measures, there were several political hints that the severe legislation would not have a smooth journey. Eventually, due to divisions within the party, immigration was struck from the list of goals within the Contract with America.

Once more, Hispanic and Asian groups relied on a left–right coalition to manipulate the legislation in favor of their policy goals. High-technology companies, including the National Association of Manufacturers, Intel, and Microsoft, also rose up against the bill, staging several high-profile "fly-ins" to the capital to argue against any limits on legal immigration.[41] The Business

Coalition explained that international operations made employment of immigration vital to the future success of their companies.

The bill was initially introduced as a reform of both legal and illegal immigration. Pro-immigration interest groups recognized the current hostility toward illegal immigration, and knew that if the two issues were joined, there was a great risk that legal immigration would be blamed for the problems of illegal immigration. Pro-growth libertarians and economic conservatives were soon persuaded by the family coalition that legal immigration must be protected, and they also joined the struggle against a bill attempting to address all types of immigration. As there was significantly less momentum attached to the issue of legal immigration, these interest groups were able to stall this portion of the legislation. A series of "dear colleague letters" went out in support of splitting the bill, tying legal immigration to free trade and free markets. Conservatives explained that they would be willing to address legal immigration at a later time, but it was necessary to separate the issues in order to address them effectively. Eventually, with the approval of the Clinton administration, support for splitting the bill was widespread, and the cuts to legal immigration were deferred for another legislative session.

Despite their importance in previous immigration reform, labor unions had a significantly diminished voice in the 1996 legislation. Without a Democratic majority, it was difficult for labor unions to gain a seat at the table. Even so, Senator Edward Kennedy lobbied aggressively on their behalf, arguing for protections to be added to the bill in favor of American workers. But with a weak political position, the unions were ultimately cut out of any significant discussions, and even the reforms added by Senator Kennedy were largely eliminated by the time the bill was passed.

Once the bill was split, the final legislation was focused on increased protection of the border, and greater responsibility for incoming immigrants and their family sponsors. A significant factor in the call for reform was a belief that the employer sanctions put in place by the 1986 legislation had failed. With no reliable method of determining the authenticity of documentation, employers could easily claim an affirmative defense against the sanction's force. Originally, it was suggested that a phone verification system should be put in place to provide certification of documents. Although a pilot version of this phone verification system was implemented, the focus of reform shifted away from a correction of the sanctions to stricter control over the border. One thousand U.S. Border police were added, alongside more severe consequences for those entering the country illegally. The proposed legislation barred admission for three years for aliens unlawfully present in the United States for 180 days, and barred admission or any legal status for ten years if an illegal immigrant was present in the country for more than a year. The legislation changed laws for excluding and removing aliens, limiting the judicial review of INS decisions.

The suggested reforms also placed greater responsibility on family sponsors to prevent increased dependence of new immigrants on public services. Financial responsibility rules limited admission of immigrants that were likely to be reliant on the welfare system by requiring sponsors of relatives to prove the requested immigrant had an income 25 percent above the poverty line. Once an immigrant had entered the United States, their family sponsor was required to sign a legally binding affidavit of support, and the sponsor's income was included with the alien's income for any qualification for public support. Under the welfare reforms of 1996, states were also delegated the authority to determine immigrant eligibility for federal benefits. Some scholars argue this authorization of state-level discretion put an end to the era of federal exclusivity that had dominated the twentieth century, inviting states into the debate on the legal status of immigrants.[42] Peter Spiro argues that the provision ensured that the alien's status would no longer be fixed in Washington, but also in the states.

In the final stages of passage, a controversial amendment arose that threatened to destroy the legislation. The Gallegy Amendment, an early attempt to increase the role of immigration federalism, granted power to states to deny public schooling to children present in the country illegally. Opponents of the bill argued that keeping immigrant children out of school would increase crime and victimize children who had no part in the illegality of their entry. Although conservative Democrats from the South favored the amendment, President Clinton came out strongly against it and threatened to veto the entire bill if the amendment was included. In the midst of the presidential election, the Republican candidate for president, Robert Dole, lobbied aggressively for inclusion of the amendment believing this would force President Clinton to either veto the bill, losing votes in California, or backtrack on his promise, losing legitimacy with the electorate. But despite the pressure from Republican leaders, Republican representatives saw the risk that the bill would fail, and stood firm on excluding the Gallegy Amendment in the final legislation.

THE BUSH ERA AND THE ATTACKS ON SEPTEMBER 11, 2001

At the commencement of the George W. Bush presidency, there was hope that more comprehensive reform would be possible. President Bush invited Mexican President Vicente Fox as the first foreign dignitary under the new administration, signaling the importance of the relationship between the two countries. As the two national leaders debated the terms of a trade agreement, pro-immigration groups remained hopeful that immigration reform within the United States would follow. On September 11, 2001, American policy goals experienced a severe and unexpected shift. An opening of American borders was taken off the table, and policies focused on tightening the border and determining who was in the United States illegally. The Department of Homeland Security was created, absorbing various units of the INS. U.S. visas dropped precipitously and the perception of illegal immigration, and even legal immigration, began to grow unfavorable.

Just two years later, immigration would become increasingly politicized. After the auspicious climate for immigration reform had faded away with the attacks on September 11, 2001, the momentum for a new guestworker program with Mexico and a possible grant of amnesty had been replaced with increased attention on border control and security. Out of frustration over delayed reforms and unfulfilled promises of possible amnesty, more than 800 people departed from the nine major cities, traveling by bus to Washington, DC.[43] In an attempt to mimic the black Freedom Rides of the 1960s, the protestors hoped to use the journey to recast amnesty and further immigration policy liberalization as the great civil rights struggle of our time, and present secure borders and effective immigration law enforcement as the new Jim Crow.[44] The protestors lobbied for the legalization of more than 10 million immigrants, and an increase in opportunities for immigrants to bring family members into the country. But rather than raising awareness of their cause, these protestors highlighted the growing size of the illegal immigrant population.[45] American citizens who had stayed out of the debate previously could no longer avoid the vivid images of immigrants boldly waving flags of their own country, fearlessly declaring their undocumented status.

In response, the general public demanded greater enforcement of existing laws, leading to the Real ID Act of 2005. The Real ID Act focused primarily on security and authentication standards for state driver's licenses and identification cards, along with various immigration issues including terrorism concerns. The act created restriction on political asylum, increased enforcement mechanisms, restricted some due process rights, and imposed federal restrictions on state driver's licenses for immigrants, making it more difficult for illegal immigrants to procure and use certain types of documents for official purposes.

On May 1, 2006, protestors once more thrust immigration issues into the public view. Mass protests had begun in the spring of 2006, with breathtakingly large turnouts in April and May. The organized rallies had continued the politicization of immigrants begun with the Freedom Rides, inadvertently raising the national consciousness about illegal immigration and the financial burdens it imposed. On May 1, immigrants coordinated an economic protest labeled A Day without Immigrants. The nationwide protest was an effort to display the necessity of immigrants to the U.S. economy, further bolstering calls for reform and amnesty. Despite the participation of more than 50 cities, from Las Vegas to Miami, the impact of the boycott was minimal. But the political significance of the protests was lasting and widespread. The sea of Mexican and Latin American flags, the language of a "stolen land" and "Reconquista," and the sight of thousands of illegal immigrants demanding citizenship shook American conceptions regarding immigration. The image presented by the protests stood in direct contradiction to earlier portraits of illegal immigrants as frightened docile people, cowering behind locked doors, never knowing if the next knock would bring deportation. Citizens became concerned, rather than empathetic.[46]

Largely in reaction to the protests, the House and the Senate passed two vastly different immigration bills. In December 2005, the House of Representatives passed a restrictionist immigration bill (H.R. 4437) that many people saw as punitive, although it seemed to be in harmony with public wishes.[47] The bill would have criminalized being in the country illegally, required the deportation of illegal aliens, and imposed new penalties on employers and service providers who offered assistance to illegals. It provided no provisions for guestworkers, nor did it offer a pathway to citizenship. In reaction to a public outcry, a few months later, the Senate passed a friendlier bill (S. 2611) that offered a tiered path to citizenship, a guestworker program, and a provision for bringing more legal immigrants into the country. It also included a controversial provision that would require private and public employers to pay the prevailing wage to guestworkers on all construction projects. The proposed bills died in the conference committee where members of both houses tried to reconcile differences to create a single bill to be voted up or down. Thus, the federal government failed in its last major attempt to reform immigration.

Perhaps in reaction to federal failure, the states increased their activism in the area of immigration reform. By July 2006, 30 states had passed 57 laws that dealt with some aspect of immigration reform. Although a few of these laws expanded benefits for noncitizens, the vast majority made it more difficult for illegal immigrants to receive government benefits such as unemployment benefits, driver's licenses, employment in government-funded projects, and gun permits.[48] Aggressive actions by state and local governments are likely to continue until Congress offers some real leadership on the issue.

THE OBAMA ERA AND THE DREAM ACT

Despite the intensity of the debate, Congress has been unable to reach consensus on the issue of immigration, with most changes in the last decade coming from the state level or through administrative channels. Even so, legislation to address immigration has been the subject of virulent debate within the legislative branch, spilling over into state legislatures. One of the most salient pieces of legislation has been the DREAM Act, a suggested program for development, relief, and education of alien minors that has lingered in Congress for years.[49] In June 2012, it was partially implemented by President Barack Obama through a presidential directive of the Department of Homeland Security that temporarily ended the deportation of thousands of illegal aliens who met certain criteria.[50]

The Obama policy became known as the Deferred Action for Childhood Arrivals (DACA), and it remained in effect until September 5, 2017, when

Attorney General Jeff Sessions found that DACA "was not statutorily authorized and was therefore an unconstitutional exercise of discretion by the executive branch."[51] In an effort to wind down the legislation in "an orderly and minimally disruptive manner," the Administration gave Congress six months to develop a legislative solution to bring relief to the population that was protected by the Obama directive.[52] As Carol Swain shows in Chapter 12, President Obama also tried unsuccessfully to shield the parents of DACA protections through the use of a second directive called Deferred Action for Parents of Americans and Lawful Permanent Residents (DAPA), but this was struck down by the Courts and has not been resurrected by the Trump administration. As of October 2017, however, there was talk of a bipartisan agreement that would enact a version of the DREAM Act described in the following paragraphs, potentially achieving a major goal of the Obama administration.[53]

The DREAM Act has been debated for more than a decade as a solution to the plight of hundreds of thousands of young illegal aliens brought to the country by their parents. Originally introduced in 2001, the initial version of the legislation was placed alongside various other immigration-related bills that eventually failed.[54] Politicians expressed concern that the bill could encourage chain migration, aggravating rather than solving the issue of illegal immigration. Other politicians agreed with the principles of the bill, but refused to act on the legislation unless it was a part of a more comprehensive immigration reform. Still others recognized the importance of the measure, but found it to be distracting in light of more pressing issues.

The act was later reformulated to address the concerns, resulting in what remains the most current version of the legislation (S.1615; as of October 2017).[55] The current version of the DREAM Act would allow illegal alien students to gain "permanent resident status on a conditional basis" if they have not participated in the persecution of others in any way; have graduated from or are enrolled in a U.S. high school, have a GED, or otherwise have gained admittance to an institution of higher education; arrived in the United States before the age of eighteen; and have lived in the country continuously for at least four years.[56] The applicant must not have been convicted of any crime with a maximum prison sentence of more than one year or of three or more crimes for which he or she has served an aggregate prison sentence of more than 90 days.[57] If an applicant meets these qualifications, they may be granted permanent resident status once they have completed two years of armed service, acquired a degree from an institution of higher learning, completed two years and are in good standing in a program for a bachelor's degree or higher, or worked at least 75 percent of the time for at least three years.[58] Previous to completion of any of these activities, participants in the program would only qualify for a conditional status. There was previously an age cap that was removed in recent changes to the bill. Furthermore, it is clearly stated that all DACA recipients are covered under this bill.[59]

Despite significant changes to the proposed act, some citizens disagree with the fundamental assumptions of the legislation, and the undesirable effects they believe it will create. Opponents also claim that the act provides an unjustified reward for illegal immigration, because not everyone benefits from the proposed legislation. Although the Act is still pending, the presidential directive (DACA) has given temporary status to more than 800,000 formerly undocumented persons who can now work openly with government-issued identifications.[60] The presidential directive was a controversial sidestepping of congressional intent. Not surprisingly, it came during an election year in which many Hispanics had voiced disappointment with the president's failure to keep his promises about reforming immigration.

The DREAM Act has also ignited state action focused on addressing the plight of young people in the affected categories. Several states have acted on the model provided by the federal bill, demonstrating the ability of states to test policies the nation is not yet prepared for. In 2011, California enacted a state version of the DREAM Act, granting access to state-funded financial aid for illegal immigrants who meet GPA requirements, graduate from a California high school, and enter the U.S. before age sixteen (A.B. 131). Later that year, Illinois followed suit, also providing privately funded scholarships for legal and illegal immigrant children (S.B. 2185). Overall, 18 states have passed laws affording in-state tuition to undocumented students.[61]

Although little was accomplished in terms of bringing about expansive immigration reform through the legislative process at the national level during the Obama administration, President Obama communicated a broad policy to reduce deportation of certain groups of immigrants. In June 2011, the administration quietly announced new rules in a memo from a top official at the U.S. Immigration and Customs enforcement agency, creating the aforementioned DACA program.[62] Many have labeled the memo as an attempt to pass the DREAM Act through an executive order, as the memo highlights the use of "prosecutorial discretion," encouraging officers to limit enforcement of immigration laws if illegal immigrants are enrolled in an education center or their relatives have volunteered for the U.S. military.

The overall Obama record on immigration enforcement is mixed. Although the administration boasted of having had an unusually high record of deportations (more than 2.7 million in the first 7 years), many of its deportations were of criminal aliens.[63] A much more lenient policy of catch and release for noncriminal aliens seems to have been the norm. Representative Lamar Smith (R-TX), chairman of the House Judiciary Committee, has questioned the administration's record of enforcement. Smith has accused the administration of inflating its numbers.[64] According to Smith, the numbers are misleading because they "include voluntary removals in the deportation statistics." Voluntary removals are not deportations because the "illegal immigrant is not then subject to penalties for returning to the United States ...

a single illegal immigrant can show up at the border and be voluntarily returned numerous times in one year – and counted each time as a removal."[65]

THE RETURN OF IMMIGRATION FEDERALISM

States have always been active in immigration regulation, occasionally enforcing sanctions against employers, and regulating immigrant access to public services. But the trend in state and local immigration legislation in the twenty-first century has been dramatic.[66] The noticeable rise of state action on immigration issues can be explained by several factors. First, since 1990 the nation has been in the midst of a demographic reordering, as the majority of immigrants now come from Asia and Latin America rather than the traditional Europe.[67] By 2006, approximately 11.5 million immigrants were also unauthorized.[68] The year 2011 brought dismally low rates of unemployment, but immigration was at the highest rate ever recorded.[69] Due to changes in border control, immigrants have been dispersed deeply and broadly across the nation, bypassing traditional urban centers. These changing immigration patterns have brought noncitizens into new regions of the country that feel the need to generate a policy response. Effective integration of new citizens has required states to adopt positions, often in tension with federal immigration policy. The city of Hazelton, PA, developed laws stricter than federal regulation, enforcing sanctions against landlords in addition to employers; whereas cities such as New Haven, CT, provided ID cards and other benefits to undocumented immigrants the federal government does not yet recognize.[70] State and local government responses to immigration are also motivated by a sense that the cost of unauthorized immigration falls unevenly across the levels of government, with some states going so far as to sue the federal government for reimbursement.[71] Lastly, since the terrorist attacks of September 11, 2001, the federal government has come to rely on law enforcement assistance from the states, which have willingly accepted the authority granted by federal agencies.

State and local governments have had a growing incentive to become involved in immigration policy as they respond to the necessity of local enforcement, the lack of federal enforcement, and the need to integrate new immigrants into their societies. Clare Huntington[72] recognizes three primary areas of growing state and local involvement in immigration policy flowing from these motivations: acceptance of delegated authority from the federal government to local governments, state enforcement of existing federal law without a delegation of authority, and laws generated by the states regarding noncitizens. The federal government began to delegate authority to state and local law enforcement with congressional enactment of the Immigration Reform and Immigrant Responsibility Act of 1996, which added Section 287(g) to the Immigration and Nationality Act. Section 287(g) authorized the federal government (most recently, the secretary of Homeland Security) to enter into agreements with state and local governments to enforce federal immigration law. This delegated authority entailed broad responsibilities, including the power to arrest and detain noncitizens for immigration violations, investigation of immigration violations, and collection of evidence in preparation for immigration cases brought before an immigration judge. Several states and localities entered into such agreements, accepting oversight by federal immigration officials. The second clear delegation over immigration authority came from the Personal Responsibility and Work Opportunity Reconciliation Act, which granted states the ability to determine immigrant eligibility for federal benefits programs. Although it was expected most states would use this authority to enforce stricter limits on access to benefits, states were commonly more generous than the federal government had been.[73] Although a few states took advantage of these opportunities in the 1990s, 23 states have signed the mutual agreement provided under 287(g) in the last ten years.[74]

The next category of growing state action is enforcement of existing federal laws that the federal government enforces either ineffectively or not at all. In a controversial opinion by the Office of Legal Counsel, the Justice Department found that states and localities possess inherent authority to enforce both the criminal and civil provisions of the INA in 2002.[75] Although this formal opinion provides more limited authority than that granted under section 287(g), there is an indication that the assistance of local and state agents in arresting noncitizens and delivering them to federal officials will be accepted in certain instances. With rising populations of undocumented immigrants, states are showing an increasing willingness to enforce existing federal law to protect the interests of their citizens.

The final category of state action is legislation that affects noncitizens either indirectly or directly. These laws range from granting in-state tuition to immigrants to forbidding businesses from employing undocumented workers. Although critics of the rise of immigration federalism fear increased discrimination against immigrants, many state laws benefit noncitizens, including unauthorized migrants, through provision of healthcare, identification cards, access to higher public education, and limits on racial profiling of employers.[76] Other states have acted in response to the federal government's failure to curb unauthorized migration, with Arizona enacting one of the more far-reaching laws in the nation to date.

CONSTITUTIONAL AUTHORITY OVER IMMIGRATION

Proponents and opponents of immigration federalism often share one basic assumption: immigration is the exclusive responsibility of the federal government. Those who oppose recent state action reason that states are legislating on a matter forbidden to them, which must be stopped. Proponents of state action argue that states are forced to act because the federal government has failed to do so. But neither side recognizes the powerful marriage of innovation and authority the federal-state-local dynamic offers in solving the issues of immigration. In order for such an arrangement to succeed, courts must abandon the political rhetoric and legal doctrine of federal exclusivity that has blocked and limited the potential for state solutions. Although immigration has been viewed as an area of exclusive federal authority, this is only an accurate description of the current legislative landscape. There is no constitutional mandate for federal exclusivity over immigration law, and the states' access to such authority is far more legitimate than the debate suggests.

There are three ways to receive federal authority over immigration: structural, with no appropriate role for state or local governments; dormant, requiring the federal government to activate underlying state authority; and statutory, where state and federal governments have initial authority to regulate, but the federal government may exclude state action through preemption. Dormant preemption requires explicit delegation, which does not apply in the case of immigration. Typically, structural preemption also requires a clear textual basis in the Constitution, as seen with copyright and bankruptcy law, although some scholars have argued that structural preemption is implied when dual regulation on an issue would be undesirable.[77]

Structural preemption is one of the more common classifications of immigration authority, as many perceive a need for a uniform standard for exit and entry into the country. But the Constitution refers only to the need for a uniform rule of naturalization, not sole authority over immigration by the federal government. Rather than rely on an explicit textual mandate, proponents for the structural view of immigration insist that the issue is comparable to the treatment of foreign affairs, and must be exclusively controlled by the federal government to preserve sovereignty and uniformity. But the classification of immigration as a purely national issue has grown increasingly outdated, and all that remains is a formal doctrine without strong constitutional justifications. Several countries with powerful central governments now allow subnational regions to control their immigration policy.[78] With the rise of non-state actors, other nations are less likely to interpret the actions of a state as indicative of broader national policy. Foreign affairs are only tangentially related to the issue of immigration, and an attempt to join the two overlooks the nuances of immigration policy. Although the federal government largely dominated immigration policy throughout the twentieth century, this was a consequence of the need for a more uniform standard, not recognition of exclusive federal authority.

If authority over immigration is viewed under statutory preemption, states would share regulatory authority, but the national government would maintain the ability to preempt through federal statute according to the Supremacy Clause. This enables the federal government to maintain a consistent federal policy while allowing for state innovation within its primary goals.[79] Broader federal protections, such as the Equal Protection Clause, First Amendment, and even landlord-tenant laws will continue to apply to state laws, ensuring that state action stays within certain bounds. Supreme Court precedent does not explicitly foreclose a statutory preemption view of federal authority; instead, it embodies the tension between an interest in a uniform rule on a national level, and states' interest in exercising police power to protect their citizens.[80]

An understanding of the basis for federal authority will influence how courts will assess substantive laws of the states, and will open up the debate about the proper allocation of authority between the various government entities. Federal delegation of authority to states will be permissible under the statutory preemption view, although it would be expressly suspect under a structural view. Even in the absence of delegation by the federal government, state and local enforcement of federal immigration laws would be permissible unless statutorily preempted under a statutory interpretation. If the constitution provides for state authority, it would not limit states to enforcement of existing law, but would also allow them to develop their own. Statutory preemption would permit states to innovate where the federal government has not already legislated, or where the federal government does not enforce. Currently most courts begin with the assumption that state laws are constitutionally proper to the extent they accord with traditional areas of state authority, such as health, safety, and other matters of local concern where Congress has not preempted through previous legislation. Structural preemption would distinguish these laws according to whether they can be labeled as alienage law or pure immigration law. Under the statutory preemption view, most state laws would be permitted, although the federal government would be able to preempt through congressional legislation.

VIEWPOINTS ON IMMIGRATION FEDERALISM

Even if state legislation is legally permissible, some scholars oppose the concept of immigration federalism and believe that individual rights will suffer under a "devolution" of immigration policy.[81] Other scholars are concerned that communities will see an increase in crime if immigrants learn to distrust local law enforcement agents.[82] Opponents of the development argue that there is a need for uniformity in immigration policy and that the national government is better able to identify and correct for market imperfections and failures, protect fundamental rights, and guard against a regulatory race to the bottom.

But gradually, scholars have come to embrace the inevitable trend of immigration federalism, and are willing to see the benefits of such a development. Immigration federalism provides the opportunity for innovation, a "quintessential force multiplier" in the resources available to address the issue,[83] and a "steam-valve function" that allows states with strong anti-immigration leaning to have a voice without swaying all national policies.[84] States provide "laboratories of democracy," as they compete with each other for residents and resources, increasing political accountability and participation as they are able to address local needs and meet the demands of a smaller constituency.[85] The full development of divergent views on the benefits and costs of immigration allow for polices to be tested before enactment on a national scale.[86] State policies often fall on either side of national policy, as states have demonstrated both hostility and openness to noncitizens. While the federal government was developing policy to build a wall along the border of the United States, states such as California were working to provide in-state tuition to undocumented immigrants.[87] By allowing states to enact such policies, the federal government acknowledges the important economic and social stake that states and local governments have in immigration. Although many fear an increasing threat to individual rights, there is no reason to think the federal government is better at protecting such fundamental rights, and if anything, the states provide a check on such expansive power.[88]

CONCLUSION AND POLICY SUGGESTIONS

The 2012 decision in *Arizona* v. *United States*[89] has given grist to the mill of Americans who argue that immigration should be the exclusive purview of the federal government. Immigration is an issue that is continuing to increase in significance and volume. *Arizona* clearly places the onus on Congress to enforce immigration laws in a reasonable and timely fashion. Clear lines of accountability could spur grassroots movements to hold the institution accountable for what often seems like a gross dereliction of duties. Something must be done. The nation's immigrant population, both legal and illegal, reached 40 million in 2010, the largest number in the nation's history.[90] With the vast expansion of immigration throughout the country, negative externalities are no longer contained in border states, and certain communities have lost more than others.[91] Limited resources and a growing dependent population have left politicians with difficult decisions on how to allocate services to legal immigrants and residents as we enter into the twenty-first century.

State participation in immigration enforcement and policy has led some to question the legitimacy of such action, whereas others have seen the promise of a solution. Once we recognize that federal exclusivity is not constitutionally mandated, classic federalism arguments will work well in determining the appropriate allocation of authority among levels of the government. The federal government may preempt states where it is necessary to have a unified policy, and broader constitutional provisions will ensure that state legislation protects individual rights. Since 1986, Congress has only been able to achieve piecemeal immigration reform. As a consequence, it is likely we will see state legislation continue to fill voids in immigration policy. As Cristina Rodriguez[92] argues, immigration is no longer a purely national issue, it is a state issue in the same vein as education, crime control, and the regulation of health, safety, and welfare; not only because immigration influences every one of those interests, but because managing the immigration movement itself is a state interest.

In order to achieve the beneficial partnership between local and federal, courts should assess potential conflicts between federal and state laws. Lawmakers should be encouraged to engage in federal-state-local cooperation, and Congress should restrain from over-regulating the issue and thereby excluding state innovation. Integration and acceptance of new citizens must be taken on as a partnership. Although federal law will control who enters the country, states must play a necessary role in integrating new immigrants. We have a national interest in seeing laws upheld that reflect legitimate state interests, while not trampling on individual rights or the lofty goals and ambitions of a national policy that often seems vague and misguided.

NOTES

1. Justice Stevens writing for the majority in *Arizona* v. *United States*, 132 S.Ct. 2492, 2510 (2012).
2. Malcolm Feeley and Edward Rubin, *Federalism: Political Identity and Tragic Compromise* (Ann Arbor: University of Michigan Press, 2008), p. 12.
3. National Conference of State Legislatures, "2011 Immigration-Related Laws and Resolutions in the States (Jan. 1–Dec. 7, 2011)." Available at: www.ncsl.org/documents/immig/2011immfinalreportdec.pdf, accessed February 28, 2018.
4. Clare Huntington, "The Constitutional Dimension of Immigration Federalism," *Vanderbilt Law Review* 61 (2008): 790.
5. Hiroshi Motomura, "Federalism, International Human Rights, and Immigration Exceptionalism," *University of Colorado Law Review* 70 (1999): 1361; Michael J. Wishnie, "Laboratories of Bigotry? Devolution of Immigration Power, Equal Protection, and Federalism," *New York Law Review* 76 (2001): 493.
6. Michael J. Wishnie, "State and Local Police Enforcement of Immigration Laws," *University of Pennsylvania Constitutional Law Journal* 6 (2004): 1084; Motomura, "Federalism, International Human Rights, and Immigration Exceptionalism," 1361.
7. Linda Bosniak, "The Undocumented Immigrant," in Carol Swain (ed.), *Debating Immigration* (New York Cambridge University Press, 2006), 85–94.
8. Bosniak, "The Undocumented Immigrant," p. 86.
9. Bosniak, "The Undocumented Immigrant," pp. 86–87.
10. Peter H. Schuck, "Taking Immigration Federalism Seriously," University of Chicago Law Forum (2007). Available at: http://ssrn.com/abstract=965338, accessed March 1, 2018.
11. *Arizona* v. *United States*, 567 U.S. ____ (2012). Available at www.supremecourt.gov/opinions/11pdf/11-182.pdf, accessed March 1, 2018.
12. See *Toll* v. *Moreno*, 458 U.S. 1, 10.
13. Tyler Anbinder, *Nativism and Slavery: The Northern Know Nothing and the Politics of the 1850s* (New York: Oxford University Press, 1992).
14. Chinese Exclusion Act, Sess. 1. Chap. 126; 22 Stat. 58. 47th Congress; Approved May 6, 1882.
15. Roger Daniels, *Guarding the Golden Door* (New York City: Hill and Wang, 2004), chapter 1.

16. Daniels, *Guarding the Golden Door*; Alejandro Portes and Ruben Rumbaut, *A Portrait of Immigrant America*, Third edition, revised (Berkeley, CA: University of California Press, 2006).

17. Portes and Rumbaut, *A Portrait of Immigrant America*, pp. 12–38.

18. Carolyn Wong, *Lobbying for Inclusion: Rights Politics and the Making of Immigration Policy* (Stanford: Stanford University Press), pp. 44–63.

19. Stephen Thomas Wagner, "The lingering Death of the National Origins Quota System: A Political History of United States Immigration Policy, 1952–1965," Ph.D. dissertation, Harvard University, Cambridge, MA (1986).

20. Wong, *Lobbying for Inclusion*, pp. 61–62; Portes and Rumbaut, *A Portrait of Immigrant America*, pp. 12–63.

21. Wagner, "The Lingering Death of the National Origins Quota System," pp. 464–465.

22. John D. Skrentny, "Obama's Immigration Reform: A Tough Sell for a Grand Bargain," in Theda Skocpol and Lawrence R. Jacobs (eds.), *Reaching for a New Deal* (New York: Russell Sage Foundation, 2011), p. 274.

23. Skrentny, "Obama's Immigration Reform," p. 270.

24. Wong, *Lobbying for Inclusion*, p. 68.

25. Wong, *Lobbying for Inclusion*, pp. 95–132.

26. Daniel J. Tichenor, *Dividing Lines: The Politics of Immigration Control in America* (Princeton: Princeton University Press, 2002), pp. 226–227.

27. Wong, *Lobbying for Inclusion*, p. 96; Skrentny, "Obama's Immigration Reform," pp. 273–320.

28. Wong, *Lobbying for Inclusion*.

29. David M. Reimers, *Still the Golden Door: The Third World Comes to America* (New York: Columbia University Press, 1992).

30. Wong, *Lobbying for Inclusion*, p. 101.

31. Wong, *Lobbying for Inclusion*, p. 102.

32. Wong, *Lobbying for Inclusion*, p. 104.

33. The Immigration Act of 1990 (Pub.L. 101–649, 104 Stat. 4978, enacted November 29, 1990).

34. Douglas S. Massey, "Borderline Madness: America's Counterproductive Immigration Policy," in Carol Swain (ed.), *Debating Immigration* (New York: Cambridge University Press, 2007), p. 132.

35. Massey, "Borderline Madness," pp. 134–135.

36. Massey, "Borderline Madness," p. 135.

37. Massey, "Borderline Madness," pp. 136–137.

38. Wong, *Lobbying for Inclusion*, p. 133.

39. Proposition 187 was ultimately overturned, but it is relevant in showing the rise of state action and its effect on national politics.

40. Peter Spiro uses this turn of events to indicate the need for the "steam-valve" function, discussed next.

41. Wong, *Lobbying for Inclusion*, p. 137.

42. Peter J. Spiro, "Learning to Live with Immigration Federalism," *Connecticut Law Review* 29 (2007): 1627.

43. Visa Law.Com. 2003. Available at: www.visalaw.com/03sep4/16sep403.html, accessed 2005.

44. "Freedom Riders' Rally for Immigrant Rights," *The Chicago Tribune*. October 5, 2003.

45. Carol M. Swain, "Introduction" in Carol Swain (ed.), *Debating Immigration* (New York: Cambridge University Press, 2007), pp. 6–9.

46. Swain, "Introduction," p. 8.

47. Swain, "Introduction," pp. 8–9.

48. "Immigration Bills Compared," *The Washington Post*, 2005. Available at: www .washingtonpost.com/wp-dyn/content/custom/2006/05/26/CU2006052600148.html, accessed March 1, 2018.

49. Yamiche Alcindor and Sheryl Gay Stolberg, "After 16 Futile Years, Congress Will Try Again to Legalize 'Dreamers,'" *The New York Times*. Available at: www .nytimes.com/2017/09/05/us/politics/dream-act-daca-trump-congress-dreamers.html, accessed March 1, 2018.

50. "U.S. to Stop Deporting Some Illegal Immigrants," *The Wall Street Journal*. Available at: http://online.wsj.com/article/SB10001424052702303822204577468 343924191180.html, accessed March 1, 2018.

51. The White House Office of the Press Secretary, "President Donald J. Trump Restores Responsibility and the Rule of Law to Immigration," September 5, 2017. Available at: www.whitehouse.gov/the-press-office/2017/09/05/president-donald-j-trump-restores-responsibility-and-rule-law, accessed March 1, 2018.

52. Office of the Press Secretary, "President Donald J. Trump Restores Responsibility and the Rule of Law to Immigration."

53. Ed O'Keefe and David Nakamura, "Trump, Top Democrats Agree to Work on Deal to Save 'Dreamers' from Deportation," *The Washington Post*, September 14, 2017. Available at: www.washingtonpost.com/news/powerpost/wp/2017/09/13/trump-top-democrats-agree-to-work-on-deal-to-save-daca/?utm_term=.df33762820be, accessed March 1, 2018.

54. Alcindor and Stolberg, "After 16 Futile Years."

55. The text of the bill can be found at www.congress.gov/bill/115th-congress/senate-bill/1615, accessed March 1, 2018.

56. Dream Act of 2017, S. 1615, 115th Cong., 2017. Available at: www.congress.gov/ bill/115th-congress/senate-bill/1615/text, accessed March 1, 2018.

57. DREAM ACT of 2017.

58. DREAM ACT of 2017.

59. DREAM ACT of 2017.

60. U.S. Citizenship and Immigration Services, "Number of I-821D, Consideration of Deferred Action for Childhood Arrivals by Fiscal Year, Quarter, Intake, Biometrics and Case Status: 2012–2016," June 30, 2016. Available at: www .uscis.gov/sites/default/files/USCIS/Resources/Reports%20and%20Studies/Immigrat ion%20Forms%20Data/All%20Form%20Types/DACA/daca_performancedata_fy 2016_qtr3.pdf, accessed March 1, 2018.

61. American Immigration Council, "The Dream Act, DACA, and Other Policies Designed to Protect Dreamers," September 6, 2017. Available at: www .americanimmigrationcouncil.org/research/dream-act-daca-and-other-policies-designed-protect-dreamers, accessed March 1, 2018.

62. Immigration and Customs Enforcement, "Exercising Prosecutorial Discretion Consistent with the Civil Immigration Enforcement Priorities of the Agency for the Apprehension, Detention, and Removal of Aliens," 2011. Available at:

www.ice.gov/doclib/secure-communities/pdf/prosecutorial-discretion-memo.pdf, accessed March 1, 2018.

63. Department of Homeland Security, *Yearbook of Immigration Statistics 2015*, May 16, 2017. Available at: www.dhs.gov/immigration-statistics/yearbook/2015, accessed March 1, 2018.

64. Lamar Smith, "Obama Deportation Numbers a 'Trick,'" *Politico*, October 25, 2011. Available at: www.politico.com/story/2011/10/obama-deportation-numbers-a-trick-066805, accessed March 1, 2018.

65. Smith, "Obama Deportation Numbers a 'Trick.'"

66. Cristina M. Rodriguez, "The Significance of Local in Immigration Regulation," *Michigan Law Review* 106 (2008): 569.

67. *Ibid.*, 574.

68. Pew Hispanic Center, Jeffrey S. Passel, 2006. "The Size and Characteristics of the Unauthorized Migrant Population in the U.S., 2006." Available at: http://pewhispanic.org/files/reports/61.pdf, accessed March 1, 2018.

69. Steven A. Camarota, "A Record-Setting Decade of Immigration: 2000–2010," Center for Immigration Studies, October 2011. Available at: https://cis.org/Report/RecordSetting-Decade-Immigration-20002010, accessed March 1, 2018.

70. Rodriguez, "The Significance of Local in Immigration Regulation," p. 579.

71. Schuck, "Taking Immigration Federalism Seriously," p. 79.

72. Huntington, "The Constitutional Dimension of Immigration Federalism," pp. 578–579.

73. Schuck, "Taking Immigration Federalism Seriously," pp. 60–61.

74. Immigration and Customs Enforcement, Fact Sheet: Section 287(g) Immigration and Nationality Act, U.S. Immigration and Customs Enforcement, 2011. Available at: www.ice.gov/news/library/factsheets/287g.htm, accessed March 1, 2018.

75. Office of Legal Counsel to the Attorney General, Jay S. Bybee, Assistant Attorney General, Non-Preemption of the Authority of State and Local Law Enforcement Officials to Arrest Aliens for Immigration Violations (2002).

76. Huntington, "The Constitutional Dimension of Immigration Federalism," pp. 803–804.

77. Huntington, "The Constitutional Dimension of Immigration Federalism," pp. 812–823.

78. Germany, Australia, Canada, and Switzerland allow subnational units to determine immigration policy. Schunk, "Taking Immigration Federalism Seriously," p. 67.

79. Where there is a desire to maintain consistent national policy, the federal government may preempt. Huntington cites *American Insurance Co.* v. *Garamendi* as an example of effective statutory preemption of undesirable state legislation. Huntington, "The Constitutional Dimension of Immigration Federalism," p. 817.

80. Huntington, "The Constitutional Dimension of Immigration Federalism," pp. 824–827.

81. Wishnie, "Laboratories of Bigotry?" p. 493.

82. Orde F. Kitrie, "Federalism, Deportation, and Crime Victims Afraid to Call the Police," *Iowa Law Review* 91 (2006): 1449–1508.

83. Schuck, Taking Immigration Federalism Seriously," p. 92.

84. Spiro argues that state action prevents a single state from pulling legislative reform in one direction – something he claims took place in the 1990s with California.

While generally diminishing pressure on the structure as a whole, immigration federalism provides alternatives. Spiro explains it is "better from an alien's perspective to be driven from a hostile California into a receptive New York than to be shut out of the United States altogether." Spiro, "Learning to Live with Immigration Federalism," p. 1635.

85. Spiro, "Learning to Live with Immigration Federalism," p. 1627.
86. Huntington explains that in the case of Colorado, citizens who were virulently opposed to any form of immigration changed their opinion once their ideas were put into practice, and they were able to experience actual costs and benefits of stricter laws. "The Constitutional Dimension of Immigration Federalism," p. 848.
87. Huntington, "The Constitutional Dimension of Immigration Federalism," p. 848.
88. Schuck, "Taking Immigration Federalism Seriously," p. 60.
89. *Arizona* v. *United States*, 132 S.Ct. 2492.
90. Camarota, "A Record Setting Decade of Immigration," p. 1.
91. George Borjas estimates that the least well-off of our society face lower wages or lost jobs as the result of the increasing presence of undocumented workers in their communities. Borjas explains that for African American men in particular, a 10 percent increase in competing laborers from illegal immigration leads to a 3 percent reduction in wages, and close to a 5 percent reduction in employment. George J. Borjas, "Immigration and the Economic Status of African-American Men," *Economica* 77 (2009): 255–282.
92. Rodriguez, "The Significance of Local in Immigration Regulation," pp. 576–589.

12

Barack Obama: Testing the Constitutional Limits on the Executive

Carol M. Swain

INTRODUCTION

During his presidency, Barack Obama tested the limits of executive action in the realm of immigration reform when he engaged in executive actions to fulfill campaign promises stymied by Congress's failure to reform immigration laws. Using stealth and the power of press releases and executive actions, President Obama changed immigration policy affecting two classes of illegal aliens: young people brought to America as children and later their undocumented parents. The first of these major initiatives was the 2012 Deferred Action for Childhood Arrivals (DACA) program, and the second was the 2014 Deferred Action for Parents of Americans and Lawful Permanent Residents (DAPA). These programs went on to be challenged in the 2016 Supreme Court case of *United States* v. *Texas*[1] where a 4–4 split left standing a national injunction against DAPA and left the fate of DACA in the hands of President Donald J. Trump, whose election was partially based on his promises to reform immigration.[2] In this chapter, I review President Obama's use of executive actions, and I conclude with a brief look at early reactions to President Trump's efforts to use the power of the office to implement change ahead of legislative action by Congress.

THE BIRTH OF DACA

On June 15, 2012, President Barack Obama issued remarks coupled with a memorandum released by former Secretary of Homeland Security Janet Napolitano creating the DACA immigration program. DACA is a discretionary initiative that allows prosecutors and immigration enforcement agents to choose to suspend or decline to bring removal actions against young people who are present in the United States without authorization.[3] In order to be eligible to apply for deferred action, applicants must have come to the United

States before their sixteenth birthdays and have been continuous residents of the U.S. for five years, and, when DACA was originally implemented, be under age 31 at the time of application.[4] They must have come to the U.S. without having their immigration statuses inspected, or their lawful immigration statuses must have expired since their residency began. They must be current students or graduates of high school, holders of GEDs, members of the U.S. armed forces, or honorably discharged veterans. Applicants must not have been convicted of any felony, "significant misdemeanor," or three or more misdemeanors, and must not otherwise "pose a threat." Finally, applicants must be present in the United States at the time the request for deferred action is made. Secretary Napolitano clarified in her memorandum that no substantive right is created by the policies expressed therein; such a substantive right can only be conferred by Congress. President Obama confirmed in his remarks that he would sign DACA into law if it were passed by Congress.

DACA was largely a response to Congress's inability or unwillingness to pass a comprehensive immigration reform bill. President Obama used congressional inaction as a justification for implementing administrative changes using executive branch agencies. Under the current conditions, DACA can be eliminated by President Trump or it can continue as stated. While the Obama administration categorized DACA as only a policy of prosecutorial discretion that does not create any substantive rights, DACA encourages eligible people to rely on its protections and "come out of the shadows." The fact that the policy may be repealed, however, has resulted in hesitancy to take advantage of its benefits. In 2014, the Pew Research Center estimated that there were 11.2 million people present in the United States without documentation.[5] Of these 11.2 million, the Migration Policy Institute estimated that, in 2016, nearly 2 million were eligible for DACA and another 3.6 million were eligible for its companion program for parents of legally present children, DAPA.[6] Although over five million people are eligible for the protections of the Obama administration's deferred action proposals, as of June 2016, just over one and a half million applications for the programs had been received.[7] Not all of those eligible for DACA or DAPA have sought their protections. Potentially eligible people may be discouraged from applying because their protected statuses could later be revoked.

SEPARATION OF POWERS

The doctrine of Separation of Powers governs the allocation of powers and abilities among the branches of federal government. Congress's powers are detailed in Article I of the Constitution, while the Executive's are found in Article II. The duties of the courts are discussed in Article III. All legislative powers are vested in Congress by the Constitution, and Article I, Section 8 enumerates such powers, most of which have been construed broadly. Among the enumerated powers is the power to establish a uniform rule of naturalization, which relates to immigration policy. Congress also enjoys the broad language of the Necessary and Proper clause, which serves as a flexible way to allow Congress to create any laws that carry out the enumerated powers.

The bulk of executive power is derived from the Take Care and Faithful Execution Clauses found in Article II. These leave in the president's hands the responsibility of implementing the laws passed by Congress. The president often accomplishes this through the use of administrative agencies. While administrative agencies are not addressed explicitly in the Constitution, their constitutionality is uncontroverted. Agencies are constrained by the constitutional limits on the executive branch as a whole and by the delegation of power granted to them by Congress. Finally, Article III of the Constitution has been interpreted to give the federal judiciary the power to interpret the law and rule on the propriety of Congressional and executive action.

The constitutionality of DACA and DAPA was vigorously challenged, with arguments that they represented a violation of the Separation of Powers doctrine. While this constitutional question has not yet been conclusively decided by the courts due to a time-honored practice by the courts to decline to reach constitutional questions if a case may be disposed of on statutory grounds, the questionable use of executive power to accomplish outcomes that are legislative in nature sends a message to future presidents that, at best, the precedent is established to circumvent constitutional constraints, and, at worst, the Constitution is not a document to be respected. In September 2017, however, the Trump Administration did declare that DACA "was not statutorily authorized and was therefore an unconstitutional exercise of discretion by the executive branch."[8] As it stands, then, both DACA and DAPA no longer remain in force. Along with the termination of DACA, President Trump also gave Congress six months to develop a legislative solution to the status of Dreamers.[9] These issues now await congressional action either comprehensively or piecemeal, depending on the circumstances, as discussed in the next section. We return to the legal challenges against DACA and DAPA in a later section.

CONGRESS'S INACTION

Failure to enact new laws is often blamed on the gridlock produced by a divided government, where Congress and the office of president are controlled by different political parties. Thought to be even less efficient is a divided Congress, where different parties control the House of Representatives and the Senate. If one house of Congress is able to pass a bill, it is unlikely that the other house will adopt the same version if it is subject to control by a competing political party. While this argument has not been subject to statistical analysis, individual examples lend support. The Obama presidency serves as such an example. During the Obama presidency, which was marked largely by Republican control of the House of Representatives, only 2.4 percent of bills introduced were enacted.[10] This is the lowest rate for any presidency in the last 50 years. The most sweeping pieces of legislation of his presidency, the Patient Protection and Affordable Care Act (ACA) and the Restoring American Financial Stability Act (Dodd-Frank), were passed by the 111th Congress. The 111th Congress was the only sitting Congress during the Obama presidency where Democrats controlled both houses.

Congressional inaction has been extremely apparent in the area of immigration law and reform. Congress has not passed a substantial immigration law since 1986, when the 99th Congress was very effective despite the fact that Democrats controlled the House while Republicans controlled the Senate and the presidency (which would tend to erode the claim that divided government is the primary cause of political gridlock).[11] The Immigration Reform and Control Act of 1986 passed by a narrow margin, however. The bill largely focused on sanctions for employers who hire undocumented immigrants.[12] Subsequent attempts at comprehensive immigration reform have also focused on employment, but with extreme variation. The proposed Comprehensive Immigration Reform Act of 2006, for example, sought to create a new non-immigrant temporary worker visa and to raise the number of employment-based visas available each year.[13] It also would have permitted employers to hire non-immigrant temporary workers upon showing that doing so would not adversely affect the wages, benefits, or working conditions of similarly situated U.S. workers. The Border Security, Economic Opportunity, and Immigration Modernization Act of 2013, alternatively, would have set caps on non-immigrant worker visas to be awarded, and would have required employers to show that hiring non-immigrant workers would not displace U.S. workers.[14] That bill would have outlawed hiring workers without authorization, mandated the use of employment verification systems, and required the government to confirm the identity and employment eligibility of employees.

Perhaps the great degree of variation with respect to individual issues in comprehensive bills contributed to the trend of disaggregation. Recently, the vast majority of immigration legislation has taken the form of subject-specific bills under a piecemeal approach. This allows for more involved debate on specific issues, such as border control, employment, or deportation. Some of the most recent piecemeal legislation has been designed to address issues related to the Separation of Powers doctrine. November 2014 was the first time in the past decade that Congressional concern about the executive branch's involvement in immigration policy was demonstrated through the introduction of legislation.[15] After President Obama announced his executive action plan in an immigration reform speech, Congress responded almost immediately (within two weeks of the speech) to defend its position as the branch of government empowered to make decisions related to border protection, high-skilled immigrant worker visas, and undocumented immigrant adjudications.

Tension between the two branches appeared to run high, as indicated in President Obama's November 21, 2014, speech announcing his expansion of the DACA program to parents in the form of DAPA. There he issued the following statement:

The actions I'm taking are not only lawful, they're the kinds of actions taken by every single Republican President and every single Democratic President for the past half century. And to those Members of Congress who question my authority to make our immigration system work better, or question the wisdom of me acting where Congress has failed, I have one answer: Pass a bill. I want to work with both parties to pass a more permanent legislative solution. And the day I sign that bill into law, the actions I take will no longer be necessary. Meanwhile, don't let a disagreement over a single issue be a deal-breaker on every issue. That's not how our democracy works, and Congress certainly shouldn't shut down our government again just because we disagree on this. Americans are tired of gridlock. What our country needs from us right now is a common purpose; a higher purpose.[16]

President Obama was correct about a few things in his statement. The American people were frustrated by Congress's ineffectiveness. During Obama's tenure, congressional approval ratings fluctuated between 9 and 39 percent, with the highest approval ratings occurring early in his presidency and the lowest toward the end.[17] The American people largely did not perceive Congress as doing its job, and they did not have much confidence in Congress. President Obama was also correct in saying that his actions were not unprecedented. Many presidents have created policy unilaterally. Most notable was Franklin D. Roosevelt, whose presidency will be discussed below. The president made an important error in his statement though; disagreements on single issues can and should derail a comprehensive piece of legislation if the issue is important enough and not sufficiently considered, which is why piecemeal legislation is preferable.

AN UNCOMMON PRESIDENCY

The Obama presidency was not remarkable when analyzed in light of the number of executive orders or vetoes. Obama's 276 Executive Orders were well within the range of orders signed by presidents since the twentieth century, and his record pales in comparison to the monumental 3,721 signed by President Franklin D. Roosevelt.[18] Additionally, he only vetoed 12 bills during his tenure; this is another figure dwarfed by the Roosevelt presidency, which holds the record for presidential vetoes at 372.[19] Obama does, however, stand out in terms of lawsuits brought against his administration. While previous administrations have been sued, Obama and his cabinet-level officials had to defend against multiple suits while watching many favored policy initiatives, including those fulfilling campaign promises, be dismantled by the courts. These lawsuits, some of which were brought by individuals disgruntled by the way the political cookie crumbled, exposed the president's level of comfort with testing the limits of the law. It is difficult to determine whether this is despite or because of the president's position as a professor of constitutional law at the University of Chicago Law School. Obama demonstrated his fascination with defining the contours of executive power through his announcement of the DACA and DAPA programs, both of which represent an impermissible use of executive authority that was characteristic of his presidency and threaten to set a dangerous precedent for future American presidents. The American people had to rely on the courts as protectors of the constitution and arbiters of statutory disputes to ensure that the president did not overstep his bounds.

The use of unilateral executive action is highly controversial, due largely to its ambiguous constitutional underpinnings.[20] Presidents throughout history have created policy without the aid of Congress in events including the Louisiana Purchase, the Emancipation Proclamation, the formation of Japanese internment camps, and the creation of government agencies such as EPA and FDA. The Constitution was designed to allow sufficient room for changed circumstances so that it could address unanticipated future situations without need for change to the constitutional language itself. This led to a great deal of vagueness in its drafting that allows for experimental application based on trial and error. These ambiguities create large opportunities for presidents to test their power and seek its outer limits. Without precise boundaries, there is a great deal of uncertainty regarding the propriety of unilateral presidential action. It rests almost entirely on the courts to say when a president has gone too far, though presidents may also be reined in through exercise of the legislature's impeachment powers. Because these remedies have been reserved for the direst of circumstances, presidents are in a unique position to test the limits of their power without much recourse. Even with this great opportunity for unilateral executive control, most presidents have largely resisted the temptation to go too far, whatever that may mean in this fluid constitutional context.

Typically, unilateral presidential action is studied in the context of a president's issuance of executive orders. This ignores the variety of other options available to presidents to announce and implement policy, such as proclamations, memoranda of understanding, letters of agreement, and more. Research on executive action has been facilitated by the Federal Register Act of 1935, which requires publication of executive branch activities. Not surprisingly, this act was created in response to the explosion of executive activity during the New Deal era. As discussed above, President Franklin D. Roosevelt holds the record for most executive orders issued by a president. This number does not even reflect other executive policymaking accomplished through means other than executive orders, and it does not account for the importance or triviality of each order. Roosevelt's presidential activism is often justified by the old adage, "desperate times call for desperate measures." Emerging from the Great Depression and entering World War II marked an extremely tumultuous time in American history, and Roosevelt believed that a strong executive would help return the nation to peace and prosperity. Roosevelt's New Deal policies included the creation of myriad agencies, commonly referred to as "Alphabet Soup" due to the proliferation of acronyms they produced. Alphabet Soup represented a great success and changed the bureaucratic landscape entirely. Less successfully, his attempt to increase the number of Justices on the Supreme Court so that he could appoint judges with political leanings consistent with his own in order to ensure future implementation of New Deal policies was recognized as court packing and failed completely. This is one of the few examples of a president pushing his power too far.

Franklin D. Roosevelt's presidency probably represents the high-water mark of unilateral executive action, but it certainly bears similarities to the Obama presidency. Various political blogs and news outlets have compared the two presidencies. Although by the numbers President Obama does not appear to have been as activist as Roosevelt, they have much in common. It is unusual to see a president create unilateral policy so boldly, but it is possible that Obama was encouraged by his own constitutional law background. Knowing the incredibly flexible standards offered by the Constitution, he demonstrated confidence in the appropriateness and legality of his actions. Unfortunately for President Obama, the American people did not consistently view him as a hero, as they did Roosevelt. Perhaps the times were not sufficiently desperate to justify his measures. While his inheritance of the financial collapse and the War on Terror represented significant challenges in his early presidency, Obama's most far-reaching initiatives were not related to those issues. Although most people would identify the healthcare and immigration landscapes in the United States as less than ideal, they do not appear to have presented the threats of nearly universal poverty and war confronted in the 1930s. Still, President Obama used his office to vindicate his frustration with an inactive Congress by using unilateral executive action, largely by employing agencies (which owe their very existence to Franklin D. Roosevelt) to carry out non-legislative policies. As we will see, the Obama administration's tendency was to use methods other than executive orders to effectuate its policy goals.

TECHNIQUES USED BY THE OBAMA ADMINISTRATION

As explained above, the Federal Register Act mandates the publication of executive orders and other executive documents. The purpose of this requirement is to produce transparency and enable the public to locate sources of executive law in one location. The Federal Register is essentially a daily newspaper, now available online, detailing the actions taken by all of the executive agencies, as well as the Office of the President. Aside from executive orders, the Federal Register contains documents related to agency rulemaking, including Notices of Proposed Rulemaking and Final Rules, also known as regulations. The public nature of the register is crucial in enabling public participation and allowing people to determine exactly what the law is. Prior to the Federal Register, there was no such repository for executive documents, and it was often unclear exactly what the law was. The landmark case of *Panama Refining Co. v. Ryan* demonstrated the need for an executive analogy to the United States Code for legislation.[21] That case represented a huge embarrassment to the Department of Justice, which was required to admit to the Supreme Court that the very executive order it was attempting to enforce had in fact already been revoked. When even the government does not know which orders are in effect, the public can hardly be expected to puzzle through the state of the law. The Federal Register goes a long way in remedying this problem because it makes available crucial executive documents. However, there are some documents that are not subject to publication in the Federal Register.

Perhaps because of their public nature, the Obama administration appeared to avoid executive orders. Therefore, President Obama's issuance of nearly 300 orders is not entirely representative of the unilateral action taken. His administration tended to favor another approach, which combined speeches and press releases made by the President with memoranda issued by secretaries of agencies. This is the approach that was used to announce DACA. In searching for the document that created DACA, it would be a naïve assumption that it would take the form of an executive order. Even with careful examination of various government websites for many hours, using every search parameter imaginable, a DACA executive order cannot be found. That is because no such executive order ever existed. Instead, on the day that DACA was announced, President Obama made a speech and issued a press release about the policy, which was confusing to both the media and the public. It implied that policy would be implemented by executive order. However, on the same day, Janet Napolitano, then-Secretary of the Department of Homeland Security, released a memorandum detailing the contents of the policy. It seemed as if the policy was entirely created by the Department, and not by the President.

The complexity of the form of DACA's creation, regardless of its intentionality, provided important benefits to the president. First, it made the law hard to find. For something controversial like immigration reform, public scrutiny is sure to follow. Such scrutiny is impeded when the public cannot locate the policy itself. Second, it allowed the president to take credit for the policy's success while maintaining the ability to blame the agency in the event of its failure. This was a political win–win. If the policy proved to work out well, the president could claim it as his own by citing the speech. If it did not, he could cite Secretary Napolitano's memorandum and call it agency action. However, the Secretary of Homeland Security is a member of the president's cabinet, and it is clear from whom cabinet members take their orders. Finally, it allowed for flexibility in the DACA program. If the president wished to change the program, he could have the Department of Homeland Security issue another memorandum detailing the ways it would exercise its prosecutorial discretion in handling undocumented immigrants. This is preferable from the president's perspective to the use of executive orders, which are modified or revoked by subsequent executive orders.[22] If the policy had initially been created in an executive order, each change made to the program would have to occur through executive order and would have to be made available to the public in the Federal Register in the section devoted to the Office of the President.

DACA, DAPA, AND THEIR QUESTIONABLE LEGALITY

The issuance of Secretary Napolitano's memorandum and President Obama's press release on June 15, 2012, probably did not produce the same media storm they would have if they had been published in the Federal Register.[23] Still, the policy was groundbreaking and caught the attention of those interested in immigration issues. While not going as far as creating a substantive right to remain in the United States, the policy pushed against the boundary of what is considered regulatory guidance and what is truly legislative in nature. Framed as a set of guidelines for the exercise of prosecutorial discretion by the Department of Homeland Security, DACA laid out certain parameters that would qualify an undocumented immigrant as low-priority and not subject to deportation proceedings, as long as the policy remained in effect and the immigrant continued to meet the parameters. Eligible immigrants were those who came to the United States before they turned 16 and had lived in the U.S. continuously for at least five years. They must have been in school, a graduate or holder of a General Education Diploma, or serving in or honorably discharged from the United States military. They could not have been convicted of a felony, significant misdemeanor, or multiple misdemeanor offenses.

When DACA was first created in 2012, it only applied to people aged 30 or younger. The policy was changed in November 2014 and made applicable to people of any age, representing a large expansion in eligibility. This DACA expansion was coupled with the announcement of a new program, DAPA. Under DAPA and the DACA expansion, Immigration and Customs Enforcement maintained discretion on an individual level over immigrants, and satisfaction of the above criteria did not guarantee that a removal proceeding would not be brought against them. Additionally, if an immigrant failed to satisfy any of the criteria, they would no longer be eligible for deferred action. In order to benefit from the protection against removal offered by DACA or DAPA, immigrants had to file an application. If they were eligible and accepted into the program, the policy of deferred action applied to them and they were generally not at risk of deportation. These changes were again effectuated through the issuance of two Department of Homeland Security memoranda, coupled with a televised announcement delivered by the president.

It was not long before a federal lawsuit was filed against the United States government seeking to halt the implementation and dispute the constitutionality of the 2014 expansion of DACA and the creation of DAPA. The lawsuit was heard in a federal trial-level court in Texas by Judge Andrew S.

Hanen.[24] The state of Texas, as plaintiff, brought claims under statutory and constitutional grounds. Due to a longstanding legal doctrine, the judge decided the case on purely statutory grounds. The Doctrine of Constitutional Avoidance states that if a case can be decided on statutory grounds, the court should refrain from considering constitutional issues. Because the judge found the statutory arguments dispositive, he did not consider the constitutionality of DACA or DAPA. The constitutional issues were fully briefed and thus were preserved for consideration upon appeal. The federal government did in fact appeal the judge's ruling, which determined that the DACA expansion and DAPA creation violated the federal Administrative Procedure Act (APA) and issued an order barring the government from implementing the programs by accepting new applications.

The decision was upheld by the Fifth Circuit Court of Appeals, split 2–1, which also declined to reach the constitutional issues. The federal government then petitioned the Supreme Court of the United States for a writ of *certiorari*, which was granted. During the pendency of the case, Justice Antonin Scalia passed away suddenly and unexpectedly, leaving only eight justices to decide. Without a tie-breaking vote, this left the Court vulnerable to a 4–4 split, which is precisely what occurred. In an astonishingly brief *per curiam* opinion, the divided Court adopted the Fifth Circuit's opinion as its own, leaving Judge Hanen's trial-court-level opinion intact. The case could have been revisited by the Supreme Court after the appointment and confirmation of a ninth Justice, but this has not occurred. Even with the confirmation of conservative Justice Neil Gorsuch to the Supreme Court, the case has not been revisited, and it seems that the ruling will stand for now. A discussion of the District Court and Circuit Court opinions is therefore in order.

As mentioned above, Judge Hanen decided the case on statutory grounds according to the provisions of the Administrative Procedure Act. The judge emphasized in his decision that prosecutorial discretion is correctly viewed as an issue best resolved by the executive branch of government, and the judiciary should be careful not to disturb agency action with respect to such discretion. Because of agency expertise, the executive's authority to exercise prosecutorial discretion must be respected unless it is in violation of a statute or the Constitution. The District Court judge determined that the DACA expansion and DAPA did not constitute an exercise of prosecutorial discretion, but rather qualified as a policy or program. The hallmark of prosecutorial discretion is case-by-case analysis, not categorical policies of exemption from the strictures of the law. This assisted the judge in determining that judicial review, rather than judicial restraint, was appropriate.

With judicial review in order, the judge was required first to examine the statutory arguments brought by the state of Texas related to the APA, as the applicability of the APA was conceded by the federal government. The APA has certain requirements related to the regulatory, or rulemaking, process. Under the definitions of the APA, the DACA expansion and DAPA qualified as "rules," which are issued through "rulemaking," and so the requirements of the Act apply to both. APA Section 553 lays out the formal requirements that must be adhered to in rulemaking. One of these requirements is publication of the proposed rule in the Federal Register. The only way this requirement would not apply is if these programs qualified as an interpretive rule, general statement of policy, or rule of agency organization, procedure, or practice. The publication requirement applies to all other substantive rules.

Whether a rule is substantive or interpretive is determined by three factors, with none being dispositive: government characterization, binding effect, and substantive change in existing law. With respect to the first factor, the Department of Homeland Security, through the Department of Justice, argued that the rule was merely a statement of policy and that the directive represented guidelines, but President Obama's speech announcing DACA deemed it to be a program and he professed to be changing the law. Analysis of this inconsistent government characterization was thus inconclusive. In consideration of the second factor, it was clear that the agency did not have the freedom to consider the facts of individual situations. The criteria were generalized, categorical, and binding, and the agency only had to determine whether an individual fit the criteria. Individuals who did not fit the criteria could not be extended DACA/DAPA protections or benefits. Finally, with respect to the third factor, substantive changes in existing law are those that adopt a new position inconsistent with existing law. DACA and DAPA were new guidelines and represented a departure from existing immigration law. Therefore, weighing the three factors together, the court concluded that the DACA extension and DAPA should have been promulgated using the rulemaking requirements of APA Section 553.

Because the policies were not properly promulgated, they could not be enforced. This meant that the Department of Homeland Security could go through the process of re-issuing the DACA expansion and DAPA in the form of rules, rather than memoranda. This process would have been extremely time-consuming, as the procedures described in the APA require much of agencies creating new rules. The hallmark of the notice-and-comment rulemaking process is public participation, and the agency must consider all public comments submitted in response to a proposed rule. This means that the new rules could not be implemented until after a final rule was promulgated, which would likely have taken a few years and required the political will to do so.

Even if a final rule were promulgated, it is not clear that it would have withstood judicial review. This is because, aside from the procedural defects noted by the court, there were unconstitutional aspects of the policy. The arguments made in the initial lawsuit could be made yet again with respect to a properly promulgated final rule. The constitutional arguments relate largely to the Separation of Powers doctrine and essentially argue that the executive branch was engaging in legislation when it created DAPA and extended DACA. Legislative functions are expressly reserved for the legislature, and if

DACA and DAPA are tantamount to legislation, then it was beyond the executive's power to create them. Another constitutional argument is that the Obama administration failed to uphold its Article II obligation to faithfully execute Congress's laws because immigration law at that time did not contemplate such prioritization of deportation cases but rather required the removal of any individuals not lawfully present in the country. Because of these and other similar arguments, the Trump administration removed what remained of DACA in September of 2017, citing that its creation was unconstitutional.[25]

It is important to note that the decisions rendered by the District Court, the Appeals Court, and the Supreme Court were limited to the procedural context in which they were issued. When the state of Texas and its 25 companion plaintiff states initially filed the lawsuit, one of the forms of relief they sought was what is known as a preliminary injunction. This was a request that the court, prior to disposing of the case on its merits, prevent the federal government from continuing to implement the policies while the case was pending. Judge Hanen's decision was a decision to prevent DAPA and the DACA expansion from being implemented while the litigation was considered. The Obama administration appealed that decision, and that decision alone. The final constitutionality of the actions was never decided by the courts, and the question was only finally resolved when further action was taken by the executive branch during the Trump administration to completely remove the policy. What legislative actions will be taken remains to be seen.

CONCLUSION

To his supporters, Barack Obama is a champion of those in need of political protection but unable to garner it on their own – the poor and the disenfranchised. To his critics, he is willing to manipulate or even disregard constitutional language in order to achieve his objectives. Regardless of political or personal opinion, it is clear that the Obama presidency was an uncommon, and in some ways remarkable, one. Whether it was remarkable in a positive or negative way is beyond the scope of this discussion. By taking unilateral executive action, President Obama sought to test or even establish the outer limits of presidential power, capitalizing on the vague and incomplete language of the Constitution. He acted when Congress was unwilling to do so in order to advance his own policy ideals, and the courts have not always treated his methodology favorably. He took controversial issues such as immigration and healthcare and used his position and available loopholes to create new policy in decisive, albeit questionably legal, ways. His presidency has been compared to that of the most activist president in national history, Franklin D. Roosevelt. While Roosevelt benefitted from unprecedented public support and justification for his extreme actions provided by extreme circumstances, President Obama did not find himself in the same situation. His presidency was instead marked by controversy and disapproval from both Congress and the American public. While many presidents have resisted the temptation to take unilateral action for fear of the appearance of imperialism, Obama used all tools available at his disposal to advance his own agenda while relying on the judicial system or Congress to tell him when he went too far, actions that may have permanently changed the nature of the presidency.

This legacy of reliance on Congress and the judiciary to dictate when the president has pushed his powers too far appears to be a pattern that continues with the election of Donald Trump. President Trump, in many ways, has not received the same level of executive latitude as his predecessor, however. In the first four months of his presidency, President Trump issued 36 executive orders,[26] four of which have already been challenged in court (as of June 2017).[27] The two most controversial and politically salient of these, like those policies challenged during the Obama administration, relate to immigration and were executed without congressional approval. Nevertheless, in both cases, they have also been successfully blocked at both the District and Circuit Court levels.

The first challenged executive order was issued on January 27, 2017. This executive order banned the entry of all immigrant and non-immigrant travelers from Iraq, Iran, Libya, Somalia, Sudan, Syria, and Yemen for 90 days; restricted the entry of all refugees for 120 days and the entry of Syrian refugees indefinitely; lowered the cap of the number of refugees to 50,000 for the year; and directed the prioritization of minority religious groups in refugee admissions. Due to an unclear plan for implementation, confusion ensued and a court in the state of Washington quickly issued a Temporary Restraining Order, or TRO. The government appealed the case to the Ninth Circuit Court of Appeals, but the court upheld the district court's decision. The Trump administration, rather than appeal to the Supreme Court, decided to re-write the current executive order to address the concerns that had spurred the Temporary Restraining Order. This second executive order was issued on March 6, 2017, revoking and replacing the first.[28] Although very similar to the first executive order, it removed Iraq from the list of banned countries, stopped the indefinite ban on Syrian refugees, and eliminated the requirement to prioritize religious minorities in refugee admissions. It also allowed for waivers on a case-by-case basis and clarified that it did not apply to those already in possession of a visa. The day before this order was to go into effect, it was also challenged in court, and a temporary injunction was issued by District Courts in Hawaii and Maryland. The Maryland injunction applied only to Section 2(c) of the order, which denied entry of immigrants and non-immigrants from the six aforementioned countries.[29] The Hawaii injunction applied to this same section, as well as the section restricting the entrance of refugees.[30] President Trump and his administration once again appealed both cases. The Maryland case was considered by the Fourth Circuit Court of Appeals. The Appeals Court upheld the District Court's decision, ruling that the executive order violated the

Establishment clause of the first amendment and was thus unconstitutional.[31] The president appealed the case to the Supreme Court on June 1, 2017, with a request to reinstate the blocked portions of the executive order.[32] On June 26, 2017, the Supreme Court upheld part of the executive order and granted *certiorari* for the case. The Court will hear oral arguments in fall 2017.[33]

In short, President Trump has also been testing the limits of his executive powers, but it remains unclear whether the judiciary branch will allow him the same freedom to do so that it gave to his predecessor. It is obvious that Barack Obama's presidency is still influencing American politics, but whether the current reaction to President Trump's actions is a result of, or in spite of, this legacy is less clear. Overall, the presidency of Barack Obama was an exceptional one, and it is already having far-reaching consequences in American politics. His presidency will surely be remembered, but the writers of history books will have much to do with the light in which it is painted.

NOTES

1. *U. S. v. Texas,*137 S.Ct. 285 (2016).
2. Chishti Muzaffar and Faye Hipsman, "Supreme Court DAPA Ruling a Blow to Obama Administration, Moves Immigration Back to Political Realm," *Migration Policy Institute*, June 29, 2016. Web. Available at: www.migrationpolicy.org/article/supreme-court-dapa-ruling-blow-obama-administration-moves-immigration-back-political-realm, accessed March 2, 2018.
3. Alejandro Mayorkas, "Deferred Action for Childhood Arrivals: Who Can Be Considered?" Blog post. *The White House*. The United States Government, 15 August 2012. Web. 11 December 2016. Available at: https://obamawhitehouse.archives.gov/blog/2012/08/15/deferred-action-childhood-arrivals-who-can-be-considered, accessed March 2, 2018.
4. United States of America. Department of Homeland Security. *Exercising Prosecutorial Discretion with Respect to Individuals Who Came to the United States as Children.* By Janet Napolitano. N.p., 15 June 2012. Web. Available at: www.dhs.gov/xlibrary/assets/s1-exercising-prosecutorial-discretion-individuals-who-came-to-us-as-children.pdf, accessed December 11, 2016.
5. Jeffrey S. Passel and D'Vera Cohn, "Unauthorized Immigrant Totals Rise in 7 States, Fall in 14," *Pew Research Center's Hispanic Trends Project*. N.p., 18 November 2014. Web. 11 December 2016. Available at: www.pewhispanic.org/2014/11/18/unauthorized-immigrant-totals-rise-in-7-states-fall-in-14/, accessed December 11, 2016.
6. "Deferred Action for Childhood Arrivals (DACA) Data Tools," *Migration Policy Institute*. N.p., 26 September 2016. Web. 11 December 2016. Available at: www.migrationpolicy.org/programs/data-hub/deferred-action-childhood-arrivals-daca-profiles, accessed March 2, 2018.; "Deferred Action for Unauthorized Immigrants Who Are Parents," *Migration Policy Institute*. N.p., 08 June 2016. Web. 11 December 2016. Available at: www.migrationpolicy.org/content/deferred-action-unauthorized-immigrants-who-are-parents, accessed December 11, 2016.

7. "Number of I-821D, Consideration of Deferred Action for Childhood Arrivals by Fiscal Year, Quarter, Intake, Biometrics and Case Status: 2012–2016," *United States Citizenship and Immigration Services*. N.p., 30 June 2016. Web. Available at: www.uscis.gov/sites/default/files/USCIS/Resources/Reports%20and%20Studies/Immigration%20Forms%20Data/All%20Form%20Types/DACA/daca_performancedata_fy2016_qtr3.pdf, accessed March 2, 2018.

8. The White House Office of the Press Secretary, "President Donald J. Trump Restores Responsibility and the Rule of Law to Immigration," September 5, 2017. Available at: www.whitehouse.gov/the-press-office/2017/09/05/president-donald-j-trump-restores-responsibility-and-rule-law, accessed March 2, 2018.

9. Office of the Press Secretary, "President Donald J. Trump Restores Responsibility and the Rule of Law to Immigration."

10. "Statistics and Historical Comparison," *GovTrack*. N.p. Web. Available at: www.govtrack.us/congress/bills/statistics, accessed December 11, 2016.

11. "Party Divisions of the House of Representatives | US House of Representatives: History, Art & Archives," *History, Art & Archives*. United States House of Representatives, n.d. Web. Available at: http://history.house.gov/Institution/Party-Divisions/Party-Divisions/, accessed December 11, 2016.

12. Carolyn Wong, *Lobbying for Inclusion: Rights Politics and the Making of Immigration Policy* (Stanford, CA: Stanford UP, 2006).

13. Comprehensive Immigration Reform Act of 2006, S. 2611, 109th Cong. (2006). Print.

14. Border Security, Economic Opportunity, and Immigration Modernization Act, S. 744, 113th Cong. (2013). Print.

15. Separation of Powers Act of 2014, H.R. 5768, 113th Cong. (2014). Print; Preventing Executive Overreach on Immigration Act of 2014, H.R. 5759, 113th Cong. (2014). Print.

16. *President Obama's Immigration Address*. CNN. 21 Nov. 2014. *CNN Politics*. Web. Available at: www.cnn.com/2014/11/20/politics/obama-immigration-speech-transcript/index.html. Transcript, accessed December 11, 2016.

17. Gallup, Inc., "Congress and the Public," *Gallup*. N.p., 28 September 2016. Web. Available at: www.gallup.com/poll/1600/Congress-Public.aspx, accessed December 11, 2016.

18. John Woolley and Gerhard Peters, "Executive Orders," *The American Presidency Project*. University of California Santa Barbara, 20 June 2017. Web. Available at: www.presidency.ucsb.edu/data/orders.php, accessed June 20, 2017.

19. John Woolley and Gerhard Peters, "Presidential Vetoes," *The American Presidency Project*. University of California Santa Barbara, 28 September 2016. Web. 11 December 2016. Available at: www.presidency.ucsb.edu/data/vetoes.php, accessed December 11, 2016.

20. McNollgast, "The Political Origins of the Administrative Procedure Act," *Journal of Law, Economics, and Organization* 15.1 (1999): 180–217. Web. 11 December 2016.

21. *Panama Refining Co. v. Ryan*. 293 U.S. 388. Supreme Court of the United States. 7 January 1935. Print.

22. United States of America. Congressional Research Service. *Executive Orders: Issuance, Modification, and Revocation*. By Vivian S. Chu and Todd Garvey. N.p.,

16 April 2014. Web. Available at: https://fas.org/sgp/crs/misc/RS20846.pdf, accessed December 11, 2016.

23. Janet Napolitano, "Exercising Prosecutorial Discretion with Respect to Individuals Who Came to the United States as Children," Memorandum to David V. Aguilar, Alejandro Mayorkas, John Morton, 15 June 2012. *United States Department of Homeland Security.* N.p., 15 June 2016. Web. Available at: www.dhs.gov/sites/default/files/publications/s1-exercising-prosecutorial-discretion-individuals-who-came-to-us-as-children.pdf, accessed December 11, 2016.

24. *United States* v. *Texas.* United States District Court for the Southern District of Texas. 16 Feb. 2015. N.p., n.d. Web. Available at: www.txs.uscourts.gov/sites/txs/files/1-14-cv-254_145X20977588_0.pdf, accessed March 2, 2018.

25. Office of the Press Secretary, "President Donald J. Trump Restores Responsibility and the Rule of Law to Immigration."

26. "2017 Donald Trump Executive Orders," *The Office of the Federal Register.* The United States of America, 2017. Web. Available at: www.federalregister.gov/executive-orders/donald-trump/2017, accessed May 31, 2017.

27. Richard Wolf, "Court Challenges to Trump Policies May Multiply," *USA Today.* 4 May 2017. Web. Available at: www.usatoday.com/story/news/politics/2017/05/04/court-challenges-trump-policies-may-multiply/101243776/, accessed May 31, 2017.

28. Maria Sacchetti and Matt Zapotosky, "Trump's New Entry Ban to Be Challenged in Courts Hours before It Takes Effect," *The Washington Post.* WP Company LLC, 14 March 2017. Web. Available at: www.washingtonpost.com/local/social-issues/lawyers-challenging-trumps-new-travel-ban-hope-for-court-action-by-wednesday/2017/03/14/2e8be98a-08c2-11e7-b77c-0047d15a24e0_story.html?utm_term=.d7f5ee714e18, accessed May 31, 2017.

29. *International Refugee Assistance Project* v. *Trump*, No. 17–1351 (4th Cir. 25 May 2017).

30. Maura Dolan, "Hawaii Asks 9th Circuit Court for an 11-judge Panel to Review Trump's Travel Ban," *The Los Angeles Times.* N.p., 12 April 2017. Web. Available at: www.latimes.com/politics/washington/la-na-essential-washington-updates-hawaii-asks-9th-circuit-for-an-11-judge-1492021688-htmlstory.html, accessed June 8, 2017.

31. *International Refugee Assistance Project* v. *Trump*, No. 17–1351 (4th Cir. 25 May 2017).

32. Bill Chappell, "Trump Asks Supreme Court to Reinstate Travel Ban on 6 Majority-Muslim Nations," *The Two-Way.* NPR, 2 June 2017. Web. Available at: www.npr.org/sections/thetwo-way/2017/06/02/531158852/trump-asks-supreme-court-to-reinstate-travel-ban-on-6-majority-muslim-nations, accessed June 8, 2017.

33. *Trump* v. *International Refugee Assistance*, 582 U. S. ____ (2017), Per Curiam. Available at: www.supremecourt.gov/opinions/16pdf/16-1436_l6hc.pdf, accessed March 2, 2018.

PART III

PHILOSOPHY AND RELIGION

13

Biblical Prudence and American Immigration

James R. Edwards, Jr.

This chapter offers an approach to some of the most important immigration policy questions confronting the United States from the perspective of biblically based Christian faith. As a Christian congressional staffer working for evangelical legislators, I faced the hard task of having to make public policy concerning many of these issues and have tried as conscientiously as I can to apply what I understand to be the insights and commands of the Bible and Judeo-Christian principles of prudence to the issues surrounding our current immigration challenges.

I stress from the outset that deriving policy prescriptions from the Bible and other Christian sources is a difficult business. Many complex issues are involved – theological, exegetical, and pragmatic. I do not claim that my own conclusions are infallible, and I acknowledge that other believers may honestly and conscientiously reach different conclusions. But I do believe that the *principles* I outline here, as distinct from their specific application, are the appropriate Christian biblical principles to apply to these policy questions. As such, I believe they are the principles best suited to guide all Christians in making public policy judgments, even if we don't always agree as to their application in specific cases.

Before addressing the specific immigration controversy, the chapter considers three aspects of the Christian faith that provide background and context to the controversy itself: the biblical role of civil government; the distinction between ancient Israel and the United States; and the role of Christianity and Reformation Protestantism in shaping America's political culture. After these issues have been addressed, the chapter looks at what the Bible specifically teaches about immigrants and immigration, and concludes with an assessment of U.S. immigration policy based on biblical principles.

WHAT IS GOD'S PURPOSE FOR CIVIL GOVERNMENT?

Christians hold the Bible, including both the Old and New Testaments, as the source of moral authority because it is considered God's own inerrant communication to His human creatures. In terms of government, the Bible indicates the purpose God intends civil government to serve. The most extensive discussion is Romans 13:1–7. Similar teachings occur elsewhere, such as at I Peter 2:13–17 and Titus 3:1. A major theme in these passages is that civil government is divinely instituted for the protection of the innocent and the punishment of the guilty. Earthly authorities, it says in Romans 13:4, act as God's agents for justice, as "agent[s] of wrath to bring punishment on the wrongdoer." Civil magistrates, in other words, are established to maintain law and order, and police forces and national armies exist to fulfill that purpose. According to the biblical view, civil magistrates hold responsibility under God for the protection of the people whom God has placed under their authority, the citizens. Jesus affirmed this godly purpose of civil authorities with, "Therefore render to Caesar the things that are Caesar's, and to God the things that are God's"[1] (Mark 12:17).

Two things to note: One, the job of civil government is to uphold justice, not award positive rights. Two, mercy and compassion are demanded of individuals, not public policy for the state. J. P. Moreland of Biola University distinguishes between the standards Scripture applies to Old Testament Israel and its neighboring, pagan countries. Those countries faced God's judgment because their civil authorities oppressed their people, rather than protecting them. Moreland says, "[T]he state is not to be in the business of showing compassion or providing positive rights for others. That is an individual moral responsibility. No, the state is the protector of negative rights."[2]

"Compassion" or "mercy" is willingly to accept an injustice. The appropriate showing of mercy by civil government comes more in tempering punishment so that it is fitting to the crime (e.g., not amounting to cruel torture or utter brutality) or is applied only in exceptional individual cases.[3] Government's attempt to enact affirmative "compassion" laws oversteps its divine bounds. The reason is because the government serves as the agent for all its citizens. Enacting "mercy" as policy easily slips into misuse of civic resources, favoring some people on the backs of other people within its jurisdiction. The government's "mercy" essentially uses coercion to force one group of people to provide a benefit to another group. This amounts to forcing injustice in the name of mercy. This exceeds government's divine authority as ensurer of justice.

Then, what are the biblical teachings of mercy and compassion? We see that showing compassion is really the personal responsibility of individuals, not a mandate for civil government. For instance, Jesus teaches, "love your enemies, do good to those who hate you, bless those who curse you, pray for those who mistreat you. If someone strikes you on one cheek, turn to him the other also. If someone takes your cloak, do not stop him from taking your tunic" (Luke 6:27–29). Christ sets forth the Golden Rule: "Do to others as you would have them do to you" (Luke 6:30).

It would be unjust of governors to turn these teachings into public policy (in their capacity as agents), though they should pursue them in their personal conduct (in their capacity as actors). Similarly, it is inappropriate for the government to try to carry out Christ's concern for "the least of these my brothers" (Matt. 25:31–46), in terms of guaranteeing "positive rights," as Moreland notes. The associated demonstrations of voluntary care and self-sacrifice (e.g., clothing the naked, feeding the hungry) are done or not done by individuals and carry moral consequences. Again, the government demanding such sacrifice as policy employs state coercion of what rightfully should remain voluntary in order to remain compassionate or merciful acts. Such "merciful" policies fall short of achieving mercy. That is why such acts must remain voluntary, individual acts.

Returning to civil authorities, such agents of justice are responsible for how they carry out this responsibility. Psalm 58:1–2 exemplifies the standard to which God holds civil authorities: "Do you rulers indeed speak justly? Do you judge uprightly among men? No, in your heart you devise injustice, and your hands mete out violence on the earth." Rulers owe God a duty faithfully to carry out this trust, just as citizens have a moral duty to obey civil authorities. The government's obligation is to protect all the citizens under its care, believers and unbelievers. Citizenship – formal relationship to, or membership in, a given state – is intended to have real meaning, with implications for both governors and the governed. This relational status of rulers and citizens within a body politic rests upon the authorities using force to serve the purpose of preserving the peace, upholding justice, and promoting the good of the state and its people.

The government's power and its duty to punish evildoers have many implications. In addition to the responsibility of punishing criminals, government has the obligation to defend the nation against foreign invaders. There is also a duty to put down insurrection and to punish treason, in the interest of protecting the life of the body politic. All of these duties of government relate to preserving the rule of law, executing justice, protecting order, and defending the law-abiding citizen. The government's obligation, moreover, is particularistic. It safeguards the public good for a particular group of people, in a particular geographic location, who belong to a particular body politic.

Throughout the Bible, government is seen as having a legitimate right to use force to protect the innocent from the result of human sinfulness. From a biblical perspective, Adam and Eve's disobedience in the Garden of Eden left human beings flawed in the depths of their nature. David writes in Psalm 53:1, for instance, "there is no one who does good." The consequences of this "sin nature" spill over beyond an individual's life; the consequences affect the health and well-being of the entire social order. Therefore, it is necessary for a human society and its earthly rulers to adopt laws for the public good, thereby keeping human evil in check. For example, laws protecting the infirm from abuse by the stronger, putting violent criminals to death or behind bars for life, ensuring fairness in trade and commerce, and deporting criminal aliens all seek to protect the innocent against wrongdoers and are appropriate activities of government – indeed, governments are *obligated* to do these kinds of things.

For justice to be served by laws designed to protect innocent citizens, the authorities must have the means to enforce those laws. For laws to achieve their moral purpose in civil society, governors must hold people to the law. There must be judgment and punishment for disobedience under the law. This standard of justice for the protection of innocent citizens requires that authorities possess the ability to enforce the law against lawbreakers, as Romans 13 indicates. The concept of keeping the peace comes through in this framework; force serves the interest of society's peace.

Just as the government has an obligation to carry out the protective purpose for which it exists, so those who are under the authority of government – its citizens – have the parallel obligation to submit to the legitimate laws and commands promulgated by their government. "Submit yourselves for the Lord's sake to every authority instituted among men," I Peter 2:13–14 says, "whether to the king, as the supreme authority, or to governors, who are sent by him to punish those who do wrong and to commend those who do right." Similarly, St. Paul in Titus 3:1 directs Christians "to be subject to rulers and authorities." And in Romans 13:1, Paul says, "There is no [civil] authority except that which God has established. The authorities that exist have been established by God." Indeed, the Lord instructed the Israelite exiles in Babylon not merely to obey their captors' laws; they were told to "seek the peace and prosperity of the city to which I have carried you into exile. Pray to the Lord for it, because if it prospers, you too will prosper" (Jeremiah 29:7). This personal investment toward the peace and prosperity of one's country may be viewed as a generally applicable biblical principle, which includes but goes beyond merely following a nation's laws.

The obligation of Christians to be subject to rulers and authorities is well summed up in the Westminster Confession of Faith: "It is the duty of people to pray for magistrates, to honor their persons, to pay them tribute and other dues, to obey their lawful commands, and to be subject to their authority for conscience' sake."[4] Christianity does not give license to disregard lawful statutes of our earthly nation, and may even require military service and other forms of public service, though our eternal citizenship after death is in Heaven (Philippians 3:20).

It is important to keep in mind that while the Bible commands us to obey legitimately constituted authority, Scripture specifies no particular form of government as favored by God. Various forms of government have stood over different peoples and nations throughout history, and there is no claim in the Bible that one form – for instance, monarchy or democracy – is alone legitimate. The God of the Old and New Testaments has used everything from theocracy[5] in ancient Israel, to the later monarchy under the Israelite kings, to the Athenian republic, to the Roman Empire, to the American republic as the agency of His purpose. Christians, Israelites, and pagans alike have served as civil magistrates. Clearly, some rulers have fulfilled their responsibility better than others – consider the Old Testament accounts of those judges and kings who were faithful and those who were not. But the civic duty of citizens to obey civil authorities, except in limited circumstances, and to promote civil peace and prosperity remains constant.

ANCIENT ISRAEL AND MODERN AMERICA

The systems of government in Old Testament Israel and the United States differ substantially in form and operation. This, however, poses no problem for the Christian, as we believe that God sanctions different forms of government for different people in different times and places. Many forms of government can be agents of justice in their particular historical setting. Christians believe that certain moral laws from the Bible such as those embodied in the Ten Commandments are universal in the sense of being binding on everyone, everywhere, and at all times. But this is not the case with the ceremonial and judicial laws in the Old Testament.

Christians generally believe that the ceremonial and judicial laws given to ancient Israel applied to that nation alone. Ephesians 2:15 says that Jesus Christ "[abolished] in his flesh the law with its commandments and regulations." This refers to the ceremonial laws of ancient Israel, but not the universal moral commandments. G.I. Williamson points to Hebrews 7–10 as evidence of the ceremonial law's passing.[6] For example, Hebrews 9, he points out, speaks of the priesthood and sacrificial system as a stopgap "until the time of the new order" (v. 10), implying Messiah's ultimate sacrifice. With the sacrifice, death, and resurrection of Jesus, the old Jewish sacerdotal system and its laws are superceded by a new dispensation under "the one Man, Jesus Christ," through whom "God's grace" did "overflow to the many" (Romans 5:15). Besides the ceremonial laws, the civil laws of Israel were also of a particularistic character as can be seen in the fact that many were clearly aimed at a specific local circumstance (e.g., Joshua 13–21, where the Hebrew tribes are assigned to a particular region of Canaan).

While some Christian sects have seen the Old Testament form of government as a universal model for all Christian peoples to follow, this is clearly not the requirement of the Bible, which provides for greater flexibility and prudential wisdom in determining what is the best form of government in different historical circumstances. Our American form of government differs greatly from that of ancient Israel, but this does not mean it is worse or strays from the biblical path. There is no single biblical model when it comes to the form of governance of different peoples, in different historical periods, under different political conditions. John Calvin, whose governance of the city of Geneva adopted many features of the Old Testament theo-political order, said civil laws should be based on "the condition of the times, place, and nation."[7] Paul Marshall, author of one of the most illuminating books on Christianity and American politics, well sums up the situation for Christians when he says, "If we want to make a law, we need not only to know about laws in general, even divine laws, but we also need to know about these [particular] citizens, this [particular] legislature, this president, this constitution, these [specific] laws."[8]

American government clearly allows for scriptural principles to inform her civil laws. This can occur because of the ingrained Christian aspects of America's history and culture, because of the influence of millions of Christian Americans being involved in civic affairs, and because of the public service of Christian officials. Yet we live in a democratic republic whose governing structure separates church and state institutionally and whose decision-making process is based on popular elections.[9] That is, though American civil laws should honor and reflect – even codify – many of God's moral laws, those civil laws are enacted through republican means that preserve the democratic process. Christians are obligated to honor that process and have a biblical obligation to obey the civil authorities under most circumstances, even if the authorities are non-Christians. Non-Christian magistrates have every right to demand obedience by Christians to lawfully enacted decrees.[10]

Here America differs not only from ancient Israel, but from more contemporary regimes like those in Iran and other Muslim countries where government is in the hands of ruling religious bodies. There, church and state are essentially one. And it would be hard to argue that America is the worse for its differentiation of spheres, providing the means of faithful Americans to bring their faith to the public square in meaningful, but unofficial ways. On the contrary, the consequences of not separating religion and state in the modern world may be very harmful, as may be seen in the heavy-handed rule of the Taliban in Afghanistan, the excesses of the "morality police" in Iran, and the harmful influence of the Wahabist clergy in Saudi Arabia.

Besides biblical principles, the civil government of the United States also reflects features of English common law, Lockean liberalism, ancient Greco-Roman ideals, and the practical political compromises agreed to by the Founding Fathers who were charged with improving upon the Articles of Confederation.[11] America's Founders appreciated the need for keeping apart church governance and state rule. America's form of representative government allows for the exercise of prudential judgment by both Christian and non-Christian citizens and seeks to be fair to all members of this society. The American republic provides an orderly process for securing the "consent of the governed" on public questions, even though universal agreement on every law cannot be obtained. The system of checks and balances that we have – e.g., the bicameral national legislature, the federated structure of the government, the separation of powers into three co-equal branches – has been generally successful in "securing the blessings of liberty" to a huge population over a vast nation. We have moved substantially from the form of government of ancient Israel, but for a Christian, that is a prudential development, in keeping with biblical providence.

THE ROLE OF CHRISTIANITY IN AMERICAN POLITICAL CULTURE

One can understand much of American government and American political culture as a synthesis of two countervailing streams of thought, one deriving from the Enlightenment and the other from Christianity, particularly the Protestant Reformation.[12]

The Enlightenment stressed individual rights and tended to downplay the need for social cohesiveness and common virtues. Taken to its extreme, the Enlightenment project can lead to the triumph of self-seeking individualism, the substitution of misplaced faith in progress for a deeper religious faith, the general secularization of society, and the destruction of tradition and stability.[13] Much of the success of the American project can be attributed to the fact that these potentially destructive consequences of the Enlightenment were offset by the influence of both Christianity and the tradition of civic republicanism about which J. G. A. Pocock and many other scholars have written. As the Christian writer Os Guinness explains, "a combination of classical republicanism and Protestantism" (that is, principles from the Roman republic and the Protestant Reformation) constrained the Enlightenment's influence. "Predominantly religious beliefs held in balance apparently irreconcilable opposites, such as self-reliance and community cooperation, daring enterprise and social stability."[14]

The Reformation, derived from Judeo-Christian principles, contributed a number of key ideals to American government. These included freedom of conscience, ordered liberty, the restraint of sinful passions, the rule of law, representative government from the bottom up rather than rule from a top-down hierarchy, and the need to restrain the governing elite no less than the governed. American civic ideals such as liberty, equality, individual responsibility, and justice under law derive from this heritage. These principles and ideals for government and society provided a means of achieving *unum* amidst *pluribus*, and constrained a free people's drifting away from their ethical moorings.

America's Founders sought to erect a limited civil government that would preserve liberty under law. But the only way limited government can work, they believed, is if the citizens display a high level of self-government and self-restraint.[15] Philosopher Francis Schaeffer has explained just how difficult it is for a government to achieve a healthy balance between order and liberty, or what he calls "form" and "freedom." We in the West, he says, "take our *form-freedom balance* in government for granted as though it were natural."[16] Historically speaking, however, it has been very unnatural, Schaeffer stresses, though America has been more successful than most other societies, he believes, in combining an emphasis on individual rights with an equally important emphasis on the fulfillment of societal obligations. The success of the

American experiment in ordered liberty, Schaeffer and others contend, can largely be attributed to the Judeo-Christian religious consensus that stresses the need for self-control and self-restraint and the need for God's guidance and God's grace in achieving these goals.[17] Proverbs 14:31 illustrates the need for high societal moral standards and their critical role to national vitality: "Righteousness exalts a nation, but sin is a disgrace to any people." The Founders knew that only a people so self-restrained could remain politically free.

WHAT DOES THE BIBLE SAY ABOUT IMMIGRANTS AND IMMIGRATION?

With the foregoing as a foundation, we can now proceed to an understanding of what the Bible has to say about immigrants and immigration. What does this base have to do with immigration? It provides a framework of the Judeo-Christian underpinnings of the United States' system of government, the role of believers as members of this society, and the motivation for promoting civil justice through, in part, individual and corporate morality. Immigration involves the civil policies for admitting new members of society from outside that society. The criteria for admission affect the future moral constitution of the citizenry and the "righteousness" necessary to "exalt [the] nation."

The first thing we notice is that the Bible speaks much more about the treatment of immigrants – that is, the treatment of the stranger, the sojourner, the foreign resident in our midst – than it does about immigration policy, in the sense of the laws and customs that should regulate the admittance of foreigners into a settled community. This distinction is important to keep in mind because some people erroneously confuse biblical teaching about the treatment of immigrants with the Bible's view of a moral and just immigration policy. Thus, we see that Scripture states principles concerning immigrant policy more so than immigration policy.

Certain Old Testament passages directly address the treatment of strangers and aliens. For instance, Leviticus 19:33–34a says, "When an alien lives with you in your land, do not mistreat him. The alien living with you must be treated as one of your native-born." A similar theme is raised in Exodus 22:21: "Do not mistreat an alien or oppress him, for you were aliens in Egypt." These and similar verses (e.g., Zechariah 7:9–10) have great significance for both Christians and Jews. The Exodus verse has particular salience for Jews because the Jewish people were once enslaved and mistreated as aliens in Egypt during biblical times, and have known similar hardship and mistreatment as foreigners during the many centuries of their Diaspora. Christians can relate to such passages in a spiritual sense because the Bible declares us "strangers and aliens" in this world (e.g., Ephesians 2:19; Philippians 3:20) – we are not finally home, even in the land of our birth, with final rest coming only in Heaven. The clear message of such passages, where public policy is concerned, is "equal justice under law" for foreign-born lawful residents. However, little in such passages spells out the grounds for aliens' and strangers' admission into or exclusion from the nation.

In the Old and New Testaments, each particular kingdom, empire, or nation controlled human movement across its political jurisdiction.[18] Territorial sovereignty has long been the rule, reaching to decisions about permission for entry, conditions for stay, and demands for departure.[19] For example, Abram (later Abraham) secured permission to sojourn in Egypt during a famine, but Pharaoh revoked that permission when it became known that Abram lied about his wife Sarai (later Sarah) (Genesis 12:10–20). Moses asked the Edomite king for permission for the Israelites to transit his territory, but was denied entry (Numbers 20:14–21). Nehemiah, tasked with restoring Jerusalem's city walls following the Israelite exile in Babylon, exercised authority over entry and exit (Nehemiah 13:15–22). By the time Palestine existed as part of the Roman Empire, Rome governed its conquered territories through a combination of local control and Roman governance. The expansive Roman Empire enabled the safer passage of individuals within the empire. Roman citizenship carried certain rights and privileges; citizenship was obtained by birth or, for some, by purchase. The Roman Empire's infrastructure, both legal and practical, facilitated the spread of Christianity by the travels of the Apostles, including St. Paul.

Old Testament scholar James Hoffmeier explains the very serious nature of ancient sovereignty and borders. "Nations small and large had clearly recognizable borders, typically demarcated by natural features such as rivers, valleys, and mountain ranges, much as they are today. Warring Egyptian Pharaohs often claimed that they went on campaigns to widen or extend Egypt's borders. Wars were fought over where boundary lines would be drawn, and forts were strategically placed on frontiers to defend the territory and to monitor movements of pastoralists. Permits akin to the modern visa were issued to people entering another land."[20]

Further, the Bible uses different Hebrew terms translated as "stranger," "foreigner," and "alien." One term (ger) refers to someone from another nation who is given permission to reside in the country, while other terms (nekhar, zar) refer to a foreigner. "The distinction between these two terms and ger is that while all three are foreigners who might enter another country, the ger had obtained legal status," says Hoffmeier.[21] They are not interchangeable terms.

Once granted admittance, lawful foreign residents (ger) of ancient Israel were assigned certain protections in and certain obligations to the community, similar to those of Jews. For instance, Deuteronomy 14:28–29 requires both Jews and Gentiles within Old Testament Israel to share part of their agricultural produce every third year with a town's Levites, aliens, orphans, and widows. This amounts to lawful resident foreigners owing the same civil obligation as native Israelites. Deuteronomy 16:9–15 places a similar requirement applicable to all residents, including Gentiles, to observe the Feast of Weeks and the Feast of Booths. This demonstrates a degree of cultural assimilation central to the nation concerning the lawfully resident alien.

Other Scriptural passages, however, assign different obligations upon Jews and certain Gentiles. While "an alien living in any of your towns" may take for food an animal that has died (Deut. 14:21), Hebrews could not eat it because they were "a people holy to the Lord your God." Similarly, while Hebrews were to relieve their fellow Israelites' debts every seven years, this commandment did not apply to transactions between Jews and Gentiles ("You may require payment from a foreigner [for credit loaned him]" it says in Deut. 15:3). In these cases, God called for distinguishing between citizens of Israel and certain noncitizens. As Hoffmeier notes, the different standards under Israelite law generally applied to the foreign visitor of more tenuous standing (nekhar, zar).

This distinction highlights what was said earlier about the difference between universal moral laws binding on all people in all places and the ceremonial, judicial, and other types of law that in the Old Testament apply only to the Israelites and their nation in that place and time. Bible commentator Matthew Henry elaborates further on the Jews' practice of giving or selling of unclean food to foreigners: "It is plain in the law itself that [these precepts] belonged only to the Jews, and were not moral, nor of perpetual use, because not of universal obligation, for what they might not eat themselves, they might give to a stranger, a proselyte of the gate, that had renounced idolatry, and therefore was permitted to live among them … "[22] In some circumstances, it was thus appropriate to treat Jews and Gentiles differently under Israelite law – indeed, this was God's command. In America, these principles of how immigrant Gentiles were lawfully to be treated – the same as Israelites in certain instances and differently in others – are reflected in the appropriate differentiation under U.S. law for U.S. citizens and lawful permanent residents and, different still, illegal aliens or visitors on a temporary visa.

Of relevance to the modern immigration debate is the biblical view of the different nationalities of the earth and the place to which God has assigned them to reside. The division of the earth into specific geographic locations and the assignment of different peoples to these different geographic regions are first described in detail in Genesis 10. It is alluded to later in Deuteronomy 32:8: "When the Most High gave the nations their inheritance, when he divided all mankind, he set up boundaries for the peoples according to the number of sons of Israel." St. Paul takes up the same theme in Acts 17:26, when, in addressing the Athenians, he explains that "from one man [God] made every nation of men, that they should inhabit the whole earth; and he determined the times set for them and the exact places where they should live." This indicates that nation-state boundaries and the division of mankind into different peoples living in different geographic locations is something God ordained and part of a providential plan. It is not something sinful, immoral, or contrary to divine intent. In a world where evil exists and corrupts human harmony, adopting different rules to govern the different peoples and their lands to meet the predominant circumstances they each face is providentially practical. That is, God provides for the care of individuals by placing them within certain people groups in specific locations. Their civic leaders hold the responsibility to rule justly, protect their innocent citizens, and punish lawbreakers. This mirrors the divine element of the social contract in every political jurisdiction.

Likewise, He holds people (governors and governed) accountable for their actions, both individually and corporately, exalting a righteous nation or disgracing an evil people (e.g., Prov. 14:34). This is seen in God's punishing the Israelites as a nation through exile, defeat, and other judgments. Nations' policies toward outsiders who wish to enter the land may reasonably differ, depending on whether the foreigners' intent is invasion, subjugation, assimilation to the native culture, peaceful and lawful residence, commerce, trade, or something else.

WHAT IS A JUST BIBLICAL IMMIGRATION POLICY?

Moving now from specific biblical passages to the immigration controversy in modern America, we see Christians divided largely between religious leaders on one side of the debate and parishioners on the other. Certain religious elites advocate for what might be called the "brotherhood of mankind" position, which elevates being human to trumping the state's authority over citizenship and immigration, and of an individual's duty of faithful citizenship. These philosophies correlate with globalism, popular among elites, and with patriotism, prevalent among average citizens, or as Wheaton's Amstutz characterizes these competing views, cosmopolitan vs. communitarian.[23] Globalists ignore the fallen nature of mankind, the common-grace provision of protectors (e.g., parents, governors) in society, and the realms where God ordains certain ties as more preeminent in certain circumstances (in civil life, one's nation, versus in church and eternity, one's relationship to God and to other human beings who belong to Him). In practice, those policies seem barely different from the immigration policies advocated by many secular political lobbies.

"Brotherhood" advocates think it morally illegitimate for a nation's government to make distinctions in public policy on the basis of a person's citizenship, nationality, residence, or place of birth. Some would stake their claim on biblical unity, though many tend to ignore other biblical teachings that are not congenial to their postmodern philosophy. The Bible does proclaim a universal message of eternal moral salvation that is available regardless of nationality, race, ethnicity, or any other human distinction. Scripture says that all human beings are created in God's image, and thus, despite their fallen sinful nature, have inherent value (e.g., Genesis 1:27). And the New Testament announces in the most forceful manner that with Christians all human distinctions of race, ethnicity, socio-economic class, and the like have little currency in the eyes of God, in terms of eternity and one's standing with God and ultimate relationship to fellow believers. The New Testament proclaims a unity among believers in Christ, based on the shared tenet that Jesus's sacrifice makes all those who call Him their Savior heirs of eternal salvation. To Christians, the differences that come into play on earth have little value in the Kingdom of God. As St. Paul says, all those who are made "sons of God through faith in Christ Jesus" are each "Abraham's seed, and heirs according to the promise" (Galatians 3:26, 29). Within the Christian community, he explains, "[T]here is neither Jew nor Greek, slave nor free, male nor female," but all are "one in Christ Jesus" (Galatians 3:28).

In the Christian message, individuals from all walks of life, from all over the globe, have become believers in Jesus Christ. They include prostitutes such as Rahab[24] (Hebrews 11:31), Roman centurions such as Cornelius (Acts 10), White House hatchetmen such as Charles Colson, and, over the centuries, untold millions from every corner of the globe. But does this spiritual universalism translate into a biblical requirement for a temporal open-borders policy of immigration, as globalists claim?

The Christians who advocate open-borders policy on immigration make, in my judgment, three cardinal mistakes from a biblical viewpoint. They simultaneously (1) fail to acknowledge the special obligations we all have toward those closest to us and to the specific communities wherein we reside; they (2) discount the biblical obligation that civil authorities have to protect the specific law-abiding people and the communities entrusted to their care; and they (3) ignore the very real pragmatic harms that the policies they advocate have on the health and well-being of American society.

PRIMARY RESPONSIBILITIES TO FAMILY, COMMUNITY, NATION

Recall the earlier discussion of the particularistic nature of nations and peoples, and about the specific geographic locations wherein they reside. In Genesis 10, Deuteronomy 32:8, and Acts 17:26, it is explained that God determined the places on the earth where the individuals who constitute humanity are each placed. That is to say, within God's common grace towards all people, we each find ourselves under the care of certain parents, community, and the state in which we are citizens. As members of different nations living in different geographic locales, our immediate responsibilities and opportunities are to those concrete persons and groups nearest us. Each of these entities – family, community, state, nation – involves human relationships. We may have concern for people in other parts of the world. We may donate our money or time to a charity after a hurricane hits a poor nation or travel with a ministry to perform a mission, giving of ourselves to build a well, a building, or give free medical treatment. However, our primary connections normally remain with the specific human beings who are part of our own circles of existence and relationship. This is a matter of God-ordered practical priority.

The situation with the family is a prime example. In I Timothy 5:8, Paul warns, "If anyone does not provide for his relatives, and especially for his immediate family, he has denied the faith and is worse than an unbeliever." Here it is made plain that we each have a primary obligation to those who are closest to us by family and blood ties – that their needs and welfare stand top in our priorities. (Yet, that primacy does not negate our civic obligations or our moral duty to obey the law.) All of us who are members of families have special obligations to our family members that are of a higher order than our obligations toward those to whom we are not related. However much we may love all human beings – and as Christians we are commanded to love our neighbor as we love ourselves – we nevertheless each have a special attachment to, and a predominant moral obligation toward, the members of our own families and their well-being.

A man who spent most of his time and money helping strangers but neglected the welfare of his own family would, in Paul's words, be denying the faith. We each have a more pressing personal obligation to provide for our family than we do for our neighbor's family, a more pressing obligation to help our relatives than to help strangers, and a more pressing obligation to be concerned with the well-being of the local civic community in which we reside and its members than to the civic community in another part of our state. The reasons are relationship and opportunity. The Good Samaritan in Jesus's parable (Luke 10:25–37) illustrates that loving one's neighbor is not confined to those with whom we have a personal tie, but extends to those in need with whom we have opportunity. The Hebrew victim of the robbers was not a relative of the despised Samaritan, but the Samaritan cared for him because of the urgent, unmet need right in his path. But generally, our best opportunity to help someone involves a person in our circle.

What is said here about our circles of relationship of family and local community can also be said about the national civic community. As American citizens, we have a greater, more immediate moral obligation to be concerned with the welfare and quality of life of our fellow Americans than citizens of other countries, just as the residents of those other countries should be more concerned with and attentive to matters there than in America. All peoples of the globe are part of various communities – nations, tribes, clans, families, local churches, etc. – and these communities have a certain corporate life, sovereignty, and corporate integrity that commands honor and respect. But politically, nations hold preeminence. Edward Erler explains that rights are only secured by national communities. Erler says the objective morality the Declaration of Independence calls the "laws of nature and of nature's God" that includes "self-evident" truths matches our rights with duties.[25] Within the nation-state, citizens owe one another "a moral obligation" to the constitutional social compact, whereby the "pursuit of happiness" doesn't include "an individual's private pleasures or imagined pleasures" that are "destructive of the public good or public happiness" in that jurisdiction.[26]

Further, the practical applies in our responsibilities toward loving our neighbor. Though God may make exceptional provision in certain cases, we generally operate on the basis of our having finite resources at our disposal. This is reflected when Paul instructs Timothy on the use of church resources in caring for widows (I Tim. 5). A widow over 60 years old, of good moral character, and lacking relatives to support her (v. 9–10) would receive help. This is the context for verse 8's directive to care for one's immediate family, followed by the stated principle: "If any woman who is a believer has widows in her family, she should help them and not let the church be burdened with them, so that the church can help those widows who are really in need" (v. 16). The concentric circles of relationship and degree of responsibility are plain, as are the practical allocation of resources. The closer the ties, the greater the responsibility.

Also, Scripture guides how and when we share our resources. The Good Samaritan parable involves the voluntary sharing of private resources. This personal, voluntary act of love for neighbor responds to an individual stranger's urgent need. The I Timothy 5 prioritization for allocating shared resources shows that true compassion may also call for prudential decisions based on people's circumstances. Allocating church (shared) resources there carries a higher burden to ensure that the recipients truly do not have relatives who should personally assume responsibility. This prudential discerning among people in differing circumstances addresses the matter in the most appropriate manner.

Further, each human being is a member of different such entities at the same time. Closer responsibilities do not erase other obligations. One may be responsible for protecting and providing for a spouse and children, caring for an aged parent, paying taxes and voting in a county, serving and financially supporting a local church, serving in the state's national guard unit, and obeying the laws of the United States and defending the country in active military duty some day. In addition, one may have joined various voluntary organizations like the Little League in which one coaches baseball, a community theater group in which one acts in plays and musicals, and a civic club such as Rotary or the Optimists. The central element is a claim on that person's commitment. Some of the circles of commitment the person voluntarily chose and others the decision was made for them. Many of these separate obligations overlap; some are longer-lasting, while others are for a limited time. But each one involves relationship among specific human beings. Most involve trust and commitment. These relationships entail both benefits and obligations. Relationships within groupings rely on fidelity and obedience to the rules of the group and mutual ascent to accepting or rejecting new members. These human relations define humanity and society. And it is through these relationships that we love our neighbors as we love ourselves.

These facts are often ignored by defenders of open borders, who oppose immigration restrictions and may see nation-state boundaries as immoral. What they say is out of tune with biblical teachings that the division of humanity and the globe into territories inhabited by different nations and people groups is part of a God-ordained order. Amstutz, who assesses modern views on immigration among the religious as falling into "cosmopolitanism" and "communitarianism," illustrates how the latter aligns with practical biblical principles for ordering human society.[27] Whatever God's ultimate plan for us may be in the triumph of His Kingdom – where our glorified existence will be quite different from our current one – in our present earthly situation, nations, families, tribes, and territorial states are a necessary component of orderly human existence and part of God's providential plan, including to secure our rights and liberties.

CIVIL AUTHORITIES' OBLIGATION TO PROTECT THE COMMUNITY

Just as we, as members of families, each have a special obligation to provide for their welfare, so statesmen and political leaders have a special obligation to look out for the well-being of the political communities entrusted to their care. The biblical basis of this view was pointed out above. As stewards of the community's welfare, political leaders have the obligation to protect the community from those who would do it harm, innocent members of that community from evildoers, members of that community from harm by nonmembers of the community, and from those whose addition to the community for one reason or another would constitute an intolerable burden or a danger. Thus, American Christians and their political leaders, from earliest colonial times, understood it as perfectly within their rights and part of their duty of moral leadership to exclude or deport public charges, prostitutes, disease carriers, anarchists, and the like.[28]

This principle extends to keeping immigration in check when the numbers or characteristics become harmful to U.S. citizens. When impoverished Chinese immigrants were flooding into the West Coast and undermining the wages of native workers in the latter part of the nineteenth century, Congress responded with legislation greatly restricting immigration from China. Similarly, in the early 1920s, after an enormous influx of immigrants from eastern and southern Europe whose assimilation into mainstream America became a daunting challenge, Congress significantly curtailed immigration. These restrictions lasted until the 1960s, when our current immigration regime was put in place. These sixties-era reforms arguably went too far in ratcheting up the volume of immigrants.[29] Again, government officials serve as ministers promoting order and the common good of their citizens, and immigration control is part of that job.

Magistrates and statesmen have an obligation to protect their own communities and, if necessary, to use the coercive power of the state to achieve this aim. This duty includes the obligation to patrol national borders and to enforce immigration laws, which are directed at the public good. Some liberal Christians believe that it is immoral for the Border Patrol to stop illegal immigrants flooding into America if all these immigrants seek is the opportunity to work and escape the impoverished conditions that exist in the lands from which they come. How can it be just or moral, they ask, to stop honest, hard-working people from coming to America when all they want is to improve their lot in life? What is wrong, they ask, with seeking a better life for oneself and one's family just as the ancestors of millions of Americans have done in the past? These are good questions – and there are good answers to them.

The problem with the huge influx of illegal immigrants into America today is that it causes many harmful consequences for the American public, particularly for the most vulnerable Americans (e.g., the less educated and lower skilled, minorities, the disabled, older citizens who need work). Some of these will be discussed shortly. Our political leaders have the obligation to enforce laws that are directed at the public good, and in regard to our immigration and naturalization laws, those who are not members of our political community have an obligation to respect those laws just as we have an obligation to observe the immigration and naturalization laws of other countries. While one can understand the desperation that motivates some illegal immigrants, there are larger matters of the public good at stake here that make the actions of the illegal immigrants morally wrong. It is similarly morally wrong for a poor person to steal from a wealthier one – an action that we may well understand, and even, in extreme circumstances, have sympathy with, but which, nevertheless, cannot be condoned. As Proverbs 6:30–31 says: "Men do not despise a thief if he steals to satisfy his hunger when he is starving. Yet if he is caught, he must pay sevenfold, though it costs him all the wealth of his house." Such circumstances do not suspend the Eighth Commandment against stealing. Illegal immigration amounts to theft of something that belongs to another, in this case to a discrete group of people who are members of a society and who rightfully control membership in that society and thus access to all benefits associated with membership.

Paul Marshall sees the maintenance of borders as one of the obligations that governments have for the well-being of those whom they govern. While sympathetic to the plight of poor immigrants, the welfare of the existing community, he believes, must be the first concern of government officials. Practical and prudential political judgments about the welfare of the community must be made through our democratic political process, and once made, the rule of law requires that appropriate officials enforce these statutes. Marshall writes:

While there are doubtless some thugs and thieves among them, as with all people, the majority of illegal immigrants entering the United States... simply desire a better life, and are willing to risk their lives in striving for it. If there were no border then who could object to what they do? It is the fact of a border, a political invention that makes their action wrong. . . . Like all borders [America's borders] are a product of war, compromise, and accident. But if governments are to be able to govern, then there needs to be some controls on who can enter a country through these borders. It is because of this necessary *political* restriction that an otherwise praiseworthy activity can become wrong.[30]

Thus the rightful power of the government includes policing the nation's borders, as well as the arrest and deportation of immigrant lawbreakers, even when their only violation is unauthorized entry or overstaying an expired visa. The state is duty-bound to act in this manner because of the illegal alien's disregard for legitimately constituted authority, and the adverse effect of his immigration upon citizens whom the civil government is duty-bound to protect. We have here again a situation that comes under the Pauline injunction: "Everyone must submit himself to the governing authorities. . . . The authorities that exist have been established by God. Consequently, he who rebels against the authority is rebelling against what God has instituted. . ." (Romans 13:1–2).

This principle, it is true, can sometimes lead to tragic situations (tragic in the classical Greek sense, where following principles leads to unavoidable suffering and even catastrophe). As seen, the Bible says it is God who establishes governments, nations, and societies. Jesus affirmed the appropriate realm and authority of civil rulers when He said to render to Caesar the things of Caesar. God places people within the care of temporal governments, imposing on them as individuals civic duties owed to that place where they hold earthly citizenship. They also are to love God and neighbor. These dual obligations may pit believer against believer, each in service under God to his own country when nations have disputes. Nevertheless, the preeminent calling to protect the best interests of their own state's citizens makes it incumbent on civil authorities to make decisions that best serve the common good of their nation.

HARMS OF OPEN BORDERS AND THE NEED FOR CONTROLLED IMMIGRATION

Immigration policy has an important effect in shaping the future of our nation. The United States issues more than a million legal immigrant visas each year – spiking to 1.5 million immigrant arrivals in 2015 – with illegal aliens adding another half million or more new residents annually.[31] These are historically high levels, rivaling the Great Wave of immigration that took place at the turn of the twentieth century.[32] What has been the result of this massive influx? While there have been net gains in certain respects, particularly with highly educated and entrepreneurially talented foreigners, in most of the country the large-scale influx of often unskilled and uneducated immigrants who pay less in taxes than they heavily draw from public services such as health and education have placed a significant burden on the communities in which they have settled. Indeed, the

National Academy of Sciences has concluded that immigrants' costs are largely borne at the state and local level, while any benefit tends to accrue at the federal level.[33] Immigrants impose a fiscal burden on citizen taxpayers, and in many areas have reduced the standard of living for citizens by increasing urban congestion and crime, particularly crime associated with foreign gang activity. Their presence in a developed nation like the United States has widened immigrants' environmental footprint significantly above what it was in their home nation.

Even in purely economic terms, the net loss to American public treasuries from the mass immigration of unskilled immigrants is quite large. Harvard economist George Borjas, the National Research Council of the National Academy of Sciences, and others have well documented this net economic cost.[34] Replicating the NRC's methodology and relying on Census Bureau data, comprehensive studies examining net fiscal impact have calculated all taxes paid and all public benefits collected and compared the net difference by education and skill level and citizenship or immigration status. Just as the NRC found in its landmark analysis, whether someone is a net contributor or a net consumer of taxpayer resources largely depends on one's education and skill levels.[35] Those households headed by someone with less than a high school diploma pay about one-third what higher-skilled families pay in taxes – $9,689 on average versus $34,629 in FY 2004. Less-than-high-skill-headed households collected between $32,138 and $43,084 a year in government fiscal outlays, compared with $21,520 to $30,819 for better educated households. That is, the low-skilled paid less than one-third what they took in public benefits, while those families headed by someone with a diploma or more paid at least $4,000 more in all forms of taxes than government spent on their household. The difference for direct benefits is even starker, with those less-than-high-schooled families annually receiving more than $22,000 net than they paid in taxes, while the higher-skilled pay more than $13,000 in taxes annually above their total direct benefits derived.[36]

A subsequent report focuses on the fiscal costs of low-skilled immigrants.[37] The authors found immigrant (both legal and illegal) households headed by someone with less than a high school education paid an average of $10,573 in FY 2004, while deriving three times ($30,160) that amount in public benefits each year. A follow-on analysis in 2013 found the same education-related phenomena associated with net fiscal impact.[38] Households headed by someone with less than a college degree, native or immigrant (legal or illegal), in 2010 averaged payment of $11,469 in all taxes while receiving $46,582 in government services and benefits, meaning they consumed a net $35,113 that year, paid by other American taxpayers. Illegal alien households netted $14,387 in government benefits. Less-educated legal immigrant families are subsidized by taxpayers for a greater net payout because unlawful aliens are excluded from certain government programs.

Legalization would significantly increase the amount formerly illegal aliens receive from the government over time, the study determined, because half of illegal alien heads of household have no high school diploma. They would eventually net $28,000 per year in government benefits beyond what they pay in all taxes. The extreme dropout rate among illegal foreign-born household heads compares with a quarter of unlawful alien heads of household having just a high school education. By comparison, one-fifth of legal immigrant heads of household are dropouts and about a quarter finished high school, in contrast with the native-born, more than 90 percent of whom have completed high school. And now, half of immigrant-headed households are on welfare.[39] It is easy to see that the sustained immigration of millions of aliens with low skill and education levels – including legal immigration – imposes a heavy price on productive Americans. These shocking figures have moral implications concerning the morality of redistributing hard-earned wealth from citizens to immigrants, the morality of sustained ultrahigh levels of immigration of ever-more-needy foreigners, the advisability of keeping the present criteria for allocating permanent visas, the ability of the country adequately to attend to the needs of its own neediest citizens, and the moralizing of advocates for ever-higher immigration for policies that allow special interests to privatize the benefit of mass immigration while socializing the huge costs imposed on society.

In addition to the cost to the public treasury, the large-scale immigration of unskilled workers has put downward pressure on low-end wages. This may be a convenient thing for the upper-class person who hires an immigrant laborer to cut his lawn or care for her elderly parent, but it is not a good thing for America's own low-skilled or disadvantaged would-be workers. Virtually uncontrolled immigration leaves low-skilled citizens, American teenagers and recent graduates, the disabled, veterans, American minority citizens, and older workers vulnerable to such harms as direct job competition, wage depression, and flooded labor markets.[40] Such immigration aids foreigners at the expense of members of the polity, thus violating the principle and moral obligation most appropriate for the state as well as the personal, first to look out for the welfare of those closest to us. Those most hurt by immigration have been America's poorest and most vulnerable, especially African American and Hispanic citizens.

The rising national security challenge of radical political Islam and its terrorists increasingly attacking innocent American citizens on U.S. soil demand a clear-eyed immigration policy response by the national government. The Obama administration's escalation of refugee resettlement in American communities,[41] exacerbated by Obama's wholesale admittance of Syrian "refugees," means more innocent Americans become potential victims of foreign radicals in our own land. President Trump campaigned on reversing this course, applying "extreme vetting" to Islamic immigrants, and taking on this serious threat in a serious manner. This involves excluding foreign political radicals from admission and deporting foreign residents who espouse subversive ideology.[42] This principle equally applies to twentieth-century Eastern European immigrants belonging to anti-American Communist organizations, German immigrant sympathizers with the Third Reich, and today's foreign-born proponents of Islamic-based totalitarianism.

Protecting American citizens from radical Islam follows the well-trod path of ideological exclusion, which dates from colonial times through the Cold War threat of Soviet Communism. With Islamic political extremism, authorities appropriately would focus on the political radicalism and its associated call for the violent overthrow of the United States. The fact that such radical beliefs derive from a religion matters little, as a policy matter. Former official John Bolton compares Communism and radical Islam: "[T]hey are ideologies driven by an obsession to force the real world to match their preconceptions."[43] Further, wrong focus leads to extending First Amendment rights to people who not only hold no allegiance to the U.S. Constitution, they are sworn enemies of our nation. The U.S. government's duty is to protect its citizens against all enemies, foreign and domestic. Exclusion and removal are the tools.

Part of the challenge posed by current immigration arises from the sheer size of the immigrant influx and its concentration in certain areas of the country. This size-effect makes assimilation much harder – it is easier for a society to deal with a small number of people who need the avenues to integrate into the wider society than it is to deal with a larger number. Immigration on the massive scale we have today impedes our ability to assimilate so many newcomers into the mainstream of American life. A key ingredient of the recipe for their success in America is immigrants' joining the ranks of the middle class, integrating into the fabric of the mainstream, and assimilating economically, patriotically, and otherwise.[44]

CONCLUSION

Current mass immigration of predominately unskilled people most directly harms our fellow Americans with fewer skills and less education.[45] An immigrant may personally command a larger paycheck, relative to earnings back in his or her home country, by immigrating, but it typically is low compared to the average American wage-earner and insufficient for the much higher U.S. cost of living. Further, these immigrants expand the pool of potential workers, especially at the lower end of the economy, and thus depress the wages of the poorest Americans and often compete directly with them for jobs.[46] The mass immigration of the unskilled places a drain on public services and threatens social stability within America. It is for these reasons that most Americans want to reduce to more manageable numbers the current large flow of immigrants.[47]

As a Christian, I believe that the governing authorities are established by God "as God's servant" to protect the population and the welfare of citizens (Romans 13:1). A civil government should not cause the citizens under its protection to suffer economic, political, social, cultural, or financial upheaval through unchecked immigration. To the extent that our current immigration policy does these things, it requires significant revision, as immigration skeptics like George Borjas and Mark Krikorian have long argued.

As citizens of the United States, we all have the obligation, regardless of our religious faith, to consider seriously the terms and conditions under which we allow aliens to enter, visit, permanently reside, or attain American citizenship. We need a course correction, guided by a high level of both prudence and sound judgment based on the whole counsel of Scripture, undoing globalist immigration policies pursued since the 1970s. We must scrupulously distinguish between that which is the Lord's commandment to each of us personally and that to us corporately as we are bound together as members of a nation-state in a given time and place on earth. In the latter case, our joint decisions have far-reaching consequences affecting our fellow citizens of this nation, to whom our shared citizenship means we owe a higher moral duty than to members of any other nation. Those of us who are Christians can bring to the table our special grounding in the wisdom of biblical principles, and the humility that comes from the recognition that we are all deeply flawed in our natures and are dependent upon God's grace to achieve whatever level of wisdom and insight we can attain. In the spirit of Christian humility, we can move forward on this issue and make genuine progress in the realm of the City of Man.

NOTES

1. Biblical citations throughout this chapter are mostly from the New International Version.
2. J. P. Moreland, "A Biblical Case for Limited Government," *Institute for Faith, Work & Economics* (2013): 7.
3. James R. Edwards, Jr., "A Biblical Perspective on Immigration Policy," Center for Immigration Studies *Backgrounder*, September 2009.
4. G. I. Williamson, *The Westminster Confession of Faith* (Philadelphia, PA: Presbyterian and Reformed Publishing, 1964), p. 240. See Williamson's entire commentary on this chapter of the Westminster Confession. Another excellent source of great value in my research was the six-volume Matthew Henry, *A Commentary on the Holy Bible* (Chicago, IL: W.P. Blessing, undated).
5. The term "theocracy" as used in this chapter means the unique, covenantal relationship between Jehovah and ancient Israel. It does not mean direct political rule by God in a given nation, and it especially does not mean the scare-mongering implications intended by antireligious political interests who invoke the term today as a rhetorical fragmentation grenade. See chapter four of Paul Marshall, *God and the Constitution: Christianity and American Politics* (Lanham, MD: Rowman & Littlefield, 2002), particularly pp. 65–70. Marshall's discussion notes that even "theocracy" in ancient Israel included human leaders chosen by the people to carry out the day-to-day functions of civil government.
6. Williamson, *The Westminster Confession*, pp. 141–143.

7. Marshall, *God and the Constitution*, p. 92.

8. Marshall, *God and the Constitution*, p. 96.

9. Religious organizations and denominational groups, in addition to faithful individuals, have throughout American history voiced moral views in the public political discourse. That role, in relation to how certain religious groups have gone on immigration, is discussed in James C. Russell, *Breach of Faith: American Churches and the Immigration Crisis* (Raleigh, NC: Representative Government Press, 2004). For an in-depth discussion of religion's role in American public affairs, there are plenty of sources available. Notable contributions to this subject include Daniel L. Dreisbach, *Thomas Jefferson and the Wall of Separation between Church and State* (New York, NY: New York University Press, 2002) and the edited volume by Daniel L. Dreisbach, Mark D. Hall, and Jeffry H. Morrison, *The Founders on God and Government* (Lanham, MD: Rowman & Littlefield, 2004), both to which I referred. In addition is the classic by Richard John Neuhaus, *The Naked Public Square* (Grand Rapids, MI: William B. Eerdmans Publishing, 1984).

10. See the Westminster Confession, chapter 23, paragraph four, which may be found in Williamson, *The Westminster Confession*, p. 240.

11. Though many sources informed this section, Russell Kirk, *The Roots of American Order*, Third Edition (Washington, DC: Regnery Gateway, 1991) was one of the most significant, as were Francis Schaeffer's "How Should We Then Live?" and "A Christian Manifesto," contained in Francis Schaeffer, *The Complete Works of Francis A. Schaeffer: A Christian Worldview* (Wheaton, Ill.: Crossway Books, 1982), and Os Guinness's *The American Hour: A Time of Reckoning and the Once and Future Role of Faith* (New York: Free Press, 1993).

12. See Schaeffer, "A Christian Manifesto," and Guinness for fuller discussions of this subject.

13. Schaeffer has expounded this subject, and Guinness furthers the discussion. Of note, Alister McGrath's *The Twilight of Atheism* (New York: Doubleday, 2004) describes some of the Enlightenment's consequences in the West via the French Revolution (chapter two) and beyond.

14. Guinness, *The American Hour*, p. 339.

15. See Daniel Dreisbach, Reading the Bible with the Founding Fathers (Oxford University Press, 2017).

16. Schaeffer, "A Christian Manifesto," pp. 427–428.

17. See, for example, Schaeffer, "A Christian Manifesto," especially chapter two, and Jeffry H. Morrison, "John Witherspoon's Revolutionary Religion," in Dreisbach, Hall, and Morrison, *The Founders on God and* Government, pp. 117–146.

18. See Edwards, "A Biblical Perspective on Immigration Policy," CIS *Backgrounder*.

19. See James K. Hoffmeier, *The Immigration Crisis: Immigrants, Aliens, and the Bible* (Wheaton, IL: Crossway, 2009) and Hoffmeier, "The Use and Abuse of the Bible in the Immigration Debate," Center for Immigration Studies *Backgrounder*, December 2011.

20. Hoffmeier, CIS *Backgrounder*.

21. Hoffmeier, CIS *Backgrounder*.

22. Henry, Vol. 2, p. 457.

23. See Mark R. Amstutz, "Two Theories of Immigration," *First Things*, December 2015.

24. Interestingly, Rahab was an ancestor of both King David and Jesus; see Matthew 1:5.

25. Edward J. Erler, "Who We Are as a People – The Syrian Refugee Question," *Imprimis* 43 (October 2016): 3.

26. Erler, "Who We Are as a People," 3.

27. Amstutz, *op. cit.* For further elaboration on Amstutz's line of thought, see James R. Edwards, Jr., Center for Immigration Studies blog, "Finally, a Prominent Christian Journal Prints Some Sense on Immigration," December 7, 2015.

28. See Marilyn C. Baseler, *"Asylum for Mankind": America, 1607–1800* (Ithaca, NY: Cornell University Press, 1998); James R. Edwards, Jr., "Public Charge Doctrine: A Fundamental Principle of American Immigration Policy," Center for Immigration Studies *Backgrounder*, May 2001; and James R. Edwards, Jr., "Keeping Extremists Out: The History of Ideological Exclusion and the Need for Its Revival," Center for Immigration Studies *Backgrounder*, September 2005.

29. See, for example, Marylin C. Baseler and Otis L. Graham, Jr., *Unguarded Gates: A History of America's Immigration Crisis* (Lanham, MD: Rowman & Littlefield, 2004), as well as Bernadette Maguire, *Immigration: Public Legislation and Private Bills* (Lanham, MD: University Press of America, 1997).

30. Marshall, *God and the Constitution*, pp. 141–142.

31. Karen Zeigler and Steven A. Camarota, "Immigration Surging: 1.5 Million Arriving Annually," Center for Immigration Studies *Backgrounder*, October 2016; Elizabeth M. Grieco, Yesenia D. Acosta, G. Patricia de la Cruz, Christine Gambino, Thomas Gryn, Luke J. Larsen, Edward N. Trevelyan, and Nathan P. Waters, "The Foreign-Born Population in the United States: 2010," *American Community Survey Reports* (Washington, DC: U.S. Census Bureau, May 2012); Office of Immigration Statistics, *2012 Yearbook of Immigration Statistics* (Washington, DC: U.S. Department of Homeland Security, July 2013); Steven A. Camarota, "Immigrants in the United States, 2010: A Profile of America's Foreign-Born Population," Center for Immigration Studies *Backgrounder*, August 2012; and James G. Gimpel and James R. Edwards, Jr., *The Congressional Politics of Immigration Reform* (Boston, MA: Allyn & Bacon, 1999), pp. 5–6.

32. See Zeigler and Camarota, "Immigration Surging," figure 1.

33. James P. Smith and Barry Edmonston, eds., *The New Americans: Economic, Demographic, and Fiscal Effects of Immigration* (Washington, DC: National Academy Press, 1997).

34. See especially George J. Borjas, *Heaven's Door: Immigration Policy and the American Economy* (Princeton, NJ: Princeton University Press, 1999); Smith and Edmonston, *The New Americans;* Roy Beck, *The Case Against Immigration: The Moral, Economic, Social, and Environmental Reasons for Reducing U.S. Immigration Back to Traditional Levels* (New York: W. W. Norton, 1996); and Mark Krikorian, *The New Case Against Immigration: Both Legal and Illegal* (New York: Sentinel, 2008) for a fuller elaboration.

35. For instance, Steven A. Camarota confirms the hugely disproportionate welfare use by immigrants along with the correlation of education level with welfare use among immigrant households. See Camarota's "Welfare Use by Legal and Illegal Immigrant Households," Center for Immigration Studies *Backgrounder*, September 2015, Tables A1 and A2.

36. Robert Rector, Christine Kim, and Shanea Watkins, "The Fiscal Cost of Low-Skill Households to the U.S. Taxpayer," *Heritage Special Report*, SR-12 (Washington, DC: Heritage Foundation, April 4, 2007), pp. 11–12. Other, more recent but less comprehensive studies confirm the significant net fiscal costs immigrants impose on the United States. See, for example, Robert Rector and Jason Richwine, "The Fiscal Cost of Unlawful Immigrants and Amnesty to the U.S. Taxpayer," Heritage Foundation *Special Report*, SR-133 (Washington, DC: Heritage Foundation, May 6, 2013).

37. Robert Rector and Christine Kim, "The Fiscal Cost of Low-Skill Immigrants to the U.S. Taxpayer," *Heritage Special Report*, SR-14 (Washington, DC: Heritage Foundation, May 21, 2007), pp. 12–13.

38. Rector and Richwine, "The Fiscal Cost of Unlawful Immigrants and Amnesty to the U.S. Taxpayer," tables 3, 5, and 6.

39. Camarota, "Welfare Use by Legal and Illegal Immigrant Households," figure 2.

40. See Camarota and Zeigler's "Immigrant Gains and Native Losses" (see note 35) and their extensive work documenting employment prospects disadvantaging Americans and benefiting immigrants during the worst economic conditions since the Great Depression, due principally to head-to-head job competition and wage constriction by mass immigration. Other sources of note include Borjas's work, particularly his *Heaven's Door*; Smith and Edmonston, *The New Americans*; and Roy Beck, "'Occupation Collapse' and Poverty Wages: Consequences of Large Guestworker Programs," testimony before the U.S. House Judiciary Subcommittee on Immigration, Border Security, and Claims, March 24, 2004.

41. Refugee resettlement programs have become money-making enterprises for many religious operations. These religiously affiliated entities pocket U.S. taxpayer money while forcing refugees from places like Somalia and Syria upon unsuspecting American towns and cities. These modern-day moneychangers are examined in my Center for Immigration Studies *Memorandum*, "Religious Agencies and Refugee Resettlement," March 2012.

42. Edwards, "Keeping Extremists Out."

43. Bolton quoted in James R. Edwards, Jr., "Islam as Ideology – and Its Exclusion," Center for Immigration Studies blog, January 10, 2016.

44. See George J. Borjas, "The Slowdown in the Economic Assimilation of Immigrants: Aging and Cohort Effects Revisited Again," National Bureau of Economic Research *Working Paper* No. 19116, June 2013; John Fonte and Althea Nagai, "America's Patriotic Assimilation System Is Broken," *Briefing Paper* (Washington, DC: Hudson Institute, April 2013).

45. See Beck, *The Case Against Immigration*, chapters five, eight, and nine, and Borjas, *Heaven's Door*. Borjas gives many sobering examples of the adverse impact that mass immigration has on vulnerable Americans, but two sufficiently illustrate the point: "In an $8 trillion economy, native earnings [lost due to immigrants' redistribution of wealth] would drop by about $152 billion" (p. 91) and "It turns out that African Americans are likely to lose from immigration . . . [b]ecause blacks own a relatively small proportion of the capital stock of the United States . . . [and,] because post-1965 immigrants tend to be disproportionately less skilled, they are much more likely to compete with black workers than with white workers" (p. 93). Also, see Karen Zeigler and Steven A. Camarota, "All Employment Growth Since 2000 Went to Immigrants," Center for Immigration Studies *Backgrounder*,

June 2014; and Steven A. Camarota and Karen Zeigler, "Immigrant Gains and Native Losses in the Job Market, 2000 to 2013," Center for Immigration Studies *Backgrounder*, July 2013.

46. James R. Edwards, Jr., "Immigration and Free Market Morality: A Christian Perspective," *The Review of Faith & International Affairs*, 9 (Spring 2011): 1.

47. Polls have consistently shown at least a plurality – and often, a majority – of the American public favoring reductions in the levels of immigration, including legal immigration. Only a bare minority – usually in single digits – supports increasing immigration levels. For instance, a 1986 CBS News/*New York Times* poll found 52 percent of respondents for cutting immigration and just 11 percent for raising it; more than 65 percent wanted immigration cuts in 1994, the American National Election Study reported, with a mere 5 percent favoring immigration increases. This pattern has held firmly for several decades. A Westhill Partners/Hotline poll of February 2005 said 37 percent favored keeping legal immigration at its present level, 39 percent wanted it cut, and 14 percent were for increasing it. Available at: www .westhillhotlinepoll.com/WHP_HotlinePoll_February.pdf, accessed November 5, 2016). A Reuters-Ipsos Poll from the summer of 2014 found 46 percent of respondents favor cutting immigration levels, 38 percent said keep it at current levels, and 16 percent prefer increasing it. Available at: www.ipsos-na.com/download/pr.aspx ?id=13859, accessed November 5, 2016). See also Gimpel and Edwards, *Congressional Politics*, chapter two.

14

The Moral Dilemma of U.S. Immigration Policy Revisited: Open Borders vs. Social Justice?*

Stephen Macedo

IMMIGRATION POLICY AS A MORAL DILEMMA

How should we think about U.S. immigration policy from the standpoint of basic justice, especially distributive justice which encompasses our obligations to the less well-off? Does a justifiable immigration policy take its bearings from the acknowledgment that we have special obligations to "our own" poor, that is, our least well-off fellow citizens? Or, on the other hand, do our moral duties simply argue for attending to the interests of the least well- off persons in the world, giving no special weight to the interests of the least well-off Americans?

There are reasons to believe that recent American immigration policy has had a deleterious impact on the distribution of income among American citizens. According to influential arguments – associated with George Borjas and others – by admitting large numbers of relatively poorly educated and low-skilled workers we have increased competition for low-skilled jobs, lowering the wages of the poor and increasing the gap between rich and poor Americans.[1] In addition to the effects on labor markets, there are other ways in which high levels of immigration may have lessened support for social welfare policies.

How should we think about the apparent ethical conflict between, on the one hand, the cosmopolitan humanitarian impulse to admit less well-off persons from abroad who wish to immigrate to the U.S. and, on the other hand, the special obligations we have to less well-off Americans, including or especially African Americans? Those with liberal sensibilities need to consider whether everything that they might favor – humanitarian concern for the world's poor, an openness to an ever-widening social diversity, and support for distributive justice within our political community – necessarily go together.

These are vexing questions in politics as much as in political theory and moral philosophy. Recent events have made them even more central. President

---

* My thanks to those who have suggested changes during the ten years since this was first published.

Donald Trump has revived the isolationist slogan "America first," and linked immigration to the loss of well-paying American jobs. His anti-immigration message is crude and cruel but he also speaks to real grievances. His message has resonated with millions of working-class Americans – especially white working-class men without a college degree – who have in many ways borne the brunt of globalization.

We have not paid sufficient attention to the domestic distributive impact of immigration (as well as globalized trade). High levels of immigration by low-skilled workers make fulfilling our moral obligations to the poorest Americans more costly and less likely. If that is true, does it mean that the borders should be closed and immigration by the poor restricted? That conclusion would be hasty: the moral terrain and the policy options are complex.

If high levels of immigration have a detrimental impact on our least well-off fellow citizens that is a reason to limit immigration, even if those who seek admission are poorer than our own poor whose condition is worsened. Citizens have special obligations to one another: we have special reasons to be concerned with the distribution of wealth and opportunities among citizens. The relative standing of citizens matters in ways that the relative standing of citizens and non-citizens does not. In this respect, I argue against "cosmopolitanism" with respect to the principles of social justice, and join Michael Walzer, John Rawls, David Miller, and Michael I. Blake, among others, in defending the idea that distributive justice holds among citizens.[2]

What is the basis of these special obligations among citizens? I argue that it is as members and co-participants in self-governing political communities that we have special obligations to our fellow members.

Distributive justice is a weighty moral consideration that bears on immigration policy, but it is not the only one. We also have significant moral duties and obligations to poor people (and others) abroad; these are different in content from what we owe to fellow citizens and they may take priority. The large external effects of our policies may dominate smaller negative effects on distributive justice.

This chapter proceeds as follows. The first part describes the reasonable grounds for thinking that we face a dilemma in shaping US immigration policy. I feature claims advanced by George Borjas and others in order to raise important moral questions while allowing that there is serious disagreement about the effects of immigration. In section two I consider the debate between "cosmopolitans" – who argue against the moral significance of shared citizenship and in favor of universal obligations of distributive justice – and those who argue for the existence of special obligations of justice among citizens. I seek to clarify the moral grounds for regarding shared membership in a political community as morally significant, but also emphasize that we have significant cosmopolitan duties. In the final section I return to the moral dilemma of U.S. immigration policy and offer some reflections on policy choices. It may be that on balance we should accept and manage ongoing high levels of movement back and forth across the U.S.–Mexico border.

One point is worth making before moving on. The perspective adopted and defended here is politically liberal. John Rawls and Michael Walzer (whose ideas I treat in some detail) are philosophers of the left in American politics. It might be thought that this limits the relevance of my argument, but this is not so. For one thing, the vast majority of Americans profess a belief in some liberal principles, such as equality of opportunity. While Americans are less supportive than Europeans of measures designed directly to reduce income disparities between the wealthy and poor, they overwhelmingly affirm that institutions such as public education should insure that every child has a good start in life, irrespective of accidents of birth.[3] The question of whether we have special obligations to our fellow citizens is important independently of the details of one's convictions about what justice requires among citizens. Even those who believe that "equality of opportunity" mandates only a modest level of educational and other social services may still think that the mandate holds among fellow citizens and not all of humanity. The general thrust of my argument should, therefore, be of relevance to those who do not accept the specific prescriptions of Rawls and Walzer.

THE CONTOURS OF THE IMMIGRATION DILEMMA

Over the past half-century, American immigration policies and practices became, in some important respects, more accommodating to the less well-off abroad. Some argue that this "generosity" has exacted a significant cost in terms of social justice at home.

The basic facts are striking. Immigration to the U.S. has trended upward since the end of World War II. Between 2001 and 2016, about one million foreign nationals per year became long-term permanent residents in the U.S. (including both new arrivals and adjustments to visa status). Whereas in 1970, less than 5 percent of the general population was foreign born, that percentage rose to 14 percent – or 45 million people – in 2015 (just under the historic record of 15 percent around the beginning of the twentieth century). Twenty-six percent of the current U.S. population – or 85 million people – are either immigrants or the children of immigrants. Over half the U.S. population growth since 1965 is due to immigration and were it not for immigration, it is estimated that the current population of the U.S. would be 252 rather than 324 million.[4]

Patterns of immigration to the U.S. were shaped deeply by amendments to the Immigration and Nationality Act passed in 1965, emphasizing the principle of family reunification. The exact formulas are complicated, but "immediate relatives" of U.S. citizens (spouses, parents, and unmarried children under 21 years of age) can enter without numerical limit (and often number nearly half a million per year). An additional 226,000 annual admission priorities are extended to adult children and adult siblings of U.S. citizens, and spouses and children of legal permanent residents ("green card" holders). In 2010, family-based preferences accounted for 66 percent of annual immigration to the US.[5]

U.S. policy also favors some migrants based on employment qualifications and skills (14 percent of the total in 2010) and others based on humanitarian grounds, as refugees and asylum seekers (13 percent of the total in 2010).[6] There are also shorter-term skills-based green card programs, including the H-1B visa program.

The composition of the growing immigrant pool changed markedly after 1965, with the skills level and earnings of immigrants declining relative to the native U.S. population. Whereas in 1960, the average immigrant man living in the U.S. earned 4 percent more than the average native-born American, by 1998 the average immigrant earned 23 percent less. Most of the growth in immigration since 1960 has been among people entering at the bottom 20 percent of the income scale. This is partly because, as George Borjas observes, "Since the immigration reforms of 1965, U.S. immigration law has encouraged family reunification and discouraged the arrival of skilled immigrants."[7]

The ethnic and racial makeup of immigration has also changed with the percentage arriving from Europe and Canada falling sharply and the percentage from Latin America and Asia rising.[8]

On Borjas's influential if controversial analysis, recent decades of high immigration have tended to lower wages overall by increasing the labor supply, with the biggest negative impact being felt by the least well-off. Immigration from 1980 to 1995 increased the pool of high school dropouts in the US by 21 percent, while increasing the pool of college graduates by only 4 percent. By 2013, half of U.S. workers with less than a high school degree were foreign born.[9] This, argues Borjas, contributed to a substantial decline in the wages of high school dropouts and to a widening of the wage gap based on education. He argues that immigration between 1980 and 2000 had the effect of lowering the wages of the average native worker by 3.2 percent, while lowering wages among those without a high school diploma (roughly the bottom 10 percent of wage earners) by 9 percent.[10] To put it another way, it is widely agreed that in the U.S. in the 1980s and 1990s there was a substantial widening of the wage gap between more and less educated workers. Borjas has argued that nearly half of this widening wage gap between high school dropouts and others may be due to the increase in the low-skilled labor pool caused by immigration.[11]

Of course, all Americans have benefited from cheaper fruits, vegetables, and the many other products and services that immigrants (including undocumented workers) help produce.[12] Firms have also benefited from cheap labor. Wealthier Americans have also benefited from increased access to cheap labor to perform service work – as nannies, gardeners, etc. By decreasing the cost of childcare and housekeeping, immigration has helped highly educated women participate in the labor force.[13] However, Borjas argues that native-born African American and Hispanic workers have suffered disproportionately because they are disproportionately low-skilled and own few firms, and often compete directly with low-skilled immigrants.[14]

Borjas also observes that nations with notably more progressive domestic policies often have immigration policies that are quite different from the U.S. While U.S. immigration policy since 1965 has emphasized family ties rather than desirable skills, Canada pioneered a system in the late 1960s that gives greater weight to educational background, occupation, and language proficiency. Canada's policy favors better-educated and high-skilled workers and this seems likely to have distributive effects that are the opposite of U.S. policy. By increasing the pool of skilled workers relative to the unskilled, Canadian policy tends to lower the wages of the better off and to raise the relative level of the worse off.[15] Australia, New Zealand, and other countries have followed Canada's lead and President Trump has argued that the U.S. should also move in that direction.[16]

It seems quite possible that Canada's policy of favoring more educated immigrants helps lessen domestic income disparities, while seeming less generous from the position of poor people abroad. U.S. policy, by admitting predominantly low-skilled and low education immigrants looks generous to poor persons abroad but may worsen the relative standing of the American poor. As is now obvious, were the U.S. to follow Canada and impose an education test on immigration this would have a substantial impact on the ethnic and racial composition and national origins of immigrants to the U.S. It would, in short, substantially and disproportionately reduce immigration from Mexico and the rest of Latin America.

We should emphasize that Borjas's arguments are controversial, and many economists argue that he exaggerates the negative effects of immigration while downplaying the positive side.[17] Economist David Card argues that "immigration exerts a modestly positive effect on the labor market outcomes of most natives," but not all, and not the least well-educated cohort.[18]

The *labor market argument* advanced by Borjas (and others including Steven A. Camarota and Karen Zeigler in this volume[19]) describes one possible way in which recent decades of immigration to the U.S. may worsen distributive justice in the United States. There are several other pathways – political, cultural, and economic – by which recent high rates of immigration may harm the relative standing of poorer Americans. I will mention these briefly.

One response to the foregoing argument is that if immigration increases our collective wealth while worsening income disparities across rich and poor, why not welcome immigration and redistribute the surplus via tax and spending policies?[20] Redistributive policies could compensate for the malign distributive effects of immigration, but immigration may undermine political support for social welfare and redistributive programs.

Nolan McCarty, Keith T. Poole, and Howard Rosenthal argue that recent patterns of immigration help explain why increasing inequality since the 1980s has come about in the U.S. without an increase in political pressure for redistribution. Since 1972, the percentage of non-citizens has risen and their income relative to other Americans has fallen. "From 1972 to 2000, the median family income of non-citizens fell from 82% of the median income of voters to 65% while the fraction of the population that is non-citizen rose from 2.6% to 7.7%."[21] Meanwhile, a "large segment of the truly poor does not have the right to vote. Whereas in 2010, noncitizens were 9.2 percent of the general population," they were 13 percent of families with incomes below $7,500 per year.[22] McCarty, Poole, and Rosenthal argue that the increasing proportion of non-citizens among the poor has shifted the position of the median voter – the voters likely to be the "swing voters" who decide close elections. Immigration to the U.S. has made the median *voter* better off relative to the median *resident*, and this has decreased median voters' likelihood of supporting redistribution.[23]

Immigration may have, thus, both worsened the relative standing of the least-well-off Americans and also made it less likely that crucial "swing voters" would support redistributive programs. McCarty, Poole and Rosenthal point out that countries with smaller portions of non-citizens among the poorest – such as France, Japan, and Sweden – have not seen the sort of sharp increases in the proportion of national wealth going to people in the top 1 percent as in the United States.[24]

This *median voter argument* suggests that recent patterns of immigration to the U.S. may not only worsen the relative lot of the least well-off Americans but also make it harder to enact redistributive policies. Excluding immigrants from social welfare services is one way to counteract these effects, but immigrants – including illegal immigrants in many places – will still be provided with a variety of social services, including education.[25]

Consider next an additional possible impact of immigration on social justice. Feelings of solidarity and mutual identification that help support social justice may be undermined, at least in the short to medium term, by the increased racial and ethnic heterogeneity associated with immigration.[26] Robert Putnam surveys a range of different forms of evidence suggesting that, "in ethnically diverse neighborhoods residents of all races tend to 'hunker down.' Trust (even of one's own race) is lower, altruism and community cooperation rarer, friends fewer."[27] The fact that immigrant groups typically have higher fertility rates than natives amplifies the effect. Putnam and others thus argue that immigration-induced increases in ethnic and racial diversity can reduce social solidarity and undermine support for the provision of public goods, including programs aimed at helping the poor.[28]

On the basis of their survey of the evidence, Stuart Soroka, Keith Banting, and Richard Johnston argue, "International migration does seem to matter for the size of the welfare state. Although no welfare state has actually shrunk in the face of accelerating international movement of people, its rate of growth is smaller the more open a society is to immigration." They further argue that, "The typical industrial society might spend 16 or 17 percent more than it does now on social services if it kept its foreign-born percentage where it was in 1970."[29]

All of these empirical claims are controversial and the impact of immigration on a society's capacity to sustain redistributive programs is bound to be complex. Just how immigration and increased ethnic and racial diversity inhibit social spending is unclear: the rise of New Right political parties in Europe is associated with controversies over immigration, and mainstream parties may need to shift to the right in response.[30]

Consider, finally, the argument advanced by John Skrentny in his contribution to this volume.[31] He joins those who think that the direct economic impact of immigration on wages is likely small. Yet he argues that native white and black workers, in particular, may be disadvantaged in local labor markets by popular stereotypes that associate Latino and Asian workers – especially immigrants – with hard work and greater reliability. The availability of Latino and Asian immigrants in a labor pool may, therefore, put white and especially African American workers at a disadvantage.

To sum up. There are reasons to believe that the specific contours of American immigration policy over the last 40 years may have lowered wages at the bottom, by increasing competition for low-wage jobs, while also reducing political support for more generous social provision targeted at low-wage workers and the poor generally. The greater ethnic and racial diversity associated with immigration may also have lowered trust among groups and support for public goods provision. And, finally, pro-immigrant workplace stereotypes may disadvantage native workers, especially whites and African Americans. Vexed empirical issues surround all of these claims.

The questions before us include the following: if U.S. immigration policies appear to be liberal and generous to the less well-off abroad (or at least some of them), does this generosity involve injustice toward poorer Native Americans, including – or perhaps, especially – African Americans? If we have special obligations to our poorer fellow citizens – obligations that are sufficiently urgent and weighty – then U.S. immigration policy may be hard or impossible to defend from the standpoint of domestic distributive justice.

Of course, the question of how we should respond to this – if it is true – is not straightforward. It does not follow that the most morally defensible policy – all things considered – is to enact more restrictive immigration policies. It might well be morally preferable to change the other laws and policies that allow the immigration of low-skilled workers to generate adverse effects on native-born poor. The inegalitarian distributive effects of immigration could be offset via publicly funded income support for low-wage workers, improved education and training for the unemployed, and other social welfare benefits for the less well-off. And yet, high levels of low-skilled immigration may also tend to lower public support for social welfare provision. This sharpens the dilemma.

We should not underestimate the complexity of the questions that surround policy choice in this area. Distributive justice is important, but other moral values are also in play, including humanitarian concern for all humans who are very badly off. Aside from the moral considerations that might help us rank various options, there is also the question of what package of policies might be politically saleable. This chapter can only scratch the surface of these issues.

COSMOPOLITAN VS. CIVIC OBLIGATIONS?

Let us step back and consider some framing moral issues. If the better-off have moral obligations to help the least well-off, why shouldn't those obligations focus on the least well-off of the world? Can we justify special obligations to our own poor, even if they are less poor than many others in the world?

Consider two ways in which we might care about the condition of the poor and seek to do something about it. We might care only about their absolute level of poverty or deprivation, or we might care about relative deprivation: the gap between the lives of the poorest and those of the richest. In response to the first concern we would engage in *humanitarian assistance* and seek to establish a floor of material well-being: a standard of decency below which no one should fall. In response to the latter concern we would articulate and enforce principles of social or *distributive justice*: standards to regulate the major institutions of taxation, inheritance, social provision, wage policies, education, etc., which help determine over time the relative levels of income, wealth, and opportunity available to different groups.

Most people seem to accept that wealthy societies owe the first sort of concern to human beings generally. Via humanitarian assistance, wealthier societies should pool their efforts and seek to lift poorer countries up at least to a level of basic decency; exactly what level is adequate or morally required is an important question. This sort of cosmopolitan moral concern has been likened to the duty we all have to be "Good Samaritans" when we can save people in distress without undue cost to ourselves.[32]

The latter species of concern – social or distributive justice – requires the establishment of institutions to regulate market inequalities: systems of progressive taxation, inheritance taxes, and the provision of social services. As noted, most Americans profess a belief that every child born in America should have a fair chance to attain good jobs – to compete based on his or her talents and effort – and this requires that governments raise taxes in order to provide good schools for all. Virtually everyone accepts some degree of progressivity in the tax structure so efforts to promote fair equality of opportunity are typically redistributive and constitute part of a system of distributive justice. Opportunity is one of the things we distribute by building public institutions – including tax-supported schools – alongside market institutions. As we have seen, immigration policies may also have an impact on the distribution of opportunities and rewards in society.

Do we have special moral obligations to our fellow citizens, especially obligations falling under the rubric of distributive justice? Do national borders matter with respect to our fundamental moral obligations to one another?

There are, roughly speaking, two opposed lines of thought. One emphasizes the moral arbitrariness of borders and the universality of our obligations to the less well-off. The other position holds that borders are morally significant, that we have special obligations to poorer fellow citizens, and that obligations of distributive justice in particular apply only among citizens. The first position is often referred to as a form of "cosmopolitanism": the idea that we are, in effect, citizens of the world. The latter position – which I argue for – goes under various names and I'll refer to it as the *civic view*.

The civic view holds that we have special obligations of mutual justification to our fellow citizens, and that the fullest obligations of distributive justice have special force among fellow citizens. With respect to people in the rest of world, our duties and obligations are different, though still quite important: fair dealing – including curbs on the exploitive potential of our corporations, and doing our fair share to address common problems (such as environmental dangers like global warming); more specific projects of historical rectification and redress in response to particular past acts of injustice; and humanitarian assistance to help lift other societies (insofar as we can) out of poverty.

Michael Walzer strikingly asserts that: "Distributive justice begins with membership; it must vindicate at one and the same time the limited right of closure, without which there could be no communities at all, and the political inclusiveness of existing communities."[33] It seems to me that Walzer is on the right track here, though he is unclear about the moral grounds. He famously argues that moral arguments in politics should take the form of interpreting "shared social meanings." Principles of justice are justified in light of "the particularism of history, culture, and membership." Social goods should be distributed according to criteria internal to their social meanings, and these shared social meanings are located within particular political communities.[34]

Given this account of the nature of moral argument and distributive justice, it is not surprising that Walzer would argue that distributive justice applies within ongoing political communities which are the natural homes of shared meanings. "[T]he political community is probably the closest we can come to a world of common meanings. Language, history, and culture come together (come more closely together here than anywhere else) to produce a collective consciousness . . . . the sharing of sensibilities and intuitions among the members of a historical community is a fact of life."[35] For Walzer, the rejection of cosmopolitan obligations of distributive justice goes hand in hand with the claim that common understandings of values are shared within particular political communities but not across them.

Walzer's argument contains part of the truth, but it is also puzzling. Achieving shared and well-justified principles of justice is surely a worthy aspiration within political communities. But while shared meanings are an important goal of public argument, an achievement to be worked toward, the extent of shared meanings is not the proper ground for circumscribing claims of social justice.

Shared social meanings – common understandings, shared assumptions of various sorts – are important for sustaining a political system based on discussion and mutual justification, but they are not the basic thing when it comes to demarcating the range of those to whom we owe justice. The range of those with whom we should seek to establish common and publicly justified principles of justice are those with whom we share a comprehensive system of binding laws. Publicly justified "common meanings" are not the basis of political obligations but rather the goal of public argument and deliberation within our political community.

Walzer lays too much emphasis on consensus and shared meanings in another way as well: what we should want is a *justified* consensus that is the result of criticism and testing. Critical argumentation is essential to public justification because what we should work toward are common understandings that are sound, and their soundness is essential to their authoritativeness. The mere fact of agreement, the mere existence of shared conventions, is not enough.

David Miller has argued eloquently for the advantages to political communities of a shared national culture and a common language, for these can help support a collective identity and bonds of mutual sympathy and understanding: "Social justice will always be easier to achieve in states with strong national identities and without internal communal divisions."[36] That again seems right, as far as it goes: social justice may be harder to achieve in very diverse societies. But justice remains an important goal in divided societies. Some societies, such as Canada, seem able to generate impressive levels of support for social justice even amidst great diversity, partly by adopting effective multicultural policies. Social scientists have more work to do to understand the relationships among heterogeneity, social capital, and social justice.[37]

Particular political societies – at least when they are well ordered rather than tyrannical, oppressive, very deeply divided, or desperately poor – will tend to generate roughly common understandings among members including standards for how disputes and disagreements should be resolved.[38] They may generate disagreements and conflicts galore, but these will be manageable if the society has working standards and practices for how disagreements should be dealt with and a reserve of rough agreement on the most important matters sufficient to sustain a common willingness to share a political order.

In his *The Law of Peoples*, John Rawls argues that the political community – or "people" – is the appropriate site of distributive justice: there are no obligations of distributive justice among human beings simply. We have humanitarian duties to relieve those in distress – as mentioned above – but we have no obligations across borders to regulate the relative well-being of better and worse off people (or to create institutions capable of doing so).

Many have found this puzzling. Rawls does not as a general matter share Walzer's emphasis on the authority of shared social meanings. Moreover, Rawls's general approach to justice encourages us to transcend morally arbitrary accidents of birth. There is a puzzle here.

When formulating principles of justice, Rawls's guiding thought is that we should put aside claims based on morally arbitrary differences and accidents of fate. We put aside claims to unequal rewards based on advantages flowing from accidents of birth: including the good fortune of being born into a well-off family, or with a superior genetic endowment. We regard these advantages as arbitrary when justifying to one another principles of justice to regulate the basic structure of society, which includes the system of property and market exchanges, incomes and inheritance taxation, and public institutions and policies of all kinds. We instead regard one another as free and equal persons, and imagine ourselves in an "original position" behind a "veil of ignorance": we ask which principles of social justice we would choose if we did not know the social position we would occupy.[39] This helps us consider which principles of justice for regulating the design of the basic structure are fair to all, and so capable of being freely accepted by reasonable people whichever position they occupy in society. To affirm mutually justified principles to regulate basic social institutions is to affirm that we regard one another as moral equals.

The upshot of Rawls's thought experiment is his argument that two basic principles of justice would be chosen by citizens of modern pluralistic democracies:

1. Each person has an equal claim to a fully adequate scheme of equal basic rights and liberties, which scheme is compatible with the same scheme for all; and in this scheme the equal political liberties, and only those liberties, are to be guaranteed their fair value.
2. Social and economic inequalities are to satisfy two conditions: (a) They are to be attached to positions and offices open to all under conditions of fair equality of opportunity; and (b), they are to be to the greatest benefit of the least advantaged members of society.[40]

Principle 2 (b) is also known as the "difference principle."

What is the relevance of all this to obligations across borders? If being born into a well-off family or with especially advantageous genes are to be regarded as morally arbitrary when thinking about justice, surely it seems equally arbitrary whether one is born in New Mexico or Mexico. One's place of birth with respect to nationality or political community seems quintessentially arbitrary. And yet, Rawls follows Walzer in arguing that obligations of distributive justice (such as the difference principle and the principle of fair equality of opportunity) apply only within the borders of political community, and only among co-participants in a shared political order. What can justify this?

Like Walzer, Rawls mentions the fact of greater diversity on the international scale: the fact of reasonable pluralism "is more evident within a society of well-ordered peoples than it is within one society alone."[41] Some have supposed that this invocation of diversity signals a retreat in Rawls's later writings with respect to his ambitions regarding justice. I think this interpretation is wrong, and, in any event, we should seek a better one if we can find it.[42]

The diversity-based argument for limiting obligations of distributive justice to particular political communities is a non-moral account of why justice's sails need trimming: a matter of bowing before unfortunate necessities, a pragmatic or prudential concession rather than a full moral justification. I believe there is a moral justification for confining obligations of distributive justice to co-participants in particular political communities. But what is it?

THE MORAL SIGNIFICANCE OF COLLECTIVE SELF-GOVERNANCE

Borders are morally significant because they bound systems of collective self-governance.[43] The arbitrariness of the location of borders does not stop them from being of great moral significance once a collectively self-governing people creates a common life within them, as Michael I. Blake, Anna Stilz, and others have emphasized.[44] Citizens of self-governing political communities – together making and being subject to the law – share a morally significant special relationship. As members of a political community we are joined in a collective enterprise across generations through which we construct and sustain a comprehensive system of laws and institutions that regulate and shape all other associations, including religious communities and families. We are born into political communities and are formed by them. From cradle to grave (and beyond) our interests, identities, relationships, and opportunities are pervasively shaped by the political system and the laws that we collectively create, coercively impose, and live within. The basic values and choices of our political order pervasively shape the lives of those who reside within it.

The governments of self-governing political communities – at least so long as they are legitimate – are recognized by members to be capable of authoritatively resolving conflicts, and of taking decisions that bind us as members of the political community: our government as our agent enters into treaties, makes alliances, declares war, and conducts various undertakings in our name. Legitimate governments are capable of putting citizens under new duties, and this is an awesome moral power.[45] We can be held collectively liable as citizens for the actions of our government, recognized by us and others to be our collective agent.[46]

Americans take responsibility – and *should* take responsibility – for what happens in North Dakota and Mississippi in a way they do not for what happens in Chihuahua and Ontario. Citizens look to one another to jointly establish collective programs concerning health and welfare: they view themselves as jointly responsible in perpetuity for their health and welfare, culture, and territory.

Citizens have powerful obligations of mutual concern and respect, and mutual justification, to one another because they are joined together – as constituent members of a sovereign people – in creating binding political institutions which determine patterns of opportunities and rewards for all.[47] A self-governing political society is a hugely significant joint venture, and we understand it as such. We have strong common obligations as fellow citizens because we collectively govern one another: we collectively make hugely consequential decisions. This could not simultaneously be true of the international society, and it is not. Membership in international bodies does not have the same significance because that membership is mediated by membership in primary political units, namely the "Member States" of the UN or its peoples: individuals are not governed directly by multilateral institutions.[48] International institutions deal with a limited range of subjects.

Cosmopolitan distributive justice (as opposed to a duty to assist other peoples to become self-governing and well-ordered) makes no sense absent a cosmopolitan state and a cosmopolitan political community, which hardly anyone seriously argues for, and which we are not obliged to bring into being; though there are good reasons for strengthening international institutions. It is, moreover, hard to understand the reasonableness of making people responsible for the welfare of others without also making them responsible for their governance. It would be strange and unreasonable to sever ongoing responsibilities for the provision of health, welfare, and education from responsibilities for governance with respect to these matters.

Federations or unions of states such as Europe may voluntarily enter into increasing cooperative relations, but we understand European peoples to be doing this as a matter of mutual advantage and choice, not as an obligation of fundamental justice. It may be good for them but it is also up to them, as the people of the United Kingdom have recently affirmed.

To argue that membership in a political collectivity is morally significant in the ways I have begun to describe raises the further question: which political collectivities qualify? Does every political community have equal moral standing, or if not, which ones? Respect for basic human rights is one crucial threshold condition of legitimacy and international respectability. Liberal democracies qualify for full respect, but so do certain not-fully liberal and democratic regimes, which Rawls calls "decent" peoples. We need not go into the details here, but suffice it to say that the theory of legitimacy at work here is the following: *we ought to fully respect states that effectively protect citizens' basic interests and provide working legal and political arrangements and within which (a) basic human rights are respected and (b) there are effective processes for giving everyone a say, for insuring that all groups within society are listened to, responded to, and effectively included in collective self-rule.*[49] To respect such political societies is to respect distinctive forms of collective self-rule, forms of collective self-rule that may deviate from some of the features that we understand to be aspects of liberal democracy, but which nevertheless observe basic rights and take all members interests seriously into account, and thereby make legitimate law. If by our lights such communities go wrong in some respects we can nevertheless say that the mistake is theirs to make. Such political communities can be regarded as the fit custodians of the interests of their own citizens.

WHAT DO WE OWE TO NON-MEMBERS?

Space does not permit an extensive discussion of what the civic view might say about obligations to non-members, but it may be helpful to round out the account before returning to the problem of immigration.

First, societies have general duties of (a) *fair dealing* with one another, and this would include non-exploitation, the avoidance of force and fraud, and the duty to curb the capacity of one's citizens or corporations to harm or exploit others. This general duty of fair dealing includes doing our share to address common problems (avoidance of free-riding), including environmental problems such as global warming, disaster relief, and humanitarian assistance.

Second, they have specific obligations to other countries or groups growing out of particular relations of exploitation, oppression, or domination, which give rise to specific obligations of *rectification and redress*. (b) If we have exploited or oppressed poorer and weaker societies, or if we have allowed our corporations to do so, then we have debts to these other societies which require some sort of recompense.

I should emphasize that these first two categories almost certainly generate strong demands to strengthen international institutions and for reform in the way that countries like the U.S. conduct themselves in the world.

Finally, it seems right to say that well-off societies have (c) general *humanitarian duties* to relieve those in destitution or distress and to respond to gross and systematic violations of human rights. Our duty is to do what we can to relieve distress, to end suffering, to stop gross violations of human rights, and to get a society on its feet so that it can look after its own affairs. These duties may involve substantial resource commitments, and they would require rich countries like the U.S. to spend more than they currently do on assistance, if it could be shown that such assistance is effective (which it very often is not[50]). The proper target of aid is helping societies to develop their own effective and legitimate political institutions which can secure the basic interests of all citizens.

Our general humanitarian duties include doing our fair share to provide safe harbor for refugees, whose basic needs are not being met in their home countries and who have no prospect for having them met as a consequence of well-founded fears of persecution.[51] If we have contributed to the creation of the conditions that generate refugees then we have special obligations to address their plight. In the absence of specific connections and special responsibilities, we still have general duties to do our part along with others: to bear some significant cost to relieve suffering abroad.

Crucially, however, members of wealthier societies do not owe to all the people of the world precisely the same consideration that they owe to fellow citizens. Full justice holds within political communities because of the special moral relation that citizens share: as the ultimate controllers and subjects of extensive institutions of shared governance.

U.S. IMMIGRATION POLICY AND DISTRIBUTIVE JUSTICE

As we have seen, it is not implausible to think that America's immigration policy has contributed to rising inequality and distributive injustice in the U.S. over the last half century. Poor immigrants are better off for having been allowed to immigrate, but many have competed for jobs with less-well-off Americans, and social programs to address inequality may have been made less politically popular. What, from an egalitarian perspective at least, could possibly be wrong in the U.S. being more like Canada, by reducing overall levels of immigration and giving greater priority to immigration by the better educated and higher skilled?

Howard Chang rightly observes that the civic, or "liberal nationalist," policy on immigration seems anomalous,

If the welfare of all incumbent residents determines admissions policies, however, and we anticipate the fiscal burden that the immigration of the poor would impose, then our welfare criterion would preclude the admission of unskilled workers in the first place. Thus, our commitment to treat these workers as equals once admitted would cut against their admission and make them worse off than they would be if we agreed never to treat them as equals. A liberal can avoid this anomaly by adopting a cosmopolitan perspective that extends equal concern to all individuals, including aliens, which suggests liberal immigration policies for unskilled workers.[52]

Chang allows, of course, that the morally justified cosmopolitan immigration policy may be politically infeasible because Americans seem unwilling to embrace the right sort of cosmopolitan moral attitude.

I have argued, however, that there are good reasons for believing that we have special responsibilities for our fellow citizens, obligations arising from membership in a self-governing community. In shaping immigration policies, concerns about distributive justice are relevant and urgent, and these concerns are inward-looking rather than cosmopolitan, emphasizing the special obligations we have to our poorer fellow citizens. If the U.S. were to move toward a more Canadian-style immigration policy this could improve the lot of less-well-off American workers. Considerations of distributive justice – taken in the abstract – argue for the superiority of the Canadian system: this would mean limiting immigration based on family re-unification (perhaps limiting that preference to spouses and minor children), placing greater weight on priorities for education and other skills, and curbing undocumented or illegal immigration.

However, sound policy recommendations in this vexed area of policy need to take into account a wider set of moral considerations and a great deal more of the relevant context, including geography and the heavy residue of historical patterns and practice. So far as the context is concerned, the United States is not Canada, and the costs of pursuing a Canadian-style immigration policy in the U.S. could be prohibitive. Empirical description, and careful analysis and prediction, must be combined with moral judgment. I can only sketch a few of the relevant considerations in concluding, and it should also be noted that patterns of migration to the U.S. are shifting rapidly.

The U.S. shares a 2,000-mile long border with Mexico, and that border has marked large differences in development, income, and wealth. For decades, there have been high levels of migration from Mexico to the U.S., and the U.S. has frequently welcomed massive influxes of migrant workers. In the period from 1965 to 1986, 1.3 million Mexicans entered the U.S. legally along with 46,000 contract workers, but 28 million entered as undocumented migrants. The vast majority subsequently returned to Mexico, yielding a net migration to the U.S. of around five million during that time.[53] Patterns of migration and return are self-reinforcing: migration prepares the way for more migration as language, labor market skills, and personal contacts are acquired.[54] Heightened border security in the late 1980s and 1990s had the perverse consequence that illegal migrants chose to remain in the U.S. far longer than they did when it was easier to leave and re-enter.

Over three million Mexicans enter the U.S. yearly on non-immigrant visas and there are well over 200 million short-term border crossings. The U.S. and Mexico (along with other Western Hemisphere nations) are committed to policies of open markets and free trade.[55] Economic growth in Mexico has narrowed the wage gap between the U.S. and Mexico: GDP in Mexico is now over $17,500 per capita, making it a middle-income country. The birth rate in Mexico has also declined.

Remittances from the U.S. undoubtedly contributed considerably to economic growth in Mexico, and Mexican migration to the U.S. has been falling since the early 2000s. In 2013, China and India surpassed Mexico as the largest senders of migrants to the U.S., though other Caribbean and Central American countries – including Cuba, the Dominican Republic, El Salvador, and Guatemala – continue to send large numbers of migrants.[56]

What is the most ethically defensible way of responding to concerns about immigration, including concerns stemming from social justice within the U.S.? We must consider the humanitarian costs of attempts to massively alter longstanding patterns of movement across our long and long-porous borders with Mexico and other Central American countries.

The approach long favored by some on the right, and now being implemented at least in part, is to try to limit legal migration and stop illegal immigration by more vigorously controlling the southern border, by constructing a security fence, and by other means, including increased arrests and deportations of undocumented persons.

Will this be effective? Policy changes in the U.S. seem to be having some effect. As this book goes to press, it appears that migration to the U.S. from Central American countries in general is down significantly: U.S. Customs and Border Protection reports that apprehensions of undocumented persons along the Southwest Border are down 64 percent from May 2016 to May 2017.[57]

But this has been partly at the cost of imposing tremendous burdens on the 11 million undocumented persons living and working in the U.S. It is estimated that 60 percent of these people have been living in the U.S. for over a decade, and a third of those have American-born children who are therefore citizens.[58] It may be that many or most of these people had no right to come here in the first place, but they came mainly for honorable and decent reasons: to help their families cope with often desperate poverty. The costs of disruption for those who have been here for any considerable amount of time, as law-abiding citizens, makes it immoral to not provide a path to regularized status.[59]

Another way of curtailing illegal migration by poor workers would focus on stemming the demand for migrant workers in the U.S. We might institute a national identification card, increase penalties for forging identification papers, and vigorously punish employers who hire undocumented people. Obviously, if such policies were implemented effectively, the cost of low-skilled labor would increase considerably in many areas, especially in agriculture, but that would appear to be good insofar as wages rise at the bottom of the income scale. It is often said that illegal migrants do work that Americans are unwilling to do, but of course they are unwilling at the prevailing low wage, and that is just the problem from the standpoint of distributive justice.[60] Suppose the wages were doubled and the work conditions improved significantly?

An alternative approach would be to accept and regularize the flow of migrant labor, as Massey, Durand, and Malone recommend. Such proposals include increasing the annual quota of legal entry visas from Mexico, and perhaps other Central American countries. In addition, instituting a temporary two-year work visa, which would be renewable once. Massey, Durand, and Malone have proposed making available 300,000 such visas per year. This would regularize and re-channel the flow of illegal migrants into a legal flow. The work visas would be awarded to workers not employers, so that workers would be free to quit. Fees for these visas plus savings in the Immigration and Naturalization Services budget could generate hundreds of millions of dollars a year that could be passed along to states and localities with high concentrations of migrants, to offset the costs of some local services. Finally, Massey and his colleagues would curtail the priorities that are now provided to family members of those who become naturalized Americans: they would eliminate the priority given to adult siblings of naturalized citizens and legal permanent residents, and they recommend making it easier for relatives of U.S. citizens to get tourist visas, so they can visit and return home more easily.[61]

It may be that the guestworker program component is most controversial. It has the advantage of directly addressing some of the underlying forces generating migration to the U.S. from Central America and elsewhere: poverty and the need for economic and social development. Massey and his colleagues emphasize that immigration is part of the development process and it is temporary. The poorest nations do not send out migrants. Developing countries typically send out immigrants for eight or nine decades, until growth at home relieves the pressures to leave. As we have seen, migration from Mexico has indeed been falling as predicted. Facilitating short-term migration and return would help promote growth elsewhere. While government-to-government foreign aid has a very poor track record, remittances sent home by migrant workers contribute considerably to economic development.

One moral problem with this approach is that it regularizes a system that would seem to impose some downward pressure on low-wage jobs in the U.S. It takes seriously the interests of poor people abroad and it benefits American employers, American consumers, and better-off Americans, but it does not fully address the special obligations we have to our poorest fellow citizens. The distributive justice problem could be dealt with by explicitly coupling these reforms with measures designed to improve the conditions of poorer and less well-educated Americans, whose economic prospects have deteriorated considerably in recent decades of globalized trade while elites have prospered. This would be appropriate and overdue in any case. While high levels of immigration by low-income people may make transfer payments less politically popular, a guestworker program, by excluding guestworkers from many public benefits, could help address this problem.

A problem with this policy is the intrinsic status of guestworkers. Adequate protections must be built into any guestworker program so that workers are not exploited and oppressed. A regulated guestworker program ought to be coupled with measures to require decent wages and work conditions, basic healthcare, protection from poisoning by pesticides, etc.[62] However, if a guestworker in the U.S. becomes seriously ill the program might be designed so that he or she is entitled to a trip to the emergency room and then a one-way ticket home. Such provisions seem likely to be part of the price of getting Americans to accept a guestworker program, and they seem legitimate so long as work conditions, wages, and protections are such that we can regard the conditions of work as humane and reasonable. (If such provisions led to workers concealing and postponing treatment of serious illnesses then we would need to re-think the acceptability of the provision.)[63]

An additional track of immigration reform can only be mentioned here: greater emphasis on skills-based migration. Such policies have spread from

Canada to many countries around the world. They may be advantageous for developed countries and have some specific advantages from the standpoint of domestic distributive justice, as discussed above. But there are serious questions concerning whether skills-based migration policies are causing a "brain drain" for sending countries. The benefits of remittances, and the likelihood that many migrants will return home, may outweigh the costs, but these issues deserve more attention than I can give them here.[64]

CONCLUSION

There is reason to believe that current patterns of immigration do raise serious issues from the standpoint of social justice: high levels of immigration by poor and low-skilled workers from Mexico and elsewhere in Central America may worsen the relative and absolute positions of poorer American citizens. Furthermore, such immigration may lessen political support for redistributive programs. Nevertheless, as we have also seen, the costs of "tightening-up" the border have been high: border security efforts have imposed great hardships and expense on migrant workers. Employer sanctions could be a more humane enforcement mechanism, but Americans have not had the political will to impose such measures.

I have argued that U.S. immigration policy presents us with the necessity of grappling with the tension between two important moral demands: justice to our fellow citizens vs. humanitarian concern with the plight of poor persons abroad. We have urgent reasons to shape major public policies and institutions with an eye to the distributive impact. Justice demands that we craft policies that are justifiable not simply from the standpoint of aggregate welfare – or the greatest good of the greatest number. We must consider the justifiability of policies from the standpoint of the least well-off among our fellow citizens. Immigration policy – as part of the basic structure of social institutions – ought to be answerable to the interests of the poorest Americans. An immigration policy cannot be considered morally acceptable in justice unless its distributive impact is defensible from the standpoint of disadvantaged Americans.

And yet, we must also consider the collateral costs of tight curbs on immigration. While domestic distributive justice is an urgent moral concern it does not, I would argue, take absolute or lexical priority over broader humanitarian concerns. Fostering development in very poor countries is a humanitarian imperative. If we can make significant contributions to this while bearing only small and uncertain costs in terms of domestic distributive justice, it seems likely that we should do so.

The proposals by Massey and his colleagues hold out the prospect of doing some real good for hundreds of thousands of migrant workers, their families, and countries of origin. It is possible that the best combination of policies would be something like the Massey proposals involving guestworkers, coupled with more generous aid to poorer Americans.

This discussion has only meant to suggest the shape of certain moral considerations relevant to any defensible immigration policy.

NOTES

1. George J. Borjas, *Heaven's Door: Immigration Policy and the American Economy* (Princeton: Princeton University Press, 1999).
2. Walzer and Rawls are discussed below. See also Thomas Nagel, "The Problem of Global Justice," *Philosophy and Public Affairs* 33.2 (2005): 113–147; David Miller, *Strangers in Our Midst: The Political Philosophy of Immigration* (Cambridge, MA: Harvard University Press, 2016).
3. See Jennifer L. Hochschild, *The American Dream and the Public Schools* (New York: Oxford University Press, 2003), pp. 9–11.
4. For a very helpful overview, see Ruth Ellen Wasem, *U.S. Immigration Policy on Permanent Admissions* (Washington, DC: Congressional Research Service, 2012), pp. 3, 7–8. Available at: www.fas.org/sgp/crs/homesec/RL32235.pdf, accessed February 23, 2018. See also Pew Research Center reports, including: "Modern Immigration Wave Brings 59 Million to U.S., Driving Population Growth and Change Through 2065: Chapter 5: U.S. Foreign-Born Population Trends," September 28, 2015. Available at:www.pewhispanic.org/2015/09/28/chapter-5-u-s-foreign-born-population-trends/; and see also Chapter 2: "Immigration's Impact on Past and Future U.S. Population Change." Available at: www.pewhispanic.org/2015/09/28/chapter-2-immigrations-impact-on-past-and-future-u-s-population-change/, accessed February 23, 2018.
5. Wasem, *U.S. Immigration Policy*; see also United States Citizenship and Immigration Services website. Available at: https://my.uscis.gov/helpcenter/search?q=sibling&tag=tag_search. And see: www.bipc.com/immigration-through-the-family-sponsored-preferences, accessed February 23, 2018.
6. Dallas Fed Report, 18–19.
7. George J. Borjas, "The U.S. Takes the Wrong Immigrants," *The Wall Street Journal*, April 5, 1990, A18; the quote continues, "75% of legal immigrants in 1987 were granted entry because they were related to an American citizen or resident, while only 4% were admitted because they possessed useful skills."
8. See Pew, "Modern Immigration."
9. Dallas Fed Report, 10.
10. George Borjas, "The Labor Demand Curve is Downward Sloping: Reexamining the Impact of Immigration on the Labor Market," *Quarterly Journal of Economics* 118.4 (November 2003): 1335–1374, 1336.
11. Borjas, *Heaven's Door.*
12. See Jorge Durand, Nolan J. Malone, and Douglas S. Massey, *Beyond Smoke and Mirrors: Mexican Immigration in an Era of Economic Integration* (New York: Russell Sage, 2003), pp. 150–151; conceding the wage effects discussed earlier, see p. 154.
13. Patricia Cortés and José Tessada, "Low-Skilled Immigration and the Labor Supply of Highly Skilled Women," *American Economic Journal: Applied Economics* 3.3 (2011): 88–123.

14. Borjas, *Heaven's Door*, pp. 11, and 22–38, 82–86, 103–104. For an update see Borjas, "The Labor Demand Curve." And see Borjas, Center for Immigration Studies, *Backgrounder*, "Increasing the Supply of Labor Through Immigration: Measuring the Impact on Native-Born Workers," April 1, 2004, which argues that immigration between 1980 and 2000, by increasing the labor supply, reduced the wages of native-born men by 4 percent; among natives without a high-school education (roughly the bottom 10 percent) he estimates the reduction at 7.4 percent. The impact on blacks and Hispanics is especially great because they form a disproportionately large share of high school dropouts; the effect holds regardless of whether immigration is legal or illegal.

15. Borjas, *Heaven's Door*, pp. 176–77.

16. See Lazaro Zamora and Jeff Mason, "Merit-Based Immigration System," Bipartisan Policy Center, April 11, 2017. Available at: https://bipartisanpolicy.org/blog/merit-based-immigration/, accessed February 23, 2018.

17. See David Card and Giovanni Peri, "Immigration Economics: A Review." See also the recent report arguing for small labor market effects, National Academies of Sciences, Engineering, and Medicine. *The Economic and Fiscal Consequences of Immigration* (Washington, DC: The National Academies Press, 2016), doi: 10.17226/23550.

18. See David Card, "How Immigration Affects US Cities," Center for Research and Analysis of Migration, Discussion Paper, November 2007, Department of Economics, University College, London. Available at: www.cream-migration.org/publ_uploads/CDP_11_07.pdf.

19. See Camarota (Chapter 3).

20. This and the next few paragraphs draw on Stephen Macedo, "When and Why Should Liberal Democracies Restrict Immigration?" in Rogers M. Smith, ed., *Citizenship, Borders, and Human Needs* (University of Pennsylvania Press, 2011), pp. 301–323.

21. Nolan McCarty, Keith T. Poole, and Howard Rosenthal, *Polarized America: The Dance of Ideology and Unequal Riches, Walras-Pareto Lectures* (Cambridge, MA: MIT Press, 2006), chapter 4.

22. Nolan McCarty, Keith T. Poole, and Howard Rosenthal, *Polarized America: The Dance of Ideology and Unequal Riches, Walras-Pareto Lectures* (Cambridge, MA: MIT Press, 2nd edition 2016), p. 137.

23. Congress restricted alien access to many federally funded welfare benefits in 1996. This would seem one way to help dampen the downward effects argued for by McCarty et al. Nevertheless, immigrants to the U.S. receive various forms of public assistance at a higher rate than Native Americans. Howard F. Chang, "Public Benefits and Federal Authorization for Alienage Discrimination by the States," *New York University Annual Survey of American Law*, Vol. 58 (2002): 357–570.

24. McCarty, Poole, and Rosenthal, *Polarized America*, 2nd edition, p. 122.

25. Malanga argues that, "Though the federal government bans illegal aliens from receiving many benefits, several states and cities have made themselves immigrant havens by providing government services through a don't-ask, don't-tell policy. New York City, for instance, offers immigrants, regardless of their status, such benefits as government-sponsored health insurance, preventive medical care, and counseling programs. Some states have moved to ensure that illegals receive in-state

tuition discounts to state colleges, even though out-of-state American citizens don't qualify for those discounts." See Malanga, *City Journal*, 2006, *ibid.*

26. As David Miller puts it, "A shared identity carries with it a shared loyalty, and this increases confidence that others will reciprocate one's own cooperative behavior," *On Nationality* (Oxford University Press, 1995), p. 92. Michael Walzer argues that the provision of social goods depends on shared social meanings, which in turn depend upon the enforcement of political boundaries, *Spheres of Justice*, chapter 2, "On Membership."

27. Robert D. Putnam, "E Pluribus Unum: Diversity and Community in the Twenty-First Century: The 2006 Johan Skytte Prize Lecture," *Scandinavian Political Studies* 30.2 (June 2007): 13, 137–174.

28. A. Alesina, E. La Ferrara, "Who Trusts Others?" *Journal of Public Economics* 85 (2002): 207–234, finding that homogeneous places tend to be more trusting; Alberto Alesina, Reza Baquir and William Easterley, "Public Goods and Ethnic Divisions," *Quarterly Journal of Economics* 114. 4 (November 1999): 1243–1284; R. La Porta, F. Lopez-de-Silanes, A. Shleifer, and R. Vishny, "The Quality of Government," *The Journal of Law, Economics, and Organization* 15.1 (1999): 222–279; Stephen Knack and Philip Keefer, "Does Social Capital Have an Economic Payoff? A Cross-Country Investigation," *The Quarterly Journal of Economics* 112.4 (1997): 1251–1288; William Easterly and Ross Levine, "Africa's Growth Tragedy: Policies and Ethnic Divisions," *The Quarterly Journal of Economics* 112.4 (1997): 1203–1250; Francis Fukuyama, "Social Capital and the Global Economy," *Foreign Affairs* 74.5 (1995): 89–103.

29. Stuart Soroka, Keith Banting, and Richard Johnston, "Immigration and Redistribution in a Global Era," in Pranab Bardhan, Samuel Bowles, and Michael Wallerstein (eds.), *Globalization and Egalitarian Redistribution* (Princeton: Princeton University Press, 2007), p. 278.

30. Soroka, Banting, and Johnston argue that the "effect seems wholly political and wholly through its direct impact on mainstream governing parties," and reflects the influence of "perceived cultural threat and economic cost," (pp. 278–279). The challenge is to devise ways to "combine openness at the global level with social integration at the domestic level," (Soroka *et al.*, p. 279). There is a large literature on ethnic diversity and public good provision, see James Habyarimana, Macartan Humphryes, Daniel N. Posner, and Jeremy M. Weinstein, "Why Does Ethnic Diversity Undermine Public Goods Provision?" *American Political Science Review* 101 (November 2007): 709–725, which notes that "the empirical connection between ethnic heterogeneity and the underprovision of public goods is widely accepted," though there is no consensus on "the specific mechanisms through which this relationship operates," (709). See also Alesina and La Ferrara, "Who Trusts Others?"; William Easterly and Ross Levine, "Africa's Growth Tragedy: Policies and Ethnic Divisions," *Quarterly Journal of Economics* 112 (1997): 1203–1250. For a contrary view, see Christel Kesler and Irene Bloemraad, "Does Immigration Erode Social Capital? The Conditional Effects of Immigration-Generated Diversity on Trust, Membership, and Participation across 19 Countries, 1981–2000," *Canadian Journal of Political Science*, 43.2 (2010): 319–347.

31. See Skrentny (Chapter 1).

32. Of course, there are important debates about whether foreign aid is efficacious. For a skeptical view, see William Easterley, *The White Man's Burden: Why the West's Efforts to Aid the Rest Have Done So Much Ill and So Little Good* (New York: Penguin, 2006).

33. Michael Walzer, *Spheres of Justice: A Defense of Pluralism and Equality* (New York: Basic, 1983), see chapter 2, "Membership."

34. Walzer has developed this argument in a number of places, perhaps most pointedly in "Philosophy and Democracy," *Political Theory*, 9 (1981): 379–399; this essay complements the approach of *Spheres of Justice*.

35. Walzer, *Spheres of Justice*, 28.

36. David Miller, *On Nationality* (Oxford University Press, 1995), p. 96.

37. For important recent efforts along these lines, see Keith Banting and Will Kymlicka (eds.), *The Strains of Commitment: The Political Sources of Solidarity in Diverse Societies* (Oxford: Oxford University Press, 2017).

38. Similarly, Philip Pettit argues that if we are to speak of "peoples" – understood as collective agents capable of taking decisions that bind all their members – then we must suppose that the persons who compose these societies "must subscribe as a matter of common awareness to certain ideas about how their affairs should be ordered. They must treat these ideas as common reasons that constitute the only currency in which it is ultimately legitimate to justify the way things are done in the collective organizing of their affairs," Philip Pettit, "Rawls's Peoples," in Rex Martin and David Reidy (eds.), *Rawls's Law of Peoples: A Realistic Utopia* (Oxford: Blackwell, 2006), pp. 38–56.

39. I paraphrase here the general approach of *A Theory of Justice* (Cambridge: Harvard, 1971).

40. John Rawls, *Political Liberalism* (New York: Columbia University Press, 1993), pp. 5–6. See also *Theory of Justice*.

41. John Rawls, *The Law of Peoples* (Cambridge: Harvard University Press, 1999), p. 18. Rawls also emphasizes that principles of justice among peoples should take seriously an international duty of toleration.

42. Some misread Rawls's *Political Liberalism* as insisting that principles of justice are limited to matters about which we can achieve an "overlapping consensus." If so, it would then seem obvious that, since in the international arena we encounter more diversity, so principles of global justice will need to be thin. However, this misreads *Political Liberalism*: the idea of an "overlapping consensus" is an account of how principles of justice can be stable given a plurality of conflicting "comprehensive" philosophical and religious views, and it is not an argument that the only justified principles are those that secure a consensus.

43. The account that follows draws on my "What Self-Governing Peoples Owe to One Another: Universalism, Diversity, and *The Law of Peoples*," *Fordham Law Review*, Symposium Issue on Rawls and the Law 72 (2004): 1721–1738. I am also indebted to various others, including Donald Moon's "Rawls's *Law of Peoples*" (unpublished manuscript); and Michael I. Blake's "Distributive Justice, State Coercion, and Autonomy," *Philosophy and Public Affairs* 30 (Summer 2001): 257–296; and Thomas Nagel's "The Problem of Global Justice," *Philosophy and Public Affairs*, 33. 2 (2005): 113–147.

44. See Blake, "Distributive Justice, State Coercion, and Autonomy," and Stilz's various recent writings, including, "Why do states have territorial rights?" *International Theory* (2009): 1.2, 185–213.

45. See Henry S. Richardson, *Democratic Autonomy: Public Reasoning About the Ends of Policy* (New York: Oxford University Press, 2002).

46. There are obviously many complexities here concerning the moral obligations of citizens – or subjects – under not fully legitimate or even illegitimate governments. And even under legitimate governments, some citizens do not recognize the authority of government to bind them.

47. Blake rightly emphasizes the central role of the mutual imposition of coercive law, but I do not think that coercion is the central consideration here. Much governance is not coercive. In addition, we are prepared to coerce outsiders, including those who try to get in illegally.

48. The UN Charter and the Universal Declaration of Human Rights are instruments created by "the peoples of the United Nations" or "Member States." See www.un .org/en/charter-united-nations/index.html. Contrast the phrasing "We the peoples of the United Nations" and "We the people of the United States," which open the preambles to the UN Charter and the U.S. Constitution. The UN Charter closes, "IN FAITH WHEREOF the representatives of the Governments of the United Nations have signed the present Charter" (capitals in original). These matters cannot of course be resolved by these textual or historical facts alone. Provinces and states within nations, autonomous territories, and plural or consociational regimes raise additional issues not covered here.

49. See the report of the International Commission on Intervention and State Sovereignty, "The Responsibility to Protect." Available at: http:// responsibilitytoprotect.org/ICISS%20Report.pdf, accessed February 23, 2018. For a valuable discussion, arguing against the idea of a human right to democracy, see Charles R. Beitz, *The Idea of Human Rights* (Oxford University Press, 2009).

50. For discussions see William Easterly, *The White Man's Burden: Why the West's Efforts to Aid the Rest Have Done So Much Ill and So Little Good* (Oxford University Press, 2006), and Angus Deaton, *The Great Escape: Health, Wealth, and the Origins of Inequality* (Princeton, NJ: Princeton University Press, 2015).

51. For a general discussion see William E. Shacknove, "Who is a Refugee?" *Ethics* 95.2 (1985): 274–284.

52. Howard F. Chang, "The Immigration Paradox: Poverty, Distributive Justice, and Liberal Egalitarianism," *DePaul Law Review*, 52 (2003), 759–776. Available at: http://ssrn.com/abstract=414561, accessed February 23, 2018.

53. Massey, *et al., Beyond Smoke*, pp. 4145.

54. *Ibid.*, 54–70.

55. Massey *et al., Beyond Smoke*, p. 158, source is *1999 Statistical Yearbook of the Immigration and Naturalization Service* (Washington, DC: Government Printing Office, 2000).

56. Muzaffar Chishti and Faye Hipsman, "In Historic Shift, New Migration Flows from Mexico Fall Below Those from China and India," Migration Policy Institute (2015). Available at: www.migrationpolicy.org/article/historic-shift-new-migration-flows-mexico-fall-below-those-china-and-india, accessed February 23, 2018.

57. See Kirk Semple, "Central Americans, 'Scared of What's Happening' in U.S., Stay Put," *New York Times*, July 3, 2017. Available at: www.nytimes.com/2017/07/03/opinion/trump-trade-war.html?action=click&contentCollection=Sports&module=Trending&version=Full&region=Marginalia&pgtype=article, accessed February 23, 2018.

58. Vivian Yee, Kenan Davis, and Jugal K. Patel, "Here's the Reality About Illegal Immigrants in the United States," *The New York Times*, March 6, 2017. Available at: www.nytimes.com/interactive/2017/03/06/us/politics/undocumented-illegal-immigrants.html?_r=0, accessed February 23, 2018.

59. See Joseph H. Carens, *The Ethics of Immigration* (Oxford University Press, 2013), chapter 5; I don't agree with Carens's larger argument for open borders.

60. Such policies would lessen the need for immigration restrictions and border security.

61. Massey *et al., Beyond Smoke*, pp. 157–163.

62. See the report by Oxfam, *Like Machines in the Fields: Workers Without Rights in American Agriculture*, 2004. Available at: www.oxfamamerica.org/static/media/files/like-machines-in-the-fields.pdf.

63. I am grateful to Ronald Dworkin for raising this question and also for supplying part of the answer.

64. For valuable discussions, see Lea Ypi, "Justice in Migration: A Closed Borders Utopia?" *Journal of Political Philosophy*, 16 (2008): 391–418; and Gillian Brock and Michael Blake, *Debating Brain Drain: May Governments Restrict Emigration?* (Oxford University Press, 2015).

15

Carved from the Inside Out: Immigration and America's Public Philosophy on Citizenship

Elizabeth F. Cohen

In 2016 Americans elected a president whose campaign made anti-immigrant rhetoric and promises a centerpiece. The tenor of the campaign could not have been a surprise in the wake of popular calls for immigration reform and a series of victories for anti-immigrant parties in European democracies. What is surprising is that this kind of election – one in which opposition to immigration was a central campaign issue – has almost never taken place in the United States. Furthermore, when they have occurred, they have not succeeded in permanently closing borders or replacing American ambivalence about immigration with a more unequivocal opposition to immigration. Immigration has shaped the country in manifold ways and yet only rarely has the government, the American republic, or the people, shaped immigration. Why is it that subjects as basic as the status of children born on American soil to undocumented immigrants, or the fairness of guestworker programs, inspire such a long-standing tradition of ambivalence in the U.S.?

Despite its lengthy history as an immigrant-receiving nation, the U.S. has, as yet, failed to produce coherent theories or practices related to immigration. Many European nations, most of which have been the recipients of large-scale immigration for less than half a century, seem as well or even better equipped than the U.S. to answer questions about the terms on which immigrants are welcome and the conditions of their continued residence and incorporation.[1] We may not like all of their answers nor may all of them be compatible with basic principles of the European Union and liberal democracy. However, that does not take away from the fact that the U.S. has a comparatively anemic sense of what role it wants immigration to play in its national identity. Twenty-first-century Americans find themselves in the position of trying to extract a reasoned set of policies to govern the border from a relatively shallow well of public policy or opinion. If we are to come to conclusions regarding how much and which sorts of immigration we ought to welcome, it seems sensible to first ask ourselves why it is that America, of all nations, asks these questions as often as any other nation and repeatedly fails to answer them.

In this essay, I will ultimately suggest that fundamental principles of American public law have contributed to an understanding of citizenship driven by concerns of difference, particularly racial difference, ascribed among native-born citizens. This internal differentiation[2] domestically produces foreignness that renders rightful citizens (including but not limited to African-Americans) foreign despite their native birth. The priority placed on managing racial distinctions through citizenship law has precluded a reconciliation of our relationship to immigrants, whose outsider or foreigner status cannot be reduced to or equated with that of the marginal native-born groups who have continually been deprived of full citizenship within the American polity.

If immigrants have not always been the most foreign members of the U.S. nation then it makes sense that immigration has not been either central to, or well attended by, existing definitions of citizenship. We have no philosophy of immigration because our understanding of citizenship is focused inward, on differences that exist within the native-born population. In the first half of the essay I will describe the contours of the problem: how immigration has been understood in the context of citizenship, and how the dilemmas created by an absence of a public philosophy of immigration manifest themselves. In the second half, I will offer an explanation for these circumstances that looks to the common law tradition we inherited from England, in particular, the jurisprudence based on *Calvin's Case*. I will argue that this jurisprudence meshed with our own commitment to racial and other internal classifications in order to produce an understanding of citizenship that was not attentive to questions of immigration.

CONTEMPORARY POLITICAL THEORIES OF IMMIGRATION AND CITIZENSHIP

Most nation-states publicly declare whether or not they consider themselves to be "countries of immigration." Patrick Weil notes that as countries begin to perceive themselves as countries of immigration they tend to invoke rhetoric and policies that are geared towards absorbing and assimilating immigrants.[3] Thus, not only can we expect to generate coherent policies and politics of immigration, but there ought to be a direct relationship between a country's philosophical approach to immigration, the mechanics of the immigration policy itself, and the treatment of the foreign-born, particularly but not exclusively through the alienage law that governs immigrants once they have arrived. In America, there is public consensus that we are a nation of immigration, and we have declared as much to the world. There is even widespread public approval of immigration, as evidenced by a number of public opinion surveys on the subject. However, there is simultaneously profound divisive disagreement about who ought to be able to immigrate, the rights they ought to enjoy, and the circumstances under which they ought or ought not be granted citizenship. In other words, while many among us view an abstract notion of immigration as integral to our politics, there still exists widespread ambivalence toward the foreigners who actually appear at our doorstep at any given point in time.

In his controversial final book *Who Are We?*, Samuel Huntington made the case that America's settlers never intended to create a nation that would be defined and continually redefined by an ever-changing cast (or caste) of immigrants. This thesis flies in the face of a voluminous and well-grounded literature that regards open immigration as central to American identity.[4] For many, the quintessential national tale is the American Dream, which speaks more directly to immigrants than perhaps any other social group.[5] While for Huntington immigration has been a process through which new members became Americanized, others view immigration itself as the defining American experience and attribute. It comes as no surprise, then, that we find ourselves so divided over the subject of our borders. We have never been entirely certain whether we were subjects of a state dedicated to accommodating the varying needs of successive generations of new members or sovereigns of an empire whose conquests are found within rather than outside of our borders.[6]

Many would protest the claim that we lack a well-articulated approach to immigration, arguing that in fact American history has engendered an intense debate over the meaning of an integrally related topic, citizenship, which is both public and self-conscious. Settlers arrived on our shores with the express purpose of founding a community in which they could enjoy rights that had not been guaranteed in their homelands. The transition from colonial settlement to nation-state instigated a set of very public and deliberate debates over the content and right to membership in the newly formed republic. These debates have replayed themselves repeatedly as Americans have come to terms with internal conflicts over the meaning of citizenship. It could therefore hardly be said that we have no public philosophy of citizenship even though this philosophy has evolved significantly since it was first conceived.

Yet, what this implies for the politics of immigration remains unclear. Many historians of American political thought who study the nature and lineage of American philosophies of citizenship examine immigration through the lens of an overarching theory of American citizenship. Rogers Smith's *Civic Ideals* details the development of multiple traditions of liberalism, republicanism and ascriptive exclusion through analysis of public law from the colonial period through the end of the nineteenth century. Smith's is the most recent in a history of venerable tomes that includes Louis Hartz's[7] defense of liberalism as the defining American ideology and Gunnar Myrdal's[8] civic republican rejoinder. Each of these texts has presumed that we can infer a great deal regarding attitudes toward immigration based on approaches to citizenship.

However, a philosophy of citizenship need not make central, or even answer, important questions regarding immigration. Indeed, an array of normative political philosophers have long noted that the theories of membership upon which practices of citizenship are founded tend to function very well when applied to bounded communities but fail the tests posed by immigration.[9] Of the ancient theorists only the Stoics envisioned cosmopolitanism, and even they did so in a limited fashion. Plato and Aristotle both set very narrow limits on the inclusion of foreigners, offering them at best the very form of second-class citizenship that Aristotle himself held.[10] Modern liberal theory invites further conundrums of inclusion by espousing principles of universal worth, while simultaneously recognizing that self-governance can occur only within well-bounded communities. Contemporary theorists, most famously John Rawls, have only replicated this internal contradiction of liberalism. Rawls qualified the entirety of *A Theory of Justice* with a statement that it only applies to nation-states. If the abstract world of normative theory cannot manage to produce theories of citizenship that accommodate immigration, then the much messier reality of public opinion and the policies it advocates can only be expected to engender further complications and contradictions.

A few scholars of citizenship explicitly acknowledge the challenges of trying to reconcile philosophies of citizenship and immigration. In her examination of the peculiar philosophies that have forged American citizenship, Judith Shklar makes an important distinction between her goal of elucidating the role of race in American citizenship and what she views as the important, but different, task of characterizing American approaches to immigration. Shklar writes, "The history of immigration and naturalization policies is not, however, my subject. It has its own ups and downs, but is not the same as the exclusion of native-born Americans from citizenship. The two histories have their parallels, since both involve inclusion and exclusion, but there is a vast difference between discriminatory immigration laws and the enslavement of a people."[11] In contrast, Smith, whose subject and spirit of inquiry is much the same as Shklar's, treats the application of the ascriptive principles, which he and Shklar indict for their effect on native-born racial minorities, to immigration laws as an extension of the same processes. He moves nearly seamlessly between discussions of the laws governing the citizenship of native-born racial minorities and women, and laws governing immigration and the rights of the foreign-born.

As Shklar indicates, this is not an illogical move since the two sets of rules are, in her words, parallel. But it might not be entirely warranted, for as parallel, or at least distinct, processes, the forging of a philosophy of citizenship is not necessarily coextensive with that of a philosophy of immigration. Not only are the two conceptually distinct, but for a variety of reasons Americans did not produce a philosophy of immigration alongside their philosophy of citizenship. The ascriptive principles guiding the exclusion of some from full citizenship prove an uneasy fit with the realities of immigrant populations and, further, the role of immigrants in, and their relationship to, American society is also different from that of native-born minorities. One can observe moments in which awkward attempts were made to fuse racial ideologies with nativism, such as the cry that the Irish would never be white, yet the experience of being an immigrant and a native-born minority in America are – and have always been –

vastly different. Indeed, evidence drawn from public law, public opinion, policy, and electoral politics indicates that even today we have not yet fully articulated our understanding of the challenges of immigration, let alone our responses to them. This evidence reveals the degree to which immigration has managed to shape American identity without being subjected to the sort of systematic philosophical scrutiny accorded to other elements of citizenship.[12]

OBSERVING AMERICAN INATTENTION TO IMMIGRATION

Indications that immigration has not received systematic thought in the context of an otherwise well-articulated and self-conscious understanding of citizenship is abundant, pervading every realm of the American political world. Together, these inconsistencies reveal the degree to which the nation is conflicted about its role as an immigrant nation and the place of immigrants in the nation.

PUBLIC LAW

Perhaps the most telling institutional evidence of American ambivalence toward immigration and border concerns is the fact that immigration was not the province of the federal government for most of U.S. history. States regulated immigration and did so in vastly divergent ways. Aristide Zolberg notes that the Passenger Act (1819) indicates early interest on the part of the federal government in limiting immigration but a federal apparatus for regulating immigration only began to emerge in a very nascent form following anti-Chinese immigration measures passed in the 1870s.[13] A full federal immigration bureaucracy only developed in 1929 as a means of implementing the 1924 National Origins Quota Act. The reasons for this delay are well rehearsed: the strong commitment to federalism evinced by many of the founders informed, and was influenced by, conflicts of interest arising from differing positions on the status of slaves and free black Americans. Internal migration therefore gave Americans as much cause for concern, and probably more, than the entry of hundreds of thousands of European nationals.[14]

One could make the claim that a laissez-faire attitude toward immigration constitutes the American approach to border control. Leaving aside the question of whether an unarticulated absence of a coherent approach to immigrants is itself any kind of philosophy of immigration, the fact remains that not all matters related to immigration can be resolved with benign neglect. Even in circumstances of open borders, the state must clarify what are the rights of non-citizens, the terms on which they may stay, and what conditions govern the continued opening of borders.

Refuge also demands proactive policies and laws. The right of refuge requires that states formulate policies and programs in order to identify and protect eligible candidates for protection. There is much to suggest that refuge is an important element of American identity – from our founding as a refuge for religious minorities to the oft-referenced inscription on the *Statue of Liberty*. And yet institutional mechanisms that define and implement such protections have only come to exist in this country recently and in an entirely ad hoc fashion. In fact, until the Cold War, America eschewed explicitly formulating a policy of refuge. While we encouraged the world to give us their tired, poor, huddled masses yearning to breathe free we weren't particularly interested in proactively rescuing anyone who might have been huddling voiceless in the dark recesses of poverty or political oppression. Only under the threat of appearing hypocritical, and with the incentive of weakening our Cold War enemies, did the federal government reluctantly institute a highly qualified policy of refuge. The terms of that policy limited the right to those fleeing Communism and oppressive regimes in the Middle East.[15] In 2017, the latter group has been singled out for exclusion by the Trump administration.

ELECTORAL POLITICS

In addition to a historically passive federal immigration apparatus, electoral politics in the U.S. have also only recently come to be shaped by conflict over immigration. While it is the case that the foreign-born have periodically been the subject of intense public scrutiny, this focus has almost never reached the levels that European countries experience. The 2016 election is the first since the 1850s, when the Know Nothings briefly held sway, in which anti-immigrant politics have held sway. The spell cast by the nativist Know Nothing rhetoric was quickly broken by internal divisions over racial politics suggesting that long-standing nativism in electoral politics is not sustainable in the U.S. Furthermore, to date, while political parties have engaged immigrants as potential citizens and threats alike, none has predicated its existence on either defending or halting immigration.[16] This stands in sharp contrast to our European peer nations, which upon discovering that they had become states of immigration following World War II, promptly generated political parties for the purpose of opposing immigration and demonizing immigrants. There is no American Marine Le Pen nor has there ever been a U.S. Front National or Golden Dawn.[17]

At the time this volume is heading to press, there is intense concern about whether the election of Donald Trump on a tide of anti-immigrant rhetoric and action marks a sea change for U.S. politics. There is no way to predict the future, but there are several reasons to believe that, despite the intense emotions and rhetoric that the 2016 election sparked, as well as Trump's own attempts to ban Muslim immigrants, it represents a continuation of our tradition of ambivalence about immigration rather than a departure from past practice. First, while the executive is currently occupied by an administration that seems uniformly hostile to undocumented immigrants, refugees, and asylum seekers, Congress has repeatedly demonstrated cleavages that stand in the way of imposing the kind of immigration reform required to return the country to the drastically limited immigration that prevailed between 1924 and 1965. This has been true for over a decade. Second, Congress seems even less motivated to spend the kind of resources that would be required to effect truly thorough deportation of undocumented immigrants and a truly sealed border. Third, the body that is most avidly in favor of restrictions on immigration, the Tea Party, is also strongly opposed to increased government spending of the sort that restrictive immigration measures would require. Both presidents Obama and Trump committed to deporting more immigrants than were deported under presidents who preceded Obama. But Trump has not yet shown that he is capable of leading Congress in a direction that would prioritize immigration restriction over fiscal conservatism. In the absence of the will to spend money on things like border fencing, monitoring, and a deeply invasive interior ICE (Immigration and Customs Enforcement) force, it seems likely that the current political fissures in both the Republican and Tea parties will continue to spout anti-immigrant rhetoric while actively blunting efforts to surpass the deportation policies of President Obama.

POLICY

Finally, as a matter of policy, the practice of consistent effective border control itself is quite new. Immigration was viewed as a necessity for much of American history – perhaps a necessary evil to some, but nonetheless inevitable. Restrictions for reasons of security, health, poverty, and criminality existed in prior centuries, but prior to 1924 they prevented only a small number of people from entering the country.[18] Americans, even at the state level, have never consistently sought or managed to control or restrict foreign-born people from crossing their borders until relatively recently. Episodic nativism occasionally has been expressed to powerful effect, as in Chinese Exclusion, the 1924 National Origins Quota Act, and the violent deportation of Mexican workers during the 1940s. But, as nativist as each of these programs was, none permanently sealed the border or returned the population to a more homogenous version of itself. Nor did any become permanently embedded in U.S. public policy as did, for example, public education once it was introduced. Instead, the exterior US border has been a consistently inconsistent place that is largely porous even when it is most heavily policed.

For most of U.S. history, undocumented immigration has been tacitly and actively encouraged not just through lax or inconsistent border enforcement but also by laws that facilitate the continued presence of undocumented or irregular immigrants and their families. Deportation, denationalization, and other forms of policing the border from the interior of the nation have been even less systematically imposed than have been restrictions on the exterior border. Only after George W. Bush's attempt to reform policies addressing immigration from Mexico failed, and the terrorist attacks of 2001 succeeded, did apprehensions at the border and deportations from the interior begin a rapid ascent. Deportations under President Obama rose precipitously but were countered by Executive Actions that stayed deportation and granted legal status to even larger numbers of people under Deferred Action for Childhood Arrivals (DACA). The net result of these recent policies is not a country with a stronger border. It is simply a differently porous border. If this indicates nothing else it ought to make clear the fact that we don't know what we want our borders or the keepers of our gates to accomplish.

EXPLAINING U.S. IMMIGRATION AMBIVALENCE: CITIZENSHIP VS. IMMIGRATION

If it is an institutional, legal, and political fact that Americans lack a public philosophy of immigration, it remains to be explained why this is so. No doubt the reasons are manifold. Having established the counterintuitive fact of American ambivalence about immigration, I will draw upon jurisprudential traditions that shaped American approaches to foreignness in order to offer an explanation of how a country so profoundly shaped by immigration has come to approach immigration in such an unsystematic manner. Immigration is an issue that cuts across otherwise well-organized material and social interest groups.[19] Yet, the moments at which immigration has been restricted and opened do not indicate that the material interests of either any given class or set of classes are being systematically pursued via border control.[20] One might also suggest that the federal nature of the republic has prevented the development of a coherent philosophy of immigration. However, the demands of federalism alone cannot explain the failure of Americans to produce a public philosophy of immigration. The period following the nationalization of immigration has been the most schizophrenic to date. Furthermore, a country such as Germany has traditionally devolved many of the powers of immigration to the Länder and yet has maintained a consistent, if objectionable, philosophy of immigration in which the rights of refuge and return are honored, while traditional immigration is discouraged.

Before turning to the circumstances that led to the divergence of philosophies of citizenship and immigration in the U.S., a word about the general principles with which we can differentiate theories of citizenship from those of immigration. Citizenship encompasses a broad and dense set of norms, policies, and laws that together govern what it means to be a member of a polity. This meaning includes rights, benefits, and expectations: the conditions of and for membership. Place of birth and/or nationality – the traits that distinguish immigrants from non-immigrants – need not hold either a singular or a central place among these conditions. One tends to assume that because nation-states are in some senses reliant on sovereign borders for their existence they must necessarily prioritize border-crossing issues in their definition of membership. Yet there is no reason that race or social class might not play a more central role in a philosophy of citizenship. That one be white or male or respectably employed in fact turns out to be crucial to many definitions of citizenship. One can be foreign without holding the passport of another nation and, at the same time, a non-native Canadian may not be perceived as, treated as, or even feel, particularly foreign.

Americans have developed a philosophy of citizenship that, while keenly sensitive to notions of foreignness, does not fully resolve issues of immigration. We understand the degree to which the nation-state has the power to determine who enjoys the status of citizen and we are extraordinarily conscious of the benefits conferred by our citizenship. But none of this dictates any particular response to entreaties from beyond our borders. One could examine this paradox through a number of lenses. Particularly illuminating is that of the distinction between immigration and alienage law discussed by Linda Bosniak.[21] This distinction refers to the degree to which we have historically regulated the immigrants in our midst, as opposed to the act of immigration itself. While there was little in the way of a nationalized immigration policy, there have long been in place powerful legal precedents that facilitated the control of aliens once admitted. Alienage law, as opposed to immigration constraints, was very well developed early on in our history. From the founding onward, the rights of aliens were subjects of public debate.[22] While we did not seek to restrict immigration, as a nation we did recognize the need to control the foreigners in our midst. Alienage law, as opposed to immigration restriction, was prioritized both by the framers, who sought to prevent those without citizenship from holding office, and by successive generations of American leaders. Even as we ignored our borders, we have always remained quite concerned with the foreigners among us.

The prioritization of debate regarding the rights of foreigners over discussion of immigration restrictions reinforces the idea that Americans have chosen to focus attention on citizenship rather than immigration. The primary concern of alienage law is the degree to which non-nationals may enjoy the rights of citizenship. To be sure, the threat of deportation looms large as an implication of alienage law, however mass deportation has not played an ongoing role in the history of immigrants in the U.S. More common has been a pattern of benign neglect of both legal and "illegal" immigration coupled with extensive use of alienage law as a tool to constrain the freedoms enjoyed by foreigners.

CALVIN'S CASE, THE ORIGINS OF THE AMERICAN CONCEPTION OF
CITIZENSHIP AND PREOCCUPATION WITH INTERNALLY GENERATED
FOREIGNNESS

That foreignness can matter so much to Americans and yet not generate a better articulated and more measured approach to border control would ostensibly seem to be unlikely if not entirely irreconcilable. However, an examination of the origins of the American approach to citizenship yields a rationale for this very striking set of circumstances. American approaches to citizenship have long reflected a preoccupation with forms of discrimination that focus on race more than nationality. Perhaps the moment at which our skepticism about immigration was at its peak was the period surrounding the passage of the 1924 National Origins Quota Act when we were concerned less with nationality and more with race. The bill itself was designed to encourage immigration from countries seen as racially and culturally in harmony with "American-ness" and simultaneously block further immigration of racially undesirable people. It was a law driven by sociobiology rather than sovereignty.

There are a number of routes to understanding why it is that race and other forms of internal differentiation have generated a philosophy of citizenship that lacks a focus on borders. I will now focus on the formative effects of the citizenship law bequeathed to America by the common law tradition of Great Britain, and in particular the influence of *Calvin's Case*. Nearly all scholarship on the origins of American citizenship acknowledges the singular importance of *Calvin's Case* in shaping the legal and philosophical principles upon which American citizenship was founded. *Calvin's Case* resolved the political status of people who had been born in Scotland after the ascent of a Scot, King James, to the British throne. The ruling accorded them subjecthood based on the principle of *jus soli* – their birth in territory considered to be a part of the British dominion. In so doing it created two categories of people: *antenati* (persons born before the joining of the two kingdoms) and *postnati* (persons born afterward). The decision rendered the latter citizens and led to the development of naturalization rules and procedures for the former. Thus, common law rules of citizenship were instantiated without any particular reference or relation to immigration across sovereign borders. In *Calvin's Case*, it was borders rather than people doing the migrating.

Insofar as it addressed the historically specific question of the citizenship of Scots who were newly incorporated into the political domain of England as result of the ascent of King James to the throne, the case appears an odd one to have served such a significant role in shaping American jurisprudence. We were not a kingdom with an empire; we were a former colony that would continue to rely upon immigration to compose its population. *Calvin's Case*, with its emphasis on *jus soli*, could not help us with that. Given the lack of an American corollary to the status of the Scottish in the British Empire, it is not entirely obvious why *Calvin's Case* became so important to American citizenship. Furthermore, the principle of *jus soli*, which *Calvin's Case* established, contradicts liberal consent, republican linkages of membership with civic virtue, or a contract-based notion of citizenship, which together embody the central philosophical influence on American citizenship doctrine.[23] Ascribing citizenship to persons based on *jus soli* (a rule based on place of birth) is almost entirely arbitrary. It deprives both the community and the individual of the opportunity to come to reasoned conclusions about membership.

It is tempting to leap to the conclusion that because America depended on mass immigration, *Calvin's Case* was crucial in establishing the means through which immigrants could become citizens since it gave the sovereign the right to naturalize non-citizens. Yet this reflects neither the spirit of *Calvin's Case*, nor the use to which it was put for much of American history. Although *Calvin's Case* defended the King's right to naturalize subjects, it did not address itself directly to questions of immigration across sovereign national borders. Rather, it provided the means through which an expanding empire and its newly acquired members could understand their membership in relation to one another and to a shared sovereign. In the decision, Coke addresses himself to foreignness, to citizenship, and to problems of alienage. He does not take up the subject of transnational immigration. *Calvin's Case* not only established an ascriptive rule of *jus soli*, it also generated a legal process of naturalization as a means through which citizenship could be granted to those not born with it. Scots born before the ascent of James had to be naturalized because the land upon which they were born had not been British territory at the time of their birth. Americans recognized that in order to remain sovereign, they too would have to engage in ascription, if only because as a newly formed nation it was imperative that some justification exist for assigning citizenship to the people of the land, particularly loyalists to the British throne whose status might otherwise be indeterminate and threatening to the new-born union.[24]

Calvin's Case therefore trained an admittedly willing American eye to look inward in order to shape the borders of the nation. The decision applied the norms of an empire intent on colonizing territories and absorbing their populations to a single nation-state. It would therefore be an imperial understanding of citizenship, and not immigration that would serve as the primary tool through which Americans would sculpt their populace. Thus, as the title of this chapter suggests, Americans have carved themselves from the inside out. This caused Europeans to remark, as Samuel Huntington notes, that we created a "consciousness among people" well before we ever formed what they would have legitimately called a state.[25]

The need to enfranchise the population following the establishment of the Union was not the only distinctly American dilemma that *Calvin's Case* resolved. It also provided a means for addressing the presence of persons who may be desirable residents but not citizens. The ruling eschewed the ascription of citizenship to all Scotsmen. Rather, the ruling applied to two sets of persons:

the *antenati* and the *postnati* – or those born respectively before and after James's accession. The decision only granted automatic citizenship to those born after his accession. Most of the *postnati* were ultimately granted naturalization, but it was not ascribed to them. It is also the case that the persons to whom citizenship was ascribed by the new rule still had to be otherwise eligible for citizenship. *Calvin's Case* did not grant the Irish full subjecthood – they remained merely denizens. Thus, to call the precedent that *Calvin's Case* establishes an ascriptive form of pure *jus soli* is to mischaracterize it. In fact, it only selectively ascribed citizenship to segments of the population. The Irish, in particular, were left in the netherworld between full and non-citizenship.

There are therefore multiple legal statuses that denote "domestic foreignness" – birthright foreignness that is not produced by movement across sovereign national borders. This is supported by the conclusion affirmed in the subsequent case indicating that the rights of non-native Scotsmen, who could be naturalized, were more extensive than those of non-native Irishmen, whose status as a conquered people accorded them a weaker set of entitlements. Coke's reasoning in *Calvin's Case* allowed that "[t]he conclusion that naturalization rested upon a legal fiction made it possible to distinguish among the various classes of subjects. Native Englishmen, *postnati* Scotsmen, and natural-born Irishmen were natural subjects."[26]

The analytical benefit of framing *Calvin's Case* thusly is that it reminds us that complicated questions of citizenship must be answered before a rule of *jus soli* can be invoked. In not automatically granting citizenship to *antenati*, *Calvin's Case* legitimized the existence of populations who would not hold citizenship despite their birth in a territory now subject to *jus soli*. It therefore raised the very likely possibility that *jus soli* leaves unanswered a range of ascriptive and substantive questions of citizenship. Understanding *Calvin's Case* thusly helps explain how Taney, in writing the *Dred Scott* decision, was able to eschew the principle of *jus soli* that the case evinces. *Jus soli* would have accorded citizenship to free blacks. But the status of the Irish following *Calvin's Case* was similar to free blacks in the U.S. Since no rule had changed it was conceivable that the principle that excluded free blacks was still in effect much in the same way that some Irish continued to be excluded even after Coke's decision in *Calvin's Case* was issued. To bring us back to the initial premise of this essay, *Calvin's Case* created an understanding of citizenship that accorded birthright citizenship based on *jus soli* to some, but not all, persons born in the territory.

Underlying the case is the presumption that rules affecting the contours of a citizenry can change and, when they do, complex negotiations will be necessary to determine to whom and how the rules ought to be applied. King James's ascent to the throne transformed the rules under which subjecthood would be awarded. A rule had changed – in this case one involving borders, and one that affected a people's relationship to citizenship. This particular rule change affected this group in a way that made many of them eligible for citizenship. However, rule changes can take many forms and one could easily imagine rule changes that would strip people of their right to citizenship. A border could contract, rather than expand, ceding the citizenship of a set of people. Furthermore, rule changes that affect citizenship need not confine themselves to questions of sovereign borders. In the twentieth century rule changes granted citizenship to American women and (temporarily) deprived Japanese Americans of theirs. In this view, therefore, the rule of *jus soli* is secondary to the larger implication of *Calvin's Case*, namely that a range of circumstances can change, and, in so doing, alter the contours of the population considered eligible for citizenship. Furthermore, when changes occur the state will require and create procedures such as naturalization in order to regularize and govern the statuses they create.

The final outcome of *Calvin's Case* was the creation of procedures to transform people into citizens when rule changes entitle them to membership. *Antenati* had to be dealt with once the decision was rendered. The idea of naturalizing noncitizens predates *Calvin's Case*, but had no legal precedent until Coke forced the issue by creating a large group of persons who needed to be naturalized. In adopting the entire jurisprudence that grew out of *Calvin's Case* America therefore adopted not only *jus soli*, but also a legitimation for multiple forms of citizenship and procedures for transforming non-citizens into citizens.

If we revisit the original question this essay posed: namely, why it is that we have such a well-articulated public understanding of citizenship that fails to answer basic questions about borders, we can now see that the jurisprudence out of which American citizenship was established was one that did not take up questions of immigration. *Calvin's Case* adopts ascriptive *jus soli* in a confined manner that does not apply universally. It actually legitimizes the simultaneous enfranchisement of immigrants and disenfranchisement of native and African Americans. Even as it dictated that a rule of *jus soli* be applied to *postnati* Scots, *Calvin's Case* simultaneously indicated that others be excluded.[27] It therefore framed questions of citizenship for the British and Americans who looked to it in ways that paid more attention to idiosyncratic and internally generated racial distinctions than to immigration. This functioned well within the unique context of the British Empire and it fed into a longstanding American tradition of legalized racial citizenship hierarchies.

But much as the British have had to execute a speedy gymnastic routine to address the influx of émigrés from former colonies following the dissolution of its empire, Americans too now find themselves forced to answer questions about immigration from within a tradition of citizenship that has more to say about how to distinguish between people of different races and nationalities than it does the question of how to make immigration law. The emphasis of race and internal differentiation within the citizenship tradition has focused attention on internal differentiation at the expense of answers to questions about whether a country of immigration ought to regularize undocumented persons, resettle proportional numbers of refugees, turn away asylees, and deal with innumerable other issues posed by the presence of large numbers of immigrants. If it seems unlikely that there are coherent legal, political, or policy traditions from which to draw answers to pressing questions about immigrants and immigration, it is because the very origins and ongoing traditions of U.S. philosophies of citizenship have not centered on answering those questions.

CONCLUSION

For much of American history our failure to develop a coherent philosophy of immigration was relatively unproblematic – in fact it may have served to allow vastly different visions of our nation to coexist. However, during the twentieth, century this lacuna led to serious repercussions, leaving us now in the position of trying to forge consensus on the basis of a set of apparently conflicting premises. Scholars of American politics must reconcile the contradictions of massive, racially defined, restrictions on immigration during the first half of the twentieth century with equally extreme liberalizations during the second half. Do we wish to remain a nation that shapes itself from within or are we in a moment of transition to a politics in which immigration controls will define the contours of future generations? Choosing the latter route will demand that the American people answer not Samuel Huntington's query of "Who Are We?" but the more fraught question, "Who do we want to be?" If the thesis of this essay is correct, then we are in for more work than Huntington acknowledges, for the reply he offers us tells us who we have been. Who we ought to be and how we ought to achieve this remain, as yet, unanswered questions.

NOTES

1. This has led scholars of immigration to study countries like France and Germany respectively as archetypes of immigration and non-immigration states. See Rogers Brubaker, *Immigration and Citizenship in France and Germany* (Cambridge: Harvard University Press, 1989).
2. K. A. Appiah and H. L. Gates, Jr., *Identities* (Chicago: University of Chicago Press, 1995).
3. Patrick Weil, "Access to Citizenship: A Comparison of Twenty-Five Nationality Laws," in T.A. Aleinikoff and Douglas Klusmeyer (eds.), *Citizenship Today: Global Perspectives and Practices* (Washington, DC: Carnegie Endowment for International Peace, 2001), pp. 17–35.
4. Appiah and Gates, Identities. Also see W. A. V. Clark, *Immigrants and the American Dream: Remaking the Middle Class* (New York: Guilford, 2003).
5. See www.palgrave.com/us/book/9781137289049, accessed February 26, 2018.
6. See http://scholarship.law.uci.edu/ucilr/vol1/iss3/16/, accessed February 26, 2018.

7. Louis Hartz, *The Liberal Tradition in America: An Interpretation of American Political Thought Since the Revolution* (New York: Harcourt, Brace and World, 1955).

8. Gunnar Myrdal, *An American Dilemma: The Negro Problem and Modern Democracy* (London: Transaction, 1996).

9. See https://books.google.com/books/about/Spheres_Of_Justice.html?id=2ndITi80Acs C&source=kp_cover; https://www.jstor.org/stable/1407506; https://www.amazon .com/Ethics-Immigration-Oxford-Political-Theory/dp/0190246790, accessed February 26, 2018.

10. See www.cambridge.org/us/academic/subjects/politics-international-relations/political-theory/semi-citizenship-democratic-politics?format=HB&isbn=9780521768993#6ezZ MDytxwZuHXXX.97, accessed February 26, 2018.

11. Judith Shklar, *American Citizenship – The Quest for Inclusion; The Tanner Lecture on Human Values* (Cambridge, MA: Harvard University Press, 1991), pp. 4–5.

12. I say systematic philosophical scrutiny because, as has been made abundantly clear during recent Congressional debates, plenty of empirical data about immigration and immigrants exist. Yet, as has also been made clear by the vast gulf that exists between the bills produced by the House and the Senate, there is little consensus on what the purpose of immigration ought to be, and which immigrants are entitled to a permanent place in American society.

13. Aristide R. Zolberg, *A Nation by Design: Immigration Policy in the Fashioning of America* (Cambridge, MA: Harvard University Press, 2006). On the Passenger Act see pp. 110–111. Zolberg's larger thesis is that immigration in the United States has been regulated more than is usually acknowledged and that the regulation of immigration was part of a larger project of nation-building. While much of what he says is true: the states did regulate immigration and zealous support for Nativist restrictions surfaces periodically throughout American history, even his detailed history of immigration regulation in the United States identifies no consistent set of political or cultural goals that constitute the nation-building mission he claims to support.

14. Anna O. Law, "Lunatics, Idiots, Paupers, and Negro Seamen – Immigration Federalism and the Early American Republic," *Studies in American Political Development* 28 (2014): 107–128; Allan Colbern, "Regulating Movement in a Federalist System: Slavery's Connection to Immigration Law in the United States" (draft on file with author).

15. Daniel J. Tichenor, *Dividing Lines: The Politics of Immigration Control in America* (Princeton, NJ: Princeton University Press, 2002).

16. Perhaps Patrick Buchanan's short-lived candidacy most closely approximates an anti-immigrant politics; however, the brevity of his run muted much of his influence and further underscored the degree to which Americans have avoided making immigration central to electoral politics.

17. I would like to reiterate that this is a limited claim: there have been racist and nativist politicians who have had a broad and deep influence on American politics. I seek only to state that none have succeeded in forcing the issue of border control.

18. T. A. Aleinikoff, *Semblances of Sovereignty: The Constitution, the State, and American Citizenship* (Cambridge, MA: Harvard University Press, 2002).

19. Tichenor, *Dividing Lines*.

20. Tichenor, *Dividing Lines*.

21. Bosniak, Linda, "The undocumented immigrant: contending policy approaches." Available at: www.amazon.com/Debating-Immigration-Carol-M-Swain/dp/0521875 609/ref=mt_hardcover?_encoding=UTF8&me=, accessed February 26, 2018.

22. Rogers Smith, *Civic Ideals: Conflicting Visions of Citizenship in U.S. History* (New Haven, CT: Yale University Press, 1997).

23. Peter Schuck and Rogers Smith, *Citizenship Without Consent* (New Haven: Yale University Press, 1985).

24. James Kettner, *The Development of American Citizenship, 1608–1870* (Chapel Hill, NC: University of North Carolina Press, 1978).

25. Samuel Huntington, *Who Are We?: The Challenges to America's National Identity* (New York: Simon & Schuster, 2004), p. 114.

26. Kettner, *Development of American Citizenship*, p. 41.

27. Indeed, references to the partial citizenship of various groups within American society can be found in a range of judicial opinions issued well into the nineteenth century (see Smith, *Civic Ideals*.) The idea of multiple, partial citizenships is one that democratic states eschew but find themselves as unable to avoid instantiating (see www.cambridge .org/us/academic/subjects/politics-international-relations/political-theory/semi-citizenship-democratic-politics?format=HB&isbn=9780521768993#6ezZMDy txwZuHXXX.97), accessed February 26, 2018.

PART IV

COSMOPOLITANISM: HOW EUROPEAN NATIONS DEAL WITH IMMIGRATION

16

The Politics of Citizenship and Belonging in Europe

Marc Morjé Howard and Sara Wallace Goodman

In historical and comparative perspective, immigration and citizenship have been viewed as two of the main features that distinguish the United States from the countries of Europe. The U.S., along with Australia and Canada, has typically been considered a "settler" country, with very open and generous policies for the admittance and integration of immigrants. Most European countries, in contrast, have been very conflicted about including immigrants in their societies, and their policies have been relatively restrictive in comparison to the U.S. But in the postwar period, the growing need for unskilled labor brought about unprecedented levels of immigration in much of Europe, leading to two distinct types of national strategies: former colonial powers (such as the United Kingdom, France, and the Netherlands) began to allow large and increasing numbers of people from their former colonies to immigrate and become citizens; while other countries (such as Germany or Austria) implemented "guestworker" models, where many ostensibly temporary workers were imported in the 1950s and 1960s, without being encouraged to integrate, bring their families, or "settle" into their host societies.[1]

While this two-type categorization of European immigration responses did fit much of the second half of the twentieth century quite well, it has considerably less utility today. Indeed, almost all of the 15 "older" countries of the European Union (EU) – regardless of their earlier model – are confronting a new reality, namely that their societies include significant minorities (usually 5–10 percent of the population, and much higher in cities) of immigrant origin, who have the intention – and the right, as enshrined in national and European law – to stay permanently. As a result, just as has been the case in the U.S. for many decades, European policymakers are beginning to distinguish more closely between their policies on *immigration* and on *integration*.

In a sense, immigration and integration are two sides of the same coin: the former involves the entry of foreigners into a country, while the latter has to do with what happens when they stay. In terms of immigration, even though the raw numbers and proportions are often very different from one country to the next, most advanced industrialized countries have come to a common conclusion: they need to restrict and better control immigration levels. As a result, ferocious debates have emerged in both the U.S. and Europe about how countries can accommodate a complex set of contradictory imperatives, including *demographic* pressures to hire more workers in order to keep pension systems afloat, the *economic* need by both businesses and consumers for low-skilled menial and/or high-skilled technical labor, and the *political* risk of either pandering to or fueling the xenophobia and anti-immigrant populism that are often seething below the surface.

Whereas the immigration policies of the U.S. and Europe now largely share common features and similar goals, integration strategies have remained very different from one another, with a tremendous amount of variation within Europe itself. The most widely accepted indicator of whether immigrants become politically incorporated into their new society is the extent to which a country allows them to become citizens. This is not a perfect measure, of course; the July 2005 terrorist attacks in London or *Charlie Hebdo* shootings in Paris provide vivid reminders that even citizens of immigrant origin may not feel loyal or welcome. Also, the increasing number of political and welfare rights attached to permanent residence across Europe calls into question the unique value of citizenship's conveyance. Still, citizenship remains exclusively important as a membership category and, therefore, the best available way of comparing the political incorporation of immigrants across countries. And a closer analysis of citizenship and membership policies shows that national traditions and responses have generally remained enduring and distinct – even in the EU.

The U.S. has long stood out as having one of the most liberal and generous policies on the granting of citizenship: ever since the 14th Amendment, any child born on American soil – even if the parents are undocumented – automatically receives American citizenship[2]; moreover, naturalization procedures are relatively transparent and automatic; language and country knowledge assessment is straightforward[3]; and dual (or multiple) citizenship is openly tolerated. Whereas many other countries in the world offer variants on each of these components of citizenship policy,[4] few if any are so free and open. Periodically, however, this generous American citizenship policy has come into question – a trend that may continue in the future, especially if illegal immigration continues, and if the perception that Hispanic minorities are not integrating continues to grow.[5] This messaging was a cornerstone to Donald Trump's successful presidential campaign. Debates over citizenship have also been occurring in many European countries. Over the past decade or two, most EU member-states have been rewriting or revising their citizenship laws, often very quietly, but sometimes to great fanfare. How these laws and policies are written and enforced across countries will have enormous consequences for the shape and character of European society in the coming decades.

While recognizing the importance of studying immigration policy itself, this chapter focuses on the integration side of the coin, as it seeks to analyze and compare the citizenship and membership policies among the countries of the EU. The goal of this focused comparison is to reach more general conclusions that will help to elucidate some of the vexing problems and contradictions in political debates about immigration, citizenship and belonging – in Europe, the U.S., and elsewhere.

The chapter starts with a discussion of the concept of citizenship and why national citizenship matters in an age of globalization. Then it turns to an empirical exploration of the historical and contemporary variation in citizenship policies in the "EU-15," focusing in particular on an explanation of continuity or change. In doing so, we develop an argument about the importance of the *politics* of citizenship, showing that while various international and domestic pressures have led to liberalization in a number of countries, these usually occurred in the absence of public discussion and involvement. In contrast, when public opinion became mobilized and engaged – usually by a well-organized far-right party, but also sometimes by a referendum or petition campaign – on issues related to citizenship reform and national belonging, liberalization was usually blocked, or further restrictions were introduced. As such, this perspective identifies a significant role not only for the public voice but also for the policy actors that corral opinion, i.e., political parties of the center- and far-right. The chapter concludes by raising some paradoxical and troubling general questions about the connection between democratic processes and liberal policy outcomes.

WHAT IS CITIZENSHIP?

What exactly is citizenship, and what does it entail? On the most basic level, citizenship bestows upon individuals membership in a national political community. In liberal democracies, this membership conveys a series of rights and obligations to an individual, including the right to vote, to run for office, and to participate freely in public activities, while also requiring the obligation of paying taxes and possibly serving in the military. It also bestows a status of belonging, capturing the way an individual identifies, feels a part of, or behaves connected to a political community. Therefore, citizenship is understood and used here to be a formal, legal category (as opposed to a feature of civil society, social capital, or state–society relations more generally[6]) that often – but not always – conveys unique membership in the national political community. This status and identity is valuable not only to the citizenship-seeking individual but also to the state. In particular, where citizenship is a formal instrument for effectively allocating resources, achieving democratic legitimacy, and even surveilling a population, belonging and membership serve to establish and strengthen social cohesion, foster common group goals, and build loyalty.

In terms of the larger international community, citizenship serves as what Rogers Brubaker calls "a powerful instrument of social closure"[7] in two respects. First, the boundary of citizenship allows rich states to draw a line that separates its citizens from potential immigrants from poor countries. Second, it allows states to create internal boundaries that separate citizens from foreign residents, by associating certain rights and privileges with national citizenship.

Citizenship therefore evokes a fundamental paradox within liberal democracies, namely, what Seyla Benhabib calls "the paradox of democratic legitimacy."[8] Liberal democracies are based on the universal language of fundamental human rights, along with the free association and participation of "the people," yet they also delineate clear and enforceable borders and boundaries. This refers not only to territorial borders, but also to the boundaries of political membership. Determining who is included in the concept of "the people" also implies at least an implicit understanding of who is excluded. In essence, the paradox is that liberal democracies are "internally inclusive" while remaining "externally exclusive."[9]

WHY NATIONAL CITIZENSHIP MATTERS

In a major contribution – one that is both theoretical and empirical – to the study of citizenship, T.H. Marshall developed a model of citizenship based on the experience of industrialization and the emergence of democracy, and his work raises questions that are still relevant for contemporary debates about the future of citizenship.[10] Marshall argued that the extension of rights and benefits go in a specific historical sequence as democracy develops and expands, starting with basic *civil rights* (freedom of conscience, protection of property, and some associational liberties), leading eventually to *political rights* (to vote, hold office, speak and associate freely), and finally culminating in *social rights* (to form labor unions, and eventually to receive the many social benefits that welfare states provide). The argument is compelling, and it fits the pre-World War II historical experience of the United Kingdom – and to some extent Western Europe in general – quite well.

In recent decades, however, the development, establishment, and contraction of the welfare state has created a new logic that is quite different from Marshall's historical account. In most liberal democracies today, wide-ranging civil as well as social rights are extended to almost all workers and legal residents, even if they are not citizens, and therefore do not have political rights. For example, in Germany, immigrants seeking permanent residence have significant access to social benefits, in which full-time employment rather than citizenship status determines eligibility for, for example, core insurance programs. In other words, political rights are no longer a prerequisite for social rights. Moreover, as previously mentioned, in an increasing number of places in both Western Europe and North America, non-citizens are being granted local or regional (but not national) voting rights.[11] At the same time as this *sub*-national political participation has been expanding, citizens of countries that are members of the *supra*-national EU can now choose to vote in European elections in their EU country of residence, rather than their country of origin.

As Marshall's historical progression no longer applies to the contemporary situation, this has led some scholars to proclaim the current or impending empirical irrelevance of citizenship in the nation-state. According to this argument, since social rights can now be achieved without political rights, and since an increasing number of political rights are now available on the sub-national and supra-national level, national citizenship no longer matters. As one proponent of this view argues, "when it comes to social services (education, health insurance, welfare, unemployment benefits) citizenship status is of minor importance in the United States and in Western Europe."[12] In short, this type of argument places great emphasis on the recent emergence of transnational and "postnational" norms based on individual human rights, which undermine the previously dominant system of nation-states.[13] It is far too early, however, to dismiss the relevance of the nation-state and national citizenship. This is particularly the case in the EU – where the broader umbrella of "European citizenship" entitles citizens of any EU member-state to have a vast set of rights and privileges across the territory of the union – since EU citizenship is itself strictly derivative of national citizenship. As a result, "third-country nationals" (people who are not citizens of an EU country) still face limitations on their rights and opportunities, and the citizen versus non-citizen distinction therefore remains very important to them and to the society in which they live. For example, to contrast the aforementioned German example (in which welfare barriers are based on employment, not citizenship), five of Austria's nine provinces do not provide their social assistance programs to people who are not citizens of Austria or another EU country. The UK also maintains a statutory prohibition on welfare benefits for immigrants.

Citizenship is also still the key to unlocking certain public sector jobs. For example, France only accepts French or EU citizens in railway, postal, and hospital jobs; in Germany, government service employment positions in such areas as public transportation and education are restricted to German or EU citizens; and in the U.S., the government can restrict such postings as public school teachers, state troopers, and probation officers to American citizens.[14] Finally, with the ebb and flow of sub-national movements and the near-constant presence of immigration politics in the fore of political debates, the question of who belongs and to what remain core to the question of democratic legitimacy and state sovereignty.

Moreover, national citizenship is still quite significant for the eventual integration of immigrants into the host society. The recent and widespread adoption of civic integration requirements that obligate immigrants to obtain language proficiency and host society knowledge for citizenship is evidence of a policy view that active and productive participation by immigrants in society and the labor market is possible through their acquiring a set of "citizen-like," or civic, skills. While modeled off of the U.S. naturalization test and oath ceremony, European counterparts have gone beyond this earlier practice by making tests more comprehensive and difficult, requiring integration and orientation courses to precede test-taking, and obliging oath-commitments through enforceable contracts (for which the penalties for noncompliance range from repeating coursework to denial of residence or citizenship). Importantly, these policies reveal that citizenship is not merely the ultimate membership category, it is also a guide for promoting inclusion at prior stages of integration, including entry and settlement.

A final, policy-oriented, dilemma facing the advanced industrialized world – and EU countries in particular – has to do with demographics. European countries have among the lowest birth rates in the world, and they desperately need more workers in order to prevent their pension systems from collapsing over the coming two decades.[15] One obvious (though partial) solution to this problem, which has been recognized by scholars and political elites for years, involves increasing levels of immigration and naturalization. Yet resistance and outright hostility to immigrants has remained high, whether measured by public opinion surveys, support for extreme-right parties and candidates, or criminal attacks against foreigners. These two countervailing pressures – the need to incorporate more immigrant workers within a context of an often xenophobic public opposition – hearkens back to Benhabib's "crisis of democratic legitimacy" and will have to be resolved, in one form or another, over time. And political elites will struggle with these contradictory demands, though politicians tend to be more responsive to the short-term nature of the electoral process. The demographic problem, however, is a longer-term one, and a key part of its eventual resolution will depend on how these countries define and enforce their citizenship policies.

In short, whether in terms of politics and elections, welfare state benefits, public sector employment, integration, or demographics and pension systems, national citizenship remains an essential and enduring feature of modern life. This is – especially, though perhaps surprisingly, the case in the "supra-national" European Union, where eligible British citizens have sought to retain benefits of European membership by seeking national citizenship elsewhere (notable examples include Ireland, Portugal, and Germany) in the wake of the successful Brexit referendum. Having established the importance of citizenship and the value in studying it, we can now turn to some important empirical and theoretical questions related to recent change of citizenship policies in Western Europe.

IDENTIFYING VARIATION, CONTINUITY, AND CHANGE

Over the past several decades, the EU has been integrating and "harmonizing" in just about every area – from economic to judicial to social issues. But has a similar development taken place in the realm of citizenship and integration policy? How have countries changed their policies, and to what extent have they converged? In order to answer these empirical questions, and as a prior step to addressing theoretical questions, we need to first establish a descriptive landscape of citizenship policies across the countries of Western Europe, specifically the "EU-15". This group of states – bound together as the original members of the European Union – constitutes a relatively coherent entity, consisting of countries that face similar pressures of immigration and globalization within the common, institutional framework of the EU. Despite this context, we observe a variety of outcomes mapping on to more global patterns of variation. In short, a careful examination of the EU-15 provides for analytically useful contrast and variation within a relatively similar set of cases with tremendous real-world importance, as highly desired destinations, thus allowing for more systematic comparisons than would be possible by looking at the entire world or the European continent.

To identify citizenship policy across countries and at different points in time, Howard developed a coding scheme that classifies and scores the citizenship policies of the 15 EU countries based on three main components: (1) whether or not it grants *jus soli*, i.e., whether children of non-citizens who are born in a country's territory can acquire that country's citizenship; (2) the minimum length of its *residency requirement* for naturalization (for both immigrants themselves and immigrant spouses who are married to citizens); and (3) whether or not *naturalized immigrants* are allowed to hold dual citizenship.[16] While this approach does not cover all aspects of citizenship policy, they cover the two, main statutory modes of citizenship acquisition (by birth and by naturalization), as well as the primary deterrent that can potentially discourage immigrants to naturalize even if they are eligible (dual citizenship). This minimalist approach also highly correlates with more detailed coding schemes, suggesting it is both sufficient and valid to reveal general patterns and trends.[17] Each component is scored on a 0–2 scale, yielding a 0–6-point range for the total index.[18]

Based on a detailed analysis of citizenship law, Table 16.1 presents updated, aggregate Citizenship Policy Index (CPI) scores for the EU-15 countries in 2016.[19] In this distribution, we see three countries (Austria, Denmark, and Spain, though just barely) maintain restrictive citizenship policies where access is highly limited, four countries (Germany, Luxembourg, Greece, and Italy) maintain moderate citizenship policies, and a majority of countries (Netherlands, Finland, Belgium, France, the UK, Portugal, Ireland, and Sweden) maintaining liberal and open citizenship policy regimes. Policy settings that typify the most restrictive cases – Austria and Denmark – include no possibility for acquisition based on birth in the territory (*jus soli*), high-residency requirements (10 and 9 years, respectively), and no allowances for dual citizenship. Since 2015 Denmark has allowed for dual citizenship but only for Danes who have sought or seek to become citizens of other countries, i.e.,

TABLE 16.1 *Citizenship policy index in 2016*

Category	Country	Score
Restrictive (0–1.5)	Austria	0
	Denmark	0
	Spain	1.50
Medium (1.51–4)	Germany	2.04
	Luxembourg	2.25
	Greece	2.43
	Italy	2.50
	Netherlands	4.22
	Finland	4.48
	Belgium	4.72
Liberal (4–6)	France	4.72
	U.K.	5.22
	Portugal	5.32
	Ireland	5.36
	Sweden	5.47

Note: For a detailed breakdown of the various components and scoring of citizenship policies, see Howard, *The Politics of Citizenship in Europe.*

not for immigrants becoming Danish. On the other end of the spectrum, policies typifying liberal citizenship countries include accessible acquisition based on *jus soli,* low residency requirements, and allowance of dual citizenship.

Figure 16.1 presents aggregate CPI in three time snapshots: the 1980s,[20] 2008, and today. The first significant pattern we observe is the stark change between scores in the 1980s and the more contemporary periods. Finland, Germany, Luxembourg, the Netherlands, Portugal, and Sweden all exhibit major liberalization between these periods, moving in the positive direction on the scale.[21] More specifically, the most common change resulted from countries beginning to accept dual citizenship for naturalized immigrants, as occurred in Finland (in 2003), the Netherlands (over the course of the 1990s),[22] and Sweden (in 2001); in all cases this was a departure from the previous policies. Germany (in 2000) and Luxembourg (in 2001) reduced their residency requirements (from 15 to 8 years and from 10 to 5 years, respectively), resulting in a liberalizing change in their scores. Of all the countries, Germany liberalized the most, as the 2000 law not only reduced the residency requirement, but it also allows for a form of *jus soli,* representing an important change from its notorious 1913 law.[23] Overall, an empirical analysis of change since the 1980s shows that many, but certainly not all, of the more restrictive countries have changed their citizenship policies significantly.

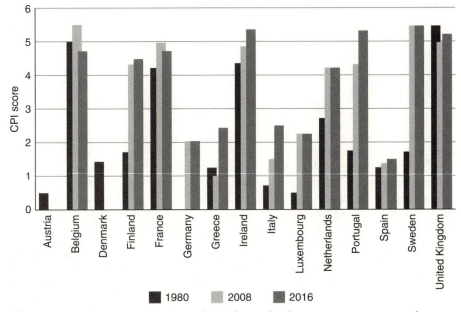

FIGURE 16.1 Changes in the citizenship policy index between 1980, 2008, and 2016
Note: Where there is no bar, a CPI score of 0 is recorded for that year.

A second meaningful pattern is how little difference we see between the 2008 and 2016 scores. While the difference between the 1980s and 2008 is marked by a significant liberalizing trend, the past eight years has seen only moderate change. Of the 15 countries examined, only three countries – Greece, Italy, and Portugal – exhibit a sizable change in CPI scores. This results not from policy change but from differences in acquisition rates of citizenship. In contrasting average acquisition rates between 2000 and 2005 (used as a weight in the 2008 CPI scores) and 2008 to 2013 (used as a weight in the 2016 CPI scores), we observe significant improvements for these countries. Greece went from an acquisition rate of 0.23 percent to 2.02 percent; Italy from 0.68 percent to 1.71 percent; and, Portugal from 0.56 percent to 5.30 percent. Our interpretation is that these improved acquisition rates illustrate the effect of earlier citizenship liberalization, in which practice inevitably lags behind policy implementation. Germany is one country where citizenship liberalization did not produce an increase in citizenship acquisition; in fact, the rate in Germany actually *decreased* from 2.09 percent to 1.54 percent. As Schönwälder and Triadafilopoulos point out, it is "reasonable to assume" that requirements such as demonstrated economic self-sufficiency and language and country knowledge, and – particularly – social benefit non–utilization rules "act as deterrents" for would-be applicants, and thereby keep naturalization rates low. Citing government figures, they estimate that between 1.5 and 2 million foreign residents in Germany are ineligible for naturalization because of dependency on unemployment assistance and welfare.[24]

Only three countries experienced a change in CPI score because of policy, and even in these instances the policy change was to civic integration requirements and not to broader categories of citizenship. Belgium posts a sizable policy change by re-introducing a language and integration requirement in 2012 that it had previously jettisoned in 2000. France's moderate policy change is also a result of civic integration, where a move from a subjective interview to an arduous language exam results in a slight decline in its CPI score. And, in 2016, Spain moved from informal interviews to standardized language and civic testing. Indeed, on the coat-tails of large-scale citizenship liberalization, civic integration policy adoption has swiftly followed as one of the most significant and widespread areas of policy change in Western Europe. Nearly every country (except Ireland and Sweden) has adopted some form of language or country knowledge testing. Not all of this change is visible in CPI scoring, primarily because CPI only captures civic integration policy *at citizenship*. What makes civic integration stand out as a policy phenomenon is the imposition of language proficiency and country knowledge conditions at membership gates *prior* to citizenship, namely permanent residence and entry. To wit, Italy introduced comprehensive integration and language requirements for permanent residence with the Security Act of 2009 (in force in 2012), but without similar changes to citizenship. As such, while CPI scores incorporate civic integration policy as a "corrective" to conditions of residence, there is sufficient reason to elevate the study of civic integration to its own distinct domain.[25]

Although cross-national differences are not quite as vast as they were a few decades ago, they are still very wide.[26] In short, there does appear to be a *relative* convergence taking place (i.e., countries are closer to one another than they used to be, rather than more distant), but it is far from the level of *absolute* convergence (or "institutional harmonization") occurring in many other areas and sectors of EU integration, and there is clearly not a common EU policy today, or – especially after the major setbacks to the EU Constitution – on the horizon. But we still need to explain why change has or has not occurred across the countries of the EU. The final section picks up this task.

EXPLAINING CITIZENSHIP POLICY VARIATION

Why have some countries liberalized while others have resisted the pressures of liberalization and remained quite restrictive? Can one identify common patterns that apply across countries, despite the national idiosyncrasies that inevitably apply to policymaking? In each case, the decisive actors who determine citizenship policy are, of course, domestic political elites and political parties, but they do not act without constraints. What, then, are the factors that have influenced them, and how?

The existing literature on immigration and citizenship is much stronger on providing theoretical reasons for liberalization than for restrictiveness. Indeed, several arguments have been developed to explain liberalization, with some emphasizing global causes and others stressing domestic factors. On the global level, scholars have stressed economic globalization,[27] neo-functional economic cooperation,[28] and new norms of "postnational" human rights.[29] At the domestic level, scholars who focus on immigration have considered interest group politics, whereby organized groups and businesses often exert influence quietly on policymakers to expand immigration,[30] or domestic courts and the judicial system in general, which have often sided with immigrants, thereby putting added pressure on political elites to adjust the policies themselves.[31] Despite the quite different points of emphasis, each of these theoretical arguments has the expectation of increasing liberalization across the countries of the EU. But what about the countries that did *not* liberalize? What explains the resistance to liberalization, and how does it play itself out politically? These questions have been less explored.

Several plausible arguments could be presented to account for resistance to liberalization, but most do not work out empirically. Structural factors such as rates of economic growth, unemployment, or immigration levels, do not shed any light on the puzzle of why, among the nine most restrictive countries with citizenship index scores in the 0–2 range in the 1980s, Finland, Germany, Luxembourg, and Sweden liberalized, but Austria, Denmark, Greece, Italy, and Spain did not. Nor do more cultural factors, such as the level of racism or xenophobia, hostility to immigrants, or general discontent with the EU – at least as measured by such public opinion surveys as the Eurobarometer or the European Social Survey – help to establish any connection to the liberalization of national citizenship policies.[32] And differences in political institutions, such as minimal percentage requirements to enter parliament, or various electoral rules and practices, explain very little as well.[33]

What is missing from these structural, cultural, and institutional factors is the actual *politics* of citizenship. How have political actors navigated the potentially treacherous waters on this volatile issue? How have they dealt with the various pressures from interest groups, social movements, and public opinion? How have they made choices, and attempted to implement them politically into new laws and policies? While lack of change can simply represent a form of institutional inertia – where the old policies continue to persist simply because they already existed – we actually observe elites pursuing conscious strategies and fighting open battles, in which these contingent political factors were decisive.

An in-depth analysis of the politics of citizenship across the EU-15 exceeds the bounds of this chapter, but even a rudimentary examination of the political dynamics within countries will help to explain why some of the restrictive countries liberalized but others did not. And it allows us to draw some more general conclusions about the mobilization of public opinion on issues connected to citizenship and belonging, which generally results in the prevention of liberalization.

One of the most prevalent explanations for the liberalization differential has been to consider whether political parties of the left or right were in power. As Christian Joppke has argued, left-of-center governments are typically in favor of increasing the citizenship rights of immigrants (what Joppke calls "de-ethnicization"), whereas right-of-center governments want to resist such impulses, while simultaneously expanding the country's connections to its émigrés (what he calls "re-ethnicization").[34] This argument certainly applies to Germany, where the 2000 citizenship law clearly resulted from the installation of a new Social Democratic–Green coalition government in 1998, and Joppke also applies it effectively to France, Spain, and Italy. Finland and Sweden also had Social Democratic governments when their citizenship laws were changed, though they had been in power for significant periods prior to this liberalization. Luxembourg, however, had a right-of-center government at the time its new citizenship law was proposed and passed, so it cannot simply be a matter of whether the left is in power. Moreover, this explanation is not sufficient, as several of the countries that did *not* liberalize their laws also had left-of-center governments in the time-period under examination. In short, the left–right orientation of the government does seem to be related to the liberalization of citizenship laws, but having a leftist government only accounts for part of the liberalization.

Building on Joppke's left–right dichotomy, Howard argues that the political orientation of the right is even more important than the constellation of forces on the left. And the issue is not simply whether a right-of-center government is in power, but whether it is *mobilized* on the issue of immigration and citizenship reform. Thus, if we accept that the liberalizing pressures mentioned above are influential in the EU-15, the question is what can counteract those forces. We point to the mobilization of public opinion – which is otherwise latently hostile to immigrants throughout the EU – either in the form of a successful far-right party, a popular movement, or a referendum of some kind on the issue of immigration or citizenship. In other words, the mobilization – essentially the "activation" – of anti-immigrant sentiment can "trump" the liberalizing pressures that other scholars have identified.

How does this argument play out empirically in the EU-15 countries? The mobilization of anti-immigrant sentiment is very difficult to measure, since it can take on different forms. The most obvious and common form is the emergence of a far-right party whose main platform emphasizes immigration and national citizenship issues. Of the four restrictive countries that liberalized their citizenship laws (Finland, Germany, Luxembourg, and Sweden), liberalization only occurred in the absence of a significant far-right party or movement. Among some restrictive countries that did not liberalize their laws at all (Austria, Denmark, Italy) we see a significant role played by strong far-right movements, in which pressures for liberalization were effectively blocked. Still, Greece had a virtually non-existent far right movement (until the entrance of Golden Dawn into Parliament in 2012) and did not liberalize until 2010. But, even this liberalization was minimal. While 2010 reforms aimed to deliver significant change, particularly in terms of *jus soli* provisions, much of the reform implementations were blocked by a decision of the Council of State in 2013. Finally, Spain has also not experienced meaningful policy liberalization, but we speculate the high salience of sub-nationalism playing a meaningful role in prohibiting significant rewrites to rules of national belonging. Also, the fact that they have not changed yet does not mean that they will never do so.

Of course, immigration and citizenship also emerge as highly polarizing political issues in countries with already-liberal citizenship policies. Belgium, France, and the Netherlands have some of the strongest and most visible far-right movements in Europe, and each has experienced some tinkering with its citizenship laws as a result of the pressure of the far right. One policy area in which we see the far right particularly active in these otherwise liberal settings is civic integration. In comparing policy adoption and change, Goodman expands upon both Joppke and Howard by noting it is not merely the politics that matter (namely, the left or right orientation of government) but the institutional setting of government that parties operate in that shapes the type of influence far-right parties can have. In the case of France and the Netherlands, both have adopted cultural requirements in the context of liberal citizenship policy. Both policies were introduced by left-wing governments to promote inclusion, and both were summarily co-opted by right-of-center governments who sought to transform them into instruments of immigration control. But Dutch requirements ended up being far more difficult and entrenched than French requirements. Goodman accounts for these divergent policy paths by looking at both politics and institutional design: the far right was influential in both cases, but in the Netherlands, politicization produced consensus (where a "consociational" democratic structure relies on broad governing coalitions) while in France it yielded polarization (where government is built by ideological families).[35]

Finally, we can see politics shape citizenship policy through other forms of public mobilization. Ireland does not have an organized far-right movement, but proponents of restrictions on citizenship acquisition succeeded in implementing a controversial referendum, which passed overwhelmingly (with 80 percent support) in June 2004, to limit the *jus soli* rights of the children of non-citizens, so that children born on Irish soil can only receive Irish citizenship if at least one of their parents has resided in Ireland or the UK for three of the previous four years.[36] This remarkable development shows the tremendous salience of this issue when it becomes publicly mobilized – and the result is almost always change in the direction of restrictiveness.[37] The UK also introduced a major overhaul to citizenship in 2009, attempting to raise the residency requirement to eight years and introduce conditions of "active citizenship" (e.g., volunteerism), in the face of mounting public discontent over immigration. However, this Labour-led initiative remained unenforced by the subsequent coalition government of Conservatives and Liberal Democrats, as often happens in single-actor systems.

To summarize, politics sit at the explanatory center of the puzzle of citizenship policy restriction in Western Europe. In some cases, far-right parties play a meaningful role in agenda-setting, contributing to existing debates in the context of anti-immigrant sentiment, and catalyzing legislation through electoral success and coalition participation. In other cases, we see citizenship policy liberalization being blocked not by the far right but by public mobilization, including referendums. In other words, while politics-based arguments about the impact of the far right help to account for variation in the type of change that has or has not occurred, it certainly does not provide the final word on the topic of citizenship policies and how they have adjusted to new pressures and circumstances.

CONCLUSION

Over the past few decades, almost every country in the EU-15 has revisited – though not necessarily revised – its citizenship law. And while the international and domestic pressures to liberalize have been significant, and sometimes decisive, they have sometimes been held in check by the countervailing pressure of a mobilized public opinion that is latently hostile to immigrants. In fact, as the evidence in this chapter suggests, it appears that when public opinion gets activated politically, with a concrete sponsor or means of expression, liberalization is usually stopped, or an existing law becomes even more restrictive. This was the case in Austria, Denmark, and Italy, where the far-right parties have played leading roles; in Ireland, where a restrictive referendum passed overwhelmingly; and in Germany, where an unprecedented petition campaign rapidly stopped the momentum of liberalization. But if, on the other hand, elites manage to pass reforms without significant public involvement – as occurred in Finland, Luxembourg, and Sweden – then liberalization will most likely be the outcome. However, considering the rising popularity of populist politics alongside continually salient immigration politics – notably including the 2015 Refugee Crisis, continued liberalization appears unlikely.

This brings us to a larger paradox, if not a serious normative problem: in terms of issues dealing with immigration and citizenship, a non-democratic, elite-driven process may lead to more liberal policy outcomes, whereas genuine popular involvement can result in more restrictive laws and institutions. In other words, proponents of liberal, inclusive policies should give more thought to the role of democracy – whether representative democracy that results in the inclusion of far-right parties in governments and policymaking, or direct democracy that takes the form of referenda and initiatives – on issues that are prone to populism, xenophobia, and racism.[38] The trend is clear, as countries are increasingly relying on referenda and popular initiatives, which advocates of the far-right view as being the ultimate expression of "true democracy." The great challenge, therefore – particularly in the EU, but also in the U.S., where populist leaders succeed on anti-immigrant, nativist platforms, where reliance on popular initiatives is increasing rapidly, and where mass opinion may also have strong, if still latent, anti-immigrant tendencies – will be for elites to surmount the much-criticized "democratic deficit" to ensure the bounties of citizenship – namely, entitlements, rights, access, and security, are fairly distributed.

NOTES

1. See, for example, Stephen Castles and Mark J. Miller, *The Age of Migration.*Third Edition (New York: Guilford Press, 2003).

2. The 14th Amendment states that "All persons born or naturalized in the United States and subject to the jurisdiction thereof are citizens of the United States and of the State wherein they reside." The one exception is for the children of foreign diplomats.

3. Applicants for naturalization need to complete a short English-language exam as well as a civic exam, which is comprised of ten questions on United States history and facts (e.g., geography). All preparatory materials are available free of charge through the United States Citizenship and Immigration Services.

4. For example, many countries offer a form of *jus soli* (the granting of citizenship to the children of non-citizens who are born in that country), but most restrict it to legal immigrants and longer-term residents, with many specific variations in practice.

5. On September 29, 2005, the Subcommittee on Immigration, Border Security, and Claims of the U.S. House of Representatives held an Oversight Hearing on "Dual Citizenship, Birthright Citizenship, and the Meaning of Sovereignty," in which these long-standing American policies were put into question. For academic treatments along the same lines, see Stanley A. Renshon, *The 50% American: Immigration and National Identity in an Age of Terror* (Washington, DC: Georgetown University Press, 2005); Samuel P. Huntington, *Who Are We?: The Challenges to America's National Identity* (New York: Simon & Schuster, 2004).

6. Although this may deviate somewhat from some contemporary discussions that use the term citizenship as a synonym for civic engagement and related concepts, it provides a more focused and grounded definition, while staying true to the theoretical and empirical debates that started with Aristotle.

7. Rogers Brubaker, *Citizenship and Nationhood in France and Germany* (Cambridge: Harvard University Press, 1992), p. 31.

8. Seyla Benhabib, "Transformation of Citizenship: The Case of Contemporary Europe," in *Government and Opposition* 37 (2002): 439–465, especially 449–453.

9. Brubaker, *Citizenship and Nationhood in France and Germany*, p. 21.

10. T. H. Marshall, *Citizenship and Social Class* (London: Cambridge University Press, 1950).

11. For updated discussions on citizen versus non-citizen voting rights in EU member-states, see "Access to Electoral Rights" country reports, available at the EUDO-Citizenship Observatory website, eudo-citizenship.eu (accessed September 19, 2014).

12. Saskia Sassen, *Losing Control? Sovereignty in an Age of Globalization* (New York: Columbia University Press, 1996), p. 95.

13. Yasemin Nuhoglu Soysal, *Limits of Citizenship: Migrants and Postnational Membership in Europe* (Chicago: University of Chicago Press, 1994).

14. T. Alexander Aleinikoff and Douglas Klusmeyer, *Citizenship Policies for an Age of Migration* (Washington, DC: Carnegie Endowment for International Peace, 2002), pp. 71–72.

15. As one EU report put it, most pension systems will be facing an "unsustainable financial burden" within 10–15 years. See European Commission, "Proposal for a Joint Report by the Commission and the Council on Adequate and Sustainable Pensions" (2002), pp. 11–12.

16. Immigrant dual citizenship, on the other hand, involves the integration of foreigners as naturalized citizens who plan to live, work, and settle permanently in the host or receiving country, and is quite distinct from whether countries allow their émigrés who naturalize elsewhere to maintain their original citizenship. For example, historical countries of emigration – Germany, Greece, Ireland, Italy, the Netherlands, Portugal, Spain, and the United Kingdom – all allow and even encouraged their ethnic descendants or diaspora to maintain their earlier citizenship, but only some of them have extended that option to immigrants within their borders.

17. See the Migrant Integration Policy Index (MIPEX) and the EUDO-Citizenship Citizenship Law Indicators ("CITLAW") for examples. For correlations, see Sara Wallace Goodman, "Concluding remarks: What we can learn from citizenship policy indices," in "How to measure immigration policies," *APSA Newsletter for Migration and Citizenship Section*, 2 (Summer 2013): 48–54.

18. To summarize briefly: *jus soli* – an average score of both at birth and after birth provisions – is coded intermittently for variation between 0 (not allowed) or 2 (allowed); residency requirements for naturalization – an average score of both individual and spousal conditions – is coded incrementally between 0 (10 years or more) and 2 (3 years or less), and also includes "correctives" for civic integration and naturalization rates; and, acceptance of dual citizenship for immigrants is coded between 0 (naturalized citizens must relinquish their prior citizenship) and 2 (naturalized immigrants can retain their previous citizenship), with intermediate scores for more complicated policy configurations and corrected by naturalization rates. For more details as well as the scoring of the individual components for each country, see Howard, *The Politics of Citizenship and Belonging in Europe*.

19. For earlier years of CPI scores – namely 2006 and 2008 – see, respectively, Howard, "Explaining Citizenship Policy Variations" and Howard, *Politics of Citizenship in*

Europe, this volume updating draws on citizenship law country reports from the EUDO-Citizenship Observatory website.

20. The use of the label "1980s" is intentional in order to account for any changes that may have occurred at any time during that decade. In a sense, therefore, the effective cut-off date for this time-period is 1990. In most cases the laws in the 1980s were identical to, or closely in line with, the historical origins of each country's laws. For historical overviews of all 15 EU countries, see the excellent chapters in Randall Hanson and Patrick Weil (eds.), *Towards a European Nationality: Citizenship, Immigration, and Nationality Law in the EU* (New York: Palgrave, 2001).

21. Italy is an unusual case, in that it became more liberal on one factor, but more restrictive on another, with no overall change to its aggregate score. It began to accept dual citizenship starting in 1992, but this was balanced by the lengthening of the residency requirement for non-EU citizens, from five to ten years.

22. Note that while the official policy of the Netherlands still does not allow for dual citizenship, numerous exceptions were established over the course of the 1990s, resulting in a very liberal dual citizenship policy in practice. See Sara Wallace Goodman, "Naturalisation Policies in Europe: Exploring Patterns of Inclusion and Exclusion." EUDO Citizenship Observatory Comparative Report, RSCAS/EDUO-Cit-Comp. 2010/7 (2010), pp. 9–11.

23. That said, despite the initial objectives of the incoming Schröder government in 1998, dual citizenship is still not permitted for immigrants, and in fact the children of long-term legal foreign residents must choose either their parents' or German citizenship by the age of 23. In other words, the change was significant, but it was still partial in comparison to the original proposal. See Simon Green, *The Politics of Exclusion: Institutions and immigration policy in contemporary Germany* (Manchester: Manchester University Press, 2004).

24. Karen Schönwälder and Triadafilos Triadafilopoulos, "A Bridge or Barrier to Incorporation? Germany's 1999 Citizenship Reform in Critical Perspective," *German Politics & Society* 30 (2012): 60–61.

25. See Sara Wallace Goodman, *Immigration and Membership Politics in Western Europe*.

26. This latter point is strongly reinforced if one incorporates the policies of the 10 recent "accession" countries, which have quite restrictive citizenship policies. For a comparison of the accession countries and the EU-15, see Howard, *The Politics of Citizenship in Europe*.

27. Sassen, *Losing Control?* and Saskia Sassen, "The de facto Transnationalizing of Immigration Policy," in *Challenge to the Nation-State*, edited by Christian Joppke (Oxford: Oxford University Press, 1998).

28. Alan Butt Philip, "European Union Immigration Policy: Phantom, Fantasy, or Fact," *West European Politics* 17 (1994): 168–191.

29. Soysal, *Limits of Citizenship*.

30. Gary P. Freeman, "Migration Policy and Politics in the Receiving States," *International Migration Review* 26 (1992): 1144–1167.

31. Christian Joppke, "Why Liberal States Accept Unwanted Immigration," *World Politics* 50 (1998): 266–293.

32. Although there is of course some variation across countries, the striking finding in these surveys is that large numbers of people across the EU are quite hostile to

immigrants. See European Monitoring Centre on Racism and Xenophobia, Majorities' Attitudes towards Minorities: Key findings from the Eurobarometers and the European Social Survey Summary (2005), available at europa.eu.

33. For rigorous testing of these hypotheses, see Howard, *The Politics of Citizenship in Europe.*

34. Christian Joppke, "Citizenship between De- and Re-Ethnicization," *European Journal of Sociology* 44 (2003): 429–458.

35. For more, see Goodman, *Immigration and Membership Politics in Western Europe,* pp. 161–201.

36. It should be pointed out, however, that while the new law is certainly more restrictive than it was previously, Ireland still grants *jus soli*, and in fact it is still more liberal than most other countries, such as Germany, which have lengthier residency requirements for the parents of children born in the host country, and which sometimes include employment requirements that many poorer immigrants lack.

37. The same phenomenon has occurred repeatedly in Switzerland – including, most recently, in June 2008 – where voters have consistently rejected referenda that would liberalize the extremely restrictive Swiss citizenship law. And it should be added that Germany was close to passing a major liberalization (including full dual citizenship for immigrants) in 1998–1999, but this proposal was shelved after the opposition Christian Democrats resorted to an extremely successful petition campaign against dual citizenship, which garnered five million signatures in a matter of weeks, and succeeded in forcing the compromise law that took effect in 2000. See Green, *The Politics of Exclusion.*

38. For a more focused argument along these lines, see Marc Morjé Howard, "Can Populism Be Suppressed in a Democracy? Austria, Germany, and the European Union," *East European Politics and Societies* 15 (2001): 18–32, especially 27–30.

17

Globalization, Migration and Governance

Susan F. Martin

INTRODUCTION

International movement of people is one of the most salient, controversial and poorly managed issues on the twenty-first-century policy agenda. International flows of people connect directly with an equally controversial issue – globalization – that is both a cause and consequence of international migration. This chapter explores the connections between migration and globalization historically and contemporaneously. It also examines a key challenge of globalization: gaining the international cooperation needed to manage movements of people from one country to another.

Only in the area of refugee movements, and more recently human smuggling and trafficking in persons, have a large number of governments agreed to binding international agreements. Yet, international cooperation is difficult even in these areas, as witnessed by the global refugee crisis that has affected countries as diverse as Germany, Lebanon, Malaysia, and Ethiopia. Although responsibility-sharing is an integral part of the UN Refugee Convention, governments have been slow in cooperating with the frontline countries receiving asylum seekers or in providing adequate financial assistance or offering durable solutions such as resettlement or local integration of refugees.

In an era of globalization, in which there are processes to manage many transnational issues, such as monetary policy, trade, the environment, pandemics, to name only a few, the system of global governance for international migration remains very weak. There are many contributing factors, notions of sovereignty among the most important. Despite these obstacles, during the past 20 years, there have been serious efforts to strengthen international cooperation in managing movements of people, as discussed later in this chapter. In one respect, the progress towards effective international cooperation among governments is very modest. The mechanisms are mostly informal processes that allow states to consult and share information. In another respect, however, the progress has been significant in building the confidence of states in multilateral approaches. Governments with widely diverging views have worked together to organize what have generally been constructive discussions. Some of these have led to concrete partnerships among States, not through formal resolutions but through recognition of common interests.

The potential for negotiating binding migration agreements that encompass a broad range of countries, some destinations and others sources of migrants, is more challenging. At present, migration agreements tend to be bilateral or regional. Even these are difficult to negotiate and, sometimes, even more difficult to implement. Yet, with further growth in confidence and small steps towards greater cooperation, such negotiations will be seen as a reasonable next step. Political leadership is needed, however, if these processes are to lead to meaningful global, multilateral action that tackles the most difficult issues on the international migration agenda: better protecting refugees and asylum seekers, improving the rights of migrant workers, combatting human smuggling and trafficking in persons, managing large-scale displacement and the potential need for relocation in the context of climate change, to name only a few challenges that will require global solutions.

This chapter places international migration trends, causes, and consequences into the context of broader aspects of globalization. It begins with an examination of the relationship between movements of people and other facets of globalization, including movements of capital and goods. The absence of a global regime for movement of people, as compared to the much more developed ones for movement of capital (e.g., the International Monetary Fund) and goods (e.g., World Trade Organization), will be analyzed. The chapter will then discuss efforts to develop a global regime on international migration. The chapter assesses two facets of global governance: (1) mechanisms for inter-state cooperation in responding to and managing an area of common interest, and (2) the emergence of international organizations to support state initiatives. The chapter concludes by examining the prospects for establishing a global migration regime to meet the needs of globalization.

GLOBALIZATION AND MIGRATION

Globalization is not a new concept; nor is large-scale international migration. Each has long historical roots. And, for as long as both have existed, there has been a complex relationship between the two phenomena. Globalization has many definitions and components. During the 1990s, as international migration grew considerably, several migration scholars attempted to define globalization as it relates to transnational movements of people. Most definitions include economic integration as an important component of globalization. Overbeek[1] defined it as the "process of structural transformation of the global political economy, historically unparalleled and with tremendous impact on the lives of billions of people. This transformation takes place in the sphere of both production

and finance, and has far-reaching repercussions for the role of the state."
Sassen (1995) described three components of globalization that had
particular import for migration: (1) territoriality – where the global
economy functions, particularly as seen in the advent of global financial
markets and sites of production; (2) the creation of new legal regimes and
practices to govern the global economy, including the movement of people;
and (3) the growing importance of electronic space, or what Sassen calls the
virtualization of the global economy.

Castles and Davidson[2] broadened the concept to include important social
and political relationships. Their definition of globalization included (1) the
emergence of a global economy of transnational corporations and international
markets for commodities, services and futures; (2) new information
technologies which have revolutionized global communications; (3) freer
movement of capital, goods and labour, particularly at the regional level; (4)
development of supra-national institutions at the regional and global levels; and
(5) growth in global, shared democratic and human rights norms and a global
commitment to a common set of values and standards. Appadurai[3] adds to the
concept by focusing on cultural diffusion as an element of globalization,
defining cultural flows to include five dimensions that he terms (a)
ethnoscapes, (b) mediascapes, (c) technoscapes, (d) financescapes, and (e)
ideoscapes. Ethnoscapes relate most directly to migration: "By ethnoscape,
I mean the landscape of persons who constitute the shifting world in which
we live: tourists, immigrants, refugees, exiles, guestworkers, and other moving
groups and individuals constitute an essential feature of the world and appear to
affect the politics of (and between) nations to a hitherto unprecedented
degree."[4]

In effect, globalization is defined by heightened mobility and requires
freer movement of labor to succeed. Statistics on international migration
bear out this perspective. Each wave of globalization has produced increased
human mobility, both within and across borders. In the modern era, four
somewhat overlapping revolutions created conditions for globalization and
migration: the mercantile revolution of the fifteenth to eighteenth centuries,
the Industrial Revolution of the nineteenth and early twentieth centuries, the
rights revolution of the late eighteenth to twentieth centuries, and the
information technology revolution of the current period. The mercantile
revolution was characterized by exploration and trade by Europeans with
other regions. Settlement followed these patterns as Europeans colonized
vast areas of the Americas, Africa, and Asia. The Industrial Revolution
produced even larger flows of people for both temporary and permanent
settlement in a new era of globalization. Timothy Hatton and Jeffrey
Williamson's seminal study,[5] looking at European migration from 1850 to
1914, argues:

The story begins with two economic shocks of enormous proportions: a resource discovery in the New World and an industrial revolution in the Old World.... The two shocks produced a profound labor market disequilibrium early in the century. Wage gaps between the labor-scarce New World and the labor-abundant Old World reached huge dimensions.... But these two shocks also produced the means by which global labor market integration could, at least eventually, be achieved.

In effect, the need for inexpensive labor and natural resources to fuel manufacturing, along with innovations in travel and communications such as the steamship, railroad and telegraph, led millions to move within and between regions during the nineteenth and early twentieth centuries.

At the same time, the rights revolution spurred migration as part of a globalization of ideas that began with the Enlightenment. The Revolutions of 1830 and 1848 led to flight from Europe when authoritarian governments suppressed the reform movements. Democracies in North America and Oceania proved attractive to many of those seeking protection of their rights, particularly since these countries were also experiencing economic growth. The process continued into the twentieth century, particularly in the aftermath of World War II and the promulgation of human rights instruments, including the UN Convention Regarding the Status of Refugees which established what became a global norm for the protection of refugees fleeing persecution.

At present, the information technology revolution is bringing both globalization and migration to new levels. Never before has it been as easy to receive information about the problems and opportunities at home and abroad. Nor has it ever been as inexpensive to travel to distant countries or to maintain contact with one's family left behind. Production is now distributed over multiple locations in multiple time zones, allowing 24-hour productivity. Rather than serve as a substitute for human mobility, this process has instead stimulated economic, social, and even cultural integration that has supported the networks that allow migration to occur. Global corporations manage global labor forces in which employees move from one location to another to get specialized training, take up new responsibilities, share knowledge and, in some cases, lower costs.

This is not to say that globalization is not without costs. As Sassen reflected looking back at 20 years of globalization, "as I had feared in 1995, the present is mostly marked by growing inequality, growing losses of citizens' rights, and growing antiimmigrant (*sic*) sentiment.[6]" She further points to a contradiction in terms of globalization's influence on economies versus migration:

Economic globalization denationalizes national economies; in contrast, immigration is renationalizing politics. There is a growing consensus in the community of states to lift border controls for the flow of capital, information, and services and, more broadly, to further globalization. But when it comes to immigrants and refugees, whether in North

America, Western Europe, or Japan, the national state claims all its old splendor in asserting its sovereign right to control its borders.[7]

This is not surprising, since migration is an issue that defines sovereignty – who enters and remains on a state's territory; who may eventually become citizens. Governments generally wish to retain unilateral national action in managing migration. As a result, relative to the other major components of globalization today – capital and trade flows – trans-border movements of people are still seen as a matter for national prerogative, not collective international action. Only in the area of refugee movements and more recently human smuggling and trafficking in persons have a large number of governments agreed to binding international laws and norms.

Yet, as discussed in the next section, globalization is driving new forms of governance regarding international migration. Managing such large and complex movements of people cannot be achieved through unilateral state action alone. By definition, migration involves at least two countries – source and destination – and, increasingly implicates numerous other countries that serve as transit points, competitors for talent, trade partners, collaborators in combatting organized crime and movement of terrorists, and participants in the global financial system that moves remittances. Moreover, migration also involves transnational non-state actors that intersect with governments and each other in managing movements of people. Some of these have formal, sanctioned roles (e.g., multinational corporations, labor recruitment agencies, humanitarian aid organizations, trade unions) whereas others are engaged in illicit activities (e.g., human smuggling and human trafficking organizations). Furthermore, international migration intersects with other transnational issues, including development, security, environmental change, conflict resolution, disaster risk reduction, human rights, and humanitarian action. But, unlike these other areas, the efforts to develop global governance systems to respond to new challenges have lagged behind in the migration area.

There are a number of barriers beyond reasons of sovereignty that help explain this lag. First, states are unclear what they want to achieve through their own immigration policies, let alone in cooperating bilaterally and multilaterally. Moreover, unlike the case of trade and capital flows, there is no consensus as to whether all parties to any immigration agreements would, on the whole, benefit from liberalization or curtailment of the movement of people. Even though the economics literature appears to indicate that migration has a positive impact on the world's economy[8], economics are not the only, or sometimes even the most important, factor in determining the effects of population movements. Social, fiscal, cultural, religious and other impacts may be as salient to governments when weighing whether liberalizing or curtailing flows of people make sense.

Public opinion also is often ambivalent, at best, about immigration and, as noted by Sassen, globalization itself has rendered negative views of migration as one of its most visible components. Sometimes publics are deeply divided as to whether migration is a problem or an opportunity.[9] Interest groups in these countries tend to take more consistent stances in favor or opposed to enlarging or contracting immigration but they may cancel each other out in the public immigration debates. Moreover, even among those who see immigration as an opportunity, there are widespread concerns that governments are unable to manage it well.[10]

A final impediment to international cooperation is the difficulty in harmonizing policies that derive from varying national interests and processes. There is a natural asymmetry in the process of building an international migration governance system. Most destination countries are global or regional hegemons in relationship to the source countries from which people migrate. They are certainly wealthier and often they are also strategically and militarily dominant. In negotiations, the destinations have disproportionate power to define the terms by which their visas will be allocated. Even among countries with similar economies and political systems, harmonization of policies is often elusive. The European Union has been working on such harmonization issues for decades and has still not achieved all of the policy coherence that it has sought.

INITIATIVES TO BUILD GLOBAL GOVERNANCE ON INTERNATIONAL MIGRATION

Efforts to increase international cooperation in managing migration date back to the early twentieth century.[11] During the past 20 years, there have been a number of initiatives aimed at strengthening both normative and institutional responses to international migration.

At the normative level, there has been recognition that binding labor migration conventions are not well ratified but governments might be more willing to sign on to non-binding principles and guidelines, especially if these were developed by governments themselves. At the institutional level, the focus has been on improving migration management at the national level and greater coordination and consultation at the regional and international levels.

Migration was an integral part of the 1994 Conference on Population and Development in Cairo and figured prominently in the Cairo Program of Action (PoA). The PoA devoted a full chapter to international migration, emphasizing the need to encourage more international cooperation.[12] There was disagreement among states, however, regarding the benefits or value of convening a conference specifically on international migration and development. Many were reluctant to support global discussions of migration. In 1997, after consulting with member governments about the desirability of an international conference on migration, United Nations Secretary General Kofi Annan found insufficient consensus to plan such a meeting.

TABLE 17.1 *National, regional and international initiatives to foster international cooperation on migration*

Initiative	Date
International Conference on Population and Development	1994
Berne Initiative	2001–2004
Doyle Report	2002
Global Commission on International Migration	2003–2005
Global Migration Group	2006
UN High Level Dialogue on Migration and Development (1)	2006
Global Forum on Migration and Development	2007+
UN High Level Dialogue on Migration and Development (2)	2013
UN High Level Meeting on Large Movements of Refugees and Migrants	2016

Instead, the focus was on regional and cross-regional consultative processes, several of which were already underway. Yet, interest in establishing mechanisms for global dialogue on migration did not fade, especially since many governments found themselves participating in multiple regional or specialized consultative mechanisms. In 2001, the Swiss government launched the Berne Initiative as a states-owned consultative process with the goal of obtaining better management of migration at the global level through cooperation between states. Through regional and international consultations, the Berne Initiative developed an *International Agenda for Migration Management* (IOM 2005). The strength of the Berne Initiative was the state-led consultative process that brought source, transit and destination countries together to build consensus on common understandings and effective practices. At the same time, the weakness of the Berne Initiative was its relative exclusion of non-state representatives. Although staff of international organizations, nongovernmental organizations and academic experts participated in the international and regional meetings, the process was dominated – purposefully – by governments. There was little opportunity for external actors to voice their concerns or recommendations. This diminished some of the credibility that the Initiative might have gained through a more inclusive process.

While the Berne Initiative was considering modes of inter-state cooperation, the United Nations was considering its own role in migration management. The Secretary-General asked his Special Adviser, Michael Doyle, Professor of International Relations at Columbia University, to convene a working group to present recommendations for future UN involvement in migration issues. In analyzing the international system, Doyle identified numerous agencies within and outside of the United Nations that worked consistently on migration issues. In particular, the UN High Commissioner for Refugees had a strong normative and institutional mandate to protect and assist refugees but not others who cross international borders. Doyle concluded that "International migration is lightly institutionalized within the United Nations system.... No organization has the broad mandate that would allow the international community better to meet the challenges of internationalization by coordinating action, developing preventive strategies, and fostering constructive solutions."[13] The one agency with broad responsibilities for migration – the International Organization for Migration[14] – was not part of the UN system and its member states were not favorable towards it joining the larger organization.[15]

Doyle recommended that the Secretary General establish a commission to make more specific recommendations about the assignment of long-term responsibilities for migration.

Following this recommendation, UN Secretary General Annan asked Switzerland and Sweden – key participants in the Berne Initiative – to provide financial and technical support for what became the Global Commission for International Migration (GCIM). The GCIM was mandated to "provide the framework of a coherent, comprehensive and global response to the issue of international migration".[16] The Commission laid out a two-phase reform process. In the long term, the Commission concluded, a fundamental overhaul would be required to bring the disparate migration-related functions of the UN into a single organization. For the short-term, GCIM recommended enhanced coordination among the existing UN international organizations with migration responsibilities.

In response, the Global Migration Group was formed to take on some of the Commission's recommended coordination activities. An outgrowth of the Geneva Migration Group, the membership was expanded to include a broad range of UN agencies, IOM and the World Bank. The aim of the GMG is to "promote the wider application of all relevant international and regional instruments and norms relating to migration, and the provision of more coherent and stronger leadership to improve the overall effectiveness of the United Nations and the international community's policy and operational response to the opportunities and challenges presented by international migration."[17]

While the GMG provided opportunities for enhancing institutional coherence among international organizations, the need for a global mechanism to foster cooperation among states remained. Towards that end, General Assembly resolution 58/208 in December 2003 called for high-level dialogue on international migration and development within the context of the 2006 General Assembly. To assist in the preparation of the HLD, Peter Sutherland was appointed in January 2006 as Special Representative of the Secretary General of the United Nations on International Migration and Development. He subsequently played an extremely important role in encouraging states to cooperate and bringing issues to their attention.

In plenary statements, states generally acknowledged that the transnational nature of migration required transnational coordination. There was disagreement, though, as to the nature of the processes to be established to foster greater cooperation. Some states preferred for it to be in the United Nations while others preferred a more informal process that was designed to be state-owned. A few states, including the United States, opposed any new process. The Belgian government announced at the HLD that it would host a Global Forum on Migration and Development (GFMD) in 2007 and invited interested governments to participate. More than 160 governments accepted the invitation.

The GFMD subsequently proceeded as a state-led process. It has two principal components. The core of the GFMD is a meeting of government officials, which relies primarily on the governments themselves to plan and execute. The second part is a gathering of nongovernmental representatives, called the Civil Society Days (CSD). The CSD precedes the government meeting with the aim of contributing recommendations on the issues to be discussed by the officials. A Common Space provides the opportunity for the two groups to meet jointly. Representatives of international organizations participate in both parts of the Forum as observers.

Much of the work of the GFMD/CSD is organized around roundtables that focus on a wide range of issues that link migration and development including human capital development and labor mobility; remittances and other diaspora resources; rights of migrants; options to increase legal admission options and reduce irregular migration; and integration and reintegration of migrants. In addition, roundtables focus on emerging issues, such as the impact of the financial crisis on migration patterns, migrant well-being, migrants in countries in crisis, and environmental change and migration. A recurring area of discussion at all GFMDs has been enhancing policy and institutional coherence and promoting partnerships for migration and development. The roundtable preparation process, by this author's observation, serves a confidence-building role in its own right, as governments bring different perspectives into the discussions about the papers while weighing which inputs are sufficiently based on evidence to merit inclusion in the final paper.

The continued enthusiasm of the participating governments, as witnessed by the successful completion of ten GFMD sessions, the establishment of a small support structure, and working groups and conferences that have allowed for discussions between formal annual meetings, indicates that many countries find it a useful way to exchange information, form partnerships and tackle difficult issues. It is not global governance in the classic sense, however, since it is not decision-making. The GFMD is not a mechanism to forge agreement on migration policy. In fact, the GFMD has been successful precisely because it has no decision-making authority. This is not to say that there is no follow-up to the recommendations that come out of the GFMD, but their implementation depends solely on the interest of individual countries.

A follow-up High Level Dialogue was held in 2013 and strongly endorsed the GFMD as a model for consultation and dialogue on migration issues. Unlike its 2006 predecessor, which issued a chair's report, the 2013 HLD was able to adopt a declaration following negotiations led by the Mexican government.[18] The success of these consultations paved the way for the 2016 UN High Level Meeting on Large Movements of Refugees and Migrants, discussed in the next section.

THE WAY FORWARD

Whether the current arrangements will result in stronger global governance is still debatable. Such a system of governance would require a strong normative framework, effective institutions, and commitment of states to cooperate in managing migration. Obtaining the first may be the most difficult. The current regime consists of a weak normative framework encapsulated in a series of international conventions with relatively few state ratifications, particularly from the major destination countries. Encouraging states to accept a stronger normative framework is highly problematic but essential to protecting the rights of migrants. Unlike its counterparts of capital flows and trade, migration directly involves humans. Global migration governance is not just a matter of protecting states from unfair practices of other states; it also requires protection of migrant rights. Years of negotiations on the UN Convention on the Rights of All Migrant Workers and Members of their Families yielded a document that few states will ratify. With no major destination country as a party, the Convention does not represent a viable framework for protection of migrant rights. Yet, many of the Convention's provisions are already in much more widely ratified legal instruments, indicating that state reluctance may be related to optics as much as substance. Binding a country to a convention that explicitly specifies that all migrants, including those in irregular status, have certain rights appears be more than many governments are willing to undertake.

Bottom-up, state-led consultative processes with multi-stakeholder involvement have become more common in addressing protection gaps in migration. Two cases are illustrative. The Nansen Initiative was launched in 2011 at a Ministerial Conference commemorating the sixtieth anniversary of UNHCR's founding and adoption of the 1951 Refugee Convention. Chaired by Norway and Switzerland, the aim was to develop an agenda for improving protection of people displaced across borders by natural disasters and the slow onset effects of climate change. In 2015, the initiative published its Agenda for Protection, which was endorsed by 109 countries at a global consultation.[19] The Migrants in Countries in Crisis (MICIC) Initiative was launched at the 2013 High Level Dialogue to address the situation of migrants who were caught in conflicts and acute natural disasters in their host country. Chaired by the

United States and the Philippines, MICIC released its Guidelines on Migrants in Countries Experiencing Crises.[20] In both cases, the primary focus was on identifying principles and practices that states could utilize in developing policies and programs that were more protective of the rights of the affected populations. In neither case is the guidance binding on states although, to the extent possible, they incorporate existing legal norms. Whether this will lead to a stronger normative framework is too soon to tell but the large number of governments that are endorsing the results of these initiatives is encouraging.

The institutional barriers to a more effective regime may be more easily overcome than the continuing weakness in the norms and principles. On September 19, 2016, at the High Level Meeting on Large Movements of Refugees and Migrants, the United Nations and the International Organization for Migration signed an agreement through which IOM enters the UN system as a related organization. A related organization is an apt designation since the other pillar of globalization – the World Trade Organization – holds the same status. Related organizations are defined by the UN as "organizations whose cooperation agreement with the United Nations has many points in common with that of Specialized Agencies, but does not refer to Article 57 and 63 of the United Nations Charter, relevant to Specialized Agencies."[21] As a related organization, IOM will be part of the UN Chief Executives Board (CEB), which is composed of heads of the specialized and related agencies. The CEB is where major decisions are made which affect the UN system. For the UN, this closes a major gap in the institution's ability to address the last remaining global issue not firmly on their agenda. It will also participate in the Global Migration Group in a new way – as a part of the UN system rather than as an outsider agency.

Although there will certainly be growing pains for both IOM and the UN in defining this new arrangement, there are reasons to be optimistic. IOM already has a close working relationship with many of the UN agencies. In particular, IOM and UNHCR have fostered much closer ties in the past few years despite differences in their focus (IOM on migrants broadly defined and UNHCR on refugees, persons displaced by conflict and statelessness) and operating styles – IOM's activities being more pragmatic, programmatic and flexible and UNHCR's tied strongly to its legal protection mandate under the UN Refugee Convention. Both understand, however, that in today's complex patterns of mobility, mixed migration is becoming more and more common, blurring the distinctions between migrants and refugees. The effective collaboration between the two organizations in responding to the 2011 emergency in Libya, which affected both migrants and refugees, was promising evidence that these two institutions – each with a key role in addressing the challenges of globalization – can and will cooperate when such collaboration is needed.

There are two major challenges to IOM as it becomes the focal point for a new global regime on migration. The first is the lack of a clear set of normative frameworks governing its activities. IOM's mission statement appears to provide such a framework ("IOM is committed to the principle that humane and orderly migration benefits migrants and society") but it also acknowledges that IOM has no legal protection mandate for migrants, as compared to UNHCR's for refugees (IOM, 2014a). IOM's Constitution references a specific list of purposes and functions of the organization, but none of the items relates to a responsibility towards migrants, stating rather a range of services that IOM would provide to states. Tying IOM to a specific Convention is not needed to establish a stronger mandate for protection of migrant rights; IOM's Constitution could be amended to establish a legal obligation for protection that would be as clear as its current mandate to assist states in their management of migration. Such a statement would not be in contradiction with recognition of the sovereign responsibility of states to protect everyone on their territory, including migrants. Rather, such a statement would recognize that once having entered a state, migrants have certain rights that must be protected and IOM's actions with regard to migrants must meet international legal standards. Having such a statement in its Constitution would give IOM more leverage in pressing states to take their protection obligations in areas such as detention and deportation into account in forming policies. It would also give greater substance to the important and often dangerous protection work that the IOM already does, such as the rescue and evacuation of migrants in countries that fall into crises resulting from conflict and acute natural hazards.

A second barrier pertains to the way in which IOM receives its financial resources from states. While state members provide for administrative costs on the basis of agreed-upon assessments, the operational budget comes mostly from voluntary, earmarked allocations for specific programs and activities. Only a small portion of the operational funding is available for discretionary activities, mostly derived from the indirect costs associated with earmarked resources. Many of the global functions of the IOM – for example, its policy, research and legal analysis units – are largely funded as a discretionary activity, as compared to its service functions, which are generally funded through earmarks. This creates a vicious cycle. As long as states are reluctant to support global governance in this area, the states are unlikely to earmark funds for this purpose, restricting IOM's activities. This in turn limits the ability of the organization to demonstrate the value of having a more robust international migration regime, which reinforces state reluctance.

Another major challenge to establishing an effective system of global governance pertains to the willingness of states to cooperate and share the responsibilities of migration. While the Global Forum on Migration and Development is a promising step in the direction of greater cooperation, there are countervailing pressures that are concerning. First, the election of Donald Trump as President of the United States on a platform of "America First" raises questions about whether the U.S. will take leadership in promoting global solutions to world problems. During the George W. Bush administration, the United States did not participate actively in the GFMD, although it continued to support regional consultative processes as well as both IOM and UNHCR's activities. The Obama administration, by contrast, engaged wholeheartedly in the global discussions. As the country with the largest number of international migrants, U.S. commitment to global engagement on migration issues is essential to any progress being made in the arena. President Trump has already given indications through public statements and, more importantly, his budget requests, that he intends to reduce funding for multilateral organizations as well as humanitarian and development aid more generally. As of this writing (March 2018), Congress has provided funding in these areas despite the President's budget request, but it is by no means certain it will continue to do so. It is also an open question as to what, if any, role the United States will play in the Executive Committees of the UNHCR and IOM or if it will provide funding and leadership in advancing initiatives to advance protection of migrants worldwide.

A second concern is the inability of the European Union to find ways in which member states would share the responsibility for protecting asylum seekers. Some countries, especially Germany and Sweden, took in hundreds of thousands of Syrians and other asylum seekers, whereas others adopted a hard-line stance, building fences rather than assisting those who were attempting to enter the country. In the meantime, few countries worldwide offered to resettle significant numbers of Syrian refugees. And, troubling for all refugees, contributions to the international organizations that assist and protect such populations worldwide were insufficient despite numerous calls for humanitarian aid. In early September 2015, the World Food Program announced that it had been forced to drop 30 percent of Syrian refugees in Jordan and Lebanon from their caseload and reduce the monthly value of food vouchers to $.14 per person per month. This occurred just as the burden on neighboring countries had reached such high levels that many of the countries in the region were closing their borders to new arrivals. Not surprisingly, such policies had ripple effects in encouraging those who could reach wealthier countries to try to do so even in the face of dangerous voyages. Nor were Syrian refugees and the countries hosting them the only ones short-changed by the international community. Crises in South Sudan, Central African Republic and elsewhere received even less attention and support.

The failures of the world community to respond to what is termed, depending on the view of the observer, the Global Migration or Global Refugee Crisis, spurred the Secretary General to call for the High Level Meeting on Large Movements of Refugees and Migrants.[22] The Secretary General's report for the High Level Meeting described its objectives: "The report calls for a more predictable and equitable way of responding to large movements of refugees through adoption of a Global Compact on responsibility-sharing for refugees, and by setting out elements of a comprehensive response plan for refugees."

A core element of the refugee compact was to be commitment "to sharing responsibility for hosting refugees more fairly," recognizing that responsibility-sharing stands at the core of the international protection regime.[23] Responsibility-sharing would manifest itself through "financial and in-kind support, technical assistance, legal or policy measures, personnel and resettlement places or other pathways for admission of refugees, and to endeavor to make contributions proportionate to the global needs of refugees and to the diverse capacities of each Member State.[24]"

The comprehensive response plan for refugees survived months of negotiation, but states did not come to agreement on the global compact on responsibility-sharing for refugees. The New York Declaration adopted at the summit did acknowledge that governments have "a shared responsibility to manage large movements of refugees and migrants in a humane, sensitive, compassionate and people-centered manner."[25] They further committed to a "more equitable sharing of the burden and responsibility for hosting and supporting the world's refugees, while taking account of existing contributions and the differing capacities and resources among States."[26] However, the refugee compact itself was deferred to 2018. Although many refugee advocates were disappointed that the High Level Meeting did not achieve greater progress on responsibility-sharing, one close observer of the process concluded that the statements in the New York Declaration were a significant achievement in themselves, noting that "the 19 September summit was the first time ever that the UN General Assembly had expressed a collective commitment to sharing responsibility for refugees (Ferris 2017)."

The Secretary General's report also called for "strengthening global governance of migration beyond refugee movements."[27] Instead of proposing language for the compact, the Secretary General asked for "a State-led process to elaborate a comprehensive international cooperation framework on migrants and human mobility, in the form of a global compact for safe, regular and orderly migration, and to hold an intergovernmental conference on international migration in 2018 to adopt the global compact." In addition, the Secretary General requested that states initiate a state-led, consultative process to improve protection and assistance for migrants in vulnerable situations and to give favorable consideration to implementing the recommendations of the Nansen and MICIC initiatives. The New York Declaration agreed that the global migration compact should set out "a range of principles, commitments and understandings among Member States regarding international migration in all its dimensions." Annex II of the declaration outlines a comprehensive set of 24 issues to be addressed in the compact. They range from the very general (cooperation at the national, regional and international levels on all aspects of migration) to the very specific (promotion of faster, cheaper, and safer transfers of remittances through legal channels).

The process for negotiating the migration compact is led by the President of the UN General Assembly, who named the governments of Mexico and Switzerland as co-facilitators. The UN Secretariat and IOM are jointly servicing the negotiations – the former providing capacity and support and the latter extending technical and policy expertise. In his final report, Sir Peter Sutherland, the former Special Representative of the Secretary General for International Migration, set out an agenda for action that highlights five policy priorities for the global compact: (1) managing crisis movement and protecting migrants in vulnerable situations; (2) building opportunities for labor and skills mobility; (3) ensuring orderly migration, including return; (4) fostering migrant inclusion and development benefits; and (5) strengthening governance capacities.[28] Others have emphasized that the global compact should primarily reinforce the human rights framework for the protection of migrants.[29] Towards that end, Louise Arbour, the former UN High Commissioner on Human Rights and Sir Peter's successor at SRSG on International Migration, is playing a prominent role in devising the global compact.

CONCLUSION

After almost 100 years of efforts to increase international cooperation on international movements of people, there has been modest success in moving towards a system of global governance that would put movements of people on par with movements of capital and goods in a globalized world. In the past two decades, progress has been made in the establishment of forums through which greater trust and consultation has been able to take place. First at the bilateral and regional level, and now increasingly at the global level, states appear willing to discuss issues of mutual concern although actual decision-making on these issues remains elusive. More promising, however, is that even governments that were most reluctant to engage on these issues 20 years ago have not only been at the tables at which the discussions of international cooperation take place, they have taken leadership roles in setting the agenda.[30] Further progress in this area will require political leadership, stronger international organizations, a broader normative framework for protection of migrant rights, and binding agreements as to how responsibilities will be allocated across countries in managing both forced and voluntary movements. These will not come easily or quickly, however, necessitating careful thought via incremental steps to build confidence in multilateral institutions and frameworks. In a time of growing nationalism and anti-immigrant populism, progress is by no means assured. Yet, the need for greater international cooperation could not be greater in the face of current and likely future trends in international migration.

NOTES

1. Henk Overbeek, "Towards a new international migration regime: globalization, migration and the internationalization of the state" in Robert Miles and Dietrich Thränhardt, *Migration and European Integration: The Dynamics of Inclusion and Exclusion* (Madison, NJ: Fairleigh Dickinson University Press, 1995), p. 22.
2. Stephen Castles and Alastair Davidson, *Citizenship and Migration: Globalization and the Politics of Belonging* (New York: Routledge, 2000).
3. Arjun Appadurai, *Modernity at Large – Cultural Dimensions of Globalization* (Minneapolis: University of Minnesota Press, 1996).
4. *Ibid.*
5. Timothy Hatton and Jeffrey Williamson, *The Age of Mass Migration: Causes and Economic Impact* (Oxford: Oxford University Press, 1998), p. 250.
6. Saskia Sassen, *Losing Control: Sovereignty in an Age of Globalization* (reissue) (New York: Columbia University Press, 2015).
7. *Ibid.*
8. World Bank, *Global Economic Prospects: Economic Implications of Remittances and Migration* (Washington, DC: World Bank, 2006).
9. German Marshall Fund of the United States, *Transatlantic Trends 2014* (Washington, DC: German Marshall Fund, 2014).
10. *Ibid.*
11. Susan F. Martin, *International Migration: Evolving Trends from the Early 20th Century to the Present* (New York and Cambridge: Cambridge University Press, 2014).
12. International Conference on Population and Development Programme of Action, 1994. Available at: www.unfpa.org/sites/default/files/event-pdf/PoA_en.pdf, accessed February 26, 2018.
13. Michael W. Doyle, "The Challenge of Worldwide Migration," *Journal of International Affairs* 57 (2004):1–5.
14. International Organization for Migration, *International Agenda for Migration Management* (Geneva: IOM, 2005).
15. The members believed that IOM was a more flexible and efficient organization than many UN agencies, as well as more willing to serve the interests of states.
16. Global Commission on International Migration, *Migration in an Interconnected World: New Direction for Action* (Geneva: GCIM, 2005).
17. Global Migration Group, *Terms of Reference* (Geneva: GMG, n.d.).
18. President of the General Assembly, *Declaration of the High-level Dialogue on International Migration and Development* (New York: UN, 2013). Available at: www.un.org/ga/search/view_doc.asp?symbol=A/68/L.5, accessed February 26, 2018.
19. Nansen Initiative, *Agenda for the Protection of Cross-Border Displaced Persons in the Context of Disasters and Climate Change* (Geneva: Nansen Initiative, 2015). Available at: www.nanseninitiative.org/global-consultations/, accessed February 26, 2018.
20. Migrants in Countries in Crisis, *Guidelines to Protect Migrants in Countries Experiencing Conflict or Natural Disaster* (Geneva: IOM, 2016). Available at: https://micicinitiative.iom.int/sites/default/files/document/MICIC_Guidelines_web.pdf, accessed February 26, 2018.

21. Article 57 says: "The various specialized agencies, established by intergovernmental agreement and having wide international responsibilities, as defined in their basic instruments, in economic, social, cultural, educational, health, and related fields, shall be brought into relationship with the United Nations in accordance with the provisions of Article 63." Article 63 in turn specifies that the Economic and Social Council may enter into agreements with any of the agencies referred to in Article 57, defining the terms on which the agency concerned shall be brought into relationship with the United Nations. Such agreements shall be subject to approval by the General Assembly. It may coordinate the activities of the specialized agencies through consultation with and recommendations to such agencies and through recommendations to the General Assembly and to the Members of the United Nations.

22. Another spur was the decision by President Barack Obama to hold a summit of world leaders on ways to increase support for refugees. The UN summit was held on September 19 and the US summit on September 20.

23. UN Secretary General, *In Safety and Dignity: Addressing Large Movements of Refugees and Migrants* (New York: United Nations, 2016), p. 25. Available at: https://refugeesmigrants.un.org/sites/default/files/in_safety_and_dignity_-_addressing_ large_movements_of_refugees_and_migrants.pdf, accessed February 26, 2018.

24. *Ibid.*

25. United Nations, *Outcome Document for 19 September 2016 High-Level Meeting to Address Large Movements of Refugees and Migrants* (New York: United Nations, 2016). Available at: www.un.org/pga/70/wp-content/uploads/sites/10/2015/08/ HLM-on-addressing-large-movements-of-refugees-and-migrants-Draft-Declaration-5-August-2016.pdf, accessed February 26, 2018.

26. *Ibid.*

27. UN Secretary General, *In Safety and Dignity.*

28. Sir Peter Sutherland, *Report of the Special Representative of the Secretary General on Migration. A/71/728* (New York: United Nations, 2017). Available at: www.un.org/en/development/desa/population/migration/events/coordination/15/ documents/Report%20of%20SRSG%;20on%20Migration%20-%20A.71.728_ ADVANCE.pdf, accessed February 26, 2018.

29. Elspeth Guild and Stefanie Grant, *Migration Governance in the UN: What is the Global Compact and What Does it Mean?* Queen Mary School of Law Legal Studies Research Paper No. 252/2017, 2017. Available at SSRN: https://ssrn.com/ abstract=2895636, accessed February 26, 2018.

30. The U.S. withdrawal from negotiations over the Global Compact on Safe, Orderly and Regular Migration does not bode well, however, for U.S. engagement on these issues during the Trump Administration.

18

The Free Economy and the Jacobin State, or How Europe Can Cope with Large-Scale Immigration

Randall Hansen

Americans and Europeans tell themselves different immigration stories. Although it is in fact exceedingly difficult to migrate legally to the US, and America's immigration policy was shot through with racist intent until the 1960s, immigration is a basic part of the country's founding myths. By contrast, with the partial exception of France, European nation-states did not base their identity on immigration. Perception is what matters here: it was always grating to see scholars, often with undisguised glee at their own cleverness, point out the supposed contradiction between Germany's official claim that it was "not a country of immigration" and the reality of substantial migration. There was in fact no contradiction: the statement was about whether Germany derived its identity from immigration and whether immigration was wanted.[1] It did not, and it was not. Neither Germany nor the rest of Europe pursued a policy of encouraging immigration; on the contrary, all European countries pursued until the late 1990s the chimerical goal of zero immigration.

This official stance changed in the late 1990s, when all governing parties in Europe's largest countries – the UK, France, Germany, Italy, and Spain – changed their rhetoric, attitude, and policies towards immigration. They had good reason to do so. If the demographers are right (and they have been spectacularly wrong about most things over the last century, so the "if" is not rhetorical), Europe will need much more immigration to stave off population decline. In the same way that growth is not an unalloyed good (indeed, we thought a few decades ago that it was a great evil), population decline is not singularly bad. It could reduce pressures on the environment, increase per capita wealth in stagnant or slow-growing economies, reduce costs of fixed stock goods (housing, for instance), and transfer powers from capital to workers (which may or may not be a good thing). Contemporary Japan is an experiment in rapid population aging and decline with very little immigration; the outcome remains unclear. But, overall, population decline seems to create more problems than solutions, particularly in aging societies with generous welfare states. European policymakers have accordingly accepted that some degree of immigration has to be part of the solution.

To a degree, the 2008 financial crisis, the consequent recession, and relatively slow economic growth since then (for those European countries that actually have growth) have dampened enthusiasm for migration and in some cases increased hostility to it. In the UK, public opinion is hostile to immigration, and the United Kingdom Independence Party (UKIP) secured its first seat in the House of Commons in October 2014 on an anti-immigration and anti-EU platform. The 2010–2015 Conservative-Liberal Democratic coalition, formed after the 2010 General Elections, attempted, with little success, to reduce net migration to under 100,000.[2] Most decisively, immigration played a key role in the June 23, 2016 referendum, which produced a 52 percent vote in favor of[3] leaving the European Union. But across the EU, parties representing far-right, anti-EU, and anti-migration views did well in the May 2014 European Parliament elections, admittedly on the back of a low turnout. UKIP secured 26.6 percent; France's Front National 19.7 percent; Austria's Freedom Party 12.9 percent; Hungary's Jobbik 14.7 percent; the Netherlands' Freedom Party 13.3 percent; the Finns Party 12.9 percent; and Greece's Golden Dawn 9.4 percent.[4] These developments have not undermined European governments' support for skilled migration, but they make the pursuit of an open immigration policy much more difficult than it was in the mid-2000s.

As support for immigration has declined, migration pressure has, if anything, increased. At the same time as Europe faces a demographic shortfall, portions of Africa and the Middle East, have a massive and growing surplus. State breakdown and instability in the Middle East, as well as in the Great Lakes region and Horn of Africa, have contributed to a record 65 million forcibly displaced migrants. By the middle decades of this century, there will be a drastic population imbalance. Stagnant, aging, and declining European populations will stand against large, growing, young populations in the developing south. Political instability in the Middle East and portions of Africa, if it continues, will only increase migration pressure on Europe. This perfect convergence of push and pull factors will in all likelihood lead to a great migration to Europe.

The question for European countries is how they can cope with these new migrations. It divides into two parts. First, how can Europe ensure the socio-economic integration of such migrants given its broad failure to integrate economically past waves of migrants? Second, how can Europe ensure that the new migrants embrace the liberal democratic values institutionalized in Europe belatedly and at the cost of so much blood and treasure? To answer these questions, this chapter considers the lessons for Europe of the world's oldest countries of immigration: the United States and France. It is divided into three parts. The first provides a brief historical overview of migration history and migration policy in Europe. The second part compares the integration experience of migrants on the two continents, attending to both its socioeconomic and cultural aspects. The third – taking inspiration from the US and France – outlines a series of steps that Europe would be behooved to take if it is to succeed as a continent of immigration.

MIGRATION TO EUROPE

Postwar migration to Europe was a market-driven phenomenon: migrants traveled to Europe in response to the needs of the buoyant postwar economy, particularly in the Franco-German core. Migrants arrived in response to this demand through two distinct channels. The first were the guestworker schemes operated by Belgium, France, Germany, Austria, Switzerland, Sweden, Denmark, and Norway. All these countries sought to fill labor shortages with migrants regarded as least troublesome and most likely to return: southern Europeans. Large numbers of Italians, Greeks, Spanish, and Portuguese migrated north for work. Once this initial pool of workers had been exhausted, labor-importing countries had to look outside Western Europe. Austria, Switzerland, and Germany had no colonies. As a result, they expanded their guestworker programs to include Yugoslavia and Turkey.

It was at this time that the second migration channel emerged. Britain, France, and the Netherlands found themselves increasingly reliant on colonial migration because they were unable to compete with Swiss and German wages. The process was a passive one insofar as none of these countries was keen to encourage large-scale, nonwhite, colonial migration. Nonetheless, they all maintained citizenship and/or migration schemes that provided privileged access for colonial migrants. The combination of labor market demand and open or relatively open immigration channels could only have one consequence: West Indians and South Asians migrated to Britain, North Africans to France, and Surinamese to the Netherlands. Most of these migrants were young men, and they later brought their wives and had families. The same process occurred in the guestworker countries. Although many guestworkers did return home, enough stayed – three million (out of fourteen million) in the case of Germany – to ensure that, following family reunification, these countries would have substantial ethnic minority populations. Some half-hearted efforts were made to ensure that guestworkers would return home and to limit family reunification once it was clear that they wouldn't, but these efforts were blocked by domestic courts. A defining case was heard in Germany.[5] It involved an Indian national who had entered Germany on a temporary work visa, which he regularly renewed. As the deadline for his departure approached in 1972, he applied for German citizenship. While his application was pending, the authorities withdrew his work permit in 1973 – on the not-unreasonable grounds that he intended to stay in Germany permanently – and ordered his departure. The matter went before the constitutional court, however, which argued in a landmark 1978 decision that the repeated renewal of the work permit had built up a "reliance interest" on his part. His deportation would thus violate the "protection of legitimate interests" principle of article 19 of the German constitution.

In this and other key legal decisions, activist courts, imbued by a postwar, post-Holocaust concern for individual rights, drew on national constitutions and jurisprudence to ensure the guestworkers' stay. For their part, colonial migrants entered mostly as citizens, and they could not be compelled to leave. Many countries introduced incentives for voluntary return, but these programs were limited, symbolic in intention (designed to placate the restrictionist right), and rarely used except by those migrants who had intended to return anyway. The result, by the mid-1970s, was a large and stable migrant population – numbering in the millions – in the larger, northern European states. When the European economy entered recession in the early 1970s, all the northern receiving countries ended primary migration (migrants who have no familial ties to the destination country), and limited new migration to family reunification.

MIGRATION POLICY IN EUROPE

From the early 1970s to the late 1990s, all European countries pursued zero-immigration policies by blocking primary migration and attempting to limit family reunification and refugee movements. Only the first was successful. With the exception of the UK (where there is no right to family reunification), domestic courts drew on domestic constitutions to defend family reunification as a basic right.[6] At the same time, all EU member states are signatories to the 1951 United Nations Convention relating to the Status of Refugees, and they all have developed complex and lengthy legal mechanisms for processing asylum claims.[7] Most individuals who apply for asylum under the 1951 Convention do not get it ("recognition rates" are 10–30 percent across the EU), but legal, financial, and moral constraints on deportation mean that they are not returned either. In practice, asylum has been, and is recognized to be by traffickers and migrants, an effective channel for lengthy if not permanent migration to Europe. The result of these two channels was net migration to Europe that ebbed and flowed not in relation to policy change but, rather, to the strength of Europe's economy (a pull factor) and economic, political, and environmental crises abroad (push factors). Figure 18.1 provides an overview of net migration to Europe since 1961.

The only way in which zero-immigration policies were effective was in blocking the one type of migration in which European states have an interest: labor migration, and particularly skilled labor migration. Until recently, it was exceptionally difficult for labor migrants without family in Europe to migrate there. In the UK, employers could apply for a temporary work permit and, after four years, the work permit holder could apply for permanent residence. Work permits were, however, only exceptionally granted and were subject to intrusive Home Office scrutiny. In Germany, post-guestworker, non-ethnic immigration

FIGURE 18.1 Net migration to the European Union, in thousands
Source: *Eurostat Yearbook* 2012, Office for Official Publications of the European Communities.
Note: Includes corrections due to population censuses, register counts, etc., which cannot be classified as births, deaths or migration.

was effectively non-existent. Across Europe, the migration "stop" of the early 1970s meant that there were only two migrant channels open: family reunification and asylum seeking. In Germany during the early 2000s, family migrants (76,000), asylum seekers (79,000) and ethnic Germans (96,000) made up 67 percent of net annual migration.[8] In France from 1993 to 1999, 78 percent of the migrants arriving annually were family members (37,600) or asylum seekers (23,000).[9] In the UK in 1994, asylum seekers (31,200) made up 40 percent of applicants and family members 25 percent (19,500), or 65 percent together.[10]

EUROPE'S NEW OPENNESS TO IMMIGRATION

In a reversal of their previous zero-immigration policies, the UK, France, Germany, Spain, and Italy all opened their doors to new immigration from the late 1990s. The change has multiple causes, but chief among them are economic and demographic ones. Starting in 1995, American economic growth accelerated. It appeared for a time that the US had managed to double its non-inflationary growth rate: from an average of 2–2.5 percent, common to most OECD countries post-OPEC oil embargo, to (albeit briefly) one of 4–5 percent. The source of the new growth potential was said to be a productivity increase occasioned by new applications of information technology (IT).

The competition from the U.S. had two effects on Europe. First, the major European economies faced labor shortages in the IT sector; during the 2000 IT boom, Germany reported 75,000 unfilled vacancies.[11] Second, policymakers saw in the labor shortage one clear source of European sluggishness vis à vis the US: the latter's immigration policy on H1B visas for highly-skilled workers, through which Indians, Koreans, Chinese and (even) brain-drained Europeans worked in the U.S. The American shadow over Germany's first attempt to attract skilled immigration was obvious: Germany's policy of issuing 20,000 visas for high-skilled, high-wage jobs, earning more than €51,129 (DM 100,000) per year, which was dubbed misleadingly (because of its five-year contractual limit) the "green card" program. Importantly, Germany announced this policy during a time of high unemployment and continued opposition to new immigration. Although the initiative was a disappointment, the German government adopted in 2004 a law allowing companies to hire highly qualified non-EU workers.[12]

The 2004 measure was partly designed to address skills shortages (still very much an issue in Germany at the time of writing) and partly to address a demographic time-bomb. In virtually all European countries, birth rates are below replacement levels: Italy and Germany's rates are especially low, at 1.4 and 1.5 births per woman, respectively.[13] Certainly, migration alone will not address Europe's reproductive shortfall. If the number of births remains constant, then Germany would actually require a net total of 600,000 to 700,000 migrants per year to make up the difference. This figure is likely beyond Germany's integration capacity.[14] But immigration can have the effect of rendering the depopulation process less difficult, and it can affect the age structure in a manner that might cushion – particularly in the context of later retirement ages – government programs under pressure through an ageing population.

INTEGRATION IN EUROPE I: ECONOMICS

Whether this new openness to migration will pay dividends for Europe and Europeans depends on how those new migrants are incorporated. Recent European history and current policy are not encouraging. In the area of economic integration, the contrast between the US and Europe could not be sharper: whereas the US integrates migrants into work, Europe integrates them into welfare.[15] The following chart provides data on ethnic minority/migrant unemployment rates on the two continents:

TABLE 18.1 *Relative unemployment as percentage of the labor force by origin,* 2012

| Country | Unemployment in % of labor force | | | Relative unemployment for-eign-born/native-born |
	"native-born"	"foreign-born"	Total	
Belgium	5.9	16.9	7.5	2.9
Canada	7.0	8.5	7.2	1.2
Denmark	6.8	14.7	7.5	2.1
France	9.2	16.0	9.8	1.7
Germany	4.9	8.7	5.5	1.8
Netherlands	4.5	10.6	5.3	2.4
Sweden	6.5	16.1	8.0	2.5
United Kingdom	7.9	9.1	7.9	1.2
United States	8.3	8.1	8.1	1.0

Source: *International Migration Data*, OECD. http://stats.oecd.org/Index.aspx?DataSetCode=MIG
Note: Total unemployment rates: http://stats.oecd.org/index.aspx?queryid=36499

The results are striking. In continental Europe, unemployment rates among immigrants are often in excess of double the national average, and at worst almost three times the national average. In North America, the gap is less than 1 percent (figure in the table has been rounded slightly up). Thus, the relative unemployment rate for foreigners in Europe – which includes both recent immigrants and long-term residents (and sometimes their children) – ranges from 1.2 in the UK to 2.9 in Belgium.

What explains this difference? One interpretation might rely on selection: migrants to North America have more skills and more education and therefore higher employment levels.[16] Although this is true of Canada (and Australia, which also selects for skill), it is not true of the United States. The vast majority of migrants to the US come through the family immigration stream, and most are unskilled. Both Europe and the US select negatively, and yet migrants to the United States work.[17]

Obvious other factors limiting migrant entry into the labour market might be higher levels of social exclusion, racism, and Islamophobia. Taking the last two first, racism no doubt plays a role, but it cannot explain why certain ethnic minorities – such as the Indians and the Chinese everywhere – do as well if not better than the overall population.[18] Racists are unlikely to distinguish between different groups of Asians. The same point applies to Islamophobia: it is doubtful that racists could differentiate Indian/Pakistani Hindus and Muslims in theory, or that they would want to in practice.[19] More importantly, racism and racists exist in North America, and recent Canadian evidence has suggested that nonwhite migrants to Canada face discrimination that limits both their employment and earnings prospects.[20] Yet, their employment levels are far higher than those in Europe.

An alternative explanation focuses on the incentive structure faced by migrants and their children. Although the pro-migrant lobby – Pro Asyl in Germany, No One is Illegal in the UK – often speaks as if migrants are invariably hapless victims, they are in most cases willful and determined actors. Migrating is not easy; it requires considerable resources – financial and personal – and, more often than not, guile. Individuals have to leave friends and family; to educate themselves on the legal (or illegal) entry points to developed countries; and to raise funds for travel or, in the case of most illegal migrants, smugglers and/or traffickers. They are, in short, rational actors who will respond to the incentives they face on arrival. In the U.S., arriving migrants receive little or no social support and have to rely on their own initiative and the support of their communities. In Europe, legal migrants are granted the full range of benefits – housing, healthcare, subsistence-level social support – that is available to permanent residents and citizens. Much the same is true of illegal migrants. If they claim asylum, as any rational migrant will do, they are entitled to extensive, if not overly generous, social support, healthcare, and housing.

The result is that a legal migrant arriving in Europe will face the choice between, on the one hand, seeking a job in an often less-than-buoyant market and (because his/her qualifications will likely not be recognized) accepting a poorly paid and unrewarding position and, on the other hand, accepting comfortable, clean social housing, and sufficient monthly support to eke out an existence. The choice should be clear. In the US, a legal migrant will face the choice between work and hunger. The choice should be equally clear, and it is borne out by the data above. Despite broadly similar educational levels, migrants to the US work, whereas migrants to Europe do not. During the 2005 riots in the Paris suburbs and elsewhere, much was made of the social deprivation affecting these areas. What was not mentioned was that the standard of housing, income support benefits, and public safety were all at a level far above that of American urban ghettoes; what was as bad, if not worse, was unemployment, often reaching 40 percent among youth.[21]

Academic studies broadly support this line of argument. Studies that examine the relationship between immigrant status and welfare dependency find higher take-up rates among immigrants, particularly in highly generous Scandinavian welfare states.[22] In mid-1990s Sweden, immigrants constituted 11 percent of the population but almost 50 percent of the country's expenditure on social assistance.[23] Many of these studies find that higher welfare dependency levels vanish in some countries, such as Germany, once controls for education and socio-economic status are added, but this is really an intellectual dodge. When scholars conclude that immigrants do not rely on welfare more when education is controlled for, they are not saying that immigrants use welfare less; they are saying that immigrants are using welfare more because they are less educated. The impact of such welfare expenditures on public budgets is not large, but the (unsurprising, given higher unemployment levels) fact is that immigrants rely on (certain forms of) welfare more than natives.[24]

The question is whether they would use it less were welfare, and specifically income support in times of unemployment, less generous. Once again the American comparison is relevant: immigrants to America have higher poverty and lower education levels, *but* they generally do not have higher welfare take-up rates.[25] Where they do, such as in California, the generosity of income support programs relative to other states appears to explain the difference. As one scholar notes "there may indeed exist a purposive clustering of less-skilled immigrants in California."[26] Other studies looking at smaller groups – poorer women, poorer women with children – also find evidence for a magnet effect.[27] Similarly, a recent study of nineteen European countries found higher take-up rates of unemployment assistance among non-EU migrants than EU migrants in twelve countries, with a particular marked difference in Norway, Finland, Austria, Italy, France, Greece, and Sweden.[28]

The question of whether migrants travel to a country or region for welfare is distinct from the question of whether migrants, whatever their motivations for migration, are more likely than natives to rely on welfare. The few, now somewhat dated, studies examining the question suggest that they are. One study of Europe found that, controlling for personal characteristics and ethnicity (that is, comparing the same ethnic groups), the probability of employment among immigrants varied inversely with the generosity of the social safety net.[29] Others have reached similar findings.[30] An early 2000s study of Canada and Australia showed that recent immigrants to Australia experienced higher unemployment than new immigrants to Canada or the US because of Australia's more generous unemployment benefits.[31] None of these studies alone closes the argument but, laid against consistently higher ethnic minority unemployment across very different European economies, they collectively suggest a powerful conclusion: more generous European welfare systems encourage the assimilation of low-skilled migrants into welfare rather than work.[32]

Given this, Europe's policy response should involve a bit of tough love: reduce or remove income support benefits for migrants, and make it clear to them that that they are welcome, but that their welcome is contingent on their willingness to enter the labor market. This recommendation, it is worth noting, refers only to income support: high levels of spending on education are fully consistent with low-skilled immigration and, indeed, will help migrants move up the income ladder.

Implementing such a policy will not be easy. Many Europeans view with repugnance the idea that migrants should be told either to work or to go hungry. More importantly, jurisprudence in Europe allows very little room for distinguishing between citizens and residents,[33] and any effort to strip legal residents of social rights enjoyed by citizens would likely face a court challenge. What this means is that a European government intent on rolling back migrant rights to social entitlements would likely have to embed this in a general rollback of welfare state provision.

This leaves Europe in a bind, but some hope lies in the fact that other pressures are pushing in this direction anyway. In France, Germany, and the UK, which collectively constitute almost two-thirds of Europe's total GDP, the pressures of international competition have created pressure in favor of a loosening of the labor market and a reduction of social provision. The UK went down this road long ago; Germany followed in 2003. In France, there is support for such reform within the conservative parties, but their opponents' ability to clog Paris's already narrow streets in reaction to any whiff of change makes it difficult to enact even modest reforms. If these countries do succeed, they may be better prepared to cope with the sort of immigration levels viewed as normal in the United States. The corollary of this is, of course, that Europe may look, in matters of social solidarity and economic inequality, more like the United States.

COMMON VALUES AND A COMMON IDENTITY

The second aspect of integration is cultural, by which I mean the incorporation of migrants into liberal values: a commitment to individual rights, to gender equality, and the rights of ethnic, religious, and sexual minorities. Several indicators, none of them without controversy, have suggested that there is a divergence in the values of Muslims and non-Muslims in Europe. In 2006, the DC-based Pew Research Center on Global Attitudes published a study on attitudes of Muslims and non-Muslims in 13 countries.[34] Clear majorities of Muslims and non-Muslims in Europe viewed the relationship between the two groups as "generally bad," and they blamed each other. Substantial minorities of Muslims in Europe appeared to hold views that appeared to be extreme, and in one case delusional. Between 35 percent (Spain) and 56 percent (Britain) of Muslims believed that Arabs were not responsible for the 9/11 attacks on the US. Between 5 percent (France) and 16 percent (Spain) of Muslims expressed "some" or "a lot" of confidence in Osama bin Laden. When asked about the relationship between Islam and modernity, between 25 percent and 50 percent of Muslims living in Europe believed that there was a basic conflict between being a devout Muslim and living in a modern society. Finally, 15 percent of British and 16 percent of Spanish and French Muslims thought that suicide bombers against civilian targets are "sometimes justified" or "often justified" in order to defend Islam against its enemies. In Germany, the figure was notably lower: 7 percent.

Like all polls, these figures should be interpreted with caution. Pew commissioned its work in the spring of 2006, when emotions were running high: the Danish cartoon controversy (over the publication of portrayals of the prophet Mohammed in a Danish paper), the US-led war in Iraq, and often heated discussions about Islam in Europe may have inflamed opinions on all sides. The questions were not repeated in 2011, likely because of the political blowback from the first poll, so it is difficult to evaluate the shift in opinions over time.[35] Subsequent polls asking different questions resulted in data that suggests a more mixed picture. A 2009 Gallup poll (based, it should be noted, on a meagre 500 respondents) found strong levels of national identification among European Muslims: 40 percent of German Muslims and 77 percent of British ones identified "strongly" or "extremely strongly" with Britain and Germany, respectively. Importantly, these numbers represented higher levels of identification than those exhibited by the general public (32 percent of Germans and 50 percent of Britons; in France, the two groups were basically equally enthusiastic, with 52 percent of Muslims and 55 percent of the overall public identifying "strongly" or "extremely strongly").[36] A 2010 study by Rahsaan Maxwell confirmed British Muslims' high degree of identification with their country and also found that UK Muslims trust their government more than do Christians.[37]

When polls asked about moral issues, European Muslims and their co-citizens continued to part company. According to the 2009 Gallup poll, "French, German, and British Muslims *all* held significantly more conservative attitudes than non-Muslims towards abortion, premarital sex, extramarital affairs, and suicide – on each item the British Muslims turning out as the most conservative of all."[38] A striking zero percent of British Muslims found homosexual acts morally acceptable.[39]

As measures of cultural integration themselves, such surveys are problematic. Many conservative Roman Catholics will hold views on abortion or homosexuality that would make them outliers among north London liberals. The important point for our purposes is not the absolute values but the comparison, as it provides a wedge into questions of integration. Two patterns emerge from the data. The first is that Germans hold an unreciprocated set of negative attitudes towards their Muslim co-citizens. Only 36 percent of Germans express favorable opinions of Muslims. On the question of Islam and modernity, fully 70 percent of the general German population think there is a natural conflict between the two (the highest in the West), whereas only 36 percent of German Muslims agree. Interestingly, 37 percent of the general German population also thinks that there is a basic conflict between being a devout Christian and living in a modern society, which was also the highest percentage in Europe. These figures suggest that Germans are more Islamophobic than the British or French; that they are highly suspicious of religion in general; and that the Turkish community's supposedly poor cultural integration – a problem to which non-Turkish Germans devote endless numbers of column inches – is in large measure constructed.

The second, and more important of the two, concerns the Franco-British contrast. British policymakers used to congratulate themselves on their more relaxed approach to integration and multiculturalism relative to the French. "Our diversity is our strength" became a common refrain. Following France's 2004 ban on the wearing of "ostentatious" symbols in schools (the hijab, kippa, and large crosses), the left-wing mayor of London, Ken Livingstone, speaking to a packed city hall, told his audience that: "The French ban is the most reactionary proposal to be considered by any parliament in Europe since the Second World War." He continued, "I am determined London's Muslims should never face similar restrictions. It marks a move towards religious intolerance which we in Europe swore never to repeat, having witnessed the devastating effects of the Holocaust." (Not long after, it might be noted, he refused to apologize to a Jewish journalist, or Holocaust survivors, after comparing the journalist to a concentration camp guard.) In the midst of the Danish cartoon controversy, prominent scholar Tariq Modood, claimed that refusal by British newspapers to republish caricatures of Mohammed reflected the fact that the UK "came to this fork in the road with the *Satanic Verses* affair. While we could not be said to have made a decisive choice there is greater understanding in Britain about anti-Muslim racism and about the vilification-integration contradiction than in some other European countries."

There might be. The British were tied with the French for the most positive attitudes towards Muslims and the most optimistic view of the prospects for Muslim integration. British Muslims did not show much gratitude. Across almost all categories, attitudes among UK Muslims were more hostile and pessimistic than anywhere else in Europe. Clear majorities of British Muslims viewed non-Muslim Britons as selfish, arrogant, violent, greedy, and immoral, and a substantial minority viewed them as fanatical (44 percent). Only a minority of British Muslims viewed their fellow citizens as respectful of women, tolerant, honest, or devout. The one bright spot was generosity: a majority (56 percent) thought that non-Muslim Britons were generous. By contrast, a majority of German, Spanish, and French Muslims viewed non-Muslims in these countries as respectful of women, generous, tolerant, and honest (but not devout), and only a minority viewed them as arrogant, violent, greedy, immoral, or fanatical. Fully 47 percent of British Muslims thought there was a natural conflict between being a good Muslim and living in a modern society. Elsewhere, the percentage was between 25 percent (Spain) and 36 percent (Germany). One half of British Muslims believed that they cannot live harmoniously in their country while being a devout Muslim.

The European country in 2006 that, overall, produced the most encouraging results was France. French non-Muslim attitudes toward Muslims were (along with the British) the most positive in Europe. Majorities of French non-Muslims viewed Muslims as generous and honest, and a substantial minority (45 percent) viewed them as tolerant. The sentiment was reciprocated: French Muslims were the most positively predisposed toward their countrymen. They are also the most self-critical: 21 percent, by far the highest in Europe, blamed Muslims for the breakdown in trust between Muslims and non-Muslims.

According to every measure, the contrast with Britain is striking. Whereas 47 percent of British Muslims had unfavourable attitudes towards Jews (relative to 7 percent of the overall population), 28 percent of French Muslims did (compared with 13 percent of the general population). Whereas 71 percent of British Muslims had a favourable view of Christians, 91 percent of French Muslims did (a figure higher than the average for the general population in the two countries – 87–88 percent). Whereas 59 percent of British Muslims believed that democracy would work well in Muslim countries, 76 percent of French Muslims held this view. Finally, whereas almost half of British Muslims believed that there is a natural conflict between Islam and modernity, only a quarter of French Muslims took this pessimistic view. Culturally, French Muslims were better integrated according to any measure than British Muslims, and they were viewed as positively by the overall population as were Muslims in the UK.

How can one explain this? As ever, many factors are at work, but most of the factors that might distinguish between the two countries – poverty, social exclusion, provenance, experience of discrimination – are common between them. French Muslims suffer high unemployment and low wages, and they are spatially segregated. France's economy offers fewer job opportunities than Britain's. Racism in France is as common as it is in the UK. The two groups originate from different parts of the world, but there is no obvious reason why Muslims from Pakistan should be more radicalized than those from Algeria, particularly as the internet, rather than mosques or madrasas, appears to be the main source of radicalization.[40] Indeed, the most recent Jihadist attacks – on the offices of the *Charlie Hebdo* magazine, Paris's Bataclan theatre, a Nice promenade, and a Berlin Christmas market – have occurred in France and Germany, not the UK. Finally, some Muslims in both countries might have reason to feel aggrieved by foreign policy. The French stayed out of the Iraq War that began in 2003, but they have consistently interfered in Algerian politics.

The clearest difference between the two countries is in their attitudes toward integration. The British have been more *laissez-faire* than the French in ensuring the incorporation of migrants. French integration is addressed in Paris; in Britain, it is left to the localities. The British have more willingly adopted multicultural policies on school dress and religious schools. France has been more uncompromising in its suspicion of claims for religious or cultural difference in public institutions. Its hijab/kippa/cross ban was fully consistent with France's republic framework and its overriding belief that difference belongs in the private sphere. The Anglo-American chattering classes were furious in their denunciations. It would inflame moderate Muslim opinion and pander to racism. It has done neither. Indeed, the most recent study shows that very large majorities of French Muslims (74 percent) identify with

France (they "feel French") and that the more integrated Muslims are (born in the country, holding French citizenship, and speaking French), the more they identify with France.[41] The degree of religiosity among Muslims (and among Christians) does play a role in reducing attachment, but it is a much smaller one. Evidence from France thus refutes both the claim that there is any inherent tension between being full French/European citizens and being Muslims *and* the claim that a more assimilationist approach to religious and ethnic differences risks alienating Muslims.

Data from France and the US provide a clear, if perhaps not popular, message. Large-scale immigration policies work when migrants are channelled into work and kept out of welfare, and integration works when the receiving countries have a clear integration framework reflecting (liberal) values they confidently hold. This should not be surprising. If we cannot be confident of our values and the society that supports them, how can we expect others to view them as objects of emulation? In different ways, France and the US have got it right. If Europe is to cope with a new century of immigration, it needs labour market policies *à l'américaine* and integration policies *à la française*.

NOTES

1. Christian Joppke, "Why Liberal States Accept Unwanted Migration," *World Politics* 50 (1998): 266–293.

2. Randall Hansen, "Paradigm and Policy Shifts: British Immigration Policy, 1997–2011," in James F. Hollifield, Philip L. Martin, and Pia M. Orrenius (eds.), *Controlling Immigration: A Global Perspective* (Stanford: Stanford University Press, 2014).

3. UNHCR. Global forced displacement hits record high. Available at: www.unhcr .org/news/latest/2016/6/5763b65a4/global-forced-displacement-hits-record-high .html, accessed February 26, 2018.

4. European Parliament Elections. House of Commons Library: Research Paper 14/32, June 11, 2014. Available at: www.parliament.uk/briefing-papers/rp14-32.pdf, accessed February 26, 2018.

5. Phil Triadafilopoulos, *Becoming Multicultural: Immigration and the Politics of Membership in Canada and Germany* (Vancouver: University of British Columbia Press, 2012), p. 122.

6. Christian Joppke, *Immigration and the Nation-State: The United States, Germany and Great Britain* (Oxford: Oxford University Press, 1999), chapters 1 and 8; Randall Hansen, *Citizenship and Immigration in Postwar Britain* (Oxford: Oxford University Press, 2000), p. 260.

7. Matthew J. Gibney and Randall Hansen, "Deportation and the Liberal State: The Forcible Return of Asylum Seekers and Unlawful Migrants in Canada, Germany and the United Kingdom," UNHCR Online, 2003. Available at: www .unhcr.org/en-us/research/working/3e59de764/deportation-liberal-state-forcible-return-asylum-seekers-unlawful-migrants.html.

8. Philip L. Martin, "Germany: Managing Migration in the 21st Century," *University of California at Berkeley Working Papers*, May 1, 2002. Available at: https://escholarship.org/uc/item/1gb6j2o3, accessed February 26, 2018.

9. James F. Hollifield, "France: Republicanism and the Limits of Immigration Control," in Wayne A. Cornelius, Takeyuki Tsuda, Philip L. Martin and James F. Hollifield (eds.), *Controlling Immigration: A Global Perspective* (Stanford: Stanford University Press, 2004), pp. 183–214; Gibney, Matthew J. and Randall Hansen, "Asylum Policy in the West: Past Trends and Future Possibilities," in *Poverty, International Migration and Asylum*, edited by George J. Borjas and Jeff Crisp (Houndmills, Basingstoke, Hampshire: New York: Palgrave Macmillan, 2005), pp. 70–96.

10. Scott Blinder, "Migration to the UK: Asylum," *The Migration Observatory Briefing* (July 23, 2014): 3. Available at: www.migrationobservatory.ox.ac.uk/sites/files/migobs/Briefing%20-%20Migration%20to%20the%20UK%20-%20Asylum_0.pdf, accessed February 26, 2018.; Carlos Vargas-Silva, "Long-Term International Migration Flows to and from the UK," *The Migration Observatory Briefing* (February 2, 2014): 5. Available at: www.migrationobservatory.ox.ac.uk/sites/files/migobs/Briefing%20-%20Long%20Term%20Migration%20Flows%20to%20and%20from%20the%20UK_0.pdf, accessed February 26, 2018.

11. *Migration News*, "Germany: Green Cards, Labor," *Migration News* 8 (2001). Available at: https://migration.ucdavis.edu/mn/more.php?id=2352_0_4_0, accessed February 26, 2018.

12. Veysel Oezcan, "Germany: Immigration in Transition," *Migration Policy Institute Profile* (July 1, 2014). Available at: www.migrationpolicy.org/article/germany-immigration-transition, accessed February 26, 2018.

13. The World Bank, *Fertility rate, total (births per woman)* (2014). Available at: http://data.worldbank.org/indicator/SP.DYN.TFRT.IN, accessed February 26, 2018.

14. The two movements are not directly comparable, but the arrival of over some 700,000 asylum seekers in 2015 overwhelmed Germany's bureaucracy, led to extremely long waits as asylum seekers sat in limbo, and exacerbated an already significant housing shortage.

15. Philip L. Martin, "Germany: Managing in the 21st Century," *Institute of European Studies, University of California at Berkeley Working Papers* (May 1, 2002), 3. Available at: www.migrationobservatory.ox.ac.uk/resources/briefings/migration-to-the-uk-asylum/, accessed November 20, 2016.

16. Frank Kalter, Nadia Granato and Cornelia Kristen, "Die strukturelle Assimilation der zweiten Migrantengeneration in Deutschland: Eine Zerlegung gegenwärtiger Trends," in Rolf Becker (ed.), *Integration durch Bildung: Bildungserwerb von jungen Migranten in Deutschland* (Wiesbaden, Germany: VS Verlag für Sozialwissenschaften, 2011).

17. Philip Martin and Elizabeth Midgley, "Immigration in America 2010," *Population Bulletin Update* (June 2010). Available at: www.prb.org/pdf10/immigration-update 2010.pdf, accessed February 26, 2018. In 2010, only 30 percent of migrants to the United States had a college degree or higher while 28 percent lacked a high school education. Matthew Hall, Audrey Singer, Gordon F. De Jong, and Deborah Roempke Graefe, "The Geography of Immigration Skills: Educational Profiles of Metropolitan Areas," *Brookings Brief* (June 9, 2011. Available at: www.brookings.edu/research/papers/2011/06/immigrants-singer, accessed February 26, 2018. In Canada,

53.5 percent of migrants had a bachelor's degree or higher. Diane Galarneau and René Morisette, "Immigrants' education and required job skills," *Statistics Canada* (2010). Available at: www.statcan.gc.ca/pub/75-001-x/2008112/article/10766-eng .htm, accessed February 26, 2018.

18. Andrew J. Fuligini, "The Academic Achievement of Adolescents from Immigrant Families: The Roles of Family Background, Attitude, and Behavior," *Child Development* 68 (1997): 351–363; David Goodhart, *The British Dream: Successes and Failures of Post-War Immigration* (London: Atlantic Books, 2014); Carola Suárez-Orozco, Francisco X. Gaytán, Hee Jin Bang, Juliana Pakes, Erin O'Connor, and Jean Rhodes, "Academic Trajectories of Newcomer Immigrant Youth," *Developmental Psychology* 46 (2010): 602–618.

19. Randall Hansen, "The Two Faces of Liberalism: Islam in Contemporary Europe," *Journal of Ethics and Migration Studies* 37 (2011): 881–897, especially 886.

20. Sheila Bock and Grace-Edward Galabuzi, *Canada's Colour Coded Labour Market: The Gap for Racialized Workers* (Toronto: Canadian Centre for Policy Alternatives, 2011).

21. "Forgotten in the Suburbs: Young, diverse and unemployed," *The Economist*, February 23, 2013. Available at www.economist.com/news/europe/21572248-young-diverse-and-unemployed-forgotten-banlieues, accessed February 26, 2018.

22. Herbert Brückner, Gil S. Epstein, Barry McCormick, Gilles Saint-Paul, Alessandra Venturini, and Klaus Zimmermann, "Welfare State Provision," in Tito Boeri, Gordon Hanson and Barry McCormick (eds.), *Immigration Policy and the Welfare State* (Oxford: Oxford University Press, 2002); Jörgen Hansen and Magnus Lofstrom, "Immigrant-Native Differences in Welfare Participation: The Role of Entry and Exit Rates," Institute for the Study of Labour Discussion Paper No. 2261 (2006). Available at: http://repec.iza.org/dp2261.pdf, accessed February 26, 2018.

23. Hansen and Lofstrom, p. 1.

24. On the weak fiscal impact, see Alan Barrett, "Welfare and Immigration," *European University Institute Migration Policy Centre Report* 07 (2012). As migrants tend to be younger, they will, all things being equal, rely on healthcare less.

25. On applying controls across Europe, see Alan Barrett and Bertrand Maïtre, "Immigrant Welfare Receipt across Europe," Institute for the Study of Labour Discussion Paper, No. 5515 (2011). On Germany, see Edward J. Castronova, Hilker Kayser, Joachim R. Frick and Gert G. Wagner, "Immigrants, Natives, and Social Assistance: Comparable Take-up under Comparable Circumstances," *International Migration Review* 35 (2006): 726–748.

26. George J. Borjas, "Immigration and Welfare Magnets," *Journal of Labour Economics* 17 (1999): 618.

27. Alan Barrett, "Welfare and Immigration," *European University Institute Migration Policy Centre Report* 07 (London: University of London, 2012); Marie E. Enchautegui, "Welfare Payments and Other Economic Determinants of Female Migration," *Journal of Labour Economics* 15 (1997): 529–554; Phillip B. Levine and David J. Zimmermann, "An Empirical Analysis of the Welfare Magnet Debate Using the NLYS," *Journal of Population Economics* 12 (1999): 391–409.

28. Alan Barrett and Bertrand Maïtre, "Immigrant Welfare Receipt across Europe," Institute for the Study of Labour Discussion Paper 5515 (2011).

29. Suzanne Model, E. P. Martnes, Justus Veenman, and Roxane Silberman, "Immigrant Incorporation in France, England and the Netherlands," Paper presented at the 50th annual meeting of RC 28, Libourne, France, May 13, 2000.

30. John Mollenkopf, "Assimilating Immigrants in Amsterdam: A Perspective from New York," *Netherlands' Journal of Social Sciences* 36 (2000): 15–34; Robert C. Kloosterman, "Amsterdamned: The Rise of Unemployment in Amsterdam in the 1980s," *Urban Studies* 31 (1994): 1324–1344.

31. Heather Antecol, Peter Kuhn, and Stephen Trejo, "Assimilation via Prices or Quantities? Labor Market Institutions and Immigrant Earnings Growth in Australia, Canada and the United States," *IZA Discussion Paper No. 802.* (2003). Available at: https://papers.ssrn.com/sol3/papers.cfm?abstract_id=422522, accessed February 26, 2018.

32. On variance across European economies, see Peter A. Hall, "Varieties of Capitalism and the Euro Crisis," *West European Politics* 37 (2014): 1223–1243.

33. Yasemin N. Soysal, *The Limits of Citizenship* (Chicago: University of Chicago Press, 1994).

34. Pew Research Center. *The Great Divide: How Westerners and Muslims view Each Other* (Washington, DC: The Pew Global Attitudes Project, 2006).

35. "Muslim–Western Tensions Persist," *Pew Research Global Attitudes Project*, July 21, 2011. Available at: www.pewglobal.org/2011/07/21/muslim-western-tensions-persist/, accessed February 26, 2018.

36. Christian Joppke, "Europe and Islam: Alarmists, Victimists, and Integration by Law," *West European Politics* 37 (2014): 1314–1335, 1321.

37. Rahsaan Maxwell, "Trust in Government among British Muslims: The Importance of Migration Status," *Political Behavior* 32 (2010): 89–109.

38. Joppke, "Europe and Islam," 1321.

39. Amusingly, *Guardian* commentator Andrew Brown took great pleasure in the results on loyalty (high) and the importance of having a job for integration (majority agreement) but was skeptical about the results on homosexuality. Brown, "Muslim attitudes survey: A closer look," *The Guardian*, May 7, 2009. Polls, one might conclude, are reliable when they tell us what we like to hear.

40. Alan Travis, "Internet Biggest Breeding Ground for Violent Extremism, Ministers Warn," *The Guardian*, February 6, 2012 (citing a House of Commons Home Affairs Committee report); Radhika Sanghani, "Forget radicalization in mosques – 'Sheikh Google' is the real threat to young Muslims," *Daily Telegraph*, October 29, 2014 (citing interviews with Muslim mothers); Ines von Behr, *Radicalisation in the Digital Age: The Use of the Internet in 15 Cases of Terrorism and Extremism* (Brussels: Rand Europe, 2013).

41. Rahsaan Maxwell and Erik Bleich, "What Makes Muslims Feel French?" *Social Forces* 93 (2014): 155–179.

19

Human Smuggling and Trafficking into Europe

Louise Shelley* and Camilo Pardo

INTRODUCTION

Human smuggling and trafficking are two of the fastest growing transnational criminal activities, and are calculated to be among the most lucrative forms of organized crime after the drug trade.[1] While most victims are located in Asia, Western Europe post-2013 has become a major destination point for smuggled and trafficked individuals as the conditions in the countries to the South and East of Europe deteriorate. The International Organization for Migration has reported that over one million people illegally crossed European borders in 2015.[2] Despite great efforts to cut off migration, in September 2016 a total of 317,228 migrants and refugees had arrived in Europe by land and sea routes since the start of the year.[3] Over 14,000 people have died attempting to cross the Mediterranean between January 2014 and May 2017. The number of deaths and disappearances across the Mediterranean peaked in 2016 as a consequence of the Syrian refugee crisis, when there was an increase of 40 percent over the previous year.[4] On average, more than 3,500 people die annually trying to get to Europe.[5]

In the absence of a resolution of conflicts in the Middle East and the worsening conditions in Africa, millions who cannot move to Europe legally seek the services of smugglers and some are trafficked. The individuals who facilitate this movement make substantial profits from the thousands of people that seek to enter Europe illicitly. Europol has estimated that in 2015 alone, criminal networks involved in migrant smuggling generated between 3 and 6 billion euros.[6] These figures are likely to show a stark increase in 2017 as there was a recorded 24 percent increase in the number of migrants entering Europe illegally.[7] Yet this human smuggling/trafficking phenomenon is not always a standalone form of illicit trade but is connected to other forms of illegal activity as those moving individuals may also engage in other violent crimes, theft, and drug trafficking and may illegally possess weapons.[8]

* Louise Shelley wrote this paper while an Andrew Carnegie Fellow of the Carnegie Corporation.

Illicit immigration has expanded but it is not a new phenomenon. The recent dramatic rise in illegal migrants is the culmination of a trend that commenced in the 1980s. Human trafficking and smuggling into Europe have grown since then as emigrants were initially attracted by generous welfare support and perceived economic advantages, as well as the demand in Western Europe for "three-D" workers – those willing to take dirty, dangerous, and/or degrading jobs that national citizens are unwilling to do. Yet the recent rise is attributable to more dramatic developments and rise of insecurity in so many regions in proximity of Europe. The conflicts and rise of terrorism in Iraq, Syria, Afghanistan, and Pakistan are major drivers of migration. The impacts of climate change and absence of employment in the Sahel, enduring conflicts in the Sudan and Somalia, widespread unemployment and underemployment in Ethiopia and countries of West Africa has fueled the rise of desperate migrants eager to flee difficult conditions at home. Furthermore, the absence of governance in North Africa, particularly in Libya, has provided an important locale from which illegal migrants destined for Europe can depart.[9] Many of those who are smuggled work as trafficked laborers to pay for their costs while in transit or on arrival. Desperate family members in the Middle East may sell a kidney to pay for the transport, so trafficking may help pay for smuggling.[10]

Europe is faced with an enormous governance challenge as it has been unable to stem the flows and has not been able to integrate those who have arrived. The difficult situation in which many migrants are living is not just a humanitarian crisis but one that has had significant political consequences within Europe. The illegal arrival of more than a million individuals in Europe has resulted in major backlashes against this population movement including the Brexit vote in the UK and the rise of right-wing nationalism in several countries in Continental Europe.

European policymakers have made great efforts to restrict illegal immigration. This is an enormous challenge given the nature of EU borders – the Mediterranean coast is lightly guarded, and the Balkan route that adjoins Turkey includes porous regions with high degrees of corruption[11] through which many migrants and trafficked people from other regions transit.[12] Ninety percent of those who are entering Europe illegally are being helped by facilitators. The illegal entry into Europe is leading to the rise of illicit networks and 40,000 people have been identified as parts of these networks from over 100 different nationalities.[13]

Payments to Turkey to deter migration to Europe[14] have reduced the numbers of migrants flowing through there, but many still arrive across the Mediterranean. The recent breakdown in EU admission talks with Turkey, which came amid increasing internal instability, has made Erdogan threaten to send more migrants to Europe.[15] The use of human beings as part of a political game is itself a form of human trafficking where human lives are subordinated to political interests.

Consequently, combating the transnational criminal groups that facilitate trade in humans has become a high priority for the Member States of the European Union. Policymakers have allocated significant resources to Europol, the European police agency, which in 2016 launched The European Migrant Smuggling Center dedicated solely to supporting member states in dismantling criminal networks dedicated to these activities,[16] and to Frontex, the European agency devoted to border control,[17] whose budget and mandate have steadily gotten bigger since its foundation in 2004.

This chapter reviews a broad range of analysis from scholars, European agencies addressing human trafficking non-governmental agencies and multilateral bodies such as the United Nations, OSCE (the Organization for Security and Cooperation in Europe), and the International Organization for Migration. The chapter has several goals: to outline the dynamics of smuggling/trafficking, their impact and the policies to address the phenomenon.

DEFINITIONS

Both human smuggling and trafficking involve the recruitment, movement, and delivery of migrants from a host to a destination state. What differentiates the two activities is whether the migrants are willing participants or not: traffickers enslave and exploit trafficked persons, while smuggled migrants have a consensual relationship with their smugglers and are free at the end of their journey. Human smuggling can transform into trafficking after the individuals move and are exploited. This is, unfortunately, increasing in Europe today as individuals are extorted for more money while en route from home to their destination in Europe.

The United Nations has adopted a legislative framework to define human smuggling and trafficking. Distinct protocols were adopted on the two crimes in 2000 in conjunction with the United Nations Convention against Transnational Organized Crime.[18] The adoption of these protocols in tandem with the convention reflects the international understanding that human smuggling and trafficking are part of organized crime.[19]

The definition of trafficking in Article 3a of the anti-trafficking protocol defines the problem in the following way:

The recruitment, transportation, transfer, harbouring or receipt of persons, by means of the threat or use of force or other forms of coercion, of abduction, or fraud, of deception, of the abuse of power or of a position of vulnerability or the giving or receiving of payments or benefits to achieve the consent of a person having control over another person, for the purpose of exploitation. Exploitation shall include, at a minimum, the exploitation or the prostitution of others or other forms of sexual exploitation, forced labour or services, slavery or practices similar to slavery, servitude or the removal of organs.[20]

This broad definition of trafficking includes sex trafficking as well as trafficking into exploitative work situations such as domestic help, agricultural work, and work in dangerous industries. It also includes the trafficking of child soldiers, of children put up for adoption or forced into begging, and the less well-known and analyzed problem of organ trafficking. Most of these types of trafficking are present in Europe, though there is no evidence of child soldiers since the wars in the Balkans.

The Protocol Against the Smuggling of Migrants by Land, Sea, and Air defines the problem in the following way:

"Smuggling of Migrants" shall mean the procurement, in order to obtain directly or indirectly, a financial or other material benefit, of the illegal entry of a person into a State Party of which the person is not a national or a permanent resident.[21]

Although human smuggling and trafficking have different definitions, the demarcation is not so clear in real life.[22] Because smuggling often occurs within the context of large-scale migration, there are numerous possibilities for abuse. In the past, smuggled women and children started off as paying clients of human smugglers but ended up as trafficking victims.[23] Now, with the rising number of male illegal migrants to Europe, men have increasingly become victims of trafficking.

SMUGGLING AND TRAFFICKING: MODELS, TRENDS, AND ROUTES

Human smuggling and trafficking are not evenly distributed across Europe. A decade ago, according to the United Nations, five countries of Western Europe – Belgium,[24] Germany, Greece, Italy, and the Netherlands – had the highest recorded number of trafficking victims. A recent report published by the statistical office of the EU shows the way these trends have changed in the past years. The Netherlands and Italy remain focal areas for victims of human trafficking but Bulgaria, Romania and Latvia have been added.[25] These additions are countries at the eastern borders of Europe with strong domestic problems of trafficking. However, in absolute numbers, countries with the most identified victims are Italy (6,572), the United Kingdom (4,474) the Netherlands (3,926), Romania (3,243) and France (2,131).[26] With the exception of Romania, all of these countries have made human trafficking a priority. Therefore, these numbers may reflect the impact of enforcement rather than a greater number of victims.

A recent Europol study found that human trafficking in Europe is mainly a European issue in that around 70 percent of both, victims and facilitators are nationals of a European country (mainly central and eastern Europe).[27] The focus of identification in these countries is on sex trafficking, which explains the dynamics described.

Many fewer cases of labor trafficking are reported. Meanwhile, human trafficking for the purpose of labor exploitation has been increasing in the past years and most of the reported victims are male citizens of Bulgaria, the Czech Republic, Estonia, Poland, Romania, and Slovakia. There has been a paucity of cases addressing labor exploitation of migrants coming from the Middle East and Africa and they appear to be very under-represented in the data.[28]

SOURCE COUNTRIES: CHANGES IN COMPOSITION

There has been very significant change in the source countries of individuals smuggled and trafficked into Europe since 2000. Before the Arab Spring, the majority of individuals were of European origin. But this has changed dramatically in the last five years as the forces of change and conflict have precipitated a flow of desperate individuals seeking the stability of Europe. Therefore, many more are arriving from conflict regions or those with low levels of economic development.

Different regions of Europe receive victims of trafficking from different source countries. In its 2012 assessment, Europol identified five major hubs of organized crime. The five hubs are: in the northwest, the Netherlands and Belgium; in the northeast, the Baltic states and Kaliningrad; in the southeast, Bulgaria, Romania, and Greece; in the south, southern Italy; and in the southwest, Spain and Portugal.[29] These have evolved since then. The Southern and Eastern hubs have become increasingly important with the rise of illegal migration from Africa and the Middle East and beyond. In 2016, Greece was the first point of entry for irregular migrants followed by Italy. A Northern route from Russia to Norway became increasingly important since the end of 2015.[30] Spain receives irregular migrants and trafficking victims from Africa and Latin America.[31] These routes are all used because of the possibility of corrupting officials, a problem that has facilitated the growth of corruption in Europe.

Irregular immigrants from Syria, Iraq, Afghanistan and Pakistan try to head to European locales such as Germany, Sweden and the UK where they may have connections and perceive the chance of success as higher. Irregular migrants from Africa originate from Senegal, Somalia, Niger, Morocco and other African countries.[32] "In addition to these nationalities, there is also a continuous flow of irregular migrants from Asian countries such as India, Bangladesh, China, and Vietnam, albeit to a lesser extent."[33] There is a significant difference in the source countries for smuggled and trafficked individuals. The major source countries of trafficking victims identified by Europol in 2015 include Albania, Brazil, China and Vietnam for the purpose of sexual exploitation and Albania, Morocco and Turkey for the purpose of forced labor. The presence of citizens of former European colonies among the victims of trafficking in Europe reveals the impact of historical legacies on contemporary exploitation. Yet it is these same former colonies that are also sources of drug flows into Europe reflecting the convergence of different forms of illicit trade – humans and narcotics.[34]

Citizens from these former colonies are increasingly identified as victims of trafficking, both for sex and labor, particularly in the Mediterranean countries. Large numbers of women from the Dominican Republic, a Spanish colony until the early nineteenth century, are trafficked to Europe.[35] Women and transgender men from Brazil and Colombia are identified as victims of sex trafficking in Europe.[36]

Italy, home to the second-largest Nigerian diaspora community in Europe, had 12,500 trafficked Nigerian women working as prostitutes in 2006, representing approximately half of the prostitutes in Italy.[37] In 2015, the figure was over 5,600 despite years of law enforcement and civil society efforts to counter the phenomenon.[38] This problem has not abated. About 3,600 Nigerian women arrived by boat into Italy in the first six months of 2016, almost double the number who were registered in the same time- period in 2015, according to the IOM. Based on past experience, IOM expects that more than 80 percent of these women will be trafficked into prostitution in Italy and across Europe.[39] Other forms of trafficking of illegal migrants receive less attention. For example, little effort has been made to address the labor exploitation that is going on in the agricultural sector of Italy where illegal migrants from Africa work, living in miserable circumstances. Locked up in farms in Southern Italy, the migrants are compelled to perform agricultural work with limited or no compensation.[40]

Before the major rush of irregular migrants and refugees, citizens from Romania, Bulgaria, the Netherlands, Hungary and Poland were those most frequently identified among European countries as sources of human trafficking. Often their movement was facilitated by citizens from their country of origin working with diaspora communities in Europe. The Netherlands, with its major focus on combating human trafficking, explains its unique representation among Western European countries.[41] Prior to the mass migration of 2014–2016, the top source countries of non-EU identified victims of human trafficking included Nigeria, Brazil, China, Vietnam, and Russia.[42]

Most of the identified trafficking victims are adults but serious problems remain in the trafficking of children. Many children are forced into begging, are compelled to engage in pickpocketing or other low level crime.[43] Among child victims, leading source regions are Eastern Europe, North Africa, and Asia.[44] The disappearance of 10,000 refugee children, primarily from Syria, suggests that they may have become victims of human trafficking. According to Europol, half of them have disappeared in Italy.[45]

ROUTES

The routes for human smugglers and traffickers resemble those for other commodities.[46] This is true because for those who engage in this activity, humans are just another form of commodity. As Tinti and Reitano have said about smugglers in Libya, human smuggling was previously an ancillary form of smuggling but has become more central as demand and profits rise.[47] But these networks were built on smuggling networks previously based on the smuggling of fuel, cigarettes, and alcohol.[48]

The smugglers are proactive and shift routes. They are flexible and exploit loopholes in the existing system. For example, when they notice that law enforcement is weaker in one area then people are increasingly moved through that locale.

The routes that were primary in the early 2000s have changed, especially in recent years. The Arab Spring had a significant impact on illegal immigration into Western Europe. Many migrants from sub-Saharan Africa who were working in North Africa when the unrest started escaped to Europe. Frontex, the European border control agency, noted that in the first nine months of 2011 there were 112,000 illegal migrants detained, compared to 77,000 for the same time-period in 2010, although not all from sub-Saharan Africa.[49] As routes across the Mediterranean were shut off through interdiction at sea, more individuals came through Turkey before transiting through Greece.[50] Greece has remained a central hub for illegal migration. Open air human trafficking markets exist, like the one that can be witnessed in Athens's Victoria Square or the one in the nearby port of Piraeus, where migrants seeking asylum and human smugglers meet and arrange illegal trips to travel further west and north.[51]

There are many routes into Europe from different regions of the world – North Africa, Latin America, and Eastern Europe and Asia. The primary transit routes are across the Mediterranean, the Balkans, Eastern Europe, and Turkey. These routes change over time as traffickers and smugglers adapt to enforcement and effective border patrols. The accession of the Czech Republic and Poland into the European Union in 2004 reduced the use of routes across these countries, as border controls were tightened with training and support from the European Union. By contrast, the accession of Romania and Bulgaria to the European Union in 2007 has not been as successful in shutting off Balkan smuggling rings. These countries still suffer high levels of corruption at the borders and in law enforcement generally. These countries were key in the smuggling of migrants from the Middle East, Afghanistan and Pakistan until barriers were established in other East European countries such as Hungary.[52] Many of the routes used for human smuggling have been used to smuggle goods since the time of the Ottoman empire.[53]

The individuals trafficked into Europe travel by air, sea, and land (most often by cars, buses, and trucks). In terms of sea travel, an important increase in the use of unseaworthy vessels and decommissioned fishing and leisure boats has become evident in recent years, as well as facilitation by train and by air, which is presumed to be related to the additional controls introduced on land and sea routes.[54]

An important identified route before it was cracked down on went from Macedonia, through Serbia and Hungary, and into Austria.[55] Entry from the Baltic Sea and through the northern parts of Europe is less common. Many routes – whether from Africa, China, or Afghanistan and Pakistan – are circuitous and involve long distances. The routes from Latin America are more direct; those smuggled and trafficked often fly straight to Spain or Portugal.

For migrants from Nigeria, there are many routes from the exit point of Lagos into Europe.[56] These routes change and reorganize on a constant basis to avoid intervention by the police or immigration patrol guards. Migrants from Nigeria use routes similar to those from other countries in the Sahel. A major route within Africa goes from Ethiopia and Sudan into Egypt and Libya.[57] During the civil conflict in Libya, new routes were used as smugglers and traffickers exploited the internal chaos in Libya to move individuals from sub-Saharan Africa to Italy's island of Lampedusa.[58] This movement out of Libya continues as this has become the central launching point for immigrants out of Africa. This exit towards Italy from Libya accelerated in 2015, placing a strain on Europe's capacity to deal with the flow.[59] Members of the Italian Coast Guard have rescued individuals from flimsy boats.[60]

Before 2014, illicit migrants did not enter Europe often by sea; only 8 percent were thought to have entered this way.[61] The recent migrant crisis resulting from conflicts in the Middle East, Afghanistan and continuous unrest in Africa changed this trend and in 2015, according to IOM, only 3 percent of migrants reached European by land; most of the rest have initially entered by sea.[62] This analysis has been questioned, suggesting that current migration patterns are based on ingenuity and combine a variety of "permutations" of transport.[63] Apart from those who enter illegally, a significant number enter legally by air, then stay on beyond their visa authorization.[64]

Frontex, the European border control agency, has identified in recent years the increasing use of large cargo ships to transport migrants directly from the Turkish coast near Syria to Italy.[65] The European police body has identified more than 230 locations where illegal facilitation or migrant smuggling takes place; the main criminal hotspots for migrant smuggling outside the EU are Amman, Algiers, Beirut, Benghazi, Cairo, Casablanca, Istanbul, Izmir, Misrata, Oran, and Tripoli. The main criminal hotspots for intra-EU movements include Athens, Berlin, Budapest, Calais, Copenhagen, Frankfurt, Hamburg, Hoek van Holland, London, Madrid, Milan, Munich, Paris, Passau, Rome, Stockholm, Tornio, Thessaloniki, Vienna, Warsaw, and Zeebrugge.[66] These are not isolated locales, as there are interactions among them. For example, recruiters in Turkey bring individuals to Libya who will be moved to Europe. Individuals in refugee camps sell their kidneys for transplants in Egypt to have family members provided smuggling transport to Europe.[67]

PROFILES OF FACILITATORS

Traffickers are logistics specialists who can move individuals across vast distances. More than 90 percent of the migrants travelling to the EU used facilitation services. In most cases, these services were offered and provided by criminal groups. A large number of criminal networks as well as individual criminal entrepreneurs now generate substantial profits from migrant smuggling.[68] They often require numerous safe houses along the way where they can lodge their human cargo until it is safe to move them further. For individuals traveling the Balkan route into Western Europe, these safe houses are often in Turkey and Eastern Europe. For those traveling from sub-Saharan Africa, there are many stations along the way.

Routes are often indirect, as traffickers carefully avoid policed roads, border checkpoints, and jurisdictions where there is efficient and honest law enforcement. While not quite as complex as the operations of large-scale narcotics traffickers, human traffickers and smugglers do require a military-like intelligence capacity to successfully avoid these obstacles. The end destinations for victims are often diaspora communities that can absorb the trafficked people, or urban areas where allied crime groups can receive and distribute the trafficked laborers.[69]

A general profile of traffickers and smugglers is hard to assemble but there are some common patterns shared by facilitators. About 70 percent of European citizens suspected to be involved in human trafficking are citizens of Bulgaria, Hungary, Romania, and Slovakia. Non-European networks often have participants of Chinese or Nigerian origin. The Chinese are known to be proficient in the production of fake documents and the Nigerians in the black market of stolen identifications.[70]

In contrast, human smuggling is a more international business. Europol has identified participants in this business from over one hundred countries. The most common countries of origin include some of the Eastern European countries associated with human trafficking but others as well such as Kosovo and Serbia that have been part of smuggling routes. It also includes participants in many more countries, from North Africa (Egypt, Tunisia), the Middle East (Turkey and Syria), and Pakistan. In contrast with trafficking, many more of the smuggling networks involve non-Europeans, with 44 percent of the networks composed of non-EU nationals and 26 percent of both Europeans and non-EU citizens. Less than a third are composed only of Europeans. This reveals the transnational nature of this phenomenon.[71] Research has revealed cases of collaboration among these groups, suggesting an existing, or at least nascent, transnational enterprise of broad reach.[72] Such criminal groups – especially the Chinese, Nigerian, and Romanian ones – work with diaspora communities overseas to limit detection. Bulgarian, Hungarian, and Turkish groups are often facilitators, moving individuals from the east through the Balkans to Western Europe, following trajectories already established in the Ottoman era. Balkan traffickers operate within family groups, often functioning within diaspora communities.[73]

Some activities are outsourced to groups that have a special skill set or a regional expertise. This is possible because for already a decade, pyramidal structures have been replaced by loose network structures."[74] The phenomenon of outsourcing has increased as the complexity of smuggling and the scale of the business has accelerated in recent years. For example, residents in a border area may take "advantage of the opportunity to profit from the presence of irregular migrants by assisting them to cross an individual border or a difficult stretch of terrain."[75]

The businesses of smuggling and trafficking regularly intersect with the legitimate world as facilitators are needed from legal businesses such as personnel of hotels, travel agencies, and groups that can process money. Employment agencies, which may be complicit, are used to facilitate the movement of victims. Apartment owners may knowingly or unknowingly rent apartments to smuggled and trafficked individuals, thus facilitating their residence in Western Europe. Nightclub owners may employ young unauthorized female workers, and some even go to great lengths to secure such employees. Hotels seeking cheap staff may hire unauthorized workers who have been smuggled or trafficked into Europe.[76] All these actors may be only tangentially involved, and sometimes may be without realizing it, but nevertheless their support is essential to the execution of the crime. Groups also hire individuals outside their communities to reduce suspicion. Belgian and Dutch women have been hired by Balkan clans engaged in trafficking to help run day-to-day operations and minimize risks.[77]

Corrupt officials include members of the military, border control agencies, consular officials, law enforcement officials and regulatory agencies. Specialized service providers include those with proficiency in new media for communications and advertising, producers of illicit documents and specialists in logistics.

Women are more active in human trafficking than other areas of transnational crime.[78] This pertains to the business of trafficking opposed to that of smuggling, where men still predominate. Analysing the business in Southern and Eastern Europe,[79] research found an important number of women "recruiters" who were encouraged by their traffickers "to invite their friends to work abroad also but were unaware of the intention to exploit." A similar situation was identified in Nigerian trafficking networks, where women tend be in charge of controlling female victims. But in some trafficking networks women enjoy less autonomy.[80] Nigerian madams are often key people in the trafficking networks. They are often former victims of sexual exploitation themselves who recruit young women in their home towns and finance their transport to European territory. Their victims will work for them until they repay the investment.[81] This dynamic has come to establish an observable cycle of victims turning into offenders.[82]

FACILITATING TECHNOLOGIES

Contemporary human smuggling and trafficking is facilitated not only by people but by technology. The following technologies have been identified in Europe through investigations of recruitment techniques of actual trafficking victims: chat rooms; SMS messaging; camera phones; mail interception software; video link; the dark web; social networking sites; computer games; and peer-to-peer networks.[83] New technologies are also contributing to the operations of human smugglers moving people into Europe. One broker for a journey in which 500 people died at sea after departing from Egypt advertised his services through Facebook. An analysis of the facilitator's Facebook page shows the connections of the recruiter to some of his victims who perished at sea.[84] The role of all these technologies has become central to understanding new trends of trafficking and smuggling in human beings, as became evident after the expansion in social media accounts devoted to such activities, which went from 141 in 2015, to 1,150 in 2016, a more than eightfold increase in just one year.[85]

KEY NETWORKS

There are now many diverse networks involved in the smuggling and trafficking of people. In 2013–2014, Europol received reports on 6,000 organized groups involved in human trafficking. The vast majority – 90 percent – were involved in sexual exploitation, 5.6 percent concerned cases of labour exploitation, 1.9 percent were involved in forced sham marriages, and 0.3 percent in forced criminality and begging. These data may be more representative of citizen concerns than the actual distribution of victims.[86]

Especially important are the groups moving people from the Southern and Eastern Mediterranean. Turkish criminal groups have become specialists in the logistics needed to move drugs and people. Groups in the eastern parts of Turkey, especially on the borders with Iraq and Syria, have helped facilitate this illicit trade.[87] In some cases, the crime groups are linked with the terrorist organization the Kurdish Workers' Party (PKK).[88] ISIS and al Nusra generate funds by individuals seeking to be smuggled out of the conflict region. The Turkish National Police revealed that many transnational criminals from different countries operated in Turkey, facilitating this trade. Already in 2008, criminals from 64 different countries operating in conjunction with different Turkish crime groups were arrested in Turkey.[89] Many of these were functioning in the drug arena, but their networks were also utilized for trade in human beings.

Turkish human smuggling follows the trade routes of the Ottoman empire. Instead of bringing spices and silks from the Orient to Western Europe, these routes bring political refugees from conflicts in Afghanistan, Iraq, Syria, Pakistan, and Somalia and labor migrants who seek to earn more in the economies of Europe. Turkish organized crime has globalized in recent decades, facilitating this trade from East to West.[90] The geographic location of Turkey on the Black Sea and its borders with Soviet successor states, Iraq, Syria, and Iran, all facilitate this trade. Moreover, its long Mediterranean border – too long to be fully policed – provides excellent points of covert entry and exit from the country.

The recent rise of smuggling/trafficking from North Africa has led to a rise of new actors. But these groups are not as well known as the Turkic and Balkan groups, which have been operational for longer. A proclaimed successful extradition of a major smuggler from North Africa has been challenged in the Italian courts because of problems of identification.[91]

THE ROLE OF CORRUPTION

Corruption is deeply connected to the problem of human trafficking in Europe: travel agencies, border guards, law enforcement, military, customs officials, consular officers, and other diplomatic personnel must be bribed or extorted for trafficking to be successful.[92] Corruption in Greece by border officials has helped facilitate the migrant flows into Europe. Migrants arriving from Turkey could pass after bribes were paid as officers simply "failed to notice that the passports being used belonged to somebody else."[93]

In other cases, corruption prevents exploited victims from receiving the protection of law enforcement authorities. Victims' narratives often point to the complicitous relationship between criminals and law enforcement authorities as one of the main reasons that prevent them from denouncing their victimizers earlier.[94] The vicious role of public officials has been detected at all of the stages of human trafficking, "indicating that bribery and abuse of power of public officials or influential people are often part of the process."[95]

Corrupt officials facilitate human trafficking and/or smuggling by providing operational information, which allows criminal networks to avoid detection. Eleven of the 23 member states of Frontex reported to have identified this type of corruption, and two more reported awareness of this problem in their country.[96]

PROFILE OF TRAFFICKED AND SMUGGLED PERSONS

A very different profile differentiates the individuals who are trafficked and those who are smuggled. The individuals who are smuggled and then become victims of trafficking come from different regions of the world and are more often male. In fact, in West and Central Europe more nationalities have been represented among human trafficking victims than in any other part of the world.[97] Furthermore, Europe identifies more adult victims than youthful ones. Globally, children account for about one-third of victims but in Europe the figure is closer to one-fifth.[98] Many of the identified child victims of human trafficking are Roma from Eastern Europe.[99] This may be a consequence of the fact that there is little local trafficking and most individuals have to travel far to reach their point of exploitation. The profiles of victims of trafficking in Europe identified a decade ago reveals an enormous range of victims: young children who are forced to sell flowers in the street, beg, or commit petty crime for their traffickers; mature women who are exploited as care providers for children and the elderly; and men forced to undertake manual labor.[100] Women and children are most often identified as the victims and they are exploited for sex and are victims of domestic servitude. This phenomenon is even broader as homosexual males were trafficked from Latin America primarily to serve male clients; however, this problem has largely been neglected in UN reports, as they rely on reported data.[101] A 2015 Eurostat report found that only 4 percent of the victims of sexual exploitation were male but men predominated in those identified as victims of labor trafficking (71 percent).[102] Yet there is significant research and analysis to suggest that male trafficking, particularly in the sexual arena, is under-reported.[103]

The irregular migrant population and those seeking refugee status come from very different countries than those who are trafficked. The motivations to enter are clear. Not only are individuals hoping to enter a safer environment, but one that allows them to send remittances home. Research suggests that undocumented immigrants typically send more remittances than legal immigrants.[104]

The diverse origins of the migrants are illustrated by a ship that left Egypt with a tragic outcome when most passengers died in transit across the Mediterranean on April 9, 2016. Among the victims were 190 people from Somalia, Ethiopia, Egypt, Sudan, Syria and other countries. Other irregular migrants come from Iraq, Pakistan, and Afghanistan.[105] Most of these attempting to make the voyage are male. According to figures released by the UNHCR and local authorities from Greece, Italy, Spain, and Malta in the first ten months of 2015, "more than one in five of over 870,000 refugees and migrants who have crossed the Mediterranean Sea to Europe is a child."[106] Almost half the children seeking asylum in Europe come from three war-torn countries – Afghanistan, Iraq, and Syria.[107] Many of these children are vulnerable to exploitation.

There are significant numbers of unaccompanied minors coming from Afghanistan and this problem has been identified since the mid-2000s. The problem has accelerated since the withdrawal of NATO forces in 2014. Families are paying between 5,000 to 8,500 euros to have the children transported.[108] This treacherous journey across many countries requires numerous facilitators. But the children are not assured entry to their destination countries. Before the abolition of the Calais camp in France, there were over 1,000 children among 10,000 adults – most from Afghanistan. Only a small number of them were certified to be fast-tracked as refugees under family unification laws.[109]

CONCLUSION

The mass numbers of people arriving in Europe who are vulnerable to exploitation by traffickers, smugglers, and facilitators is very significant. Many embark on the voyage to Europe, believing that they are leaving for a better situation. But the reality which awaits them is far different and there is a limited capacity within Europe to process and absorb refugees. While some Europeans are ready to help smuggle migrants to safety,[110] there is a mounting resistance in many countries to Europe to settling these individuals.[111] Therefore, for many who were not initially victims of trafficking, their inability to become legal residents of Europe forces them into a situation of illegality. This compounds the risk and the reality of human trafficking.

The human tragedy of these desperate individuals is just one element of the problem. There are broader consequences for Europe from human smuggling and trafficking that include reduced quality of governance as a result of Europe's inability to police its borders, violence against individual victims, and increased anti-immigrant sentiment that is having major political consequences on Continental Europe and contributed to the Brexit vote in the UK and the anti-referendum vote in Italy. The economic costs of providing the needs for impoverished migrants and the diversification of organized crime into the business of human smuggling and trafficking has dramatically increased profits, further embedding crime into the economic life of European countries and exacerbating problems of corruption.

Not only do the practices of smugglers and traffickers violate basic human rights, but, once arrived, the unauthorized status of the transported irregular migrants challenges democratic processes. The significant numbers of unauthorized immigrants, including trafficked people now living and working in Europe do not enjoy the rights of citizenship or legal residency. Refugee status is hard to obtain even for those deserving of this status. Few countries in Europe, apart from Germany and Sweden, are willing to regularize their status or provide residence permits, since this could be seen as rewarding illegal behavior.[112] Legislation[113] has made victims of trafficking a vulnerable group in the European Union entitled to special asylum seeking procedures. But determining the extent of coercion, deception, and exploitation that qualify an individual for this status is not well defined.[114]

At present there are no long-term strategies to control irregular migrant flows other than greater and often authoritarian controls of Europe's borders. The problem of irregular migration and the illicit and corrupt actors that facilitate this activity are no longer just crime problems for Europe. They are concerns that go to the core of European politics, identity, and the future economy of the region. The abuse that is associated with the smuggling and trafficking results in widespread human suffering and victimization and has made the criminal law and justice system and asylum processes increasing arbiters of the conditions of human existence. But these overburdened systems are ill-adapted to dealing with major inflows that have broader consequences for the future of Europe.

NOTES

1. United Nations Office on Drugs and Crime, *2007 UN World Drug Report* (Vienna: United Nations, 2007).

2. Irregular Migrant, Refugee Arrivals in Europe Top One Million in 2015: IOM. Available at: www.iom.int/news/irregular-migrant-refugee-arrivals-europe-top-one-million-2015-iom, accessed November 21, 2016.

3. See www.iom-nederland.nl/images/Migration_Response/Europe-Mediterranean-Migration-Response-Situation-Report.pdf, accessed November 21, 2016.

4. See https://missingmigrants.iom.int/, accessed November 20, 2017.

5. International Organization for Migration – Global Migration Data Analysis Center, *Dangerous Journeys. International Migration Increasingly unsafe in 2016*, (Geneva: IOM-GMDAC, 2016), 1. Available at: https://missingmigrants .iom.int/, accessed November 22, 2016.

6. Europol, *Migrant Smuggling in the EU*, 13. Available at: www.europol.europa.eu/publications-documents/migrant-smuggling-in-eu, accessed November 21, 2016.

7. Europol-Smuggling Centre, *Activity Report First Year Jan. 2016–Jan. 2017*, p. 13. Available at: www.europol.europa.eu/publications-documents/emsc-first-year-activity-report, accessed June 19, 2017.

8. Conny Rijken, Julia Muraszkiewicz, and Pien van de Ven, "Report on the Features and Incentives of Traffickers and on the Social Interactions Among Them," 18. Available at: http://trace-project.eu/wp-content/uploads/2015/06/TRACE_Deliverable-3.1_Final.pdf, accessed August 15, 2016.

9. Peter Tinti and Tuesday Reitano, *Migrant Refugee Smuggler Saviour* (London: Hurst and Co., 2016), pp. 101–126.

10. Arnold Ahlert, "ISIS Trafficking Human Organs?" February 19, 2015. Available at: www.frontpagemag.com/fpm/251753/isis-trafficking-human-organs-arnold-ahlert, accessed November 22, 2016; Campbell Fraser "Human Organ Trafficking." Available at: https://vimeo.com/156708248, accessed November 22, 2016.

11. Center for the Study of Democracy "Anti-corruption measures in EU border control," 2012. Available at: http://frontex.europa.eu/assets/Publications/Research/AntiCorruption_Measures_in_EU_Border_Control.pdf, accessed November 23, 2016.

12. Frank Laczko, Irene Stacher, and Amanda Klekowski von Koppenfels, *New Challenges for Migration Policy in Central and Eastern Europe* (Cambridge: Cambridge University Press, 2002).

13. Europol, *Migrant Smuggling in the EU*, 17.

14. Patrick Kingsley, "Refugee crisis: What does the EU's deal with Turkey mean?" March 18, 2016. Available at: www.theguardian.com/world/2016/mar/18/eu-deal-turkey-migrants-refugees-q-and-a, accessed November 22, 2016.

15. Safak Timur and Rod Nordland, "Erdogan Threatens to Let Migrant Flood Into Europe Resume," *The New York Times*, November 25, 2016. Available at: www.nytimes.com/2016/11/25/world/europe/turkey-recep-tayyip-erdogan-migrants-european-union.html?_r=0, accessed November 28, 2016. See also Nick Gutteridge, "'We'll Blow Your Minds': Turkey threatens to allow 15,000 migrants a month to EU," *Express*, March 17, 2017. Available at: www.express.co.uk/news/politics/780509/Migrant-Crisis-Turkey-threatens-scrap-EU-deal-refugees-Erdogan-Brussels-Netherlands, accessed June 19, 2017.

16. "Europol launches European Migration Smuggling Centre," February 22, 2016. Available at: www.europol.europa.eu/newsroom/news/europol-launches-european-migrant-smuggling-centre, accessed November 23, 2016.

17. Frontex is a specialized and independent body based in Warsaw to provide operational cooperation on border issues; see Frontex, "Origin." Available at: http://frontex.europa.eu/about-frontex/origin/, accessed December 1, 2016.

18. Kara Abramson, "Beyond Consent, Toward Safeguarding Human Rights: Implementing the United Nations Trafficking Protocol," *Harvard International Law Journal*, 44 (2003): 473-502; Janice G. Raymond, "The New UN Trafficking Protocol," *Women's Studies International Forum* 25 (2002): 491–502.

19. Anne Gallagher, "Human Rights and the New UN Protocols on Trafficking and Migrant Smuggling: A preliminary Analysis," *Human Rights Quarterly* 23 (2001): 975–1004.

20. UNODC, "United Nations Convention on Transnational Organized Crime and the 2 Protocols Thereto." Available at: www.unodc.org/documents/treaties/UNTOC/ Publications/TOC%20Convention/TOCebook-e.pdf, accessed November 29, 2016.

21. United Nations, "Protocol Against the Smuggling of Migrants by Land, Sea, and Air, Supplementing the United Nations Convention Against Transnational Organized Crime (2000)." Available at:www.uncjin.org/Documents/Conven tions/dcatoc/final_documents_2/convention_smug_eng.pdf, accessed November 29, 2016.

22. For a discussion of this, see Bridget Anderson and Julia O'Connell Davidson, *Is Trafficking in Human Beings Demand Driven? A Multi-Country Pilot Study* (Geneva: International Organization for Migration, 2003). Available at: www .iom.int/jahia/webdav/site/myjahiasite/shared/shared/mainsite/published_docs/ serial_publications/mrs15b.pdf, accessed November 3, 2016.

23. Benjamin S. Buckland, "Smuggling and Trafficking: Crossover and Overlap," in Cornelius Friesendorf (ed.), *Strategies Against Human Trafficking: The Role of the Security Sector*, (Vienna and Geneva: National Defense Academy and Austrian Ministry of Defense and Sports, 2009), pp. 146, 151.

24. Stef Janssens, Patricia Le Cocq, and Koen Dewulf, *La Traite et Le Trafic des être$ humain$: Lutter avec des personnes et des ressourcés. Rapport Annuel 2008* (Bruxelles: Centre pour l'égalité des chances et la lutte contre racisme, 2009).

25. Eurostat, *Trafficking in Human Beings, Statistical Working Paper* (Luxemburg: Publications Office of the European Union, 2015). Available at: https://ec.europa .eu/anti-trafficking/sites/antitrafficking/files/eurostat_report_on_trafficking_in_hu man_beings_-_2015_edition.pdf, accessed July 28, 2016; UNODC, *Global Report on Trafficking in Persons 2014* (Vienna: United Nations Publications, 2014).

26. *Ibid.*, 23.

27. This proportion is corroborated by Eurostat, *Trafficking in Human Beings, Statistical Working Paper,* 41, which suggests that 65 percent of victims have European origin, and also by UNODC, *Global Report on Trafficking in Persons 2014,* 39, that states that 61 percent of victims have European citizenship.

28. International Labour Office (ILO), *Hard to See, Harder to Count: Survey Guidelines to Estimate Forced Labour of Adults and Children* (Geneva: ILO, 2011). Available at: www.ilo.org/global/docs/WCMS_182084/lang–en/index.htm, accessed November 23, 2016.

29. Europol, *Situation Report. Trafficking in Human Beings in the European Union,* (The Hague: Europol, 2016), 12. Available at: https://ec.europa.eu/anti-trafficking/ sites/antitrafficking/files/situational_report_trafficking_in_human_beings-_europol .pdf, accessed September 26, 2016.

30. Europol, *Migrant Smuggling in the EU*, p. 5; Tinti and Reitano, pp. 83–84.

31. Europol, *Migrant Smuggling in the EU*, p. 5.

32. *Ibid.*, p. 5 and Tuesday Reitano, "Human Smuggling from West Africa to Europe," in *Illicit Financial Flows: The Economy of Illicit Trade in West Africa*, forthcoming report, OECD 2016. Available at: www.oecd.org/dac/accountable-effective-institutions/Economy-Illicit-Trade-West%20Africa.pdf, accessed December 7, 2016.

33. Europol, *Migrant Smuggling in the EU*, p. 5.

34. Europol, *Situation Report Trafficking in Human Beings in the EU,* p. 14.

35. International Organization for Migration (IOM), Migration Information Program, *Trafficking in Women from the Dominican Republic for Sexual Exploitation*

(Geneva: IOM, 1996). Available at: www.oas.org/atip/country%20specific/TIP%20DR%20IOM%20REPORT.pdf, accessed November 23, 2016; US Department of State, "Dominican Republic," in Trafficking in Persons Report 2016 (Washington, DC: Department of State, 2016). Available at: www.state.gov/j/tip/rls/tiprpt/countries/2016/258758.htm, accessed November 23, 2016.

36. Liz Kelly, *Journeys of Jeopardy: A Review of Research on Trafficking in Women and Children in Europe* (Geneva: IOM, 2002), p. 26. See also: The US Department of State 2015 Trafficking in Persons Report on Brazil and Colombia. Available at: www.state.gov/j/tip/rls/tiprpt/countries/2015/243402.htm and www.state.gov/j/tip/rls/tiprpt/countries/2015/243416.htm, accessed November 23, 2016.

37. John Picarelli, "Organised Crime and Human Trafficking in the United States and Western Europe," in Cornelius Friesendorf (ed.), *Strategies Against Human Trafficking: The Role of the Security Sector* (Vienna: National Defense Academy and Austrian Ministry of Defense and Sport, 2009), p. 134; Jørgen Carling, "Trafficking in Women from Nigeria to Europe," July 2005. Available at: www.migrationpolicy.org/article/trafficking-women-nigeria-europe, accessed November 23, 2016; Jørgen Carling, *Migration, Human Smuggling and Trafficking from Nigeria to Europe* (Geneva: IOM, 2006). Available at: www.iom.int/jahia/webdav/site/myjahiasite/shared/shared/mainsite/published_docs/serial_publications/mrs23.pdf, accessed November 25, 2016.

38. Annie Kelly, "Trafficked to Turin: Nigerian women forced to work as Prostitutes in Italy," August 7, 2016. Available at: www.theguardian.com/global-development/2016/aug/07/nigeria-trafficking-women-prostitutes-italy, accessed November 9, 2016.

39. Annie Kelly and Lorenzo Tondo, "Trafficking of Nigerian women into Prostitution in Europe At Crisis Level," August 8, 2016. Available at: www.theguardian.com/global-development/2016/aug/08/trafficking-of-nigerian-women-into-prostitution-in-europe-at-crisis-level, accessed November 20, 2016.

40. Interviews with specialists in Italy, Naples, November 2016; "African Migrants Exploited in Italian Orange Farms," CCTV. Available at: www.youtube.com/watch?v=CKgkc5_eCec, accessed November 23, 2016.

41. Eurostat, *Trafficking in Human Beings, Statistical Working Paper*, p. 34.

42. *Ibid.*, 11.

43. Combating Trafficking in Human Beings for the Purpose of Forced Criminality, April 11–12, 2016. Available at: www.osce.org/event/alliance16, accessed December 7, 2016.

44. United Nations Children's Fund (UNICEF) Innocenti Research Center, *Child Trafficking in Europe: A Broad Vision to Put Children First* (Florence, Italy: UNICEF, 2008). Available at: www.unicef-irc.org/publications/pdf/ct_in_europe_full.pdf, accessed October 23, 2016.

45. Darrin Zammit, "More than 10,000 Refugee Children Missing in Europe," January 31, 2016. Available at: www.aljazeera.com/news/2016/01/10000-refugee-children-missing-europe-160131164555450.html, accessed September 12, 2016.

46. Mark Shaw and Fiona Mangan, *Illicit Trafficking and Libya's Transition: Profits and Losses* (Washington, DC: United States Institute of Peace, 2014).

47. Tinti and Reitano, 109–112.

48. *Ibid.*, p. 113.

49. Agence France-Presse (AFP), "Arab Spring Prompts Surge of Illegal Immigrants to EU," November 16, 2011. Available at: www.timesofmalta.com/articles/view/20111116/local/arab-spring-prompts-surge-of-illegal-immigrants-to-eu.3 94158, accessed November 9, 2016.

50. EurActiv, "Greece Measures Arab Spring Immigration Impact," November 22, 2011. Available at: www.euractiv.com/justice/greece-measures-arab-spring-immigration-impact-news-509109, accessed November 9, 2016.

51. Diego Cupolo, "Asylum-seekers weigh options in Athens," December 12, 2015. Available at: www.dw.com/en/asylum-seekers-weigh-options-in-athens/g-1891 7994, accessed October 23, 2016; Nektaria Stamouli, "Inside the Migrant-Smuggling Trade: Escapes Start at €1,000," March 19, 2016. Available at: www .wsj.com/articles/european-border-crackdown-kick-starts-migrant-smuggling-busi ness-1459260153, accessed October 23, 2016; Helena Smith, "Athens under Pressure: City Races to Clear Port's Refugee Camp before Tourists Arrive," April 26, 2016. Available at: www.theguardian.com/cities/2016/apr/26/athens-under-pressure-city-port-refugee-camp-tourists, accessed October 23, 2016.

52. "Hungary's PM Plans 'More Massive' Fence to Keep Out Migrants," August 26, 2016. Available at: www.theguardian.com/world/2016/aug/26/hungarys-pm-plans-more-massive-fence-to-keep-out-migrants, accessed December 7, 2016.

53. Mostafa Minawi, *The Ottoman Scramble for Africa: Empire and Diplomacy in the Sahara and the Hijaz* (Stanford: Stanford University Press, 2016).

54. European Migrant Smuggling Centre, *Activity Report First Year Jan. 2016–Jan. 2017*, p. 10.

55. AFP, "Arab Spring Prompts Surge of Illegal Immigrants to EU," *Times of Malta*, November 16, 2011. Available at: www.timesofmalta.com/articles/view/20111116/local/arab-spring-prompts-surge-of-illegal-immigrants-to-eu.394158, accessed November 28, 2016.

56. The air routes include direct flights from Lagos to Italy, Lagos–France–Italy, Lagos–London–Italy, Lagos–Accra (by road)–Italy (by air), Lagos–the Netherlands–Italy, and Lagos–any Schengen country–Italy. Other land and sea routes include Lagos–Togo–Morocco–Spain–Italy, Lagos–Togo–Libya–Italy, Lagos–Togo, Morocco–Spain–France–Italy, and Lagos–Togo–Burkina Faso–Mali–Spain–France–Italy. See: United Nations Interregional Crime and Justice Research Institute (UNCJRI), "Trafficking of Nigerian Girls to Italy," 2003. Available at: www.unicri.it/services/library_documentation/publications/unicri_series/trafficking_nigeria-italy.pdf, accessed October 23, 2016.

57. Tinti and Reitano, p. 94.

58. Sabina Castelfranco, "Italian Island of Lampedusa Sees Increase of North African Refugees," March 7, 2011. Available at: www.voanews.com/english/news/europe/Italian-Island-of-Lampedusa-sees-Increase-of-North-African-Refugees-117510933 .html, accessed November 20, 2016.

59. Tinti and Reitano, p. 143.

60. Susana Capeluoto, "Newborn Twins Among 6,500 Migrants Rescued," August 31, 2016. Available at: http://www.cnn.com/2016/08/30/europe/libya-migrants-rescued/, accessed November 20, 2016.

61. UNODC, *The Role of Organized Crime in the Smuggling of Migrants from West Africa to the European Union* (Vienna: UNODC, 2011), p. 8. Available at:

www.unodc.org/documents/human-trafficking/Migrant-Smuggling/Report_SOM_
West_Africa_EU.pdf, accessed October 23, 2016.

62. See www.iom.int/news/irregular-migrant-refugee-arrivals-europe-top-one-million-
2015-iom, accessed October 23, 2016.

63. Tinti and Reitano, p. 87.

64. See, "Statistics on Enforcement of Immigration Legislation." Available at: http://ec
.europa.eu/eurostat/statistics-explained/index.php/Statistics_on_enforcement_of_
immigration_legislation, accessed December 3, 2016.

65. Frontex, *Annual Risk Analysis* (Warsaw: Frontex, 2015). Available at: http://
frontex.europa.eu/assets/Publications/Risk_Analysis/Annual_Risk_Analysis_2015
.pdf, accessed August 9, 2016.

66. Europol, *Migrant Smuggling in the EU*, p. 7.

67. Discussions with Campbell Fraser after participation in EU mission in Libya,
November 2016; "Egypt Arrests 'organ trafficking ring'," December 6, 2016.
Available at: www.bbc.com/news/world-middle-east-38224836, accessed
December 7, 2016.

68. Europol, *Migrant Smuggling in the EU*, pp. 2, 4.

69. Financial Action Task Force, *National Money Laundering and Terrorist Financing
Risks Assessment* (Paris: FATF/OECD, 2013). Available at: www.fatf-gafi.org/media/
fatf/content/images/National_ML_TF_Risk_Assessment.pdf, accessed November 26,
2016, pp. 35–36.

70. Europol, *Situation Report Trafficking in Human Beings in the EU*, p. 17.

71. Europol, *Migrant Smuggling Report*, p. 7.

72. Europol, *Situation Report. Trafficking in human beings in the EU*, p. 14.

73. Jana Arsovska and Stef Janssens, "Human Trafficking and Policing: Good and Bad
Practices," in Cornelius Friesendorf (ed.), *Strategies against Human Trafficking:
The Role of the Security Sector* (Vienna: National Defence Academy and Austrian
Ministry of Defence and Sport, 2009), p. 213.

74. Rebecca Surtees, "Traffickers and Trafficking in Southern and Eastern Europe
Considering the Other Side of Human Trafficking," *European Journal of
Criminology* 5 (2008): 39–68.

75. Michael Collyer, "Cross-Border Cottage Industries and Fragmented Migration,"
in Sergio Carrera and Elspeth Guild (eds.), *Irregular Migration, Trafficking and
Smuggling of Human Beings Policy Dilemmas in the EU* (Brussels: Center for
European Policy Studies, 2016), 19. Available at: www.ceps.eu/system/files/
Irregular%20Migration,%20Trafficking%20and%20SmugglingwithCovers.pdf,
accessed October 23, 2016.

76. Alexis Aronowitz, Gerda Theuermann, and Elena Tyurykanova, *Analysing the
Business Model of Human Trafficking to Better Prevent the Crime* (Vienna: Office
of the Special Representative and Co-ordinator for Combating Trafficking in
Human Beings, 2010).

77. *Ibid.*, p. 184.

78. Dina Siegel and Sylvia de Blank, "Women Who Traffic Women: The Role of
Women in Human Trafficking Networks – Dutch Cases," *Global Crime* 11
(2010): 436–447; Alexis Aronowitz, *Human Trafficking, Human Misery:
The Global Trade in Human Beings* (Westport, CN: Praeger, 2009), pp. 52–55.

79. Rebecca Surtees, "Traffickers and Trafficking in Southern and Eastern Europe Considering the Other Side of Human Trafficking," *European Journal of Criminology* 5 (2008): 39–68.

80. Marina Mancuso, "Not All Madams Have a Central Role: Analysis of a Nigerian Sex Trafficking Network," *Trends in Organized Crime* 17 (2014): 66–88; Paolo Campana, "The Structure of Human Trafficking: Lifting the Bonnet on a Nigerian Transnational Network," *British Journal of Criminology* 56 (2016): 68–86.

81. Finnish Immigration Service –FIS– (2015), "Human Trafficking of Nigerian Women to Europe 2016." Available at: www.migri.fi/download/60332_Suu ntaus_NigSuuntaus_HumanTraffickingfromNigeriaFINAL200415.pdf?b3ecfe879 399d388, accessed August 8, 2016.

82. C. S. Baarda, "Human Trafficking for Sexual Exploitation from Nigeria into Western Europe: The Role of Voodoo Rituals in the Functioning of a Criminal Network," *European Journal of Criminology* 13 (2016): 257.

83. Hayley Watson, Ann Donovan, and Julia Muraszkiewicz, "Role of Technology in Human Trafficking," *Trace* (October 2015). Available at: race-project.eu/ wp-content/uploads/2015/11/TRACE_D4.2_Role-of-Technologies-in-human-trafficking_Briefing-Paper_FINAL.1.pdf, accessed December 11, 2016.

84. Stephen Gray and Amina Ismali, "The Forgotten Shipwreck," December 6, 2016. Available at: www.reuters.com/investigates/special-report/migration/#story/60, accessed December 7, 2016.

85. European Migrant Smuggling Centre, *Activity Report First Year Jan. 2016–Jan. 2017*, p. 16.

86. Europol, Situation Report, "Trafficking in Human Beings in the EU," p. 19.

87. Mark Galeotti, "Turkish Organized Crime: Where State, Crime, and Rebellion Conspire," *Transnational Organized Crime* 4 (1998): 25–42.

88. Janssens *et al.*, *La Traite et Le Trafic des être$ humain$*.

89. Turkish National Police, *Turkish Organized Crime Report* (Ankara: Department of Anti-Smuggling and Organized Crime, 2008).

90. Stef Janssens and Jana Arsovska, "People Carriers: Human Trafficking Networks Thrive in Turkey," *Jane's Intelligence Review* (December 2008): 44–47; Xavier Raufer, "Une maffya symbiotique: traditions et évolutions du crime organisé en Turquie," *Sécurité Globale*, 10 (2009–2010): 91–119.

91. Lorenzo Tondo and Patrick Kingsley, "'They Got the Wrong Man' Says People-Smuggling Suspect," *The Guardian*, November 22, 2016. Available at: www .theguardian.com/law/2016/nov/22/people-smuggling-suspect-sends-facebook-message-that-man-on-trial-is-not-him, accessed November 26, 2016.

92. John Pomfret, "Bribery at Border Worries Officials," *Washington Post*, July 15, 2006. Available at: www.washingtonpost.com/wp-dyn/content/article/2006/07/14/ AR2006071401525.html, accessed February 26, 2018; Transparency International, "Corruption and Human Trafficking" (working paper No.3/2011, Transparency International, Berlin, 2011). Available at: www.transparency.org/publications/ publications/working_papers/wp_03_11_corruption_human_trafficking, accessed February 26, 2018.

93. Philip Gounev, Rositsa Dzhekova, and Tihomir Bezlov, "Study on anti-corruption measures in EU Border control, 2012." Available at: http://frontex.europa.eu/

assets/Publications/Research/Study_on_anticorruption_measures_in_EU_border_control.pdf, accessed December 11, 2016.

94. "On Holiday in Greece as a 14-year-old, Megan Stephens Fell in Love. But Her Boyfriend Turned Out to be a Pimp Who Trafficked Her for Six Years. She Tells Her Story to Elizabeth Day." Available at: www.theguardian.com/law/2015/jan/18/i-was-sold-into-sexual-slavery?CMP=fb_gu, accessed December 1, 2016.

95. UNODC (2011), "The Role of Corruption in Trafficking in Persons." Available at: www.unodc.org/documents/human-trafficking/2011/Issue_Paper__The_Role_of_Corruption_in_Trafficking_in_Persons.pdf, accessed December 7, 2016.

96. Philip Gounev, Rositsa Dzhekova, and Tihomir Bezlov, "Study on anti-corruption measures in EU Border control," 2012. Available at: http://frontex.europa.eu/assets/Publications/Research/Study_on_anticorruption_measures_in_EU_border_control.pdf, accessed December 7, 2016.

97. UNODC, *The Globalization of Crime. A Transnational Organized Crime Threat Assessment* (Vienna: Division for Policy Analysis and Public Affairs, UNODC, 2010), 44. Available at: www.unodc.org/documents/data-and-analysis/tocta/TOCTA_Report_2010_low_res.pdf, accessed December 7, 2016.

98. UNODC, *Global Report on Trafficking in Persons 2014*, pp. 29–37. Available at: www.unodc.org/documents/data-and-analysis/glotip/GLOTIP_2014_full_report.pdf, accessed December 7, 2016.

99. Europol, *Situation Report. Trafficking in Human Beings in the European Union*, 18. See also Center for the Study of Democracy, "Child Trafficking Among Vulnerable Roma Communities Results of country studies in Austria, Bulgaria, Greece, Italy, Hungary, Romania and Slovakia," 2015. Available at: http://childrentrafficking.eu/wp-content/uploads/2014/04/CONFRONT_NEW_WEB.pdf, accessed December 7, 2016.

100. Kristiina Kangaspunta, "Trafficking in Persons: Global Patterns" (presentation at International Symposium on International Migration and Development, UNODC, Turin, June 28–30, 2006), p. 20. Available at: www.un.org/esa/population/migration/turin/Turin_Statements/KANGASPUNTA.pdf; Europol, *Trafficking in Human Beings in the European Union, 18*, accessed December 7, 2016.

101. Raphael Minder, "Spain Breaks Up a Trafficking Ring for Male Prostitution," August 31, 2010. Available at: www.nytimes.com/2010/09/01/world/europe/01iht-spain.html?_r=0, accessed December 7, 2016.

102. Sofija Voronova and Anja Radjenovic, "The Gender Dimension of Human Trafficking," European Parliament Research Service, Feb. 2016, 3. Available at: www.europarl.europa.eu/RegData/etudes/BRIE/2016/577950/EPRS_BRI(2016)577950_EN.pdf, accessed December 7, 2016.

103. Jessica Jackman, "Male Human Trafficking as an Unrecognised Problem," *The BSIS Journal of International Studies*, 9 (2012). Available at: www.kent.ac.uk/brussels/documents/journal/2012/Jessica%20Jackman%20-%20Male%20Human%20Trafficking%20as%20an%20Unrecognised%20Problem.pdf, accessed December 7; USAID, "Trafficking of Adult Men in the Europe and Eurasia Region: Final Report," July 2010. Available at: http://pdf.usaid.gov/pdf_docs/Pnadw368.pdf, accessed December 7, 2016.

104. Pia Orrenius and Madeline Zavodny, "Undocumented Immigration and Human Trafficking," in Barry R. Chiswick, and Paul W Miller (eds.), *Handbook of the Economics of International Migration* (Amsterdam: Elsiever, 2015), p. 708.

Available at: www.sciencedirect.com/science/handbookA, accessed December 7, 2016.

105. Gray and Ismali, "The Forgotten Shipwreck".

106. IOM, "Migration of Children to Europe," November 30, 2015. Available at: www .iom.int/sites/default/files/press_release/file/IOM-UNICEF-Data-Brief-Refugee-and-Migrant-Crisis-in-Europe-30.11.15.pdf, accessed December 7, 2016.

107. *Ibid.*, 3.

108. Enza Roberta Petrillo, "The Securitisation of the EU External Borders and the Rise of Human Smuggling Along the Eastern Mediterranean Route: The Case of Afghan Unaccompanied Minors," in Elena Ambrosetti, Donatella Strangio, and Catherine Wihtol de Wenden (eds.), *Migration in the Mediterranean: Socio-economic Perspectives* (New York: Routledge, 2016).

109. Lisa O'Carroll and Carmen Fishwick, "Calais Camp Charity Threatens UK with legal Action over Vulnerable Children," October 19, 2016. Available at: www .theguardian.com/uk-news/2016/oct/19/calais-camp-charity-threatens-uk-with-legal-action-over-vulnerable-children, accessed December 7, 2016.

110. Adam Nossiter, "A French Underground Railroad Moving African Migrants," October 4, 2016. Available at: www.nytimes.com/2016/10/05/world/europe/france-italy-migrants-smuggling.html, accessed December 7, 2016.

111. Jim Yardley, "In Italy, Anguish on Both Sides of Asylum Pleas," *The New York Times,* December 11, 2016, p. 6.

112. Cornelius Friesendorf (ed.), *Strategies against Human Trafficking: The Role of the Security Sector* (Vienna and Geneva: National Defence Academy and Austrian Ministry of Defence and Sport, 2009), pp. 444–510.

113. European Migration Network Study, "Identification of Victims of Trafficking in Human Beings in International Protection and Forced Return Procedures." Available at: http://ec.europa.eu/dgs/home-affairs/what-we-do/networks/european_migration_network/reports/docs/emn-studies/emn_synthesis_identification_victims_trafficking_final_13march2014.pdf, accessed December 7, 2016.

114. Vladislave Stovanova, "Victims of Human Trafficking – A Legal Analysis of the Guarantees for 'Vulnerable Persons' under the Second Phase of the EU Asylum Legislation," in Celine Bauloz, Meltem Ineli-Ciger, Sarah Singer, and Vladislava Stoyanova (eds.), *Seeking Asylum in the European Union. Selected Protection Issues Raised by the Second Phase of the Common European Asylum System* (Leiden: Brill Nijhoff, 2015), p. 78.

PART V

CONCLUSION

20

Concluding Thoughts

Carol M. Swain

Democracy must be built through open societies that share information. When there is information, there is enlightenment. When there is debate, there are solutions.

–Kosovar President Atifete Jahjaga, 2012[1]

Democracy is only as strong as the people and the ideas that support it. In this volume, authors from many different academic backgrounds have shared information, all seeking to impart knowledge and wisdom about immigration and its impact around the world. Although we do not agree on the best solutions, we recognize that continued debate is needed and we approach the subject with optimism that by grappling with the issue and engaging in cross-national, cross-disciplinary conversations, we will come closer to a solution that will strengthen our democracies and move toward the development of more effective policies.

We have expressed our viewpoints and pointed to a variety of immigration-related issues and, in some cases, disagreed as to their causes and consequences. We have challenged each other to think critically about all aspects of immigration – even some that are often taken for granted, such as the legal–illegal dichotomy. We come from different backgrounds and express different opinions of both immigrants and immigration itself. Even among such a diverse group, however, there are some similar themes.

Throughout this work, it is clear that immigration produces winners and losers; some groups benefit, while others pay the costs. Consequently, the immigration concerns that citizens express are almost always based in real, legitimate concerns. While it is frequently convenient or easy to dismiss these worries as simply racism or nativism, this is rarely the case. Thus, these concerns must be taken into consideration when seeking to develop policy outcomes that benefit our nations as a whole. Furthermore, the contributors in this volume all agree that creating immigration policy has never been, is not now, and likely will never be easy. It creates unique challenges for each country and none have yet developed a perfect immigration system. In order to make progress, new, innovative policy options must be developed, and new approaches tried.

It is crucial to review the flaws in the current immigration system that various contributors identified. This will aid in understanding why changes must be made to improve outcomes. Only then can we focus on what we see as the consequences of the systemic flaws. Lastly, we offer our sense of the positive aspects that can and often do flow from a system that allows individuals to leave the nations of their birth to pursue opportunities in other parts of the world.

SYSTEMIC FLAWS

With respect to such flaws, each contributor offers a unique perspective, and together we help form a more complete picture of a system in need of help. When speaking of the United States, the authors disagree both on what *causes* today's problems and also what *constitutes* a problem.

Douglas Massey and Karen Pren dedicate themselves to the first of these points and contend that the most salient immigration issues facing the country today are largely the unintended consequences of past policy failures. They claim that past and current immigration laws were made without a sound understanding of the processes involved in migration, causing increased net inflows of both legal and illegal immigrants. The ultimate result of these policies is the ever-increasing immigrant population that the United States and other Western nations must face each day.

Rogers Smith similarly focuses on the ways in which past immigration policies have failed to achieve their stated goals, causing a different modern immigration challenge. In his contribution, he notes that recent immigration policy has often succeeded only in reducing immigrant (and sometimes citizen) rights, without successfully curtailing immigration in any way. As a result, these policies are unsuccessful in meeting their stated goals and, ultimately, undermine rights that should be guaranteed.

Such failures as the aforementioned could be due to the lack of a coherent philosophy of immigration in the United States, as Elizabeth Cohen notes. She emphasizes that the absence of a consistent immigration doctrine has undoubtedly led to erratic, and often conflicting, immigration policies. During the tenure of Barack Obama, for example, the administration was simultaneously conducting mass deportations and introducing policies to allow certain illegal immigrants to remain. In her view, this is one of the major problems facing the United States today, as well as a cause of many of the other issues that the nation faces.

It is possible that this lack of a consistent philosophy has further contributed to the lack of legislative action that I note in my chapter on President Obama's executive overreach. It certainly makes policymaking more difficult. This is problematic in and of itself; as Congress has not enacted any significant immigration legislation in recent years, I mention, it puts added pressure on the president to enact policies, often leading to actions that go beyond the power of the executive branch. This points to another flaw in the current system.

Furthermore, both Jim Edwards and Stephen Macedo use moral and philosophical arguments to claim that the state is not currently doing enough to protect its citizens from the negative effects of immigration, as is its duty. According to these two authors, the costs of immigration too often fall on those who can least afford to pay them, resulting in an unjust situation for the poorest members of society. The government's job is to correct this injustice, and in the current flawed system it is not doing so.

THE DARK SIDE OF IMMIGRATION

But what exactly are the negative effects of immigration mentioned above? The contributors in this volume also spend much time considering, and sometimes disagreeing on, this issue.

Many of the most salient negative ramifications noted in the chapters are economic in nature. Speaking to these economic effects, Steven A. Camarota and Karen Zeigler present evidence that most job gains in the past 17 years have gone to immigrants, not to native workers. John Skrentny notes a similar trend and seeks to explain why this is the case, especially among low-skilled workers. These workers constitute a group that is often cited as the one most affected by immigration to the United States today. He posits that this is due to systematic bias shown by employers; they view immigrants, especially those who have recently arrived, as harder workers than natives and are consequently more likely to hire these immigrant workers (despite the fact that this is illegal under current civil rights law). Such bias can lead to disastrous effects for low-skilled native workers. Going beyond employment measures, Philip Cafaro further notes that immigration simultaneously correlates with increased economic inequality in America and decreased support for the redistribution policies that could help reduce such inequality. This further exacerbates the problem for low-skilled, low-income U.S. workers. Many of the contributors to this volume also note the decline in wages that increased immigration causes.

Although economic concerns are the most oft-cited, there are other considerations, as well. Several authors mention the importance of the security and social justice issues that mass immigration creates. Philip Cafaro also contends that large numbers of immigrants exacerbate natural resource scarcity and urban sprawl. Moreover, the contributors present abundant examples of the ways in which immigration worsens an already difficult situation for blacks in America. As I assert in my chapter on the Congressional Black Caucus, immigration has begun to divide the interests of those that claim to represent African Americans. As a result, the CBC is not taking the leadership position that it should with regard to immigration; despite the fact that it harms the job opportunities for black Americans, they have taken little to no action to protect them. John Skrentny further emphasizes the importance of such action on behalf of African Americans when he notes that black Americans are among those that are most harmed by employers' biased selection of workers. Along with Skrentny, other contributors also note how immigrants take the civil rights advantages intended for blacks, leaving them with diminished opportunities. Overall, these contributors contend that black Americans pay many of the costs of immigration while reaping very few of the rewards.

In Europe, a large variety of issues also come into play, some similar to and others different from those faced by the United States, as the contributors presented in this volume emphasize. Louise Shelley and Camilo Pardo focus on the important role that corruption often plays in European immigration, especially in relation to both human trafficking and human smuggling. This is an aspect that goes unmentioned in the chapters that relate to the issues facing the United States today. Susan F. Martin views the lack of a strong global migration regime as one of the most salient modern immigration problems facing both Europe and the world as a whole. Such a regime could perhaps decrease the trafficking and smuggling noted by Shelley and Pardo and create better immigration outcomes worldwide. Marc Morjé Howard and Sara Wallace Goodman take yet another approach while also emphasizing one difficulty in forming a global regime – they focus on the differing views of citizenship (and the policies that result) in different European countries. They further highlight the difficulty in coming to one idea of citizenship, and especially one that can successfully incorporate immigrants (a conundrum with which Elizabeth Cohen also grapples in relation to the United States). Looking at a different aspect of this multi-faceted issue, Randall Hansen underscores the difficulties that Europe has in integrating large waves of immigrants. He contends that this is because of the welfare programs that the governments provide to migrants and because of the lack of hands-on integration programs in most countries, pointing to the United States and France as models for how to better integrate those that enter a country's borders. He does admit, however, that this may lead to the levels of inequality seen in the United States today, a challenge that Philip Cafaro would readily agree with.

On the whole, there are a variety of challenges facing both the United States and Europe with respect to immigration today. It is clear that a truly successful immigration policy must take into consideration and address a multitude of issues.

A POSITIVE VIEW

Despite these challenges, the situation is not entirely bleak; some authors also affirm that immigrants do much good for the countries in which they reside. In general terms, most authors agree that immigrant labor does have the effect of creating lower costs for many goods and services; this is beneficial for at least some portion of the population. Speaking specifically of the United States, Amitai Etzioni contends that immigrants bring a variety of other benefits as well. He indicates that immigrants help refocus America on communitarian values that have been lost in recent years; specifically, immigrants help foster a culture of commitment to family, community, and nation, as well as morality and respect for authority. Etzioni claims that immigrants are thereby helping rehabilitate some of the country's core values. He further acknowledges that immigration helps protect the United States from the demographic decline that is so common in European and Asian nations today. Additionally, he notes that immigrants are helping to depolarize American society by shifting the focus from a black–white dichotomy to a more varied ethnic and racial environment. On a more individual level, Noah Pickus and Peter Skerry reference the fact that many immigrants seek to act as good neighbors and be contributing members of society. This will help in the integration process of these people if only they can be told what exactly is expected of them, they posit. In the end, these positive results of immigration should also be noted and considered carefully, as they allow one to see the value of immigrants. Understanding such value helps underscore the importance of creating a truly just immigration policy.

POLICIES AND SOLUTIONS

What would such a just immigration policy look like? The contributors in this volume paint diverse pictures in response to this query. Overall, they demonstrate the complexity of the issue and the many ways in which the United States and other countries may begin to alter their immigration systems to produce more positive outcomes for all.

An oft-cited solution in modern political discourse in the United States involves a wall or fence along the border with Mexico and increased border enforcement in order to control the flow of illegal immigrants into the country. In my policy suggestions, I advocate for this as one piece of a more complex immigration reform plan. Other contributors, however, disagree with this option. Douglas Massey and Karen Pren, for example, note that such policies were part of what ultimately resulted in an increase in net inflows of immigrants. They contend that a softer border policy would actually be more effective in reducing the inflow of immigrants into the country. Peter Skerry also notes strong disagreement with this policy. In his view, such actions have been a part of the immigration debate for far too long and are limiting the innovation of more creative solutions to the issues at hand. All in all, this is still a contested policy choice, both in this volume and in the political sphere.

Another frequently disputed policy option is that of a guestworker program, in which workers come on temporary visas to perform tasks for which there is insufficient native labor supply. Massey and Pren allege that the removal of such a policy in the form of the former Bracero Program led in part to the high levels of illegal immigration that the country saw in the years following that time. Does this mean that a similar program should be reinstituted in the United States? Some authors would agree, while others offer a resounding "no." Stephen Macedo notes at the end of his contribution that a guestworker program could be a potential solution to the lack of prioritization given to the poorest Americans today if it is combined with protections for these citizens. I also mention such a program in my policy suggestions, noting that it could be part of a larger solution if it is properly reformed. Peter Skerry, on the other hand, feels that this particular policy option should also be abandoned in favor of more innovative actions.

Looking to other popular policy choices, both Peter Skerry and I advocate for some form of an employment verification program. With employment verification, employers would no longer be able to hire undocumented workers, and consequently, the employment opportunities for both native workers and legal immigrants would increase. This is not a complete solution for either party, however. Peter Skerry further advocates for programs to help immigrants learn English, actively working to help immigrants integrate into society. This would help them be the "good neighbors" that Skerry mentions in his piece with Noah Pickus. I include employment verification as one part of a complex set of solutions; also included are registration of illegal immigrants, stiffer penalties for immigration-related offenses, and background checks. Similar to Peter Skerry, Randall Hansen also advocates for hands-on integration practices, as well as active attempts to integrate immigrants into the employment system.

Other contributors opt for a simpler solution: a reduction in the number of immigrants allowed into the country. Philip Cafaro believes that this is absolutely necessary to achieve progressive political goals. A reduction in immigration would help with such diverse objectives as resource conservation, improved wages, and a reduction in income inequality, he claims. Jim Edwards argues for this same reduction for similar reasons, but with different logic. He notes that immigration tends to harm the most vulnerable members of society and argues that, according to the Bible, the government's first duty is to protect those citizens. Immigration, then, should be held at lower levels that will not cause harm to those least able to defend themselves against it. On a related note, but with another focus, I argue for policies that will encourage undocumented immigrants to self-deport, voluntarily removing themselves from the country. This helps lower the cost of deportation.

Focusing on a different aspect of immigration policy, some authors choose to spotlight the way policies are formed, rather than what those policies should look like. Virginia Yetter and I emphasize one way in which this could be done: federalism. We posit that certain aspects of immigration policy, especially those related to the way immigrants are treated following their entry into the country, are well within the scope of authority given to the states. Immigration policy does not have to be strictly created at the federal level, and we contend that much more innovative policies will result from immigration federalism. At a more international level, Susan F. Martin notes the power that a global migration regime could have. The use of one major governing body in global migration could help countries better coordinate their immigration policies, leading to improved outcomes overall. These would both be unique methods of policy formation that would change the way policies are currently created.

However, there is still another component of the immigration policy path that other authors emphasize. Noah Pickus and Peter Skerry, in particular, stress the need to re-frame the entire debate before creating any sort of policy. While many politicians today focus on a very clear legal-illegal dichotomy, Pickus and Skerry argue that this makes much more sense politically (as an action to gain support) than it does in policymaking. Most Americans are more concerned with whether immigrants can be good neighbors – law-abiding, contributing members of society – than whether they are here legally or illegally. Consequently, to fully address the concerns that citizens express, the United States and those that inhabit it must re-frame the current debate and look at what can be done to help those who are good neighbors assimilate without admitting those who are not.

Similarly, other contributors also underscore the importance of giving thorough consideration to what citizens want from immigration policy before creating it. Elizabeth Cohen focuses on the fact that the U.S. does not currently have a coherent philosophy of immigration. She notes that because the country's definition of citizenship focuses on the black–white divide, it does not address how immigrants are to be treated. To form consistent policies, the United States must first address this issue and decide what type of immigration policy citizens truly want. Too often in the past, policies have been made too hastily, and this has led to multitudinous unintended consequences, as Douglas Massey and Karen Pren highlight in their contribution. Rogers Smith mentions one such unintended consequence that goes beyond those that are traditionally considered. He focuses on citizen and immigrant rights and notes that these must both be carefully examined when making future policies.

In short, there are many considerations when forming immigration policy, and without careful thought and deliberation, this process cannot be successful. The contributors to this volume as a whole have highlighted this point and sought to suggest both ideas to contemplate and policies to implement. There have been points of agreement and points of disagreement, allowing space for much further discussion. Through this dialogue, we will one day find the solutions we need to the challenges we are facing.

SUMMARY

All the authors of this volume agree that the immigration issue is immensely complex; there will never be one "miracle bill" that can fix all of the world's immigration problems. The current system undeniably has flaws, and there are clear costs, and even some benefits, that come with immigration. Moreover, immigration is an issue that will remain for many years to come. For these reasons, we have offered solutions, entering into a debate with the aim of creating a more just immigration system. In the end, the answer lies neither in closing the borders entirely nor in leaving them completely open. Rather, the solution must be a middle ground that can only be arrived at through discussions such as those presented here. Only when scholars, politicians, and regular people from all parts of the political spectrum begin to dialogue together and work to find a solution can true progress begin. So, let us continue debating immigration, hearing each other's opinions, and working to find an ideal outcome.

NOTES

1. A. Jahjaga, "Kosovar President Atifete Jahjaga: The four key ingredients for peace," *The Hill*, 14 June 2012. Available at: http://thehill.com/policy/international/232703-kosovar-president-atifete-jahjaga-the-four-key-ingredients-for-peace, accessed September 18, 2017.

Index